Have you ever met someone you feel you have known forever? This is most often because there is an easy flow of communication or the two of you tend to "think alike," "feel like twins," or otherwise feel an instant knowing and attraction. These people are familiar to you at some subconscious level. Things just feel right between you, and you tend to think that because of the likeness of the past, your futures can be brighter together. And, in most cases, this turns out to be true.

Or have you ever met someone for whom you had an instant dislike? You can't relate to this person, you two have nothing in common, and you seem to be at cross-purposes in life. Sometimes we meet people who are "opposites" of us, just like our astrological opposites. We know they are all wrong for us and yet we can't seem to resist them.

The disharmonious energies are harder to work with and yet can certainly make for interesting, challenging, and very romantic relationships just the same. . . .

The harmonies of love aspects are important, and they are one of the many tools you can use in life to assist your relationships. But keep in mind, as Linda says, that "love can conquer all."

BANTAM BOOKS
NEW YORK
TORONTO
LONDON
SYDNEY
AUCKLAND

*

★ LINDA ★ GOODMAN'S Relationship ★ Signs ★

by Linda Goodman

Companion Text by
Carolyn Reynolds

Edited by Crystal Bush

This edition contains the complete text of the original hardcover edition.
NOT ONE WORD HAS BEEN OMITTED.

LINDA GOODMAN'S RELATIONSHIP SIGNS
A Bantam Book

PUBLISHING HISTORY
Bantam hardcover edition / 1998
Bantam paperback edition / June 1999

ISBN 0-553-58015-9

Bantam Books are published by Bantam Books, a division of Bantam
Doubleday Dell Publishing Group, Inc. Its trademark, consisting of the words
"Bantam Books" and the portrayal of a rooster, is Registered in U.S. Patent and
Trademark Office and in other countries. Marca Registrada. Bantam Books,
1540 Broadway, New York, New York 10036.

PRINTED IN THE UNITED STATES OF AMERICA

OPM   10   9   8   7   6   5

★ Dedications ★

From Crystal

First, to Linda Goodman, the Goddess of Astrology, for her undeniable trust and faith in me, that in her absence I would complete this legacy of work and share it with the Universe. My dear Linda, my heartfelt thanks.

To my wonderful daughter Kate, whose unconditional love, support, and faith in me and the Linda Goodman mission made all things possible. I thank you.

To her lovely husband, Daren, for being by our sides throughout, for always being patient, never complaining. I thank you; we needed you so much.

To the other jewels in my crown of happiness, my daughters Karen Maria and Kelly-Anne, I am truly blessed to have your love, support, and understanding when time has been so limited. I thank you.

To my stalwart friend and partner, Jim, the grounding element in my Universe, who remained confident throughout that we would achieve the impossible dream. I thank you.

To the lovely Carolyn, whose knowledge of astrology and love of Linda Goodman helped us achieve this final product. I thank you.

To my earth angel Cheri, my fortress, my friend, I thank you.

Last but not least, to Cathi, for all your long hours of typing and for always being available for me. I thank you.

From Carolyn

First, for now and always, to my beloved mother, who has gone on to a higher plane. And to my wonderful husband, Patrick, who is my shining star in broad daylight, and to our doggie son, Stevie. Finally for Crystal, with gratitude for bringing this project to me.

To Linda's Fans

Well, our beloved and enlightened Linda is gone. Not too far away, for she is here for those of us who worked with her last project daily with subtle little nudges along our way. For her fans—and she has millions—she left a final story, about how to make our love relationships better, stronger, and easier to understand. Her insights are now our keys to unlock the workings of relationships astrologically.

In our work together we wanted to honor one of Linda's last wishes. Linda wanted to be remembered as a poet, and so we interjected appropriate verses into her last manuscript to commemorate Linda Goodman the spiritual poet.

Linda Goodman was courageous and defiant in her search for truth in all aspects of life. She spread her love of astrology throughout the world and touched all of us; we were smitten by her work, her depth, her humor, and we understood for the first time how the planets affected our personalities, our lives. Her valiant efforts will live forevermore in our hearts, minds, and souls. Linda, we are so glad you came, so glad you spent some time here with us.

★ ★ Contents ★

Section Three: Linda Goodman's Interpretations of Your Relationship Signs

Section Four: How to Find Your Ascendant or Rising Sign

Section Five: How to Find Your Planets

Appendices

★ Crystal's ★ Preface

My earliest memories of my childhood in Ireland are of happy times. I am the youngest of six children, the offspring of a very strong, independent, hardworking mother. My little Irish mother's objective was to help me value the person I am, believe in the unbelievable, and settle for nothing less than that which is honest and true.

Money was certainly not plentiful, but the things important to a child were: family, friends, and a close-knit community. Everyone knew everyone and had stories to tell about your father's father, your uncle Tom, aunt Jane, and cousin Sarah. At times this could be aggravating, but mostly it was fun listening to the old cronies telling the same tales time and time again. My mother was very well read and always had time for me. I can remember sitting on her knee while she stressed life's most important values to me: going to church every Sunday and belief in God. She impressed upon me that education was supreme, that life was simply a path of learning, and that through our most difficult struggles we learn the most about ourselves.

One of her favorite statements was, "Education travels with you, increases daily, and no one can take it from you, but money, on the other hand, darling, can be here today and gone tomorrow!"

We explored Irish folklore together, fairies, leprechauns, banshees, the Giant's Causeway, and of course much more. Daily I was reminded of that special angel I had watching over me and that I would never come to any harm. As I write this, I think what an enchanted childhood I had; humble, yes, but forever filled with love and a vision that set me on a path of questioning, salivating for more knowledge about the mysticism of the Universe. The cosmos had decided early on to set the stage for my future involvement in the world of metaphysics and the wonderful world of Linda Goodman and astrology.

Growing up, life was very busy. With this strict Christian upbringing and education, I sang in the church choir, was a medical cadet for the St. John's Ambulance Brigade, a girl guide, and an Irish dancer. Each day overflowed with family life, education, and hobbies; there was never a boring moment. Television was a luxury, not a normal appliance in every household as it is today.

When I was about eleven years old and on my way home from school (in those days we walked everywhere; only my brother had the luxury of a car), I was stopped by a very elderly gentleman, probably around seventy years old, maybe older. It was difficult to tell then, and even more difficult on reflection. This elderly man was "a man of the road." I hesitate to call him a tramp, as "tramp" conjures up a vision of someone down and out, dirty and shabbily dressed. Not this old man. I had seen him several times before, maybe once or twice a year on my walks to and from school. He was rather strange looking but in a nice sort of way, and I had no fear of him. When he looked at me it was as though he saw my eyes and then went past them into my soul. He stood straight and tall and wore a long Harris Tweed overcoat, which was in good condition and came almost to his ankles. On his feet he wore what seemed like cowboy boots, most unusual to see in those days in Ireland. He had a beard, which was extremely long—a mixture of white and gray with some yellowish, smoke-stained parts around the mouth—and it came down to his waist, but his eyes were the most captivating aspect of the whole ensemble. They were so special. Today I still have a clear memory of those gentle, smiling, loving eyes, with such depth, wrinkling at the corners, framed by very bushy eyebrows and set in a weather-beaten face.

He chatted to me about school and my studies, gaining my confidence, then he asked me if I would like to know what was going to happen in my lifetime. He said he would like to tell me. He took my hand, held it, and looked into the palm. I think besides reading my palm he was also reading my energy, and I was mesmerized by the concept that someone could tell me such a thing; I listened attentively to his every word. I have repeated this story so many times since that day that I remember all he said clearly, like it was yesterday. He told me that I would finish my education in England, marry, have a family, and spend the first half of my life there. The second half of my life would be spent mostly in America working on something completely different than my chosen path or career. He spoke about other things that I did not know or understand then. However, now I have a greater knowledge and understanding. Today, I believe I was talking to a guru, or an angel, or an avatar— certainly someone very special. If only I had the opportunity to speak to him again today; boy, would I have a lot of questions to ask!

He was so right in prophesying my future; the first half of my life was spent in England, and now I'm here in America working on this very special project: *Linda Goodman's Relationship Signs*.

Linda Goodman's first book, *Sun Signs*, was published in the late 1960s and first grabbed my interest in astrology. In the late 1970s, I treasured Linda's second book, *Love Signs*, which was so in-depth and so accurate about relationships and how the various signs complement one another, it became my bible for relationships and my family's continual reference. During the late eighties I was given *Star Signs* as a Christmas gift. The book was so captivating I could not put it down. Her work on numerology and lexigrams in this book fascinated me. A whole new world of understanding had been opened up for me. I was glued to this book from the moment I started to read it until I finished it, and have continued to refer to it since then. I remember thinking that if only I could meet this lady, if only I could meet Linda Goodman, I could learn so much. The manner in which she wrote was so very special. It wasn't just the phrases and the message contained therein but the extraordinary beauty of her words, the spirit in her every sentence, and the musical way she presented her information—that is what was so unique about Linda. She was a guru. Her writing opened the mind and soul, introducing another arena of learning in a manner that everyone could understand, and with such humor—because relationships are humorous, wouldn't you agree? That was 1987. Sadly, my marriage came to an end, and, in a state of great unhappiness and personal confusion, I threw myself into my career. I was a workaholic trying to keep up a hectic schedule so I would not to have to think, not allowing myself time to reflect, to feel emotions, or to grieve.

However, I thought back to the old man who prophesied so much of what had already happened and wondered if my future was to be in America, though I couldn't see how that could be. I had a successful career. It was most challenging living and working in London, but it had its compensations. However, on a March day in 1992 I was walking from my home in Eaton Place to meet with some clients. The sun was shining, and it was a beautiful, crisp, sunny London day. I raised my face up to the sun to "inhale" it, for we see sun so seldom in London, and a strange thing happened: I looked up at this wonderful ray of gold, soaked in the warmth, and then, as if a realization came over me, I said, "Good-bye, London, the love affair with you is over. I'm going to the States." It took me several months to wind down my affairs and to make that gigantic step to move to America. My three daughters thought I had flipped, but nothing could deter me. I had no idea what I was going to do, I just knew I had to do it—I had to make this change. I would take a year off and see what the Universe would provide. This was a big gamble by all appearances!

Now, I am sure that how I came to meet Linda Goodman is a burning question for all you readers and fans.

My youngest daughter, Kate, one of life's greatest treasures—who, strangely enough, was born on the same day as Linda: April 9—followed me to the States and introduced me to a lady astrologer. Through this introduction I began to look at astrology from a much wider viewpoint: not just my own personal gratification, but how having more direct access to astrologers could assist people in their everyday lives. My plan was to create a live astrological network. Thereafter, I was introduced to a friend of Linda's who was working on the software for what turned out to be her last work, *The Love Signs Profile*. He asked me if I would like to meet the Goddess of Astrology. I replied, "That can only be Linda Goodman." Can you imagine how I felt? I was ecstatic, I was delighted. After all these years of reading this lady's work and wishing I could meet with her, my wish was now granted.

Never underestimate the power of thought, the energy of a wish, when we put it out there.

I was introduced to Linda's manager, Jim McLin, and after I passed that test, he decided that I should have an audience with Lady Linda.

The meeting took place in Cripple Creek, Colorado, 10,000 feet above sea level with the snow-capped mountains in sight. The day was cloudy and cold with the occasional ray of sun breaking through. Linda's house was very warm and cozy, with a log fire burning in the grate and wonderful views overlooking the valleys below. In the living room I noticed that there were many books about Abraham Lincoln. I remember thinking that Linda must be a historian or a Lincoln scholar, besides all her other attributes. However, the story that unfolded much later about this great man and his connection with Linda is truly incredible and shall be told in another book at another time.

Linda's wonderful mountain retreat had all the hallmarks of a somewhat reclusive hideaway. This was understandable, as she needed her space in order to meditate and to channel information for her books. This place was ideal.

Later Linda told me that she spent time daily in meditation in an altar room next to her living room. During my visit there, she showed me how the beautiful stained-glass windows caught the rays of the sun, spreading them throughout the room and creating a heavenly atmosphere through which one expected to see angels appear. Linda had many special moments there. In a place such as this, one would truly be able to take one's meditation to a very profound level.

Initially I was told that Miss Goodman could only allow me one hour of her time, and my appointment was at 10 A.M. We had to travel up the mountain for over three hours, and it was quite a trek, but we arrived on time. The altitude and probably the excitement of at last meeting the lady whose writing I had so enjoyed over the past thirty years was making me headachy. When Linda made her entrance into the living room I was surprised by her petite stature. She was so much smaller than I had imagined—around five feet two inches. How could such a tiny person have so much to offer us in our understanding of one another and our planetary influences?

When we were introduced, she held my hand for a moment and looked deeply into my eyes, and past them and into my soul. Then a smile came across her face and I tried to recall where had I had a similar experience before. Oh yes, I remembered!

She was obviously pleased that I had made the journey to meet her. The meeting was fascinating; my whole body was filled with that fresh excitement one gets when one fulfills a dream and achieves something one thought would be impossible. Here I was at last, in the presence of this great knowledge.

We talked and talked, though Linda did most of the talking. She laughed a bit, and twirled her hair as she talked. We forgot about the time, we forgot about lunch, we forgot about everything else. Sometimes she'd sit cross-legged, at other times she'd simply curl up on the chair, using her hands to express or emphasize a particular point. The hours passed by (maybe it was finbar time, as mentioned in her book *Star Signs*), and finally the warmth of the room, the early start to the day, and the altitude caught up with me. It was approaching 6 P.M., and my headache had developed into a full-blown migraine. With an arduous three-hour journey down the mountain still ahead of me, I was thankful that I had Jim there to drive me back to my hotel. We said our good-byes and I made my way down the mountain, with so many thoughts swirling around in my head. This was an incredible experience, a once-in-a-lifetime event and the beginning of several years of friendship and lengthy daily chats with a wonderful teacher, a master, in our time.

Much later Jim told me of a conversation he had with her the day after that meeting. Linda told Jim that she knew who I was within the first two minutes. Perhaps that knowledge was why the meeting was allowed to continue so long. She agreed to work with me on what turned out to be her last project: the contents of this book. Although she was working on several projects at the same time, Linda really wished to be known to the world as a poet, and her wonderful book of prose, *Gooberz*, a story of love, life, and beyond, is certainly proof that she was just that. One of her greatest wishes was also to write simplified astrology books for children.

Her last request was that I and I alone should be responsible for her name and image throughout the world. This is a very humbling experience for me; having someone with her great insight, her great knowledge and incredible gift with words, which have helped so many people, entrust all that she has created to me, is a big responsibility. I shall endeavor to live up to her expectations.

Linda wrote a brief note to me a few days before she died. The contents of that note thanked me for the miracles and reminded me once again of this responsibility.

So enjoy reading Linda's last works, her last love affair with the typewriter, and let's take that final journey together.

This is her last gift to you!

— CRYSTAL

The
Planets

we've fought a long and bitter war, my Twin Self and I
lost and lonely, fallen angels—exiled
from a misty, long-forgotten Oober galaxy of stars

caught in Neptune's tangled web
wounded cruelly by the painful thrust of Mars
tortured by the clever lies of Mercury

shocked and nearly torn asunder
by Vulcan's distant, raging thunder
shattered by the lightning
of the sudden, awful violence of Uranus

crushed beneath the weight of stern, unyielding
Saturn
who lengthened every hour into a day . . .
each day into a year
each year . . . into millenniums of waiting

scorched by the Sun's exploding bursts of
pride as those wandering angels, stilled and
helpless deep within us, cried
still we fought on, in unrelenting fury
striking blow for blow

driven by the pounding drums of Jupiter's giant,
throbbing passions
stumbling at the precipice of the Moon's enticing
madness

to fall, at last, in trembling fear
before the ominous threat of Pluto's tomb-like silence
consumed by inconsolable sadness
and the bleakness of despair

we bear . . .

the wounds and scars of furious battle,
my Twin Self and I

but now we walk in quiet peace . . . with all our
scattered pieces whole
together, hand-in-hand . . . full serpent circle
back into the pyramid-shaped rainbow of tomorrow's
brighter Eden
crowned by gentle Venus with the Victory of Love

that did not die, but has survived
the night of selfish seeking

to wait for morning's soft forgiveness

and the dawn of understanding

—FROM *GOOBERZ*, BY
LINDA GOODMAN

Linda Goodman's
Relationship Signs

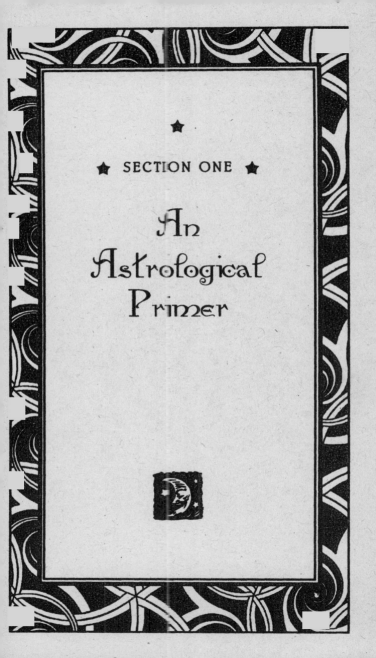

★

★ SECTION ONE ★

An
Astrological
Primer

★

★ 1 ★

How to Use This Book

We are going to make this book simple to understand, like all of Linda's work. While Linda's report is complex and the conclusions a culmination of Linda's genius, *you don't have to know a thing about astrology to figure out your chart, the chart of your lover or loved one, and your relationship comparison.*

All the work has been done for you. Just write down your birthday (month, day, year, and time) and the birthday (month, day, year, and time) of the person for whom you want a relationship reading. Everything else you'll need to create your own personal astrological charts is in this book.

In no time at all, you'll become your own instant astrologer. And you won't feel like a novice for long, because after a few relationship comparisons you'll recognize the Doodles, i.e. the signs, the planets, and the aspects, and you'll know what they mean to you and your relationships. Section One of this book is an astrological primer on these basics. Read through it if you are unfamiliar with any part of the charting process. To begin your comparison charts, turn to Section Two: How to Chart Your Relationship.

Most importantly, have fun uncovering the mysteries of your closest relationships.

★

★ 2 ★

What Is Astrology?

Astrology is the study of man in relation to celestial bodies or, to be precise, the planets. It is a system of thought that attempts to show a relationship between man and all things.

Long ago, about 10,000 B.C., hunters noted the phases of the moon by carving notches on reindeer horns. Of all the many things I have read about the history of astrology, I find this the most fascinating.

Why? Because it tells the story of ancient man, who lived without maps, telescopes, and sophisticated equipment. He is trying to plan his life, to get in tune with the environment and in harmony with nature.

The caveman understands that there is a relationship among all parts of nature: animal, human, vegetable, and celestial. He has to find a tool to help him know when to plant, when to hunt, how to understand the cycles of cause and effect — or he won't survive.

He records the phases of the moon for predictive astrology. He times harvest cycles and, as he evolves, he translates these findings to help him live in harmony: man to animal, husband to wife, and physical beings to spiritual beings.

Perhaps these notches were used for more than hunting information. Much like our popular astrology columns today, these same moon positions could have given early man daily answers about life and his surroundings from the patterns of the Moon, Sun, and stars.

WHAT IS ASTROLOGY? 5

Looking to the skies, our navigator ancestors could have foreseen the ebbing of the tides, and our hunter ancestors could have foreseen the phases of the moon and the patterns of the herds.

If man was aware of the Moon phases, he also, no doubt, noticed the likelihood of a rising birthrate with the full Moon (drawn with a circle) or in the month of September.

The increasing Moon could have been drawn like the "right-hand Moon," as it is known. This can be symbolized by curving the index finger and thumb on the right hand to create a crescent. Could early man have noticed the chance for happier unions at this time?

The decreasing Moon and the "left-hand Moon" symbol also signify changes. Did man observe and record that as the moon gets smaller, the sap in trees shrinks and enables easier cutting and faster drying?

Today, with advanced technology that the ancients could not comprehend, we ask the same questions the man of 10,000 B.C. asked: (1) "When is the best time to undertake major business decisions?" What was hunting, planting, and harvesting is now profits, losses, and business ventures. (2) "How can we live more harmoniously with one another?" What were neighboring tribes and villages have become networks of people and relationships.

Did early man acknowledge the blueprint in the skies, enabling him to understand his environment and kinship with his tribes? We can only guess, but one thing remains clear: Early man's relationship to the skies was acknowledged, utilized, and communicated.

Not too different from our own daily horoscopes, is it?

So the use of astrology is old. Very old, in fact.

What Is a Birth Chart?

Man's conception of the Universe is both physical and mystical. In order for man to visualize the sky and the planets within it, he views it as a circle. This celestial circle, like any other, consists of 360 degrees. The planets are located within this celestial circle.

In astrology, we also use a circle — 360 degrees — to diagram the position of the planets, and we call this circle a birth chart. How the planets influence your life depends on where they fall in your birth chart. Each planet is drawn in a specific place in this chart to represent its location at the time you were born. Where you were born also affects the position of the planets in your chart. Therefore, a birth chart is unique to each individual.

For us to interpret our birth charts, we needed to be able to describe where the planets were in the chart, and what their positions meant. An order had to be created that everyone could use. So the 360 degrees of the birth chart were divided into twelve equal parts, called houses. Each house corresponds to one of the twelve signs of the zodiac, depending on your time of birth. And each house governs a different area of your life, like family, finances, or relationships.

This order works for each and every one of us, which goes back to astrology being a system of thought. Astrology is very well organized.

How Does the Movement of the Planets Affect Us?

The word planets comes from the Greek word *planes*, which means "the wanderer." Planets roam around the sky in different directions and through different zodiac signs. As the planets move and rotate, their energies change and affect us on earth. Man reacts to these vibrations, just as plants are sensitive to the Sun's movement from morning to afternoon.

We can see examples of how cosmic rhythms are linked with man and his body. We know that our body temperature changes from night to day, and that seasonal changes assist us in planting in spring and gathering in fall. We know that human beings need sunlight for vitamin D. And we know that some of us get depressed when winter dulls the sun's rays. All the planets work their energies on us in different ways, but with the same principle. It is part of man's relationship with nature.

Are the Signs of the Zodiac the Same as the Signs of the Constellations?

Astrologers use the signs of the zodiac, not the signs of the constellations, when they talk about the positions of the planets.

I only tell you this because there is an age-old debate about astrologers being one sign off — which astronomers bring up when they want to pick a fight. So if you just happen to be talking to an astronomer and you say, "I am a Capricorn," he or she will no doubt want to inform you that you were born under the constellation of Sagittarius. You can agree. You are both right, but about two different things.

Until about 200 A.D., the Earth was considered the center of our solar system, rather than the Sun. Then increased mathematical understanding brought new insights about the paths of the Earth and Sun. Because the constellations are part of the fixed stars, their positions in the new map of the heavens were affected by this shift: They ended up a sign away from their original positions.

But astrology is based on the movement of the planets, so astrologers' interpretations were unaffected by the discovery. The meaning of the signs of the zodiac remained unchanged.

So you are still a Capricorn. But you *were* born under the sign of Sagittarius.

What Are Aspects?

Aspects are the mathematical degrees that describe where one planet is in relation to another and, therefore, how their energies are interacting. They tell us the difference between a good and a not-so-good day. They also tell us whom we get along with best, least, and whom we love regardless, so what next?

Aspects are favorable when: the planets are in the same signs (conjunction), two signs — 60° — from one another (sextile), or four signs — 120° — from one another (trine). Aspects are harder to deal with when: the planets are three signs — 90° — apart (square) or six signs — 180° — away from one another (opposition).

So if a good planet like Jupiter is in the fifth house of speculation and makes a good aspect (like a trine) to another favorable planet, it could be time to buy that lottery ticket. That's how aspects work.

And I can't say this enough: Jupiter is one of the good planets and it is doing something nice every day. So no matter how bad the rest of the aspects are on a certain day, Jupiter is there to give you faith, luck, and hope. And if you are like me, there have been days when you've had to focus on the good just to keep believing.

So you remember, if you ever get a negative reading from an astrologer (and a good one won't give one, by the way), just say, "Yeah, well what about Jupiter?"

Okay, What Next?

Now that you've been given an overview of how astrology works, you are ready to move on to the symbols, the tables — and how to chart your own relationship dynamics.

★
★ 3 ★

An Introduction to Symbology

Signs	Planets	Aspects
♈ Aries	☉ Sun	☌ Conjunction
♉ Taurus	☽ Moon	⚹ Sextile
♊ Gemini	☿ Mercury	△ Trine
♋ Cancer	♀ Venus	□ Square
♌ Leo	♂ Mars	☍ Opposition
♍ Virgo	♃ Jupiter	
♎ Libra	♄ Saturn	
♏ Scorpio	♅ Uranus	
♐ Sagittarius	♆ Neptune	
♑ Capricorn	♇ or ♇ Pluto	
♒ Aquarius		
♓ Pisces		

★

★ 4 ★

The Twelve Zodiac
Signs and Doodles

There are twelve signs in your astrological chart. These signs look like doodles or hieroglyphics. They are picture symbols. Astrologers call them glyphs. Each of the following glyphs represents an astrological sign.

The Astrological Doodles and the Zodiac Signs

Aries	♈	The Ram's Horns Fire Sign
Taurus	♉	The Bull's Horns Earth Sign
Gemini	♊	Roman Numeral Two The Sign of the Twins Air Sign
Cancer	♋	The Crab Water Sign
Leo	♌	The Lion's Mane Fire Sign

Virgo	♍	An M with a downward slash (/) The Sign of the Virgin Earth Sign
Libra	♎	The Balance Scales A long, flat loop with a line under it Air Sign
Scorpio	♏	The Scorpion *Be careful — This looks like Virgo, but Virgo ends in a downward slash (/). The Scorpio symbol has a stinging arrow. Water Sign
Sagittarius	♐	The Archer's Arrow Fire Sign
Capricorn	♑	The Goat with a fish tail — or a V with an S beside it for "Very Sturdy" Earth Sign
Aquarius	♒	The Water Bearer Two sets of squiggles on top of each other like ripples of water Air Sign
Pisces	♓	Two Fishes Water Sign

What Is a Sun Sign?

A Sun Sign is a particular zone of the zodiac — Aries, Taurus, Gemini, etc. — in which the Sun was located at the moment you drew your first breath, an exact position taken from a set of tables called an ephemeris, calculated by astronomers.

The Sun is the most powerful of all the stellar bodies. It colors the personality so strongly that an amazingly accurate picture can be given of the individual who was born when it was exercising its power through the known and predictable influences of a certain astrological sign. These electromagnetic vibrations (for want of a better term in the present stage of research) will continue to stamp a person with the characteristics of his or her Sun Sign as he or she goes through life. The Sun isn't the only factor in analyzing human behavior and traits, but it is easily the most important single consideration.*

Most people are familiar with the signs of the zodiac because they know their Sun Sign. Won't it be fun to find out what sign all your other planets are in.

The Astrological Elements and the Four Temperaments

Fire	Earth	Air	Water
Aries	Taurus	Gemini	Cancer
Leo	Virgo	Libra	Scorpio
Sagittarius	Capricorn	Aquarius	Pisces

The concept of the four elements has been used by early cosmologies to describe the basic building blocks of all organic life. Astrologically, we use the same principle to describe the four "elements" of man. As mentioned earlier, each sign of the zodiac is ruled by one of the temperaments. See the chart above.

We acknowledge the four elements every day in our slang:

"She's so practical and down to earth."
"He's the salt of the earth."
"She's an airhead."
"You know what they say about still waters."
"She's the fiery redhead."

* By Linda Goodman — extract from *Sun Signs*.

The Fire Element or Temperament

This element relates to the active, vital energies. These are the independent spirits, the pioneers, the more aggressive temperaments.

The Earth Element or Temperament

This element relates to the real, the tangible, the physical, and things of value. These are the practical, cautious, plodding, and persistent temperaments.

The Air Element or Temperament

This element relates to the social, mental, and often restless energies. These are the logical, friendly, versatile, and communicative temperaments.

The Water Element or Temperament

This element relates to the intuitive, feeling, emotional energies. These are the ever-changing, impressionable, and often mysterious temperaments.

5

The Planetary Symbols and What They Say About Themselves

Each of These Glyphs Represents a Planet

Sun	☉	Jupiter	♃
Moon	☽	Saturn	♄
Mercury	☿	Uranus	♅
Venus	♀	Neptune	♆
Mars	♂	Pluto	♇

The Sun and Moon are called planets, although we all know they are not. They are luminaries. But they are so important to us that they seem like planets. The eleventh "planet" is not a planet but a point in time based on the moment of our birth. It is considered of third importance in our charts, after the Sun and Moon. This is called our Ascendant or our Rising Sign. The Rising Sign always appears in the first house on an individual's chart, as shown on the following page. This will be explained more fully on page 33. Tables for determining your rising sign begin on page 207.

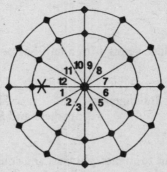

☉

The Sun
A Circle with a Dot in the Center

Rules
Physical Force, Life Force, Character

Reveals
The Father, Males in General, The Masculine Side of Woman

"I represent the life force and the physical body, and I am at the center of everybody's chart. What sign are you? Or what *Sun* are you? The dot is to remind you to try to keep yourself centered. Life forces need to be centered, not off kilter or misplaced."

☽

The Moon
A Crescent Symbol

Rules
Emotions, Empathy, Receptivity in Subconscious Needs

Reveals
The Mother, Women in General, The Feminine Side of Man

"I represent emotional needs. And I am changeable. Sometimes I have more needs than at other times. I am drawn like a crescent, but in a chart I can be a sliver or a full Moon, depending on how much attention I need."

☿
Mercury
Mercury looks like Venus with a half-hat on the top.

Rules   **Reveals**
Mental Activity, Intelligence,   Short Journeys,
Reasoning and   Brothers and Sisters, Studies
Communication

"I represent the thoughts, phrases, and sounds of the way you speak. I am the way you talk to your lover, inspired by your unique astrological planetary aspects."

♀
Venus
A Circle with a Cross Underneath

Rules .   **Reveals**
Love, Marriage, Attraction   Our Capacity for Love,
                                                      Beauty and Harmony

"I represent the colors, sound, music, and varieties of love. I also am there to provide you with smooth sailing through the stormy seas of life. I bring beauty and blessing."

♂
Mars
An Arrow with a Circle on the Bottom

Rules   **Reveals**
Energy, Physical   How We Act Out Our Sexual
Stamina,   Impulses, Passion and Challenges,
Motivation   Sexual Expression in Men

"I represent your physical energy, how you act and react."

♃
Jupiter
A Big Fat 4

Rules	**Reveals**
Benefits, Good Future, Expansive Ideas, Social Adaptation	Personal Ethics, Philosophies, Personal Growth

"I represent the promise of all good things. I am your good luck charm. I am always there in your chart to give you something nice, even when the going is rough, and to remind you that you are never forsaken."

♄
Saturn
A Tall 7 with a Hat on the Top
Saturn is also drawn as a cross with a half-circle on the bottom.

Rules	**Reveals**
Careers, Philosophies, Personal Growth, Public Recognition	Sense of Responsibility, Loyalties, Commitment to Family, Stability

WHY DID I DREAM OF SATURN LAST NIGHT?

Yes, why Saturn?
the stern, stony and silent
planet of Karma
of death and discipline
Why did I dream of ... Saturn?
In the few brief hours I am able to sleep
why are my restless dreams about Saturn?
Saturn does not bring reprieve....

When I first learned to draw
the astrological symbol of Saturn

stern, stony, silent planet
I found a trick, so I wouldn't forget
how to draw it
What was that
Saturn symbol drawing trick?

Oh yes, I remember!
now I remember
you just draw the figure seven — you draw a 7
then you make it taller — like this
and then you take the taller 7 ... being now
and place upon it, a small hat
like that!
7,7 taller   then a hat   like that!
and you have it:
... the symbol for Saturn

— FROM *GOOBERZ,* BY
LINDA GOODMAN

Like the rest of us, Linda had to have a beginning in astrology. She had to learn the symbols too. And she left this poem to help us remember the symbol for Saturn.

♅
Uranus
An H with a Line Through the Middle, Then a Circle on the Bottom

Rules	Reveals
Ability to Experiment, Innovate, and Change; Sudden and Unexpected	Our Reckless Side, Where We Seek Our Thrills, Our Eccentricities

"I represent the planet of change. I come in and make electrifying, sweeping changes. I am the rock-and-roll of your chart. I am always unplanned and uninvited. But I am not unpleasant unless you try to resist me totally."

Ψ
Neptune
A Fork with a Cross at the Bottom

Rules	**Reveals**
Illusions, Imagination,	Romantic Side,
Vision, Misconceptions,	Romantic Fantasies,
and Fantasies	Where We Can Be Deceived,
	Where We Like to Escape

"I am the planet of deception. Sometimes I bring confusion and mix-ups. Sometimes I tell lies or try to trick you. I can bring dreams and illusions. Everybody needs me for a little magic sometimes. Imagine life served straight up; what you see is what you get. Sometimes we all need rose-colored glasses. Yes, that's it: I prefer to be considered rose-colored glasses."

♀ ♇
Pluto
A Cross with a Fat Half-Circle on Top to Support a Full Circle on Top of That. Or a Capital P with a Foot — Nice and Direct

Rules	**Reveals**
Transformation,	Rejuvenation, Crisis,
Our Ability to Reinvent	Beginnings and Endings
Ourselves,	
Subconscious Drives and	
Forces, Change	

"Hello, I am Pluto and I am here to change your life. Wherever I land in your chart is what I tear down to rebuild. I am here for your ultimate good, or at least try to be, if you will not resist my energies. I am the planet of life and death, of the new you and the old you. I repair and resurrect. I cause you to reinvent yourself every now and then."

★

★ **6** ★

Aspect Symbols: The Last of the Astrological Doodles

Each of these glyphs is used to represent a mathematical degree that shows how far apart two planets are, and how harmonious things are between two or more people.

Conjunction (planets are in same sign) ☌
Sextile (planets are 60° apart) ✳
Trine (planets are 120° apart) △
Square (planets are 90° apart) ☐
Opposition (planets are 180° apart) ☍

☌ Conjunction: The conjunction looks like an exclamation point gone astray. It's a positive, reinforcing aspect. It's two planets, or signs, almost smack dab on top of each other.

✳ Sextile: The sextile looks like a snowflake, or an asterisk. It's a good thing to have in your chart.

△ Trine: The trine looks like a triangle. It's considered lucky. Very lucky. It promises great things. Sometimes, though, it makes people take each other for granted in relationships.

☐ Square: The square looks like, well, a square. It represents energies that do not flow easily. It's hard to deal with. But don't be misled. Squares can create great things if you work on them.

♂ Opposition: The opposition looks like two circles on a slash. The opposition is considered challenging. Relationships between people with a lot of opposition are frequently at odds. However, this is the romance of "opposites attract."

The Conjunction   ♂

A conjunction is when a planet in your chart is in the same sign as another person's planet. See the chart wheel below.

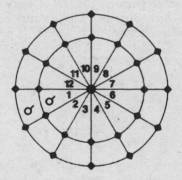

When the planets are this close, their energies intensify. If two people have planets that are conjunct in the sign of Pisces, for example, you have twice the sensitivity and introversion in the relationship. Your personalities reflect like a mirror or a pool of shimmery water. Your relationship can be intuitive, and you'll often read each other's minds.

If the two planets are in the sign of Cancer, the relationship can become as changeable as the weather — sunny one minute and cold the next — and even dark like the dark side of the Moon.

When you stress the positive side of the doubled energies, you find couples who can accomplish the near impossible, activate and energize each other, and understand each other without words.

If you are a Sagittarius and your partner's Sun is in the first house in the same sign, you have conjunct Suns. Knowing this, you can refer to the "Sun Aspects" pages in Section Two and understand more about your relationship with this person. To help you master the process of reading aspects, I have set up examples with our very own Romeo and Juliet, Ryan and Maria. See Maria's Pluto conjunct Ryan's Venus in their comparison charts on page 41.

The Sextile ✳

The sextile occurs when a planet in your chart is two signs away from another person's planet, or sixty degrees (each house contains thirty degrees). This is considered favorable. See the chart wheel below.

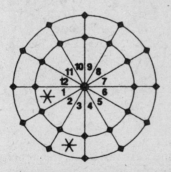

While the sextile is not as powerful as the conjunction, it is complementary. The planets in sextile become partners and cooperate. I think of the sextile as friendly, helpful energy. Wherever the energies unite, it creates a certain harmony.

With a sextile between the Aries Sun and the Gemini Sun, for example, there will be a joint effort to produce ideas and find new outlets for creative expression.

Sextiles require a little work, for their energies are not as strong as some of the other aspects.

If you have the Moon in Capricorn and your person of comparison has the Moon in Pisces, you have a Moon sextile. They are two signs apart. There is a sextile between Ryan's Venus in Virgo and Maria's Venus in Scorpio (page 41). Here, Linda says that "the two of you tend to express affection in the same way, and there are probably few differences between you when it comes to your social lives and cultural interests. You will agree most of the time about spending or saving money."

Other sextiles:

Aries is sextile Gemini and Aquarius.
Taurus is sextile Cancer and Pisces.
Gemini is sextile Leo and Aries.
Cancer is sextile Virgo and Taurus.
Leo is sextile Libra and Gemini.
Virgo is sextile Cancer and Scorpio.
Libra is sextile Sagittarius and Leo.
Sagittarius is sextile Libra and Aquarius.
Capricorn is sextile Scorpio and Pisces.
Aquarius is sextile Aries and Sagittarius.
Pisces is sextile Taurus and Capricorn.

The Trine   △

Trines occur when a planet in your chart is four signs away from another person's planet. Since each house contains 30 degrees, you count to 120. Example: From Aries Sun it's 30 degrees to Taurus, 60 to Gemini, 90 to Cancer, and 120 to Leo. Aries Sun trines Leo Sun or planets. See the chart on the next page for reference.

This configuration is viewed as a lazy one. Its energies come so easily; where is the challenge and growth?

For example, if the trine is created by a Virgo Sun and Capricorn Sun, you find that business matters often come to fortunate solutions without the usual work and worry involved. Success is usually a by-product of this configuration.

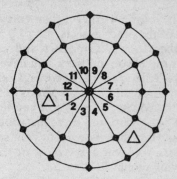

For a trine example, see Maria's and Ryan's charts on page 41. Maria's Saturn in Aries trines Ryan's Leo Sun (four signs away).

Other trines:

Aries is trine Leo and Sagittarius.
Taurus is trine Virgo and Capricorn.
Gemini is trine Libra and Aquarius.
Cancer is trine Scorpio and Pisces.
Leo is trine Sagittarius and Aries.
Virgo is trine Capricorn and Taurus.
Libra is trine Aquarius and Gemini.
Scorpio is trine Pisces and Cancer.
Sagittarius is trine Aries and Leo.
Capricorn is trine Taurus and Virgo.
Aquarius is trine Gemini and Libra.
Pisces is trine Cancer and Scorpio.

The Square   □

A Square occurs when a planet in your chart is three signs away from another person's planet. Squares box us in. They tend to create energy blocks and make you feel at odds. See the chart wheel on the next page.

This configuration is considered difficult and conflicting, and the strife is often not as outward as it is inward.

For example, if the square is created by a Taurus Sun and

Leo Sun, there might be conflicts over money and power. Neither person can rest with this situation until one or the other accepts it for what it is.

On the positive side, it can teach us to adjust or limit, and to accept restrictions.

On page 41, you can see that Ryan's moon in Taurus squares Maria's Mars in Aquarius.

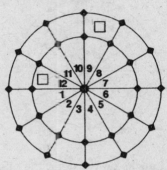

Other squares:

Aries is squared to Cancer and Capricorn.
Taurus is squared to Leo and Aquarius.
Gemini is squared to Pisces and Virgo.
Cancer is squared to Aries and Libra.
Leo is squared to Taurus and Scorpio.
Virgo is squared to Gemini and Sagittarius.
Libra is squared to Cancer and Capricorn.
Scorpio is squared to Aquarius and Leo.
Sagittarius is squared to Virgo and Pisces.
Capricorn is squared to Aries and Libra.
Aquarius is squared to Scorpio and Taurus.
Pisces is squared to Sagittarius and Gemini.

The Opposition ☍

The opposition occurs when a planet in your chart is six signs away from another person's planet. These are 180 degrees apart, and this is considered stressful and challenging. See the chart wheel on the following page.

Opposites attract. Opposites can be mirror images. In relationship charts oppositions lead to challenges. You know about opposites. You have nothing in common, see everything differently, and can't get enough of one another. That's an opposition.

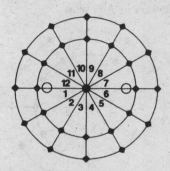

If the square knocks on the door, the opposition breaks the door down. The energies of opposition are more intensified and demanding. The opposition is usually associated with outward rather than inward conflicts. This aspect requires action.

If, for example, you have a Libra/Aries opposition aspect in your own individual chart, you express the dilemma of being on your own versus being joined at the hip with another person. You view relationships as either/or. An opposition reminds us to look at both sides and learn the art of compromise.

For an opposition, see Maria's and Ryan's charts on page 41. Maria's Scorpio Venus is opposite Ryan's Taurus Moon. Other oppositions:

Aries is opposite Libra.
Taurus is opposite Scorpio.
Gemini is opposite Sagittarius.
Cancer is opposite Capricorn.
Leo is opposite Aquarius.
Virgo is opposite Pisces.

★
★ 7 ★

An Overview of Harmony – and Disharmony

Harmonious Combinations

Aries	*Taurus*	*Gemini*	*Cancer*
Leo	*Virgo*	*Libra*	*Scorpio*
Sagittarius	*Capricorn*	*Aquarius*	*Pisces*

When planets are harmonious, they create mutual understanding between people, the likelihood of happiness, and ease in relationships. This influence inclines toward mutual interests, shared goals, and, most often, a comfortable home. Planets that are harmonious are the least likely to promote critical misunderstandings. Disagreements are settled with simple adjustments and compromises. Matters are usually resolved readily and without a lot of fuss and hidden agendas. This harmonious flow of trines and sextiles, or favorable energies, seems to attract equally shared relationships where the balance of power is good and each helps the other succeed in all endeavors. All conjunctions add emotional sensitivity and a very strong bond of affection between the two people involved.

Disharmonious Combinations

Aries	*Gemini*	*Taurus*
Cancer	*Virgo*	*Leo*
Libra	*Sagittarius*	*Scorpio*
Capricorn	*Pisces*	*Aquarius*

When planets are disharmonious, they create more confrontation and there is less likelihood of an easy relationship. These individuals are at odds. Feelings, when injured, can create combative situations, and solutions are more complex and less straightforward. These couples usually have dissimilar tastes, interests, and characters. Because of the basic differences, quarrels are often long lasting and estrangements are more frequent than with the more favorable aspects and energies. Yet there is the potential for two strong-willed individuals to force each other to look at things from a different perspective and create both positive change and growth for each person.

Why do the aspects tend to create harmonious or disharmonious energies? Because when planets are in the same signs, or compatible signs, we are similar to one another or have an innate understanding of each other.

Have you ever met someone you feel you have known forever? This is most often because there is an easy flow of communication or the two of you tend to "think alike," "feel like twins," or otherwise feel an instant knowing and attraction. These people are familiar to you at some subconscious level. Things just feel right between you, and you tend to think that because of the likeness of the past, your futures can be brighter together. And, in most cases, this turns out to be true.

Or have you ever met someone for whom you had an instant dislike? You can't relate to this person, you two have nothing in common, and you seem to be at cross-purposes in life. Sometimes we meet people who are "opposites" of us, just like our astrological opposites. We know they are all wrong for us and yet we can't seem to resist them.

The disharmonious energies are harder to work with and yet can certainly make for interesting, challenging, and very romantic relationships just the same. Think of the great stuff of romantic novels where the heroine can't stand the hero and yet finds him irresistible. Over time they make adjustments, learn to appreciate their differences, and manage to live happily ever after. It won't come easy. But then don't we tend to appreciate most the things we work the hardest for?

The harmonies of love aspects are important, and they are one of the many tools you can use in life to assist your relationships. But keep in mind, as Linda says, that "love can conquer all."

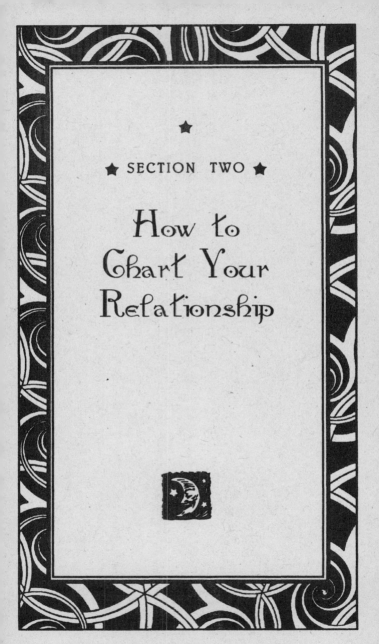

★

★ SECTION TWO ★

How to Chart Your Relationship

★

★ 1 ★

How to Begin

Step One: The Ascendant or Rising Sign

Using the blank charts on page 49, write your Ascendant or Rising Sign next to the first house (or piece of pie #1). You might want to take a look at the example comparison charts of Ryan and Maria on page 41 before you get started. Each of the houses (piece of pie) on the chart is identified by the number in the center of the chart.

If you do not know your Ascendant or Rising Sign, follow the directions on page 207.

Only by having your chart done by a professional astrologer can you get the precise degrees of your Rising Sign; however, these tables are usually accurate.

The Ascendant or Rising Sign is the sign of the zodiac that was above your birth location at the time of your birth.

The Rising Sign is the beginning point of the astrological chart and is considered one of the three most important factors in determining the entire focus of the horoscope. The other two are the zodiac position of the Sun, or your Sun Sign, and the zodiac position of the Moon on the day you were born. The Rising Sign represents the way we approach life, how we meet its challenges, and how we express ourselves to others. While our Sun Sign represents our basic character, the Ascendant or Rising Sign is the active manifestation of this persona.

Do you rush headlong into life like the Aries rising? Are

you sensitive and ever changing like Cancer? Or dramatic and glamorous like the Leo rising?

If two persons' Ascendants are in the same sign, you often deal with matters in a similar fashion.

If the Rising Signs are in square or opposition to each other, you find your approaches radically different and often disharmonious. The opposition aspect, however, will in some cases act like mirror opposites (see Section Two: "Linda Goodman's Interpretations of Your Relationship Aspects"). And that can be ultimately complementary.

When the Rising Signs trine or sextile, there is a basic harmony and a wonderful feeling of togetherness, understanding, and support.

With a conjunction (when two Ascendants are in the same sign), there is a wondrous harmony, sameness, and often very karmic feelings of knowing each other without words. Things happen to each of you that are similar when you are not even near one another.

The Rising Sign is the starting place for understanding the people in your life, whether lovers or friends. To understand more about what your Rising Sign means, refer to "Rising Signs for Men" and "Rising Signs for Women" in Section Three, "The Rising Sign." The Rising Sign profiles can also give quick insights into the other people in your life, as well.

Step Two: The Twelve Houses

Fill in the rest of the signs counterclockwise next to the rest of the houses, remembering that the order of the signs is permanently fixed. The order of the Signs is always Aries, Taurus, Gemini, Cancer, Leo, Virgo, Libra, Scorpio, Sagittarius, Capricorn, Aquarius, and Pisces.

So if you have Sagittarius in the first house, you will have Capricorn in the second, Aquarius in the third, Pisces in the fourth, Aries in the fifth, etc., around the rest of the circle, according to the order of the signs.

The astrological houses divide the 360-degree circle into twelve houses. Each house represents a Department of Life. Here is a list of all the houses (or pieces of pie) and which area or life each one rules:

First House

This house is the Ascendant. It contains the Rising Sign, or the zodiac sign, on the horizon at the time of your birth. This is the house of your personality, the way you present yourself to the world, and your physical appearance. This house begins your astrological chart, and the houses move counterclockwise from this starting point.

Second House

This house rules your possessions, finances, and how you handle money.

Third House

This house rules short-distance travel, correspondence, communications and studies, and neighbors and relatives, such as cousins, brothers, and sisters.

Fourth House

This house rules your environment, home, and the mother.

Fifth House

This house rules creative ideas, romance, speculation and amusements, recreation, children, and sex.

Sixth House

This house rules your service to others, your work and daily routine, and is your house of health.

Seventh House

This house rules marriage and partnerships; it is where the first house merges with the world and you become more public. Here you find your spouse and business partner.

Eighth House

This house rules joint finances, taxes, inheritances, your partner's money (whether business or marriage partner). The finances of other people and how you handle them are also found here. This also rules sex or bonding of a spiritual nature.

Ninth House

This house rules long-distance travel, religion, ethics, and your in-laws.

Tenth House

This house looks like noon on a clock. It is called the Midheaven, and it rules your career, your standing in the community, and your social status. It also refers to the father.

Eleventh House

This house rules friends, hopes, and wishes. It also represents associations.

Twelfth House

This house rules secrets, confinements, subconscious thinking, and restrictions.

Step Three: Begin a Chart for Your Person of Comparison

Once you have completed Step Two, take a breath, pat yourself on the back, and start thinking about the comparison chart. You will need to do the same thing for your person of comparison in the outer ring of the circle.

Remember to start with his or her Rising Sign. It doesn't have to be the same as yours and most probably isn't.

Step Four: Look up Your Planets

Everything you need is in the tables starting on page 249. Write down the position of the planets and those of your person of comparison on the worksheets provided. Then fill them in in the appropriate sign on the chart you have already labeled. You'll want to draw your planet symbols in the inner ring, to leave room for your comparison.

To review the signs, let's look at the symbols one last time before you start your own relationship charts.

Aries	♈	Taurus	♉	Gemini	♊	Cancer	♋
Leo	♌	Virgo	♍	Libra	♎	Scorpio	♏
Sagittarius	♐	Capricorn	♑	Aquarius	♒	Pisces	♓

For practice, we'll use Ryan and Maria for our relationship example. Let's start with Maria's planets. Maria was born at 12:36 P.M. on December 15, 1967.

The Sun is in Sagittarius.	☉	♐
The Moon is in Gemini.	☽	♊
Mercury is in Sagittarius.	☿	♐
Venus is in Scorpio.	♀	♏
Mars is in Aquarius.	♂	♒
Jupiter is in Virgo.	♃	♍
Saturn is in Aries.	♄	♈
Uranus is in Virgo.	♅	♍
Neptune is in Scorpio.	♆	♏
Pluto is in Virgo.	♇	♍
Ascendant is Pisces*	ASC.	♓

---

* We can see in our Ascendant tables (p. 211) that the Ascendant was in Pisces from 11:45 A.M. to 12:54 P.M. on December 15th.

Reader Worksheet

Name: _Maria_

The Sun was in _Sagittarius_

The Moon was in _Gemini_

Mercury was in _Sagittarius_

Venus was in _Scorpio_

Mars was in _Aquarius_

Jupiter was in _Virgo_

Saturn was in _Aries_

Uranus was in _Virgo_

Neptune was in _Scorpio_

Pluto was in _Virgo_

The Ascendant or Rising Sign was _Pisces_

Ryan was born at 11:30 A.M. on August 18, 1965. Ryan's Planets run thus:

The Sun is in Leo.	☉ ♌
The Moon is in Taurus.	☽ ♉
Mercury is in Leo.	☿ ♌
Venus is in Virgo.	♀ ♍
Mars is in Libra.	♂ ♎
Jupiter is in Gemini.	♃ ♊
Saturn is in Pisces.	♄ ♓
Uranus is in Virgo.	♅ ♍
Neptune is in Scorpio.	♆ ♏
Pluto is in Virgo.	♇ ♍
Ascendant is Libra.*	ASC. ♎

Just for fun, I took a quick peek at their Ascendants, and I think they are going to have nice relationship signs.

Ryan is popular and has a strong sense of honor about him, according to his rising profile on page 227. This works really well for Maria, who will stand by her man when he loses his job or his car, but not if he loses his self-respect. And Maria is very feminine (with Pisces Rising), which is something every Libra Rising man looks for in a woman.

* See p. 215 for Ryan's Ascendant table.

Reader Worksheet

Name _Ryan_

The Sun was in _Leo_

The Moon was in _Taurus_

Mercury was in _Leo_

Venus was in _Virgo_

Mars was in _Libra_

Jupiter was in _Gemini_

Saturn was in _Pisces_

Uranus was in _Virgo_

Neptune was in _Scorpio_

Pluto was in _Virgo_

The Ascendant or Rising Sign was _Libra_

Comparison Charts

Name *Maria*

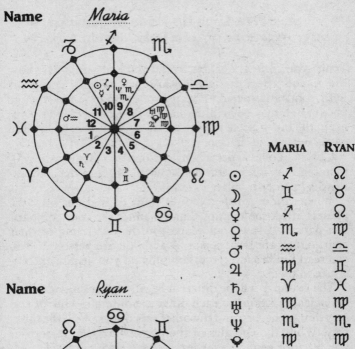

	MARIA	RYAN
☉	♐	♌
☽	♊	♉
☿	♐	♌
♀	♏	♍
♂	♒	♎
♃	♍	♊
♄	♈	♓
♅	♍	♍
♆	♏	♏
♇	♍	♍
Asc.	♓	♎

Name *Ryan*

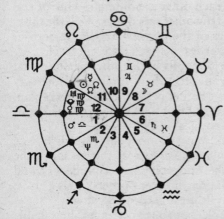

Planets

Sun	☉	Venus	♀	Saturn	♄	Pluto ♀ or ♇
Moon	☽	Mars	♂	Uranus	♅	
Mercury	☿	Jupiter	♃	Neptune	♆	

Step Five: Look Up Linda Goodman's Interpretations of Your Relationship Aspects

When you compare charts, you'll want to know first how the planets affect the relationship dynamics for you. Start with yourself as person A and your comparison partner as person B. It may be helpful to mark the other person's planets in the outer circle of your chart, so you can quickly and easily determine the aspects.

Check "Love Aspects" in Section Two first (page 55), then read the interpretations of each aspect in the comprehensive, planet-by-planet sections.

When you're finished, you'll want to find out how the planets affect the relationship dynamics for your comparison partner. Draw your planets in the outer ring of their chart—they are now person A and you are person B. You can read Linda's interpretation of what you inspire and energize in them.

The readings will be different because your individual astrological reactions to each other are different. One of you sees things one way and the other sees things, well, the other way. While the energies of the planets are felt by both of you, each of you experiences this on a different level.

For example, if your Sun falls in the other person's first house, or ascendant, you affect their vitality and the way they present themselves to other people. Of the two of you, you are the leader in determining how you appear as a couple. You bring out the physical in this person.

If the other person's Sun falls in your twelfth house, which rules secrets, you may tend to keep this person in the background. You might find you share confidences and hide much of your relationship from others. This person will bring out a more reflective, deeper side in you.

You are the same couple, but you experience things in different ways. It is important to consider what each of you brings to the other in your relationship—and fun to look at things from your comparison partner's perspective. Linda's insights provide an overview for each of you.

Here is Linda Goodman's interpretation of Ryan and Maria's Relationship Chart:

♀ ☍ ☽

Maria's Venus is opposite (is six signs away from) Ryan's Taurus Moon and Linda would say, "The Law of Polarity is at work between you, creating a magnetic vibration that causes you to encourage one another and blessing your relationship with a calm, soothing, and comforting undercurrent. Each of you may have certain interests or activities the other doesn't share, but it is likely that you'll resolve this by the Moon exposing Venus to interests Venus learns to enjoy."

♄ ♈ △ ☉ ♌

Maria's Saturn is in Aries and trines (is four signs away from) Ryan's Leo Sun. Here Linda advises, "Usually two people with this aspect have some sort of shared goal and are able to achieve it together. Because your approaches to duty and responsibility are compatible, you tend to agree and cooperate in meeting both total and individual obligations. You'd make a great team in any project concerning security, insurance, finances, real estate, or scientific research."

♇ ☌ ♀

Maria's Pluto conjuncts (is in the same sign as) Ryan's Venus. Linda says, "There is an indisputable karmic tie between you, and it's a powerful one, to be sure. Perhaps you don't 'believe in' reincarnation, the cause of such things as karmic ties. It doesn't matter. Not believing in it doesn't cancel its reality or keep it from working. Anyone who tries to come between you will not succeed. No way."

Sounds like Maria and Ryan have a lot going for them. Including, maybe, a past life.

Now, let's see what your Relationship Signs have to say about you and your relationships.

★

2

Relationship Chart Worksheets

Reader Worksheet

Name ....

The Sun was in ....

The Moon was in ....

Mercury was in ....

Venus was in ....

Mars was in ....

Jupiter was in ....

Saturn was in ....

Uranus was in ....

Neptune was in ....

Pluto was in ....

The Ascendant or Rising Sign was ....

Reader Worksheet

Name ....

The Sun was in ....

The Moon was in ....

Mercury was in ....

Venus was in ....

Mars was in ....

Jupiter was in ....

Saturn was in ....

Uranus was in ....

Neptune was in ....

Pluto was in ....

The Ascendant or Rising Sign was ....

Reader Worksheet

Name ....

The Sun was in ....

The Moon was in ....

Mercury was in ....

Venus was in ....

Mars was in ....

Jupiter was in ....

Saturn was in ....

Uranus was in ....

Neptune was in ....

Pluto was in ....

The Ascendant or Rising Sign was ....

Reader Worksheet

Name ....

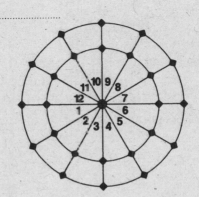

Name ....

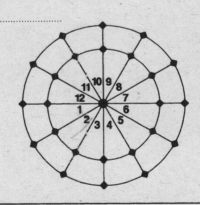

Signs (read across, from left to right: Aries, Taurus, Gemini . . .)

Aries	♈	Taurus	♉	Gemini	♊	Cancer	♋
Leo	♌	Virgo	♍	Libra	♎	Scorpio	♏
Sagittarius	♐	Capricorn	♑	Aquarius	♒	Pisces	♓

Planets

Sun	☉	Venus	♀	Saturn	♄	Pluto	♇ or ♇
Moon	☽	Mars	♂	Uranus	♅		
Mercury	☿	Jupiter	♃	Neptune	♆		

Aspects

Conjunction	☌	Trine	△	Square	□	Opposition	☍
Sextile	✳						

Reader Worksheet

Name ....

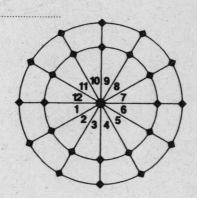

Name ....

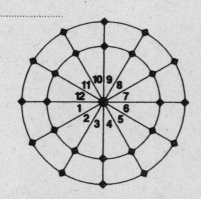

Signs (read across, from left to right: Aries, Taurus, Gemini...)

Aries	♈	Taurus	♉	Gemini	♊	Cancer	♋
Leo	♌	Virgo	♍	Libra	♎	Scorpio	♏
Sagittarius	♐	Capricorn	♑	Aquarius	♒	Pisces	♓

Planets

Sun	☉	Venus	♀	Saturn	♄	Pluto	♇ or ⯓
Moon	☽	Mars	♂	Uranus	♅		
Mercury	☿	Jupiter	♃	Neptune	♆		

Aspects

Conjunction	☌	Trine	△	Square	□	Opposition	☍
Sextile	✳						

Reader Worksheet

Name ....

The Sun was in ....

The Moon was in ....

Mercury was in ....

Venus was in ....

Mars was in ....

Jupiter was in ....

Saturn was in ....

Uranus was in ....

Neptune was in ....

Pluto was in ....

The Ascendant or Rising Sign was ....

Reader Worksheet

Name ....

The Sun was in ....

The Moon was in ....

Mercury was in ....

Venus was in ....

Mars was in ....

Jupiter was in ....

Saturn was in ....

Uranus was in ....

Neptune was in ....

Pluto was in ....

The Ascendant or Rising Sign was ....

Reader Worksheet

Name ....

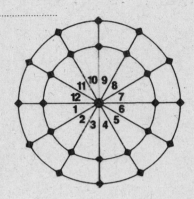

Name ....

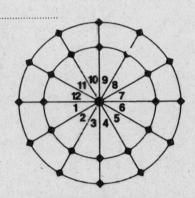

Signs (read across, from left to right: Aries, Taurus, Gemini...)

Aries	♈	Taurus	♉	Gemini	♊	Cancer	♋
Leo	♌	Virgo	♍	Libra	♎	Scorpio	♏
Sagittarius	♐	Capricorn	♑	Aquarius	♒	Pisces	♓

Planets

Sun	☉	Venus	♀	Saturn	♄	Pluto	♇ or ♇
Moon	☽	Mars	♂	Uranus	♅		
Mercury	☿	Jupiter	♃	Neptune	♆		

Aspects

Conjunction	☌	Trine	△	Square	□	Opposition	☍
Sextile	✶						

Reader Worksheet

Name ....

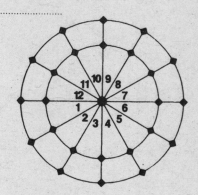

Name ....

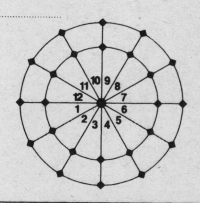

Signs (read across, from left to right: Aries, Taurus, Gemini . . .)

Aries	♈	Taurus	♉	Gemini	♊	Cancer	♋
Leo	♌	Virgo	♍	Libra	♎	Scorpio	♏
Sagittarius	♐	Capricorn	♑	Aquarius	♒	Pisces	♓

Planets

Sun	☉	Venus	♀	Saturn	♄	Pluto	♇ or ♉
Moon	☽	Mars	♂	Uranus	♅		
Mercury	☿	Jupiter	♃	Neptune	♆		

Aspects

Conjunction	☌	Trine	△	Square	□	Opposition	☍
Sextile	✶						

★

★ SECTION THREE ★

Linda Goodman's Interpretations of Your Relationship Signs

★

★ 1 ★

Love Aspects

People who are in a relationship together combine charts, and this combination tells their "togetherness" story, or what they are like together.

In relationships we act differently with various people because they bring out different parts of ourselves, or different energies are ignited in us because of our interaction with them.

Each planet has a vibration, and each vibration "pulls" energies to us in different ways. Venus gives a different flavor to romance for the Pisces (not so practical) than it does to the Capricorn (practical).

The results of these different vibrations can be mismatched emotional needs. With a lot of squares there may be one person who causes constant stress or can't make concessions. Or one person may need more space and the other can't stand separations. All this shows up in the planets and the signs.

Linda separated the Love Aspects from the other aspect interpretations in this book because she wanted to emphasize how especially important they are in the charts of lovers. In astrology the planets can be read for all types of relationships, as well as for love and marriage vibrations.

The readings on the following aspects give special attention to astrological clues of a more romantic love, such as a love affair or a marriage.

"Love Aspects" also provides a special reading for people

who are in an actual relationship or marriage, during which time the contact is going to produce sexuality on a deeper level, commitment on a more spiritual level, and challenges in many areas of one's life.

Astrologers emphasize Love Aspects because they suggest the strength of the sexual passions, who has the power, who loves the deepest, and how secure are the ties that bind.

Linda looked to the Moon for emotional responses, to Venus and Mars for sexual attraction, and to Mercury for understanding. When the Love Aspects are read, Linda has considered how Jupiter expands the other planets; for example, with Venus which rules warmth and love, the capacity to love is magnified by Jupiter. The planet Saturn can add endurance to the union. Uranus conjunct Moon keeps you going back for more and not knowing why. Neptune can help you keep romance alive, and Pluto, a favorite of Linda's, might be the clue to the soulmate or a love that is stronger than any other. For example:

Sun Conjunct, Sextile, or Trine Mercury
☉ ☌ ✳ △ ☿

Here are the aspects of friendship, intellectual cooperation, and the power of potentials. They will help you to solve problems together. You may meet through work, or you may work together as a result of your meeting or relationship. Either way, you inspire and advise one another. Your interests run to the cultural, educational, philosophical. The sages believed that since the Sun is the center of the solar system, the person whose Sun is aspecting the other person's Mercury has the power in this relationship.

Sun Opposed or Square Mercury
☉ ☍ □ ☿

This aspect acts well in platonic relationships because there is a feeling of brotherly or sisterly love. If there is not a lot of Mars/Venus activity, the sexual attraction may be weak. The allure with this combination is in the mind. Mental activity, multiple ideas, challenging scientific discoveries, and musical works often accompany this configuration. These aspects promote accomplishments, activity, and work. But there are also tensions, and this may affect both of your nervous systems. Because you are inclined to be more keyed up around one another, you may find the other person's quirks annoying. There is an old saying, "You like someone because; you love someone in spite of." When you have this combination the "in spite of" becomes more obvious. The more romantic feelings—tenderness, harmony, and sexual attraction—are usually lessened unless there are other strong aspects that promote romantic love.

The following astrological Love Aspects are Linda's special interpretation of common aspects as they relate specifically to love relationships.

Love Aspects ★ ★ ★ ★

Sun Conjunct, Sextile, or Trine Moon
Sun Opposed or Square Moon
Sun Conjunct, Sextile, or Trine Venus
Sun Opposed or Square Venus
Sun Conjunct Mars
Sun Opposed or Square Mars
Sun Conjunct, Sextile, or Trine Jupiter
Sun Square Saturn
Sun Sextile or Trine Uranus
Moon Opposed Moon
Moon Conjunct, Sextile, or Trine Venus
Moon Opposed Venus
Moon Conjunct Mars
Moon Sextile or Trine Mars
Moon Opposed or Square Mars
Moon Conjunct, Sextile, or Trine Jupiter
Moon Sextile or Trine Saturn
Moon Square, or Opposed Saturn
Moon Conjunct, Sextile, or Trine Uranus
Moon Opposed or Square Uranus

Moon Opposed or Square Pluto
Mercury Square Mercury
Mercury Conjunct, Sextile, or Trine Venus
Venus Conjunct, Sextile, or Trine Mars
Venus Opposed or Square Mars
Venus Conjunct, Sextile, or Trine Jupiter
Venus Conjunct Saturn
Venus Sextile or Trine Saturn
Venus Opposed or Square Saturn
Venus Conjunct, Sextile, or Trine Uranus
Venus Opposed or Square Uranus
Venus Conjunct Neptune
Venus Sextile or Trine Neptune
Venus Opposed or Square Neptune
Venus Conjunct, Sextile, or Trine Pluto
Venus Opposed or Square Pluto
Mars Conjunct Uranus
Mars Opposed or Square Uranus
Mars Conjunct, Sextile or Trine Neptune
Mars Square or Opposed Neptune
Mars Square or Opposed Pluto
Jupiter Conjunct, Sextile, or Trine Jupiter

Sun Conjunct, Sextile, or Trine Moon   A's Sun, B's Moon
☉ ☌ ✳ △ ☽

Any of these three aspects is the best possible indication of radical harmony between lovers and an excellent foundation for marriage. If troubles arise, causing occasional separations, they'll almost surely be temporary. The door is always open for reconciliation, if that's your desire. And it will be.

Sun Opposed or Square Moon   A's Sun, B's Moon
☉ ☍ □ ☽

There could be quite a few "lovers' quarrels" and much petty bickering between you. If this occurs too often, it could rather quickly lead to a breakup, and chances are it will be permanent. Therefore, you are both advised to retreat; go on a brief vacation or stay with friends for a few days (separately) until the planetary transits causing the problems pass over and stop triggering irritations between you. It's best to avoid these annoyances if you want to remain together forever. Another way is to take a vow of silence when either of you is tempted to say something you'll surely be sorry for later, when you've cooled off.

Sun Conjunct, Sextile, or Trine Venus   A's Sun, B's Venus
⊙ ☌ ✶ △ ♀

Because you are mutually encouraging, this aspect goes a long way toward bringing domestic peace, fidelity, and affection. It also sometimes indicates financial stability through marriage.

Sun Opposed or Square Venus   A's Sun, B's Venus
⊙ ☍ □ ♀

Because of certain astrological energy and polarity rules, this is (surprise!) usually a favorable vibration for love and marriage, assuming that one of you controls a tendency toward extravagance and the other controls a tendency toward false pride.

Sun Conjunct Mars   A's Sun, B's Mars
⊙ ☌ ♂

I don't suppose you need astrology to tell you that there's a great deal of sexual chemistry and passion between you. It can be really overwhelming at times. In addition, one of you contributes vital energy to mutual or separate business goals, increasing ambition and bringing financial success. One of you (guess which one!) can be a little impatient and demanding at times but simultaneously protective and affectionate. You are a blend of vices and virtues, one might say. But, generally speaking, you should find living together more than satisfying—except for those occasional flare-ups caused by the Sun's pride and Mars's willfulness!

Sun Opposed or Square Mars
⊙ ☍ □ ♂

A's Sun, B's Mars

When it comes to love and marriage, the two of you may frequently lock horns, and mutual hostility can become emotionally explosive. Anger is too easily aroused, and you seem to put each other on the defensive too often, which naturally causes frequent arguments, with each trying to prove that he or she is right and that the other one is wrong. A marriage between you will endure only if you share several strongly positive aspects between other planets in your birth charts—and if you exercise lots of patience and tolerance. One of you will simply have to give in to the other in your quarrels, since compromise won't work. At least try to be fair and take turns giving in.

Sun Conjunct, Sextile, or Trine Jupiter
⊙ ☌ ⚹ △ ♃

A's Sun,
B's Jupiter

These aspects don't relate to the physical passion and emotional affection between you, but they do bring your union much good luck in a general way. They often indicate money or social prestige through marriage, and the vibration is capable of smoothing out many minor difficulties.

Sun Square Saturn
⊙ □ ♄

A's Sun, B's Saturn

When two lovers share this aspect, there's often a wide difference in age, causing one to be more mature and experienced than the other. However, this person is not necessarily always the one who is chronologically older. The more mature partner is the one whose Saturn squares the other's Sun. Saturn is the teacher in your relationship, and so the Sun must learn lessons that Saturn imparts, never mind how reluctantly.

In marriage, the bond between you is hard to break, if not impossible. This aspect binds you together despite yourselves. It will help heaps if Saturn uses more of a cheerful and light touch when teaching those lessons, so they'll be more acceptable and less bitter for the Sun to swallow.

If outside influences or your own personalities should cause you to separate, as they very well may (part of the soul testing), even though the bond between you can't be broken, the length of time before reconciliation could be very long indeed. The Sun's pride is one reason. The other is that the planet delays everything, simply everything. Try not to risk separation because it isn't worth the loneliness for such a long time, especially when your stars tell you the break isn't destined to be permanent.

The soul-testing limitations you both experience under this influence can take several forms: the illness of one or both, difficulties in cutting ties with a former lover or mate, brief periods of impotency or frigidity, brief financial restrictions, and so on. But note the word *brief*. That's the key. Hang on to that and forget the rest. If you're both reasonably enlightened souls, you'll be able to conquer these vibrations and enjoy the rich rewards of true happiness, which is gained only after a long struggle and testing for worthiness. That's why genuine happiness is so rare in love. Few possess the required patience—or faith in the promises for tomorrow.

Sun Sextile or Trine Uranus   A's Sun, B's Uranus
⊙ ✳ △ ♅

In a love affair or marriage, this aspect strongly increases the romance in the relationship and also greatly increases the friendship vibrations between you, so that you will always be romantic lovers as well as good friends—an ideal situation. There is something glamorous and strange (in a nice way) about your meeting, and this same aura of the unusual will continue when you become intimate. This aura makes life together interesting, which is always a decided plus, especially when it's founded on that "friendly lovers" gift from your planets. Neither of you will forget the anniversary of your first encounter or your wedding anniversary (the romantic angle), and you'll always be one another's "best friend." Sun sextile or trine Uranus is a rare and harmonious astrological blessing.

Moon Opposed Moon   A and B
☽ ☍ ☽

Because of astrology's "polarity law," an opposition between your Moon Signs can be an excellent augury for marriage, making your daily togetherness pleasant and adding harmony through your emotional understanding of each other's different moods and attitudes. The vibrations are also helpful to the sexual chemistry between you.

Moon Conjunct, Sextile, or Trine Venus   A's Moon,
☽ ☌ ✳ △ ♀   B's Venus

Moon conjunct, sextile, or trine Venus is a strong vibration for marriage because you have a calm and soothing effect on each other, much affection, and mutual devotion. As a couple, you'll find that this aspect goes a long way toward mitigating any personality conflicts in your intercharts.

Moon Opposed Venus   A's Moon, B's Venus
☽ ☍ ♀

You may not have many interests in common, but nevertheless, due to the astrological "law of polarity" regarding oppositions, there is much genuine affection and harmony between you, and you're emotionally well mated. Venus has a comforting and soothing effect on the Moon's cranky or depressed moods.

Moon Conjunct Mars   A's Moon, B's Mars
☽ ☌ ♂

Your relationship contains powerful stimulations, not the least of which is physical attraction. This vibration strongly encourages propagating and conception. You both probably desire parenthood, and with the kind of sexual magnetism you share, it's a good thing you do! The longing to become a family can be lessened by other aspects in your intercharts but never completely negated. It's rather like the little ditty we sang in school: "First comes love, then comes marriage, then comes a stroll with a baby carriage!" There could also be an urge to adopt a child or children. If for any reason you don't desire to create a human infant, you're supercapable of creating a "brainchild" together, like a co-authored book or some splendid project related to one of the arts. After all, creation is creation. Should the conjunction be in the sign of Gemini, it's possible that you could either be the parents of twins or "give birth" simultaneously to two of those "brainchildren" projects!

Moon Sextile or Trine Mars   A's Moon, B's Mars
☽ ✶ △ ♂

Like the conjunction between these planets, either the sextile or the trine strongly stimulates mutual reproductive urges and greatly encourages conception, even when, for one reason or another, it seems unlikely. Both of you long to create, whether it be the producing of children and a family or an artistic project related to one of the arts, just so you create something together, a desire considerably strengthened by the genuine affection and sexual passion underlying your love. If either Moon or Mars in this aspect is in the sign of Gemini, it's an indication that you could become the parents of twins or two almost simultaneous "brainchild" artistic projects, doubling your happiness!

Moon Opposed or Square Mars   A's Moon, B's Mars
☽ ☍ □ ♂

In the beginning the physical chemistry is powerful, which may or may not be sustained in a permanent relationship, because following the initial sexual magnetism there could be personality conflicts and disturbing emotional discords. Indiscretions by one or both of you are a possibility (not a probability, a possibility. There's a difference, you know). Difficulty in producing a family may be a factor. Also, one person tends to nag excessively, the other to behave in a hasty, rude, and critical manner. The only way to mitigate these difficult vibrations is to have many positive, harmonious aspects between your other planets. Study your entire analysis carefully.

Moon Conjunct, Sextile, or Trine Jupiter

☽ ☌ ✶ △ ♃

A's Moon, B's Jupiter

In the birth charts of lovers or mates, this is an excellent omen for fertility and raising a family, whether through natural parenthood or adoption. If there is some fertility problem on one side or the other, this vibration promises considerable help toward a happy ending, never mind what the medical profession professes to know. The Higher Selves of the two who share this aspect between their birth charts are much wiser—and also far more powerful than doctors. Expect a miracle!

Moon Sextile or Trine Saturn

A's Moon, B's Saturn

☽ ✶ △ ♄

Your emotional harmony is pronounced and stable most of the time. The Moon sees Saturn as more wise, kindly, and protective than stern and demanding. Saturn recognizes that the Moon has the rare ability to smooth over pain and depression, providing the kind of gentle affection and optimism Saturn needs—and appreciates. The romance between you will not slowly fade away after marriage, but has a very good chance of lasting, of surviving the daily annoyances of living together.

This is an excellent support of endurability, which indicates that a marriage between you will be binding, regardless of any problems initiated by other planetary aspects between you. You'll share both emotional and financial stability, although the latter depends on the Moon being willing to follow Saturn's wiser counsel in this area. Mutual loyalty and protectiveness are also the gifts of this vibration. It steadies the affections and creates a harmonious interdependence.

Moon Square or Opposed Saturn   A's Moon, B's Saturn
☽ □ ☍ ♄

Regardless of how basically harmonious your physical attraction may be as indicated by other planetary aspects between you, this one can at some time cause periodic coldness or disinterest in sexual union. I said periodic. Look it up in the dictionary. It is not a synonym for permanent. Therefore, you shouldn't allow yourselves to be unduly disturbed by it, to rush into separation or the divorce court. Saturn may be inclined to place the responsibility for any kind of problems you have on the Moon, when Saturn is equally to blame, which tends to limit the Moon emotionally. As for those occasional periods of sexual disinterest, they could be caused by temporary feminine frigidity or masculine impotence, whichever applies (sometimes both). The one who is the recipient of the other's coolness should avoid making an issue of it. Just wait quietly until the fires of passion are rekindled—and be astrologically assured that they will be, but not while the response is resentful accusation. That will never reignite the flame.

Patience, patience, patience! What is that old English rhyme? "Patience is a virtue, hard to understand, seldom found in woman, and never found in man!" All right, okay, I won't deny it. I'm a feminist—except when I need a macho male to lift something heavy.

Moon Conjunct, Sextile, or Trine Uranus   A's Moon,
☽ ☌ ⚹ △ ♅   B's Uranus

A spontaneous, inexplicable, and powerful magnetic attraction brought you together in some kind of unusual and unconventional situation. Your relationship will always be intensely romantic, and the romance will continue after marriage. So will the magnetic attraction—and unorthodox situations. You will positively never bore each other but, on the contrary, will permanently fascinate each other. This vibration encourages conception, and there will be something strange or curious and unexpected about it. If not a child, then you will create a "brainchild" together, such as a collaboration relating to one of the arts, which would likewise be strange, curious, and unexpected!

Moon Opposed or Square Uranus   A's Moon, B's Uranus
☽ ☍ □ ♅

A love affair between you or a romantic attraction can result in an indiscreet or unconventional relationship of a kind not usually condoned by traditional society. Although a romance can be intensely interesting and full of surprises, marriage may hold a few unpleasant ones. Wedlock brings problems, such as separations that are sudden and could end up being permanent. Also in marriage, common law or orthodox, along with many moves and changes, which are disturbing and frustrating, friction can occur related to the career ambitions of one or perhaps both of you. If other planetary aspects in your intercharts indicate genuine love, well, I keep telling you that real love can overcome any difficulties. There could be a delay or frustration in achieving a family, but the chances are equally strong for an unexpected happy ending. Not all friends, but certain ones, could be the source of occasional trouble. Stay away from them.

Moon Opposed or Square Pluto   A's Moon, B's Pluto
☽ ☍ □ ♀

Problems relating to sexual matters could surface on occasion, and there may be serious misunderstandings regarding domestic or family situations. Marriage will not be trouble free. Much patience and tolerance are needed to reach any degree of harmony with this vibration, but other planetary aspects between your birth charts of a positive nature will mitigate the vibrations of this one—assuming there are enough of the latter—and love can make miracles. One of the difficult areas could involve children: whether or not to have them, and how to raise them once they've arrived. The Moon could be more harmed by this aspect than Pluto. And so it's Pluto's responsibility to make the miracle of transforming negative to positive. Pluto can do anything through the awesome power Pluto possesses.

Mercury Square Mercury   A and B
☿ □ ☿

To keep your relationship from becoming one continual battle, you're both warned to stop being so critical of each other and to try being more tolerant. There are pronounced differences in your mental approaches to nearly everything, but have you ever heard of compromise? It's a talent diplomats must (and do) cultivate. Admittedly, it isn't easy. How would you like the task of getting Israel to agree with the PLO? But if a diplomat can pull it off, albeit with hard work, so can you. Have you ever tried the art of diplomacy—or compromise? Probably not.

If your relationship or marriage means something to you, try it. If it doesn't, you may not want to make the effort. Only you can know if what you feel for each other is worth the energy. Assuming that you truly love, it's well worth both of you spending the time to see the other's viewpoint. With differences like yours, one is not 100 percent right and the other 100 percent wrong. Each of you is partially right and partially wrong. Somewhere in the middle of these percentages, you can agree. Compromise. Diplomacy. Peace is the reward, unless you enjoy constant quarrels. And if you do, you're both masochists. Or would it be sadists? It doesn't matter because intelligent persons don't choose to be either. Right? Right. Don't argue with me!

Mercury Conjunct, Sextile, or Trine Venus   A's Mercury,
☿ ☌ ⚹ △ ♀   B's Venus

You're considerate of one another's emotions; therefore a marriage between you will be founded on a harmonious blend of mutual affection and sympathy. Another bonus is that you'll probably basically think alike about financial matters, so a joint checking account should present no problems. As my great aunt used to say, "Little birds in their nests agree"—and so do you.

Venus Conjunct, Sextile, or Trine Mars

♀ ☌ ✶ △ ♂

A's Venus,
B's Mars

One important facet of your relationship is passion, passion, passion! You're blessed with the gift of combining romantic and tender affection with intense sexual desire, causing your physical union to be both a profoundly erotic and a trembling experience, a powerful blend of innocence and mystery. If you have any conflicts from other planetary vibrations in your intercharts, they'll usually disappear in the bedroom! Couples who share any one of these three aspects between Venus and Mars usually don't wait until marriage to "become one." Is that phrase too old-fashioned for the New Age? Then let me state it in another way by telling you a story I once heard at Scout camp:

A girl was in a store choosing a gown to wear for her approaching wedding, her first. She turned to the saleslady and said, "I'm not sure what color my bridal gown should be." "Well," the saleslady replied, "if you've never been married before, it's traditional to wear white. If you have been married before, you should wear purple." The bride-to-be hesitated for a moment, then asked, "Uh ... do you have something in white with a small touch of lavender?"

There is only one minor warning note: If the aspect the two of you share is the conjunction, Mars may harbor hidden jealousy, a secret lack of self-esteem, and bossy behavior, but Venus can usually soothe it all away.

In the ancient texts, famed astrologer Ptolemy writes that any of these three aspects between Venus and Mars "lead to entire love and affection, which will be so marked as to attract attention and comment." Unquote!

Venus Opposed or Square Mars

♀ ☍ □ ♂

A's Venus, B's Mars

The sexual chemistry between you is powerful but, unfortunately, that's not the end of the story. Both before and after marriage, the strong stimulation of the passionate nature of both tends to break down restraint barriers, and there could be excessive sexuality in one or both partners, which may lead to indiscretions. Naturally, this can destroy harmony. Jealousy could bring serious friction to your relationship, and you're both overly emotional. You'll need plenty of positive aspects from the other planets in your birth charts to dilute this one. A commitment is a commitment, so don't make one unless you intend to keep it. Subdue any latent urges toward promiscuity if you want love to last. The future of your relationship is yours to protect and nourish—or to destroy. Astrology can't make that decision for you. This vibration is a soul test. As the poet Kahlil Gibran wrote, "Think not that you can direct the course of love ... for love if it finds you worthy, will direct your course."

Venus Conjunct, Sextile, or Trine Jupiter   A's Venus,
♀ ☌ ✶ △ ♃   B's Jupiter

I don't know how the two of you behave with others (I'd need to have checked your complete charts for that), but together you're a couple of loving, happy-go-lucky, eternal optimists. Talk about a fun couple! Is that great news or what? You both enjoy challenges, your affectionate natures are similar, your emotions are generally harmonious, you're willing to take chances, you like animals and sports, and a marriage between you will be most fortunate in a financial sense. Just don't blow all your savings on some big gamble. But what am I saying? Although I suppose it's possible for you to have a savings account, with this vibration it's unlikely. Never mind, whether you do or don't, you'll just tell yourselves that "there's always more where that came from!" You know what? With you two, there usually will be.

Venus Conjunct Saturn   A's Venus, B's Saturn
♀ ☌ ♄

This vibration between you can become either a curse or a blessing. I'm not going to predict which, since the outcome is up to you. I won't comment also because, to be astrally cautious, this aspect could end up touching your relationship with a combination of positive and negative alternate experiences. On the negative side, one of you could be either chronologically older or more experienced and therefore adopt a bossy or superior attitude toward the other. Saturn may depress Venus and considerably chill Venus's affections by being overly cautious and conservative, or by not being sufficiently emotionally demonstrative, restricting Venus's expressions of love. On the positive side, Venus is able to cheer and uplift Saturn out of all these personality flaws. Also, there's probably a marked loyal protectiveness of each other against outsiders, and a marriage between you has a good chance of enduring. (I didn't intend to imply that an age difference is negative, as long as the older one doesn't use age as a control weapon.)

Venus Sextile or Trine Saturn   A's Venus, B's Saturn
♀ ✳ △ ♄

Venus sextile or trine Saturn is one of the strongest indications of permanent love and endurability of marriage. The vibrations stabilize the emotions, as well as increase loyalty and faithfulness. Saturn will be solicitous of Venus's welfare, and Venus is equally protective of Saturn's happiness. Physical passion will grow rather than diminish after marriage. You each feel a sense of responsibility for the other, which is only one of the reasons this aspect causes a binding relationship.

Venus Opposed or Square Saturn   A's Venus, B's Saturn
♀ ☍ □ ♄

In a love or marital relationship, Venus will experience some kind of sorrow or hurt initiated by Saturn either intentionally or involuntarily, through the interference of others. Saturn could be unduly critical of traits in Venus that Saturn views as flaws, whether they are or not, and if these are not corrected by Venus, then Saturn will feel extremely annoyed and frustrated. Venus could consider escaping the relationship if Saturn becomes too domineering, depressing, and pessimistic. Admittedly, this can be a seriously discordant vibration if the two of you allow it to be. But if you make a genuine mutual effort, based on the sympathetic understanding of real love and boosted by the positive aspects between other planets in your birth charts, you can considerably dilute its power over you and take firm control of your relationship yourselves.

Venus Conjunct, Sextile, or Trine Uranus   A's Venus,
♀ ☌ ✶ △ ♅   B's Uranus

Your attraction is founded on a rather remarkable magnetism that excites your romantic feelings and arouses your emotions easily. In the beginning you may define this attraction as "only a curious infatuation," but you soon discover it to be far more—and there is something strange and unusual about it. Maybe the right word is *unconventional*? Or *bizarre*? Or just plain *weird*? The romantic fascination you first experienced has an excellent chance of remaining after you marry. Although you may have to hopscotch through a few sudden separations and equally sudden reconciliations, your relationship will probably bring much happiness and an exciting companionship. Just watch those spasmodic, unexpected separations after some silly quarrel. Uranus may wander off in a huff, secretly intending to return, then forget your mutual address and unlisted phone number. Don't laugh. It's been known to happen when Uranus is part of any aspect! Uranus is the planet of amnesia and is associated with so-called absentminded professors.

Venus Opposed or Square Uranus   A's Venus, B's Uranus
♀ ☍ □ ♅

Unless there are other strongly harmonious aspects between you, this aspect is unfortunate for a permanent relationship or marriage. There can be many changes of heart and disappointing changes of mind, bringing on sudden, unexpected separations. Lacking other positive vibrations in your intercharts, it's best that you remain friends. One bright note: Any breakup should not be deeply painful, because you'll both forget about it fairly quickly. Check your entire analysis before you make a decision. Other aspects may allow you to "tame" this one successfully.

Venus Conjunct Neptune   A's Venus, B's Neptune
♀ ♂ ♆

Depending upon how mature and responsible you are, and assuming that other planetary aspects indicate harmonious endurability, this aspect can be extremely favorable, although there may be something unconventional about your romance. You may, for example, choose a "common law" marriage instead of a traditional, legalized union. Neptune may bewitch, entice, or seduce Venus, but Venus probably won't mind, as long as Neptune doesn't behave in an elusive manner, arousing suspicions of deception in Venus. Since sympathy sometimes masquerades as love, and because there's a great amount of mutual sympathy between you (which is normally an ideal situation), be sure that what you feel really is love. You'll know in your hearts. The gentleness with which you usually treat each other makes your relationship especially comforting. You often read one another's thoughts, thanks to the intense psychic link between you.

Venus Sextile or Trine Neptune   A's Venus, B's Neptune
♀ ⚹ △ ♆

The ESP bond between you is powerful—and reliable. With all the kindness, consideration, generosity, affection, and devotion you share, your relationship is wonderfully harmonious (except for temporary periods when other discordant aspects between you vibrate briefly). Adopt a few pets, investigate mystical matters together, and don't be afraid to expect the miracle of happiness. You're both silently aware of a fantasy aura around you, with hints of a magical fairy tale, whether you've spoken of it or not. You know it's there.

Venus Opposed or Square Neptune   **A's Venus,**
♀ ☍ □ ♆   **B's Neptune**

This vibration places some degree of unavoidable stress on romantic harmony. Should the stress become unbearable, instead of breaking it off for any specific reason or mutual decision, it's more likely that you'll simply drift apart—gradually. There could be unfaithfulness on one side or the other, or, if not, the mistaken suspicion of it. Either way, there may be unpleasant confrontations and true or false accusations of various kinds of deception. Whatever friction occurs, it's probable that Venus will suffer more than Neptune. It's the debt payment demanded of both of you for negative actions toward each other in past lives, and karma must always be balanced in some manner. Remember that this aspect brings the possibility of infidelity or some other kind of deception, but it also brings the probability (two different words) of something more harmful to your relationship: the suspicion of infidelity (or some other form of deception) when it doesn't actually exist.

The reason suspicion is so dangerous to love is because it can cause deception to manifest when otherwise it wouldn't have, because the one unjustly suspected becomes weary of being falsely accused. When anything untrue is repeatedly imagined, it can become a reality: "What I feared has come upon me." If you want to salvage what you feel for one another, memorize the words of this verse.

oh! hard, hard karmic lesson ... trust in love the kind that
"casts out all fear" by far the most difficult and soul searching
one all lovers must eventually master

the gift of trust may be given without pain only
when the recipient of such trust makes love and
loyalty plain ... to be seen and heard through
loving glance and tender word

for a constant reassurance of affection and devotion is the
necessary foundation of trust ... and it must! yes, it must be
given freely before the need to ask arises

*could Romeo or Juliet ever have been mistrustful? which of
them would dream to doubt the other with both lovers offering
such constant declaration of devotion?*

*but lacking this, then trust must tarnish with
the rust of jealousy and suspicion which
are only lonely synonyms for fear*

*yet a rust so easily removed by love in
word and deed and glance made clear
neither time nor tide nor sea can keep my own
away from me ... as the poet wrote*

*nor take my own away from me, he might have added if "my
own" declares repeatedly that he is, indeed "my own" or if she
declares, as the case may be, the same ... to him*

—FROM GOOBERZ, BY
LINDA GOODMAN

In your sharing of this vibration's disturbing karmic burden (which will be lightened somewhat by other positive aspects in your intercharts), try to practice mutually the
formula in this verse for creating trust, and eventually you'll
be able to transform it from "dangerous" into what astrologers call "a mild, powder-puff" planetary aspect.
When was the last time you said "I love you"?

Venus Conjunct, Sextile, or Trine Pluto   A's Venus,
♀ ☌ ✶ △ ♇   B's Pluto

Whatever the connection—family, business, or friendship—these three aspects are evidence of a deep karmic
bond from numerous past associations.

Found in the charts of lovers or mates, the bond is different and more profound. (In other associations, the same
tie exists, but it's not a sexual one, see page 155–156.)

These aspects indicate either Twin Souls or Soul Mates.

Two people who were once the same individual are referred to as Soul Mates. One person was the male half of the soul and the other was the female half. As the Universe evolved and man's relationship to God changed the souls were separated. They have an innate longing for the other, and both of them sense that a part of themselves is missing or incomplete. From lifetime to lifetime, these souls unite and feel the joy of completion. They find the twin half of themselves.

This aspect, and in particular the conjunction, reveals the possibility of Soul Mates.

Soul Mates are fully absorbed in the other, and may experience extreme tension when your emotions can't be fully expressed. The sexual chemistry between you is magnetic and deep, and was so from your first meeting. It may or may not be consummated under the sextile or trine between these planets, but is not likely to be resisted under the conjunction.

With any of these three aspects (especially the conjunction), you will meet involuntarily, and cannot be separated on Earth except for temporary periods. Not even death can separate you in the astral existence, because you will rush into mutual flesh rebirth to be reunited. These are powerful karmic vibrations of love, the kind of relationship called "love at first sight," which is not a fable, but attributable to karma. When apart you both feel an inexpressible longing for one another, however much you may try to deny it for personal reasons. With the sextile or trine, if you choose to postpone union until another incarnation, your mutual feelings will nevertheless be intense. With the conjunction it's doubtful that you'll choose postponement. The ancient marriage ceremonial words "That which God hath joined together, let no man put asunder" apply to such lovers, not to all brides and grooms. Because such aspects are a precious gift from the Universe, and from the Higher Selves of the man and woman, they can't be taken lightly. They require deep meditation and thoughtful analysis.

The following brief verse comes to mind regarding these Venus-Pluto vibrations.

I'd like to give you a Christmas gift
a pair of glasses with multiple lens
to help the eyes see long ago
then you would know
the reason for the music.

Soul Mates usually have other aspects in common like the Moon conjunct the Sun or ascendant in the other's chart, as well as multiple ties and conjunctions shown in both charts. In addition, they meet after a major crisis in one or the other's life. True Soul Mates are much more complex and rare than the idea that is commonly referred to in our culture.

Venus Opposed or Square Pluto   A's Venus, B's Pluto
♀ ☍ □ ♇

Pluto may be demanding and in some way impose on Venus, upsetting Venus's emotional stability. There could be problems kept secret until some event forces them to surface. Unrequited love is a possibility, and adjustments in your sexual relations could be necessary. Stress could be caused by difficulty in parenting children or quarrels about how to raise them, and the personal values of both of you may undergo strenuous revision or reconstruction. Pluto should be very careful in dealing with Venus's gentler, more delicate, affectionate nature, and Venus must allow Pluto sufficient distance and space to be alone and meditate. Even so, you're bound to experience friction between you on occasion, which, as always, will be less of a strain on your relationship if you also share a number of harmonious aspects between other planets in your charts.

Mars Conjunct Uranus   A's Mars, B's Uranus
♂ ☌ ♅

To be candid, there will be troublesome times when you irritate each other, but to what degree depends on both the discordant and the harmonious aspects between other planets in your birth charts. If a large number of them are strongly positive, this one will annoy you only now and then and not create serious problems, or at least not permanently damaging ones. Because the emotions you feel for each other are so intense and you both have such independent and proud spirits, the more you love, the more explosive your disagreements will be when they do occur. You can comfort yourselves with the knowledge that your reconciliations will be as swift and unexpected as your quarrels. Considering the chaos caused periodically by the upsets, outside interferences, sudden changes, and uncertainties your relationship experiences from time to time, it's no wonder that both your nervous systems can be affected occasionally. You have a good chance of eventually controlling this vibration and achieving harmony should either one of you (though preferably both) be even slightly developed spiritually, and if you're both willing to master your emotional responses and tempers. If you're as strong and intelligent as you believe yourselves to be, you should be able to do that. Unless you're too weak—there! That reached you, right?

Mars Opposed or Square Uranus   A's Mars, B's Uranus
♂ ☍ □ ♅

A marriage between you will have a better chance of enduring if you're careful not to combine it with any sort of business partnership or association, which could adversely affect your personal relationship. The best way to soften this unpredictable and rather explosive vibration is to promise you'll take frequent vacations apart, to separate periodically—and keep that promise. It will go a long way toward restoring harmony and quieting the stress between you. Otherwise, proceed with caution.

Mars Conjunct, Sextile, or Trine Neptune   A's Mars,
♂ ☌ ✶ △ ♆   B's Neptune

Do you recite poetry together or play music during your lovemaking? Whether you do or not, your sexual union will sometimes be more mystical than erotic or sensual, more tenderly affectionate than fiercely passionate. Not always, but occasionally. And what's wrong with that? Nothing. Titania and Oberon—absolutely nothing.

Mars Square or Opposed Neptune
♂ □ ♂ ♆

A's Mars,
B's Neptune

Neptune may confuse Mars and dissipate Mars's energy, while Mars may stimulate and influence Neptune but at the same time tread on Neptune's sensitive nature with hobnail boots. Nevertheless, Mars may suffer more in a love affair or marriage because Neptune will eventually wear down Mars's vitality and courage, as one drop of water a day, falling steadily over the years on a rock, will finally split the stone in half. There's also a danger that one or both of you may at some time be tempted to excess regarding alcohol, drugs, procrastination, or wastefulness. The negative vibrations of this aspect won't totally or permanently disappear, but favorable aspects between your other planets can subdue them—and your own free-will determination is capable of exerting an even stronger influence to mitigate the stressful soul testing possible when Mars is thus aligned with Neptune. The aspect is not one you'd want to celebrate with champagne (you two are better off celebrating with iced tea, anyway) and it's definitely not a piece of cake (or even two slices of apple pie), but it won't destroy your relationship if you don't allow it to do so. Just don't be careless. Remain alert to gathering storms, and separate temporarily before the downpour begins.

Mars Square or Opposed Pluto
♂ □ ♂ ♇

A's Mars, B's Pluto

With this vibration, some form of sexual perversion is possible (not probable, only possible), as are other kinds of sexual difficulties, such as frigidity, impotency, or infertility on one side or the other. Various adjustments will have to be made, for this is one of those aspects of past karma needing to be balanced. There are some couples sharing this vibration who find that the difficulties they endure in their relationship have the effect of drawing them closer together. There can be no compassion where there is no pain. And compassion is a sublime healer—of anything. Anything at all. Avoid confrontation at any cost, whatever you do, because a simple argument or disagreement between you two can quickly erupt into full-scale war, featuring minefields that make the ones in Vietnam and the Gulf seem like the flower-strewn meadows in *The Sound of Music*! Mars and Pluto are natural enemies, but they're only planets. Your Higher Selves have absolute power over such electromagnetic influences if you tune into them.

Jupiter Conjunct, Sextile, or Trine Jupiter   A and B
♃ ☌ ✳ △ ♃

The ancient texts say this is an excellent planetary aspect to find in the charts of marriage partners. It blesses your union with material success, mental compatibility, and emotional harmony most of the time. Not all of the time, gentlepeople; nothing remains the same all of the time, not even things this positive. In fact, especially not positive things, since constant happiness can change from exciting to boring. Continuity takes the edge off. You need something to compare the joy to so you can really appreciate it. Be satisfied that your personal happiness when you're together lasts longer than most people's and, best of all, will inevitably return. With such an insurance policy, don't complain. Be grateful. Whatever rain other aspects between your planets may bring to your relationship, this one will always bring out the Sun again. You're tolerant and considerate of one another more often than not, but you may occasionally need to learn to forgive your mutual trespasses. You'd make great married lawyers or a stockbroking team. Spending a vacation on safari would appeal to you, and you possibly have a house full of pets. With Jupiter ruling both idealism and expansion, your lovemaking is probably frequent, and the old adage that "each time is like the first time" applies to you.

★

2

Sun Aspects

Sun conjunct, sextile, or trine Moon
Sun square Moon
Sun opposed Moon
Sun conjunct, sextile, or trine Mercury
Sun square Mercury
Sun opposed Mercury
Sun conjunct, sextile, or trine Venus
Sun opposed or square Venus
Sun conjunct Mars
Sun sextile or trine Mars
Sun square Mars
Sun opposed Mars
Sun conjunct, sextile, or trine Jupiter
Sun opposed or square Jupiter
Sun sextile or trine Saturn
Sun conjunct Saturn
Sun square Saturn
Sun opposed Saturn
Sun conjunct Uranus
Sun sextile or trine Uranus
Sun opposed or square Uranus
Sun conjunct Neptune

Sun sextile or trine Neptune
Sun opposed or square Neptune
Sun conjunct Pluto
Sun sextile or trine Pluto
Sun opposed or square Pluto

Sun Conjunct, Sextile, or Trine Moon   A's Sun, B's Moon
☉ ♂ ✳ △ ☽

Any of these three aspects between the luminaries (Sun and Moon) represent the strongest of all harmonies between two people, especially the conjunction, although the sextile and trine are big boosters to compatibility in their own way. Not always (nothing in the realm of existence is always), but at least 95 percent of the time, those who have such a luminary aspect between their birth charts can count on a cosmic insurance policy against an acrimonious or permanent destruction of their relationship, whether it be that of lovers, mates, friends, relatives, or business associates.

This (Sun-Moon) vibration won't totally prevent quarrels, arguments, and various problems initiated by so-called negative (actually energizing) aspects between your other planets, but it will powerfully assist resolutions of upsetting events. With this astrological gift, should the two of you temporarily break off your relationship for any reason, you're guaranteed repeated opportunities for reconciliation. These aspects are nearly always found between men and women who divorce then remarry each other, sometimes more than once, and between friends, relatives, and business partners who angrily end their associations, then "kiss and make up," with mutual apologies.

The reason for the excellent harmony bestowed by these luminary aspects is that the Moon's emotional nature and the Sun's personality are compatible; therefore the entire relationship is basically harmonious, regardless of discordant vibrations from other planetary aspects in your intercharts.

Sun Square Moon   A's Sun, B's Moon
☉ □ ☽

With this mutual aspect, there is a difference in basic temperaments, a clash between the natures and personalities, even with two people of the same sex, but especially so between two people of the opposite sex, in any kind of relationship or association. The Sun may be too bossy and thoughtless or arrogant, ignoring the Moon, bringing on tears and withdrawal. On the other hand (Libra insists on sneaking into these compatibility aspects), the Moon may be overly sensitive and exaggerate a lack of consideration displayed at times by the Sun, taking the relationship far too seriously for harmony. The cosmic counsel to the Sun is: Try to realize that you are not the only important person in this association; you are only half of it. The cosmic counsel to the Moon is simplicity itself. For you I have two words: Lighten up!

Sun Opposed Moon   A's Sun, B's Moon
☉ ☍ ☽

The vibration here is half negative, half positive. The choice belongs to both of you. It reflects the familiar question concerning the optimist and the pessimist: "Is the glass half full or half empty?"

To prevent the relationship from becoming, in some degree, a kind of sadist-masochist vibration (the Sun the former, the Moon the latter), both of you must make an effort: the Sun to soften attitudes and behavior, the Moon to be more assertive. I didn't say domineering, I said assertive. There is no need to go from one extreme to the other! Despite the occasional opposed views between you, there is also the positive side of the opposition to consider, meaning that this aspect can operate through bringing a strong magnetic attraction (polarity always does!) and gradually pulling forth the best qualities of each, blending them into mutual achievements. But this does take work—and careful analysis of each minor and major clash of wills.

Sun Conjunct, Sextile, or Trine Mercury
⊙ ♂ ⚹ △ ☿

A's Sun,
B's Mercury

If the two people possessing this aspect between them are teacher and student, parent and child, or boss and employee, your association will probably be unusually cooperative and successful, and it also makes a congenial and satisfying love affair or marriage, cutting down on mental disputes between you.

Mercury understands where the Sun is coming from most of the time (and nothing pacifies the Sun more than being understood), while the Sun empathizes and sympathizes with Mercury's ideas, encouraging and stimulating them (nothing pleases Mercury more than being able to play exciting games of mental challenge in any and all mutual discussions). Instead of disagreeing with each other's concepts, you'll blend them into harmony, and share lots of common interests, which naturally makes agreement easy between you and collaboration free from major conflict. Even though the two of you are totally different in your mental and emotional natures and personalities, you still seem to think alike on most matters, and that makes a strong foundation for a cozy, comfortable association or relationship.

Sun Square Mercury
⊙ □ ☿

A's Sun, B's Mercury

Don't forget what you were told before regarding the nature of various mutual astrological aspects between you, such as that a square creates stress and tension but is also an energizer, which means it's what makes the car or plane or whatever machine go into gear, so to speak. Without tension and energizing vibrations, everything would stand still. With this particular aspect between you, the stress it brings involves the different outlook of Mercury, which is always intellectual, mental, or analytical, and that of the Sun, which is more creative in seeing things as a whole. The Sun must try not to project, even silently, a patronizing attitude toward Mercury's more intellectual and analytical approach to ideas, while Mercury would be well advised to give a more conciliatory response to the Sun's creative way of fitting the puzzle pieces together to form a complete picture. It might be interesting if you bought two identical picture puzzles and each tried to complete one in separate rooms, with your divergent methods, to see which one first managed to—no, scratch that. A bad idea. Competition would only create more controversy. Sorry. The thought just popped into my head. As an astrologer, I should be ashamed of myself.

On the other hand (here comes Libra poking around again), such an exercise might be jolly fun and help you both become more tolerant of each other's different approaches. Just so the one who wins by completing the puzzle first doesn't brag to the other. That's a definite no-no for harmony.

Sun Opposed Mercury   A's Sun, B's Mercury
☉ ☍ ☿

This aspect relates to your mutual creative and mental energies, which will be either frequently opposed or nicely balanced. The choice is up to you! The effect is never neutral. There may occasionally be clashes of viewpoints, even when the creative and mental energies are well balanced, but such differences can usually be discussed and resolved. At some time in your relationship, you may work together in a business sense or share an interest in publishing, advertising, or salesmanship matters. The mental projects will be initiated by Mercury, the creative projects by the Sun. In either case, one may accuse the other of being a "workaholic," or of being expected to be one herself or himself.

Sun Conjunct, Sextile, or Trine Venus   A's Sun, B's Venus
☉ ☌ ✶ △ ♀

You can count on mutual admiration and encouragement, except when temporarily veiled by any other possible so-called negative aspects between your birth charts. Even then, you won't lose the basic goodness of any one of these three aspects between the Sun and Venus (especially the conjunction, although the sextile and trine perform their own marvelous magic). Friendship, companionship, and loyalty are beaded on a silvery blue cord connecting you, even when you're physically not in the same room. You'll likely have the same or similar goals and ambitions. Often this aspect indicates that the association or relationship brings financial benefits, with the money usually (not always) belonging to Venus. It doesn't matter which one of you is responsible for the financial security because you're both strongly inclined to share everything with one another, including money, unless some other planetary aspect in your charts lessens the generous urges. Even if this happens, your basic simpatico regarding mutual giving will periodically return. You'll be fortunate in earning money together, and more than fair about dividing it.

Sun Opposed or Square Venus   A's Sun, B's Venus
☉ ☍ □ ♀

There is a great deal of affection between you, even with this so-called negative (stressful) aspect of a square or opposition. Because the Sun and Venus are such benefic planets, no contact between them is seriously antagonistic or dangerous to a relationship. However, with the square or opposition, there may be some accusations from one of you to the other of extravagance (or stinginess), and perhaps frequent disputes over money. Differences in cultural backgrounds may cause some friction, and you may have different life-styles, such as one of you preferring a more retiring and simple life-style with little socializing and the other preferring a more gregarious, outgoing, and social life-style, all the way to minor disagreements, such as one wanting to turn up the lamps at night all over the house, flooding it with bright light, and the other wanting the peaceful, restful feeling of dim lighting at night. Or one might like to hear music playing throughout the day on the stereo, while the other desires quiet, listening to music only occasionally. But such conflicts are relatively minor when viewed as only a facet of the entire relationship. There could be marked differences in taste, again a minor matter, whether in the area of home decor, clothing, or entertainment. As for the cultural background differences, each of you can learn from the other. If one of you comes from Poverty Gulch or a blue-collar background and the other was born into upper-class-type surroundings, look at the interesting possibilities. One of you can invite a homeless person to dinner the same night the other invites the governor of the state. It could be a real happening.

Sun Conjunct Mars   A's Sun, B's Mars
☉ ☌ ♂

Sometimes you powerfully stimulate and encourage each other, moving aggressively toward any mutual or individual goal with awesome energy and intensity, resulting in impressive success together. At other times a tad of envy can rear its ugly little green head, a rivalry to see who gets to the top of the mountain first! Your progress will always be rapid when each of you fully cooperates with the other, so control the occasional urge to outclass one another. Your winnings and victories will be far greater when they're achieved as a team rather than separately. Don't waste your energies in competition. Pool them, and the sky's the limit! In your day-to-day association, Mars will often incite the Sun to outbursts of angry words but will also trigger the Sun into positive action, bringing out all of the Sun's creative abilities. There are two sides to every coin in astrology just as in daily life experience. The Sun can likewise bring forth angry outbursts in Mars, but can also act as the rash Mars's benevolent protector, helping Mars to avoid the pitfalls of impulsiveness by looking before leaping. When the two of you are together, it will seldom be peaceful and quiet; more likely the atmosphere around you will be charged with magnetic energy, for better or for worse. It will more often be for better if you avoid mutual overstimulation.

Sun Sextile or Trine Mars   A's Sun, B's Mars
⊙ ⚹ △ ♂

The Sun stimulates self-confidence, energy, and enthusiasm in Mars. Mars stimulates the same qualities in the Sun.
The Sun brings out an enterprising spirit and the courage to
initiate in Mars. Mars brings out the same qualities in the
Sun. Being made aware of this, you don't need astrology to
tell you that the two of you, in any sort of relationship or
association, are often, if not always, in harmonious agreement when it comes to achieving any goal, meeting any
challenge, or climbing any mountain, from Pike's Peak to
Mount Everest. You create a powerful sense of ambition between you; therefore you can run, not walk, up the success
ladder together. But be careful. There could be aspects between other planets in your charts that might cause you to
slip on one of the rungs. Perhaps it's best to walk up that
ladder, just in case.

Sun Square Mars   A's Sun, B's Mars
⊙ □ ♂

Unless there are other extremely positive planetary aspects between your birth charts, it may be wiser to balance
your mutual karma in another lifetime. If you do have other,
strongly positive aspects between you, then this powerful
vibration of trouble can be diluted to a degree, and maybe
even finally be overcome. You can make a more informed
decision after you've studied this analysis of your entire relationship.

The problems created by the Sun and Mars in a square
position between your charts may not be immediately apparent and naturally won't surface every day. But when the
transiting planets trigger this sensitive aspect from time to
time (you'll need a human astrologer to calculate the tim-
ing), then things can become dangerously explosive between two people in any kind of relationship or association.

Your separate ambitions could conflict, resulting in a
reaction of anger and unconcealed hostility. Tempers are
easily aroused, and then each of you becomes intensely

defensive, inciting frustration on both sides. The only way to erase the damage from this aspect completely is for one of you to give in totally and submit to the stronger one, turning the other cheek repeatedly. The problem is that the hidden resentment resulting from such masochistic behavior can eventually cause the health of the one who submits to be seriously affected, unless the submission is motivated by love and humility. Assuming this, please apply to the Vatican for canonization as a saint! But love can solve all difficulties and if there's enough of it around, the struggle between the Sun and Mars when they "square" off like this will bow to its awesome power and influence. There is no pain that enough love cannot heal. If only you could love enough, you would be the wisest, happiest, and most powerful beings on the planet. The key word is *enough*.

Sun Opposed Mars   A's Sun, B's Mars
⊙ ☍ ♂

Storm warnings! There could be "trouble in River City," as the song goes in *The Music Man*. There are periodic tugs-of-war when one or the other becomes too aggressive and domineering, or when your individual viewpoints differ and clash like a cymbal! True, you stimulate each other's ideas, but at times there may be too much stimulation. Then your temperaments (and tempers!) make compromise difficult, if not impossible. You'll need lots of harmonious aspects between your other planets to offset this vibration of serious conflict. Study your entire relationship in this analysis and make a careful judgment with your own intuitive abilities. You're on your own with this one. No one else possesses enough personal knowledge to offer a reliable final assessment.

Too often, you each adopt a stance of resistance, with little desire for cooperation. You need to hire a referee, but neither of you would be inclined to listen to him or her, any more than you listen to each other. Impatience, pride, rivalry, and jealousy could leave deep scars in your relationship. If the majority of your other planetary aspects is disharmonious, you might find life to be more peaceful by working out your karma with this person in a future incarnation and avoiding intimate contact in this one. But if the majority of your other mutual planetary aspects is harmonious, they can dilute this one into only occasional disputes. As with everything else in astrology, it's up to you. *You* are always in control of the final round. It's called free will, and exercising it strengthens the character. Overcoming problems is good for you, as your mother used to say about eating your broccoli and brussels sprouts.

Sun Conjunct, Sextile, or Trine Jupiter
☉ ♂ ⚹ △ ♃

A's Sun,
B's Jupiter

Regardless of how you behave with others, you bring out something of the clown and the eternal optimist in each other when you're together. You'll often find that some giggles and a good laugh can cause most of the frustrations of your lives to disappear. You have a knack for cheering up one another, to lift each other out of depression and the gloomies with little effort. If other planetary aspects between your birth charts should indicate religious, legal, intellectual, or educational disagreements, you'll usually be fortunate in working them out smoothly in the final analysis, since this aspect has the power to decrease any disharmony between you involving these areas.

Although the Sun is astrologically guaranteed to reap major monetary benefits from an association with Jupiter, you'll both offer financial support to each other, and you can count on lots of general good luck in several areas, mutually given and received. The loyalty and trust you share brings out your finest qualities. Instinctively, you'll assist each other in both material and spiritual ways. As a team, with concerted effort, you can realize just about any mutual goal, from founding a successful business or a new religion to climbing Mount Everest.

Your ambitions are probably more expansive than most, and it's likely that you both enjoy all kinds of sports, especially the ones presenting a challenge. Since the chances are good that you share an attachment to animals, from dogs and cats to horses and elephants, why not adopt a pet pig?

That should jolly you both and provide lots of Jupiter laughter!

Sun Opposed or Square Jupiter   •   A's Sun, B's Jupiter
⊙ ☍ □ ♃

It's difficult to define this vibration as totally positive or totally so-called negative. It's certain to bring benevolent influences, but the benevolence may be somewhat one-sided at times, which is not the same as discordant. If chords of conflict do appear, it will likely be when your dreams and goals are different. Jupiter leans toward more ethical and idealistic goals, while the Sun is more interested in material ambitions. The Sun may too often shift responsibility to Jupiter, and Jupiter will nearly always assist and help, but may also on occasion promise more than can be realistically delivered, complaining that "you expect too much of me" to the Sun. Assuming any sort of mutual financial endeavors or situations between you, even though Jupiter is more idealistic than materialistic and the Sun usually the opposite, there could be times when the Sun accuses Jupiter of being too extravagant. This aspect is an odd blend of mutual benefit and lopsided helpfulness, working itself out through the personal idiosyncrasies of the two of you. Depending on your individual involvements, there could be minor disagreement in religious beliefs, educational matters, publishing, stock market, or legal situations. Not in all, of course, but perhaps at least one of these areas.

Sun Sextile or Trine Saturn   A's Sun, B's Saturn
⊙ ⚹ △ ♄

The two of you are capable of combining and balancing confidence, enthusiasm, and optimism (the Sun) with the stability, patience, and organizational qualities needed for long-lasting success (Saturn). Most of the time, you'll be in agreement relating to the responsibility of who minds the store, which one takes the reins of authority in various situations, the disbursing of duties, and so forth. Saturn will accept suggestions to be looser, more expansive, and willing to take a few chances if they come from the Sun rather than from other people, while the Sun will gracefully accept the beneficial limiting cautions and restraints suggested by Saturn (unless other mutual planetary aspects seriously overshadow this one) without feeling stifled, as would be the case if anyone else tried to do the same. However, the Sun may often lecture Saturn to be more open and less conservative, and whatever Saturn may do to restrict the Sun's pride and overconfidence will work toward the ultimate good and benefit of both of you rather than create conflict. Very nice.

You both should also know that you've had some sort of relationships or associations in former incarnations, since Saturn is the planet of karma. When it is linked with the Sun (or any planet) in two birth charts, whatever the nature of the aspect, it indicates either minor or major contacts in earlier existences. Whether these contacts were minor or major depends on other planetary aspects between your charts. This vibration of Sun sextile or trine Saturn is particularly excellent for family harmony, permanent friendships, and enduring financial benefits from marriage or business partnerships. Usually with this aspect, but not always, there is a chronological age difference, either calendar-wise or through the maturity-from-experience of one person and the lack of worldly wisdom in the other.

Sun Conjunct Saturn   A's Sun, B's Saturn
☉ ☌ ♄

This conjoining of the Sun and Saturn can be helpful or unfortunate, depending on whether the majority of other aspects in your intercharts are stressful or harmonious. Study your entire planetary compatibility analysis to discover which general effect this conjunction will have on your relationship. As with most things in life, it will probably be a little of each.

One thing you can count on: Whatever your individual behavior patterns may be separately, when your efforts are combined and you operate as a team, you're both so consumed by duty and responsibility you may need to join

Workaholics Anonymous! Obviously, this falls on the positive side of the vibration—I think.

One frictional facet of the aspect could be that Saturn may try to "sit on" or hold down the Sun's enthusiastic desire to move forward, and the Sun won't appreciate being held down, even (and especially) when told "Slow down . . . it's good for you"—which it is. On the plus side, the Sun will encourage Saturn's ambitions, which will help to alleviate Saturn's fears, worries, pessimistic negativity, and suchlike; as always with these planetary aspects, despite the Sun Sign of the Saturn individual, because even when a person is a cheerful, puppy-dog-friendly Aries Sun Sign, the position of Saturn in the birth chart reveals the serious and depression-prone portion of that person's (or anyone's) whole personality.

The influence of a Sun conjunct Saturn mutual aspect causes the Sun to make many excellent suggestions to Saturn, which Saturn would be wise to accept, since one of the Sun's virtues is a knack for creative concepts. But the Sun may have to wait an eternity for Saturn to accept the Sun's beneficial ideas, Saturn being so very slow to act on anything (or so it seems to the more aggressive Sun).

If this aspect can be considered a "good" one (read the first paragraph again, please), there will be a great deal of loyalty between you, a sort of two-against-the-world link. Whether the relationship is that of friends, relatives, business associates, lovers, or mates, there will usually be a difference in chronological age between you—or it may be only that Saturn's attitudes and behavior from time to time make it seem that one of you is chronologically older or more mature!

The Sun is more tolerant and forgiving than Saturn, which is fortunate, since in your relationship the Sun will have to ensure harmony by making most of the concessions and doing most of the compromising.

Before the Sun complains about it, remember this eternal Universal Law: The Sun conjunct Saturn (just as with the square and opposition between these two planets) means that there are karmic lessons to be taught, and the teacher, the one in charge of the wisdom to be exchanged, is always the one whose Saturn aspects the other's Sun, not the other way around. I don't know if this makes the discipline and teaching easier to accept or not, but it does, I trust, make clear that it's useless to fight it. It's better—and wiser—to practice "grace under pressure." Otherwise, the lessons will have to be learned in some future incarnation, since there's no escape from the inflexible "for every action there is a reaction" law of the masters of karma—unless you've read Chapter 9 in my book *Star Signs* and don't plan to allow your present body to die. In that case, the lessons must be learned at some point in time of the existence of your "Physical Immortality" on this Earth. A word to the wise is sufficient.

Sun Square Saturn   A's Sun, B's Saturn
⊙ □ ♄

I'll begin by counseling both of you to fight your frustrations because, in a cosmic and karmic sense, you have no choice. Accepting the irritations of this aspect will make it easier. It's all your fault anyway, not the fault of the stars. Your mutual behavior in a former life (or lives) created the problems that need to be resolved in this incarnation. So pay your karmic dues and stop struggling against the inevitable. You can be sure that Saturn's concepts of security and stability will, at some time, clash with the Sun's concepts. Now and then Saturn could chip away, sometimes coldly, at the Sun's self-confidence with criticisms and limitations, which will periodically so discourage and depress the Sun that physical illness is a real possibility. Much of the frustration results from the Sun's repeated refusal at least to try to follow Saturn's life-style. Saturn, in response and retaliation, will treat the Sun with hurtful coolness when the Sun refuses to play follow-the-leader, with Saturn, of course, as the leader. The other way around is what the Sun has in mind! Even if these matters aren't expressed in words, they'll be made clear through the experiences of your relationship.

Saturn's haughty, superior manner is difficult for the proud and equally haughty Sun to adjust to. Eventually, the

Sun will comprehend the rewards of acceptance and adjustment, but until then it can be the pits—for both of you, since Saturn is as frustrated by the Sun's insistence on independence as the Sun is by the limitations Saturn places on the relationship. Listen, you caused this together who knows how many centuries, millennia, or eons ago, so you'll have to suffer it together. In astrology this aspect is considered the most important one of all, which I suppose is why it's interpretation is so complex.

Whatever kind of relationship you share, there may be a difference in chronological age. That's to be expected between parent and child, but it's also frequently the case between business associates, friends, lovers, and mates.

A Saturn contact with any planet indicates that the two persons have shared one or more close relationships in former lives, Saturn being the planet of karma. Should your intercharts reveal more than one Saturn aspect, the former reincarnational experiences have been plural and profound, especially if they're accompanied by aspects involving Neptune, or a Pluto-Venus contact.

I'm sorry to burden the Sun with the following, but Universal Law remains immutable in that, when there are karmic soul-testing lessons to be learned by both, it's the person whose Saturn aspects the Sun who is the teacher in charge of the wisdom mutually needed—not the other way around. The Sun is probably bristling and boiling at learning this, but since there's no avoiding it, the Sun might as well settle down, relax, and submit to Saturn's role as teacher. In a rather subtle way, it's analogous to the counsel Queen Victoria gave to young people regarding the wedding night: "Just lie back and think of England."

In similar fashion, the Sun must "lie back" (figuratively) and think of the rewards of happiness after your mutual karmic scales are balanced! Eventually you'll both realize that the way to resolve your heavy karma and pass your much-needed soul testing is to practice "grace under pressure." As the poet wrote, "It's grace that's brought me safe so far ... and grace will lead me home."

True, this aspect demands occasional sacrifices of the ego,

but anything worth keeping forever requires mutual self-sacrifice, and, after all, love is eternal.

Saturn is secretly aware of a deep need for what the Sun can give. Likewise, the Sun is secretly aware of a deep need for what Saturn can give. Consequently, both of you may try to possess and hold on, each reluctant to permit the other to leave, regardless of friction, which is the main reason this vibration creates such a strong bond that is so difficult to break. The keynote of the strain between you could accurately be called "Who's the boss?" Both of you believe you know the answer. Unfortunately, it's not the same answer!

Should you be among those rare few with a double influence of this aspect between you (A's Saturn squares B's Sun, while at the same time B's Saturn squares A's Sun) then the bond linking you together, instead of being difficult to break, may be impossible to break, no matter how hard you may try to do so. If the latter is the case, good luck, and may you earn a thousand stars in your karmic crowns!

Postscript: Do you know who "the boss" really is? Answer: your Higher Selves.

Sun Opposed Saturn   A's Sun, B's Saturn
⊙ ☍ ♄

There is a strong tug of almost automatic resistance between you. Undoubtedly, you've felt it frequently. Saturn's limiting, cautious, and conservative attitudes in various areas of your relationship will be intensely and keenly felt by the Sun, making it appear that Saturn is being unnecessarily demanding, stubbornly uncompromising, and needlessly taking an opposite stance to whatever the Sun desires or suggests. Not always, but on rare occasions, Saturn can behave in a suspicious and exacting manner, which humiliates and hurts the Sun's pride and self-confidence and causes an explosive response born of resentment long held within. Of course, the friction isn't one sided. Saturn may complain that the Sun is overbearing and uncooperative, refusing to be instructed.

But your problems could be overcome by the Law of

Polarity. When two people possess opposite viewpoints and opposing temperaments, there can still be congenial vibrations between them. Therefore, if you make an effort, your differences can blend harmoniously because each can supply what the other one lacks. Whether the Sun opposed Saturn in your intercharts creates continual and endless mutual resistance or results in successfully "pulling out" magnetically the polarity position of these two planets is your free will choice. You're in charge. But both of you should be doing the work. Only one person willing to make the adjustment could turn it into a sado-masochist vibration. Still, it's also possible that if one of you initiates the effort necessary to bring out the positive side, it may influence the other to do the same. Halfway measures won't work. They're like "hope," a four letter, weak, and impotent word admitting the possibility of failure. What makes miracles is to know that negative doesn't really exist, except in the world of illusion—and to sing in your heart the wise lyrics of an old popular song: "You have to accentuate the positive / eliminate the negative / latch on to the affirmative, and don't mess with Mister In-Between!" Fair dinkum! (In Australia, that means "It's true, mate!") So throw another shrimp on the barbee and remember that the magnetism of the Law of Polarity can manifest magic!

Here's another fair dinkum bit of astrological information concerning this aspect: Saturn is the planet of karma. When it aspects any planet between two people, whether conjunct, square, opposed, sextile, or trine, you can be sure that you've shared one or more relationships in former lives. With several Saturn contacts in your intercharts, the reincarnational experiences in the past are increased relative to the number of Saturn aspects between you, especially if there are also Neptune aspects and a Pluto-Venus aspect. When there are no Saturn aspects between the birth charts of two people, they are meeting for the first time in this particular lifetime in a meaningful relationship; in past lives they have only touched one another briefly or lightly, like two ships that pass in the night.

And speaking of ships, a true sailor prefers to be captain of a ship that's seaworthy, rather than a brand-new and untried vessel. Seaworthy means that the ship has successfully sailed through several storms without serious or permanent damage. When you separate the word that describes your association, *relationship*, making it *relation* and *ship*, you can see why periodic storms between you, which have left you still together, should be considered a positive rather than a negative influence. Fair dinkum!

Sun Conjunct Uranus   A's Sun, B's Uranus
⊙ ☌ ♅

There's something vaguely upsetting and unusual about your relationship. Get used to it, because there always will be! It's an interesting association, no doubt about it. The only stressful facet of this vibration is that more than once you'll probably be separated by circumstances out of your control, for example, the unavoidable necessity of one of you traveling more than either of you likes. Then, too, there could be sudden (and probably brief) separations caused by your temperaments when Uranus flashes irritation like a bolt of lightning or the Sun's pride causes exhibitions of arrogant behavior. But it won't happen frequently, just periodically. Between you two there's always a surprise around the corner, and it's likely to be unique or unconventional. Any mutual endeavor you engage in will be progressive, innovative, and never, never prosaic or dull. The Sun's creative talents, exciting concepts, and large-scale ambitions will inspire more of the same in Uranus. And the Sun will probably respond with gracious hospitality when Uranus (to whom friendship is a sacred rite) pops up with unannounced dinner guests who could be the corner cop, a bag lady, the mayor, the governor, a stray Saint Bernard, or Prince Charles.

Sun Sextile or Trine Uranus   A's Sun, B's Uranus
⊙ ✶ △ ♅

This vibration often signifies an association founded on common unconventional or inventive projects involving politics, astrology, metaphysics, or scientific research. Both of you will benefit in several ways from your relationship. You tend to stimulate each other's originality through your exchange of progressive and Utopian ideas, and you awaken one another's intellectual and creative talents; consequently you're always interested in each other. The aspirations you share may be considered bizarre and eccentric by others, but they form the "tie that binds" between you, and if the world ridicules or ignores you, it only draws you closer in the kind of empathy that creates a feeling of "no one else really understands me," causing an interdependence that builds a lasting companionship.

The Sun won't find it strange if Uranus keeps a jar of pencils in the freezer so they'll stay sharp, and Uranus will comprehend the Sun's determined pursuit of any number of odd and peculiar projects. You'd make a fascinating couple to invite to a party, but you'd probably prefer to stay home together and discuss *Star Trek*, the rain forests, saving the elephants from poachers, or establishing a biosphere on Mars. If you blend your dreams as a team, you could establish a new political party, patent some marvelous invention, produce an innovative film or maybe a musical album—extremely avant-garde, of course!

The Sun's huge plans for the future will intrigue and delight Uranus, encouraging some matching gigantic ambitions, and Uranus can wear one of those bright red plastic clown noses while sitting in freeway traffic and waving merrily at other drivers without shocking the Sun in the slightest! Sharing compatible idiosyncrasies can be a really fun experience, even when others think you're a couple of harmless dorks. Why should you care? At least you have each other, like Barnum's Alligator Man and three-headed goat!

Sun Opposed or Square Uranus   A's Sun, B's Uranus
☉ ☍ □ ♅

The mildest effect of these tense aspects between the Sun and Uranus will be a sporadic, off-again, on-again relationship with periodic explosions followed by unexpected reconciliations, followed by periodic explosions, followed by unexpected reconciliations, and so on. You see the general picture. The more serious effect is an association in which there's a strong conflict of individualities. Uranus's frequent unorthodox and totally unpredictable behavior will keep the Sun nearly dizzy with confusion, never knowing what to anticipate next The Sun will try to boss or influence Uranus in some manner, which will trigger the latter's resentment and rebellion against the Sun's attempt to display authority in the relationship. Both of you will, at times, be impatient with and rebel against one another. Cooperation may occur occasionally, but only rarely, and it is difficult to achieve. If you'll both attempt to be more introspective, to project poise, balance, and self-discipline, you can reduce this stressful vibration to one of minor annoyance. It depends a great deal upon other mutual aspects between your birth charts. If they are strongly harmonious, then you can be victorious over the problems this one brings because you'll eventually realize it's worth some mutual tolerance and humility, with a large dash of forgiveness, to save the happiness you experience in other ways.

Sun Conjunct Neptune   A's Sun, B's Neptune
☉ ☌ ♆

Whatever other difficulties may arise between you periodically, for whatever planetary reason, your relationship is based on an endless supply of mutual compassion, born of many mountains climbed together in the sharing of living, loving, and forgiving in countless former incarnations. The spiritual tie between you is profound and unbreakable. This is especially true if the conjunction of these planets in your intercharts is less than one degree apart, but regardless of the degree of the orb of influence astrologically allowed when calculating this aspect, the understanding and sympathy between you is remarkable. According to the ancients, the Sun conjunct Neptune (and also a sextile or trine between them), whether found in a comparison of two birth charts or in an individual's chart, indicates more than one past incarnation in a convent or monastery as a high priest or priestess or a life as a religious leader long ago.

As a result of the karmic implications of this planetary contact, there is much shared sensitivity in your relationship, an amazing psychic tie that allows you to read each other's minds frequently and, whether you realize it consciously or not, the two of you are able to communicate without benefit of the post office or the telephone. You may or may not have developed this potential, but you should try to do so. It's a valuable asset for several reasons.

You have a sort of invisible crystal ball between you, and ESP experiments could prove astonishing. There is much devotion, tolerance, and idealism in your relationship or association, and often, for reasons beyond the control of either, some form of personal sacrifice may be required. But don't be overly concerned about such a vibration. The subtle influence of this aspect will forge a strong link with the power to overcome any such temporary karmic demands. The only so-called negative facet of the Sun conjunct Neptune is that there may be rare occasions when Neptune is deeply hurt if the Sun finds it necessary to break a promise, however minor, or when Neptune appears to be frustratingly mysterious and unfathomable to the Sun. Even so, the natural sympathy your relationship is blessed with will heal the hurt, so that your mutual trust is constantly renewed. It would take many powerfully disharmonious aspects in your intercharts to dilute this one.

Sun Sextile or Trine Neptune   A's Sun, B's Neptune
☉ ✶ △ ♆

As with the conjunction between these two planets, the sextile or trine bestows a powerful psychic tie, common spiritual interests, and a great deal of mutual sympathy and understanding. Each of you provides self-confidence and emotional support to the other. You'll probably share an interest in art, music, dancing, poetry, drama, and metaphysical matters. There's also a possibility of a common tie relating to health, hygiene, or medicine. Both of you are likely kind to animals and unfortunate Earthlings. You may also share, at some time, an interest in the sea, dolphins, and the environment-threatening issue of acid rain. Ecological goals could be part of your relationship or association, as could a religious involvement together. If you teamed up to produce a film about the saving of the Earth and her creatures, it would be successful. It's easy for you to anticipate one another's desires and wishes, and, odd as it seems, you can probably interpret each other's dreams, not to mention nightmares!

Sun Opposed or Square Neptune   A's Sun, B's Neptune
☉ ☍ □ Ψ

Neptune will continually try to escape the Sun's attempts to exhibit authority and issue commands, expecting obedience. The Sun will often be baffled and even angered by Neptune's evasive actions, interpreting them as deception. In a way, this is correct, because Neptune can appear to be submissive while simultaneously, in a subtle manner, eluding the Sun's influence. Naturally, such behavior can be misleading and, in the Sun's opinion, downright sneaky. There could be accusations of disloyalty in family, friendship, or business associations, or suspicions of infidelity between lovers or mates. These irritations are seldom as serious as they seem, however, and much of the time the situations provoked by the Sun's bossy arrogance and Neptune's "slippery" techniques in dealing with it will neutralize themselves before becoming insurmountable. Or once both of you recognize the source of the trouble, if you each tone it down a bit (the behavior that mutually annoys you), you can reach some sort of a truce, albeit a slightly uneasy one. Why not face the truth? If Neptune would be less elusive, the Sun would be less accusatory and suspicious, and if the Sun would stifle those expectations of obedience, Neptune would be free to be more up-front and direct.

Sun Conjunct Pluto   A's Sun, B's Pluto
☉ ☌ ♇

Even though it may be dormant and unexpressed, each of you wants some form of power over the relationship. The Sun itself is all powerful. So is the planet Pluto. When this immense power is combined without envy or competition, it can just about literally move mountains. Otherwise, if the two of you struggle for authority, you can destroy each other's confidence, not to mention the projects you launch together. Pluto may try to force changes on the Sun that drastically affect the relationship. Generally, the Sun should try to compromise with Pluto because—well, because it's less stressful. Pluto's essence is not a naturally accommodating one. You are both equally fascinated by the secrets and ancient mysteries of the Universe, and peruse them together down whatever path they may lead you. (You'd make a great investigative team, like Holmes and Watson, never mind gender!) However, secrets may also be a source of conflict. The Sun will not appreciate it if Pluto keeps any secrets, however innocent.

Your association is deeply karmic, and this is not the first time you've met, by any means. You've traveled many worlds and eons together in a myriad of relationships. You may or may not sense this. Perhaps you do when you retain eye contact. The eyes are the windows of the soul. And the soul knows. The soul remembers. This aspect may create periodic difficulties if there is a generation gap between you, which will only intensify any struggle for supremacy of outlooks, ideas, and life-styles. Inherent in your relationship is an awesome ability to build, or to destroy. Now, wouldn't it be foolish of both of you to transmute it into the latter instead of the former? Think about this.

Sun Sextile or Trine Pluto   A's Sun, B's Pluto
☉ ✶ △ ♀

An extremely favorable reward for your good behavior in past lives together is given to both of you by this excellent score on your karmic report card. It promises considerable harmony between you in the exchange of ideas and the solving of mysteries or problems. You stimulate ambition and enterprise in each other, resulting in substantial benefits. In the charts of individuals involved in business, politics, research, or promotional activities, it can bring great success. Between lovers or mates it can cause them to analyze and probe the depths of their relationship, creating an awareness of who they are and *why* they are. There will usually be a mutual interest in unsolved mysteries of existence in all areas of life.

Sun Opposed or Square Pluto   A's Sun, B's Pluto
☉ ♂ □ ♀

The closer you are, the more friction results from this aspect. There will be periodic testing of mutual loyalty and mutual tolerance. Even when other interchart planetary aspects are mostly harmonious, this vibration can be a troublemaker at times. In one way or another, Pluto will try to change the Sun, which the Sun will fiercely resent. Conversely, Pluto is sure to resist any attempted authority or dominance by the Sun. Pluto may now and then be jealous, demanding, and, on occasion, even revengeful or vindictive, while the Sun will be rebellious and fight against any change or control attempted by Pluto. Neither one of you accepts being corrected by the other. It sounds like what is called a Mexican standoff, doesn't it? Each of you possesses a great deal of personal power, which is why you both resist anyone, even someone with whom you are otherwise compatible, trying to lead the parade. Your equally strong personalities create the competitive stubbornness that threatens to damage your relationship. How can I help you make this vibration easier to soften and finally resolve? All right, let's try this:

When Pluto is behaving dreadfully, before the Sun explodes in fiery rebellion, the Sun should meditate on the lyrics to a little tune sung by Mr. Rogers on his children's television program, *Mr. Rogers' Neighborhood*. The words sparkle with a basic truth no one ever seems to realize.

"The people you know who are sometimes bad / are the very same people who can make you feel glad." The message is simple and clear and doesn't need explaining. Comprehend it and you'll see how wasteful and unnecessary those struggles for power and control between you really are.

As for Pluto, well, when Pluto feels an urge to try to change the Sun, Pluto should say to the Sun instead the closing words of each Mr. Rogers program: "I like you just the way you are!" I've quoted them in interpreting another aspect, but truth can't be repeated too often.

Since Pluto has such a hang-up about power, it's well to remember that those words have profound power to create harmony in any relationship between two people. Try them. You have nothing to lose except the Sun's rebellion. Listen closely with your heart and you'll hear the Sun saying, "Please stop trying to change me. I need you to like me, to love me, just the way I am."

★

★ 3 ★

Moon Aspects

Moon conjunct Moon
Moon sextile or trine Moon
Moon opposed Moon
Moon square Moon
Moon conjunct, sextile, or trine Mercury
Moon opposed Mercury
Moon square Mercury
Moon conjunct, sextile, or trine Venus
Moon opposed Venus
Moon square Venus
Moon conjunct Mars
Moon sextile or trine Mars
Moon opposed or square Mars
Moon conjunct, sextile, or trine Jupiter
Moon opposed or square Jupiter
Moon sextile or trine Saturn
Moon conjunct or square Saturn
Moon opposed Saturn
Moon conjunct Uranus
Moon sextile or trine Uranus
Moon opposed or square Uranus
Moon conjunct, sextile, or trine Neptune

Moon opposed or square Neptune
Moon conjunct Pluto
Moon sextile or trine Pluto
Moon opposed or square Pluto

Moon Conjunct Moon   A and B
☽ ☌ ☽

In astrology, the Sun rules the personality, and the Moon rules the emotions. Normally, an individual will behave most of the time as the Sun Sign indicates, but when the emotions are aroused or involved, the individual will behave temporarily according to the sign the Moon was in at birth.

Since your Moons were in the same sign when you were born, any time your emotions are aroused you'll both behave in more or less the same manner, according to the traits of the Moon sign you share.

This vibration can produce a telepathic exchange of thoughts, making you sensitive to each other's moods and sympathetic to each other's feelings.

All of the nice things above apply when your individual emotions are temporarily aroused at different times. If the emotions of both of you are involved simultaneously, a little cautionary warning may be required.

Why? Because when you become emotional at the same time and behave in basically the same way, there's a good chance the traits of the sign your Moons were in at birth will be emphasized and increased (both the positive and negative traits of your shared Moon Sign).

With two people whose mutual Moon Sign is Taurus, for example, both will become uncommonly stubborn. If the mutual Moon Sign is Cancer, both people will become weepy, possessive, cross, and cranky. If in Leo, both will swell up like balloons with pride and bossiness, and, well, you see what I mean. This lunar conjunction is a great smoother and harmony builder when your emotional moments occur apart but a bit sticky when they occur together. However, you've been advised how to keep the latter from causing serious problems, so do as you're told (be careful) and all will be well!

Here's an interesting facet to this aspect: You're likely to discover that your mothers treated you basically the same as children, and probably still do.

Moon Sextile or Trine Moon   A and B
☽ ⚹ △ ☽

In astrology, the Sun Sign influences the outward personality seen by others, but the Moon Sign influences the inner emotions. Therefore, when an individual becomes strongly emotionally involved with anything, the individual temporarily behaves in a manner matching the qualities of the sign the Moon was in at birth.

Because your Moons were in compatible and harmonious signs when you were born, when either of you becomes emotional separately at different times, or when your emotions are aroused simultaneously, things will work out smoothly between you.

With your Moon harmoniously aspected at birth, your dispositions and temperaments are markedly congenial, and your emotional responses to most situations and events involving yourselves or others are similar, causing you to sympathize with one another's moods and feelings.

There is often a telepathic exchange of thoughts between you. Your tastes are similar, likewise your "likes and dislikes," and you'll usually be in agreement in both major matters and the minor ones, little day-to-day things others quarrel about. If additional planetary aspects in your intercharts indicate conflicts, this one will help you both be more understanding of them. So Moon sextile or trine Moon is a great little booster to have in your relationship.

Moon Opposed Moon   A and B
☽ ☍ ☽

Your moods and feelings are very different, nevertheless there is much sensitivity to each other's moods and feelings. That sounds like a contradiction, but it isn't, really, and the experiences of your relationship have already made this clear to you. In fact, the differences are mutually helpful, because you have a basic sympathy and understanding of your divergent emotional approaches to situations and events, so there is seldom any serious tension or conflict. Unless you share a lot of planetary aspects in your birth charts, your dispositions adjust smoothly most of the time, allowing you to cooperate and balance the polarity of your emotional natures. Remember that the Law of Polarity can work in a beneficial way because each possesses what the other lacks, and the magnetic pull between two opposed planets can cause your natures to balance smoothly in a pleasant exchange of attitudes toward day-to-day problems, especially in disagreements with others outside your relationship.

Moon Square Moon   A and B
☽ □ ☽

When there is a Moon opposed Moon aspect between two birth charts, it causes different emotional attitudes and responses, but there is also usually a mutual sympathetic understanding of the differences. This aspect of the square between your two Moons at birth presents the same differences, but lacks the mutual sympathetic understanding of these differences in your moods and feelings, causing inconsiderate behavior and impatience on both sides when you respond differently to the same situation. Usually, this vibration doesn't create any really serious stress or tension. It will more likely manifest itself in petty bickering or trifling irritations and annoyances, which may occur frequently but leave no lasting scars to destroy your relationship. One of you may accuse the other of "making much ado about nothing," and probably with good reason.

It is possible that the two of you secretly enjoy this planetary vibration. It gives you the opportunity to experience the stimulus of minor disagreements and energizing discussions, followed by "making up" with apologies and bear hugs. The latter expression of atonement does not, of course, apply to a couple of macho males in a business association as it does to other kinds of relationships, because males are forbidden by custom to demonstrate affection between themselves in this manner. Custom is wrong. Bear hugs are needed by and are good for both sexes. When "society" comprehends this, our planet will become a brighter and happier place to "do our karmic time," since, in the words of Beatle John Lennon, "Life is what happens to you when you're busy making other plans."

Moon Conjunct, Sextile, or Trine Mercury   A's Moon, ☽ ☌ ⚹ △ ☿   B's Mercury

The Moon's sensitive, intuitive qualities blend smoothly with Mercury's curiosity and quick intelligence, so that your concepts of a situation are nearly always in harmonious agreement. Together, you create a kind of Sherlock Holmes (Moon)–Dr. Watson (Mercury) team in penetrating puzzling matters of all sorts. You probably have a number of common interests and encourage each other in them. Because of your pronounced mental and emotional affinity, there's excellent understanding between you. When the Moon's deep feelings combine with Mercury's mental alertness, some startling results could occur, of decided benefit to both of you.

You love traveling together and should do so as often as possible, since mutual hegiras bring you good luck. Keep your suitcases packed so you can fasten the wings on your heels and fly toward the clouds on short notice! Computers probably fascinate you, including the one called the human brain. There's an extra bonus to this harmonious vibration: You can very likely interpret each other's dreams, which is a handy little knack to possess in any kind of relationship.

Moon Opposed Mercury
A's Moon, B's Mercury

☽ ☍ ☿

From the beginning of your relationship, you've shared some fascinating conversations and stimulating discussions, which is one of the reasons for the attraction between you. Whatever the nature of the relationship, you both find it more exciting than boring. However, there may be some friction caused by a different attitude toward communication and the exchange of ideas. Mercury needs to express thoughts with a shower of words, which can make the Moon impatient, sometimes rudely so, while the Moon's more introverted approach to communication, using few words, could make Mercury equally impatient and annoyed because Mercury needs the Moon to communicate and express thoughts verbally or orally, not with silence.

Try a little less criticism and a little more mutual respect for one another's different manner of expressing. Then you can use the Law of Polarity to pull out or magnetize your opposed attitudes of expression, blending them into a harmonious and compatible vibration, since there is merit in both behaviors, divergent as they are. Aside from this occasional stress between you, the Moon-Mercury opposition in your intercharts has a positive side. When Mercury's gift for words and mental quickness combine with the Moon's ultrasensitive perceptions, you can use the opposition to make your ambitions manifest instead of harping at each other. Understanding and tolerance, minus criticism, can transform this aspect from a problem into an asset.

Although the Moon may grumble that Mercury, when asked what time it is, will explain how to make a watch and Mercury may complain that the Moon often discusses important issues in monosyllables, the mutual irritation can be decreased if Mercury tries not to express the same thought several times when one carefully spoken declaration will suffice, and if the Moon will try harder to respond to Mercury with a few more words than a brief "Yes," "No," or "Maybe," playing an exasperating lunar guessing game with Mercury. It's the old battle between enthusiastic extroversion and subdued introversion. Each attitude benefits from borrowing a little of the other. As with all truth and wisdom, the solution is simple but not always easy to recognize.

Moon Square Mercury   A's Moon, B's Mercury
☽ □ ☿

Mercury's glibness, mental quickness, and sometimes contradictory speech and behavior (Shall we say double-talk? Yes, let's!) will frequently be misunderstood by, and therefore upsetting to, the Moon's extremely sensitive nature. The Moon wishes Mercury would play those mental chess games and perform those quick changes with someone else. Mercury often becomes annoyed and impatient when the Moon doesn't comprehend thoughts or grasp ideas quickly, and angrily envious when the Moon, using the latent lunar intuition and imagination, manages to perceive matters far ahead of Mercury's initial recognition of them. Result? Mercury becomes defensive and retaliates by using the mercurial weapons of critical sarcastic speech against the hypersensitive Moon, which can leave deep scars. Other favorable or harmonious aspects in the intercharts can patch up the hurts this one brings and make it less antagonistic. Actually, the vibration is not a seriously negative one, and the worst trouble it can cause the two of you is some measure of bickering and snappiness. If Mercury will watch that caustic speech in response to the Moon's differing taste and interests and the Moon will try harder not to misinterpret the ideas and concepts Mercury is trying to project, you'll achieve a reasonable degree of harmony by becoming more—well, more reasonable!

Moon Conjunct, Sextile, or Trine Venus   A's Moon,
☽ ☌ ⚹ △ ♀   B's Venus

Assuming that most of the other planetary aspects in your intercharts are harmonious, this one will bless your relationship with deep mutual devotion and affection, inspiring a permanent attachment. If there are antagonistic and tense aspects in your intercharts, this one will soften and lighten any differences in your personalities and behaviors toward one another. Your relationship will be comfortably congenial the majority of the time. You will both benefit not only from mutual consideration and sympathy, but also in financial matters. You have so much in common that it's difficult for the seeds of disagreement, which will rarely crop up, to grow into real problems. They quietly fade away with each morning's new sunrise and will seldom be serious enough or last long enough to cause bitterness or grudges. Both of you are inclined to forgive small hurts easily, tend to be generous to one another with money, and are usually in agreement regarding creative endeavors, traveling, and social activities. Aren't you glad your fairy godmothers waved this astrological wand over your cribs?

Moon Opposed Venus   A's Moon, B's Venus
☽ ☍ ♀

The Law of Polarity is at work between you, creating a magnetic vibration that causes you to encourage one another and blessing your relationship with a calm, soothing, and comforting undercurrent. Each of you may have certain interests or activities the other doesn't share, but it's likely that you'll resolve this by the Moon exposing Venus to interests Venus learns to enjoy, and through Venus enticing the Moon to experience activities the Moon discovers are fun and exciting. "You teach me to ski, and I'll teach you to play tennis," "I'll teach you to paint, and you teach me to dance," or whatever. If one of you possesses a natural talent the other doesn't, it's more likely to inspire respect and admiration than to spawn competitive urges.

Moon Square Venus   A's Moon, B's Venus
☽ □ ♀

Especially in very close and intimate relationships, there's a strong possibility (let's be honest and say probability) of periodic tension caused by petty jealousy, most likely imaginary and unnecessary. Both of you will be jealous to some degree, but one of you is painfully open and direct about it, expressing your jealousy in occasional outbursts of hurt and anger followed by withdrawal, and the other is equally troubled by the fear of losing love through a third person stealing it away but will tend to try to hide such feelings and deny they exist. With this aspect, an astrologer can't tell which person responds which way, but the two of you will know. There could also be some conflicting patterns in your life-styles involving social inclinations and recreational preferences, but if other interchart aspects indicate basic mutual affection and harmony, these minor matters can be smoothly adjusted between you. Although the square is not as favorable as other Moon-Venus configurations, it can't be considered seriously harmful to compatibility. It should help both of you to remind yourselves to realize that jealousy, when kept under reasonable control, is a compliment, and instead of being an annoyance, can, in a very subtle manner, increase the self-confidence of the one toward whom it's directed.

A cosmic message for both of you: After all, it should be more pleasant than troubling to know someone you care about can be upset over anything that might take you away. It would be a sight more upsetting if the other person wished you would go away or didn't care if you switched your loyalty to someone else. Whether your association is family, friendship, business, or romantic, never lose sight of this basic truth: Whether the jealousy is career founded or emotionally seeded, in every situation without exception jealousy is deeply rooted in fear and therefore should be met with compassionate reassurance, not resentment. In fact, that's the only way to cause it to permanently disappear. Repeat: the only way.

Moon Conjunct Mars
☽ ☌ ♂

A's Moon, B's Mars

In all kinds of associations or relationships, Mars needs to curb the tendency to be bossy, argumentative, impatient, and demanding with the Moon. And the Moon must control a tendency to be evasive, secretive, and moody, crawling into a shell of self-protection or weeping waterfalls of sensitivity over every minor and usually imaginary hurt. The two of you who share this aspect will face periods in your relationship when it may seem that you're from different planets altogether, even different solar systems or galaxies. First, one of you will claim to be a normal Earthling and accuse the other of being a Vulcanite. Then you switch roles—and labels. The sometimes harsh and aggressive behavior Mars exhibits can be unbearably abrasive to the ultrasensitive Moon, while the Moon's occasional moody silences can be intensely frustrating to Mars. But wait, what is that strange magnetism between you that causes the two of you to stick together against the cold, unfeeling world? I guess it could be called empathetic mutual support. Empathetic support won't prevent the flaring of tempers and disagreements, but it does make it easier to make up and say "I'm sorry." When one of you is genuinely sorry, the other should accept it. To ignore a heartfelt apology is cruel and will only deepen the conflict. To forgive even before someone apologizes is the most blessed of all traits a human can possess. How about remembering that? Also remember to try to understand instead of trying to be understood. It's a miracle-making formula.

Moon Sextile or Trine Mars ☽ ✳ △ ♂   A's Moon, B's Mars

You can take your choice of terms. Physical chemistry. Sexual magnetism. Irresistible passion. Whatever it's called, it forms a powerful bond between lovers or mates, and it even intensifies the platonic loyalty tie between relatives, friends, or business associates. Any way you view it, this is a strongly positive planetary aspect between two birth charts. Mars bolsters the Moon's self-confidence, stimulating the Moon's latent imagination, ideas, and ideals. The Moon is able to gently guide and direct Mars's forceful drive into productive channels. When you work together as a team, there's an ancient cooperation that makes things happen and brings projects or endeavors to a successful conclusion. With this vibration between you, there will usually be a determination to follow through and avoid procrastination, moving straight ahead instead of in circles.

Moon Opposed or Square Mars   A's Moon, B's Mars
☽ ☍ □ ♂

As you've undoubtedly already discovered, along with the strong mutual attraction of this vibration (sexual with lovers or mates, mental in other associations), there is an equally strong emotional reaction between you, producing serious personality conflicts. Mars's impulsive behavior may topple the Moon's poise and adversely affect the Moon's more tranquil disposition. The Moon will irritate Mars by being hypersensitive when Mars meant no harm. It's a frustrating trick of the planets to give you this aspect that so powerfully pulls you together, almost irresistibly, for the evident purpose of forcing you to work out difficult karma together. But planets do that, because they are in charge of your mutual karmic soul testing, you know. There could be back-and-forth accusations of nagging, rudeness, abruptness, and refusals to talk things over calmly. The only cosmic wisdom to heal the hurts this aspect causes is the same given to those who have the Moon and Mars conjunct in their intercharts.

I've quoted it elsewhere, but I'll repeat it here, since it also applies to both of you. The healing wisdom lies in the last lines of the prayer of *Francesco di Bernadone* of Assisi: "Grant that I may not so much seek to be understood as to understand / then miracle shall follow miracle, and wonders shall never cease." Say these words aloud every single day of your life together, and you will see how true they are. Oh, yes—and also practice what they advise you both to do!

Moon Conjunct, Sextile, or Trine Jupiter   A's Moon,
☽ ☌ ✶ △ ♃   B's Jupiter

Even those whose intercharts reveal a predominance of discordant aspects and who, later, for whatever reason, terminate their relationship won't hold grudges or harbor any permanent ill will if they share this one.

Assuming that the two of you have an adequate number of harmonious additional aspects between your birth charts, this one will pack a powerful positive punch! When the Moon requests a favor from Jupiter, it will nearly always be granted without question. Any one of these three aspects will bestow substantial financial benefits and "luck" from Jupiter on the Moon. Most of the time the Moon will be co-operative with Jupiter's expansive ideas and concepts, adaptable to those gigantic goals and ambitions. There is normally agreement in all educational, legal, or religious matters (unless other mutual planetary aspects create friction in these areas, but even then this Moon-Jupiter contact will ease any such tension). Jupiter will tend to be generous and protective toward the Moon while, in turn, the Moon is wonderfully able to stir Jupiter's imagination and self-confidence. This is probably not needed by Jupiter, but every little bit helps! Even when one already possesses an abundance of imagination and self-confidence, it certainly doesn't hurt for another person to intensify and increase it just by being around. It's been said that more is not necessarily better. But in this case, it is.

Moon Opposed or Square Jupiter   A's Moon, B's Jupiter
☽ ☍ □ ♃

Yes, you do have your share of disagreements and arguments, especially in two areas: religion and/or finances. Some of these quarrels may involve family matters, in-laws, or other relatives, but basically you are, to some degree, at odds with each other's religious concepts and money viewpoints. You may bicker over the budget frequently, and there could be conflict over spending money either too economically (usually the Moon) or too extravagantly (usually Jupiter). Stress could occasionally involve, in some way, matters relating to the stock market or legal entanglements, attorneys, etc. Jupiter may, with all good intent, make expansive promises, causing the Moon to expect too much, and be deeply disappointed when a promise or two is broken now and then. The Moon is not innocent of initiating trouble either, by taking advantage of Jupiter's generous and benevolent disposition to make constant demands. None of these problems need be serious enough to cause a break in the relationship, but they can be emotionally disturbing to both of you and can considerably disrupt harmony, especially if you both live under the same roof.

Look, so one of you goes to Synagogue and the other goes to daily Mass, or one is into astrology and the other is a born-again Christian, or one of you thinks the other's mother is the Witch of Endor and the other thinks your mother is Lizzie Borden. Keep your opinions and beliefs to yourself, because you are *not*, in all likelihood, going to change your viewpoints—either of you. Therefore, it's best to observe silence on the painful subjects. Otherwise you may win the battle but lose the war. Of course, all wars are a dreadful waste, even to the victor.

Moon Sextile or Trine Saturn   A's Moon, B's Saturn
☽ ✶ △ ♄

This is not a planetary aspect of passion, but one of stability. Saturn is like the proverbial Rock of Gibraltar to the Moon, providing a strong shoulder for the Moon to lean on and weep on (which the Moon may do with fair frequency). The harmony between you is based on mutual need and mutual fulfillment. Saturn steadies the Moon's changing emotions and provides a safe port following any storm caused by outsiders. The Moon finds Saturn to be steadfast, loyal, and dependable, offering wise counsel when the Moon's moods are depressed and the dreams are troubled. But the gifts exchanged between you are not one-sided by any means. The Moon expands Saturn's goals, softening Saturn's behavior, and demonstrates to Saturn what can be accomplished when imagination is added to practicality, a combination Saturn will find to be most beneficial. This is a planetary vibration guaranteed to add a comforting sense of quiet harmony to any relationship, whether involving lovers, mates, family members, or business associates. There may be a difference in age between the two of you, which is hardly worth noting, since chronological calendar age is an illusion anyway.

Note: Read Chapter 9 in Linda Goodman's *Star Signs*.—*Editor*

Moon Conjunct Saturn   A's Moon, B's Saturn
☽ ☌ ♄

One might call this vibration somewhat paradoxical as far as breaking up and making up are concerned. As you're probably already aware, your relationship is not always a garden path of lilacs and sweet peas. There are a few thorns and pebbles along the way, tripping you up now and then, however strong the bond linking you may be, and this aspect, as I said, paradoxically, makes that bond even stronger, although at times it may seem more like double handcuffs than "the golden tie that binds"!

Remember that Saturn is the planet of karma; therefore, the person whose Saturn conjuncts the Moon (or any planet) of the other is the one who's in charge of the karmic lessons to be learned by both of you. This may upset the Moon, but there's about as much use fighting it as trying to stop the sunrise. Saturn's attempts to discipline the Moon and take charge of the relationship can make the Moon feel stifled and restricted, even suffocated. Also, Saturn, when in a negative mood, may exaggerate trifles and turn cool, injuring the Moon's sensitive feelings. Periodically, Saturn will place some sort of limitation on the relationship and be overly critical, which naturally depresses the Moon. When the Moon responds with resentful, hurt withdrawal, Saturn, instead of sympathizing, is capable of becoming even colder. This aspect sometimes causes one of your relatives to interfere in some way and dampen your spirits, adding to the frustrations.

Admittedly, the planet Saturn is a strict master of karma, but Saturn can't help playing the assigned cosmic role, and the Moon should try to keep this in mind. Now and then each of you feels like saying to the other, "Lighten up!" although for different reasons. Actually, those two words will go a long way toward lifting the burden of this planetary conflict: Lighten up, lighten up, lighten up, lighten up! Because of the heavy karma of this aspect, the stress of the learning process is not as painful as the loneliness would be if you parted. I warned you at the beginning, in the first sentence, that this is a paradoxical vibration with a capital P!

Moon Opposed or Square Saturn   A's Moon, B's Saturn
) ♂ □ ♄

The Moon will resent Saturn's disciplinary behavior, unjust criticisms, and inconsiderate, selfish attitudes. Saturn will resent the Moon's moody disposition, flights of impractical fancy, oversensitivity, and tearful responses to imaginary hurts. Saturn will periodically arouse worry and anxiety or cause discouragement to the Moon, while the Moon frustrates Saturn by crawling into a protective shell of silence or retreating into weeping spells, becoming emotional instead of rational when problems arise. You have opposite ways of handling everything from stress and conflict to the spending of money and life-styles.

Still, as in Nature, in human nature the Sun does manage to break through the clouds now and then, and rainbows can appear after your storms. To bring out the Sun and the rainbows of your relationship, try to seek the positive promise of any two opposed planets or polarized viewpoints. It's a delicate and complex task but definitely worth the effort. Since Saturn sees the conservative, safe, and practical side of any situation and the Moon sees the intuitive, imaginative, and magical side, when you blend your two opposite views, realizing that each of you possesses what the other lacks and needs, the combination can be a powerful vibration for success. Such a balance infallibly produces harmony. That's why an opposition has such magnetism. It draws you together, then forces you to face your individual shortcomings. What each needs to balance your nature is found in the other; it's there for the taking. Why allow this conflict of attitudes to create warfare between you when you can mutually choose to guide it into a powerfully energizing vibration?

Moon Conjunct Uranus   A's Moon, B's Uranus
) ☌ ♅

The intellectual stimulation between you is exciting and powerful. The moment you met, both of you felt a spontaneous, unexpected, and magnetic attraction, rather like a bolt of lightning, creating an unconventional friendship, business association, or romantic union—unconventional to others but as natural as rain to the two of you. However, friction and irritation can change attraction into repulsion or disinterest, also like a bolt of lightning! There's nothing predictable about your association. Sometimes Uranus's bizarre behavior clashes with the Moon's more conventional attitudes. There is tremendous fascination here, but it's an extremely changeable vibration and doesn't do much for permanency of a relationship unless other planetary aspects between your natal charts bind you together. Still, there are always those thrilling lightning bolts to consider, and boredom will never be one of your problems. If you link your minds and hearts, the two of you could patent an invention that might change the world! In astrology, that's called channeling energy (whether so-called positive or so-called negative energy) into a laser beam of power instead of dissipating it into the ethers haphazardly. So use this admittedly tricky aspect to become a double laser beam!

Moon Sextile or Trine Uranus   A's Moon, B's Uranus
☽ ⚹ △ ♅

Your relationship is certain to be highly unusual and unorthodox in some way, and perhaps in several ways. Whatever your relationship is, it's definitely not ordinary or conventional. Your emotions are stimulated by the rather far-out events you continually experience, creating a powerful magnetic pulse between you. It's an inspirational and stimulating vibration in business, friendship, or family associations, but when found in the charts of lovers or mates, Moon sextile or trine Uranus bestows a rare blessing. In addition to loving each other, you also like each other. You are friends as well as romantic lovers, which is an ideal situation. You'll probably move unexpectedly many times during your relationship, but these sudden changes of residence are likely to be more exciting than stressful. Uranus awakens the spirit and inspires idealism in the Moon, while the

Moon's natural imagination will stimulate and increase
Uranus's originality, versatility, and creative ability. Uranus
will frequently assist the Moon in unexpected ways. You'll
have a rollicking time together—reading a symphony or listening to a book. Leaving tact aside, you are both quite
weird, you know. Well, at least one of you is, for sure!

Moon Opposed or Square Uranus   A's Moon, B's Uranus
☽ ☍ □ ♅

If your interchart aspects between other planets do not
offer strong promises of permanency, this one can cause an
abrupt and unexpected breakup, like a flash of lightning
(which, by the way, Uranus happens to rule). If your other
interchart aspects do indicate a permanent association or
relationship, then this one will not necessarily cause a final
break but could cause periodic (and noisy, weepy) sudden
separations, later reconciled almost as quickly as they oc-
curred.

The Moon's sensitive moods, emotions, and feelings are
often disturbed by Uranus's changeable and unpredictable
behavior. It's true that Uranus will stimulate ideas and such
to the Moon's undeniable benefit, but it's equally true that
the stimulation will test the Moon's ability to adapt and
puts considerable strain on the Moon's poise and stability.
If yours is the opposition rather than the square aspect between these two planets, you can save the day by drawing
on the astrological rule of the magnetism of polarity, meaning that you can each fill up the holes, so to speak, in the
other, with one supplying what the other needs and lacks.

However, whether these two heavenly bodies are opposed
or square, the result may be anything but heavenly—and
more often unsettling. Moon opposed or square Uranus can
be an undeniably chaotic vibration at times, but to some people that's a challenge. So if you like challenges, this planetary aspect will not disappoint you. One of the ways it could
channel its energy is into many changes of careers and/or
residence.

Moon Conjunct, Sextile, or Trine Neptune   A's Moon,
☽ ☌ ⚹ △ ♆   B's Neptune

If you choose, the two of you can save lots of money on your AT&T, Sprint, or MCI long-distance calls and on your U.S. Post Office, Federal Express, or UPS expenses. Why pay out all that cash to communicate when the two of you possess such an incredible telepathic tie? If you hone and sharpen and improve what you already have between you instinctively, you can reach each other any time you feel the need tugging on the pulsing cords and chords that link your minds, hearts, and spirits. There is much mutual sympathy and inspiration in your association or relationship. You both frequently answer the phone before it rings (when the other is on the line). You share consolation and comfort when life is disappointing and ever-spiraling ideals and ideas when life is stable.

You'd be an absolutely splendid team in dancing, acting, or any of the arts; founding a new religious or spiritual movement; investigating or writing about mysteries; and suchlike. Any esoteric, mystical, or occult studies probably fascinate you mutually. If you haven't visited the Great Pyramid in Egypt together yet, you should. Your experience there will be most enlightening. But don't try to visit or investigate the Bermuda Triangle; your friends may never see you again! The only small irritation between you with this aspect may be that both of you may seem to be slightly distant or aloof to the other at times (a natural result when two people are always taking astral trips, both together and separately), but with the spiritual wisdom and illumination you share, that should be easy for you to resolve. All of the foregoing applies to family, friendship, and business associations, but with lovers or mates, Moon conjunct, sextile, or trine Neptune can be a regular Elizabeth Barrett–Robert Browning vibration! Have you ever written poems to one another?

Moon Opposed or Square Neptune
A's Moon, B's Neptune
☽ ☍ □ ♆

Admit it! You're both ultrasensitive and moody. And you both overreact to (usually) imagined hurts from each other. You're equally easily disturbed by trifles, and you both tend to respond with brief or lengthy disappearances into silence, although the Moon may sometimes dampen the silences with anything from sniffles to waterfalls of tears (even the men). It should be realized that this mutual behavior is not the way you, as individuals, behave with others, only with one another.

Neptune can cause a great deal of mental confusion in the Moon, which escalates misunderstandings that began as difficult to clarify. Many issues seem to be evasive and cloudy—foggy. Each of you appears to be mysterious to the other from time to time, impossible to penetrate, leading to mutual suspicions of deception, usually not real but imagined. Nevertheless, suspicions, whether true or fantasized, can result in prickly irritations on both sides.

You should both drop the wounded silence routine and try talking things over. Let the fresh air of honesty blow through the windows of your minds, and vocalize your fears and resentments. Retreating never works; it only deepens frustrations. Open up! And try to curb your mutual tendency to secrecy (not to others, remember, but to each other). If there's anything that vastly increases suspicion, it's secrecy. You both pride yourselves on your ability to keep secrets, but no one is going to give you an award, a medal, or a blue ribbon for this "talent." If you can't resist the temptation, drop the relationship and join the CIA.

Moon Conjunct Pluto
A's Moon, B's Pluto
☽ ☌ ♇

This aspect can have a strongly positive or strongly negative effect on your relationship, through your free-will choice. But whichever way the relationship's energy is channeled, it will be strong—and this strength emanates from past karma together in former incarnations.

Pluto can be possessive and absorbing, sometimes needlessly jealous, arousing resentment in the Moon. Also, Pluto can probe into secrets the Moon would rather keep private, and perhaps attempt to change or drastically reform something in the Moon's character or behavior patterns. Still, the Moon will often benefit from the way Pluto increases the Moon's already considerable imagination and greatly enlarges the Moon's viewpoints and conceptions of life.

This planetary aspect in the intercharts can create a powerful physical attraction when the two are lovers or mates. In other relationships and associations, the attraction will be mental.

Moon Sextile or Trine Pluto   A's Moon, B's Pluto
☽ ⚹ △ ♇

Like all Pluto (and Saturn) mutual aspects, this one initiates from past karma in former incarnations. It powerfully stimulates your imaginations, dreams, and intuitions when you're together. A magnetic mental attraction is felt from the beginning of a family, friendship, or business association, and between lovers or mates the chemistry is profoundly sexual. It bestows ESP on you, and telepathy and compassion for each other's pain and disappointments. It's an excellent vibration for any kind of professional or political association. If the two of you ever become involved in investigative or research projects, especially in esoteric fields, ecology projects, or real estate, you'll make excellent partners.

Moon Opposed or Square Pluto   A's Moon, B's Pluto
☽ ☍ □ ♇

This is another one of those Pluto (or Saturn) karmic patterns from something one of you did against the other in earlier lifetimes that needs to be worked out and balanced in this one. It will take lots of gentle patience, tolerance, understanding, and forgiveness to ease the stress and strain of this vibration.

Pluto may expect the Moon to make all or most of the adjustments, so the relationship or association may possibly cause serious emotional disturbance or physical illness in the Moon, unless a conscious attempt is made by both of you to smooth out your disagreements before they grow into mountains of misery. Be kind to each other; life is so much more comfortable that way. It might help to take separate retreats alone now and then to renew your inner spiritual energy.

4

Mercury Aspects

Mercury conjunct, sextile, or trine Mercury
Mercury opposed Mercury
Mercury square Mercury
Mercury conjunct, sextile, or trine Venus
Mercury opposed or square Venus
Mercury conjunct Mars
Mercury sextile or trine Mars
Mercury opposed or square Mars
Mercury conjunct, sextile, or trine Jupiter
Mercury opposed or square Jupiter
Mercury conjunct Saturn
Mercury sextile or trine Saturn
Mercury opposed or square Saturn
Mercury conjunct, sextile, or trine Uranus
Mercury opposed or square Uranus
Mercury conjunct Neptune
Mercury sextile or trine Neptune
Mercury opposed or square Neptune
Mercury conjunct Pluto
Mercury sextile or trine Pluto
Mercury opposed or square Pluto

Mercury Conjunct, Sextile, or Trine Mercury   A and B
☿ ☌ ✶ △ ☿

You have the ability to read each other's minds, not so much through telepathy as because your minds are so often thinking the same thoughts! Your mental affinity is marked, which causes your perceptions of people and events to be, if not identical, at least very similar.

You like playing mind games with one another, a favorite mutual pastime, even when it's practiced unconsciously. You'd be fortunate in endeavors involving writing, publishing, health, advertising, radio, and newspapers, to name only a few areas—actually in any job or career requiring verbal dexterity.

You probably enjoy traveling together, anyplace and anytime, because to both of you the grass always looks greener in faraway pastures. When you're not traveling geographically, you're probably astral traveling, or making imaginative trips into each other's minds. You have no trouble communicating ideas, and you greatly enjoy your conversations and discussions, which are likely to be numerous.

This is a blessed vibration, not in any sense a minor one, since it insures that you'll never lose interest in your relationship, never run out of things to talk about, and will fascinate each other forever. Another gift of this aspect is that, when any troubles or problems arise between you, if you express yourselves by talking things over, you can find a solution, however impossible it may seem. Words have magical powers!

Mercury Opposed Mercury   A and B
☿ ☍ ☿

You have an enthusiastic interest in testing each other's mental agility and alertness, which is why you're always playing mental chess games with one another, in both obvious and subtle ways. When one checkmates the other, it's not always just for the sheer fun of it. More often than not, the hidden motive is to win an intellectual victory. Since your mental outlooks are polarized, the games are always exciting. When you blend your opposite viewpoints, you can solve just about any problem in math or human behavior. When you don't, well, after an exercise in mental powers, the one who wins will project a rather superior attitude while the one who loses will feel a need to continue the challenges by instigating more of the same. There are few times in your relationship when one of you is not attempting to top the other. This contributes to interesting fireside chats, even mutual talking in your sleep! You may argue about short trips—one wants to take the train, the other wants to drive—but the disagreements are all on the surface, for the purpose of stimulation. This opposition of your Mercury birth positions serves to make you hard to beat as a team in any endeavor that requires mental superiority. I wouldn't want to play Trivial Pursuit against the two of you! They wrote that travel song for you, the one that goes, "I'll take the high road/you take the low road/and I'll get to Scotland before ye!/On the bonny, bonny banks of Loch Lomond..."

I'm not sure about the spelling of the last word in the previous sentence. I know how to spell *loch*, the Scottish word for lake, but I'm not certain about "Lomond." If my spelling is right, fine. If not, one (or both) of you will be sure to catch the error and quickly correct it mentally, so I won't bother to look it up at the library. You see I have Mars-in-Gemini (the sign ruled by Mercury), so I'm able to play your mental chess games too—right along with you!

Mercury Square Mercury   A and B
☿ □ ☿

You share a bushel of differences of opinion, some of them serious, some just plain silly. You're capable of criticizing everything from the way one of you brushes his or her teeth or how the toilet paper should go on the roll to the way money is spent and the best time to vacation, let alone the place. You'll probably argue about politics, quarrel about what music to listen to or what movie to see. There's just no denying the difference in your taste in entertainment, lifestyle, the news, and food. But you can try to make those differences work for harmony, instead of against it, and become happy campers despite this vibration. Sometimes differences create perfect solutions, like the old Mother Goose nursery rhyme "Jack Sprat could eat no fat, / His wife could eat no lean. / And so you see, between them both / They licked the platter clean." Look on the bright side.

Mercury Conjunct, Sextile, or Trine Venus   A's Mercury,
☿ ☌ ✳ △ ♀   B's Venus

Unless many of the mutual aspects between your other natal planets are strongly tense or stressful in some way, there are probably few areas of real conflict between you (every relationship has some!). You probably cooperate well in most financial matters, encourage each other's talents and creative aspirations, and respect one another's intellectual abilities. Even your secret dreams of happiness are similar because your understanding springs from genuine mutual sympathy and affection. Things should be easy and smooth if you choose to work together on any kind of project, whether the endeavor is practical or cultural. But don't let your natural harmony cause you to drift gradually into an emotionless vacuum.

Pick an argument now and then, just for the fun of it! An occasional mild dispute allows the cool, fresh breezes of mental and emotional stimulation to blow through the stale air of constant and eternal absolute agreement. As the Sun Sign of Libra teaches (even to non-Librans), the answer to happiness is neither positive nor negative, but a perfect balance of each. So-called positive energy can have its downside of exaggerated optimism, and so-called negative energy can have its bright side of comfortable security and soothing passivity. Balance is the answer. You wouldn't be able to rejoice in the sunlight if you had never experienced rain, nor would spring be so magical if it were not for winter. Mother Nature knows what she's doing. Trust her. Imitate her wisdom in your human nature. In the mirror world of perfect balance, the reverse is always also true. For example, personally, I love rain, whereas continual sunlight depresses me. Others adore sunshine and are depressed by rain. That's how the miracle of perfect balance works. Do you understand? Do you agree? Please, just this once, will one of you not understand and not agree? Thank you.

Mercury Opposed or Square Venus
☿ ☍ □ ♀

A's Mercury,
B's Venus

In a close association or an intimate relationship, there will be periodic minor annoyances and disagreements. The reason for such occasional conflicts is that the two of you do not always view things the same way; therefore, one of you may keep trying to change the other's outlook (creating the irritation). It won't work, because each viewpoint has both its flaws and its virtues. It's best to ignore the entire matter, as much as possible. Mercury tends to lack sympathy with the Moon's emotional needs, which results in the Moon seeing Mercury as cold and unresponsive. Mercury's complaint is that the Moon is frustratingly evasive, moody, cranky at times, tending to vacillate and to live in a fantasy world. Mentally agile and changeable, Mercury's sometimes sharp and sarcastic criticism can cause the Moon to escape into wounded, silent retreat. Mercury must learn to recognize the Moon's hypersensitivity to unkindness, whether intentional or not, and the Moon must learn to respect and tolerate Mercury's absolute need to communicate with words and face issues mentally rather than emotionally. Then all will be smooth and lovely. Does it hurt to try? You have nothing to lose and a whole lot to gain by each of you attempting to understand and tolerate the divergent outlook and behavior of the other. This is not a joyous vibration, but it's a mild aspect and won't cause a serious threat to your relationship.

Mercury Conjunct Mars
☿ ☌ ♂

A's Mercury, B's Mars

I will not pussyfoot or tippy-toe around the truth. The responsibility for whether this aspect in your intercharts showers joy and excitement or misery and discontent upon your relationship lies not with the stars, but with *you*. On the sunny side of the street, this planetary conjunction can greatly enliven your association, quicken and intensify your mutual abilities to "make things happen," allowing your mental awareness and talents for self-expression and communication to become powerful arrows for hitting the bull's-eye of success, turning ideas into ideals, then into the manifestation of reality. It can carry you far, very far—toward your mutual dreams, adding the fire of Mars to the intellectual organizing of Mercury.

On the shady side of the street, aside from the undeniable stimulation of this aspect, anything from minor irritation to major annoyance can occur when Mars becomes impatient, headstrong, and argumentative, insisting on immediate action when Mercury needs and desires to plan in a rational, reasonable manner. Mars feels that Mercury takes a frustrating length of time changing opinions and decisions before acting, while Mercury can be appalled by Mars's reckless, impulsive way of acting without first counting to ten. (In the army, the philosophy is "Ready-Aim-Fire!" With Mars, often the philosophy is "Fire-Aim-Ready!") Well, there you have it. Remember the song lyric "Life can be so sweet / on the sunny side of the street" and choose it over the shady side.

Mercury Sextile or Trine Mars   A's Mercury, B's Mars
☿ ✶ △ ♂

How nice! One might call this aspect a recipe for success. It bestows the same powerful stimulation as the conjunction of these two planets, without the conjunction's possibilities of irritation and annoyance. With this vibration humming between you, Mercury is able to encourage Mars's intense ambition and at the same time curb Mars's impatience—and quell Mars's fiery, impulsive energy in an intelligent, thoughtful direction, preventing Mars from becoming a misguided missile, scattering energies like confetti to the winds. An extra blessing is Mars's ability to inspire self-expression and expanded learning in Mercury. These qualities are already possessed by Mercury, but they may need Mars's booster punch to manifest in their totality. You sympathize with and support each other's efforts, sharing your individual talents. As I said at the beginning, nice!

Mercury Opposed or Square Mars   A's Mercury, B's Mars
☿ ☍ □ ♂

It will be difficult for you to achieve compromise, but achieve it you must, at whatever cost of individual self-control and mutual tolerance. Otherwise, this vibration could cause planetary warfare to erupt between Mars and Mercury with your relationship as the battlefield. It's undeniably an exciting and stimulating aspect in an intellectual sense, causing you to respect and admire each other's minds and intelligence.

However, as you've probably already discovered, there is frequent friction between Mars's impulsive, aggressive behavior and Mercury's more rational, reasonable approach. Stressful misunderstandings and sudden quarrels are a result of a mutual refusal to compromise, as you've been warned to try to do. (The square aspect is more frictional than the opposition.) Mars's rash, impulsive speech and naive viewpoints will intrigue Mercury and arouse Mercury's latent tender, protective urges but could also be disturbing at times to Mercury's more realistic approach to life. It's difficult, if not impossible, to fool Mercury. It's easy to fool Mars, due to an inner gullibility based on innocence with which Mercury often has little patience.

Further, Mercury's occasional sharp-tongued sarcasm could ignite the short fuse of Mars's temper—and so it goes. Both of you should cool it, because when the tension becomes too hot it can explode into a blaze. That's the only counsel the stars have to offer to dilute and eventually control this aspect between you. In the cosmic code: Cool it, cool it, cool it, cool it—Cool it!

Minor Postscript: Relatives or in-laws of one of you could be a possible source of trouble, but not seriously damaging to your relationship, just frustrating and annoying. When and if this should occur, the solution is obvious: Avoid the source of trouble. After all, you do possess free will, you know!

Mercury Conjunct, Sextile or Trine Jupiter   A's Mercury,
☿ ☌ ✳ △ ♃   B's Jupiter

The conjunction has the strongest effect, but the sextile and trine between these two planets in your intercharts add similar magic to your relationship. Jupiter inspires and expands ambitious urges and optimism in Mercury, while Mercury tactfully, without offending, keeps the sweeping vision of Jupiter's ideals from getting hung up in the clouds, using logic and intelligence to keep them from crash-landing when Jupiter flies too high. (Mercury here is more tactful than usual, and will tend to refrain from the typical mercurial sarcasm when interacting with Jupiter.) This is an especially excellent vibration for all kinds of partnership associations: parent and child, teacher and student, business partners, and marriages. Jupiter is tolerant of and sympathizes with Mercury's desire for learning and education, and Mercury admires and respects Jupiter's moral, spiritual, and intellectual abilities, in some ways even intensifying these qualities in Jupiter. You'll undoubtedly agree on educational, religious, and legal matters, and travel. There is much general goodwill, humor, and understanding underlying your relationship, and you'll enjoy plenty of harmony together, along with several bushels of luck from the elves, leprechauns, and druids who dance through your dreams.

Mercury Opposed or Square Jupiter   A's Mercury,
☿ ☍ □ ♃   B's Jupiter

The two of you may have disputes about subjects like religion, education, legal matters, or your ethical backgrounds (not all of these, of course, Lord forbid; just one or two provide enough frictional food for chewing!). It's possible (not for certain, just possible) that one of you will persuade the other to change religious or spiritual views. Relatives or in-laws could create problems between you, but not serious ones, just frustrating. Mercury could have an edge on the benefits of your association, but if you stifle the stress, join forces, and work as a team, you could reach success in any of the areas ruled by these two planets, such as: salesmanship, broadcasting, advertising, travel, newspapers, the stock market, educational institutions, telemarketing, publishing, and media promotion. One small pocket of irritation may be that Mercury's chatter and general concepts may seem inconsequential to Jupiter, who tends to see the larger picture. Another potential source of annoyance could be that Jupiter's large, expansive goals may cause a promise or two to be unintentionally broken on rare occasions, giving Mercury a chance to say "I told you so"—and that's not what Jupiter needs to hear when a dream crashes from its own weight. Whatever the seeds of trouble, they can be weeded out of your relationship. If you work together, you can win last-minute victories.

Mercury Conjunct Saturn ☿ ☌ ♄   A's Mercury, B's Saturn

Because Saturn is the planet of karma, its effect on the planet Mercury is more noticeable than the reverse. The planet Saturn is the teacher of karmic lessons needed to be learned by both of you, and therefore it is more or less in charge of them.

Mercury can learn much of benefit from Saturn, although the learning is not always pleasant. Saturn is either chronologically older than Mercury or else appears to be the more mature one of the two because of more experience, resulting in a tendency to try to discipline Mercury. However disparaging and critical of Mercury's shifting reasoning and judgments Saturn may be, nevertheless, Saturn possesses wisdom it would behoove Mercury to respect and absorb, not resent.

True, Saturn's inclination to instruct can make Mercury feel inadequate and "put down," which isn't a barrel of fun. But karmic lessons are not designed to be "fun," so don't blame poor Saturn, who can't help playing the cosmic role assigned by the masters of karma. Mercury won't be thrilled by the pressure of responsibilities demanded, or by Saturn's sometimes cold disapproval of Mercury's habit of changing ideas and opinions on short notice (or with no notice), resulting in hastily made promises that are later broken. Mercury calls it mental versatility. Saturn calls it unreliable and irresponsible behavior.

It can be frustrating when Saturn frowns on Mercury's need for self-expression and higher learning, and even when Saturn approves of such urges, there can be a critical watchfulness of any progress made. Saturn may privately call Mercury a mental tap dancer. Mercury may privately call Saturn an impossible stuffed shirt.

But there's good news too! Mercury is able to talk Saturn cheerfully out of those periodic spells of depression and melancholy, while Saturn blesses Mercury with a comforting sense of mental and emotional stability and financial security. Of course, to reverse the old truism, "Every silver lining has a cloud." So what to do?

Accentuate the affirmative side of those words and, as the song says, "Look for the silver lining / whenever dark clouds come into view. / Remember somewhere the sun is shining / and it will shine again for you" (if you both pay your karmic dues with smiles instead of with the coins of complaining).

Mercury Sextile or Trine Saturn   A's Mercury, B's Saturn
☿ ✶ △ ♄

Congratulate yourselves for having behaved nicely toward each other in one or more previous lives together. Now you're being rewarded with this karmic vibration, which has a comfortable, steadying effect on your relationship. Unlike the stressful aspects between these planets, the sextile and trine cause Saturn to offer wise suggestions to Mercury rather than to criticize and make demands, so that Mercury, instead of resenting Saturn's guidance, appreciates and respects the knowledge and counsel being offered. Saturn is more mature than Mercury, if not chronologically then through wisdom gained by experience. It's also a bonus that Mercury frequently gives Saturn positive energy to lighten periodic discouragement. This is an interplanetary indication of a long-lasting relationship and a rare mental compatibility.

Mercury Opposed or Square Saturn
☿ ☍ □ ♄

A's Mercury,
B's Saturn

Saturn can be a harsh judge of Mercury's ideas, sternly disapproving and critical of Mercury's achievements. Naturally, this chips away at Mercury's self-confidence and creates resentment. Saturn may be in some way responsible for delays and limitations to Mercury's goals and ambitions. Obviously, there's a shortage of cooperation between you, since most of the time neither wants to give an inch. It's as though one of you says (in George Bush's silly, blustering words), "I have drawn a line in the sand," and the other replies, "Big deal. So what?" Mercury seems careless, irritating, and annoying to Saturn from time to time, and Saturn can appear to be cold, stuffy, and bossy to Mercury at times, but there's a good reason for it.

There is? Yes, there is. Saturn is the planet of karma, so that all aspects between Saturn and any other planet in your intercharts emanate from one or more former lives together. Obviously, you two alienated each other in some way in the dim and misty, long-forgotten past. It's called karma, and the way to erase it is that most sacred of all words: forgiveness. On both sides. It may not occur simultaneously, but if one person makes the first move, the other will eventually follow. Why not make that person you? Mercury: "Does she mean me?" Saturn: "Does she mean me?" How should I know? You're the only ones who know the answer. But remember that the masters of karma have "a method to their madness." The friction between you is a mutual challenge that will, in the final analysis, help you both to grow in wisdom. Don't be dorky. Forgive those long-ago trespasses, even if you don't remember exactly what they were. That doesn't matter, because defining hurt is the least important part of the game of life. Forgiveness is the only sure way of winning it.

Mercury Conjunct, Sextile, or Trine Uranus
☿ ☌ ⚹ △ ♅

A's Mercury,
B's Uranus

You stimulate each other mentally, and are as snug as two bugs in a rug when you're exchanging ideas (usually unconventional ones) in your conversations, which are frequent! If there are no other planetary aspects between your birth charts to dilute this one substantially, communication flows smoothly and nearly constantly between you, whether you're awake or asleep. You may have had more than one experience of meeting astrally in your dreams, which was recalled vividly later by both of you. Uranus awakens Mercury's already agile and alert mind to new and challenging concepts (some of them pretty far out!), and Mercury is able to bring the flying carpet Uranus rides to a lower level of practical application of all those wild, unorthodox conceptuals. There's a great deal of intuition and ESP between you, and sometimes your friends, family members, and business associates don't quite comprehend what you're talking about. That figures, because occasionally the two of you speak a strange language, normally spoken only aboard UFOs. Yes, you! And admit it, you are somewhat "spaced out." Remember E.T.'s famous, desperate plea, "E.T. phone home! E.T. phone *home*!" Both of you feel you're home when you're with each other.

If you're willing to make the effort, you could combine your talents and ideas into a project that brings recognition and awards. You both love to be around people, have bushels of friends from every walk of life, and probably love taking lots of short trips—together, of course! Inexplicably, you have a mysterious and strongly beneficial influence on each other's health.

Mercury Opposed or Square Uranus   A's Mercury,
☿ ☍ □ ♅   B's Uranus

Sometimes Mercury feels like a spinning top in this association. It's no wonder, since Uranus stimulates, excites, and irritates Mercury's mind simultaneously, which is naturally upsetting. Uranus frequently seems unstable and erratic to Mercury. On the other hand, Mercury often seems elusive, shallow, and contradictory to Uranus. The two of you do have a "meeting of the minds," but when your minds meet, they usually create fiery sparks! The friction is more intense when the relationship is a close one. If you live under the same roof, there could be a number of unexpected separations and reconciliations, spasmodic disagreements, and such. Mercury can't seem to understand the complex convolutions churning in Uranus's mind, and if a way can't be found to ignore this, it can seriously upset Mercury's nervous system. The same thing can happen to Uranus, who can't bear Mercury's "flitting around like a tipsy firefly." It may be (indeed, will be) difficult, but the two of you simply must try to understand and adjust to each other's eccentricities. You don't have to be mental Siamese twins to achieve harmony. Try respecting and listening to each other's ideas, and some wild and profitable concepts could be the result. When Uranus's inherent gift of envisioning the future combines with Mercury's quick and clever intellectual abilities, magic can explode! All it takes to wave your wands and create it is a tad of tolerance and patience.

Mercury Conjunct Neptune   A's Mercury, B's Neptune
☿ ☌ ♆

One positive result of this planetary aspect in your intercharts is a definite, strong, and unbreakable psychic tie, resulting in powerful telepathic communication between you. This you can rely on. So, Mercury, at those times when Neptune seems to you to be elusive, evasive, and apparently deceptive, why don't you just yank on that ESP cord you share, read Neptune's mind, and settle down? As for you, Neptune, why don't you do the same when Mercury hurts your sensitive feelings with sometimes stinging and sarcastic speech? When you penetrate deeply into Mercury's heart and true self, you'll discover that those impulsive words were regretted as soon as they were spoken. What's the good of having such an amazingly profound telepathic link if you don't use it to read each other's minds and find out what really matters to both of you?

Mercury Sextile or Trine Neptune   A's Mercury,
☿ ✶ △ ♆   B's Neptune

This is one of those blessed vibrations that can considerably soften or dilute other stressful ones between you, making their effect less upsetting. Neptune is able to inspire Mercury, to elevate and encourage those mercurial ideas and concepts, because of the strong psychic tie between you, of which you're both probably already aware and have been since you first said "Hello." You share an almost visible telepathic communication, sometimes sending messages to each other through the ethers without the necessity of written or spoken words. Mercury can find practical outlets and expressions for Neptune's imagination and intuition, and that can be a lovely thing whether your relationship is business, friendship, family, or love. Aren't you blessed? You needn't be grateful to astrology for this wonderfully harmonious vibration because you earned it in a past incarnation when your souls were still in their childhood and your spirits were "younger." Remember the lyrics from the song in *The Sound of Music*? "There you are, standing there, loving me / whether or not you should. / Yes, somewhere in my youth or childhood / I must have done something good."

Mercury Opposed or Square Neptune   A's Mercury,
☿ ☍ □ ♆   B's Neptune

All right, so which one of you, on occasion, lies to the other? Probably both. So it isn't lying. It's simply that you're each inclined to keep secrets. Okay, okay, okay, okay. But don't play semantics games, especially not with an astrologer! Don't you see how keeping secrets is a first cousin to lying? Most lies are lies of commission. Your kind of mutual lies are lies of omission. Granted, there's a difference between them, but it's a fine line, and do consider that both kinds of "lies" are equally painful and equally likely to cause suspicion to raise its knobby head in both your minds. You may look on this as a continual but harmless game of mental chess, but it isn't as "harmless" as you've convinced yourselves it is. Suspicion can cut the heart like a knife. Tell you what. Remember when both of you were Scouts (if you were—and even if you weren't!)? Play a daily courtroom taking-the-oath scene and recite: "I promise to tell the truth, the whole truth, and nothing but the truth, so help me God!

Scout's Honor!" Give each other a polygraph for Christmas, and look up the word *trust* in the dictionary. Then consider that trust vibrates to the number 19 in the Chaldean numerological system. Check the meaning of the double number 19 in *Star Signs*. If you follow this multilayered recipe for contentment, you'll reach the 19 vibration of trust and eventually stop doubting each other.

Mercury Conjunct Pluto   A's Mercury, B's Pluto
☿ ☌ ♇

You may not have a lot of interests in common (depending, of course, on other mutual aspects between your birth charts), but you are capable of causing sweeping changes in each other's ambitions, goals, and dreams. Pluto can greatly expand Mercury's viewpoints, and Mercury can broaden Pluto's range of interest in various areas of life. There are too many possibilities of the changes you bring to one another to list them all, so I'll just give you one example. If it doesn't fit, you'll find your own path to becoming a successful team. That example (and remember that it's not the only one) is that you could form a great partnership in anything even remotely occult or esoteric. Pluto can train Mercury to be a powerful public speaker on anything from the Great Pyramid to ancient Greek mythology, and Mercury can train Pluto to develop into a compelling author of mysteries or mystical matters, all part of the perhaps unawakened, latent essence within Pluto. But Mercury may be needed to teach Pluto the magic trick of how to string words together into a chain of imagery. An extra suggestion: You could both become private investigators and open a PI agency. You have a mutual talent for uncovering buried secrets (including each other's). A minor but vital warning concerning this aspect: Pluto is by far the stronger of the two of you, so Mercury must be careful that Pluto doesn't attempt to dominate Mercury's mind because it comes naturally to Pluto to try. Especially since Mercury is so incredibly intellectually alert, which can become an irresistible challenge to Pluto. Don't tease!

Another facet of this warning is that Pluto, if allowed, can have a truly explosive effect on Mercury's mind, and Mercury must be watchful because, as the old saying goes, when given an inch, Pluto will take a mile. Still Mercury can be amazingly adept at dancing out of danger like quicksilver, usually faster than Pluto can follow! Mercury can be a regular twinkletoes at escaping—anything.

Mercury Sextile or Trine Pluto   A's Mercury, B's Pluto
☿ ⚹ △ ♇

You have a strong influence on each other's minds, which leads to lots of changes in your life-styles. It's more likely that Pluto will change Mercury's viewpoints and way of thinking than the other way around, but there will definitely be changes. Your discussions are occasionally profound, regardless of the subject matter. As always, depending on your entire compatibility analysis including all of the planets involved between your birth charts and assuming there are no other vibrations to dilute the strength of this one, the two of you can combine your minds into a great intellectual powerhouse that could build any mutual project, goal, or dream into a giant success, especially in the areas of transportation, writing, publicity, newspaper and radio media, advertising, and agent representation, especially, but not exclusively, because just about anything you seriously set your combined minds to can miraculously manifest.

Mercury Opposed or Square Pluto   A's Mercury, B's Pluto
☿ ☍ □ ♇

This is a strange vibration, but then everything about the planet Pluto is strange. Profound. Mysterious. Secret. Buried. And so on. One of the reasons for the strangeness of this aspect is that much of the time the two of you intensely stimulate one another's minds, occasionally reaching awesome heights in both intellectual and spiritual illumination. And yet, at other times you seem to be worlds apart in your opinions, your outlooks, and your methods of dealing with a situation. These divergent ways of thinking and mental attitudes could surface when you least expect it in the areas of health (one of you needs lots of sympathetic attention when ill; the other wants to be left alone and totally isolated to heal), the siblings or in-laws of one or both of you, anything to do with publicity or the media, teaching and learning, various facets of salaried employment, and perhaps a few others. The square aspect normally creates more tension than the opposition, but the latter is not exactly a jar of jelly beans either. Whichever one of these aspects you share in your intercharts, the only way to remove its teeth, so to speak (or should I say "fangs"?) is to practice the ancient counsel of the magical blend of tolerance and understanding. I'm sure you're weary of hearing such advice, but it truly is effective. Until you've tried it you can't prove me wrong, right? A bright spot is that if other aspects between your birth charts indicate mental affinity, they will greatly soften and dilute this one. But you don't want to lose the vibration described in the beginning of this paragraph. That's a "keeper."

5

Venus Aspects

Venus conjunct, sextile, or trine Venus
Venus opposed or square Venus
Venus conjunct, sextile or trine Mars
Venus opposed or square Mars
Venus conjunct, sextile, or trine Jupiter
Venus opposed or square Jupiter
Venus conjunct Saturn
Venus sextile or trine Saturn
Venus opposed or square Saturn
Venus conjunct Uranus
Venus sextile or trine Uranus
Venus opposed or square Uranus
Venus conjunct Neptune
Venus sextile or trine Neptune
Venus opposed or square Neptune
Venus conjunct, sextile, or trine Pluto
Venus opposed or square Pluto

Venus Conjunct, Sextile, or Trine Venus   A and B
♀ ♂ ✶ △ ♀

The two of you tend to express affection the same way, and there are probably few differences between you when it comes to your social lives and cultural interests. You'll also agree most of the time about spending or saving money, indeed on anything of a financial nature. You're both either slightly cool or warmly passionate in your emotional natures, compared with others you know. Whichever it is, your responses are similar. This vibration greatly increases harmony, comfortable companionship, mutual sympathy, and the ability to enjoy the same pleasures. It doesn't have any effect on your mental affinity or other matters involving your association, but it will help to untangle many of the emotional pretzels in your shared experiences caused by other planetary aspects between your birth charts.

Venus Opposed or Square Venus   A and B
♀ ♂ □ ♀

Your affection for each other is equal, although you express it differently, which can cause occasional misunderstandings. Also, it could sometimes be difficult to compromise on financial matters, and your life-styles may clash now and then. But these are inconsequential discords and will never seriously or permanently damage your relationship. Time will eventually soften these little annoyances if you learn to play the wise game of taking turns. That is, first one of you expresses affection in the manner of the other, then vice versa. You'll be surprised how effective this can be. Let's say that one of you expresses affection in a cool and controlled, quiet manner and the other in a warmer, more demonstrative and outgoing way. Try switching. I guarantee the one who (by turns) first switches to the other's usual way of expressing will find it unexpectedly easy, as well as fun—when the response is shocked delight, as it will always be. It's an exercise in empathy that's sure to expand the emotional horizons of both of you, so there's mutual benefit from such taking turns in switching your different manners of expressing affection.

Then, after a while, any minor negative effects of this aspect will become milder, and milder, and milder—and one day may all but disappear. When? Don't rush it. Remember the ancients teach that "all things come when time intends ... and patience is a blessing."

Venus Conjunct, Sextile, or Trine Mars ♀ ♂ ✳ △ ♂

A's Venus, B's Mars

Whether between members of the same or the opposite gender, this is a peaches-and-cream vibration you share. Your emotional attitudes and behaviors are as compatible as April showers and May flowers! Speaking of flowers, like the daffodils and tulips the two of you may tippy-toe through under this vibration, you'd best be warned to look out for a few bumblebee stings when Venus doesn't pay sufficient attention to Mars and Mars becomes a tad jealous, impetuous, or bossy. But it won't happen very often, and it's surely a small price to pay for all the smooth emotional harmony this aspect blesses you with.

With obvious sarcasm, my high school English teacher, Ms. Helen Fay, used to try to train us to remember proper word usage by making us repeatedly write in our notebooks, "A preposition is a poor thing to end a sentence with." Some got the message, some didn't. I got it, but just now broke it—deliberately, so that doesn't count, right? I know the correct way: "not a small price to pay for all the smooth emotional harmony with which this aspect blesses you." See? The point is, dear gentlepeople, that either way the sentence is true and should be remembered!

Venus Opposed or Square Mars ♀ ☍ □ ♂

A's Venus, B's Mars

It wouldn't be honest to duck the issue here. Depending as always on other aspects in your entire analysis, although this one can create a tremendous amount of mutual stimulation, it also has the potential of possible serious conflict. (With lots of other harmonious aspects in your intercharts, this can be considerably lightened.)

What do I mean by possible "serious conflict?" Well, let's see. I mean that this vibration indisputably acts as an intensely magnetic stimulant in the beginning (especially between lovers, but actually, leaving out the sexual chemistry, also in family, friendship, and business associations), but this is just the planets' way of seducing you into thinking everything is always going to be whipped-creamy smooth and delicious. It is not. It can occasionally be more like sour pickles mixed with that hot stuff in Mexican food, or meat dishes called "blackened" that fool you until the first bite turns your unsuspecting tongue into a flaming barbecue. (Serves you right: you should be vegetarians.)

As for the stimulation, there's stimulation—and then there's stimulation. In this case, it could become overstimulation that turns into a mutual stance of stubborn resistance with little attempt at compromise. There could be clashes of temperament—and tempers!—and periodic annoyance and hurtful words, later regretted. If you'll forgive my being logical, words never spoken don't need to be later regretted. So bite your tongues (metaphorically speaking, of course) and try unbending a bit. Mars could at times feel smothered by Venus's possessiveness, or by the way Venus takes unintentional hurt so seriously. Venus can be deeply wounded by Mars's sometimes rash behavior or thoughtless speech.

Tell you what. Mars, tone down your tendency to domineering behavior. Venus, curb your unnecessary oversensitivity. Then both of you hold hands, go out at midnight, and wish on a star together. Have you ever meditated on the words to the song, "When You Wish Upon a Star"? They ring with indisputable cosmic truth: "When each star is born/they possess a gift or two/one of them is this/they have the power/to make a wish come true!" And they do. They really, really, not nearly, but really do! With only the tiniest bit of help from you, which is that you must sincerely mean your wish. Intensely ordain it. This is quite simple, once you get the hang of it. Then you can both wink back at Mars and Venus. In a karmic and cosmic sense, they're your friends. Dismiss them from your minds and invite them into your hearts.

Venus Conjunct, Sextile, or Trine Jupiter   A's Venus,
♀ ☌ ⚹ △ ♃   B's Jupiter

The two of you probably enjoy the same pastimes, cultural interests, social life, hobbies, and forms of entertainment. You both like to read, to travel to foreign countries, and may be involved in some way with educational matters, the stock market, or publishing. If not involved, then you have a mutual excellent understanding of these areas.

You'd make a good team as professional attorneys because, when you hold discussions about any subject at all, you're both surprisingly good amateur lawyers, adept at logical deduction. You also quite likely have good relationships with each other's relatives (and if you're related yourselves, family ties are probably more comfortable than most).

This vibration often blesses both people with better-than-average good health, optimism, and self-confidence, the reason being that you bring out these qualities in each other.

You're unusually generous with one another, fortunate with mutual financial endeavors, mutually sympathetic, and encouraging. Unless other aspects between your birth charts strongly interfere, it's doubtful that you disagree about religion, since your spiritual beliefs, whether deeply devotional or agnostic, are similar. Your friends may feel it's a pleasure to be around you, because the very essence of your relationship seems somehow to uplift them into believing in themselves and their own aspirations.

Jupiter tends to expand the horizons of Venus, and Venus returns the favor by sincerely believing in Jupiter's sweeping goals and visions. You have more chance than most people of imitating the flight to Never-Never Land made by Peter, Wendy, and her two brothers. Go ahead, just raise your arms and fly! Last, but not least, Tinker Bell herself showers your togetherness with sparkles of sheer good luck.

Venus Opposed or Square Jupiter   A's Venus, B's Jupiter
♀ ☍ □ ♃

The opposition of these planets is not as likely to trip up a relationship as the square between them. Still, either aspect carries a warning of extravagance on the part of one or the other, sometimes both. There could be differences of opinion in handling finances, although it's not as likely that the disputes will involve accusations of stinginess as of "throwing money away unnecessarily." Whichever one of you accuses the other of this shortcoming, it's rather like the pot calling the kettle black, right? Confess. Although one of you might at times be somewhat careful with money, it's doubtful that either of you could be accused of being overly cautious with cash as a general rule.

Jupiter may occasionally accuse Venus of not being entirely open and honest, and Venus may accuse Jupiter of being too open and honest, of making blunt statements that are undeniably truthful but also hurtful. If Jupiter would practice a little more tact, it would help the tension between you considerably. So would it help to ease the friction if Venus would become more direct, putting all the cards on the table, candidly, instead of making Jupiter guess what's really happening. It may be like walking a tightrope, Jupiter, but could you make an attempt to rein in your admirable trait of honesty while at the same time toning down the sharp edges of your expression of it? And Venus, you should realize that playing games like "seeking the denial" can be unintentionally unkind. Like making exaggerated negative statements about yourself only for the purpose of hearing Jupiter deny them. That's not honest.

In addition to finances and brutal-truth-that-hurts, other trouble areas could be religion, education, publishing, legal matters, and relatives. But since both planets are called, in astrology, "benefics," their ability to cause friction is limited to minor disputes, not serious ones. Both of these aspects also bestow mutual good luck from time to time. So grab the brass ring on the carousel, then stop traveling in circles!

Venus Conjunct Saturn   A's Venus, B's Saturn
♀ ☌ ♄

You've heard the familiar statement and question "I have good news and I have bad news. Which do you want to hear first?"

Well, let's consider the good news first. It will act as a soft pillow to cushion the bad news, which isn't really all that bad, just a smidgeon difficult, not really unbearable.

The "good news" is that Saturn is inclined to provide Venus with much-needed mental, emotional, and financial stability, while Venus has a capacity for sympathy and affection that can stimulate Saturn's confidence and decrease Saturn's tendency to submit to pessimism and depression. This aspect also strongly encourages mutual loyalty, as Saturn feels a responsibility for Venus's welfare and Venus will be compassionate and solicitous of Saturn's unspoken needs. This aspect also tends to make any kind of relationship or association binding and enduring. So far, fine.

Now for the "bad news," but remember that nothing is so bad it can't be overcome. There is the possibility that Saturn can become overly possessive of Venus, behaving in a selfish and strict manner, insistently demanding obedience, which can, understandably, considerably chill Venus's normally affectionate nature. Venus will sometimes feel smothered and restricted by Saturn's criticism and attempts to discipline, and yet, if Saturn is stifled from expressing these natural Saturnine inclinations, it can be frustrating to the point of causing Saturn to suffer inwardly. The solution to the problems presented by this conjunction is a puzzlement. But surely the well-known and recognized wisdom of the Saturn essence, combined with the even deeper wisdom and understanding of love, which is synonymous with the Venus essence, gives you the power to solve any kind of puzzlement.

Venus Sextile or Trine Saturn   A's Venus, B's Saturn
♀ ⚹ △ ♄

There's an excellent chance that yours will be a mutually beneficial and long-lasting relationship or association. Whether the aspect is a sextile or a trine, the favorable effect is the same. Whatever additional planetary aspects in your intercharts may be stressful and frictional or difficult to handle, this one will support the two of you through many an emotional storm, as it gentles the controversies caused by other vibrations between your birth charts. It's rather like a cool hand on a fevered brow.

Regardless, then, of any possible negative Venus-Saturn aspect between you, this one promises that at least part of the time Venus will be graced by Saturn's demonstration of such positive Saturn traits as steady reliability and kindly wisdom. Consequently, Venus will often feel more protected than possessed by Saturn, more "free just to be" than sternly restricted, more cherished than dominated, more respected and admired than criticized and disciplined. At the same time, Venus will contribute a soft and sympathetic nature that has a near magical quality in its ability to melt the sometimes cool and aloof attitude Saturn projects to others. One of the nicest results of sharing this sextile or trine is that you trust each other. I mean really trust each other, somewhere deep down within, no matter how things appear to be on the surface, and it's not likely that either of you would ever abuse that trust. This is a rare and precious part of your relationship.

Of course other mutual planetary aspects between you may allow an occasional unfounded suspicion to tug on such trust temporarily, but it will always return. It's an astral insurance policy, a gift from your fairy godmothers.

As with all aspects involving the planet Saturn (and the planets Neptune and Pluto), this one is an echoed chord of your mutual karma from the long ago and far away, a cosmic protection against the harshest vibrations of all other aspects between you, considerably softening them.

Venus Opposed or Square Saturn   A's Venus, B's Saturn
♀ ☍ □ ♄

Saturn has many lessons to teach Venus, and Venus won't be anxious to learn them. It will occasionally be a struggle, but it's your karmic destiny (every Saturn aspect is), so you may as well make the best of it. Venus will endure some unhappy experiences in this relationship, especially when Saturn blames Venus for problems they encounter together. This is decidedly unfair. But there's nothing fair about karmic lessons unless you happen to know the primordial cause of them, which requires total recall of many "yester-days." If you're able to remember the original reincarnational misbehavior that started it all, the balancing of the karmic scales is easier to bear. Should you be fortunate enough to possess this rare gift of total recall of one or more past lives, I congratulate you. Should you not possess it, I sympathize with you.

Check this long string of adjectives. No use avoiding them! Saturn may not always, but periodically behave toward Venus in a disciplinary, limiting, selfish, condemning, resentful, critical, and disapproving manner. Quite naturally, it's difficult at such times for Venus to give affection to Saturn, except when it's inspired by anxiety or fear. Venus could feel frustrated and dominated, or just plain unhappy. It should make the burden lighter if we remind Venus that Saturn's sometimes admittedly harsh lessons are rooted in Saturn's unexpressed but very real concern and caring, an urge to guide a "lost soul" protectively. Believe it or not, this is the way Saturn demonstrates genuine love—in a sort of parent/child pattern. And so, Venus, tell yourself that you are loved beneath the occasional cold front of Saturn's personality. Does that comfort you? It doesn't? Well, then try to recall what you did eons ago to Saturn to deserve this karma. Because you did do something, or it wouldn't be happening. The plus side is that Saturn will probably never leave you but will hang around to provide you with a large measure of stability and emotional security. And this you very much need, right? Right. You agree. That's good. Let's quit while we're ahead.

Venus Conjunct Uranus   A's Venus, B's Uranus
♀ ☌ ♅

Should the two of you be involved with an innovative or creative endeavor in music or any of the arts, or have in mind inventing something, you'll find that you naturally stimulate one another's original ideas.

Even if you're not involved with any of the foregoing, your association will be exciting and you'll be constantly contributing to each other's goals, ambitions, and dreams.

Although Uranus will be tolerant and encouraging toward Venus, Uranus may also be responsible for swift and unexpected changes in the relationship and the environment, which can cause Venus some anxiety and nervous twinges.

There's certain to be something highly unusual or unconventional about your relationship, like maybe you're trapeze artists? Or you both have pet pigs or pet monkeys? Whatever it is, the bizarre facet of your association probably makes Michael Jackson's behavior patterns seem as tame as the life-styles of Grover Cleveland and Calvin Coolidge.

Venus has the blessed ability to hang on when Uranus is jogging about six feet above the ground, which is no small talent—and this is a calm and comforting thing to Uranus. I mean, when a person can't resist taking off on an occasional hegira of fancy, it's good to have a jolly "buddy" willing to tag along. It's entirely possible (not probable, just possible) that Venus may wonder how to cure what might be a case of daily amnesia in Uranus. Advice to Venus: Just tie a sky blue ribbon or string around Uranus's finger, big toe, ear, or whatever. That will eventually cause Uranus to remember your name and to stop forgetting things like what year it is, let alone what day it is!

Venus Sextile or Trine Uranus   A's Venus, B's Uranus
♀ ✷ △ ♅

There's something highly unusual about your relationship, or something extremely unorthodox about the way you first met. Maybe at the circus, with one dressed as a clown, the other munching cashew nuts in the monkey cage? No? I guess you could have bumped into each other crossing the street in the middle of a parade, or at a party at Michael Jackson's house. But wherever it was, I stand by the basic truth that your first "encounter of a third kind" was very far-out. Decidedly dorky.

And then what? Well, it became, like, Alice's adventures in Wonderland, "curiouser and curiouser." This aspect always indicates a mystical or glamorous aura defining the association or relationship, a certain exciting rhythm that makes others envious, especially when they can't figure it out. Even your arguments are bizarre, unlike anyone else's quarrels. As for your reconciliations, they can sometimes be as disruptive as your separations! Together, you bring out the latent creative genius in each other. Mutual achievement awards or honors are quite possible. Uranus is always surprising or shocking Venus in one way or another.

Venus has a pleasant way of toning down Uranus's eccentricities, acting as a sort of emotional leveler when Uranus is flying a kite and lets go of the string. When one of you stumbles, the other is always there with a safety net, a cone of pink cotton candy, and two tickets for a ride on the Ferris wheel!

Venus Opposed or Square Uranus   A's Venus, B's Uranus
♀ ☍ □ ♅

There's no shortage of stimulation between you, but most of it initiates from Uranus stimulating or seducing Venus into thinking patterns, activities, and behavior not natural to the more placid and passive Venus. Periodic bursts of eccentric behavior can occur, and minor or major disappointments in each other can cause sudden and unexpected temporary separations. When this aspect is vitalized and manifested by the transiting planets, Uranus will seem undependable, unpredictable, and just plain old-fashioned crazy to Venus—but never boring. Venus can, on occasion, make Uranus feel compelled to win a race with a hundred-pound weight attached to his ankles. It's a lively vibration, full of surprises, like the passing vaudeville show of life Itself.

Venus Conjunct Neptune   A's Venus, B's Neptune
♀ ☌ ♆

I know you're annoyed by astrological equivocation, and I don't blame you, but this is one of those aspects that gives a different effect, depending entirely on the other planetary aspects you share between your birth charts. So I apologize in advance on behalf of the planets for being so equivocal in the interpretation.

If a majority of your other mutual aspects is strongly stressful or cautionary, then this one can punctuate your relationship with incidents of one seducing the other into a weakness for drugs or alcohol, and there could be occasions of deception and disillusion. But if a majority of your other mutual aspects is strongly positive, this one can create an ideal relationship for lovers, or a perfect compatibility for business, family, or friendship associations. There is extraordinary sympathy, understanding, and devotion between you. An unusual amount of compassion enters into your relationship in some manner, and the astral link between you is so strong you could literally hypnotize each other simultaneously if you tried. (Better have a third person around to bring you out of it!)

Mutual hypnotism is a mite dangerous, for obvious reasons. The vibration produced by the conjoining of these two planets is excellent for an association involved in the areas of medicine, research, metaphysics, investigation, or religion. Still, with all the virtues of this aspect, Neptune may involuntarily entice or bewitch Venus in some way, and Venus may encourage in Neptune any latent leanings toward procrastination, self-sacrifice, and, well, laziness. But if you're both mature and reasonably sensible individuals, there will be far more benefits than disappointments in your lives together. Incidentally, you probably share a love for the arts, for the theater, film, drama, dancing, music, poetry; and painting. Also, oddly, you both are interested in convents, monasteries, and ancient ruins.

Venus Sextile or Trine Neptune   A's Venus, B's Neptune
♀ ⚹ △ ♆

Did you meet in a monastery or a hospital? Whether you are lovers, mates, relatives, friends, or business associates, a mutual interest in religion or medicine, occult or esoteric studies, music, the theater, or investigative work may have drawn you together. A mutual love of nature and ecology may also be a shared interest. The two of you seem to bring forth in each other the virtues of generosity, sympathy, and kindness—toward both yourselves and others. Whatever type of relationship you enjoy, there's an aura of quiet affection and devotion between you in all of your mutual endeavors. You may stimulate each other's natural love of the arts in all forms, including modeling and photography. This is one of those aspects you can rely on to smooth out the wrinkles in other, less harmonious, vibrations between you.

Venus Opposed or Square Neptune
♀ ☍ □ ♆

A's Venus,
B's Neptune

As planetary aspects go, this one is more subtle than strong, more delicate than powerful. What makes it a disturbing vibration to deal with is the way it can sometimes wrap its threads around you when you least suspect anything is wrong. Although Neptune's intentions may be basically honorable, Venus can feel deceived or misled in minor and major matters. And vice versa. This vibration carries various degrees of misconception and confusion. Regardless of how much essential integrity you both possess, a vague suspicion of deceit can snake through your relationship if you aren't alert. The problems may occur because of your different interpretations of the word *honesty*. You can avoid much of the pain by simply promising each other never to deceive or mislead, always to tell the entire truth, however much it may hurt. Never lie to one another about even the smallest thing, and that will transform the effect of this aspect into mutual spiritual or astral experiences and a strong telepathic bond between you. Like any other difficult aspect between the planets in your intercharts, this one is, essentially, a challenge to be overcome. And what is life without challenges? Dreadfully dull and boring.

Venus Conjunct, Sextile, or Trine Pluto
♀ ☌ ✶ △ ♇

A's Venus,
B's Pluto

There's an indisputable karmic tie between you, and it's a powerful one, to be sure. Perhaps you don't "believe in" reincarnation, the cause of such things as karmic ties. It doesn't matter. Not believing in it doesn't cancel its reality or keep it from working. It's just that certain matters are a whole lot easier to deal with when you comprehend the why of them.

Even when occasional disagreements occur between you, whether initiated by yourself or by outsiders, it's next to impossible to separate the two of you permanently. One way or another, you'll be magnetized back together, whatever the nature of the relationship. If siblings are separated at birth, through adoption, the two are almost sure to find one another eventually, either by intent or so-called accident. The same is true of any kind of business association you share, and of all family matters. Anyone who tries to come between you will not succeed. No way. Even if attempts to sever the silver-blue cord (and chord) between you appear to succeed temporarily, wait. You'll be back together as surely as the darkness of night is eternally banished by sunrise, and that's as "surely" as anything can be! The "grace" of this vibration can't be avoided.

Should your relationship be that of lovers or mates, these aspects have the same foregoing effect, as they likewise have for friends, family, or business associates, but they have also an additional profound and complex meaning, as you saw in "Love Aspects," the first aspect discussed in Section Two.

Venus Opposed or Square Pluto   A's Venus, B's Pluto
♀ ☌ □ ♇

What did you two do to each other in one or more past lives? It had to be serious to be so strongly reflected now in this one through such a potent mutual karmic aspect.

When your relationship explodes now and then, it will usually be Venus who gets the worst of the bargain. Why? Because in any kind of conflict or confrontation, Pluto has more strength and staying power. The problems may often—not always, but often—begin when Venus finds a dozen ways to frustrate Pluto, maybe not deliberately, but the result is the same.

Of course it would be helpful if you could both have total recall of former lives together, so you could remember just what was said and done by each to the other. That would make it easier to balance the scales of atonement between you.

But without such total recall, you'll just have to deal with the stress and tension by realizing that something went wrong "back then" and making an effort to cancel it as best you can.

One way would be for Pluto to loan some of that strength to Venus instead of using it as a weapon of control, and for Venus to stop fearing Pluto's tendency to get even, and to replace resentment with charm. Pluto can use lots of lessons in charm!

Or, if all else fails, just say to each other, "I'm very sorry for whatever I did to you that I can't remember, but whatever it was, please forgive me, and let's get on with our trip down the Yellow Brick Road together." Who could resist such lovely logic?

6

Mars Aspects

Mars Aspects

Mars conjunct Mars
Mars sextile or trine Mars
Mars opposed or square Mars
Mars conjunct, sextile, or trine Jupiter
Mars opposed or square Jupiter
Mars conjunct Saturn
Mars sextile or trine Saturn
Mars opposed or square Saturn
Mars conjunct Uranus
Mars sextile or trine Uranus
Mars opposed or square Uranus
Mars conjunct Neptune
Mars sextile or trine Neptune
Mars opposed or square Neptune
Mars sextile or trine Pluto
Mars conjunct, opposed, or square Pluto

Mars Conjunct Mars   A and B
♂ ☌ ♂

It's difficult to explain this aspect, so it might be easier
if we begin with an astrological fact. The planet Mars, in
everyone's individual chart, influences or "rules" self-
expression. Your speech and actions. Your verbal patterns.
These will follow the kind of expression exhibited by the
sign in which Mars was located at birth. This doesn't cancel out your Sun Sign personality, Moon Sign emotional attitudes, or your general character involving the other
planets; it just influences the way you speak and express
yourself much of the time. For example, the basic You-of-
You doesn't change, but if Mars is in Aries in your individual birth chart, you'll speak and express yourself more
forcefully and directly. If Mars is in Pisces in your birth
chart, you'll be a mite more soft-spoken and gentle in your
expression, perhaps also a little more evasive. See?

So what happens with two people when each person's
Mars was in the same sign when each was born, forming a
Mars conjunct Mars aspect in their planetary interchart
comparisons? Let's use an analogy, somewhat imperfect,
but then all analogies are somewhat imperfect. Still, it might
help to clarify this aspect's vibrations.

In a manner of speaking, the effect is similar to the rule
of mating the same breed of horses, dogs, and other animals, that is, an increase of both the desirable and undesir-
able hereditary genes. Likewise, when Mars was conjunct
(in the same sign) when each of you was born, the result will
be a strong emphasis on the positive virtues of that sign—
and also a strong emphasis on the not-so-positive traits of
the sign. As with the rules of animal breeding, everything is
increased or doubled. I'll give you only three examples of
this. There are, of course, twelve possible examples, since
there are twelve signs in which both your Mars planets
could have been deposited at birth, making them conjunct.
But three examples should be sufficient to illustrate why
Mars conjunct Mars in your intercharts carries with it a
warning.

Since, at this writing, I've no way of knowing which of

the twelve signs Mars was in at your births, these examples will have to do for the nonce, as Will, the Bard, would say.

Example 1: Mars Conjunct Mars in the Sign Taurus

The stability, devotion, practicality, patience, and humor of the Taurus expression will be greatly increased in your relationship. But so will the bullheaded stubbornness of the Taurus expression. The solution? Take full advantage of the former and make an extra effort to tone down the latter.

Example 2: Mars Conjunct Mars in the Sign Leo

The generosity, warmth, and creativity of the Leo expression will be greatly increased in your relationship. But so will the Leo traits of arrogance, pride, and bossiness. Again, the solution is to take full advantage of the former and make an extra effort to tone down the latter.

Example 3: Mars Conjunct Mars in the Sign Gemini

The versatility, intelligence, and irresistible charm of the Gemini expression will be greatly increased in your relationship. But so will the negatives, such as Gemini double-talk, sarcasm, repetitive speech, and breathlessly swift changes of opinions and attitudes. Once more, the solution is to take full advantage of the former and make an extra effort to tone down the latter.

However, those with Mars conjunction in the Sign of Gemini face a few more than the usual problems of those with a Mars conjunction in any of the other eleven signs. Gemini is the sign of the Twins, duality, two-people-in-one. Consequently, with two people who share Mars conjunction in Gemini, the vibration is quadrupled, since each person's individual double vibration of Mars in Gemini is once again doubled. See? Two times two people equals four something! Is that chaotic confusion or what? These poor souls often can't figure out with which one of the four of them one of them is communicating. You'd best read that sentence again.

Since both frequently change their admittedly brilliant minds (often in the middle of a sentence), each person's expression on one day may be completely reversed the next day (or the next hour—or sometimes even the next minute), leaving both continually trying to guess the other's next move in this unending game. Who will win? No one. That's why it's unending!

To add to the convolutions, true to Gemini speech patterns, both tend to repeat themselves. Example: "I'll call you at noon. [brief pause] I'll call you at noon." Response: "Okay. [brief pause] Okay." Like that.

There's one bit of astral counsel I can share that might ease some of the frictional frustration of this multiple vibe. Even though your ways of expressing yourselves are similar, and could be harmonious, if one tries to take the lead in a situation, rather than both together, fiery sparks of rivalry, impatience, and anger could result. So you two should cooperate on mutual endeavors with no one playing the role of leader. Follow-the-leader is definitely not the favorite pastime of Mars, whatever sign it was in when both of you arrived on Earth. Your best chance (indeed, your only chance) to achieve the harmony possible with this conjunction between you is cooperation. Walk side by side so that no one is in front or behind. Speak and act in the same way. Side by side, as equals. Then you can face all the outside influences—and win every time! Since Gemini rules writing, perhaps people sharing a double Mars-in-Gemini aspect could become authors and collaborate on a book.

If your own Mars-conjunct-Mars aspect is not in one of the three foregoing example signs but in one of the other nine signs, I suggest that you read *Sun Signs* to learn what particular positive/negative traits this conjunction will increase, depending on which sign may be involved. That will help.

All right, I've done my part. The rest is up to you. Incidentally, you should know that the "increase" caused by the conjunction applies only to Mars. A conjunction of any other two planets (Venus conjunct Venus, Moon conjunct Moon, and so on) does not give the same results. Only the Mars conjunction. Thank goodness!

Mars Sextile or Trine Mars   A and B
♂ ✶ △ ♂

A decided plus for harmony! The way you speak, the way you express your thoughts, may not be identical, but will definitely be similar and follow the same general pattern. In other words, this aspect is harmonious. The two of you co-operate effectively in any endeavor requiring your combined energies and actions. Your desires and dreams are very much alike; furthermore, you'll both find it easy to en-courage and inspire each other's goals and ambitions. This aspect may not remove every trace of rivalry and competi-tion between you (depending on other mutual aspects), but it will considerably reduce the amount of tension caused by any such vibrations. You're well suited for business, friend-ship, or marriage partnerships. If you are relatives, you probably run to each other for sympathy when other fam-ily members have insulted, angered, or hurt you in a minor or a major way. As any kind of a team, you fit the words to the familiar "friendship song" (with the bad grammar): "It's friendship, friendship / just a perfect friendship. / When other friendships have been forgot / ours will still be hot!"

Mars Opposed or Square Mars   A and B
♂ ☍ □ ♂

Even if you don't always exhibit it openly, there's a sub-tle conflict of wills between you. Well, maybe not so subtle when you express the differences in your thoughts verbally, because your speech patterns are also in conflict! Even when you both want the same thing, you don't want it at the same time. Many of your disputes are initiated when one of you tries to interfere with and obstruct the other's work or life-style—or at least "the other" will believe this is so, whether true or imaginary.

Yes, there will many occasions for Mars-type fiery flare-ups and flurries of furies, but no, they needn't be the end of the world—or the end of your relationship or association. Instead of behaving like bad boys—or bad girls, or a bad boy and girl—you can turn this aspect into a marvelous opportunity to earn lots of glittering stars in your karmic crowns! Every time you overcome the inner resentment that is a natural response to submitting to the other person's desires at the expense of your own, another star is born in that karmic tiara!

In business associations, each of you may prefer a different technique or procedure. But since both methods will probably achieve the same result, what difference does it make in the final analysis other than your mutual pride? So take turns. It's the same with lovers or mates. One wants to see Arnold What's-His-Name's latest epic of violence, the other wants to watch Bugs Bunny cartoons. Take turns. Gradually, as you accumulate those stars, you'll learn how to be in command of your individual emotional natures, and that achievement is worth a whole galaxy of asteroids. Here's the astral sermon, the cosmic credo of the day for you: Harmony is happier than hostility, and compromise is more creative than conflict.

Mars Conjunct, Sextile, or Trine Jupiter   A's Mars,
♂ ☌ ✶ △ ♃   B's Jupiter

Mars provides a foundation of aggressive action and forceful drive for Jupiter's dreams, goals, large ambitions, and aspirations. You may both have an unusual interest in sports or animals. This is a great vibration for partnerships of all kinds, whether marriage or business. Jupiter promotes a desire for all kinds of expansion in Mars, and, perhaps best of all, you constantly encourage optimism in each other, both of you exhibiting Scarlett O'Hara's philosophy: "After all, tomorrow is another day!"

In some manner, the two of you will have smooth agreement in matters of the law, education, and religion. No arguments about these subjects! Unless they're caused by other planetary aspects between you, and, if so, this one will make them mild and minor. You complement one another very nicely in most things, and as a team (if your aspect is the sextile or trine) you have a rare ability to achieve prosperity and financial security together.

All of these happy harmonies are true of any of the above three aspects, including the conjunction, but if your aspect is the conjunction, although you will enjoy the same blessings as are given by the sextile and trine, there may be an occasional stirring of stress in the area of money, that is, its unexpected and unwelcome disappearance due to the unwise spending of it. At times, you seem to stimulate excessive spending in each other. First, Mars accuses Jupiter of extravagance, then Jupiter accuses Mars. You know what? You're both rather free spenders, if the truth be told. Get a business manager and keep separate checking accounts. Then you can settle down to the pleasures of this vibration!

I almost forgot another note of warning in your symphony if yours is the conjunct aspect. In the same way that the god Jupiter enjoyed teasing the god Mars in Greek mythology, likewise the Jupiter and Mars conjunction can cause Jupiter to enjoy teasing Mars, which Mars does not always find amusing. So Jupiter should curtail the clowning around, while Mars should lighten up and realize that no harm is meant. (Hint: The way to stop anyone's teasing is to ignore it and not respond because that takes away all the fun!)

Mars Opposed or Square Jupiter   A's Mars, B's Jupiter
♂ ☍ □ ♃

There could be periodic discord between you when your ambitions are in conflict. This could create rivalry, or perhaps cause one of you to do something against the other's best judgment. Your differences of opinion will mostly involve moral or ethical viewpoints, usually regarding relatives, publishing, the law, education, or religious issues. You could also tend to be mutually impatient, either expecting or demanding too much of each other. In family or romantic affairs, one person could make promises that somehow fail to be completely fulfilled. In business associations, one could accuse the other of impulsively taking foolish risks, leading to financial reverses. Another unpleasant facet of this vibration is that it often brings out any latent extravagant or wasteful traits in both Mars and Jupiter, so in all fairness, the blame should be mutual, since neither one of you could be called weak-willed. You can't honestly claim that you were forced or "led into" later regretted actions because you do most things with your eyes wide open. (All four of them: both pairs.)

Don't give up the ship yet! There are solutions to these problems, as there are to all conflicts between Earthlings. In this case, you'll need to try to respect each other's opinions and judgments when they differ, each allowing the other the freedom to act independently, and if one of you goofs, don't say "I told you so." Be tolerant. Don't ever try to influence one another; keep your separate ways, congratulate each other when one of you wins, and give sympathetic support when one of you makes a serious mistake. Another magic wand to wave over the occasional ripples of disharmony with this vibration is the same astral counsel given to those who share a conjunction between these planets, which is: Get a couple of good business managers (one for each) and let the managers fight it out! Also, get separate checking accounts. *Please* get separate checking accounts, preferably in different banks. Then meditate on the profound wisdom in television's Mr. Rogers's theme song: "I like you just the way you are." That means warts, tempers, faux pas, goofs, boils, crankiness, extravagance (a synonym for which, remember, is generosity plus!), foolishness, and the whole ball of wax. Concentrate on each other's virtues. If you look for them, you'll find bushels.

Mars Conjunct Saturn   A's Mars, B's Saturn
♂ ☌ ♄

Most astrological textbooks give dire warnings to those who share this planetary aspect, as dire as those they give when they're interpreting Mars conjunct in an individual's horoscope alone. But the ancient texts lack a certain degree of, shall we say, optimism. They lean a bit too heavily on the dangers in the layers of human communication. Not that this aspect is strawberry shortcake all the way, but the challenges it offers to enlightened people who can see the glass as half full instead of half empty, once faced and conquered, can result in lots of good for both of you. The trick is in learning how to bring out the positive benefits of this vibration, and it's easier than you may think.

Let's chew on the so-called negative side first and get it out of the way. Then we can consider all the lollipops. We'll eat our veggies, then have dessert, all right? Here are the main warning sirens: A planet always restricts in some way the self-expression of any planet it conjuncts, regardless of the sign in which the conjunction occurs. This means that Saturn will in some manner limit Mars's behavior and/or activities, forcing Mars to relinquish one or several personal dreams or goals, some of them temporarily, some permanently. Saturn will delay them by placing obstacles in their way, frustrating Mars into fierce resentment that could quickly grow into some fiery temper tantrums on occasion.

As for Saturn's challenges in the relationship, Mars can be, at times, extremely irritating to Saturn's slower, more careful, and practical nature by demanding immediate answers, instant results, and being unwilling to wait. Definition of wait: Patience. In truth, Mars typically does not have much of the stuff, but Saturn has a spiritual warehouse full of it for life's emergencies.

Now for the positive benefits of this aspect, which lie over the rainbow for the two of you. Mars's courage and ingenuity can rise up to assist Saturn in a crisis and help Saturn overcome those blue indigo moods of discouragement and depression. And Saturn will restrain Mars's tendency to act too impulsively without sufficient foresight or preparation, and by so doing (if Mars will listen) cause their mutual projects to be successful and help Mars transform those sky-rocket concepts into financial profits. In short, Saturn can keep Mars from becoming a misguided missile, and Mars can fire the sometimes slow-pokey Saturn off the launch pad, toward Saturn's stable and practical dreams.

If Mars is properly appreciative, Saturn's careful counsel will not be sternly dictated, but wisely and kindly offered.

And if Saturn is properly appreciative, Mars's urgent, helpful-in-the-long-run pushing and shoving will not be so harsh, but more soft and gentle.

Saturn has much to learn from Mars's aggressive spirit, and Mars has much to learn from Saturn's quiet, patient caution. Since Saturn is the planet of karma, any aspect involving it always indicates mutual karmic dues to be paid. Pay them together with "grace under pressure," and you'll enjoy many unexpected benefits. Trust me.

But remember that Mars (both the planet and the person) is the one in charge of the mutually needed soul-testing lessons. I know that's tough to take, Mars, but fighting it is futile.

Mars Sextile or Trine Saturn   A's Mars, B's Saturn
♂ ✶ △ ♄

In any kind of partnership association, whether business or marriage, and also in family relationships, this planetary vibration between you should make all endeavors you undertake together run serenely and smoothly (unless the two of you share a multitude of stressful aspects from other planets, which could somewhat weaken this one but won't eliminate it).

Mars's strong mental and physical drive complements Saturn's careful caution, so that mutual efforts can be successfully accomplished. A blend of Saturnine patience and stability with Martian aggressive enthusiasm is clearly an ideal combination. This vibration graces both of you when you're working toward a common goal or mutual dream together by bringing out the very best in your natures. Mars stimulates Saturn's ambition and self-confidence, while Saturn's practicality restrains Mars's tendency to act too impulsively. The influence of this planetary aspect creates what has been called "the best of two worlds." In both love and business unions, it increases endurance and permanency because the planet Saturn is the ruler of karma and always binds. Saturn can teach Mars to prepare for possible emergencies, how to achieve financial security, the value of stability and cool serenity, and Mars can teach Saturn how to overcome obstacles, ride carousels, find four-leaf clovers in the grass, and make magic. All things considered, that adds up to a neat relationship, regardless of any other annoying aspects that create occasional friction between you.

Mars Opposed or Square Saturn   A's Mars, B's Saturn
♂ ☍ □ ♄

Saturn may not be able to control an urge to depress or restrict Mars's energetic initiative, which will eventually cause Mars to rebel defiantly. Saturn doesn't mean harm toward Mars, it's just that Mars's sometimes impetuous, impulsive, and thoughtless behavior disturbs Saturn's inherent instinct to be prudent, believing that it's better to be safe than sorry. Naturally, these different attitudes create a certain amount of discord between you.

When Saturn criticizes and tries to limit Mars's reckless and rash actions, Mars will angrily resist such restriction, not realizing until much later that it was motivated by Saturn's concern and desire to protect Mars against loss and disappointment. Mars's appreciation of the benefits of Saturn's wisdom and practicality develops only after long periods of frustration, and sometimes not even then. When Mars is rebellious, it can unsettle Saturn's usually unshakable cool. When Saturn tries to teach Mars the rewards of patience and caution, Mars feels that Saturn is behaving like a dictator and makes it clear that this person will not be controlled by anyone for any reason—and such defiance can cause Saturn to become physically ill.

This vibration is especially difficult in a parent/child relationship because if Saturn is the parent's planet in the aspect, the child can see the parent as overly strict and severe. When Saturn is the child's planet and Mars the parent's planet, the parent can push the child too hard because the child seems "too slow," which can cause the child to resent and even fear the parent. But in this family relationship, as well as with friends, business associates, lovers, and mates, either one of these aspects between the planet Saturn and the planet Mars flows from events set into motion in a past life, Saturn being the planet of karma. Therefore, a sufficient amount of forgiveness for long-ago hurt and lots of love and affection exchanged in the present incarnation can cancel the conflicts. You mean you didn't know the tremendous magical power of love? Then I guess that's the lesson your stars intend to teach you through this vibration. Learn it.

Mars Conjunct Uranus
A's Mars, B's Uranus

C♂ ♅

When your dreams, goals, or ambitions are the same, the two of you can reach for the stars and grab whole galaxies of them! Translation: Together you have the independence of spirit, aggressive drive, originality, and courage necessary for really huge success. However, if your dreams, goals, or ambitions are different, those stars of success may slip through your fingers. You'll find cooperation and compromise hard to achieve. Sooner or later, one of you will irritate and frustrate the other, although the intensity of the friction depends on how many other stressful aspects exist in your intercharts. If the two of you are by chance involved in jobs, careers, or endeavors involving any kind of scientific, environmental, literary, inventive, or mechanical activities, this vibration will stimulate and bring good fortune to such projects. Otherwise, it tends to bring out everything rebellious and unpredictable in your natures, requiring strict control over your emotions.

There will be times, perhaps frequent, when both of you will feel the other is not dependable and cannot be counted on to keep promises. Mostly it will be Uranus who exhibits this kind of erratic, unconventional behavior, which infuriates Mars. Then Mars will break a few promises also (plus a few dishes!). Mars may rebel and balk when Uranus spends too much time with friends and outsiders and doesn't give Mars the attention needed. Uranus considers such behavior childish and will not hesitate to say so, which is hardly the way to restore harmony, since Mars does not cotton to criticism. This vibration can bring on sudden and unexpected quarrels and breakups, but they usually disappear as swiftly as a bolt of lightning—and that's swift! If you don't like what's happening between you, just wait. It's certain to change. If there's anything you can count on in your relationship, it's change.

Mars Sextile or Trine Uranus ♂ ✶ △ ♅   A's Mars, B's Uranus

Each of you stimulates the other's originality, inventiveness, creative ability, and independence, influencing you as a team to be both progressive and productive. You encourage confidence, initiative, and aggressive drive in one another, and your relationship is usually harmonious, even if a bit bizarre and unconventional. You're fortunate to share a vibration that is so dynamic, exciting, and full of positive surprises. Unless your association is a family one between relatives, your meeting was probably not planned by either, but totally unexpected, and strange in some way. And here's an extra bonus: If your mutual efforts are sincere in their intent, cooperative, and free of doubt and inhibition, you could win rewards and recognition together for creating something to benefit the Earth and its Earthlings. The two of you are not Earthlings, however. You are clearly from the outer limits of space. If a UFO ever lands near you and you're invited aboard, go! You'll feel right at home.

Mars Opposed or Square Uranus ♂ ☌ □ ♅   A's Mars, B's Uranus

Whether or not it shows on the outside, you're both strong-willed, very independent individuals. So it's little wonder that you'll experience occasional clashes of those strong wills, initiated by your uniquely independent minds. Clash! Crash! Smash! Bash! Flash! It may not be quite that bad, but it's likely to be noisy. Neither of you could be called a shrinking violet, or the type to run from confrontation. When it's there, you'll both face it, for better or for worse. Sometimes it's for the better, and clears the air of cloudy, unspoken frustrations. But when it's for the worse, with words and actions later deeply regretted, don't fret. You can reconcile your differences and try again, if you want to. Those last four words make all the difference in the Universe.

Mars resents the impersonal, unemotional side of Uranus, and Uranus resents the overemotional, abrasive side of Mars. The mutually irritating result of such resentment can actually and literally affect the nervous system of one or both of you. On these occasions, each of you should take a shower to cleanse the aura of negative vibrations (it really works!) but not at the same time, of course. Then leave and see a movie (separately), and spend the night at a hotel or a friend's house. (Not together—don't wish that on a friend, for goodness sake.) If you give yourselves a chance to cool off and calm down, breakfast can return reasonable harmony between you.

The final score? Dear gentlepeople, that's entirely up to you. The stars have relinquished their control of this one and passed the responsibility to you. You can't blame them. Where the planet Uranus is concerned, things are no more predictable than an electrical storm. Of course there's always the chance of a rainbow. But even so, the two of you wouldn't be satisfied until you flew over it to the other side! I guess there's nothing wrong with such a goal. And when you achieve it (which you can if you believe you can), may your troubles melt like lemon drops!

Mars Conjunct Neptune   A's Mars, B's Neptune
♂ ☌ ♆

Mars will constantly excite Neptune's emotions, sometimes in a negative way, but mostly in a positive sense. Neptune is able to inspire Mars to the pure idealism buried near the surface of Mars's naive and trusting nature and veiled by an aggressive personality. Neptune can gently lift those veils, exposing Mars's benevolent, spiritual aspirations, and urge Mars to believe that dreams can come true.

A negative note in your mutual musical concert is that Mars can overstimulate and thereby confuse Neptune's more delicate mental and emotional nature. Also, Neptune may periodically seem deceptive or evasive to Mars, and in some manner wear down Mars's vitality and courage, while Mars, unless careful to be gentle, may unintentionally cause anxiety and fear in Neptune, who will, in turn, sap Mars's energy with such anxieties and fears.

If the two of you are involved in a joint endeavor involving medicine or dramatic, artistic, or musical interests, this aspect has great creative value and encourages mutual achievement. If you both behave yourselves nicely, then Neptune's intuition and spirituality blended with Mars's inner strength and courage can manifest a formidable vibration for personal and public success. I must tell you, however, that two people sharing this planetary aspect in their birth charts are sternly warned by the stars and the ancients against self-indulgences of any kind, especially drugs and alcohol. Also, far-out psychic experiments, such as seances and so forth, are dangerous for both of you.

Mars Sextile or Trine Neptune   A's Mars, B's Neptune
♂ ✳ △ ♆

Neptune's subtle influence on restless Mars is a multiple blessing. For example, Neptune not only inspires Mars to ever greater achievements, but it is also able to soothe Mars's ruffled emotional feathers and heal the hurts inflicted by the rest of the world. Mars returns the favors by helping Neptune fight a tendency toward inertia or procrastination, stimulating Neptune into action with an infusion of energy. Mars's initiative and leadership qualities combine with Neptune's uncanny intuition and vision, which can stimulate powerful creative potentials in both of you.

The combination is especially effective if there is a common interest in psychic phenomena, ecology, astrology, medicine, investigative work, religious concepts, archaeology, or mystical research of any kind. The study of spacecraft could be a satisfying mutual hobby, as could anything to do with water. You're both pro—animal life, loving whales, dolphins, forests, and Mother Earth in general. This is an excellent vibration for sympathy and compassion equally exchanged, which makes being together deeply comforting even when you share other aspects that are more stressful.

Unlike others, Mars won't accuse Neptune of mysterious or evasive behavior, because Mars is able to penetrate directly into Neptune's private world of shimmering Neptunian daydreams.

A most unusual facet of this aspect between two people is that, according to the ancients, it gives irrefutable evidence that at least one past incarnation you shared was intensely religious. Not in the sense of nuns or monks, convents or monasteries (other planetary aspects you may or may not have in your intercharts indicate that vibration), but in the sense of dynamic spiritual leadership of some kind, perhaps founding or heading an esoteric movement in an aggressive manner. So the sounds of chants and tolling bells weave through your personal astrological compatibility symphony. Have you heard them? Listen!

Mars Opposed or Square Neptune   A's Mars,
♂ ☍ □ ♆   B's Neptune

Mars can sometimes exhibit abrupt, impatient, and rash behavior, which will inevitably result in Neptune's hurt silence or elusive withdrawal, a reaction that only makes Mars behave even more aggressively. The basic problem is Mars's direct approach to a situation, which can be at war with Neptune's detached response. Neptune detachment infuriates Mars, and Mars's angry determination to "fight it out to the finish" causes Neptune to swim away from confrontation and hide behind the seaweed. Fire is fire (Mars) and water is water (Neptune), and each is capable of destroying the other. It happens with fire-water combinations in the Sun Signs of any two people; this planetary aspect you share has the same influence. Too much water can extinguish the brightest flame, and too much fire can evaporate water.

Those whose intercharts indicate this vibration are warned to avoid alcohol and drugs, or mutual dissipation could result. There could also be accusations of wasteful spending or the opposite: extreme stinginess. Neptune's mental and emotional health and psychic equilibrium can be seriously afflicted by the disputes between you, so Mars must genuinely try to have calmer responses to irritation and Neptune must learn to face disagreements openly instead of avoiding the issues. That's the only way to bring harmony to your relationship. If Mars would borrow a little of Neptune's essence and Neptune would borrow a little of Mars's essence, the two of you could meet somewhere in the middle of courage and honesty and Neptune gentleness—and there wouldn't be as many broken rhythms in your theme song.

Mars Sextile or Trine Pluto   A's Mars, B's Pluto
♂ ✶ △ ♀

There is such incredible energy between you for building ideas into eventual huge empires or large-scale operations that it's hard to visualize your relationship as ordinary. It's more like extraordinary. You greatly influence each other's already strong willpower, and you'd make an impressive team in politics, scientific research, penetrating hidden matters, or unearthing buried secrets in some area. Whatever type of association you share, you're both intensely devoted to any cause or project you undertake together. Truly, your mutual potential is awesome, although it may take some time and familiarity to realize it fully yourselves.

Mars Conjunct, Opposed, or Square Pluto   A's Mars,
♂ ☌ ☍ □ ♀   B's Pluto

This is a tough nut to crack, as they say. A couple of saints could handle it smoothly, but as for ordinary humans, well, it's a rocky road. Each of you has a strong will. Very strong. In a dispute between Mars and Pluto, the odds as to who will win are exactly even. No experienced gambler would take a chance on betting. The disputes will involve the resistance by each of you to any display of authority or command by the other. If there is a majority of other planetary aspects between you indicating stress or disharmony, the effect of this one can bring mutually violent reactions to any "bossy" behavior from either of you.

It's possible for Mars to hinder or interfere with Pluto's plans and projects, and for Pluto to be either mildly or strongly vindictive toward Mars in response, due to Pluto's latent urges for revenge. The often thoughtless and hasty speech that is a part of Mars's personality pattern is capable of infuriating Pluto. It's risky for anyone to anger Pluto seriously, but courageous, impulsive Mars will likely not be daunted by such risks and will instead plunge forward, following the old adage "Fools rush in where angels fear to tread." The treading, however, will more resemble stomping in where angels are too wise to go. Dear me, what to do? What to do?

You have only two choices—and no more—if you want to avoid the powerful stresses this vibration can bring. I assume you're both rational enough to want to avoid them. Here are the two choices:

1. Make certain that your association is not a close one if you both live, day after day, under the same roof. If you communicate only now and then in whatever association you share, this vibration will be much milder than if you're involved in a more intimate relationship on a daily basis, in which this aspect is definitely dangerous, or at least a threat to tranquillity.
2. Assuming that you have other harmonious (and therefore neutralizing) aspects in your intercharts, use them to (a) bite your respective tongues; and (b) take turns accepting each other's efforts at dominance gracefully.

"All well enough," I can hear Mars saying, "but Pluto is too selfish." Now I hear Pluto grumbling, "Me, selfish? Ha! Mars is the selfish one."

You know what? You're both selfish! You should each try a tad of tolerance because tolerance rhymes with tranquillity and the Universe is a poem. Uni-verse. See? "One verse."

Actually, becoming a saint needn't be a dreary process. It can be jolly fun. It makes you feel glowing and good, and can't help but make you superior to ordinary mortals.

Superior? Now there's a word that gets your attention! It's what both of you have been seeking all along, right? I trust you get the message that becoming a saint is the most reliable way to achieve it, even if you only succeed in becoming a junior saint (the kind who don't quite deserve a halo ... yet). It's kind of like the junior and senior Scouts. You have to work for those cosmic merit badges. They're not given away unless they're earned. So go for it! I send you two shamrocks for luck, and Ireland's St. Patrick sprinkles you with holy water and his blessings. Amen. A women.

7

Jupiter Aspects

Jupiter conjunct, sextile, or trine Jupiter
Jupiter opposed or square Jupiter
Jupiter conjunct, sextile, or trine Saturn
Jupiter opposed or square Saturn
Jupiter conjunct, sextile, or trine Uranus
Jupiter opposed or square Uranus
Jupiter conjunct, sextile, or trine Neptune
Jupiter opposed or square Neptune
Jupiter conjunct Pluto
Jupiter sextile or trine Pluto
Jupiter opposed or square Pluto

Jupiter Conjunct, Sextile, or Trine Jupiter　　　**A and B**
♃ ☌ ✶ △ ♃

The planet Jupiter in your birth charts represents the
clown, the philosopher, and the eternal optimist in each of
you. Since your two Jupiters are in harmonious aspect,

you'll often find that a good laugh together can make life's frustrations disappear. You're able to cheer one another up, lift each other out of the gloomies with little effort. You're both happy campers—literally. When life gets boring, you can grab a couple of sleeping bags, head for the woods, and sleep under the stars. This is known in astrology as a very lucky vibration for financial benefits and general good fortune. As a team, you'd be successful in publishing or educational projects, legal partnerships, or any kind of spiritual endeavor.

You may occasionally offend outsiders with tactless (but honest) remarks, yet when you're equally candid with each other there's no resentment because you both respect the integrity of such frankness. If you travel out of the country together, you'll have a rollicking good time. It's likely that one or both of you owns a pet—or several of them—because you share a love for all animals. Do you breed horses? Or work with PETA (People for the Ethical Treatment of Animals)? It's certainly possible. It's also possible that you're vegetarians. You probably also share a strong dislike for zoos, and would, if you could, free all the caged animals. Actually, you're unusually good people. This aspect usually removes mistrust on the part of either, since honesty is your guiding star in all matters, especially with one another.

As if all the foregoing isn't enough, you probably also share an intense interest in and fascination for UFOs and space travel. One could say that your relationship is a "close encounter" of the very happiest kind. It would take a bushel of disharmonious planetary aspects between you to dilute this one. It's just about impregnable.

Jupiter Opposed or Square Jupiter ♃ ☍ □ ♃   A and B

Your concepts of morals and ethics conflict, not always, but periodically. Your fundamental aspirations or spiritual leanings often clash and can cause frequent misunderstandings, especially if one of you is fanatical about religion. Disagreements about what is or isn't ethical in business dealings will place stress on your association, creating a need for adjustment and for compromise. You each tend to exaggerate the qualities you don't like in each other and don't hesitate to make your disapproval clear. Your mutual criticisms are neither hidden nor tactful, and this naturally seeds a great deal of irritation, annoyance, and frustration.

It will help to discuss your differences, to talk them over, but only if you do so with courtesy and tact, not bluntly. If all else fails, you might find a solution to your tensions in three words frequently repeated by a wise and wonderful Italian "mama mia" I know, who is always shouting at her noisy family: "Shudda da mouth!" Another helpful golden rule is to take care to travel separately. It's doubtful that you'll enjoy doing it together. One might be tempted to toss the other overboard. (Just joking.) Separately, you're rather nice humans; it's only when you spend every day under the same roof that conflicts begin to spark. The very best cosmic counsel from the stars is, in the final analysis, the advice of "mama mia," but say it to yourself in front of a mirror, not to each other, which would obviously only serve to ignite the flames of anger. Since most of your ideas are not the same, why not try adding an "L" for love, turning them from ideas into ideals? It could give you some common ground and make more of a difference than you might think. And uh, once more: Shudda da mouth! (Even if you're not Italian.)

Jupiter Conjunct, Sextile, or Trine Saturn ♃ ☌ ✷ △ ♄

A's Jupiter, B's Saturn

Favorable contacts between these planets are especially excellent in business associations, but they also represent very positive vibrations in other kinds of relationships, whether friendship, family, lovers, or mates.

Instead of clashing, Saturn's prudent and conservative practicality blends harmoniously with Jupiter's optimistic, expansive ideas and gambling spirit. Your respective qualities may be widely different, but when they operate together under this aspect rather than conflicting, they cause your team efforts to be surprisingly effective, your long-term goals to be successful. Even your wildest dreams have a good chance of coming true when they're united in mutual aspirations.

Any one of these three planetary contacts, by astrological tradition, promise (or at least strongly indicate) a probability of the accumulation of substantial wealth and financial security. Evidently, then, the universal ingredients of success consist of a union of the conservative with the liberal, caution with daring, and patience with aggressive drive. You are a perfect balance of opposing qualities, the secret of the Sun Sign of Libra, ruled by peacemaker Venus, the planet of both love and money. That's something worth mulling over in your minds since it contains seeds of primordial wisdom.

If your particular Jupiter-Saturn aspect happens to be a conjunction rather than a sextile or trine, you'll be blessed with all the foregoing gifts in your relationship, but the conjunction, in addition to the harmonies of this vibration, carries a minor warning. Minor, yes, but still important to remember: Saturn must try to stifle any overly stuffy caution and criticism of Jupiter, or Jupiter's natural, buoyant enthusiasm could be shattered, and we don't want that, do we? The conjunction also brings a strong possibility that Jupiter's tactless, uncompromising way of speaking the truth, however much it hurts, can deeply wound Saturn's self-confidence and cause spells of depression and brooding. But these petty pitfalls are not powerful enough to create any serious conflict between you. They'll cause only occasional tiffs, adding a sprinkle of spice to all that harmony!

Jupiter Opposed or Square Saturn   A's Jupiter, B's Saturn
♃ ☍ □ ♄

Financial security is not denied by this aspect, but money may be periodically difficult to attain because of disagreements about how to accumulate, spend, or save the stuff. Jupiter will probably not be big on saving it but is extremely talented at spending it. And Saturn will probably not be big on spending but is extremely talented at saving. You can see the problem. As for how to accumulate money, your concepts are frequently as far apart as the North Pole from the South Pole. Saturn may undermine Jupiter's enthusiastic faith by sometimes seeming to be selfish, critical, and demanding. Also, Saturn has little patience with Jupiter's Pollyanna-type optimism, which from time to time conflicts with the practical caution that's part of Saturn's outlook on life. Saturn's caution is in direct opposition to Jupiter's confidently expansive views and gambling spirit, with the result of causing Jupiter to feel confined and restrictive and Saturn to feel frustrated.

Saturn could accuse Jupiter of having no sense of responsibility, while Jupiter may accuse Saturn of delaying and limiting Jupiter's aspirations by unjustly building obstacles to their achievement. Jupiter has enough inner strength to overcome such disappointments, but only after a mighty struggle.

If your intercharts have a good number of harmonious aspects between these or other planets, this one will create tension only once in a while, and not enough of it to cause serious disturbances. However, if its vibrations are increased by a majority of discordant additional aspects, you needn't (and shouldn't) avoid or cancel your relationship, but you might consider living for occasional brief periods in nearby but separate residences, with lots of fresh air between your meetings. In either case it will help considerably for Saturn to stop dwelling on Jupiter's shortcomings and start appreciating Jupiter's honesty, a quality that Saturn certainly can't help but approve of, respect, and admire, and for Jupiter to curb tactless comments about Saturn's stuffiness and try to concentrate on Saturn's matching honesty, a trait that Jupiter can't help but approve of, respect, and admire.

So you see, the two of you have one thing in common: honesty. Surely that's a rock strong enough to build a bridge of harmony on, with a degree of tolerance on both sides. If Saturn will only allow it, Jupiter can raise Saturn's self-confidence and courage to take chances. And if Jupiter will only allow it, Saturn can prevent Jupiter's often impulsive, reckless behavior from going too far.

Jupiter: Be grateful for the blessing of Saturn's comforting reliability and protectiveness.

Saturn: Be grateful for the blessing of Jupiter's idealism and clownlike humor. It won't crack you in half to laugh now and then, you know.

Under the Universal Law of the "Divine Sense of Comedy," everything in life is funny, even your relationship. Especially your relationship!

Come on, you two—laugh your way into lightness. Your problems are only as heavy as you make them.

Jupiter Conjunct, Sextile, or Trine Uranus   A's Jupiter,
♃ ☌ ✳ △ ♅   B's Uranus

When you're together you bring out all the humanitarian qualities in each other. Even if other planetary aspects between you create a degree of mutual limitation or possessiveness, they will be tempered by this one because beneath it all you basically respect each other's need for freedom and individuality of expression. It's a vibration that makes you, when all is said and done, tolerant of any differences in your personalities. There's a pronounced desire to encourage one another's talents, ideals, and altruistic outlooks. You inspire each other in so very many ways, and this naturally leads to the possibility of causing most of your mutual dreams to materialize, as well as your individual and different dreams. Jupiter will expand Uranus's goals and creativity, while Uranus adds originality and excitement to Jupiter's plans and projects. As a team in any kind of association or relationship, you're capable of some mighty achievements and successes, which could bring much happiness to many people on Earth—and to Earth herself. One might say that, together, you can become an exploding rocket to the Moon, and beyond. When Jupiter's outspoken honesty and sweeping visions combine with Uranus's far-out, unconventional showers of genius, those around you are fascinated. They find you interesting, to say the very least! You find each other the same.

The conjunction between these two planets, however, in addition to bestowing all of the above harmonies of compatibility, may need some control, or it could cause you both to become overconfident at times, or perhaps bring out any latent recklessness lurking around in your characters. The sextile and trine aspects don't contain such a warning. And even this minor possible vibration with the conjunction is easily controlled once you've been made aware of it. Forewarned is forearmed!

Jupiter Opposed or Square Uranus ♃ ☍ □ ♅

A's Jupiter, B's Uranus

If either of you has any radical social or religious views, these aspects tend to excite them into excess. You could also overstimulate extravagance and irresponsibility in each other, or at least in one of you. Which one of you I'm not about to say, because I don't choose to be in the middle. It's not a safe place to stand! There may be occasions when Jupiter's idealistic aspirations will conflict with Uranus's more materialistic and unconventional goals. At such times Uranus will seem rebellious, inconsistent, and even unstable to Jupiter. In turn, Uranus will see Jupiter as unrealistic and be sharply critical of Jupiter's behavior. Obviously such attitudes do not promote peace and harmony. A lot of tolerance is needed, and tolerance normally is easier for Uranus to acquire than it is for Jupiter. Yet Jupiter is basically a generous, usually forgiving soul, and with some effort you can smooth out the tensions between you since they don't occur every day. When you feel stress coming on, each of you should find something interesting to do—separately—until the crankiness blows over. And it always will. Change will forever define your relationship. Therefore, patience is what you both need to practice.

Jupiter Conjunct, Sextile, or Trine Neptune ♃ ☌ ✳ △ ♆

A's Jupiter, B's Neptune

If the aspect between these planets in your intercharts is the conjunction, it's only prudent to warn you to be careful that your relationship does not lead you to seduce one another into bad habits involving extravagance, drugs,

alcohol, laziness, or self-indulgence. But if you are both reasonably spiritually developed and disciplined individuals,
this will be a minor or inconsequential flaw in your association. It's just a word to the wise, you know?

On the happier side, even if your personal mutual aspect
is the conjunction, you'll also enjoy all the following harmonies of the sextile or trine aspect involving these two planets:

You encourage idealism in one another and stimulate
your mutual charitable instincts and urges. Jupiter's expansive dreams can combine with Neptune's intuition and per-
ceptive visions to create not only enlightenment and success
in religious or educational endeavors, but also the possibility of the realization of material ambitions, perhaps even the
accumulation of wealth. Any of these three aspects is excellent for two people involved in medicine, publishing, the
law, the stock market, or large corporate ventures.

Whatever the type of your association, both your minds
and your emotions are strongly linked in a psychic sense.
The vibration of what is called ESP is either constantly displayed or subliminal. If the latter, it would be advisable to
cultivate it. ESP can be extremely useful in many areas.

Although you'd be wise to stay away from the race track
and slot machines if your aspect is the conjunction, if it's a
sextile or trine you might win on a shared lottery ticket or
the Irish Sweepstakes. Why? Because this vibration between
you creates lots of luck!

Last but certainly not least, you probably share a deep
and genuine love for animals, which can greatly benefit
Mother Earth, who is a living part of all her creatures, not
just humans. Even better, you're both likely to be vegetarians. If not, try it; you'll like it!

Jupiter Opposed or Square Neptune   A's Jupiter,
♃ ☍ □ ♆   B's Neptune

Both of these aspects carry the same warning as the conjunction of Jupiter and Neptune, which is that you must be
careful that your relationship doesn't lead you to encourage
in one or the other (or both) bad habits involving gambling,

extravagance, drugs, alcohol, laziness, or self-indulgence. Don't fret. Assuming you are reasonably disciplined and spiritually evolved individuals, this flaw in your relationship will be minor because you'll be able to control it each time it rears its lumpy little head.

Another frictional possibility could occur if Jupiter doesn't exert a real effort to avoid hurting Neptune's sensitive feelings with those occasional tactless and painful "arrows of truth." Stifle yourself, Jupiter. And, dear gentle Neptune, do try not to be so thin-skinned. When Jupiter is clowning around playing that eternal "honesty game," don't cry, dear gentle Neptune. Laugh! After all, you must admit that it's amusing when Jupiter periodically bumps into doors and lampposts and stumbles over cracks in the sidewalk, right?

Another area of trouble could arise when Jupiter becomes offended or angry over Neptune's elusive behavior from time to time. This can be innocent, a part of Neptune's nature, but Jupiter will see it as downright deceptive, and since Jupiter has this really big thing about truthfulness and honesty, it can create serious conflict.

To lighten the disharmony this vibration can bring, you should both avoid, at least as a team, the areas of religion, education, publishing, the stock market, slot machines, the race track, and lotteries. Instead, concentrate on both your individual and mutual visions of the future. You're equally blessed with the ability to manifest them, although you may disagree on how to do it. One solution to such a deadlock is for each to take turns trying the other's method. That way you double your chances to abracadabra your daydreams into reality and avoid much of the conflict.

Jupiter Conjunct Pluto   A's Jupiter, B's Pluto
♃ ☌ ♇

The planet Pluto tends, in an astrological sense, to veil both methods and outcomes, which is why the result of this vibration between you is somewhat unpredictable and depends to a large extent on the other planetary aspects in your intercharts. This aspect can be positive or negative.

In the negative area, any benefits from it are more likely to accrue to Pluto than to Jupiter. Also, it's possible that Pluto will behave in a possessive and domineering manner toward Jupiter, while Jupiter's stabbing comments or "arrows of truth" will arouse both Pluto's resentment and urges for revenge.

Skipping into the positive arena, this can be a markedly favorable vibration for financial achievements in business and success in politics. If your relationship is that of lovers or mates, it indicates a strong physical chemistry between you, and you can expect mutual stimulation in your shared endeavors. In addition, it's a powerful augury for achievement as a team in religious, legal, or educational areas, and especially in stock market or travel ventures. Pluto adds invisible and silent but immense energy to Jupiter's visions and plans, while Jupiter brings luck and optimistic expansion to Pluto's sometimes unexpressed dreams and goals. When the vibrations described in the second paragraph of this interpretation surface now and then, the two of you can probably accumulate enough money between you in your joint ventures to afford occasional separate vacations until the planetary influences pass, which they always do! Nothing in astrology is permanent; the vibrations come and go, then come again, and pass again. Everything moves in a circle.

Jupiter Sextile or Trine Pluto   A's Jupiter, B's Pluto
♃ ✳ △ ♇

If you take full advantage of this powerfully beneficial aspect, the two of you together could build large-scale projects, even an empire! There's a mighty force behind your combined endeavors. You encourage in one another spiritual enlightenment and tend to improve each other's basic characters in various ways. Depending upon how intense your mutual efforts are, the assistance you'll get from this vibration will be abundant related to material matters and an increase in your financial status. Whether you decide as a team to build a new religion, a new university, a new brokerage firm, a new airline, a chain of car washes, or a newspaper chain, this aspect should give you a very large head start!

Jupiter Opposed or Square Pluto   A's Jupiter, B's Pluto
♃ ☍ □ ♇

There's a serious conflict between your individual aspirations, goals, and ideals. Cooperation and compromise are both difficult to achieve, but keep trying. Practice makes perfect! The ancient texts refer to this vibration as a much-needed soul test. The problem is that Jupiter is probably the one to experience the soul testing while Pluto is the one to administer it. We all pass through generation-gap frictions of the same kind with parents and/or teachers. They always say, "Someday you'll thank me for this." (Do they expect us to spend the rest of our lives looking them up to say "Thank you"? Really.) However, that philosophy might be helpful with the two of you, who struggle under this aspect's stern testing. For instance, Jupiter could display—now, not later—gratitude to Pluto for the character lessons received. Yes, I know, Jupiter, I know. But who said it would be easy? I didn't say that. Did anyone else say that? If they did, they lied! It's hard, but when Pluto realizes that you're really trying to be gracious about the entire matter, it could considerably soften Pluto's vulnerable heart. Yes, in case you haven't noticed it, Pluto's heart is vulnerable, although Pluto would literally prefer to die rather than to reveal or admit it. That's only a metaphor, Jupiter; no, I was not suggesting that you help Pluto achieve that preference! Shame on you.

★

8

Saturn Aspects

★ ★ ★

Saturn conjunct Saturn
Saturn sextile or trine Saturn
Saturn opposed or square Saturn
Saturn conjunct Uranus
Saturn sextile or trine Uranus
Saturn opposed or square Uranus
Saturn conjunct Neptune
Saturn sextile or trine Neptune
Saturn opposed or square Neptune
Saturn sextile or trine Pluto
Saturn conjunct, square, or opposed Pluto

★ ★ ★

Saturn Conjunct Saturn   **A and B**
ħ ☌ ħ

Your attitudes toward ambition and how to achieve success are similar; therefore, you can help each other build constructively toward a common goal. You have the same kind of sense of responsibility and are likely to experience

much the same kind of problems, restrictions, and limitations with your parents in childhood, and employers, the
government, or other superiors in maturity. In whatever
area of life one of you feels held back or deprived, the other
will feel the same.

There's a danger that you may increase each other's tendency toward depression and pessimism and place too
much emphasis on your mutual fears, worries, and lack of
self-esteem, which can hamper your progress. Your best
healing remedy is to make a conscious and constant effort
to lighten your emotions, tell each other jokes, nurture a
mutual sense of humor, and don't take life so seriously.
When the gloomies get you down (and I'm speaking to both
of you here), instead of deepening the melancholy mood by
discussing it, write down your feelings on paper secretly,
then force yourself to speak aloud of nothing but happy
things for the next twenty-four hours. That should help.

Another suggestion: I've mentioned in other of these
compatibility aspects the optimist/pessimist test (Is the glass
half full or half empty?), but here's something the two of
you can do. Fill any glass (might as well make it a beautiful
crystal glass) halfway with water, then place it on a table or
on the mantel, where you both see it every day and can be
reminded that the glass is, true, half empty, but it is equally
true that the glass is half full. Which perception do you
choose? Why not the positive one? It's just as true as the
negative one. And therein lies the secret of the Universe,
waiting for you to discover it and unlock its mystery.

Saturn Sextile or Trine Saturn   A and B
ħ ⚹ △ ħ

Usually two people with this aspect have some sort of a
shared goal and are able to achieve it together. Because your
approaches to duty and responsibility are compatible, you
tend to agree and cooperate in meeting both mutual and individual obligations. You'd make a great team in any project concerning security, insurance, finances, real estate, or
scientific research. It's an excellent vibration for all kinds of
partnerships, whether business or marital, and also between

parent and child, and this aspect increases the longevity of the relationship. As with Peter Pan and his shadow, you're more or less stuck together, like it or lump it. You'll probably like it.

If your aspect is the trine rather than the sextile, and if the trine occurs in the water signs (Pisces, Cancer, or Scorpio), you could be involuntarily drawn into some sort of covert or secret tenth-house (government) activities. But don't worry. This vibration between your two Saturns is a protection against lasting harm to your relationship from any such possible entanglement. Nevertheless, maybe you shouldn't challenge the IRS, even though astrology says you'd win any conflict related to government matters. I wouldn't be too sure, because, well, does anyone ever win against the IRS? I suppose it's all a matter of semantics. Winning, that is.

Time and age are both illusions, but until everyone is enlightened to this great truth, if there's a chronological or calendar age difference between you (as there often is with this aspect), it won't cause any problems. Either you'll both ignore it or you'll discover the solid benefits of blending the innocence of inexperience with the wisdom of experienced maturity. Nothing is more ideal than a combination of innocence and wisdom. When you're together, you'll each feel you're with a chronological contemporary with no generation gap. This can be especially true after you've both learned to master physical immortality and age reversal through cell regeneration.

This revelation is explained in detail in Chapter 9 of the book *Linda Goodman's Star Signs*.   —*Editor*

Saturn Opposed or Square Saturn   A and B
♄ ☍ □ ♄

Your concepts of attaining security are poles apart! Both of you seek stability, but your ideas of what it should be and how to achieve it differ greatly. There's also a considerable difference in the way you handle responsibility, which may alternately discourage and frustrate both of you equally.

There could be a shadow of mistrust between you now and then, probably imaginary, based on a lack of understanding of one another's motives. Eventually, this can become devitalizing, and if you don't make a mutual attempt to adjust to your differences, the vibration is disharmonious enough to cause one or both of you to become physically ill or depleted of energy.

To transform such results of this planetary aspect into a reasonably comfortable and harmonious truce in your relationship, you'll both need a bushel of tolerance, forgiveness, patience, and grace. But your two Saturns are strong enough to handle it. There's always a way around the negativity of any vibration, and this is no exception. Try challenging yourselves to overcome your discords. After all, Saturn is the planet of wisdom and maturity, certainly capable of surmounting difficulties. True, the capability was deposited in two discordant signs when you were born, expressing itself differently, but that allows you two ways to use its surmounting abilities, a doubling up of Saturnine power influences; you have twice the wisdom, twice the maturity. So you have no excuse for not solving at least most of the problems this aspect periodically presents! As long as you do it together. That's the secret.

Saturn Conjunct Uranus   A's Saturn, B's Uranus
♄ ☌ ♅

No two planets are as widely divergent in the matters they influence as these. One of them (Saturn) is associated with the old and the past, while the other (Uranus) is associated with the new and the future. On the surface of it, these two planets have nothing in common.

However, when their divergent influences combine in a conjunction aspect between the birth charts of two people, the vibration becomes highly advantageous, blending the best of both influences into a possibly powerful harmony. Saturn's wise practicality can help Uranus's ingenuity find constructive channels, and Uranus's brilliant (if unconventional) concepts can help to stimulate Saturn's material ambitions, Saturn's long-term goals. When Saturn drifts into anxiety and apprehension, Uranus can be of great help in breaking Saturn's bonds of melancholy and depression.

Uranus can gradually persuade Saturn to be more liberal, progressive, and adaptable to change, while Saturn's prudent planning can prevent Uranus's unorthodox and independent urges from becoming irresponsibly eccentric.

In all of these ways, the old and the new symbolized by these two planets work beneficially and harmoniously when blended in a conjunction between two people. But to take full advantage of the vibrations; to receive the mutual benefits possible, Saturn must try to be a little more flexible, and Uranus must learn to be a little more reliable and responsible. Not a lot—just a little! In other words, to change slightly the American Indian saying, you two should periodically walk a few miles in each other's Moon boots.

Saturn Sextile or Trine Uranus   A's Saturn, B's Uranus
♄ ✶ △ ♅

In any kind of relationship, you have marvelous possibilities for achieving your dreams, Uranus's often being unconventional, innovative, and unorthodox, and Saturn's usually being long-term and wrapped in security blankets. The wonderful thing about the success you two are capable of attaining together is that, however weird and far-out Uranus's dreams may be, they'll be supported and backed by a solid and practical foundation, thanks to Saturn. Uranus's symphony is wild and soaring, with chords of genius. Saturn's concert is accompanied by the percussion of caution and stability, with a soothing chorus of the wisdom of ancient experience. When these two planets are harmonizing between you, how can you lose? It's a perfect blend of the eccentric progressive and the reliable conservative, as is the Music of the Spheres.

Saturn Opposed or Square Uranus   A's Saturn,
♄ ☍ □ ♅   B's Uranus

All right, let's face the challenge honestly, without flinching. Saturn requires a certain amount of stability in life and can become shaken and disorganized by the Uranus's occasional unexpected, shocking, unorthodox, and off-the-wall behavior. Uranus may view Saturn as cold, overly cautious, stern, and domineering. Then the planetary friction begins. But it isn't present all the time, just now and then, on a bad day. You need to level with each other about your individual needs. Agree to allow mutual freedom of expression to be yourselves, and try to be tolerant of your different attitudes when they flash between you. Uranus isn't really as dorky as Saturn sometimes believes, and Saturn isn't as much of a stuffed potato as Uranus sometimes believes. Think of the bright side. Working out this vibration together will give you both a chance to mature emotionally and spiritually. Don't you just hate preachy truisms when you're annoyed?

Saturn Conjunct Neptune   A's Saturn, B's Neptune
♄ σ ♆

Your relationship or association won't be seriously harmed by this planetary aspect; neither will it be substantially helped.

The benefits, mild as they are, include the ability of Neptune to add a degree of idealism and spirituality to Saturn's practical ambitions and Saturn's ability to restrain Neptune's imagination when it needs a touch of reality. The stress, minor as it is, includes mutual doubt and misunderstanding, perhaps suspicions of deception where none exists, and Saturn's attempts to force responsibility on Neptune, which Neptune may strongly resent or, at the very least, definitely not appreciate. Also, Saturn may look upon Neptune as a foolish dreamer, thereby exercising a restrictive, limiting influence. These are frictional possibilities, but they probably won't seriously damage your relationship, just cause little irritations and annoyances, like buzzing bumblebees on a hot summer day. Shoo them away! But be careful you don't get stung while you're shooing.

Saturn Sextile or Trine Neptune   A's Saturn, B's Neptune
ħ ⚹ △ Ψ

Here's a planetary aspect interpretation that's short and sweet! Neptune provides the imagination and inspiration Saturn very much needs. Saturn provides the practical wisdom and stability Neptune very much needs. A nice exchange. The vibration here is certainly harmonious, but not of great importance, relatively, compared with others. Still, it does help your canoeing together when the wind ruffles the lake, not to mention when you're caught in a storm and lose your paddles!

Saturn Opposed or Square Neptune   A's Saturn,
ħ ☍ □ Ψ   B's Neptune

If either of you plans a career as a stockbroker or banker or intends to become a senator, member of Congress, or the President, you'd best say, "Good-bye, it was nice meeting you," and go your separate ways because there's a probability that you'll bring misfortune of some kind to each other in the areas of finance, government, or politics.

Otherwise, assuming that neither of you aspires to any of the foregoing, you can go ahead and hang out together for as brief or extensive period of time as you choose and try to untangle the knots of this aspect.

There could be seeds of suspicion and misunderstanding, planted by Saturn's sometimes domineering and restrictive behavior or by Neptune's sometimes evasive, aloof attitude. Saturn may accuse Neptune of deception, which may or may not be true, but if it is, it probably stems from Neptune's fear that speaking openly will bring on Saturn's stern and judgmental criticism. Saturn may see Neptune as a sneaky, impractical, and foolish dreamer. Neptune may privately see Saturn as cold, stuffy, and selfish. Neptune is likely the one who will have to make turn-the-other-cheek concessions, since accommodation and compromise are not usually among Saturn's virtues.

However, if there are harmonious aspects between other planets in your intercharts, and if both of you equally and sincerely want to smooth out the creases and wrinkles in this vibration, you can change its influence into something satisfying rather than disturbing. For example, Neptune can soften and gentle Saturn's disposition and lighten Saturn's occasional spells of deep depression, while Saturn can wrap Neptune's anxieties and careless nature in a cozy blanket of protection and security. If you love enough.

Saturn Sextile or Trine Pluto   A's Saturn, B's Pluto
ħ ⚹ △ ♇

Although it's helpful in general, if your relationship is that of relatives, lovers, or mates, you probably won't notice any specific influence from this aspect. But if your association is that of business partners, there should be a more noticeable effect.

Pluto is capable of conceiving of and planning huge empires or large-scale enterprises when backed by Saturn's practical wisdom and experience. When you combine your harmonious qualities and natural talents, which include Pluto's silent but immense power and Saturn's steady and patient practicality, the world is your oyster. There's very little you aspire to that you can't successfully achieve together, with a team effort. Very little. All this won't fall into your lap or drop down the chimney, of course. It won't be a piece of cake. It will require hard work, which, fortunately, is also a part of your natures.

Saturn Conjunct, Square, or Opposed Pluto   A's Saturn,
ħ ☌ □ ☍ ♇   B's Pluto

Pluto may try to change or reform Saturn's strict and serious attitudes toward life, which Saturn will rebel against intensely. Assuming the two of you share harmonious vibrations from other planetary aspects in your intercharts, this one will not be apt to create serious trouble. Otherwise, mutual resentments could be fierce and gradually grow into temporary periods of actual dislike on both sides. There are only two ways to avoid such a danger: (1) assistance, as just noted, from favorable aspects between other planets in your birth charts; or (2) the kind of all-encompassing, repeated forgiveness born of genuine love. If only Earthlings would realize the power of love to conquer any kind of misery or unhappiness like a mighty magic wand, it wouldn't matter whether two people's birth charts were full of positive or so-called negative aspects because love can conquer the influences of the planets. It can even eliminate karma. Yes, if only humans truly understood this. Well, it's the Aquarian age of serendipity, so maybe someday soon.

Uranus Aspects

★ ★
★

Uranus conjunct Uranus
Uranus conjunct Neptune
Uranus conjunct Pluto

★ ★
★

Uranus Conjunct Uranus   **A and B**
♅ ☌ ♅

Until recently, most astrologers did not emphasize the importance of Uranus conjunct Uranus because many people of the same generation will have this aspect.

But Uranus is very important in relationships because it can cause sudden attractions or separations. Also, which house Uranus falls in tells how we like to live a little outside convention. If you have Uranus on the Ascendant or Seventh house, you are inclined to attract partners who are younger, more eccentric. Your ideas of marriage are not conventional. No white picket fences for you.

The planet Uranus can be disruptive in your home life or in regard to career matters if it falls in the fourth or tenth house, as sudden changes will often occur wherever it lands. But excitement is always just around the corner for both of you.

Don't worry about the effects of the other houses, as they are not that significant by comparison. Most often this aspect simply means that both of you experience sudden happenings at about the same time in a similar fashion. You may meet at organizations or through friends, become instant and fast friends, and just as suddenly become lovers.

Uranus Conjunct Neptune   A's Uranus, B's Neptune
♅ ☌ ♆

This is an unusual combination where Uranus acts as the conduit for Neptune. Uranus stimulates the dreamy Neptune to do something about all his or her ESP, imaginative ideas, religious reforms, and unpublished poetry. Together you read one another's minds, pursue interests in the occult, and escape to New Age retreats.

Uranus Conjunct Pluto   A's Uranus, B's Pluto
♅ ☌ ♇

No doubt about it, together you are involved in reform and dramatic sociological changes. Paired, you become very able in matters of survival, and restore one another to health and add strength and vitality to each other. The wonders and mysteries of the Universe fascinate both of you. As a couple, you explore vortexes and Sanskrit, and are a most exciting partnership. Who can resist you?

Neptune Aspects

Neptune conjunct Neptune
Neptune conjunct Pluto

Neptune Conjunct Neptune   **A and B**
Ψ ♂ Ψ

Because this is a generational planet, it is slow moving, and many of you who are near the same age will have this aspect together. While you share many similar interests and social conditions, when paired romantically you sometimes slide into excess together. Neptune conjunct Neptune can lead to too much idealizing of each other, getting obsessive, daydreaming, and the like. But when the other aspects are strong, like having lots of planets in the earth signs or other favorable indications, you will find balance for your escapist tendencies.

Neptune Conjunct Pluto   A's Neptune, B's Pluto
Ψ ♂ ♇

Both of you are on a spiritual path together. You may not always realize this because Neptune comes from an intuitive and sensitive place, while Pluto acts like the atomic bomb in the relationship much of the time. But Neptune leads Pluto toward a gentler path. The gift to Neptune in return for the lessons on a quieter, more spiritual life is Pluto's ability always to help his mate gain personal power. Pluto will help Neptune to improve her lot in life. You share destiny and make profound changes in the life path of one another.

★ 11 ★

Pluto Aspects

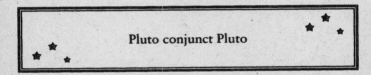

Pluto conjunct Pluto

Pluto Conjunct Pluto
♇ ☌ ♇

A and B

Pluto, as you have learned by now, is a planet of transformation and power. Everyone in a relationship with someone who is near the same age will have this aspect. When this aspect is near the Ascendant, you have tremendous, silent power as a couple. There is nothing you can't accomplish when you set your minds to it. The caution here is not to be ruthless in your power. If your Plutos fall in the seventh house, there may be power struggles over who wears the pants in the family. Face it: You both will. Ever changing, you go through many of these changes together. You may even look markedly different as a couple every seven years. But that can be exciting. And your willpower and ability to solve life's crises together is nothing short of remarkable.

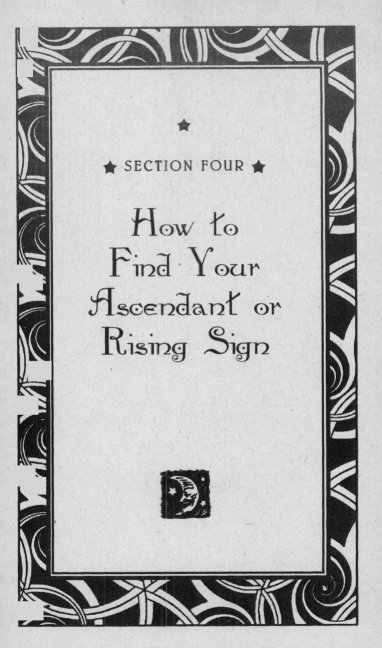

★

★ SECTION FOUR ★

How to
Find Your
Ascendant or
Rising Sign

How to Use the Ascendant Tables

1. Locate your birth date in the Rising Sign tables that follow. Notice that days 1 through 14 of each month are grouped together, as are days 15 through the end of the month. These tables apply to your birth date no matter what year you were born in.

2. The times you see listed under each set of dates are the times at which the Ascendant moved into the sign indicated. To find your Rising Sign, find the time closest to your birth that is still *before* it. The sign noted next to this time is your Ascendant or Rising Sign. If you were born during the summer, you'll need to subtract one hour from your birth time to account for daylight saving time. If you were born in the United States during wartime (March 31–October 27, 1918; March 30–October 26, 1919; or February 9, 1942–September 30, 1945), you'll also need to subtract an hour from the time of your birth.

3. Turn to the Rising Sign profiles for men and women that follow these tables and check out the characteristics of your Ascendant—and get some quick insight into others by reading their profiles, too! If your birth time is very

close to the time the Ascendant changed signs, you may want to read both profiles and determine which one sounds more like you.

4. A word about Ascendants: While time is predictable, man has created some irregularities. For example, some states adopted daylight saving time immediately and others didn't. During World War I and World War II, the United States used daylight saving time all year round to conserve energy for the war effort. Even the accuracy of the Sun Sign tables varies a little bit from year to year, which affects those of you born on the cusp of a sign.

The following tables are accurate a high percentage of the time. They are most accurate for births in North America. However, only by having your chart done by a professional astrologer can you be certain of the Ascendant. If you have had your chart done, use the Ascendant given by the astrologer as the starting point for your relationship chart, even if it differs from the Ascendant shown next to your birth time in these tables.

Of course, Linda had a simple solution for this. When she was uncertain of the time of birth for any reason (Mom was sleepy, the records were lost or the doctor forgot to record it), she considered the Ascendant the same as the Sun Sign.

★

2 ★ ★

The Ascendant Tables

JANUARY 1–14
ANY YEAR
APPROXIMATE TIME OF BIRTH

....

A.M.		P.M.	
12:25	Libra	1:10	Taurus
3:00	Scorpio	2:45	Gemini
5:30	Sagittarius	5:05	Cancer
7:45	Capricorn	7:25	Leo
9:30	Aquarius	10:00	Virgo
10:45	Pisces	11:40	Libra
11:50	Aries		

★ ★ ★

JANUARY 15–31
ANY YEAR
APPROXIMATE TIME OF BIRTH

A.M.		P.M.	
1:00	Scorpio	12:10	Taurus
4:35	Sagittarius	1:50	Gemini
6:50	Capricorn	4:05	Cancer
8:25	Aquarius	6:10	Leo
9:45	Pisces	9:05	Virgo
10:55	Aries	11:30	Libra

*　*　*

FEBRUARY 1–14
ANY YEAR
APPROXIMATE TIME OF BIRTH

A.M.		P.M.	
2:05	Scorpio	12:50	Taurus
4:35	Sagittarius	1:05	Gemini
6:50	Capricorn	4:05	Cancer
8:25	Aquarius	6:30	Leo
9:55	Pisces	9:05	Virgo
10:55	Aries	11:30	Libra

*　*　*

FEBRUARY 15–29
ANY YEAR
APPROXIMATE TIME OF BIRTH

....

A.M.		P.M.	
12:05	Scorpio	2:05	Cancer
2:40	Sagittarius	4:30	Leo
4:50	Capricorn	7:05	Virgo
6:25	Aquarius	9:30	Libra
7:45	Pisces	11:05	Scorpio
8:55	Aries		
10:10	Taurus		
11:50	Gemini		

★   ★   ★

MARCH 1–14
ANY YEAR
APPROXIMATE TIME OF BIRTH

....

A.M.		P.M.	
1:35	Sagittarius	1:05	Cancer
3:50	Capricorn	3:30	Leo
5:25	Aquarius	6:05	Virgo
6:45	Pisces	8:30	Libra
7:55	Aries	11:05	Scorpio
9:10	Taurus		
10:50	Gemini		

★   ★   ★

MARCH 15–31
ANY YEAR
APPROXIMATE TIME OF BIRTH

A.M.		P.M.	
12:35	Sagittarius	12:05	Cancer
2:50	Capricorn	2:30	Leo
4:25	Aquarius	5:05	Virgo
5:45	Pisces	7:30	Libra
6:55	Aries	10:05	Scorpio
8:10	Taurus	11:55	Sagittarius
9:50	Gemini		

* * *

APRIL 1–14
ANY YEAR
APPROXIMATE TIME OF BIRTH

A.M.		P.M.	
1:50	Capricorn	1:30	Leo
3:25	Aquarius	4:05	Virgo
4:45	Pisces	6:30	Libra
5:55	Aries	9:05	Scorpio
7:10	Taurus	11:35	Sagittarius
8:50	Gemini		
11:05	Cancer		

* * *

APRIL 15–30
ANY YEAR
APPROXIMATE TIME OF BIRTH

....

A.M.		P.M.	
12:30	Capricorn	12:30	Leo
2:55	Aquarius	3:05	Virgo
3:45	Pisces	5:30	Libra
4:55	Aries	8:05	Scorpio
6:10	Taurus	10:35	Sagittarius
7:50	Gemini	11:40	Capricorn
10:05	Cancer		

*   *   *

MAY 1–14
ANY YEAR
APPROXIMATE TIME OF BIRTH

....

A.M.		P.M.	
1:25	Aquarius	2:05	Virgo
2:45	Pisces	4:30	Libra
3:55	Aries	7:05	Scorpio
5:10	Taurus	9:35	Sagittarius
6:50	Gemini	11:50	Capricorn
9:05	Cancer		
11:30	Leo		

*   *   *

MAY 15–31
ANY YEAR
APPROXIMATE TIME OF BIRTH

A.M.		P.M.	
12:25	Aquarius	1:05	Virgo
1:45	Pisces	3:35	Libra
2:55	Aries	6:05	Scorpio
4:10	Taurus	8:35	Sagittarius
5:50	Gemini	10:50	Capricorn
8:00	Cancer		
10:30	Leo		

* * *

JUNE 1–14
ANY YEAR
APPROXIMATE TIME OF BIRTH

A.M.		P.M.	
12:45	Pisces	12:05	Virgo
1:55	Aries	2:30	Libra
3:10	Taurus	5:05	Scorpio
4:50	Gemini	7:35	Sagittarius
7:05	Cancer	9:55	Capricorn
9:35	Leo	11:25	Aquarius

* * *

JUNE 15–30
ANY YEAR
APPROXIMATE TIME OF BIRTH

A.M.		P.M.	
12:55	Aries	1:30	Libra
2:10	Taurus	4:05	Scorpio
3:50	Gemini	6:35	Sagittarius
6:05	Cancer	8:50	Capricorn
8:30	Leo	10:25	Aquarius
11:05	Virgo	11:45	Pisces

* * *

JULY 1–14
ANY YEAR
APPROXIMATE TIME OF BIRTH

A.M.		P.M.	
1:10	Taurus	12:30	Libra
2:50	Gemini	3:00	Scorpio
5:05	Cancer	5:35	Sagittarius
7:30	Leo	7:50	Capricorn
10:05	Virgo	9:25	Aquarius
		10:45	Pisces
		11:35	Aries

* * *

JULY 15–31
ANY YEAR
APPROXIMATE TIME OF BIRTH

A.M.		P.M.	
12:10	Taurus	2:05	Scorpio
1:50	Gemini	4:30	Sagittarius
4:00	Cancer	6:50	Capricorn
6:30	Leo	8:25	Aquarius
9:00	Virgo	9:45	Pisces
11:30	Libra	10:55	Aries

* * *

AUGUST 1–14
ANY YEAR
APPROXIMATE TIME OF BIRTH

A.M.		P.M.	
12:50	Gemini	1:05	Scorpio
3:05	Cancer	3:35	Sagittarius
5:30	Leo	5:50	Capricorn
8:05	Virgo	7:25	Aquarius
10:30	Libra	8:45	Pisces
		9:55	Aries
		11:10	Taurus

* * *

AUGUST 15–31
ANY YEAR
APPROXIMATE TIME OF BIRTH

....

A.M.   **P.M.**

2:05   Cancer   12:00   Scorpio
4:30   Leo   2:35   Sagittarius
7:05   Virgo   4:50   Capricorn
9:30   Libra   6:25   Aquarius
                                7:45   Pisces
                                8:55   Aries
                               10:10   Taurus
                               11:50   Gemini

★   ★   ★

SEPTEMBER 1–14
ANY YEAR
APPROXIMATE TIME OF BIRTH

....

A.M.   **P.M.**

1:05   Cancer   1:30   Sagittarius
3:30   Leo   3:50   Capricorn
6:10   Virgo   5:25   Aquarius
8:30   Libra   6:45   Pisces
11:05   Scorpio   7:55   Aries
                                9:10   Taurus
                               10:50   Gemini

★   ★   ★

SEPTEMBER 15–30
ANY YEAR
APPROXIMATE TIME OF BIRTH

A.M.		P.M.	
12:05	Cancer	12:35	Sagittarius
2:30	Leo	2:50	Capricorn
5:05	Virgo	4:25	Aquarius
7:30	Libra	5:50	Pisces
10:05	Scorpio	6:55	Aries
		8:10	Taurus
		9:50	Gemini

* * *

OCTOBER 1–14
ANY YEAR
APPROXIMATE TIME OF BIRTH

A.M.		P.M.	
1:30	Leo	1:50	Capricorn
4:05	Virgo	3:15	Aquarius
6:30	Libra	4:45	Pisces
9:05	Scorpio	5:55	Aries
11:35	Sagittarius	7:10	Taurus
		8:50	Gemini
		11:00	Cancer

* * *

OCTOBER 15–31
ANY YEAR
APPROXIMATE TIME OF BIRTH

A.M.		P.M.	
12:30	Leo	12:50	Capricorn
3:05	Virgo	2:25	Aquarius
5:30	Libra	3:45	Pisces
8:05	Scorpio	4:50	Aries
10:35	Sagittarius	6:10	Taurus
		7:50	Gemini
		10:05	Cancer

★   ★   ★

NOVEMBER 1–14
ANY YEAR
APPROXIMATE TIME OF BIRTH

A.M.		P.M.	
2:05	Virgo	1:25	Aquarius
4:30	Libra	2:45	Pisces
7:05	Scorpio	3:55	Aries
9:35	Sagittarius	5:10	Taurus
11:50	Capricorn	6:50	Gemini
		9:05	Cancer
		11:30	Leo

★   ★   ★

NOVEMBER 15–30
ANY YEAR
APPROXIMATE TIME OF BIRTH

....

A.M.		P.M.	
1:05	Virgo	12:25	Aquarius
3:30	Libra	1:45	Pisces
6:15	Scorpio	2:55	Aries
8:35	Sagittarius	4:10	Taurus
10:50	Capricorn	5:50	Gemini
		8:00	Cancer
		10:30	Leo

*   *   *

DECEMBER 1–14
ANY YEAR
APPROXIMATE TIME OF BIRTH

....

A.M.		P.M.	
12:05	Virgo	12:45	Pisces
2:30	Libra	1:55	Aries
5:05	Scorpio	3:10	Taurus
7:35	Sagittarius	4:50	Gemini
9:50	Capricorn	7:00	Cancer
11:25	Aquarius	9:30	Leo

*   *   *

DECEMBER 15–31
ANY YEAR
APPROXIMATE TIME OF BIRTH

....

A.M.		P.M.	
1:30	Libra	12:55	Aries
4:05	Scorpio	2:10	Taurus
6:35	Sagittarius	3:50	Gemini
8:50	Capricorn	6:00	Cancer
10:25	Aquarius	8:30	Leo
11:45	Pisces	11:05	Virgo

★   ★   ★

★

★ *3* ★

Rising Signs for Men

Aries Rising

"Was I the first?"

Was he the first to make you feel this way, to share your special secrets, to meet the family, to see you in that red bustier? Of course not. But while this man claims to be wild about honesty, he is far more crazed to hear how he has no predecessor and no equal. Aries is the first sign of the Zodiac, and here you find a man who is all impulse, energy (unless he is hooked up to a ventilator), and raging enthusiasm for living. He is ambitious and in a hurry. If you want to poke along and smell the roses, find yourself a mate with another Rising Sign. If you mosey out of bed, blow-dry your hair for more than ten minutes, and simply must have that first cup of coffee before you start your day, you will not be able to sustain his interest. And you will have more to sustain than his interest. While he is one of the four motivating Ascendants and can inspire others to almost anything, he sometimes cannot keep his own motor running at peak. Since he continually pours out his energies to others, he often comes up short and his cup runs low. Enter the woman of his life. She will be his coach and his trainer: "Of course you can sell the most stocks, get in the finals for Mr. Universe, and start your own business before the end of the week." He knows his boundaries: infinity. Once you understand that he wants to be the man from Krypton instead of Ohio, you will begin to see the task ahead of you. He will have disappointments and setbacks from time to time as reality challenges him with swats on the nose as if he were a frisky puppy in training. Get him to remove his imaginary cape and you will find an able breadwinner, an innovative self-starter, a trusting copartner, and a sentimental softy. I know of one tough guy with boundless dreams who was nearly broke on Christmas. He gave his wife a record, "You Needed Me" by Anne Murray. They both cried and mushed it up. Then she went back to tap dancing in the kitchen. You can fall into the pit with him, but a good coach always knows when to pick up the pace. The secret of his success is that he always gravitates toward the top of infinity. Be ready to soar with him. And don't forget to tell him he is the only one you've flown with.

Taurus Rising

"I need to call for a stock quote."

Regardless of his humble beginnings or his obvious charm upon meeting you, if you don't meet his standards of style, Taurus Rising won't embark upon a serious relationship with you. He may live with you, promise you something more in the future, and meet your family, yet he will be saving himself for Ms. Right. His idea of the perfect woman may lie in the fact that his favorite movie stars are Grace Kelly, Gene Tierney, and Greer Garson. Barely out of his teens, he'd see an old movie and get fixated on the forties woman with the sterling silver hairbrush, white gloves, and the "Oh, my gosh, my dance card is full" expression. While he's delightfully playful with his acquaintances who look like they're on MTV, he longs for something more. His entire life is a series of wistful desires for the finer things. He's saving his money for the house on the hill, dreaming of the girl who'd dance cheek to cheek at the ball with him in his tuxedo, her gloved hand draped across his shoulder. These flights of fancy are like blueprints for life with him, no matter how meager his finances. His outward calm hides his turmoil over a future where candle-lit dinners are the norm. He can't take risks with his plans, and he can't be with a woman who will embarrass him in public. This trait carries well into the golden years, where he prefers a widow over a divorcee, old money versus new, and blue chip over blue sky. Taking the stroll through life at a leisurely pace, his footing steady and sturdy, you'll find he needs a lot of rest and time to roam free. Show him this profile and he'd snort and say, "That is not at all like me." Let him win the lottery and watch the transformation. Wear lilac, lace, and the bearing of a lady, and tour the good life with a man of faithful heart and solid future.

Gemini Rising

"Let's go to both parties tonight."

Gemini Rising men are world-class travelers even if confined to their own neighborhoods. They are restless and active and have some marvelous characteristics. They have the rare quality of being able to throw themselves into work and yet totally forget it and shift into play with 100 percent abandon. Sometimes, after a late night of partying, the alarm is ringing about the time they come in. Not a problem for this guy; he will shower, shave, and proceed to work with his usual enthusiasm. That could explain why he often looks peculiar in the mornings. He is this way with women as well. And when "he's not near the one he loves, he loves the one he's near." If you can cope with that fact or are of the same inclination, things should be cool. If not, brace yourself for some turmoil. Another thing: To cover his tracks, he has a lot of stories to tell. Stories like the goat ate his divorce papers. Therefore, don't take his word as gospel. And speaking of his word, there will be lots of them, late into the night. Words are his foreplay, afterplay, and, surprisingly, his verbal fantasies during can be a humdinger of an experience. Blind dates with Gemini Rising are not often regretted. He could show up at your door in any attire topped with a baseball cap and his beeper placed on his hip, or wearing a tuxedo with a cummerbund that advertises his business. The real reason for his incongruity is that he is always on the way to or from something else. He is fussy about the way he dresses, no matter how odd it may appear to the rest of us. GQ he is not, but his clothes are meaningful to him nonetheless. As for the girl of his dreams, she'd better be feminine in appearance and less scattered than he. If he really takes an interest, he may buy you a matching cap or something he has bonded with in the way of apparel. He could take you anywhere; his destinations depend on his emotions. Even if you aren't interested in pursuing the relationship, you will have had an exciting, memorable time. Relationships with this man are punctuated with periods of upheaval (he is still seeing his ex), disappearing acts (he is seeing someone new), and absentmindedness (he has two dates tonight). Somehow he is able to get away with these antics for quite a while because he is fun. A lot of us grow up leaving the child in us behind, and Gemini Rising is delightfully childlike. He even maintains a youthful appearance well into middle age. If you don't see the beauty of being swept off your feet to an amusement park or having barbecues in your living room on rainy days, hurry on to the stodgy old Capricorn Rising and leave room for the absolute tons of women who can't resist this man. The wonder of the Gemini Rising is the delight he takes in the universe. Living is fascinating business for this man. He will always have a cause, a project, an adventure in the works. It's contagious. Get crazy with him and even when it's over you can take the lessons in living with you. What better gift?

Cancer Rising

"I'd rather stay at home."

Cancer Rising men almost go into shock when they hear other men say that home is where you go when there's nowhere else to go. It's all they can do to leave, and yet once they are out there in the business world they're some of the best moneymakers and, like shooting stars, soar through the skies of competition at work. There is really no contradiction here about home and work; they just become attached to their surroundings. Habits are their roots, strong as crabgrass. At home he won't replace his old recliner; he'll reupholster it. At work he'll use words like "expand," not relocate. The Cancer Rising man is clinging—things mean so much to him. They are part of where he's been and who he is. Garage sales should be listed before the obits in the paper, in his way of thinking. It'd be a serious breach in your relationship with this man should you not appreciate his need to be surrounded by his habits. He hangs on to his people in much the same manner. Should a loved one leave his life for whatever reason, he'll still hang on to his feelings even when they cause him anguish. While he is an excellent counselor, he's not an excellent patient because he never lets go of the garbage he totes around. He is sensitive, and you can share your innermost thoughts with him; he won't hurt you by using your weaknesses or abusing your trust. No matter. He will, however, insist on living exactly as he wants to live. It may be near his childhood home, his mother, or something of significance concerning his past. He will also have bouts with the blues. He worries about the end of the world. He worries about his health. Free-floating anxiety is as much a part of his life as it is for a Woody Allen character. So when he asks you "Why don't we just have dinner at home tonight?" he isn't really looking for an answer or debate, he's looking for more time under his 1,600-square-foot security blanket of stucco and time to drop his shell away from the demands of the world. Since security, home, and hearth are so important to him, a woman who wants to pull up roots every few years and immerse herself in another culture for the sake of experience will not entice him. Changing your hair color every now and then will make him nervous, and when he gets nervous he gets crabby. And when he gets crabby my only suggestion is to pull the covers over both your heads until it passes. He won't be cajoled, consoled, or talked out of his moods. Remember that, if you think you can mold or manipulate him because he comes across so sweet and gentle. While he is changeable, he does not change.

Leo Rising

"Is this the top of the line?"

Leo Rising men come in two primary categories: the beautiful ones who don't have to roar to be heard—a simple toss of the lion's mane will do (or the steady gaze of the hazel eyes); or the less magnificent ones who roar and bellow constantly, striving for the limelight. These lesser Leo Risings don't have the animal magnetism and grace of the beautiful ones to charm their audience, but this will not stop them in their desire to overwhelm everyone at any gathering. This is how you spot one. Another way to tell them apart from the other combinations is to ask them about anything. They'll have an answer, have been there, or know the person the subject was named for. This sounds like a lot of baloney, but chances are he's telling the truth. It's as if Nature conspired to introduce Leo Rising to everyone of prominence and educate him on all the glitzy conversational tidbits. If you want to bask in this for all eternity you'll have to make sure your orbital spin revolves around his. In other words, don't ever upstage him. That means in your career as well. While he admires the two-career family, he needs a one-man woman who allows him to dictate on matters of dress and life-style. Not that this is all bad. He'll have better taste and a finer sense of style than your latest fashion magazine. In a recent movie, Burt Reynolds refers to his rival in romance as "His Gucciness." The rival is the epitome of a Leo Rising. This man's relentlessness in pursuit of excellence extends to the selection of a mate. He would tidy up his injuries for the ambulance driver unless he was comatose. He is always perfecting his image. Muhammad Ali's (a Leo Rising) constant prefight speeches repeated the theme "I am the greatest." Wonder how he's going to be in romance? Fabulous, if you aren't offended by the mirrors above the bed. Heavenly, if you can honestly put him in the center of your Universe. He'll certainly notice you; forget postponing your pedicure. He'll be devoted. Never express your crush on the men on the Chippendales calendar. And for your own safety don't look for bargains from the local discount store for either of you. He is beyond all this. He's also beyond petty, disloyal, mundane character flaws. He is bright rays of glamour, intrigue, drama, passion, excitement, and sweetness shining down on one special person.

Virgo Rising

"Let's finish working first."

Virgo Rising looks for the women in his life much like the horse breeder looks for a future champion. He wants good sturdy stock, nice teeth—not stained—good intellect, strong hands to hold the plow. He's a sturdy, meticulous man who actually enjoys work and worry. If you've got problems, he won't hesitate to help if he judges you to be someone worth rescuing. He doesn't wear rose-colored glasses and doesn't delude himself. He deals with the facts and loves to sort through the data. Being precise, practical, and of service is exciting for him. While the rest of the world finds the laborious to be tedious and wants to put off such tasks for as long as humanly possible, for Virgo Rising this is the stuff of which dreams are made. Not that he's boring. He is intelligent and has a lot more to say than he is given credit for in most cases. Not only is he choosy about how he deals with life and with women, but being alone for great periods of time doesn't bother him. He is therefore often overlooked in the dating scene. Getting him to warm up is another matter. He is slow to respond, and even when awestruck by beauty and intelligence he'll manage to find a flaw or two to dwell on—problem areas like a disturbing lack of knowledge in Greek history or legs with cellulite. Even if you pass the majority of tests, instant wild abandon is foreign to him. He'll offer you a love that is unselfish, thoughtful, and committed. Aggressive, liberated women won't usually gain his admiration. Structured, subtle ladies who are in need of some sort of fixing up usually find him in quiet, steady pursuit. He won't write lavish poetry or send flowers, but he'll balance your checkbook and help you plant herbs. It's not the stuff that romance novels are made of, but it is the stuff that makes for long-lasting relationships. Teach him that love doesn't mean sacrifice, that simple reciprocal consideration will do, and he can excel as a partner.

Libra Rising

"I try to get along with everybody."

Lively and intelligent, always with a well-chosen word or two, this man can convince you of almost anything. Libra Rising is successful at work, popular with everyone, and has a reputation for changing his mind and his girlfriends in the bat of an eyelash. If you don't pay attention, this may be confusing. Let me lay it out for you: Whatever he changes his mind about doesn't involve a basic value. He can con anyone, but when his emotions are involved he dwells on things like honor. Ashley Wilkes in *Gone With the Wind* is the epitome of a Libra Rising man. When he stands at the woodpile and Scarlett talks to him about running away, she asks what there is to stop them. Ashley answers, "Nothing, except honor." Scarlett could have saved herself years of agony when he gave her longing looks and half promises of lust. Later, she is given another clue when he speaks of Melanie being the only dream that did not die in the face of reality. Dreams and honor, such are the things that bind and tie him. Yes, he is flirtatious, and yes, he will go from one relationship to another because he cannot stand to be alone. A connoisseur of beauty, he has been known to marry bone structure. But when he finds his dream, he commits.

Let me give you two examples of distorted honor. Upon meeting the woman of his dreams, one Libra Rising man discovered that this woman had a child from another marriage. Out of respect for the child's loss of her father he refused to visit when the child was around. Only after he made his commitment to the woman in marriage did he establish a relationship with the daughter. His reasoning: He did not want the child to experience the loss of another father figure and wanted to make sure of his position first. Another man had several mistresses and kept lifelong contact with them even after their marriages. Why? His sense of honor required him to keep tabs on their well-being since he felt guilty that he had never offered them marriage. His motives twist and wind through the T-maze but he always curves back to respect and dignity. Share the dream of perfect mates, gracious living, and getting along harmoniously with everyone, and he will provide you a comfortable home with old-world charm where love is gentle and sweet.

Scorpio Rising

"I can do anything I put my mind to."

There is no point in mincing words: This man is strong-willed. He's turbulent and volatile. He's also commanding and astute. He can excel in business where a take-control personality is needed. His intensity is shown in his line of work. He is attracted to danger and excels in investigative, political, religious, or medical careers. He's not timid in his choice of work. He can soar to the heights or fall to the depths, depending on how involved he is and what his goals are. A sturdy friend, he's not the kind you classify as a buddy. He doesn't pal around and spends much time alone. But he'll always remember a kind deed. He's best at building and rebuilding, whether it's his business, his relationships, or his list of things to master. Perhaps one of his strongest abilities to rebuild is shown in his recuperative powers. He can bounce back from years of abusing his health, a major accident, or an illness as if by pure willpower. And more than anything else, willpower is his key word. Detonating bombs won't scare him. Losing the object of his affections, however, is frightening and can lead to melancholy, brooding, and compulsive, obsessive behavior. His powers of persuasion with you are amazing. All your common sense is dissolved. Does he hypnotize you as you sleep? In your lucid moments you actually wonder how he can have such a hold on you. He prefers to dominate and control, even if only for a short time, even if the control is benevolent. When he concentrates on the woman of his choice, it is total. He'll plan romantic days for you. If he misses work to take you sailing for lunch, so be it. He'll schedule your days and evenings so tightly you won't have time to sleep. The planets are in the process of changing him now, and he's more cautious and somewhat more leery than usual. Can he be faithful? Yes. Can he make money? Yes. Can he fulfill your every dream? Yes. But only if he wants to.

Sagittarius Rising

"I'm thinking about moving on."

Whatever his faults, there is no malice in this man. You might have to repeat this line over and over when you try to rebound from his cutting remarks and insensitive behavior toward you. He is difficult to understand, like the other dual Rising signs of Gemini, Virgo, and Pisces. There is a dichotomy about these four signs and therefore each of them is more complicated—and difficult to understand—than the other eight rising signs. Look at it from his point of view. He met someone new, or someone old, or maybe he just wanted to go hunting for the week. He never realized you'd take it so hard. He doesn't think in terms of commitment. Basically he is a man who likes friendship with women. He told you from the beginning that he just wanted to be friends, that he likes to hang loose and believes that mankind was really designed for serial relationships. He is not vague about what he wants in a relationship with you. He told you what he was like, you just didn't listen. So what? Is it his fault now that two weeks after you applied for a new social security card with his last name he informs you he is moving to Idaho—without you? He is as shocked as you are that you are in this mess. He told you right up front that he was a travelin' man and that he'd always thought about getting away from the city to a nice little place like Idaho. You kept thinking you'd change him. That is why he is so dismayed. What more could he have done to make you realize he never meant to stay? "My God," he says, as his large hands fling about, "I told you we were friends and that one day I'd be moving on. But you never listened." Women never do listen to him, and it confuses him to no end. They don't fail to hear because they are hearing impaired but because they see him with their hearts. And their hearts are saying that this is a kind and gentle man. That he is baseball, Chevrolets, and apple pie. There is a boyish charm with Sagittarius Rising that could melt Aunt Elvira's heart. No one is immune—no one. That is why someone in Idaho is waiting for him. But I'll tell you what happened to Idaho. He made it through California, but by the time he hit Nevada he found this cute little thing (Sagittarius Rising tends to like the petite ones; he can just sort of grab them up in his long dangling arms, you know) and thought he'd hang out with her awhile. He is easily distracted. I think the one way to have the best of him is to think of the words of a song: "It's just knowing that your door is always open and your path is free to walk, that keeps / you ever gentle on my mind." Don't ask a lot of questions, if this is the man for you. Give him space. Don't issue ultimatums unless you mean them. Don't give his already itchy feet a rash by having your cousins over for a spaghetti feed just so they can look him over. He is likely to hide in the bathtub until he can make his escape. If he feels unrestricted by your love, he'll be dragging you home for the holidays. What he wants is a companion. A commitment is something he falls into like a black hole. He doesn't give up his wanderings, but he does take a pal along the way. At this point in the relationship you discover that walking alongside him beats trying to follow or lead. It can be a wondrous thing.

Capricorn Rising

"My mother and I are really close."

Capricorn Rising can't stop the eventual limelight his accomplishments will bring. He is shy—even when he runs for mayor. He'd make a few self-deprecating jokes (it helps him psychologically to beat his detractors to the punch) and heehaw about his flaws. Fact is, he is very sensitive to criticism and self-conscious in public situations. Why does he push himself? Because he must show everyone he can do anything. Accomplishment is what he breathes for. Nothing else matters if he cannot prove to himself that he can scale the great heights just like his zodiac symbol. Nothing is too great a price to pay to achieve and acquire. Ulcers? There are drugs for that. Broken relationships? He will settle for his memories. It's desperate, this need to produce. It is how he proves his self-worth. For him, being is not enough. So why bother with anyone this driven? Because here you have quality. Good old-fashioned values like honesty, dependability, sincerity. He may not always be faithful, but he will be devoted to his chosen one. This is an odd combination of standards. What it means to you is that he will always be there in spirit for the one he loves, but he won't spend a lot of time pining about her when he is by himself. He is afraid of the dark and does not have any plans to endure long nights alone. If you have to spend the summer in the Himalayas with your guru, his heart is the only part of himself he'll be saving for you. He makes money, he loves his mother (hope you resemble her), he takes responsibility better than most men, he is intelligent, reliable, and a general non-nerd socially. Relaxed, he has a killer sense of humor. Very relaxed, he has a hearty sexual appetite. How do you get this guy to lighten up? You spin tales of his stocks increasing, his real estate appreciating, and his agent selling his textbook for a bedtime story. When he feels secure he will express it with a well-stocked pantry, prepaid insurance, and he'll get so crazy with glee he'll go the other way and party until you beg for mercy. Since capriciousness is a well-hidden facet of his personality, you may find yourself regretting this swinging as too far to the other side. If he has enough money he'll retreat into solitude and self-indulgence. Your first tip-off could be the trapeze in the bedroom. Watch for signs. Once he becomes a wild and crazy guy it will take a lot to get him back into mundanity again. He only needs to achieve the heights once. Getting there with him could bring you the most dizzying experiences of your life. He is not your ordinary man. His highs and lows are stupendous, but he never forgets the one who rode the crests with him. And the way he'll spend forever trying to show his appreciation can leave a girl pretty breathless. And don't forget what he said about his money.

Aquarius Rising

"Let's be friends."

Cerebral, scientific, and flying his own time machine, Aquarius Rising does not have a great deal of time to dwell on emotion. His knack for understanding the connections between time and emotion allows for his not getting stuck in the moment and being able to move his mind to a point in the future where opportunities are better and brighter. Do you still wonder why he is so dispassionate when you cry over his forgetting to show for dinner? This cool and impersonal approach to all matters, including romance, leaves his acquaintances bewildered from time to time, which is the way he wants it. This man's ruler is the planet of the unexpected, and he has episodes where his actions are so unpredictable that it's as though he wants to be bad. In spite of the confusion on a personal level, his intentions for the group or fellowman are usually good. He provides fascination, something many men are unable to spark in their relationships. He offers relationships based on a flow of communication and ideas. He is the free-spirited prophet forced to work as a radio repairman until he can prove his theories about the greenhouse effect who captures many women in their midlife crises. He is a seductive change and intriguing adventure for the bored. His boldness is hypnotic for the shy. For himself he is independent, idealistic, unique. Yet for all his unpredictable, unorthodox behavior, he is fixed. Determined. Because he has such incredible willpower he is often emotionally blocked in discussions. Prepare to lose in the battle of wits with this man, not because he is brighter, but because he cannot be penetrated. The spell this man can cast in spite of his oddities is one of the fourth dimension. You learn of the vision, brotherhood, curiosity, and possibilities that are so quickly forgotten in the nine-to-five world. When he says "Let's just be friends" and you head back to mundanity, remember the flights to the unknown aboard his fantastic time machine and your momentary insight into the land of tomorrow. Wasn't the glimpse worth it all?

Pisces Rising

"I've got this feeling."

Esoteric subjects, healing crystals, and tarot cards may sound like psychobabble to your average man, but to Pisces Rising this can sound like a possible way to get in touch with his feelings. His efforts to get in touch with himself often lead to acquaintances with mystics, psychics, and modern-day therapists. He feels with such intensity that he needs people in his life who share the quest for more than the material or mundane. While he is a delightful companion, he can be enigmatic and dual. The slippery fish swimming in two directions is his sign ruler for a reason. Pleasant, caring, and sensitive, he is popular with nearly everyone—popular, but not necessarily a part of the crowd. After all, he would really rather be experiencing something life-altering than cheering with the guys over *Monday Night Football*. His mind is always searching for something more; oftentimes his body is, too. Elusive women haunt him sexually. Something within his depths keeps him from open pursuit when his feelings are involved. The object of his affections, at a loss to understand his behavior after two emotion-packed days together, does not hear from him and assumes he is no longer interested. He, playing the waiting game, assumes the same and finds himself in another broken relationship.

Must he punish himself? Yes. What he wants most is to be swept off his feet in romance, astral travel, or far-fetched dreams. The woman who captures him is bold enough to create seismographic excitement and understand his moods. This man needs to find companions who offer stability while encouraging emotional growth and responsibility, companions who are highly evolved, yet fascinating and energetic. He bores easily, and his attention span is very short. But he offers a rare gift of insight, sensitivity, and gentleness that is nearly irresistible. Also, there is a magic about him, and an ability to make dreams come true that leaves the most daring of women slightly breathless.

★

★ *4* ★

Rising Signs for Women

Aries Rising

"I'm pretty independent."

Shining, sunny, bright, there's a teeny touch of arrogance about the Aries Rising woman. Sounds of "I am woman" thunder in her heart. She likes to trespass into traditional male-dominated tasks, from plant management to her own auto maintenance. She likes to win, to be first. She can tackle sports, mechanics, and most left-brain functions. What she can't do is relax and let things happen naturally. In romance her mating call is "I'm installing my lawn sprinklers Saturday, wanna help?" Her values are in her accomplishments, competence, mastery. She looks for a man who is impressed by this. Not all are. Naturally this creates a few relationship problems for her. Quite frankly, she's very capable of living her life without a man, and she flaunts that ability. Underneath all this confidence and independence flutters a heart that fears domination and control. She isn't timid about romance, nor is she cold-hearted. What she longs for is a man who can run his own race and allow her spirit to roam about a bit. She wants a man who prefers a tank top and shorts to lacy lingerie. Feminine wiles are out of the question with Aries Rising. She could never respect a man who couldn't see through such silly games, and, above all, she needs a man she can admire and respect. When she finally finds such a knight, she'll happily give her heart, barbecue his steaks, and, if necessary, fight to defend him against the world.

Taurus Rising

"I'm good with money."

The steel magnolia of the Rising Signs, the Taurus Rising woman has a strong backbone and an iron will. Possessed of an extraordinary amount of self-control, she can contain her emotions admirably and yield to a man's apparent domination. Here's one Ascendant that's happy to let her man beat his chest. She'll let you be your eccentric self, notice the pretty passing ladies, and listen enchantingly to all your stories of bygone days. But while she may seem to know no bounds in her quiet adoration of you, she does indeed have her limits. Push her too far and she'll dig in her heels, create a cloud of sullen, white-hot dust, and simmer for days. Her anger, though not easily aroused, is an unforgettable sight. Most of her emotions aren't squandered on causes and concerns but are saved for the practical issues of her life like preparing enticing meals for her man, wearing sensuous fabrics next to her body, and the appeasement of her strong sexual nature. Money is also an issue in her life. Since money affords creature comforts, it holds a strong attraction for her. Like her temper, she hides the extent of her lust for material things and steadily plods along on the acquisition path. Calm and surefooted, she's willing to wait for her good fortune. She's not flighty, flashy, or whimsical. She's Mother Earth, the smell of fresh-baked bread, and lazy afternoons on white cotton sheets.

Gemini Rising

"I'm busy tonight."

The Gemini Rising woman is still delightfully part child. She jabbers, she jiggles, she jogs. She doesn't sit still for long stretches unless, of course, she's talking on the phone. Entertaining, she's often the best of hostesses, throwing parties extraordinaire. Her enthusiasm is contagious and her charm offsets the harsh feelings caused by her flirtatious eye. A possessive man will simply be driven nuts by her restless nature. The best of companions, she has a host of friends. She was born for fun and adventure. She's witty and can keep you up all night talking. Surprisingly, family is important to her and she's a ready friend in a crisis. Her money is spent on action, travel, entertainment, and life's pleasures. The man who attracts her must be energetic (nearly frantic is all right), sociable, intelligent, and committed to an idea or cause. He won't mind having his house invaded by new friends, old family, neighbors, and stray dogs. He'll submit to endless photographs of their life together and to telephones in the cars. He'll enjoy her becoming a blond, redhead, or brunette sooner or later, depending on her moods. It may be for this reason alone that most men find her the most irresistible of the Rising Signs. If you don't treat her right she'll move on quietly, taking only memories.

Cancer Rising

"I'm close to my family."

This is the woman of principles, the mistress of change. Looking for Mr. Right is almost an obsession, and she'll travel to China to be with him. She is nearly rooted to her home base, however, so he can expect to end up right back in the Midwest where it all began with Daddy and Mum. Nearly crazed for decorating and remodeling, she turns her home or apartment into a showplace. Since she attracts men of money, her apartment may be at the Plaza, where she'll drag in pumpkins and fix her own turkey for her honey on Thanksgiving. She has one of the strongest nesting instincts of the Rising Signs. She's intuitive, a natural therapist, and finds men nestling up to her with long, tall tales of woe about former relationships. You won't leave this relationship unchanged. She has a knack for remodeling, remember, and that means you too. She's not shallow but her anxiety over everything from flash floods to broken fingernails may make her appear so. One of the most attractive in a fragile, translucent sort of way, she nonetheless has her share of disappointments in love and gets really complicated in romance—complicated like after a year of what you think is a good relationship she stops taking your calls because of an imagined slight. Or after you settle down and start a career, she decides she needs more security. Sweet-talk her with words like *security, roots, mortgages*. She doesn't sparkle or shine; she glows. She isn't action, but reaction. She doesn't adorn, but she clings. She's déjà vu and warm memories.

Leo Rising

"I love jewelry."

A mane of hair glistening in the sunlight, a sunny smile, and an abundance of baubles and jewels are part of the aura of Leo Rising, the star of the Rising Signs. If she sounds spoiled, she is. Attention comes to her naturally, and she inspires and leads as if by birthright. She's not a standard model but a luxury one. Men who need to dominate or manipulate had better steer clear. She has only icy contempt for such attempts at control. She requires equal billing in her relationships. She's capable in many fields but will always manage to perform even the most mundane chores in some sort of creative, dramatic fashion. She prides herself on being a breed apart. For all her drama and excitement, she has the wonderful ability to enjoy life like a child, laughing, frolicking, and playful. In relationships she's generous and loving to those she admits into her inner circle but aloof to those she does not. Those exiled from her court can expect the bone-chilling indifference that comes after dismissal. She's determined, headstrong, and a challenge few men can resist. But there's a surprise for the man who wins her respect: She can be tamed. Tamed, but never conquered. As long as she believes her mate is admirable and worthy she'll be his most steadfast and loyal friend. She can be dragged through the mud; she can weather marital storms few women could endure. You can be a brief tornado in her life, but her mate cannot be cheap, petty, or unimaginative. And the man of her dreams can't spend too many Friday nights at Joe's Bar and Grill.

Virgo Rising

"I need a routine."

Here is the woman who puts you back in touch with the Earth. Her values lie in work and Nature. She writes haiku, reads *Prevention*, rides bicycles, and reminds you that you don't do too many things quite right. Curious, delving, asking for perfection, she has a wonderful flaw: She idealizes her mate. Lucky for you; even though you mess up her kitchen, botch the roofing, and hum off key, she thinks you're a wonderful human being. She won't commit to "you're adorable" (only children are), she won't admire your buns, but she'll appreciate that you work out. She has no intention of fawning over you, but she'll take great care in watching your cholesterol count, typing your exam papers, and knitting funny things for your mother. The "Virgo the Virgin" stuff is only symbolic, so you may as well forget it and come to terms with the fact that she'll leave you for someone else if you don't love and appreciate her in return. She wants romance as much as any of her zodiac sisters, but she expresses it differently. Her passion commingles with devotion and unity. She is what she appears to be: determined to pursue solid, lasting happiness and the simple things in life. Not realizing how difficult and complex relationships can become, her expectations are not easily met. She's wonderful for the man who is secure enough to appreciate the beauty of a sturdy, solid rock and forsake the glitter of fool's gold.

Libra Rising

"I'm not afraid of relationships."

Dimpled and delightful, she comes across pliant and compromising. She may be unsure, even indecisive. She'll call on you, her "friend," "daddy," "squizzle toes," to help her through the week's crisis. She's unable to manage by herself. Whoa! Get a grip on yourself, fella. Isn't she running her own business? Isn't she the doctoral candidate? This is part of her seduction. It's wonderful to play the game, but never mistake her helplessness for anything less than her carefully calculated plan to entrap you. This woman is very strong. Not that she isn't desirable, or even a terrific catch. But she's going to have you jumping through hoops if that's what she wants. She's an expert at persuasion and will have no qualms at getting you to marry her, move to another city, change your religion, your vocation. There is no other woman in the Rising Signs who can compare to her when it comes to taming her man. If you dream of a benevolent dictator, look no further. In turn you'll get a home that's cozy, a wife who's unusually attractive and intelligent, and a top-notch hostess. She'll never admit to her manipulations, and no one will ever guess that you're not guiding her through life. You can even play boss in front of your friends. She won't talk bad about you to her friends unless she's in crisis. Of course by that time she may be ready to leave. She idealizes her mate, is in love with love, and offers you dinner by candlelight. She'll camp with you, ride on your motorcycle, help you study for your exams, make herself indispensable. When she offers her affection it is without reserve. She does this because life without a mate for the Libra Rising is unbearable. She quite simply exists for love.

Scorpio Rising

"Where there's a will, there's a way."

Sensuous, alluring, mysterious, she is the predator of the zodiac. She's not afraid of life or death, and therefore the most exotic man in the room won't phase her. She'll go after what she wants from life with the strategy of a general, the daring of a skydiver. If, upon meeting her, she doesn't lock eyes with you, chances are that you, even at your most enticing best, won't get to first base. She's the steam from fire and ice, the allure of musk, the sexual chemist. She has the power to take you to the depths of despair and send you soaring back to ecstasy. She can read your mind, leave you in a sexual stupor, solicit your secrets, and yet you may not know her past, her friends, her family. She doesn't invite you over for roast dinners, or to sleep on cotton sheets. She is love potions, smoked oysters, and fur rugs before crackling fires. She is screaming fights and stupendous lovemaking. When she mates she wants it to be for life. She'll stop at nothing to defend you, to honor you, and to stand by you. Infidelities on your part are simply out of the question. While she has the strongest endurance of the Rising Signs, your involvement with another woman may leave her shattered and nearly beyond repair. Temporarily. She'll recover, mumble curses about your grave, and rise again. Her willpower is a magnificent thing.

Sagittarius Rising

"I need a lot of freedom."

It's not that she forgot her Girl Scout oath about being clean and tidy and good, but she really won't have time for a lot of the wifely things. Scattered energies and her enthusiasm for life override her desire to bake you carrot cake or start the war on dust balls. Here is the woman of enthusiasm, the bubbles in the champagne of life. If I had to pick the most outstanding characteristic of this Rising Sign I would say it is her love of living life to the fullest. Naturally, with this being her priority, she may have episodes of adventure that get her in some trouble, like forgetting to come back from her two-week vacation, hiding her new sale dresses under dry-cleaning bags ("I stayed on my budget, but cleaning costs have just gone sky high"), selling her heirloom china to pay for dance costumes. When it's all said and done, she'll have had a host of friends and twenty jobs, attracted the most admirers, and loved a dozen men. Who can resist the genuinely good-natured, the eternal optimist, the prom queen who stayed home with her best friend who had the measles? She never quite grows older, refusing to accept limitations on fun or adventure. She's hard to resist, harder yet to pin down. She does a lot of things in haste, and while marrying is not usually one of them, several marriages are in store for this firecracker.

Capricorn Rising

"I like to set goals."

Capricorn Rising will be busy setting goals, writing lists, stocking the pantry, but she's still asking her mom to go to the mall to help her pick out clothes, even though she's already in her thirties. She's the woman of substance. Anxiety ridden, no stranger to the night crazies, she's fearful and timid underneath the layers of control. She loves Woody Allen movies because he voices her fears. She's afraid to make the wrong choice, to love the wrong man, to present a paper with a dangling participle. Yet despite this, she exudes supreme confidence. Understanding this dichotomy allows you to proceed into the sacred territory of her heart. Verbalizing her fears, assessing her shortcomings, demeaning her plans, excludes you from her life. Once you understand the formula for friendship with her she's an easy friend, a loyal and loving partner. She'll keep your trust, share your dreams. She's aloof, distant, but never cold or uncaring. Slow in romance, she unfolds like a flower in spring, gently. Men sense this hesitancy and therein lies her allure. What better mating call than reluctance? Convincing her is half the excitement. She may or may not be the prettiest; men seldom notice. Refusing to market herself, she won't tell you she has an MBA, is also an interior decorator, and is one of the wittiest people you'll ever meet. Here is the woman of depth. Shallow men repel her. Aimless, unsteady men leave her chilled to the bone. She is high cheekbones and high aspirations. She looks for sincerity, decency, and, yes, some money in the bank.

Aquarius Rising

"I'm a bit of a visionary."

Aquarius Rising doesn't pay attention, yet she notices everything. Paradoxical, she never sways from loyalty, humanitarian ideals, and her basic good nature. You can be poor in material things, but the man of her dreams must be rich in talent, ideas, and achievements. Detached romantically, she can forget your anniversary or what you take in your coffee, but she'll never doubt you or ask you to compromise your beliefs. She's a banker in love, tallying your intellectual assets and good breeding against your liabilities. Feminine wiles and fits of passion are foreign to her. If she heads off for an exotic adventure you may not hear from her until she returns. She rarely suffers from homesickness or loneliness. If you haven't gathered by now, I can tell you that she is the most unusual of the Rising Signs. Needless to say, she doesn't seek a conventional man, nor will she endure a coupling that is not punctuated with excitement, chemistry, or good solid friendship. For all this, she has sudden endings or beginnings in her relationships with the opposite sex. So warning's fair: while she doesn't want to be possessed or fenced in, she does require attention. If you become detached or preoccupied (like she is) she may decide you're not worth the effort. Remember, she's a paradox. But she's witty, fun, intelligent, and progressive. Strains of H. G. Wells are in her genes. Boring she will never be.

Pisces Rising

"I have ESP."

Here is a woman who wants to be loved, protected, and cared for. Eternally feminine and devastatingly appealing, she's the hope of spring, the romance of summer, and the beauty of fall. She may not make it all the way until winter, however, because she doesn't bear up under the strain of reality very well. She can and will endure many hardships, heartbreaks, and crises, but they'll take their toll. She believes in ideals and dreams, and dreams can and do shatter in the face of reality. She'll stand by you when you lose your job or your car, but not when you lose your self-respect. The enormity of her faith in you is what you find so enduring in the beginning and so crushing in the end. Who can live up to men on the silver screen, men who don't get sick, who fill the house with flowers, and who bring boxes from Tiffany? She's short on practicality, so if you don't mind providing her shelter from the harsher realities of life and you can supply a nearly endless source of affection and attention, you can get a woman not altered by today's standards. She is eternal, not trendy. She is ethereal and volatile. She can rise above and sink to the depths, fascinating you all the while. Her attraction lies in her vagueness. Men reach out wanting to capture the elusive. Count the seasons and secure her in winter.

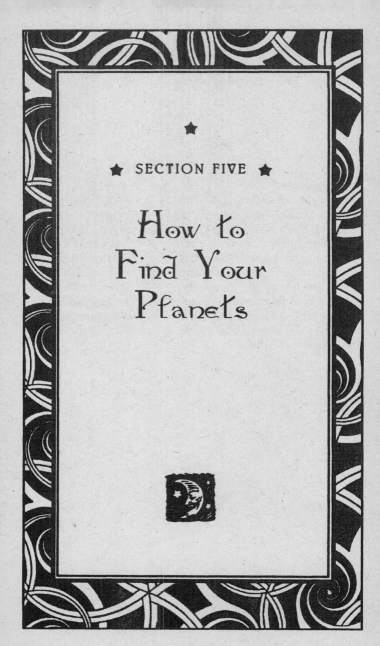

★

★ SECTION FIVE ★

How to Find Your Planets

★

★ **1** ★

A Note on the Tables

I don't know about you, but I was never good at math. I never got better at it, but I got worse the longer I was out of school.

When I first started to study astrology, I almost dropped out because I heard it required math. Well, it does but it doesn't. That is to say, it requires math and lots of it, but the math has all been done for us. I compiled these tables for you on my computer.

I have my Moon in Sagittarius which means I like things to be done quickly. Out of respect for you fire signs, I have made these tables easy and quick. Just turn to each planetary page, point your finger to your birthday, and you have the answer to where your Mars, Venus, and other planets are located.

But if you like to dwell on these things, like a Virgo Mercury would, then I will tell you all that the original tables were done by careful and methodical planetary calculations and can be found in the *Simplified Scientific Ephemeris*. (I wish I could find these guys when I need my checkbook balanced.)

Anyway, you could pay an astrologer a lot of money to look up these planets for you, or you can use this book until you can afford the luxury. And besides, it's fun to do this yourself because it broadens your understanding of the wonderful world of astrology. And if you let the stars help you in life and relationships, you'll be amazed at the results.

★

★ 2 ★

The Sun Tables

How to Find the Position of the Sun at the Time of Your Birth

IF YOUR BIRTHDATE IS BETWEEN:	YOUR SUN SIGN IS:	ASTROLOGICAL SYMBOL
Mar. 21–Apr. 20	Aries	♈
Apr. 21–May 21	Taurus	♉
May 22–Jun. 21	Gemini	♊
Jun. 22–Jul. 23	Cancer	♋
Jul. 24–Aug. 23	Leo	♌
Aug. 24–Sep. 23	Virgo	♍
Sep. 24–Oct. 22	Libra	♎
Oct. 23–Nov. 22	Scorpio	♏
Nov. 23–Dec. 21	Sagittarius	♐
Dec. 22–Jan. 20	Capricorn	♑
Jan. 21–Feb 19	Aquarius	♒
Feb. 20–Mar. 20	Pisces	♓

★ 3 ★

The Moon Tables

How to Find the Position of the Moon at the Time of Your Birth

Simply turn to the table which corresponds to your year, month and date of birth. The sign next to your date is your Moon Sign. The time noted is the time that the Moon moved into that sign.

For example, our friend Ryan's birthdate is August 18th, 1965. In the tables you will see that there is no separate listing for August 18th in that year, but do not worry. The Moon is in Taurus from the evening of the 17th to the 20th, when it changes to the sign of Gemini.

1900

JANUARY		
2	16:26	AQU
4	17:09	PIS
6	18:46	ARI
8	22:26	TAU
11	04:37	GEM
13	13:06	CAN
15	23:31	LEO
18	11:27	VIR
21	00:07	LIB
23	11:55	SCO
25	20:50	SAG
28	01:47	CAP
30	03:13	AQU

FEBRUARY		
1	02:48	PIS
3	02:38	ARI
5	04:42	TAU
7	10:08	GEM
9	18:50	CAN
12	05:49	LEO
14	18:00	VIR
17	06:37	LIB
19	18:45	SCO
22	04:54	SAG
24	11:33	CAP
26	14:16	AQU
28	14:05	PIS

MARCH		
2	13:02	ARI
4	13:25	TAU
6	17:05	GEM
9	00:46	CAN
11	11:39	LEO
14	00:04	VIR
16	12:39	LIB
19	00:35	SCO
21	11:03	SAG
23	18:57	CAP
25	23:25	AQU
28	00:42	PIS
30	00:13	ARI

APRIL		
1	00:01	TAU
3	02:14	GEM
5	08:17	CAN
7	18:11	LEO
10	06:25	VIR
12	19:01	LIB
15	06:38	SCO
17	16:39	SAG
20	00:37	CAP
22	06:06	AQU
24	08:59	PIS
26	10:00	ARI
28	10:34	TAU
30	12:30	GEM

MAY		
2	17:24	CAN
5	02:01	LEO
7	13:36	VIR
10	02:10	LIB
12	13:42	SCO
14	23:08	SAG
17	06:20	CAP
19	11:31	AQU
21	15:01	PIS
23	17:22	ARI
25	19:21	TAU
27	22:06	GEM
30	02:55	CAN

JUNE		
1	10:45	LEO
3	21:34	VIR
6	10:00	LIB
8	21:46	SCO
11	07:06	SAG
13	13:31	CAP
15	17:38	AQU
17	20:27	PIS
19	22:57	ARI
22	01:54	TAU
24	05:52	GEM
26	11:28	CAN
28	19:15	LEO

JULY		
1	05:43	VIR
3	17:59	LIB
6	06:12	SCO
8	16:05	SAG
10	22:27	CAP
13	01:41	AQU
15	03:12	PIS
17	04:38	ARI
19	07:17	TAU
21	11:48	GEM
23	18:20	CAN
26	02:49	LEO
28	13:18	VIR
31	01:30	LIB

AUGUST		
2	14:09	SCO
5	01:01	SAG
7	08:14	CAP
9	11:32	AQU
11	12:10	PIS
13	12:09	ARI
15	13:25	TAU
17	17:14	GEM
19	23:56	CAN
22	09:03	LEO
24	19:57	VIR
27	08:13	LIB
29	21:03	SCO

SEPTEMBER		
1	08:49	SAG
3	17:27	CAP
5	21:53	AQU
7	22:47	PIS
9	22:00	ARI
11	21:45	TAU
13	23:58	GEM
16	05:40	CAN
18	14:39	LEO
21	01:53	VIR
23	14:19	LIB
26	03:06	SCO
28	15:10	SAG

OCTOBER		
1	00:57	CAP
3	07:04	AQU
5	09:22	PIS
7	09:06	ARI
9	08:17	TAU
11	09:02	GEM
13	13:02	CAN
15	20:53	LEO
18	07:52	VIR
20	20:25	LIB
23	09:05	SCO
25	20:50	SAG
28	06:47	CAP
30	14:02	AQU

NOVEMBER		
1	18:06	PIS
3	19:27	ARI
5	19:25	TAU
7	19:50	GEM
9	22:32	CAN
12	04:49	LEO
14	14:48	VIR
17	03:09	LIB
19	15:48	SCO
22	03:09	SAG
24	12:26	CAP
26	19:30	AQU
29	00:24	PIS

DECEMBER		
1	03:22	ARI
3	05:01	TAU
5	06:27	GEM
7	09:04	CAN
9	14:19	LEO
11	23:04	VIR
14	10:49	LIB
16	23:34	SCO
19	10:54	SAG
21	19:33	CAP
24	01:34	AQU
26	05:47	PIS
28	09:02	ARI
30	11:55	TAU

1901

JANUARY		
1	14:54	GEM
3	18:36	CAN
5	23:59	LEO
8	08:04	VIR
10	19:07	LIB
13	07:52	SCO
15	19:43	SAG
18	04:30	CAP
20	09:47	AQU
22	12:41	PIS
24	14:45	ARI
26	17:16	TAU
28	20:54	GEM
31	01:50	CAN

FEBRUARY		
2	08:12	LEO
4	16:33	VIR
7	03:18	LIB
9	15:56	SCO
12	04:26	SAG
14	14:10	CAP
16	19:50	AQU
18	22:06	PIS
20	22:44	ARI
22	23:41	TAU
25	02:22	GEM
27	07:20	CAN

MARCH		
1	14:30	LEO
3	23:37	VIR
6	10:37	LIB
8	23:12	SCO
11	12:04	SAG
13	22:56	CAP
16	05:56	AQU
18	08:52	PIS
20	09:06	ARI
22	08:41	TAU
24	09:37	GEM
26	13:15	CAN
28	20:00	LEO
31	05:29	VIR

APRIL		
2	16:57	LIB
5	05:38	SCO
7	18:31	SAG
10	06:02	CAP
12	14:27	AQU
14	18:56	PIS
16	20:06	ARI
18	19:33	TAU
20	19:18	GEM
22	21:11	CAN
25	02:28	LEO
27	11:20	VIR
29	22:54	LIB

MAY		
2	11:43	SCO
5	00:27	SAG
7	11:54	CAP
9	20:58	AQU
12	02:55	PIS
14	05:43	ARI
16	06:16	TAU
18	06:07	GEM
20	07:03	CAN
22	10:47	LEO
24	18:19	VIR
27	05:18	LIB
29	18:07	SCO

JUNE		
1	06:44	SAG
3	17:43	CAP
6	02:30	AQU
8	08:55	PIS
10	13:01	ARI
12	15:10	TAU
14	16:10	GEM
16	17:22	CAN
18	20:23	LEO
21	02:41	VIR
23	12:42	LIB
26	01:14	SCO
28	13:51	SAG

JULY		
1	00:31	CAP
3	08:34	AQU
5	14:22	PIS
8	18:36	ARI
9	21:45	TAU
12	00:10	GEM
14	02:31	CAN
16	05:54	LEO
18	11:43	VIR
20	20:55	LIB
23	09:00	SCO
25	21:45	SAG
28	08:33	CAP
30	16:09	AQU

AUGUST		
1	20:59	PIS
4	00:16	ARI
6	03:07	TAU
8	06:08	GEM
10	09:37	CAN
12	14:04	LEO
14	20:17	VIR
17	05:14	LIB
19	16:58	SCO
22	05:54	SAG
24	17:18	CAP
27	01:13	AQU
29	05:36	PIS
31	07:44	ARI

SEPTEMBER		
2	09:17	TAU
4	11:32	GEM
6	15:11	CAN
8	20:26	LEO
11	03:33	VIR
13	12:52	LIB
16	00:31	SCO
18	13:33	SAG
21	01:44	CAP
23	10:45	AQU
25	15:43	PIS
27	17:29	ARI
29	17:47	TAU

OCTOBER		
1	18:28	GEM
3	20:54	CAN
6	01:52	LEO
8	09:28	VIR
10	19:26	LIB
13	07:19	SCO
15	20:22	SAG
18	09:01	CAP
20	19:18	AQU
23	01:46	PIS
25	04:26	ARI
27	04:34	TAU
29	04:01	GEM
31	04:42	CAN

NOVEMBER		
2	08:09	LEO
4	15:06	VIR
7	01:15	LIB
9	13:30	SCO
12	02:32	SAG
14	15:09	CAP
17	02:04	AQU
19	10:04	PIS
21	14:31	ARI
23	15:52	TAU
25	15:24	GEM
27	15:02	CAN
29	16:43	LEO

DECEMBER		
1	22:02	VIR
4	07:24	LIB
6	19:38	SCO
9	08:45	SAG
11	21:04	CAP
14	07:42	AQU
16	16:12	PIS
18	22:09	ARI
21	01:23	TAU
23	02:22	GEM
25	02:23	CAN
27	03:18	LEO
29	07:04	VIR
31	14:56	LIB

1902

JANUARY		
3	02:30	SCO
5	15:36	SAG
8	03:47	CAP
10	13:48	AQU
12	21:40	PIS
15	03:44	ARI
17	08:06	TAU
19	10:49	GEM
21	12:21	CAN
23	13:56	LEO
25	17:16	VIR
27	23:58	LIB
30	10:28	SCO

FEBRUARY		
1	23:17	SAG
4	11:38	CAP
6	21:27	AQU
9	04:29	PIS
11	09:31	ARI
13	13:26	TAU
15	16:43	GEM
17	19:37	CAN
19	22:37	LEO
22	02:44	VIR
24	09:18	LIB
26	19:05	SCO

MARCH		
1	07:27	SAG
3	20:04	CAP
6	06:22	AQU
8	13:16	PIS
10	17:21	ARI
12	19:55	TAU
14	22:13	GEM
17	01:04	CAN
19	04:54	LEO
21	10:12	VIR
23	17:31	LIB
26	03:20	SCO
28	15:24	SAG
31	04:12	CAP

APRIL		
2	15:20	AQU
4	23:03	PIS
7	03:11	ARI
9	04:50	TAU
11	05:37	GEM
13	07:04	CAN
15	10:18	LEO
17	15:57	VIR
20	00:05	LIB
22	10:28	SCO
24	22:36	SAG
27	11:26	CAP
29	23:16	AQU

MAY		
2	08:16	PIS
4	13:30	ARI
6	15:23	TAU
8	15:21	GEM
10	15:15	CAN
12	16:54	LEO
14	21:36	VIR
17	05:42	LIB
19	16:33	SCO
22	04:58	SAG
24	17:47	CAP
27	05:50	AQU
29	15:50	PIS
31	22:35	ARI

JUNE		
3	01:46	TAU
5	02:10	GEM
7	01:26	CAN
9	01:39	LEO
11	04:44	VIR
13	11:45	LIB
15	22:22	SCO
18	10:58	SAG
20	23:46	CAP
23	11:37	AQU
25	21:50	PIS
28	05:39	ARI
30	10:26	TAU

JULY		
2	12:14	GEM
4	12:07	CAN
6	11:54	LEO
8	13:43	VIR
10	19:16	LIB
13	04:56	SCO
15	17:17	SAG
18	06:04	CAP
20	17:38	AQU
23	03:24	PIS
25	11:15	ARI
27	16:57	TAU
29	20:16	GEM
31	21:34	CAN

AUGUST		
2	22:06	LEO
4	23:43	VIR
7	04:15	LIB
9	12:43	SCO
12	00:26	SAG
14	13:10	CAP
17	00:38	AQU
19	09:51	PIS
21	16:57	ARI
23	22:20	TAU
26	02:13	GEM
28	04:50	CAN
30	06:45	LEO

SEPTEMBER		
1	09:13	VIR
3	13:42	LIB
5	21:26	SCO
8	08:25	SAG
10	21:01	CAP
13	08:44	AQU
15	17:53	PIS
18	00:14	ARI
20	04:31	TAU
22	07:39	GEM
24	10:23	CAN
26	13:16	LEO
28	16:58	VIR
30	22:19	LIB

OCTOBER		
3	06:07	SCO
5	16:40	SAG
8	05:06	CAP
10	17:19	AQU
13	03:07	PIS
15	09:30	ARI
17	12:56	TAU
19	14:40	GEM
21	16:10	CAN
23	18:39	LEO
25	22:53	VIR
28	05:14	LIB
30	13:46	SCO

NOVEMBER		
2	00:26	SAG
4	12:44	CAP
7	01:22	AQU
9	12:16	PIS
11	19:44	ARI
13	23:24	TAU
16	00:19	GEM
18	00:14	CAN
20	01:06	LEO
22	04:24	VIR
24	10:49	LIB
26	20:01	SCO
29	07:12	SAG

DECEMBER		
1	19:33	CAP
4	08:16	AQU
6	20:01	PIS
9	05:03	ARI
11	10:11	TAU
13	11:38	GEM
15	10:55	CAN
17	10:13	LEO
19	11:40	VIR
21	16:46	LIB
24	01:39	SCO
26	13:09	SAG
29	01:44	CAP
31	14:20	AQU

1903

JANUARY			FEBRUARY			MARCH			APRIL		
3	02:12	PIS	1	17:52	ARI	3	07:00	TAU	1	17:50	GEM
5	12:14	ARI	4	01:36	TAU	5	12:16	GEM	3	21:00	CAN
7	19:09	TAU	6	06:27	GEM	7	15:34	CAN	5	23:39	LEO
9	22:19	GEM	8	08:25	CAN	9	17:23	LEO	8	02:27	VIR
11	22:28	CAN	10	08:33	LEO	11	18:47	VIR	10	06:11	LIB
13	21:27	LEO	12	08:41	VIR	13	21:18	LIB	12	11:45	SCO
15	21:32	VIR	14	10:53	LIB	16	02:26	SCO	14	19:56	SAG
18	00:47	LIB	16	16:43	SCO	18	11:01	SAG	17	06:49	CAP
20	08:14	SCO	19	02:29	SAG	20	22:33	CAP	19	19:15	AQU
22	19:15	SAG	21	14:46	CAP	23	11:06	AQU	22	07:01	PIS
25	07:55	CAP	24	03:20	AQU	25	22:24	PIS	24	16:07	ARI
27	20:27	AQU	26	14:31	PIS	28	07:13	ARI	26	21:55	TAU
30	07:55	PIS	28	23:45	ARI	30	13:29	TAU	29	01:07	GEM

MAY			JUNE			JULY			AUGUST		
1	03:02	CAN	1	13:45	VIR	1	00:19	LIB	1	22:21	SAG
3	05:02	LEO	3	18:18	LIB	3	06:58	SCO	4	09:49	CAP
5	08:08	VIR	6	01:28	SCO	5	16:31	SAG	6	22:21	AQU
7	12:52	LIB	8	10:46	SAG	8	03:56	CAP	9	10:50	PIS
9	19:26	SCO	10	21:47	CAP	10	16:21	AQU	11	22:23	ARI
12	04:02	SAG	13	10:06	AQU	13	05:00	PIS	14	07:52	TAU
14	14:46	CAP	15	22:42	PIS	15	16:36	ARI	16	14:15	GEM
17	03:05	AQU	18	09:43	ARI	18	01:28	TAU	18	17:12	CAN
19	15:21	PIS	20	17:17	TAU	20	06:26	GEM	20	17:37	LEO
22	01:22	ARI	22	20:46	GEM	22	07:47	CAN	22	17:13	VIR
24	07:40	TAU	24	21:12	CAN	24	07:06	LEO	24	18:01	LIB
26	10:27	GEM	26	20:35	LEO	26	06:33	VIR	26	21:46	SCO
28	11:10	CAN	28	21:04	VIR	28	08:13	LIB	29	05:22	SAG
30	11:42	LEO				30	13:27	SCO	31	16:14	CAP

SEPTEMBER			OCTOBER			NOVEMBER			DECEMBER		
3	04:45	AQU	3	00:24	PIS	1	19:37	ARI	1	13:14	TAU
5	17:07	PIS	5	11:11	ARI	4	03:36	TAU	3	17:56	GEM
8	04:12	ARI	7	19:34	TAU	6	08:39	GEM	5	19:55	CAN
10	13:22	TAU	10	01:41	GEM	8	11:50	CAN	7	20:58	LEO
12	20:11	GEM	12	06:00	CAN	10	14:24	LEO	9	22:47	VIR
15	00:27	CAN	14	09:03	LEO	12	17:16	VIR	12	02:22	LIB
17	02:30	LEO	16	11:24	VIR	14	20:55	LIB	14	07:56	SCO
19	03:20	VIR	18	13:49	LIB	17	01:42	SCO	16	15:19	SAG
21	04:28	LIB	20	17:23	SCO	19	08:06	SAG	19	00:34	CAP
23	07:33	SCO	22	23:15	SAG	21	16:50	CAP	21	11:48	AQU
25	13:53	SAG	25	08:14	CAP	24	04:09	AQU	24	00:35	PIS
27	23:45	CAP	27	19:58	AQU	26	16:55	PIS	26	13:08	ARI
30	11:59	AQU	30	08:35	PIS	29	04:42	ARI	28	22:57	TAU
									31	04:33	GEM

1904

JANUARY		
2	06:25	CAN
4	06:18	LEO
6	06:23	VIR
8	08:25	LIB
10	13:20	SCO
12	21:03	SAG
15	06:58	CAP
17	18:32	AQU
20	07:18	PIS
22	20:10	ARI
25	07:09	TAU
27	14:26	GEM
29	17:32	CAN
31	17:38	LEO

FEBRUARY		
2	16:45	VIR
4	17:01	LIB
6	20:08	SCO
9	02:49	SAG
11	12:41	CAP
14	00:37	AQU
16	13:27	PIS
19	02:10	ARI
21	13:31	TAU
23	22:05	GEM
26	03:00	CAN
28	04:36	LEO

MARCH		
1	04:16	VIR
3	03:53	LIB
5	05:24	SCO
7	10:18	SAG
9	19:03	CAP
12	06:47	AQU
14	19:43	PIS
17	08:13	ARI
19	19:09	TAU
22	03:52	GEM
24	09:55	CAN
26	13:16	LEO
28	14:31	VIR
30	14:54	LIB

APRIL		
1	16:04	SCO
3	19:41	SAG
6	02:57	CAP
8	13:49	AQU
11	02:38	PIS
13	15:04	ARI
16	01:31	TAU
18	09:31	GEM
20	15:22	CAN
22	19:27	LEO
24	22:10	VIR
27	00:05	LIB
29	02:07	SCO

MAY		
1	05:36	SAG
3	11:58	CAP
5	21:50	AQU
8	10:17	PIS
10	22:51	ARI
13	09:12	TAU
15	16:30	GEM
17	21:21	CAN
20	00:50	LEO
22	03:49	VIR
24	06:48	LIB
26	10:08	SCO
28	14:29	SAG
30	20:53	CAP

JUNE		
2	06:13	AQU
4	18:15	PIS
7	07:02	ARI
9	17:50	TAU
12	01:06	GEM
14	05:10	CAN
16	07:26	LEO
18	09:26	VIR
20	12:11	LIB
22	16:09	SCO
24	21:31	SAG
27	04:40	CAP
29	14:07	AQU

JULY		
2	01:58	PIS
4	14:55	ARI
7	02:29	TAU
9	10:32	GEM
11	14:41	CAN
13	16:10	LEO
15	16:48	VIR
17	18:14	LIB
19	21:34	SCO
22	03:10	SAG
24	11:01	CAP
26	21:01	AQU
29	08:58	PIS
31	21:59	ARI

AUGUST		
3	10:13	TAU
5	19:30	GEM
8	00:44	CAN
10	02:30	LEO
12	02:25	VIR
14	02:25	LIB
16	04:12	SCO
18	08:51	SAG
20	16:37	CAP
23	03:02	AQU
25	15:16	PIS
28	04:17	ARI
30	16:44	TAU

SEPTEMBER		
2	02:59	GEM
4	09:46	CAN
6	12:53	LEO
8	13:18	VIR
10	12:44	LIB
12	13:05	SCO
14	16:05	SAG
16	22:45	CAP
19	08:55	AQU
21	21:20	PIS
24	10:20	ARI
26	22:33	TAU
29	08:59	GEM

OCTOBER		
1	16:50	CAN
3	21:38	LEO
5	23:36	VIR
7	23:45	LIB
9	23:43	SCO
12	01:25	SAG
14	06:31	CAP
16	15:39	AQU
19	03:50	PIS
21	16:51	ARI
24	04:44	TAU
26	14:38	GEM
28	22:24	CAN
31	04:04	LEO

NOVEMBER		
2	07:40	VIR
4	09:27	LIB
6	10:20	SCO
8	11:54	SAG
10	15:56	CAP
12	23:47	AQU
15	11:14	PIS
18	00:14	ARI
20	12:06	TAU
22	01:25	GEM
25	04:17	CAN
27	09:26	LEO
29	13:27	VIR

DECEMBER		
1	16:33	LIB
3	19:01	SCO
5	21:38	SAG
8	01:46	CAP
10	08:53	AQU
12	19:30	PIS
15	08:19	ARI
17	20:33	TAU
20	05:57	GEM
22	12:08	CAN
24	16:04	LEO
26	19:01	VIR
28	21:56	LIB
31	01:12	SCO

1905

JANUARY
2	05:08	SAG
4	10:20	CAP
6	17:43	AQU
9	03:57	PIS
11	16:29	ARI
14	05:11	TAU
16	15:25	GEM
18	21:56	CAN
21	01:13	LEO
23	02:46	VIR
25	04:09	LIB
27	06:35	SCO
29	10:44	SAG
31	16:51	CAP

FEBRUARY
3	01:08	AQU
5	11:39	PIS
8	00:03	ARI
10	13:00	TAU
13	00:17	GEM
15	08:05	CAN
17	12:00	LEO
19	13:05	VIR
21	13:03	LIB
23	13:42	SCO
25	16:31	SAG
27	22:19	CAP

MARCH
2	07:05	AQU
4	18:12	PIS
7	06:46	ARI
9	19:42	TAU
12	07:35	GEM
14	16:48	CAN
16	22:19	LEO
19	00:18	VIR
21	00:03	LIB
22	23:26	SCO
25	00:26	SAG
27	04:40	CAP
29	12:47	AQU

APRIL
1	00:03	PIS
3	12:52	ARI
6	01:44	TAU
8	13:35	GEM
10	23:28	CAN
13	06:30	LEO
15	10:13	VIR
17	11:04	LIB
19	10:30	SCO
21	10:28	SAG
23	13:04	CAP
25	19:41	AQU
28	06:15	PIS
30	19:03	ARI

MAY
3	07:52	TAU
5	19:21	GEM
8	05:01	CAN
10	12:34	LEO
12	17:40	VIR
14	20:12	LIB
16	20:50	SCO
18	21:05	SAG
20	22:56	CAP
23	04:12	AQU
25	13:34	PIS
28	01:53	ARI
30	14:41	TAU

JUNE
2	01:55	GEM
4	10:57	CAN
6	17:59	LEO
8	23:17	VIR
11	02:53	LIB
13	05:01	SCO
15	06:29	SAG
17	08:47	CAP
19	13:34	AQU
21	21:57	PIS
24	09:33	ARI
26	22:16	TAU
29	09:37	GEM

JULY
1	18:17	CAN
4	00:27	LEO
6	04:53	VIR
8	08:16	LIB
10	11:04	SCO
12	13:46	SAG
14	17:12	CAP
16	22:29	AQU
19	06:36	PIS
21	17:39	ARI
24	06:16	TAU
26	18:01	GEM
29	03:00	CAN
31	08:47	LEO

AUGUST
2	12:09	VIR
4	14:20	LIB
6	16:28	SCO
8	19:24	SAG
10	23:45	CAP
13	06:00	AQU
15	14:34	PIS
18	01:30	ARI
20	14:02	TAU
23	02:18	GEM
25	12:12	CAN
27	18:31	LEO
29	21:32	VIR
31	22:33	LIB

SEPTEMBER
2	23:12	SCO
5	01:04	SAG
7	05:13	CAP
9	12:02	AQU
11	21:20	PIS
14	08:35	ARI
16	21:05	TAU
19	09:40	GEM
21	20:37	CAN
24	04:17	LEO
26	08:07	VIR
28	08:54	LIB
30	08:22	SCO

OCTOBER
2	08:35	SAG
4	11:20	CAP
6	17:36	AQU
9	03:09	PIS
11	14:49	ARI
14	03:25	TAU
16	15:59	GEM
19	03:29	CAN
21	12:33	LEO
23	18:03	VIR
25	19:55	LIB
27	19:24	SCO
29	18:34	SAG
31	19:37	CAP

NOVEMBER
3	00:19	AQU
5	09:06	PIS
7	20:48	ARI
10	09:32	TAU
12	21:54	GEM
15	09:14	CAN
17	18:50	LEO
20	01:47	VIR
22	05:29	LIB
24	06:18	SCO
26	05:47	SAG
28	06:03	CAP
30	09:11	AQU

DECEMBER
2	16:26	PIS
5	03:24	ARI
7	16:06	TAU
10	04:25	GEM
12	15:14	CAN
15	00:19	LEO
17	07:30	VIR
19	12:25	LIB
21	15:01	SCO
23	16:00	SAG
25	16:53	CAP
27	19:32	AQU
30	01:30	PIS

1906

JANUARY
1	11:16	ARI
3	23:33	TAU
6	11:58	GEM
8	22:38	CAN
11	06:57	LEO
13	13:11	VIR
15	17:48	LIB
17	21:08	SCO
19	23:36	SAG
22	01:59	CAP
24	05:26	AQU
26	11:13	PIS
28	20:06	ARI
31	07:45	TAU

FEBRUARY
2	20:17	GEM
5	07:21	CAN
7	15:32	LEO
9	20:50	VIR
12	00:08	LIB
14	02:34	SCO
16	05:08	SAG
18	08:32	CAP
20	13:17	AQU
22	19:52	PIS
25	04:45	ARI
27	15:58	TAU

MARCH
2	04:31	GEM
4	16:19	CAN
7	01:16	LEO
9	06:34	VIR
11	08:53	LIB
13	09:48	SCO
15	11:01	SAG
17	13:54	CAP
19	19:07	AQU
22	02:38	PIS
24	12:10	ARI
26	23:27	TAU
29	11:58	GEM

APRIL
1	00:20	CAN
3	10:31	LEO
5	16:53	VIR
7	19:26	LIB
9	19:29	SCO
11	19:08	SAG
13	20:23	CAP
16	00:39	AQU
18	08:10	PIS
20	18:15	ARI
23	05:56	TAU
25	18:28	GEM
28	07:02	CAN
30	18:09	LEO

MAY
3	02:03	VIR
5	05:53	LIB
7	06:23	SCO
9	05:25	SAG
11	05:12	CAP
13	07:45	AQU
15	14:06	PIS
17	23:54	ARI
20	11:49	TAU
23	00:27	GEM
25	12:54	CAN
28	00:14	LEO
30	09:11	VIR

JUNE
1	14:38	LIB
3	16:35	SCO
5	16:15	SAG
7	15:40	CAP
9	16:56	AQU
11	21:40	PIS
14	06:21	ARI
16	17:55	TAU
19	06:35	GEM
21	18:51	CAN
24	05:50	LEO
26	14:50	VIR
28	21:13	LIB

JULY
1	00:43	SCO
3	01:53	SAG
5	02:06	CAP
7	03:12	AQU
9	06:52	PIS
11	14:12	ARI
14	00:55	TAU
16	13:25	GEM
19	01:38	CAN
21	12:09	LEO
23	20:29	VIR
26	02:38	LIB
28	06:46	SCO
30	09:17	CAP

AUGUST
1	10:58	CAP
3	12:57	AQU
5	16:37	PIS
7	23:07	ARI
10	08:55	TAU
12	21:03	GEM
15	09:23	CAN
17	19:50	LEO
20	03:31	VIR
22	08:40	LIB
24	12:10	SCO
26	14:55	SAG
28	17:39	CAP
30	20:56	AQU

SEPTEMBER
2	01:28	PIS
4	08:04	ARI
6	17:21	TAU
9	05:05	GEM
11	17:40	CAN
14	04:37	LEO
16	12:18	VIR
18	16:39	LIB
20	18:53	SCO
22	20:35	SAG
24	23:02	CAP
27	02:58	AQU
29	08:34	PIS

OCTOBER
1	15:56	ARI
4	01:21	TAU
6	12:53	GEM
9	01:38	CAN
11	13:27	LEO
13	22:02	VIR
16	02:34	LIB
18	04:00	SCO
20	04:14	SAG
22	05:14	CAP
24	08:24	AQU
26	14:11	PIS
28	22:18	ARI
31	08:18	TAU

NOVEMBER
2	19:56	GEM
5	08:44	CAN
7	21:13	LEO
10	07:10	VIR
12	13:00	LIB
14	14:54	SCO
16	14:29	SAG
18	13:58	CAP
20	15:23	AQU
22	19:59	PIS
25	03:53	ARI
27	14:18	TAU
30	02:16	GEM

DECEMBER
2	15:01	CAN
5	03:37	LEO
7	14:30	VIR
9	22:00	LIB
12	01:31	SCO
14	01:55	SAG
16	01:02	CAP
18	01:03	AQU
20	03:48	PIS
22	10:17	ARI
24	20:15	TAU
27	08:23	GEM
29	21:11	CAN

1907

JANUARY		
1	09:29	LEO
3	20:19	VIR
6	04:41	LIB
8	09:55	SCO
10	12:07	SAG
12	12:21	CAP
14	12:20	AQU
16	13:55	PIS
18	18:42	ARI
21	03:21	TAU
23	15:04	GEM
26	03:56	CAN
28	16:00	LEO
31	02:12	VIR

FEBRUARY		
2	10:10	LIB
4	15:55	SCO
6	19:34	SAG
8	21:35	AQU
10	22:51	CAP
13	00:41	PIS
15	04:39	ARI
17	11:58	TAU
19	22:46	GEM
22	11:31	CAN
24	23:41	LEO
27	09:29	VIR

MARCH		
1	16:31	LIB
3	21:26	SCO
6	01:04	SAG
8	04:04	CAP
10	06:50	AQU
12	09:56	PIS
14	14:20	ARI
16	21:10	TAU
19	07:10	GEM
21	19:36	CAN
24	08:07	LEO
26	18:11	VIR
29	00:46	LIB
31	04:33	SCO

APRIL		
2	06:59	SAG
4	09:24	CAP
6	12:35	AQU
8	16:47	PIS
10	22:16	ARI
13	05:36	TAU
15	15:24	GEM
18	03:34	CAN
20	16:25	LEO
23	03:17	VIR
25	10:22	LIB
27	13:47	SCO
29	15:02	SAG

MAY		
1	15:59	CAP
3	18:07	AQU
5	22:12	PIS
8	04:20	ARI
10	12:29	TAU
12	22:41	GEM
15	10:50	CAN
17	23:53	LEO
20	11:37	VIR
22	19:54	LIB
25	00:03	SCO
27	01:05	SAG
29	00:54	CAP
31	01:26	AQU

JUNE		
2	04:10	PIS
4	09:47	ARI
6	18:12	TAU
9	04:55	GEM
11	17:16	CAN
14	06:21	LEO
16	18:35	VIR
19	04:05	LIB
21	09:43	SCO
23	11:42	SAG
25	11:30	CAP
27	11:00	AQU
29	12:07	PIS

JULY		
1	16:14	ARI
3	23:56	TAU
6	10:41	GEM
8	23:16	CAN
11	12:18	LEO
14	00:29	VIR
16	10:35	LIB
18	17:34	SCO
20	21:11	SAG
22	22:06	CAP
24	21:46	AQU
26	22:00	PIS
29	00:37	ARI
31	06:53	TAU

AUGUST		
2	16:56	GEM
5	05:27	CAN
7	18:26	LEO
10	06:17	VIR
12	16:07	LIB
14	23:35	SCO
17	04:32	SAG
19	07:05	CAP
21	08:00	AQU
23	08:33	PIS
25	10:28	ARI
27	15:26	TAU
30	00:19	GEM

SEPTEMBER		
1	12:22	CAN
4	01:20	LEO
6	12:56	VIR
8	22:07	LIB
11	05:01	SCO
13	10:07	SAG
15	13:46	CAP
17	16:12	AQU
19	18:02	PIS
21	20:25	ARI
24	00:55	TAU
26	08:49	GEM
28	20:09	CAN

OCTOBER		
1	09:05	LEO
3	20:49	VIR
6	05:40	LIB
8	11:38	SCO
10	15:47	SAG
12	19:07	CAP
14	22:13	AQU
17	01:20	PIS
19	04:57	ARI
21	10:00	TAU
23	17:39	GEM
26	04:25	CAN
28	17:14	LEO
31	05:28	VIR

NOVEMBER		
2	14:43	LIB
4	20:23	SCO
6	23:25	SAG
9	01:24	CAP
11	03:38	AQU
13	06:52	PIS
15	11:24	ARI
17	17:31	TAU
20	01:43	GEM
22	12:24	CAN
25	01:04	LEO
27	13:50	VIR
30	00:09	LIB

DECEMBER		
2	06:35	SCO
4	09:28	SAG
6	10:18	CAP
8	10:53	AQU
10	12:44	PIS
12	16:48	ARI
15	12:24	TAU
17	08:24	GEM
20	07:31	CAN
22	10:09	LEO
25	09:06	VIR
27	10:27	LIB
29	16:25	SCO
31	05:04	SAG

1908

JANUARY		
2	21:25	CAP
4	20:58	AQU
6	21:03	PIS
8	23:24	ARI
11	05:05	TAU
13	14:10	GEM
16	01:45	CAN
18	14:33	LEO
21	03:23	VIR
23	15:03	LIB
26	00:17	SCO
28	06:08	SAG
30	08:33	CAP

FEBRUARY		
1	08:32	AQU
3	07:50	PIS
5	08:31	ARI
7	12:24	TAU
9	20:23	GEM
12	07:48	CAN
14	20:47	LEO
17	09:28	VIR
19	20:48	LIB
22	06:14	SCO
24	13:15	SAG
26	17:29	CAP
28	19:04	AQU

MARCH		
1	19:05	PIS
3	19:20	ARI
5	21:50	TAU
8	04:13	GEM
10	14:39	CAN
13	03:28	LEO
15	16:09	VIR
18	03:04	LIB
20	11:52	SCO
22	18:45	SAG
24	23:48	CAP
27	02:57	AQU
29	04:33	PIS
31	05:41	ARI

APRIL		
2	08:04	TAU
4	13:26	GEM
6	22:43	CAN
9	10:58	LEO
11	23:41	VIR
14	10:33	LIB
16	18:44	SCO
19	00:41	SAG
21	05:10	CAP
23	08:40	AQU
25	11:25	PIS
27	13:57	ARI
29	17:16	TAU

MAY		
1	22:44	GEM
4	07:23	CAN
6	19:01	LEO
9	07:46	VIR
11	19:00	LIB
14	03:12	SCO
16	08:26	SAG
18	11:44	CAP
20	14:15	AQU
22	16:49	PIS
24	20:04	ARI
27	00:30	TAU
29	06:48	GEM
31	15:38	CAN

JUNE		
3	02:59	LEO
5	15:42	VIR
8	03:34	LIB
10	12:30	SCO
12	17:52	SAG
14	20:25	CAP
16	21:35	AQU
18	22:51	PIS
21	01:27	ARI
23	06:10	TAU
25	13:16	GEM
27	22:44	CAN
30	10:14	LEO

JULY		
2	22:58	VIR
5	11:20	LIB
7	21:23	SCO
10	03:49	SAG
12	06:40	CAP
14	07:07	AQU
16	06:58	PIS
18	08:02	ARI
20	11:46	TAU
22	18:48	GEM
25	04:45	CAN
27	16:38	LEO
30	05:24	VIR

AUGUST		
1	17:56	LIB
4	04:53	SCO
6	12:47	SAG
8	16:57	CAP
10	17:53	AQU
12	17:09	PIS
14	16:50	ARI
16	18:56	TAU
19	00:48	GEM
21	10:26	CAN
23	22:32	LEO
26	11:23	VIR
28	23:47	LIB
31	10:56	SCO

SEPTEMBER		
2	19:52	SAG
5	01:40	CAP
7	04:06	AQU
9	04:04	PIS
11	03:22	ARI
13	04:11	TAU
15	08:28	GEM
17	16:57	CAN
20	04:42	LEO
22	17:35	VIR
25	05:46	LIB
27	16:31	SCO
30	01:28	SAG

OCTOBER		
2	08:13	CAP
4	12:16	AQU
6	13:50	PIS
8	14:01	ARI
10	14:43	TAU
12	17:55	GEM
15	01:00	CAN
17	11:51	LEO
20	00:33	VIR
22	12:43	LIB
24	22:59	SCO
27	07:12	SAG
29	13:34	CAP
31	18:12	AQU

NOVEMBER		
2	21:10	PIS
4	22:58	ARI
7	00:43	TAU
9	04:01	GEM
11	10:18	CAN
13	20:07	LEO
16	08:23	VIR
18	20:44	LIB
21	07:04	SCO
23	14:39	SAG
25	19:55	CAP
27	23:40	AQU
30	02:39	PIS

DECEMBER		
2	05:26	ARI
4	08:37	TAU
6	13:01	GEM
8	19:33	CAN
11	04:52	LEO
13	16:39	VIR
16	05:12	LIB
18	16:12	SCO
21	00:02	SAG
23	04:38	CAP
25	07:01	AQU
27	08:38	PIS
29	10:48	ARI
31	14:24	TAU

1909

JANUARY		
2	19:54	GEM
5	03:25	CAN
7	13:01	LEO
10	00:34	VIR
12	13:11	LIB
15	01:02	SCO
17	10:02	SAG
19	15:09	CAP
21	17:00	AQU
23	17:09	PIS
25	17:36	ARI
27	20:02	TAU
30	01:22	GEM

FEBRUARY		
1	09:32	CAN
3	19:50	LEO
6	07:36	VIR
8	20:10	LIB
11	08:30	SCO
13	18:48	SAG
16	01:28	CAP
18	04:08	AQU
20	04:00	PIS
22	03:08	ARI
24	03:45	TAU
26	07:33	GEM
28	15:08	CAN

MARCH		
3	01:41	LEO
5	13:48	VIR
8	02:23	LIB
10	14:41	SCO
13	01:37	SAG
15	09:46	CAP
17	14:09	AQU
19	15:08	PIS
21	14:17	ARI
23	13:50	TAU
25	15:55	GEM
27	21:55	CAN
30	07:44	LEO

APRIL		
1	19:51	VIR
4	08:31	LIB
6	20:33	SCO
9	07:17	SAG
11	15:57	CAP
13	21:44	AQU
16	00:26	PIS
18	00:51	ARI
20	00:43	TAU
22	02:03	GEM
24	06:35	CAN
26	15:02	LEO
29	02:33	VIR

MAY		
1	15:11	LIB
4	03:05	SCO
6	13:16	SAG
8	21:26	CAP
11	03:26	AQU
13	07:14	PIS
15	09:13	ARI
17	10:24	TAU
19	12:13	GEM
21	16:15	CAN
23	23:36	LEO
26	10:14	VIR
28	22:39	LIB
31	10:38	SCO

JUNE		
2	20:32	SAG
5	03:54	CAP
7	09:04	AQU
9	12:40	PIS
11	15:22	ARI
13	17:50	TAU
15	20:53	GEM
18	01:28	CAN
20	08:32	LEO
22	18:29	VIR
25	06:36	LIB
27	18:52	SCO
30	05:03	SAG

JULY		
2	12:04	CAP
4	16:14	AQU
6	18:41	PIS
8	20:45	ARI
10	23:29	TAU
13	03:30	GEM
15	09:08	CAN
17	16:42	LEO
20	02:32	VIR
22	14:26	LIB
25	03:01	SCO
27	14:00	SAG
29	21:32	CAP

AUGUST		
1	01:22	AQU
3	02:42	PIS
5	03:22	ARI
7	05:05	TAU
9	08:55	GEM
11	15:08	CAN
13	23:29	LEO
16	09:42	VIR
18	21:36	LIB
21	10:24	SCO
23	22:17	SAG
26	07:02	CAP
28	11:37	AQU
30	12:45	PIS

SEPTEMBER		
1	12:19	ARI
3	12:27	TAU
5	14:55	GEM
7	20:35	CAN
10	05:12	LEO
12	15:55	VIR
15	04:00	LIB
17	16:50	SCO
20	05:13	SAG
22	15:13	CAP
24	21:22	AQU
26	23:32	PIS
28	23:07	ARI
30	22:14	TAU

OCTOBER		
2	23:04	GEM
5	03:10	CAN
7	10:58	LEO
9	21:42	VIR
12	10:01	LIB
14	22:47	SCO
17	11:02	SAG
19	21:37	CAP
22	05:13	AQU
24	09:09	PIS
26	10:02	ARI
28	09:27	TAU
30	09:27	GEM

NOVEMBER		
1	11:57	CAN
3	18:10	LEO
6	04:04	VIR
8	16:19	LIB
11	05:04	SCO
13	16:58	SAG
16	03:09	CAP
18	11:05	AQU
20	16:20	PIS
22	19:02	ARI
24	19:57	TAU
26	20:31	GEM
28	22:27	CAN

DECEMBER		
1	03:17	LEO
3	11:50	VIR
5	23:30	LIB
8	12:17	SCO
11	00:01	SAG
13	09:31	CAP
15	16:39	AQU
17	21:48	PIS
20	01:25	ARI
22	03:57	TAU
24	06:05	GEM
26	08:46	CAN
28	13:17	LEO
30	20:50	VIR

1910

JANUARY		
2	07:38	LIB
4	20:19	SCO
7	08:20	SAG
9	17:40	CAP
11	23:53	AQU
14	03:51	PIS
16	06:46	ARI
18	09:39	TAU
20	12:58	GEM
22	17:03	CAN
24	22:24	LEO
27	05:52	VIR
29	16:05	LIB

FEBRUARY		
1	04:33	SCO
3	17:05	SAG
6	03:04	CAP
8	09:14	AQU
10	12:13	PIS
12	13:41	ARI
14	15:20	TAU
16	18:19	GEM
18	23:03	CAN
21	05:29	LEO
23	13:41	VIR
25	23:59	LIB
28	12:16	SCO

MARCH		
3	01:10	SAG
5	12:12	CAP
7	19:23	AQU
9	22:33	PIS
11	23:10	ARI
13	23:15	TAU
16	00:39	GEM
18	04:31	CAN
20	11:04	LEO
22	19:57	VIR
25	06:46	LIB
27	19:07	SCO
30	08:06	SAG

APRIL		
1	19:56	CAP
4	04:32	AQU
6	09:01	PIS
8	10:05	ARI
10	09:33	TAU
12	09:27	GEM
14	11:34	CAN
16	16:56	LEO
19	01:35	VIR
21	12:44	LIB
24	01:19	SCO
26	14:14	SAG
29	02:12	CAP

MAY		
1	11:46	AQU
3	17:51	PIS
5	20:24	ARI
7	20:33	TAU
9	20:03	GEM
11	20:50	CAN
14	00:32	LEO
16	07:58	VIR
18	18:46	LIB
21	07:27	SCO
23	20:17	SAG
26	07:57	CAP
28	17:33	AQU
31	00:31	PIS

JUNE		
2	04:38	ARI
4	06:19	TAU
6	06:40	GEM
8	07:16	CAN
10	09:52	LEO
12	15:52	VIR
15	01:42	LIB
17	14:08	SCO
20	02:57	SAG
22	14:15	CAP
24	23:15	AQU
27	05:59	PIS
29	10:44	ARI

JULY		
1	13:48	TAU
3	15:38	GEM
5	17:09	CAN
7	19:44	LEO
10	00:55	VIR
12	09:41	LIB
14	21:35	SCO
17	10:26	SAG
19	21:41	CAP
22	06:06	AQU
24	11:57	PIS
26	16:08	ARI
28	19:27	TAU
30	22:21	GEM

AUGUST		
2	01:11	CAN
4	04:40	LEO
6	09:58	VIR
8	18:13	LIB
11	05:34	SCO
13	18:27	SAG
16	06:05	CAP
18	14:31	AQU
20	19:40	PIS
22	22:42	ARI
25	01:02	TAU
27	03:44	GEM
29	07:14	CAN
31	11:49	LEO

SEPTEMBER		
2	17:57	VIR
5	02:22	LIB
7	13:29	SCO
10	02:22	SAG
12	14:39	CAP
14	23:53	AQU
17	05:12	PIS
19	07:30	ARI
21	08:29	TAU
23	09:49	GEM
25	12:37	CAN
27	17:26	LEO
30	00:22	VIR

OCTOBER		
2	09:29	LIB
4	20:45	SCO
7	09:37	SAG
9	22:26	CAP
12	08:51	AQU
14	15:22	PIS
16	18:06	ARI
18	18:27	TAU
20	18:18	GEM
22	19:26	CAN
24	23:08	LEO
27	05:54	VIR
29	15:30	LIB

NOVEMBER		
1	03:12	SCO
3	16:06	SAG
6	05:01	CAP
8	16:19	AQU
11	00:26	PIS
13	04:43	ARI
15	05:47	TAU
17	05:12	GEM
19	04:53	CAN
21	06:45	LEO
23	12:08	VIR
25	21:17	LIB
28	09:13	SCO
30	22:15	SAG

DECEMBER		
3	10:57	CAP
5	22:17	AQU
8	07:20	PIS
10	13:22	ARI
12	16:14	TAU
14	16:39	GEM
16	16:12	CAN
18	16:48	LEO
20	20:25	VIR
23	04:10	LIB
25	15:36	SCO
28	04:41	SAG
30	17:14	CAP

1911

JANUARY			FEBRUARY			MARCH			APRIL		
2	04:02	AQU	3	00:58	ARI	2	07:49	ARI	2	20:49	GEM
4	12:50	PIS	5	05:36	TAU	4	11:22	TAU	4	22:53	CAN
6	19:33	ARI	7	09:03	GEM	6	14:23	GEM	7	02:15	LEO
9	00:01	TAU	9	11:28	CAN	8	17:24	CAN	9	07:23	VIR
11	02:17	GEM	11	13:33	LEO	10	20:45	LEO	11	14:36	LIB
13	03:03	CAN	13	16:39	VIR	13	01:05	VIR	14	00:07	SCO
15	03:50	LEO	15	22:22	LIB	15	07:19	LIB	16	11:46	SAG
17	06:31	VIR	18	07:39	SCO	17	16:21	SCO	19	00:34	CAP
19	12:47	LIB	20	19:53	SAG	20	04:05	SAG	21	12:33	AQU
21	23:06	SCO	23	08:38	CAP	22	16:54	CAP	23	21:41	PIS
24	11:54	SAG	25	19:18	AQU	25	04:13	AQU	26	03:03	ARI
27	00:30	CAP	28	02:51	PIS	27	12:41	PIS	28	05:13	TAU
29	10:57	AQU				29	16:52	ARI	30	05:39	GEM
31	18:55	PIS				31	19:14	TAU			

MAY			JUNE			JULY			AUGUST		
2	06:07	CAN	2	19:14	VIR	2	08:59	LIB	1	01:44	SCO
4	08:09	LEO	5	02:07	LIB	4	18:27	SCO	3	13:21	SAG
6	12:50	VIR	7	12:21	SCO	7	06:39	SAG	6	02:10	CAP
8	20:26	LIB	10	00:37	SAG	9	19:32	CAP	8	14:02	AQU
11	06:36	SCO	12	13:28	CAP	12	07:34	AQU	11	00:01	PIS
13	18:33	SAG	15	01:44	AQU	14	18:04	PIS	13	08:02	ARI
16	07:21	CAP	17	12:27	PIS	17	02:35	ARI	15	14:12	TAU
18	19:40	AQU	19	20:32	ARI	19	08:34	TAU	17	18:24	GEM
21	05:53	PIS	22	01:14	TAU	21	11:42	GEM	19	20:43	CAN
23	12:41	ARI	24	02:46	GEM	23	12:30	CAN	21	21:54	LEO
25	15:48	TAU	26	02:20	CAN	25	12:25	LEO	23	23:26	VIR
27	16:12	GEM	28	01:54	LEO	27	13:26	VIR	26	03:06	LIB
29	15:37	CAN	30	03:35	VIR	29	17:32	LIB	28	10:16	SCO
31	16:03	LEO							30	21:01	SAG

SEPTEMBER			OCTOBER			NOVEMBER			DECEMBER		
2	09:37	CAP	2	05:56	AQU	1	01:12	PIS	2	23:43	TAU
4	21:35	AQU	4	16:00	PIS	3	08:49	ARI	5	01:18	GEM
7	07:17	PIS	6	22:56	ARI	5	12:54	TAU	7	00:55	CAN
9	14:31	ARI	9	03:13	TAU	7	14:29	GEM	9	00:39	LEO
11	19:49	TAU	11	05:56	GEM	9	15:11	CAN	11	02:27	VIR
13	23:47	GEM	13	08:12	CAN	11	16:39	LEO	13	07:36	LIB
16	02:48	CAN	15	10:55	LEO	13	20:06	VIR	15	16:09	SCO
18	05:18	LEO	17	14:42	VIR	16	02:04	LIB	18	03:08	SAG
20	08:05	VIR	19	20:05	LIB	18	10:28	SCO	20	15:24	CAP
22	12:22	LIB	22	03:37	SCO	20	20:54	SAG	23	04:06	AQU
24	19:17	SCO	24	13:34	SAG	23	08:55	CAP	25	16:18	PIS
27	05:21	SAG	27	01:37	CAP	25	21:40	AQU	28	02:37	ARI
29	17:39	CAP	29	14:14	AQU	28	09:32	PIS	30	09:31	TAU
						30	18:36	ARI			

1912

JANUARY
1	12:29	GEM
3	12:25	CAN
5	11:17	LEO
7	11:23	VIR
9	14:42	LIB
11	22:07	SCO
14	08:57	SAG
16	21:28	CAP
19	10:07	AQU
21	22:06	PIS
24	08:41	ARI
26	16:52	TAU
28	21:42	GEM
30	23:15	CAN

FEBRUARY
1	22:47	LEO
3	22:23	VIR
6	00:13	LIB
8	05:53	SCO
10	15:36	SAG
13	03:52	CAP
15	16:34	AQU
18	04:13	PIS
20	14:17	ARI
22	22:26	TAU
25	04:15	GEM
27	07:30	CAN
29	08:43	LEO

MARCH
2	09:14	VIR
4	10:54	LIB
6	15:25	SCO
8	23:44	SAG
11	11:12	CAP
13	23:50	AQU
16	11:28	PIS
18	20:59	ARI
21	04:16	TAU
23	09:37	GEM
25	13:22	CAN
27	15:54	LEO
29	17:59	VIR
31	20:40	LIB

APRIL
3	01:16	SCO
5	08:48	SAG
7	19:24	CAP
10	07:48	AQU
12	19:42	PIS
15	05:15	ARI
17	11:51	TAU
19	16:03	GEM
21	18:53	CAN
23	21:22	LEO
26	00:18	VIR
28	04:15	LIB
30	09:48	SCO

MAY
2	17:30	SAG
5	03:42	CAP
7	15:50	AQU
10	04:08	PIS
12	14:20	ARI
14	21:04	TAU
17	00:33	GEM
19	02:04	CAN
21	03:18	LEO
23	05:41	VIR
25	10:00	LIB
27	16:27	SCO
30	00:54	SAG

JUNE
1	11:17	CAP
3	23:19	AQU
6	11:55	PIS
8	23:03	ARI
11	06:47	TAU
13	10:33	GEM
15	11:24	CAN
17	11:16	LEO
19	12:09	VIR
21	15:33	LIB
23	21:58	SCO
26	06:58	SAG
28	17:50	CAP

JULY
1	05:58	AQU
3	18:40	PIS
6	06:30	ARI
8	15:33	TAU
10	20:34	GEM
12	21:55	CAN
14	21:16	LEO
16	20:49	VIR
18	22:37	LIB
21	03:52	SCO
23	12:34	SAG
25	23:41	CAP
28	12:01	AQU
31	00:40	PIS

AUGUST
2	12:40	ARI
4	22:37	TAU
7	05:10	GEM
9	07:57	CAN
11	08:00	LEO
13	07:14	VIR
15	07:48	LIB
17	11:28	SCO
19	18:59	SAG
22	05:43	CAP
24	18:07	AQU
27	06:40	PIS
29	18:21	ARI

SEPTEMBER
1	04:20	TAU
3	11:45	GEM
5	16:06	CAN
7	17:43	LEO
9	17:51	VIR
11	18:18	LIB
13	20:54	SCO
16	02:59	SAG
18	12:43	CAP
21	00:52	AQU
23	13:25	PIS
26	00:45	ARI
28	10:04	TAU
30	17:12	GEM

OCTOBER
2	22:09	CAN
5	01:11	LEO
7	02:55	VIR
9	04:25	LIB
11	07:05	SCO
13	12:19	SAG
15	20:56	CAP
18	08:31	AQU
20	21:08	PIS
23	08:29	ARI
25	17:15	TAU
27	23:23	GEM
30	03:36	CAN

NOVEMBER
1	06:46	LEO
3	09:34	VIR
5	12:32	LIB
7	16:17	SCO
9	21:44	SAG
12	05:48	CAP
14	16:45	AQU
17	05:24	PIS
19	17:17	ARI
22	02:13	TAU
24	07:41	GEM
26	10:37	CAN
28	12:34	LEO
30	14:55	VIR

DECEMBER
2	18:26	LIB
4	23:22	SCO
7	05:48	SAG
9	14:10	CAP
12	00:51	AQU
14	13:26	PIS
17	02:00	ARI
19	11:57	TAU
21	17:51	GEM
23	20:11	CAN
25	20:44	LEO
27	21:27	VIR
29	23:56	LIB

1913

JANUARY
1	04:50	SCO
3	12:02	SAG
5	21:10	CAP
8	08:07	AQU
10	20:39	PIS
13	09:36	ARI
15	20:46	TAU
18	04:07	GEM
20	07:14	CAN
22	07:26	LEO
24	06:48	VIR
26	07:26	LIB
28	10:50	SCO
30	17:30	SAG

FEBRUARY
2	02:59	CAP
4	14:25	AQU
7	03:03	PIS
9	16:00	ARI
12	03:47	TAU
14	12:38	GEM
16	17:29	CAN
18	18:47	LEO
20	18:08	VIR
22	17:37	LIB
24	19:11	SCO
27	00:11	SAG

MARCH
1	08:52	CAP
3	20:22	AQU
6	09:10	PIS
8	21:57	ARI
11	09:35	TAU
13	19:00	GEM
16	01:21	CAN
18	04:28	LEO
20	05:08	VIR
22	04:55	LIB
24	05:37	SCO
26	09:00	SAG
28	16:09	CAP
31	02:54	AQU

APRIL
2	15:39	PIS
5	04:22	ARI
7	15:32	TAU
10	00:31	GEM
12	07:09	CAN
14	11:31	LEO
16	13:53	VIR
18	15:03	LIB
20	16:14	SCO
22	19:03	SAG
25	00:56	CAP
27	10:33	AQU
29	22:54	PIS

MAY
2	11:39	ARI
4	22:35	TAU
7	06:50	GEM
9	12:43	CAN
11	16:58	LEO
13	20:10	VIR
15	22:44	LIB
18	01:15	SCO
20	04:38	SAG
22	10:13	CAP
24	19:00	AQU
27	06:47	PIS
29	19:36	ARI

JUNE
1	06:46	TAU
3	14:43	GEM
5	19:41	CAN
7	22:52	LEO
10	01:31	VIR
12	04:27	LIB
14	08:01	SCO
16	12:31	SAG
18	18:41	CAP
21	03:21	AQU
23	14:46	PIS
26	03:38	ARI
28	15:23	TAU
30	23:47	GEM

JULY
3	04:30	CAN
5	06:40	LEO
7	08:01	VIR
9	10:00	LIB
11	13:26	SCO
13	18:37	SAG
16	01:39	CAP
18	10:48	AQU
20	22:13	PIS
23	11:07	ARI
25	23:30	TAU
28	08:58	GEM
30	14:23	CAN

AUGUST
1	16:25	LEO
3	16:44	VIR
5	17:13	LIB
7	19:23	SCO
10	00:03	SAG
12	07:25	CAP
14	17:10	AQU
17	04:52	PIS
19	17:47	ARI
22	06:31	TAU
24	17:03	GEM
26	23:54	CAN
29	02:55	LEO
31	03:16	VIR

SEPTEMBER
2	02:47	LIB
4	03:21	SCO
6	06:32	SAG
8	13:07	CAP
10	22:56	AQU
13	10:58	PIS
15	23:56	ARI
18	12:34	TAU
20	23:35	GEM
23	07:45	CAN
25	12:27	LEO
27	14:02	VIR
29	13:47	LIB

OCTOBER
1	13:31	SCO
3	15:08	SAG
5	20:11	CAP
8	05:09	AQU
10	17:07	PIS
13	06:09	ARI
15	18:31	TAU
18	05:13	GEM
20	13:45	CAN
22	19:45	LEO
24	23:07	VIR
27	00:18	LIB
29	00:30	SCO
31	01:30	SAG

NOVEMBER
2	05:09	CAP
4	12:44	AQU
7	00:02	PIS
9	13:02	ARI
12	01:17	TAU
14	11:24	GEM
16	19:17	CAN
19	01:18	LEO
21	05:40	VIR
23	08:30	LIB
25	10:13	SCO
27	11:54	SAG
29	15:12	CAP

DECEMBER
1	21:43	AQU
4	08:01	PIS
6	20:46	ARI
9	09:12	TAU
11	19:09	GEM
14	02:12	CAN
16	07:09	LEO
18	11:00	VIR
20	14:19	LIB
22	17:21	SCO
24	20:28	SAG
27	00:36	CAP
29	07:01	AQU
31	16:38	PIS

1914

JANUARY		
3	04:58	ARI
5	17:44	TAU
8	04:13	GEM
10	11:12	CAN
12	15:13	LEO
14	17:40	VIR
16	19:53	LIB
18	22:44	SCO
21	02:40	SAG
23	07:59	CAP
25	15:13	AQU
28	00:54	PIS
30	12:57	ARI

FEBRUARY		
2	01:55	TAU
4	13:20	GEM
6	21:16	CAN
9	01:27	LEO
11	03:00	VIR
13	03:37	LIB
15	04:55	SCO
17	08:04	SAG
19	13:38	CAP
21	21:41	AQU
24	08:01	PIS
26	20:09	ARI

MARCH		
1	09:08	TAU
3	21:15	GEM
6	06:34	CAN
8	12:03	LEO
10	14:02	VIR
12	13:57	LIB
14	13:40	SCO
16	15:01	SAG
18	19:23	CAP
21	03:15	AQU
23	14:01	PIS
26	02:30	ARI
28	15:27	TAU
31	03:42	GEM

APRIL		
2	13:59	CAN
4	21:06	LEO
7	00:37	VIR
9	01:12	LIB
11	00:27	SCO
13	00:23	SAG
15	02:59	CAP
17	09:31	AQU
19	19:53	PIS
22	08:30	ARI
24	21:28	TAU
27	09:29	GEM
29	19:50	CAN

MAY		
2	03:53	LEO
4	09:02	VIR
6	11:14	LIB
8	11:20	SCO
10	11:04	SAG
12	12:31	CAP
14	17:29	AQU
17	02:40	PIS
19	14:54	ARI
22	03:52	TAU
24	15:37	GEM
27	01:28	CAN
29	09:22	LEO
31	15:13	VIR

JUNE		
2	18:51	LIB
4	20:30	SCO
6	21:13	SAG
8	22:41	CAP
11	02:47	AQU
13	10:45	PIS
15	22:12	ARI
18	11:01	TAU
20	22:44	GEM
23	08:07	CAN
25	15:14	LEO
27	20:35	VIR
30	00:33	LIB

JULY		
2	03:20	SCO
4	05:26	SAG
6	07:54	CAP
8	12:11	AQU
10	19:33	PIS
13	06:15	ARI
15	18:49	TAU
18	06:47	GEM
20	16:12	CAN
22	22:43	LEO
25	03:01	VIR
27	06:05	LIB
29	08:45	SCO
31	11:36	SAG

AUGUST		
2	15:14	CAP
4	20:27	AQU
7	04:04	PIS
9	14:25	ARI
12	02:46	TAU
14	15:07	GEM
17	01:11	CAN
19	07:52	LEO
21	11:30	VIR
23	13:19	LIB
25	14:44	SCO
27	17:00	SAG
29	20:58	CAP

SEPTEMBER		
1	03:04	AQU
3	11:26	PIS
5	22:00	ARI
8	10:15	TAU
10	22:54	GEM
13	09:56	CAN
15	17:41	LEO
17	21:42	VIR
19	22:52	LIB
21	22:53	SCO
23	23:36	SAG
26	02:35	CAP
28	08:37	AQU
30	17:33	PIS

OCTOBER		
3	04:38	ARI
5	16:58	TAU
8	05:40	GEM
10	17:26	CAN
13	02:37	LEO
15	08:02	VIR
17	09:49	LIB
19	09:21	SCO
21	08:41	SAG
23	09:55	CAP
25	14:40	AQU
27	23:14	PIS
30	10:35	ARI

NOVEMBER		
1	23:08	TAU
4	11:44	GEM
6	23:33	CAN
9	09:37	LEO
11	16:42	VIR
13	20:10	LIB
15	20:36	SCO
17	19:43	SAG
19	19:42	CAP
21	22:43	AQU
24	05:53	PIS
26	16:44	ARI
29	05:22	TAU

DECEMBER		
1	17:54	GEM
4	05:19	CAN
6	15:13	LEO
8	23:03	VIR
11	04:09	LIB
13	06:23	SCO
15	06:40	SAG
17	06:46	CAP
19	08:48	AQU
21	14:25	PIS
24	00:03	ARI
26	12:19	TAU
29	00:53	GEM
31	12:02	CAN

1915

JANUARY
2	21:12	LEO
5	04:28	VIR
7	09:53	LIB
9	13:25	SCO
11	15:25	SAG
13	16:52	CAP
15	19:17	AQU
18	00:15	PIS
20	08:42	ARI
22	20:13	TAU
25	08:48	GEM
27	20:08	CAN
30	04:55	LEO

FEBRUARY
1	11:10	VIR
3	15:33	LIB
5	18:48	SCO
7	21:33	SAG
10	00:25	CAP
12	04:09	AQU
14	09:40	PIS
16	17:46	ARI
19	04:37	TAU
21	17:05	GEM
24	04:58	CAN
26	14:11	LEO
28	20:04	VIR

MARCH
2	23:15	LIB
5	01:05	SCO
7	02:59	SAG
9	05:59	CAP
11	10:41	AQU
13	17:17	PIS
16	01:55	ARI
18	12:38	TAU
21	00:58	GEM
23	13:22	CAN
25	23:38	LEO
28	06:13	VIR
30	09:10	LIB

APRIL
1	09:49	SCO
3	10:05	SAG
5	11:47	CAP
7	16:04	AQU
9	23:08	PIS
12	08:32	ARI
14	19:38	TAU
17	07:57	GEM
19	20:37	CAN
22	07:54	LEO
24	15:53	VIR
26	19:47	LIB
28	20:24	SCO
30	19:37	SAG

MAY
2	19:40	CAP
4	22:23	AQU
7	04:41	PIS
9	14:10	ARI
12	01:41	TAU
14	14:09	GEM
17	02:48	CAN
19	14:32	LEO
21	23:47	VIR
24	05:16	LIB
26	07:02	SCO
28	06:27	SAG
30	05:39	CAP

JUNE
1	06:49	AQU
3	11:32	PIS
5	20:07	ARI
8	07:31	TAU
10	20:07	GEM
13	08:38	CAN
15	20:12	LEO
18	05:53	VIR
20	12:39	LIB
22	16:03	SCO
24	16:45	SAG
26	16:22	CAP
28	16:55	AQU
30	20:15	PIS

JULY
3	03:24	ARI
5	14:02	TAU
8	02:30	GEM
10	14:57	CAN
13	02:06	LEO
15	11:22	VIR
17	18:21	LIB
19	22:51	SCO
22	01:06	SAG
24	02:04	CAP
26	03:10	AQU
28	06:04	PIS
30	12:06	ARI

AUGUST
1	21:40	TAU
4	09:43	GEM
6	22:11	CAN
9	09:08	LEO
11	17:42	VIR
13	23:56	LIB
16	04:17	SCO
18	07:19	SAG
20	09:38	CAP
22	12:03	AQU
24	15:35	PIS
26	21:21	ARI
29	06:08	TAU
31	17:39	GEM

SEPTEMBER
3	06:12	CAN
5	17:25	LEO
8	01:42	VIR
10	07:00	LIB
12	10:15	SCO
14	12:41	SAG
16	15:21	CAP
18	18:50	AQU
20	23:32	PIS
23	05:56	ARI
25	14:35	TAU
28	01:43	GEM
30	14:21	CAN

OCTOBER
3	02:13	LEO
5	11:05	VIR
7	16:09	LIB
9	18:20	SCO
11	19:21	SAG
13	20:57	CAP
16	00:15	AQU
18	05:38	PIS
20	12:57	ARI
22	22:09	TAU
25	09:15	GEM
27	21:53	CAN
30	10:27	LEO

NOVEMBER
1	20:31	VIR
4	02:29	LIB
6	04:37	SCO
8	04:36	SAG
10	04:34	CAP
12	06:23	AQU
14	11:05	PIS
16	18:40	ARI
19	04:29	TAU
21	15:57	GEM
24	04:34	CAN
26	17:23	LEO
29	04:33	VIR

DECEMBER
1	12:09	LIB
3	15:33	SCO
5	15:47	SAG
7	14:53	CAP
9	15:01	AQU
11	17:57	PIS
14	00:30	ARI
16	10:15	TAU
18	22:03	GEM
21	10:45	CAN
23	23:24	LEO
26	10:51	VIR
28	19:42	LIB
31	00:56	SCO

1916

JANUARY		
2	02:44	SAG
4	02:26	CAP
6	01:58	AQU
8	03:22	PIS
10	08:07	ARI
12	16:43	TAU
15	04:18	GEM
17	17:07	CAN
20	05:33	LEO
22	16:33	VIR
25	01:26	LIB
27	07:43	SCO
29	11:18	SAG
31	12:43	CAP

FEBRUARY		
2	13:09	AQU
4	14:16	PIS
6	17:45	ARI
9	00:50	TAU
11	11:30	GEM
14	00:13	CAN
16	12:39	LEO
18	23:09	VIR
21	07:14	LIB
23	13:09	SCO
25	17:21	SAG
27	20:13	CAP
29	22:18	AQU

MARCH		
3	00:27	PIS
5	03:56	ARI
7	10:08	TAU
9	19:46	GEM
12	08:04	CAN
14	20:41	LEO
17	07:13	VIR
19	14:38	LIB
21	19:27	SCO
23	22:48	SAG
26	01:44	CAP
28	04:47	AQU
30	08:19	PIS

APRIL		
1	12:49	ARI
3	19:11	TAU
6	04:20	GEM
8	16:11	CAN
11	05:01	LEO
13	16:07	VIR
15	23:41	LIB
18	03:48	SCO
20	05:53	SAG
22	07:34	CAP
24	10:07	AQU
26	14:05	PIS
28	19:35	ARI

MAY		
1	02:49	TAU
3	12:12	GEM
5	23:53	CAN
8	12:52	LEO
11	00:45	VIR
13	09:15	LIB
15	13:42	SCO
17	15:10	SAG
19	15:31	CAP
21	16:34	AQU
23	19:35	PIS
26	01:04	ARI
28	08:54	TAU
30	18:54	GEM

JUNE		
2	06:46	CAN
4	19:47	LEO
7	08:15	VIR
9	17:59	LIB
11	23:40	SCO
14	01:40	SAG
16	01:33	CAP
18	01:17	AQU
20	02:40	PIS
22	06:55	ARI
24	14:26	TAU
27	00:44	GEM
29	12:55	CAN

JULY		
2	01:57	LEO
4	14:33	VIR
7	01:06	LIB
9	08:16	SCO
11	11:44	SAG
13	12:21	CAP
15	11:46	AQU
17	11:55	PIS
19	14:33	ARI
21	20:46	TAU
24	06:36	GEM
26	18:53	CAN
29	07:56	LEO
31	20:18	VIR

AUGUST		
3	06:54	LIB
5	14:56	SCO
7	19:57	SAG
9	22:08	CAP
11	22:28	AQU
13	22:30	PIS
16	00:02	ARI
18	04:46	TAU
20	13:27	GEM
23	01:21	CAN
25	14:24	LEO
28	02:30	VIR
30	12:34	LIB

SEPTEMBER		
1	20:25	SCO
4	02:06	SAG
6	05:44	CAP
8	07:39	AQU
10	08:42	PIS
12	10:18	ARI
14	14:09	TAU
16	21:38	GEM
19	08:45	CAN
21	21:41	LEO
24	09:47	VIR
26	19:22	LIB
29	02:21	SCO

OCTOBER		
1	07:28	SAG
3	11:23	CAP
5	14:28	AQU
7	17:00	PIS
9	19:41	ARI
11	23:45	TAU
14	06:38	GEM
16	16:58	CAN
19	05:40	LEO
21	18:04	VIR
24	03:46	LIB
26	10:09	SCO
28	14:07	SAG
30	17:01	CAP

NOVEMBER		
1	19:50	AQU
3	23:05	PIS
6	03:00	ARI
8	08:07	TAU
10	15:19	GEM
13	01:20	CAN
15	13:45	LEO
18	02:33	VIR
20	13:03	LIB
22	19:48	SCO
24	23:12	SAG
27	00:45	CAP
29	02:06	AQU

DECEMBER		
1	04:30	PIS
3	08:35	ARI
5	14:35	TAU
7	22:41	GEM
10	09:00	CAN
12	21:18	LEO
15	10:19	VIR
17	21:50	LIB
20	05:53	SCO
22	09:58	SAG
24	11:07	CAP
26	11:05	AQU
28	11:42	PIS
30	14:26	ARI

1917

JANUARY			FEBRUARY			MARCH			APRIL		
1	20:04	TAU	2	21:31	CAN	2	03:52	CAN	3	12:33	VIR
4	04:39	GEM	5	10:16	LEO	4	16:36	LEO	5	23:54	LIB
6	15:35	CAN	7	23:09	VIR	7	05:29	VIR	8	08:55	SCO
9	04:03	LEO	10	11:04	LIB	9	17:01	LIB	10	15:51	SAG
11	17:02	VIR	12	21:06	SCO	12	02:41	SCO	12	21:08	CAP
14	05:05	LIB	15	04:23	SAG	14	10:18	SAG	15	00:57	AQU
16	14:32	SCO	17	08:24	CAP	16	15:39	CAP	17	03:25	PIS
18	20:18	SAG	19	09:32	AQU	18	18:33	AQU	19	05:10	ARI
20	22:28	CAP	21	09:06	PIS	20	19:31	PIS	21	07:31	TAU
22	22:19	AQU	23	09:00	ARI	22	19:54	ARI	23	12:05	GEM
24	21:41	PIS	25	11:20	TAU	24	21:35	TAU	25	20:08	CAN
26	22:34	ARI	27	17:35	GEM	27	02:29	GEM	28	07:32	LEO
29	02:35	TAU				29	11:28	CAN	30	20:19	VIR
31	10:26	GEM				31	23:39	LEO			

MAY			JUNE			JULY			AUGUST		
3	07:52	LIB	2	01:35	SCO	1	17:14	SAG	2	07:50	AQU
5	16:39	SCO	4	07:28	SAG	3	20:25	CAP	4	07:20	PIS
7	22:44	SAG	6	10:45	CAP	5	21:25	AQU	6	07:19	ARI
10	03:00	CAP	8	12:46	AQU	7	21:53	PIS	8	09:37	TAU
12	06:18	AQU	10	14:43	PIS	9	23:25	ARI	10	15:24	GEM
14	09:11	PIS	12	17:31	ARI	12	03:13	TAU	13	00:40	CAN
16	12:04	ARI	14	21:49	TAU	14	09:48	GEM	15	12:19	LEO
18	15:38	TAU	17	04:02	GEM	16	19:00	CAN	18	01:02	VIR
20	20:53	GEM	19	12:34	CAN	19	06:17	LEO	20	13:42	LIB
23	04:49	CAN	21	23:27	LEO	21	18:52	VIR	23	01:16	SCO
25	15:43	LEO	24	12:00	VIR	24	07:33	LIB	25	10:28	SAG
28	04:21	VIR	27	00:26	LIB	26	18:41	SCO	27	16:15	CAP
30	16:20	LIB	29	10:37	SCO	29	02:39	SAG	29	18:28	AQU
						31	06:48	CAP	31	18:11	PIS

SEPTEMBER			OCTOBER			NOVEMBER			DECEMBER		
2	17:20	ARI	2	04:25	TAU	2	23:09	CAN	2	17:32	LEO
4	18:06	TAU	4	07:14	GEM	5	08:43	LEO	5	05:07	VIR
6	22:19	GEM	6	14:06	CAN	7	20:56	VIR	7	17:42	LIB
9	06:40	CAP	9	00:50	LEO	10	09:27	LIB	10	04:53	SCO
11	18:13	LEO	11	13:32	VIR	12	20:13	SCO	12	13:11	SAG
14	07:02	VIR	14	01:59	LIB	15	04:36	SAG	14	18:35	CAP
16	19:33	LIB	16	12:54	SCO	17	10:55	CAP	16	22:00	AQU
19	06:55	SCO	18	22:01	SAG	19	15:38	AQU	19	00:31	PIS
21	16:32	SAG	21	05:14	CAP	21	19:04	PIS	21	03:07	ARI
23	23:37	CAP	23	10:17	AQU	23	21:36	ARI	23	06:26	TAU
26	03:34	AQU	25	13:03	PIS	25	23:56	TAU	25	11:03	GEM
28	04:39	PIS	27	14:09	ARI	28	03:13	GEM	27	17:29	CAN
30	04:16	ARI	29	14:59	TAU	30	08:48	CAN	30	02:15	LEO
			31	17:26	GEM						

1918

JANUARY		
1	13:24	VIR
4	01:57	LIB
6	13:50	SCO
8	22:58	SAG
11	04:27	CAP
13	06:56	AQU
15	07:54	PIS
17	09:04	ARI
19	11:49	TAU
21	16:52	GEM
24	00:17	CAN
26	09:45	LEO
28	20:59	VIR
31	09:27	LIB

FEBRUARY		
2	21:52	SCO
5	08:15	SAG
7	14:57	CAP
9	17:46	AQU
11	17:57	PIS
13	17:31	ARI
15	18:31	TAU
17	22:30	GEM
20	05:51	CAN
22	15:53	LEO
25	03:33	VIR
27	16:01	LIB

MARCH		
2	04:33	SCO
4	15:48	SAG
7	00:05	CAP
9	04:23	AQU
11	05:12	PIS
13	04:15	ARI
15	03:48	TAU
17	05:58	GEM
19	11:58	CAN
21	21:37	LEO
24	09:31	VIR
26	22:07	LIB
29	10:28	SCO
31	21:47	SAG

APRIL		
3	06:59	CAP
5	12:56	AQU
7	15:22	PIS
9	15:19	ARI
11	14:40	TAU
13	15:37	GEM
15	19:58	CAN
18	04:19	LEO
20	15:46	VIR
23	04:25	LIB
25	16:37	SCO
28	03:31	SAG
30	12:33	CAP

MAY		
2	19:13	AQU
4	23:08	PIS
7	00:41	ARI
9	01:05	TAU
11	02:06	GEM
13	05:31	CAN
15	12:31	LEO
17	23:01	VIR
20	11:26	LIB
22	23:38	SCO
25	10:09	SAG
27	18:28	CAP
30	00:38	AQU

JUNE		
1	04:54	PIS
3	07:37	ARI
5	09:30	TAU
7	11:36	GEM
9	15:14	CAN
11	21:36	LEO
14	07:11	VIR
16	19:10	LIB
19	07:30	SCO
21	18:05	SAG
24	01:51	CAP
26	07:01	AQU
28	10:27	PIS
30	13:05	ARI

JULY		
2	15:44	TAU
4	19:04	GEM
6	23:42	CAN
9	06:21	LEO
11	15:33	VIR
14	03:09	LIB
16	15:41	SCO
19	02:49	SAG
21	10:46	CAP
23	15:20	AQU
25	17:32	PIS
27	18:59	ARI
29	21:07	TAU

AUGUST		
1	00:48	GEM
3	06:22	CAN
5	13:49	LEO
7	23:17	VIR
10	10:46	LIB
12	23:27	SCO
15	11:23	SAG
17	20:17	CAP
20	01:11	AQU
22	02:48	PIS
24	02:56	ARI
26	03:35	TAU
28	06:20	GEM
30	11:50	CAN

SEPTEMBER		
1	19:53	LEO
4	05:56	VIR
6	17:35	LIB
9	06:20	SCO
11	18:51	SAG
14	05:02	CAP
16	11:15	AQU
18	13:27	PIS
20	13:07	ARI
22	12:27	TAU
24	13:31	GEM
26	17:45	CAN
29	01:25	LEO

OCTOBER		
1	11:46	VIR
3	23:44	LIB
6	12:28	SCO
9	01:05	SAG
11	12:07	CAP
13	19:54	AQU
15	23:42	PIS
18	00:14	ARI
19	23:21	TAU
21	23:11	GEM
24	01:40	CAN
26	07:55	LEO
28	17:42	VIR
31	05:45	LIB

NOVEMBER		
2	18:32	SCO
5	06:52	SAG
7	17:50	CAP
10	02:26	AQU
12	07:52	PIS
14	10:12	ARI
16	10:27	TAU
18	10:20	GEM
20	11:47	CAN
22	16:23	LEO
25	00:51	VIR
27	12:25	LIB
30	01:13	SCO

DECEMBER		
2	13:21	SAG
4	23:41	CAP
7	07:52	AQU
9	13:48	PIS
11	17:33	ARI
13	19:36	TAU
15	20:49	GEM
17	22:35	CAN
20	02:25	LEO
22	09:33	VIR
24	20:10	LIB
27	08:49	SCO
29	21:04	SAG

1919

JANUARY			FEBRUARY			MARCH			APRIL		
1	07:02	CAP	2	02:38	PIS	1	12:15	PIS	1	23:40	TAU
3	14:16	AQU	4	05:02	ARI	3	13:29	ARI	3	23:56	GEM
5	19:19	PIS	6	07:22	TAU	5	14:14	TAU	6	02:23	CAN
7	23:01	ARI	8	10:31	GEM	7	16:10	GEM	8	07:48	LEO
10	02:02	TAU	10	14:46	CAN	9	20:09	CAN	10	16:07	VIR
12	04:49	GEM	12	20:18	LEO	12	02:19	LEO	13	02:43	LIB
14	07:56	CAN	15	03:32	VIR	14	10:26	VIR	15	14:54	SCO
16	12:16	LEO	17	13:07	LIB	16	20:29	LIB	18	03:52	SAG
18	18:57	VIR	20	01:04	SCO	19	08:25	SCO	20	16:14	CAP
21	04:43	LIB	22	13:57	SAG	21	21:24	SAG	23	02:09	AQU
23	17:00	SCO	25	01:08	CAP	24	09:25	CAP	25	08:17	PIS
26	05:35	SAG	27	08:36	AQU	26	18:12	AQU	27	10:40	ARI
28	15:54	CAP				28	22:46	PIS	29	10:36	TAU
30	22:44	AQU				30	23:58	ARI			

MAY			JUNE			JULY			AUGUST		
1	10:01	GEM	1	23:26	LEO	1	14:06	VIR	2	18:08	SCO
3	10:51	CAN	4	05:19	VIR	3	22:35	LIB	5	06:58	SAG
5	14:38	LEO	6	14:58	LIB	6	10:19	SCO	7	18:52	CAP
7	22:01	VIR	9	03:16	SCO	8	23:13	SAG	10	03:57	AQU
10	08:32	LIB	11	16:12	SAG	11	10:57	CAP	12	09:59	PIS
12	20:58	SCO	14	04:05	CAP	13	20:14	AQU	14	13:59	ARI
15	09:54	SAG	16	13:59	AQU	16	03:06	PIS	16	17:05	TAU
17	22:07	CAP	18	21:32	PIS	18	08:06	ARI	18	20:03	GEM
20	08:24	AQU	21	02:38	ARI	20	11:44	TAU	20	23:14	CAN
22	15:45	PIS	23	05:29	TAU	22	14:20	GEM	23	03:00	LEO
24	19:47	ARI	25	06:42	GEM	24	16:25	CAN	25	08:08	VIR
26	21:03	TAU	27	07:28	CAN	26	19:00	LEO	27	15:42	LIB
28	20:53	GEM	29	09:24	LEO	28	23:28	VIR	30	02:16	SCO
30	21:05	CAN				31	07:06	LIB			

SEPTEMBER			OCTOBER			NOVEMBER			DECEMBER		
1	14:58	SAG	1	11:29	CAP	2	14:19	PIS	2	04:03	ARI
4	03:21	CAP	3	22:03	AQU	4	18:31	ARI	4	06:34	TAU
6	12:54	AQU	6	04:44	PIS	6	19:31	TAU	6	06:36	GEM
8	18:46	PIS	8	07:44	ARI	8	19:04	GEM	8	05:55	CAN
10	21:48	ARI	10	08:33	TAU	10	19:03	CAN	10	06:28	LEO
12	23:36	TAU	12	08:59	GEM	12	21:14	LEO	12	10:07	VIR
15	01:35	GEM	14	10:39	CAN	15	02:41	VIR	14	17:48	LIB
17	04:39	CAN	16	14:32	LEO	17	11:32	LIB	17	05:01	SCO
19	09:08	LEO	18	20:59	VIR	19	22:59	SCO	19	17:59	SAG
21	15:15	VIR	21	05:51	LIB	22	11:48	SAG	22	06:49	CAP
23	23:25	LIB	23	16:53	SCO	25	00:46	CAP	24	18:20	AQU
26	10:00	SCO	26	05:31	SAG	27	12:38	AQU	27	03:56	PIS
28	22:37	SAG	28	18:35	CAP	29	22:03	PIS	29	11:06	ARI
			31	06:08	AQU				31	15:29	TAU

1920

JANUARY

2	17:13	GEM
4	17:19	CAN
6	17:30	LEO
8	19:46	VIR
11	01:48	LIB
13	11:58	SCO
16	00:44	SAG
18	13:34	CAP
21	00:40	AQU
23	09:34	PIS
25	16:32	ARI
27	21:43	TAU
30	01:06	GEM

FEBRUARY

1	02:54	CAN
3	04:06	LEO
5	06:18	VIR
7	11:20	LIB
9	20:14	SCO
12	08:21	SAG
14	21:14	CAP
17	08:20	AQU
19	16:39	PIS
21	22:37	ARI
24	03:06	TAU
26	06:42	GEM
28	09:41	CAN

MARCH

1	12:23	LEO
3	15:41	VIR
5	20:53	LIB
8	05:10	SCO
10	16:35	SAG
13	05:25	CAP
15	16:58	AQU
18	01:25	PIS
20	06:43	ARI
22	09:58	TAU
24	12:26	GEM
26	15:02	CAN
28	18:21	LEO
30	22:48	VIR

APRIL

2	05:00	LIB
4	13:34	SCO
7	00:42	SAG
9	13:25	CAP
12	01:32	AQU
14	10:50	PIS
16	16:29	ARI
18	19:08	TAU
20	20:15	GEM
22	21:22	CAN
24	23:49	LEO
27	04:22	VIR
29	11:19	LIB

MAY

1	20:37	SCO
4	08:00	SAG
6	20:39	CAP
9	09:09	AQU
11	19:32	PIS
14	02:24	ARI
16	05:35	TAU
18	06:13	GEM
20	06:01	CAN
22	06:50	LEO
24	10:11	VIR
26	16:50	LIB
29	02:33	SCO
31	14:21	SAG

JUNE

3	03:05	CAP
5	15:38	AQU
8	02:43	PIS
10	10:58	ARI
12	15:35	TAU
14	16:57	GEM
16	16:27	CAN
18	16:02	LEO
20	17:45	VIR
22	23:06	LIB
25	08:19	SCO
27	20:15	SAG
30	09:06	CAP

JULY

2	21:31	AQU
5	08:37	PIS
7	17:39	ARI
9	23:46	TAU
12	02:40	GEM
14	03:03	CAN
16	02:32	LEO
18	03:12	VIR
20	07:03	LIB
22	15:03	SCO
25	02:31	SAG
27	15:22	CAP
30	03:37	AQU

AUGUST

1	14:18	PIS
3	23:10	ARI
6	05:56	TAU
8	10:15	GEM
10	12:11	CAN
12	12:41	LEO
14	13:28	VIR
16	16:28	LIB
18	23:13	SCO
21	09:45	SAG
23	22:22	CAP
26	10:36	AQU
28	20:55	PIS
31	05:03	ARI

SEPTEMBER

2	11:20	TAU
4	15:58	GEM
6	19:04	CAN
8	21:02	LEO
10	22:55	VIR
13	02:11	LIB
15	08:19	SCO
17	17:58	SAG
20	06:09	CAP
22	18:33	AQU
25	04:58	PIS
27	12:35	ARI
29	17:49	TAU

OCTOBER

1	21:32	GEM
4	00:29	CAN
6	03:14	LEO
8	06:23	VIR
10	10:44	LIB
12	17:14	SCO
15	02:31	SAG
17	14:17	CAP
20	02:53	AQU
22	13:57	PIS
24	21:53	ARI
27	02:34	TAU
29	05:00	GEM
31	06:35	CAN

NOVEMBER

2	08:37	LEO
4	12:04	VIR
6	17:23	LIB
9	00:50	SCO
11	10:27	SAG
13	22:03	CAP
16	10:45	AQU
18	22:40	PIS
21	07:46	ARI
23	13:48	TAU
25	15:00	GEM
27	15:12	CAN
29	15:33	LEO

DECEMBER

1	17:45	VIR
3	22:50	LIB
6	06:51	SCO
8	17:10	SAG
11	05:00	CAP
13	17:39	AQU
16	06:04	PIS
18	16:30	ARI
20	23:22	TAU
23	02:15	GEM
25	02:13	CAN
27	01:16	LEO
29	01:38	VIR
31	05:07	LIB

1921

JANUARY			FEBRUARY			MARCH			APRIL		
2	12:27	SCO	1	05:04	SAG	3	00:04	CAP	1	20:22	AQU
4	22:58	SAG	3	17:14	CAP	5	12:46	AQU	4	08:28	PIS
7	11:10	CAP	6	05:59	AQU	8	00:44	PIS	6	18:31	ARI
9	23:50	AQU	8	18:04	PIS	10	10:58	ARI	9	02:00	TAU
12	12:11	PIS	11	04:52	ARI	12	19:15	TAU	11	07:16	GEM
14	23:15	ARI	13	13:45	TAU	15	01:29	GEM	13	10:59	CAN
17	07:40	TAU	15	19:55	GEM	17	05:36	CAN	15	13:48	LEO
19	12:24	GEM	17	22:58	CAN	19	07:52	LEO	17	16:21	VIR
21	13:36	CAN	19	23:34	LEO	21	09:08	VIR	19	19:25	LIB
23	12:45	LEO	21	23:21	VIR	23	10:50	LIB	21	23:54	SCO
25	12:04	VIR	24	00:21	LIB	25	14:34	SCO	24	06:45	SAG
27	13:47	LIB	26	04:28	SCO	27	21:34	SAG	26	16:28	CAP
29	19:25	SCO	28	12:37	SAG	30	07:58	CAP	29	04:26	AQU

MAY			JUNE			JULY			AUGUST		
1	16:47	PIS	2	20:04	TAU	2	10:23	GEM	2	22:11	LEO
4	03:14	ARI	5	00:17	GEM	4	11:56	CAN	4	21:19	VIR
6	10:32	TAU	7	01:47	CAN	6	11:34	LEO	6	21:52	LIB
8	14:51	GEM	9	02:19	LEO	8	11:26	VIR	9	01:33	SCO
10	17:19	CAN	11	03:41	VIR	10	13:28	LIB	11	09:00	SAG
12	19:17	LEO	13	07:10	LIB	12	18:43	SCO	13	19:30	CAP
14	21:52	VIR	15	13:11	SCO	15	03:05	SAG	16	07:42	AQU
17	01:47	LIB	17	21:28	SAG	17	13:43	CAP	18	20:20	PIS
19	07:22	SCO	20	07:39	CAP	20	01:44	AQU	21	08:30	ARI
21	14:53	SAG	22	19:24	AQU	22	14:24	PIS	23	19:07	TAU
24	00:35	CAP	25	08:04	PIS	25	02:42	ARI	26	02:58	GEM
26	12:17	AQU	27	20:03	ARI	27	12:58	TAU	28	07:18	CAN
29	00:51	PIS	30	05:14	TAU	29	19:37	GEM	30	08:31	LEO
31	12:05	ARI				31	22:18	CAN			

SEPTEMBER			OCTOBER			NOVEMBER			DECEMBER		
1	08:07	VIR	2	20:37	SCO	1	11:08	SAG	1	03:32	CAP
3	08:06	LIB	5	01:22	SAG	3	18:38	CAP	3	13:42	AQU
5	10:24	SCO	7	09:45	CAP	6	05:18	AQU	6	02:04	PIS
7	16:21	SAG	9	21:13	AQU	8	17:51	PIS	8	14:37	ARI
10	01:58	CAP	12	09:51	PIS	11	05:52	ARI	11	00:46	TAU
12	14:01	AQU	14	21:34	ARI	13	15:20	TAU	13	07:08	GEM
15	02:39	PIS	17	07:08	TAU	15	21:41	GEM	15	10:12	CAN
17	14:29	ARI	19	14:21	GEM	18	01:41	CAN	17	11:35	LEO
20	00:41	TAU	21	19:32	CAN	20	04:32	LEO	19	13:03	VIR
22	08:42	GEM	23	23:08	LEO	22	07:17	VIR	21	15:52	LIB
24	14:06	CAN	26	01:40	VIR	24	10:32	LIB	23	20:33	SCO
26	16:58	LEO	28	03:49	LIB	26	14:38	SCO	26	03:02	SAG
28	18:02	VIR	30	06:34	SCO	28	20:03	SAG	28	11:17	CAP
30	18:41	LIB							30	21:32	AQU

1922

JANUARY

2	09:45	PIS
4	22:42	ARI
7	09:59	TAU
9	17:27	GEM
11	20:47	CAN
13	21:21	LEO
15	21:13	VIR
17	22:21	LIB
20	02:02	SCO
22	08:33	SAG
24	17:29	CAP
27	04:17	AQU
29	16:34	PIS

FEBRUARY

1	05:36	ARI
3	17:41	TAU
6	02:42	GEM
8	07:30	CAN
10	08:40	LEO
12	07:58	VIR
14	07:35	LIB
16	09:23	SCO
18	14:32	SAG
20	23:05	CAP
23	10:12	AQU
25	22:45	PIS
28	11:42	ARI

MARCH

2	23:52	TAU
5	09:49	GEM
7	16:19	CAN
9	19:10	LEO
11	19:23	VIR
13	18:44	LIB
15	19:13	SCO
17	22:34	SAG
20	05:41	CAP
22	16:18	AQU
25	04:56	PIS
27	17:50	ARI
30	05:38	TAU

APRIL

1	15:29	GEM
3	22:46	CAN
6	03:13	LEO
8	05:09	VIR
10	05:36	LIB
12	06:07	SCO
14	08:26	SAG
16	14:02	CAP
18	23:28	AQU
21	11:44	PIS
24	00:38	ARI
26	12:08	TAU
28	21:20	GEM

MAY

1	04:12	CAN
3	09:05	LEO
5	12:19	VIR
7	14:22	LIB
9	16:01	SCO
11	18:32	SAG
13	23:26	CAP
16	07:46	AQU
18	19:21	PIS
21	08:13	ARI
23	19:46	TAU
26	04:29	GEM
28	10:27	CAN
30	14:34	LEO

JUNE

1	17:48	VIR
3	20:44	LIB
5	23:42	SCO
8	03:18	SAG
10	08:30	CAP
12	16:25	AQU
15	03:25	PIS
17	16:13	ARI
20	04:09	TAU
22	13:02	GEM
24	18:27	CAN
26	21:28	LEO
28	23:37	VIR

JULY

1	02:05	LIB
3	05:30	SCO
5	10:05	SAG
7	16:12	CAP
10	00:27	AQU
12	11:16	PIS
14	23:59	ARI
17	12:28	TAU
19	22:10	GEM
22	03:56	CAN
24	06:27	LEO
26	07:22	VIR
28	08:27	LIB
30	10:59	SCO

AUGUST

1	15:35	SAG
3	22:22	CAP
6	07:19	AQU
8	18:23	PIS
11	07:06	ARI
13	19:57	TAU
16	06:43	GEM
18	13:40	CAN
20	16:45	LEO
22	17:16	VIR
24	17:05	LIB
26	18:02	SCO
28	21:26	SAG
31	03:54	CAP

SEPTEMBER

2	13:12	AQU
5	00:42	PIS
7	13:29	ARI
10	02:24	TAU
12	13:51	GEM
14	22:13	CAN
17	02:48	LEO
19	04:08	VIR
21	03:44	LIB
23	03:28	SCO
25	05:11	SAG
27	10:16	CAP
29	19:03	AQU

OCTOBER

2	06:41	PIS
4	19:36	ARI
7	08:20	TAU
9	19:44	GEM
12	04:52	CAN
14	11:02	LEO
16	14:04	VIR
18	14:43	LIB
20	14:26	SCO
22	15:06	SAG
24	18:34	CAP
27	02:00	AQU
29	13:07	PIS

NOVEMBER

1	02:05	ARI
3	14:40	TAU
6	01:34	GEM
8	10:23	CAN
10	17:06	LEO
12	21:37	VIR
15	00:01	LIB
17	00:59	SCO
19	01:53	SAG
21	04:32	CAP
23	10:36	AQU
25	20:40	PIS
28	09:21	ARI
30	22:00	TAU

DECEMBER

3	08:34	GEM
5	16:34	CAN
7	22:33	LEO
10	03:09	VIR
12	06:40	LIB
14	09:14	SCO
16	11:28	SAG
18	14:35	CAP
20	20:08	AQU
23	05:14	PIS
25	17:23	ARI
28	06:13	TAU
30	17:03	GEM

1923

JANUARY		
2	00:40	CAN
4	05:34	LEO
6	09:00	VIR
8	11:59	LIB
10	15:05	SCO
12	18:34	SAG
14	22:57	CAP
17	05:06	AQU
19	13:58	PIS
22	01:37	ARI
24	14:34	TAU
27	02:08	GEM
29	10:19	CAN
31	14:57	LEO

FEBRUARY		
2	17:12	VIR
4	18:39	LIB
6	20:37	SCO
8	23:59	SAG
11	05:08	CAP
13	12:19	AQU
15	21:44	PIS
18	09:20	ARI
20	22:15	TAU
23	10:31	GEM
25	19:58	CAN
28	01:31	LEO

MARCH		
2	03:42	VIR
4	04:01	LIB
6	04:16	SCO
8	06:06	SAG
10	10:34	CAP
12	18:02	AQU
15	04:08	PIS
17	16:06	ARI
20	05:00	TAU
22	17:33	GEM
25	04:06	CAN
27	11:14	LEO
29	14:37	VIR
31	15:07	LIB

APRIL		
2	14:26	SCO
4	14:34	SAG
6	17:19	CAP
8	23:49	AQU
11	09:51	PIS
13	22:09	ARI
16	11:07	TAU
18	23:33	GEM
21	10:28	CAN
23	18:51	LEO
25	23:56	VIR
28	01:49	LIB
30	01:33	SCO

MAY		
2	00:59	SAG
4	02:15	CAP
6	07:05	AQU
8	16:07	PIS
11	04:13	ARI
13	17:15	TAU
16	05:27	GEM
18	16:03	CAN
21	00:41	LEO
23	06:54	VIR
25	10:25	LIB
27	11:35	SCO
29	11:38	SAG
31	12:28	CAP

JUNE		
2	16:04	AQU
4	23:43	PIS
7	11:03	ARI
9	23:57	TAU
12	12:03	GEM
14	22:10	CAN
17	06:12	LEO
19	12:23	VIR
21	16:44	LIB
23	19:21	SCO
25	20:47	SAG
27	22:20	CAP
30	01:44	AQU

JULY		
2	08:28	PIS
4	18:51	ARI
7	07:25	TAU
9	19:37	GEM
12	05:34	CAN
14	12:54	LEO
16	18:10	VIR
18	22:06	LIB
21	01:09	SCO
23	03:43	SAG
25	06:33	CAP
27	10:43	AQU
29	17:23	PIS

AUGUST		
1	03:11	ARI
3	15:22	TAU
6	03:48	GEM
8	14:08	CAN
10	21:19	LEO
13	01:44	VIR
15	04:27	LIB
17	06:38	SCO
19	09:12	SAG
21	12:49	CAP
23	18:03	AQU
26	01:25	PIS
28	11:15	ARI
30	23:12	TAU

SEPTEMBER		
2	11:51	GEM
4	22:59	CAN
7	06:54	LEO
9	11:17	VIR
11	13:03	LIB
13	13:47	SCO
15	15:06	SAG
17	18:14	CAP
19	23:53	AQU
22	08:03	PIS
24	18:24	ARI
27	06:23	TAU
29	19:06	GEM

OCTOBER		
2	07:01	CAN
4	16:15	LEO
6	21:41	VIR
8	23:36	LIB
10	23:25	SCO
12	23:09	SAG
15	00:43	CAP
17	05:30	AQU
19	13:43	PIS
22	00:33	ARI
24	12:48	TAU
27	01:29	GEM
29	13:39	CAN

NOVEMBER		
1	00:00	LEO
3	07:07	VIR
5	10:24	LIB
7	10:38	SCO
9	09:37	SAG
11	09:38	CAP
13	12:40	AQU
15	19:47	PIS
18	06:25	ARI
20	18:53	TAU
23	07:32	GEM
25	19:28	CAN
28	06:02	LEO
30	14:19	VIR

DECEMBER		
2	19:25	LIB
4	21:15	SCO
6	20:57	SAG
8	20:31	CAP
10	22:10	AQU
13	03:36	PIS
15	13:08	ARI
18	01:22	TAU
20	14:03	GEM
23	01:40	CAN
25	11:40	LEO
27	19:51	VIR
30	01:52	LIB

1924

JANUARY

1	05:23	SCO
3	06:48	SAG
5	07:22	CAP
7	08:54	AQU
9	13:14	PIS
11	21:23	ARI
14	08:49	TAU
16	21:28	GEM
19	09:06	CAN
21	18:34	LEO
24	01:49	VIR
26	07:14	LIB
28	11:09	SCO
30	13:53	SAG

FEBRUARY

1	16:03	CAP
3	18:43	AQU
5	23:12	PIS
8	06:37	ARI
10	17:10	TAU
13	05:35	GEM
15	17:34	CAN
18	03:09	LEO
20	09:46	VIR
22	13:57	LIB
24	16:47	SCO
26	19:16	SAG
28	22:13	CAP

MARCH

2	02:11	AQU
4	07:45	PIS
6	15:26	ARI
9	01:36	TAU
11	13:44	GEM
14	02:08	CAN
16	12:32	LEO
18	19:27	VIR
20	23:00	LIB
23	00:28	SCO
25	01:29	SAG
27	03:37	CAP
29	07:47	AQU
31	14:13	PIS

APRIL

2	22:46	ARI
5	09:12	TAU
7	21:13	GEM
10	09:53	CAN
12	21:15	LEO
15	05:21	VIR
17	09:27	LIB
19	10:24	SCO
21	10:05	SAG
23	10:33	CAP
25	13:30	AQU
27	19:39	PIS
30	04:39	ARI

MAY

2	15:37	TAU
5	03:48	GEM
7	16:31	CAN
10	04:30	LEO
12	13:57	VIR
14	19:29	LIB
16	21:11	SCO
18	20:34	SAG
20	19:49	CAP
22	21:05	AQU
25	01:50	PIS
27	10:16	ARI
29	21:23	TAU

JUNE

1	09:48	GEM
3	22:27	CAN
6	10:29	LEO
8	20:41	VIR
11	03:41	LIB
13	06:57	SCO
15	07:17	SAG
17	06:29	CAP
19	06:43	AQU
21	09:52	PIS
23	16:56	ARI
26	03:28	TAU
28	15:52	GEM

JULY

1	04:28	CAN
3	16:11	LEO
6	02:16	VIR
8	09:55	LIB
10	14:37	SCO
12	16:32	SAG
14	16:49	CAP
16	17:11	AQU
18	19:31	PIS
21	01:12	ARI
23	10:37	TAU
25	22:37	GEM
28	11:12	CAN
30	22:38	LEO

AUGUST

2	08:05	VIR
4	15:20	LIB
6	20:24	SCO
8	23:32	SAG
11	01:21	CAP
13	02:52	AQU
15	05:29	PIS
17	10:32	ARI
19	18:54	TAU
22	06:15	GEM
24	18:48	CAN
27	06:19	LEO
29	15:19	VIR
31	21:38	LIB

SEPTEMBER

3	01:55	SCO
5	05:01	SAG
7	07:41	CAP
9	10:33	AQU
11	14:17	PIS
13	19:42	ARI
16	03:39	TAU
18	14:24	GEM
21	02:55	CAN
23	14:53	LEO
26	00:07	VIR
28	05:54	LIB
30	09:00	SCO

OCTOBER

2	10:55	SAG
4	13:03	CAP
6	16:20	AQU
8	21:07	PIS
11	03:31	ARI
13	11:50	TAU
15	22:23	GEM
18	10:48	CAN
20	23:22	LEO
23	09:33	VIR
25	15:49	LIB
27	18:27	SCO
29	19:03	SAG
31	19:39	CAP

NOVEMBER

2	21:53	AQU
5	02:35	PIS
7	09:40	ARI
9	18:44	TAU
12	05:35	GEM
14	17:57	CAN
17	06:51	LEO
19	18:11	VIR
22	01:52	LIB
24	05:18	SCO
26	05:38	SAG
28	04:58	CAP
30	05:26	AQU

DECEMBER

2	08:39	PIS
4	15:11	ARI
7	00:34	TAU
9	11:53	GEM
12	00:21	CAN
14	13:13	LEO
17	01:07	VIR
19	10:15	LIB
21	15:26	SCO
23	16:56	SAG
25	16:19	CAP
27	15:41	AQU
29	17:06	PIS
31	21:57	ARI

1925

JANUARY			FEBRUARY			MARCH			APRIL		
3	06:31	TAU	2	00:33	GEM	1	08:26	GEM	2	17:33	LEO
5	17:53	GEM	4	13:11	CAN	3	20:38	CAN	5	04:55	VIR
8	06:33	CAN	7	01:50	LEO	6	09:23	LEO	7	13:05	LIB
10	19:14	LEO	9	13:01	VIR	8	20:24	VIR	9	18:04	SCO
13	06:55	VIR	11	22:06	LIB	11	04:44	LIB	11	21:06	SAG
15	16:33	LIB	14	04:55	SCO	13	10:38	SCO	13	23:32	CAP
17	23:12	SCO	16	09:28	SAG	15	14:52	SAG	16	02:23	AQU
20	02:34	SAG	18	12:02	CAP	17	18:07	CAP	18	06:03	PIS
22	03:23	CAP	20	13:21	AQU	19	20:51	AQU	20	10:45	ARI
24	03:09	AQU	22	14:37	PIS	21	23:34	PIS	22	17:00	TAU
26	03:46	PIS	24	17:22	ARI	24	03:04	ARI	25	01:33	GEM
28	07:00	ARI	26	23:04	TAU	26	08:35	TAU	27	12:46	CAN
30	13:58	TAU				28	17:08	GEM	30	01:37	LEO
						31	04:43	CAN			

MAY			JUNE			JULY			AUGUST		
2	13:38	VIR	1	07:31	LIB	3	01:55	SAG	1	12:47	CAP
4	22:26	LIB	3	13:22	SCO	5	02:24	CAP	3	12:41	AQU
7	03:22	SCO	5	15:34	SAG	7	01:49	AQU	5	12:23	PIS
9	05:28	SAG	7	15:45	CAP	9	02:06	PIS	7	13:46	ARI
11	06:30	CAP	9	15:54	AQU	11	04:53	ARI	9	18:25	TAU
13	08:09	AQU	11	17:40	PIS	13	11:05	TAU	12	02:57	GEM
15	11:24	PIS	13	22:03	ARI	15	20:38	GEM	14	14:39	CAN
17	16:35	ARI	16	05:16	TAU	18	08:33	CAN	17	03:41	LEO
19	23:42	TAU	18	14:57	GEM	20	21:32	LEO	19	16:13	VIR
22	08:51	GEM	21	02:37	CAN	23	10:18	VIR	22	03:06	LIB
24	20:08	CAN	23	15:31	LEO	25	21:30	LIB	24	11:45	SCO
27	08:59	LEO	26	04:22	VIR	28	05:57	SCO	26	17:50	SAG
29	21:36	VIR	28	15:15	LIB	30	10:56	SAG	28	21:19	CAP
			30	22:33	SCO				30	22:41	AQU

SEPTEMBER			OCTOBER			NOVEMBER			DECEMBER		
1	23:03	PIS	1	10:06	ARI	2	04:44	GEM	1	22:19	CAN
4	00:02	ARI	3	13:20	TAU	4	14:06	CAN	4	10:13	LEO
6	03:28	TAU	5	19:35	GEM	7	02:16	LEO	6	23:14	VIR
8	10:39	GEM	8	05:33	CAN	9	15:07	VIR	9	10:53	LIB
10	21:35	CAN	10	18:09	LEO	12	01:52	LIB	11	19:04	SCO
13	10:30	LEO	13	06:44	VIR	14	09:06	SCO	13	23:23	SAG
15	22:57	VIR	15	16:58	LIB	16	13:13	SAG	16	00:59	CAP
18	09:18	LIB	18	00:13	SCO	18	15:39	CAP	18	01:36	AQU
20	17:18	SCO	20	05:12	SAG	20	17:48	AQU	20	02:52	PIS
22	23:17	SAG	22	08:58	CAP	22	20:38	PIS	22	05:57	ARI
25	03:37	CAP	24	12:13	AQU	25	00:32	ARI	24	11:25	TAU
27	06:29	AQU	26	15:15	PIS	27	05:46	TAU	26	19:19	GEM
29	08:19	PIS	28	18:24	ARI	29	12:51	GEM	29	05:27	CAN
			30	22:29	TAU				31	17:27	LEO

1926

JANUARY
3	06:26	VIR
5	18:44	LIB
8	04:20	SCO
10	10:02	SAG
12	12:09	CAP
14	12:07	AQU
16	11:48	PIS
18	13:04	ARI
20	17:16	TAU
23	00:55	GEM
25	11:30	CAN
27	23:52	LEO
30	12:49	VIR

FEBRUARY
2	01:11	LIB
4	11:40	SCO
6	19:02	SAG
8	22:50	CAP
10	23:37	AQU
12	22:57	PIS
14	22:48	ARI
17	01:09	TAU
19	07:22	GEM
21	17:28	CAN
24	06:00	LEO
26	19:00	VIR

MARCH
1	07:04	LIB
3	17:28	SCO
6	01:40	SAG
8	07:07	CAP
10	09:40	AQU
12	10:04	PIS
14	09:52	ARI
16	11:07	TAU
18	15:42	GEM
21	00:31	CAN
23	12:36	LEO
26	01:37	VIR
28	13:27	LIB
30	23:17	SCO

APRIL
2	07:08	SAG
4	13:05	CAP
6	17:01	AQU
8	19:04	PIS
10	20:03	ARI
12	21:31	TAU
15	01:21	GEM
17	08:55	CAN
19	20:07	LEO
22	08:59	VIR
24	20:52	LIB
27	06:19	SCO
29	13:19	SAG

MAY
1	18:33	CAP
3	22:32	AQU
6	01:32	PIS
8	03:55	ARI
10	06:34	TAU
12	10:46	GEM
14	17:53	CAN
17	04:20	LEO
19	16:55	VIR
22	05:04	LIB
24	14:42	SCO
26	21:14	SAG
29	01:24	CAP
31	04:19	AQU

JUNE
2	06:53	PIS
4	09:46	ARI
6	13:29	TAU
8	18:43	GEM
11	02:15	CAN
13	12:29	LEO
16	00:49	VIR
18	13:19	LIB
20	23:40	SCO
23	06:35	SAG
25	10:18	CAP
27	12:01	AQU
29	13:14	PIS

JULY
1	15:14	ARI
3	18:59	TAU
6	00:57	GEM
8	09:17	CAN
10	19:51	LEO
13	08:08	VIR
15	20:52	LIB
18	08:08	SCO
20	16:11	SAG
22	20:28	CAP
24	21:48	AQU
26	21:46	PIS
28	22:13	ARI
31	00:47	TAU

AUGUST
2	06:25	GEM
4	15:08	CAN
7	02:13	LEO
9	14:39	VIR
12	03:27	LIB
14	15:18	SCO
17	00:40	SAG
19	06:24	CAP
21	08:31	AQU
23	08:14	PIS
25	07:30	ARI
27	08:25	TAU
29	12:40	GEM
31	20:49	CAN

SEPTEMBER
3	08:01	LEO
5	20:41	VIR
8	09:23	LIB
10	21:16	SCO
13	07:22	SAG
15	14:37	CAP
17	18:23	AQU
19	19:07	PIS
21	18:20	ARI
23	18:13	TAU
25	20:51	GEM
28	03:35	CAN
30	14:11	LEO

OCTOBER
3	02:49	VIR
5	15:29	LIB
8	02:59	SCO
10	12:54	SAG
12	20:47	CAP
15	02:03	AQU
17	04:30	PIS
19	04:56	ARI
21	05:01	TAU
23	06:50	GEM
25	12:09	CAN
27	21:31	LEO
30	09:43	VIR

NOVEMBER
1	22:23	LIB
4	09:38	SCO
6	18:52	SAG
9	02:11	CAP
11	07:42	AQU
13	11:22	PIS
15	13:28	ARI
17	14:54	TAU
19	17:10	GEM
21	21:55	CAN
24	06:10	LEO
26	17:36	VIR
29	06:14	LIB

DECEMBER
1	17:40	SCO
4	02:32	SAG
6	08:53	CAP
8	13:22	AQU
10	16:44	PIS
12	19:33	ARI
14	22:23	TAU
17	02:00	GEM
19	07:20	CAN
21	15:17	LEO
24	02:03	VIR
26	14:31	LIB
29	02:29	SCO
31	11:50	SAG

1927

JANUARY

2	17:52	CAP
4	21:11	AQU
6	23:06	PIS
9	01:00	ARI
11	03:56	TAU
13	08:31	GEM
15	14:59	CAN
17	23:32	LEO
20	10:10	VIR
22	22:27	LIB
25	10:54	SCO
27	21:21	SAG
30	04:12	CAP

FEBRUARY

1	07:22	AQU
3	08:07	PIS
5	08:20	ARI
7	09:51	TAU
9	13:55	GEM
11	20:51	CAN
14	06:12	LEO
16	17:16	VIR
19	05:31	LIB
21	18:09	SCO
24	05:35	SAG
26	13:56	CAP
28	18:14	AQU

MARCH

2	19:06	PIS
4	18:19	ARI
6	18:07	TAU
8	20:29	GEM
11	02:30	CAN
13	11:52	LEO
15	23:23	VIR
18	11:49	LIB
21	00:21	SCO
23	12:07	SAG
25	21:39	CAP
28	03:39	AQU
30	05:53	PIS

APRIL

1	05:31	ARI
3	04:36	TAU
5	05:25	GEM
7	09:43	CAN
9	18:00	LEO
12	05:19	VIR
14	17:54	LIB
17	06:20	SCO
19	17:49	SAG
22	03:36	CAP
24	10:43	AQU
26	14:38	PIS
28	15:44	ARI
30	15:29	TAU

MAY

2	15:53	GEM
4	18:52	CAN
7	01:39	LEO
9	12:03	VIR
12	00:27	LIB
14	12:52	SCO
16	23:58	SAG
19	09:11	CAP
21	16:16	AQU
23	21:02	PIS
25	23:38	ARI
28	00:51	TAU
30	02:03	GEM

JUNE

1	04:50	CAN
3	10:38	LEO
5	19:56	VIR
8	07:50	LIB
10	20:16	SCO
13	07:16	SAG
15	15:52	CAP
17	22:05	AQU
20	02:25	PIS
22	05:29	ARI
24	07:54	TAU
26	10:27	GEM
28	14:04	CAN
30	19:49	LEO

JULY

3	04:27	VIR
5	15:48	LIB
8	04:17	SCO
10	15:37	SAG
13	00:07	CAP
15	05:31	AQU
17	08:43	PIS
19	10:58	ARI
21	13:24	TAU
23	16:46	GEM
25	21:31	CAN
28	04:01	LEO
30	12:42	VIR

AUGUST

1	23:44	LIB
4	12:16	SCO
7	00:14	SAG
9	09:23	CAP
11	14:46	AQU
13	17:05	PIS
15	17:58	ARI
17	19:12	TAU
19	22:09	GEM
22	03:19	CAN
24	10:39	LEO
26	19:56	VIR
29	07:03	LIB
31	19:36	SCO

SEPTEMBER

3	08:10	SAG
5	18:29	CAP
8	00:50	AQU
10	03:16	PIS
12	03:18	ARI
14	03:03	TAU
16	04:29	GEM
18	08:50	CAN
20	16:13	LEO
23	02:02	VIR
25	13:30	LIB
28	02:06	SCO
30	14:54	SAG

OCTOBER

3	02:13	CAP
5	10:07	AQU
7	13:50	PIS
9	14:15	ARI
11	13:18	TAU
13	13:12	GEM
15	15:50	CAN
17	22:07	LEO
20	07:43	VIR
22	19:28	LIB
25	08:09	SCO
27	20:48	SAG
30	08:23	CAP

NOVEMBER

1	17:27	AQU
3	22:56	PIS
6	00:54	ARI
8	00:37	TAU
10	00:04	GEM
12	01:16	CAN
14	05:49	LEO
16	14:14	VIR
19	01:41	LIB
21	14:26	SCO
24	02:54	SAG
26	14:01	CAP
28	23:07	AQU

DECEMBER

1	05:37	PIS
3	09:20	ARI
5	10:47	TAU
7	11:11	GEM
9	12:11	CAN
11	15:32	LEO
13	22:25	VIR
16	08:55	LIB
18	21:32	SCO
21	09:59	SAG
23	20:38	CAP
26	04:55	AQU
28	11:00	PIS
30	15:19	ARI

1928

JANUARY		
1	18:15	TAU
3	20:20	GEM
5	22:28	CAN
8	01:53	LEO
10	07:54	VIR
12	17:18	LIB
15	05:27	SCO
17	18:07	SAG
20	04:50	CAP
22	12:28	AQU
24	17:25	PIS
26	20:48	ARI
28	23:43	TAU
31	02:47	GEM

FEBRUARY		
2	06:22	CAN
4	10:53	LEO
6	17:10	VIR
9	02:04	LIB
11	13:42	SCO
14	02:32	SAG
16	13:54	CAP
18	21:47	AQU
21	02:06	PIS
23	04:09	ARI
25	05:42	TAU
27	08:08	GEM
29	12:05	CAN

MARCH		
2	17:38	LEO
5	00:52	VIR
7	10:05	LIB
9	21:31	SCO
12	10:25	SAG
14	22:34	CAP
17	07:31	AQU
19	12:20	PIS
21	13:54	ARI
23	14:06	TAU
25	14:54	GEM
27	17:42	CAN
29	23:05	LEO

APRIL		
1	06:54	VIR
3	16:47	LIB
6	04:28	SCO
8	17:20	SAG
11	05:57	CAP
13	16:07	AQU
15	22:20	PIS
18	00:40	ARI
20	00:36	TAU
22	00:09	GEM
24	01:14	CAN
26	05:12	LEO
28	12:29	VIR
30	22:36	LIB

MAY		
3	10:38	SCO
5	23:33	SAG
8	12:09	CAP
10	22:58	AQU
13	06:35	PIS
15	10:30	ARI
17	11:26	TAU
19	10:57	GEM
21	10:58	CAN
23	13:17	LEO
25	19:07	VIR
28	04:37	LIB
30	16:41	SCO

JUNE		
2	05:38	SAG
4	18:00	CAP
7	04:41	AQU
9	12:55	PIS
11	18:14	ARI
13	20:46	TAU
15	21:24	GEM
17	21:35	CAN
19	23:03	LEO
22	03:27	VIR
24	11:43	LIB
26	23:17	SCO
29	12:14	SAG

JULY		
2	00:24	CAP
4	10:32	AQU
6	18:23	PIS
9	00:04	ARI
11	03:49	TAU
13	06:00	GEM
15	07:20	CAN
17	09:06	LEO
19	12:53	VIR
21	20:02	LIB
24	06:48	SCO
26	19:35	SAG
29	07:47	CAP
31	17:34	AQU

AUGUST		
3	00:35	PIS
5	05:33	ARI
7	09:19	TAU
9	12:22	GEM
11	15:04	CAN
13	17:57	LEO
15	22:08	VIR
18	04:53	LIB
20	14:57	SCO
23	03:29	SAG
25	15:59	CAP
28	01:57	AQU
30	08:31	PIS

SEPTEMBER		
1	12:27	ARI
3	15:07	TAU
5	17:43	GEM
7	20:52	CAN
10	00:50	LEO
12	06:02	VIR
14	13:13	LIB
16	23:05	SCO
19	11:24	SAG
22	00:16	CAP
24	11:02	AQU
26	18:02	PIS
28	21:31	ARI
30	23:00	TAU

OCTOBER		
3	00:10	GEM
5	02:21	CAN
7	06:18	LEO
9	12:14	VIR
11	20:15	LIB
14	06:29	SCO
16	18:45	SAG
19	07:51	CAP
21	19:34	AQU
24	03:50	PIS
26	08:05	ARI
28	09:16	TAU
30	09:11	GEM

NOVEMBER		
1	09:41	CAN
3	12:14	LEO
5	17:42	VIR
8	02:05	LIB
10	12:54	SCO
13	01:21	SAG
15	14:26	CAP
18	02:40	AQU
20	12:20	PIS
22	18:14	ARI
24	20:31	TAU
26	20:24	GEM
28	19:44	CAN
30	20:29	LEO

DECEMBER		
3	00:17	VIR
5	07:53	LIB
7	18:46	SCO
10	07:30	SAG
12	20:30	CAP
15	08:36	AQU
17	18:49	PIS
20	02:16	ARI
22	06:25	TAU
24	07:40	GEM
26	07:17	CAN
28	07:07	LEO
30	09:13	VIR

1929

JANUARY			FEBRUARY			MARCH			APRIL		
1	15:09	LIB	2	20:59	SAG	2	05:03	SAG	1	02:03	CAP
4	01:10	SCO	5	10:01	CAP	4	17:55	CAP	3	14:18	AQU
6	13:50	SAG	7	21:35	AQU	7	05:45	AQU	5	23:52	PIS
9	02:51	CAP	10	06:43	PIS	9	14:44	PIS	8	05:58	ARI
11	14:33	AQU	12	13:41	ARI	11	20:52	ARI	10	09:17	TAU
14	00:22	PIS	14	19:02	TAU	14	01:05	TAU	12	11:13	GEM
16	08:07	ARI	16	23:02	GEM	16	04:24	GEM	14	13:05	CAN
18	13:37	TAU	19	01:45	CAN	18	07:24	CAN	16	15:51	LEO
20	16:44	GEM	21	03:41	LEO	20	10:28	LEO	18	20:06	VIR
22	17:52	CAN	23	05:59	VIR	22	14:05	VIR	21	02:14	LIB
24	18:17	LEO	25	10:15	LIB	24	19:12	LIB	23	10:35	SCO
26	19:48	VIR	27	17:54	SCO	27	02:50	SCO	25	21:16	SAG
29	00:19	LIB				29	13:26	SAG	28	09:43	CAP
31	08:57	SCO							30	22:19	AQU

MAY			JUNE			JULY			AUGUST		
3	08:51	PIS	2	00:58	ARI	1	14:32	TAU	2	03:16	CAN
5	15:51	ARI	4	05:35	TAU	3	17:14	GEM	4	03:11	LEO
7	19:18	TAU	6	06:57	GEM	5	17:21	CAN	6	03:23	VIR
9	20:22	GEM	8	06:35	CAN	7	16:37	LEO	8	05:56	LIB
11	20:45	CAN	10	06:25	LEO	9	17:10	VIR	10	12:22	SCO
13	22:03	LEO	12	08:20	VIR	11	20:54	LIB	12	22:45	SAG
16	01:34	VIR	14	13:39	LIB	14	04:45	SCO	15	11:21	CAP
18	07:53	LIB	16	22:33	SCO	16	16:00	SAG	17	23:50	AQU
20	16:54	SCO	19	10:03	SAG	19	04:48	CAP	20	10:46	PIS
23	04:04	SAG	21	22:45	CAP	21	17:20	AQU	22	19:47	ARI
25	16:35	CAP	24	11:24	AQU	24	04:40	PIS	25	02:56	TAU
28	05:18	AQU	26	22:59	PIS	26	14:13	ARI	27	08:03	GEM
30	16:38	PIS	29	08:22	ARI	28	21:25	TAU	29	11:04	CAN
						31	01:43	GEM	31	12:27	LEO

SEPTEMBER			OCTOBER			NOVEMBER			DECEMBER		
2	13:27	VIR	2	01:10	LIB	2	23:47	SAG	2	18:26	CAP
4	15:51	LIB	4	06:40	SCO	5	10:57	CAP	5	06:58	AQU
6	21:21	SCO	6	15:19	SAG	7	23:33	AQU	7	19:28	PIS
9	06:39	SAG	9	02:50	CAP	10	11:31	PIS	10	05:58	ARI
11	18:45	CAP	11	15:26	AQU	12	20:43	ARI	12	12:50	TAU
14	07:17	AQU	14	02:40	PIS	15	02:19	TAU	14	15:49	GEM
16	18:07	PIS	16	11:02	ARI	17	04:53	GEM	16	16:05	CAN
19	02:31	ARI	18	16:29	TAU	19	05:53	CAN	18	15:35	LEO
21	08:46	TAU	20	19:55	GEM	21	06:58	LEO	20	16:22	VIR
23	13:25	GEM	22	22:24	CAN	23	09:32	VIR	22	20:03	LIB
25	16:52	CAN	25	00:55	LEO	25	14:23	LIB	25	03:12	SCO
27	19:28	LEO	27	04:09	VIR	27	21:40	SCO	27	13:12	SAG
29	21:52	VIR	29	08:39	LIB	30	07:08	SAG	30	00:56	CAP
			31	15:02	SCO						

1930

JANUARY		FEBRUARY		MARCH		APRIL	
1	13:30 AQU	2	19:23 ARI	2	01:09 ARI	2	22:43 GEM
4	02:05 PIS	5	04:49 TAU	4	10:19 TAU	5	03:11 CAN
6	13:28 ARI	7	11:08 GEM	6	17:16 GEM	7	06:09 LEO
8	21:59 TAU	9	13:56 CAN	8	21:35 CAN	9	08:11 VIR
11	02:35 GEM	11	14:01 LEO	10	23:26 LEO	11	10:17 LIB
13	03:35 CAN	13	13:14 VIR	12	23:54 VIR	13	13:45 SCO
15	02:38 LEO	15	13:51 LIB	15	00:44 LIB	15	19:50 SAG
17	01:57 VIR	17	17:45 SCO	17	05:04 SCO	18	05:08 CAP
19	03:45 LIB	20	01:49 SAG	19	10:24 SAG	20	16:59 AQU
21	09:25 SCO	22	13:13 CAP	21	20:40 CAP	23	05:24 PIS
23	18:56 SAG	25	01:57 AQU	24	09:05 AQU	25	16:10 ARI
26	06:53 CAP	27	14:13 PIS	26	21:24 PIS	28	00:09 TAU
28	19:35 AQU			29	08:00 ARI	30	05:26 GEM
31	07:59 PIS			31	16:24 TAU		

MAY		JUNE		JULY		AUGUST	
2	08:54 CAN	2	19:37 VIR	2	04:47 LIB	2	23:25 SAG
4	11:32 LEO	4	23:04 LIB	4	09:56 SCO	5	09:35 CAP
6	14:11 VIR	7	04:30 SCO	6	17:50 SAG	7	21:27 AQU
8	17:30 LIB	9	11:56 SAG	9	03:50 CAP	10	10:03 PIS
10	22:07 SCO	11	21:21 CAP	11	15:23 AQU	12	22:33 ARI
13	04:39 SAG	14	08:39 AQU	14	03:58 PIS	15	09:38 TAU
15	13:40 CAP	16	21:12 PIS	16	16:26 ARI	17	17:46 GEM
18	01:04 AQU	19	09:15 ARI	19	02:55 TAU	19	22:02 CAN
20	13:34 PIS	21	18:36 TAU	21	09:40 GEM	21	22:58 LEO
23	00:56 ARI	24	00:01 GEM	23	12:23 CAN	23	22:14 VIR
25	09:16 TAU	26	01:58 CAN	25	12:19 LEO	25	21:58 LIB
27	14:07 GEM	28	02:07 LEO	27	11:35 VIR	28	00:11 SCO
29	16:26 CAN	30	02:29 VIR	29	12:18 LIB	30	06:05 SAG
31	17:45 LEO			31	16:05 SCO		

SEPTEMBER		OCTOBER		NOVEMBER		DECEMBER	
1	15:36 CAP	1	10:10 AQU	2	18:35 ARI	2	13:32 TAU
4	03:28 AQU	3	22:48 PIS	5	04:38 TAU	4	20:32 GEM
6	16:07 PIS	6	10:52 ARI	7	11:59 GEM	7	00:32 CAN
9	04:22 ARI	8	21:15 TAU	9	17:05 CAN	9	02:53 LEO
11	15:18 TAU	11	05:30 GEM	11	20:46 LEO	11	05:04 VIR
14	00:01 GEM	13	11:30 CAN	13	23:42 VIR	13	08:05 LIB
16	05:43 CAN	15	15:20 LEO	16	02:27 LIB	15	12:20 SCO
18	08:19 LEO	17	17:26 VIR	18	05:37 SCO	17	17:55 SAG
20	08:46 VIR	19	18:44 LIB	20	10:01 SAG	20	01:12 CAP
22	08:44 LIB	21	20:33 SCO	22	16:42 CAP	22	10:44 AQU
24	10:08 SCO	24	00:23 SAG	25	02:23 AQU	24	22:36 PIS
26	14:35 SAG	26	07:27 CAP	27	14:33 PIS	27	11:30 ARI
28	22:49 CAP	28	17:54 AQU	30	03:07 ARI	29	22:52 TAU
		31	06:23 PIS				

1931

JANUARY		
1	06:35	GEM
3	10:21	CAN
5	11:32	LEO
7	12:06	VIR
9	13:49	LIB
11	17:41	SCO
13	23:51	SAG
16	08:02	CAP
18	18:04	AQU
21	05:55	PIS
23	18:55	ARI
26	07:10	TAU
28	16:19	GEM
30	21:10	CAN

FEBRUARY		
1	22:25	LEO
3	21:57	VIR
5	21:55	LIB
8	00:05	SCO
10	05:22	SAG
12	13:39	CAP
15	00:15	AQU
17	12:24	PIS
20	01:21	ARI
22	13:54	TAU
25	00:13	GEM
27	06:47	CAN

MARCH		
1	09:25	LEO
3	09:21	VIR
5	08:33	LIB
7	09:03	SCO
9	12:30	SAG
11	19:39	CAP
14	06:04	AQU
16	18:27	PIS
19	07:24	ARI
21	19:45	TAU
24	06:19	GEM
26	14:05	CAN
28	18:29	LEO
30	19:58	VIR

APRIL		
1	19:50	LIB
3	19:51	SCO
5	21:52	SAG
8	03:21	CAP
10	12:40	AQU
13	00:49	PIS
15	13:48	ARI
18	01:51	TAU
20	11:56	GEM
22	19:43	CAN
25	01:04	LEO
27	04:10	VIR
29	05:35	LIB

MAY		
1	06:26	SCO
3	08:14	SAG
5	12:36	CAP
7	20:37	AQU
10	08:02	PIS
12	20:57	ARI
15	08:55	TAU
17	18:27	GEM
20	01:26	CAN
22	06:28	LEO
24	10:07	VIR
26	12:51	LIB
28	15:08	SCO
30	17:48	SAG

JUNE		
1	22:08	CAP
4	05:24	AQU
6	16:01	PIS
9	04:44	ARI
11	16:55	TAU
14	02:22	GEM
16	08:38	CAN
18	12:37	LEO
20	15:33	VIR
22	18:23	LIB
24	21:35	SCO
27	01:27	SAG
29	06:35	CAP

JULY		
1	13:57	AQU
4	00:10	PIS
6	12:40	ARI
9	01:14	TAU
11	11:14	GEM
13	17:31	CAN
15	20:42	LEO
17	22:22	VIR
20	00:06	LIB
22	02:57	SCO
24	07:19	SAG
26	13:23	CAP
28	21:25	AQU
31	07:46	PIS

AUGUST		
2	20:10	ARI
5	09:05	TAU
7	20:02	GEM
10	03:11	CAN
12	06:31	LEO
14	07:26	VIR
16	07:45	LIB
18	09:11	SCO
20	12:47	SAG
22	18:59	CAP
25	03:38	AQU
27	14:28	PIS
30	02:57	ARI

SEPTEMBER		
1	15:59	TAU
4	03:44	GEM
6	12:15	CAN
8	16:48	LEO
10	18:04	VIR
12	17:43	LIB
14	17:41	SCO
16	19:40	SAG
19	00:48	CAP
21	09:18	AQU
23	20:29	PIS
26	09:10	ARI
28	22:07	TAU

OCTOBER		
1	10:04	GEM
3	19:38	CAN
6	01:50	LEO
8	04:35	VIR
10	04:50	LIB
12	04:17	SCO
14	04:51	SAG
16	08:19	CAP
18	15:39	AQU
21	02:33	PIS
23	15:21	ARI
26	04:12	TAU
28	15:48	GEM
31	01:27	CAN

NOVEMBER		
2	08:40	LEO
4	13:08	VIR
6	15:03	LIB
8	15:21	SCO
10	15:39	SAG
12	17:52	CAP
14	23:41	AQU
17	09:33	PIS
19	22:09	ARI
22	11:00	TAU
24	22:12	GEM
27	07:10	CAN
29	14:06	LEO

DECEMBER		
1	19:17	VIR
3	22:45	LIB
6	00:43	SCO
8	02:04	SAG
10	04:18	CAP
12	09:10	AQU
14	17:51	PIS
17	05:50	ARI
19	18:46	TAU
22	06:00	GEM
24	14:22	CAN
26	20:17	LEO
29	00:41	VIR
31	04:18	LIB

1932

JANUARY			FEBRUARY			MARCH			APRIL		
2	07:24	SCO	2	20:39	CAP	1	02:07	CAP	2	00:05	PIS
4	10:16	SAG	5	02:49	AQU	3	09:01	AQU	4	11:53	ARI
6	13:37	CAP	7	11:15	PIS	5	18:16	PIS	7	00:44	TAU
8	18:44	AQU	9	22:18	ARI	8	05:36	ARI	9	13:27	GEM
11	02:50	PIS	12	11:05	TAU	10	18:20	TAU	12	00:47	CAN
13	14:08	ARI	14	23:28	GEM	13	07:03	GEM	14	09:22	LEO
16	03:03	TAU	17	09:03	CAN	15	17:46	CAN	16	14:22	VIR
18	14:48	GEM	19	14:49	LEO	18	00:56	LEO	18	16:00	LIB
20	23:23	CAN	21	17:25	VIR	20	04:19	VIR	20	15:34	SCO
23	04:40	LEO	23	18:22	LIB	22	04:57	LIB	22	14:58	SAG
25	07:47	VIR	25	19:20	SCO	24	04:35	SCO	24	16:15	CAP
27	10:08	LIB	27	21:39	SAG	26	05:07	SAG	26	21:05	AQU
29	12:43	SCO				28	08:08	CAP	29	05:56	PIS
31	16:07	SAG				30	14:31	AQU			

MAY			JUNE			JULY			AUGUST		
1	17:47	ARI	3	01:33	GEM	2	19:07	CAN	1	10:57	LEO
4	06:46	TAU	5	12:21	CAN	5	03:19	LEO	3	16:15	VIR
6	19:20	GEM	7	21:15	LEO	7	09:33	VIR	5	19:56	LIB
9	06:35	CAN	10	04:07	VIR	9	14:13	LIB	7	22:50	SCO
11	15:47	LEO	12	08:42	LIB	11	17:28	SCO	10	01:32	SAG
13	22:14	VIR	14	11:00	SCO	13	19:38	SAG	12	04:39	CAP
16	01:33	LIB	16	11:46	SAG	15	21:36	CAP	14	08:54	AQU
18	02:15	SCO	18	12:31	CAP	18	00:45	AQU	16	15:14	PIS
20	01:48	SAG	20	15:12	AQU	20	06:35	PIS	19	00:18	ARI
22	02:13	CAP	22	21:26	PIS	22	15:52	ARI	21	11:56	TAU
24	05:31	AQU	25	07:34	ARI	25	03:55	TAU	24	00:34	GEM
26	12:58	PIS	27	20:08	TAU	27	16:27	GEM	26	11:50	CAN
29	00:09	ARI	30	08:35	GEM	30	03:08	CAN	28	20:03	LEO
31	13:05	TAU							31	00:59	VIR

SEPTEMBER			OCTOBER			NOVEMBER			DECEMBER		
2	03:32	LIB	1	13:44	SCO	1	23:55	CAP	1	11:47	AQU
4	05:06	SCO	3	14:03	SAG	4	03:06	AQU	3	17:08	PIS
6	07:00	SAG	5	16:00	CAP	6	10:07	PIS	6	02:35	ARI
8	10:12	CAP	7	20:44	AQU	8	20:25	ARI	8	14:42	TAU
10	15:16	AQU	10	04:27	PIS	11	08:34	TAU	11	03:26	GEM
12	22:31	PIS	12	14:36	ARI	13	21:14	GEM	13	15:28	CAN
15	08:01	ARI	15	02:24	TAU	16	09:32	CAN	16	02:13	LEO
17	19:34	TAU	17	15:03	GEM	18	20:36	LEO	18	11:09	VIR
20	08:14	GEM	20	03:27	CAN	21	05:09	VIR	20	17:32	LIB
22	20:14	CAN	22	13:57	LEO	23	10:08	LIB	22	20:53	SCO
25	05:32	LEO	24	21:03	VIR	25	11:38	SCO	24	21:43	SAG
27	11:07	VIR	27	00:16	LIB	27	10:59	SAG	26	21:31	CAP
29	13:22	LIB	29	00:31	SCO	29	10:17	CAP	28	22:23	AQU
			30	23:40	SAG				31	02:17	PIS

1933

JANUARY			FEBRUARY			MARCH			APRIL		
2	10:14	ARI	1	05:40	TAU	3	02:18	GEM	1	22:50	CAN
4	21:37	TAU	3	18:05	GEM	5	14:43	CAN	4	10:17	LEO
7	10:20	GEM	6	06:14	CAN	8	01:18	LEO	6	18:33	VIR
9	22:17	CAN	8	16:17	LEO	10	08:42	VIR	8	23:01	LIB
12	08:27	LEO	10	23:43	VIR	12	13:03	LIB	11	00:32	SCO
14	16:42	VIR	13	04:59	LIB	14	15:28	SCO	13	00:52	SAG
16	23:03	LIB	15	08:47	SCO	16	17:19	SAG	15	01:54	CAP
19	03:25	SCO	17	11:43	SAG	18	19:47	CAP	17	05:03	AQU
21	05:55	SAG	19	14:23	CAP	20	23:39	AQU	19	10:54	PIS
23	07:18	CAP	21	17:29	AQU	23	05:16	PIS	21	19:14	ARI
25	08:57	AQU	23	21:56	PIS	25	12:50	ARI	24	05:31	TAU
27	12:31	PIS	26	04:43	ARI	27	22:32	TAU	26	17:18	GEM
29	19:21	ARI	28	14:20	TAU	30	10:14	GEM	29	05:59	CAN

MAY			JUNE			JULY			AUGUST		
1	18:07	LEO	2	18:15	LIB	2	05:57	SCO	2	16:41	CAP
4	03:41	VIR	4	21:25	SCO	4	07:32	SAG	4	17:22	AQU
6	09:17	LIB	6	21:32	SAG	6	07:16	CAP	6	19:11	PIS
8	11:07	SCO	8	20:33	CAP	8	07:05	AQU	8	23:41	ARI
10	10:43	SAG	10	20:41	AQU	10	09:02	PIS	11	07:45	TAU
12	10:15	CAP	12	23:50	PIS	12	14:31	ARI	13	18:58	GEM
14	11:46	AQU	15	06:51	ARI	14	23:49	TAU	16	07:33	CAN
16	16:34	PIS	17	17:12	TAU	17	11:45	GEM	18	19:23	LEO
19	00:46	ARI	20	05:26	GEM	20	00:25	CAN	21	05:08	VIR
21	11:27	TAU	22	18:07	CAN	22	12:19	LEO	23	12:30	LIB
23	23:32	GEM	25	06:17	LEO	24	22:36	VIR	25	17:45	SCO
26	12:12	CAN	27	17:01	VIR	27	06:45	LIB	27	21:21	SAG
29	00:34	LEO	30	01:11	LIB	29	12:22	SCO	29	23:52	CAP
31	11:06	VIR				31	15:27	SAG			

SEPTEMBER			OCTOBER			NOVEMBER			DECEMBER		
1	02:00	AQU	2	17:51	ARI	1	08:53	TAU	1	01:45	GEM
3	04:44	PIS	5	01:18	TAU	3	19:02	GEM	3	13:53	CAN
5	09:15	ARI	7	11:18	GEM	6	07:05	CAN	6	02:49	LEO
7	16:35	TAU	9	23:30	CAN	8	19:58	LEO	8	15:00	VIR
10	03:01	GEM	12	12:02	LEO	11	07:24	VIR	11	00:19	LIB
12	15:25	CAN	14	22:25	VIR	13	15:13	LIB	13	05:27	SCO
15	03:31	LEO	17	05:08	LIB	15	18:52	SCO	15	06:49	SAG
17	13:14	VIR	19	08:28	SCO	17	19:35	SAG	17	06:08	CAP
19	19:52	LIB	21	09:54	SAG	19	19:24	CAP	19	05:38	AQU
22	00:00	SCO	23	11:14	CAP	21	20:21	AQU	21	07:15	PIS
24	02:49	SAG	25	13:49	AQU	23	23:50	PIS	23	12:16	ARI
26	05:23	CAP	27	18:18	PIS	26	06:13	ARI	25	20:43	TAU
28	08:27	AQU	30	00:41	ARI	28	15:03	TAU	28	07:43	GEM
30	12:27	PIS							30	20:07	CAN

1934

JANUARY		
2	08:56	LEO
4	21:09	VIR
7	07:21	LIB
9	14:11	SCO
11	17:18	SAG
13	17:37	CAP
15	16:56	AQU
17	17:18	PIS
19	20:28	ARI
22	03:27	TAU
24	13:54	GEM
27	02:24	CAN
29	15:12	LEO

FEBRUARY		
1	03:01	VIR
3	13:00	LIB
5	20:32	SCO
8	01:15	SAG
10	03:24	CAP
12	03:57	AQU
14	04:28	PIS
16	06:40	ARI
18	12:04	TAU
20	21:17	GEM
23	09:23	CAN
25	22:14	LEO
28	09:46	VIR

MARCH		
2	19:02	LIB
5	01:59	SCO
7	06:59	SAG
9	10:22	CAP
11	12:36	AQU
13	14:26	PIS
15	17:00	ARI
17	21:46	TAU
20	05:52	GEM
22	17:13	CAN
25	06:03	LEO
27	17:45	VIR
30	02:37	LIB

APRIL		
1	08:36	SCO
3	12:37	SAG
5	15:46	CAP
7	18:43	AQU
9	21:52	PIS
12	01:40	ARI
14	06:56	TAU
16	14:42	GEM
19	01:27	CAN
21	14:10	LEO
24	02:20	VIR
26	11:33	LIB
28	17:07	SCO
30	20:02	SAG

MAY		
2	21:54	CAP
5	00:06	AQU
7	03:26	PIS
9	08:09	ARI
11	14:24	TAU
13	22:38	GEM
16	09:18	CAN
18	21:55	LEO
21	10:36	VIR
23	20:43	LIB
26	02:52	SCO
28	05:29	SAG
30	06:12	CAP

JUNE		
1	06:56	AQU
3	09:07	PIS
5	13:32	ARI
7	20:17	TAU
10	05:14	GEM
12	16:14	CAN
15	04:53	LEO
17	17:52	VIR
20	04:59	LIB
22	12:25	SCO
24	15:50	SAG
26	16:25	CAP
28	16:03	AQU
30	16:38	PIS

JULY		
2	19:39	ARI
5	01:48	TAU
7	10:56	GEM
9	22:21	CAN
12	11:08	LEO
15	00:07	VIR
17	11:48	LIB
19	20:31	SCO
22	01:28	SAG
24	03:04	CAP
26	02:44	AQU
28	02:21	PIS
30	03:46	ARI

AUGUST		
1	08:25	TAU
3	16:49	GEM
6	04:13	CAN
8	17:08	LEO
11	05:59	VIR
13	17:33	LIB
16	02:51	SCO
18	09:12	SAG
20	12:27	CAP
22	13:19	AQU
24	13:08	PIS
26	13:44	ARI
28	16:55	TAU
30	23:56	GEM

SEPTEMBER		
2	10:41	CAN
4	23:32	LEO
7	12:17	VIR
9	23:23	LIB
12	08:20	SCO
14	15:04	SAG
16	19:36	CAP
18	22:07	AQU
20	23:14	PIS
23	00:13	ARI
25	02:47	TAU
27	08:34	GEM
29	18:15	CAN

OCTOBER		
2	06:45	LEO
4	19:31	VIR
7	06:21	LIB
9	14:32	SCO
11	20:32	SAG
14	01:04	CAP
16	04:32	AQU
18	07:10	PIS
20	09:29	ARI
22	12:35	TAU
24	17:58	GEM
27	02:46	CAN
29	14:43	LEO

NOVEMBER		
1	03:36	VIR
3	14:41	LIB
5	22:33	SCO
8	03:33	SAG
10	06:57	CAP
12	09:52	AQU
14	12:57	PIS
16	16:26	ARI
18	20:47	TAU
21	02:48	GEM
23	11:26	CAN
25	22:54	LEO
28	11:52	VIR
30	23:39	LIB

DECEMBER		
3	08:06	SCO
5	12:53	SAG
7	15:09	CAP
9	16:34	AQU
11	18:31	PIS
13	21:51	ARI
16	02:57	TAU
18	09:58	GEM
20	19:11	CAN
23	06:38	LEO
25	19:32	VIR
28	08:00	LIB
30	17:42	SCO

1935

JANUARY			FEBRUARY			MARCH			APRIL		
1	23:27	SAG	2	13:26	AQU	2	00:16	AQU	2	10:32	ARI
4	01:44	CAP	4	12:47	PIS	4	00:13	PIS	4	11:18	TAU
6	02:04	AQU	6	12:49	ARI	5	23:41	ARI	6	14:35	GEM
8	02:18	PIS	8	15:23	TAU	8	00:43	TAU	8	21:49	CAN
10	04:03	ARI	10	21:36	GEM	10	05:12	GEM	11	08:52	LEO
12	08:25	TAU	13	07:24	CAN	12	13:52	CAN	13	21:47	VIR
14	15:43	GEM	15	19:35	LEO	15	01:48	LEO	16	10:01	LIB
17	01:38	CAN	18	08:33	VIR	17	14:52	VIR	18	20:10	SCO
19	13:27	LEO	20	21:03	LIB	20	03:08	LIB	21	04:06	SAG
22	02:20	VIR	23	08:05	SCO	22	13:45	SCO	23	10:14	CAP
24	15:00	LIB	25	16:41	SAG	24	22:24	SAG	25	14:44	AQU
27	01:46	SCO	27	22:05	CAP	27	04:49	CAP	27	17:40	PIS
29	09:11	SAG				29	08:42	AQU	29	19:27	ARI
31	12:48	CAP				31	10:15	PIS			

MAY			JUNE			JULY			AUGUST		
1	21:10	TAU	2	15:44	CAN	2	09:13	LEO	1	04:07	VIR
4	00:26	GEM	5	01:20	LEO	4	21:09	VIR	3	16:55	LIB
6	06:51	CAN	7	13:26	VIR	7	09:53	LIB	6	04:57	SCO
8	16:55	LEO	10	02:00	LIB	9	21:15	SCO	8	14:25	SAG
11	05:26	VIR	12	12:36	SCO	12	05:28	SAG	10	20:10	CAP
13	17:48	LIB	14	19:57	SAG	14	10:03	CAP	12	22:22	AQU
16	03:55	SCO	17	00:21	CAP	16	11:54	AQU	14	22:19	PIS
18	11:13	SAG	19	02:56	AQU	18	12:31	PIS	16	21:55	ARI
20	16:21	CAP	21	04:56	PIS	20	13:33	ARI	18	23:08	TAU
22	20:09	AQU	23	07:21	ARI	22	16:21	TAU	21	03:26	GEM
24	23:14	PIS	25	10:54	TAU	24	21:42	GEM	23	11:17	CAN
27	01:59	ARI	27	16:07	GEM	27	05:44	CAN	25	22:01	LEO
29	04:59	TAU	29	23:27	CAN	29	16:04	LEO	28	10:21	VIR
31	09:11	GEM							30	23:08	LIB

SEPTEMBER			OCTOBER			NOVEMBER			DECEMBER		
2	11:22	SCO	2	03:41	SAG	2	23:38	AQU	2	09:03	PIS
4	21:49	SAG	4	12:03	CAP	5	03:21	PIS	4	11:53	ARI
7	05:08	CAP	6	17:21	AQU	7	04:54	ARI	6	14:04	TAU
9	08:44	AQU	8	19:27	PIS	9	05:29	TAU	8	16:37	GEM
11	09:15	PIS	10	19:21	ARI	11	06:53	GEM	10	20:54	CAN
13	08:21	ARI	12	18:54	TAU	13	10:57	CAN	13	04:07	LEO
15	08:11	TAU	14	20:18	GEM	15	18:51	LEO	15	14:33	VIR
17	10:48	GEM	17	01:21	CAN	18	06:11	VIR	18	02:59	LIB
19	17:27	CAN	19	10:36	LEO	20	18:53	LIB	20	15:03	SCO
22	03:50	LEO	21	22:45	VIR	23	06:36	SCO	23	00:45	SAG
24	16:19	VIR	24	11:32	LIB	25	16:09	SAG	25	07:28	CAP
27	05:06	LIB	26	23:15	SCO	27	23:29	CAP	27	11:46	AQU
29	17:06	SCO	29	09:18	SAG	30	05:00	AQU	29	14:42	PIS
			31	17:31	CAP				31	17:16	ARI

1936

JANUARY			FEBRUARY			MARCH			APRIL		
2	20:11	TAU	1	05:39	GEM	1	17:26	CAN	2	19:08	VIR
5	00:04	GEM	3	11:58	CAN	4	02:21	LEO	5	07:31	LIB
7	05:29	CAN	5	20:26	LEO	6	13:18	VIR	7	20:05	SCO
9	13:02	LEO	8	06:48	VIR	9	01:26	LIB	10	08:03	SAG
11	23:05	VIR	10	18:46	LIB	11	14:04	SCO	12	18:23	CAP
14	11:11	LIB	13	07:25	SCO	14	02:06	SAG	15	01:49	AQU
16	23:39	SCO	15	18:57	SAG	16	11:52	CAP	17	05:38	PIS
19	10:12	SAG	18	03:21	CAP	18	17:52	AQU	19	06:21	ARI
21	17:19	CAP	20	07:47	AQU	20	19:59	PIS	21	05:37	TAU
23	21:03	AQU	22	08:56	PIS	22	19:32	ARI	23	05:38	GEM
25	22:35	PIS	24	08:35	ARI	24	18:38	TAU	25	08:23	CAN
27	23:36	ARI	26	08:51	TAU	26	19:32	GEM	27	15:04	LEO
30	01:38	TAU	28	11:30	GEM	28	23:52	CAN	30	01:22	VIR
						31	08:04	LEO			

MAY			JUNE			JULY			AUGUST		
2	13:43	LIB	1	09:12	SCO	1	04:27	SAG	2	04:26	AQU
5	02:17	SCO	3	20:38	SAG	3	13:34	CAP	4	07:36	PIS
7	13:54	SAG	6	06:03	CAP	5	19:57	AQU	6	09:22	ARI
9	23:57	CAP	8	13:18	AQU	8	00:11	PIS	8	11:12	TAU
12	07:48	AQU	10	18:27	PIS	10	03:10	ARI	10	14:12	GEM
14	12:53	PIS	12	21:47	ARI	12	05:46	TAU	12	18:52	CAN
16	15:14	ARI	14	23:49	TAU	14	08:39	GEM	15	01:20	LEO
18	15:48	TAU	17	01:30	GEM	16	12:28	CAN	17	09:45	VIR
20	16:12	GEM	19	04:09	CAN	18	17:58	LEO	19	20:17	LIB
22	18:20	CAN	21	09:06	LEO	21	01:54	VIR	22	08:36	SCO
24	23:42	LEO	23	17:16	VIR	23	12:31	LIB	24	21:10	SAG
27	08:48	VIR	26	04:24	LIB	26	00:54	SCO	27	07:35	CAP
29	20:39	LIB	28	16:53	SCO	28	12:56	SAG	29	14:13	AQU
						30	22:24	CAP	31	17:06	PIS

SEPTEMBER			OCTOBER			NOVEMBER			DECEMBER		
2	17:43	ARI	2	03:25	TAU	2	15:01	CAN	2	04:44	LEO
4	18:04	TAU	4	03:37	GEM	4	19:37	LEO	4	11:31	VIR
6	19:55	GEM	6	06:29	CAN	7	04:00	VIR	6	21:56	LIB
9	00:16	CAN	8	12:45	LEO	9	15:15	LIB	9	10:28	SCO
11	07:13	LEO	10	22:02	VIR	12	03:52	SCO	11	23:07	SAG
13	16:20	VIR	13	09:19	LIB	14	16:34	SAG	14	10:26	CAP
16	03:13	LIB	15	21:47	SCO	17	04:21	CAP	16	19:43	AQU
18	15:33	SCO	18	10:38	SAG	19	14:11	AQU	19	02:44	PIS
21	04:25	SAG	20	22:38	CAP	21	21:04	PIS	21	07:27	ARI
23	15:53	CAP	23	08:00	AQU	24	00:37	ARI	23	10:06	TAU
25	23:53	AQU	25	13:28	PIS	26	01:29	TAU	25	11:25	GEM
28	03:39	PIS	27	15:10	ARI	28	01:12	GEM	27	12:37	CAN
30	04:10	ARI	29	14:34	TAU	30	01:40	CAN	29	15:14	LEO
			31	13:50	GEM				31	20:46	VIR

1937

JANUARY		
3	05:55	LIB
5	17:58	SCO
8	06:43	SAG
10	17:54	CAP
13	02:25	AQU
15	08:29	PIS
17	12:49	ARI
19	16:07	TAU
21	18:54	GEM
23	21:38	CAN
26	01:08	LEO
28	06:31	VIR
30	14:50	LIB

FEBRUARY		
2	02:11	SCO
4	14:59	SAG
7	02:34	CAP
9	11:00	AQU
11	16:10	PIS
13	19:12	ARI
15	21:35	TAU
18	00:23	GEM
20	04:04	CAN
22	08:51	LEO
24	15:05	VIR
26	23:27	LIB

MARCH		
1	10:23	SCO
3	23:08	SAG
6	11:23	CAP
8	20:36	AQU
11	01:50	PIS
13	04:00	ARI
15	04:54	TAU
17	06:19	GEM
19	09:26	CAN
21	14:36	LEO
23	21:44	VIR
26	06:47	LIB
28	17:51	SCO
31	06:33	SAG

APRIL		
2	19:17	CAP
5	05:39	AQU
7	12:00	PIS
9	14:29	ARI
11	14:40	TAU
13	14:35	GEM
15	16:03	CAN
17	20:12	LEO
20	03:16	VIR
22	12:51	LIB
25	00:21	SCO
27	13:05	SAG
30	01:57	CAP

MAY		
2	13:09	AQU
4	20:57	PIS
7	00:48	ARI
9	01:32	TAU
11	00:57	GEM
13	01:01	CAN
15	03:28	LEO
17	09:19	VIR
19	18:35	LIB
22	06:18	SCO
24	19:10	SAG
27	07:54	CAP
29	19:13	AQU

JUNE		
1	03:58	PIS
3	09:22	ARI
5	11:36	TAU
7	11:46	GEM
9	11:32	CAN
11	12:45	LEO
13	17:01	VIR
16	01:08	LIB
18	12:31	SCO
21	01:26	SAG
23	13:58	CAP
26	00:54	AQU
28	09:37	PIS
30	15:51	ARI

JULY		
2	19:35	TAU
4	21:16	GEM
6	21:54	CAN
8	22:59	LEO
11	02:16	VIR
13	09:04	LIB
15	19:36	SCO
18	08:20	SAG
20	20:51	CAP
23	07:20	AQU
25	15:21	PIS
27	21:16	ARI
30	01:32	TAU

AUGUST		
1	04:29	GEM
3	06:34	CAN
5	08:36	LEO
7	11:54	VIR
9	17:59	LIB
12	03:37	SCO
14	15:59	SAG
17	04:38	CAP
19	15:05	AQU
21	22:29	PIS
24	03:24	ARI
26	06:57	TAU
28	10:02	GEM
30	13:04	CAN

SEPTEMBER		
1	16:21	LEO
3	20:35	VIR
6	02:48	LIB
8	12:00	SCO
10	23:59	SAG
13	12:52	CAP
15	23:51	AQU
18	07:19	PIS
20	11:31	ARI
22	13:50	TAU
24	15:46	GEM
26	18:25	CAN
28	22:14	LEO

OCTOBER		
1	03:29	VIR
3	10:32	LIB
5	19:55	SCO
8	07:44	SAG
10	20:47	CAP
13	08:38	AQU
15	17:04	PIS
17	21:33	ARI
19	23:10	TAU
21	23:40	GEM
24	00:47	CAN
26	03:43	LEO
28	09:02	VIR
30	16:47	LIB

NOVEMBER		
2	02:49	SCO
4	14:46	SAG
7	03:50	CAP
9	16:19	AQU
12	02:08	PIS
14	08:00	ARI
16	10:12	TAU
18	10:10	GEM
20	09:48	CAN
22	10:55	LEO
24	14:56	VIR
26	22:22	LIB
29	08:46	SCO

DECEMBER		
1	21:06	SAG
4	10:08	CAP
6	22:41	AQU
9	09:22	PIS
11	16:55	ARI
13	20:50	TAU
15	21:43	GEM
17	21:03	CAN
19	20:49	LEO
21	22:57	VIR
24	04:53	LIB
26	14:45	SCO
29	03:12	SAG
31	16:17	CAP

1938

JANUARY			FEBRUARY			MARCH			APRIL		
3	04:32	AQU	1	20:59	PIS	1	04:14	PIS	1	23:43	TAU
5	15:07	PIS	4	04:55	ARI	3	11:17	ARI	4	02:34	GEM
7	23:29	ARI	6	10:59	TAU	5	16:30	TAU	6	05:08	CAN
10	05:06	TAU	8	15:08	GEM	7	20:34	GEM	8	08:05	LEO
12	07:50	GEM	10	17:26	CAN	9	23:46	CAN	10	11:51	VIR
14	08:22	CAN	12	18:34	LEO	12	02:23	LEO	12	17:02	LIB
16	08:10	LEO	14	19:57	VIR	14	05:06	VIR	15	00:21	SCO
18	09:13	VIR	16	23:28	LIB	16	09:08	LIB	17	10:20	SAG
20	13:28	LIB	19	06:37	SCO	18	15:54	SCO	19	23:32	CAP
22	21:55	SCO	21	17:34	SAG	21	02:01	SAG	22	11:11	AQU
25	09:52	SAG	24	06:28	CAP	23	14:32	CAP	24	21:54	PIS
27	22:58	CAP	26	18:36	AQU	26	02:56	AQU	27	05:09	ARI
30	11:00	AQU				28	12:52	PIS	29	09:02	TAU
						30	19:34	ARI			

MAY			JUNE			JULY			AUGUST		
1	10:45	GEM	1	21:09	LEO	1	07:24	VIR	2	01:50	SCO
3	11:51	CAN	3	23:22	VIR	3	11:09	LIB	4	12:02	SAG
5	13:42	LEO	6	04:36	LIB	5	18:49	SCO	7	00:34	CAP
7	17:17	VIR	8	13:01	SCO	8	05:46	SAG	9	13:15	AQU
9	23:06	LIB	10	23:58	SAG	10	18:22	CAP	12	00:45	PIS
12	07:16	SCO	13	12:21	CAP	13	07:06	AQU	14	10:35	ARI
14	17:41	SAG	16	01:08	AQU	15	18:56	PIS	16	18:26	TAU
17	05:51	CAP	18	13:03	PIS	18	05:03	ARI	18	23:51	GEM
19	18:38	AQU	20	22:40	ARI	20	12:31	TAU	21	02:40	CAN
22	06:09	PIS	23	04:50	TAU	22	16:43	GEM	23	03:27	LEO
24	14:36	ARI	25	07:25	GEM	24	17:55	CAN	25	03:43	VIR
26	19:17	TAU	27	07:28	CAN	26	17:26	LEO	27	05:26	LIB
28	20:52	GEM	29	06:46	LEO	28	17:17	VIR	29	10:26	SCO
30	20:53	CAN				30	19:35	LIB	31	19:28	SAG

SEPTEMBER			OCTOBER			NOVEMBER			DECEMBER		
3	07:30	CAP	3	03:58	AQU	2	00:09	PIS	1	19:03	ARI
5	20:11	AQU	5	15:27	PIS	4	09:35	ARI	4	02:01	TAU
8	07:29	PIS	8	00:23	ARI	6	15:41	TAU	6	05:19	GEM
10	16:41	ARI	10	06:43	TAU	8	19:04	GEM	8	06:08	CAN
12	23:54	TAU	12	11:11	GEM	10	21:00	CAN	10	06:18	LEO
15	05:23	GEM	14	14:31	CAN	12	22:50	LEO	12	07:38	VIR
17	09:10	CAN	16	17:20	LEO	15	01:38	VIR	14	11:28	LIB
19	11:26	LEO	18	20:09	VIR	17	06:04	LIB	16	18:13	SCO
21	13:01	VIR	20	23:43	LIB	19	12:26	SCO	19	03:31	SAG
23	15:19	LIB	23	05:00	SCO	21	20:57	SAG	21	14:39	CAP
25	19:57	SCO	25	12:54	SAG	24	07:38	CAP	24	02:59	AQU
28	04:02	SAG	27	23:39	CAP	26	19:59	AQU	26	15:41	PIS
30	15:21	CAP	30	12:09	AQU	29	08:30	PIS	29	03:15	ARI
									31	11:48	TAU

1939

JANUARY
2	16:20	GEM
4	17:20	CAN
6	16:32	LEO
8	16:08	VIR
10	18:11	LIB
12	23:54	SCO
15	09:10	SAG
17	20:44	CAP
20	09:15	AQU
22	21:51	PIS
25	09:42	ARI
27	19:29	TAU
30	01:50	GEM

FEBRUARY
1	04:22	CAN
3	04:06	LEO
5	03:03	VIR
7	03:30	LIB
9	07:22	SCO
11	15:24	SAG
14	02:42	CAP
16	15:22	AQU
19	03:52	PIS
21	15:24	ARI
24	01:19	TAU
26	08:48	GEM
28	13:07	CAN

MARCH
2	14:30	LEO
4	14:17	VIR
6	14:26	LIB
8	17:00	SCO
10	23:23	SAG
13	09:36	CAP
15	22:02	AQU
18	10:32	PIS
20	21:41	ARI
23	06:59	TAU
25	14:15	GEM
27	19:20	CAN
29	22:15	LEO
31	23:39	VIR

APRIL
3	00:49	LIB
5	03:22	SCO
7	08:48	SAG
9	17:47	CAP
12	05:34	AQU
14	18:05	PIS
17	05:14	ARI
19	13:57	TAU
21	20:17	GEM
24	00:44	CAN
26	03:55	LEO
28	06:27	VIR
30	09:02	LIB

MAY
2	12:36	SCO
4	18:11	SAG
7	02:34	CAP
9	13:41	AQU
12	02:10	PIS
14	13:41	ARI
16	22:28	TAU
19	04:07	GEM
21	07:23	CAN
23	09:34	LEO
25	11:51	VIR
27	15:06	LIB
29	19:48	SCO

JUNE
1	02:15	SAG
3	10:50	CAP
5	21:41	AQU
8	10:05	PIS
10	22:11	ARI
13	07:43	TAU
15	13:33	GEM
17	16:07	CAN
19	16:58	LEO
21	17:57	VIR
23	20:31	LIB
26	01:25	SCO
28	08:39	SAG
30	17:54	CAP

JULY
3	04:54	AQU
5	17:18	PIS
8	05:50	ARI
10	16:27	TAU
12	23:21	GEM
15	02:16	CAN
17	02:31	LEO
19	02:08	VIR
21	03:11	LIB
23	07:04	SCO
25	14:10	SAG
27	23:51	CAP
30	11:15	AQU

AUGUST
1	23:42	PIS
4	12:23	ARI
6	23:48	TAU
9	08:06	GEM
11	12:21	CAN
13	13:10	LEO
15	12:19	VIR
17	12:04	LIB
19	14:20	SCO
21	20:14	SAG
24	05:34	CAP
26	17:09	AQU
29	05:43	PIS
31	18:15	ARI

SEPTEMBER
3	05:48	TAU
5	15:02	GEM
7	20:52	CAN
9	23:12	LEO
11	23:09	VIR
13	22:39	LIB
15	23:44	SCO
18	04:02	SAG
20	12:11	CAP
22	23:24	AQU
25	12:00	PIS
28	00:22	ARI
30	11:29	TAU

OCTOBER
2	20:38	GEM
5	03:17	CAN
7	07:10	LEO
9	08:46	VIR
11	09:16	LIB
13	10:19	SCO
15	13:36	SAG
17	20:22	CAP
20	06:40	AQU
22	19:06	PIS
25	07:28	ARI
27	18:09	TAU
30	02:31	GEM

NOVEMBER
1	08:42	CAN
3	13:02	LEO
5	15:57	VIR
7	18:03	LIB
9	20:14	SCO
11	23:42	SAG
14	05:42	CAP
16	15:01	AQU
19	03:00	PIS
21	15:36	ARI
24	02:23	TAU
26	10:09	GEM
28	15:12	CAN
30	18:34	LEO

DECEMBER
2	21:23	VIR
5	00:23	LIB
7	03:57	SCO
9	08:33	SAG
11	14:51	CAP
13	23:43	AQU
16	11:14	PIS
19	00:03	ARI
21	11:32	TAU
23	19:37	GEM
26	00:03	CAN
28	02:05	LEO
30	03:29	VIR

1940

JANUARY		
1	05:44	LIB
3	09:36	SCO
5	15:13	SAG
7	22:30	CAP
10	07:42	AQU
12	19:03	PIS
15	07:56	ARI
17	20:16	TAU
20	05:32	GEM
22	10:35	CAN
24	12:11	LEO
26	12:12	VIR
28	12:43	LIB
30	15:18	SCO

FEBRUARY		
1	20:36	SAG
4	04:27	CAP
6	14:22	AQU
9	01:59	PIS
11	14:50	ARI
14	03:36	TAU
16	14:10	GEM
18	20:47	CAN
20	23:19	LEO
22	23:12	VIR
24	22:29	LIB
26	23:14	SCO
29	02:55	SAG

MARCH		
2	10:03	CAP
4	20:08	AQU
7	08:08	PIS
9	21:01	ARI
12	09:45	TAU
14	20:53	GEM
17	04:57	CAN
19	09:15	LEO
21	10:21	VIR
23	09:48	LIB
25	09:34	SCO
27	11:31	SAG
29	17:00	CAP

APRIL		
1	02:14	AQU
3	14:11	PIS
6	03:10	ARI
8	15:39	TAU
11	02:33	GEM
13	11:04	CAN
15	16:44	LEO
17	19:35	VIR
19	20:23	LIB
21	20:33	SCO
23	21:49	SAG
26	01:50	CAP
28	09:39	AQU
30	20:56	PIS

MAY		
3	09:52	ARI
5	22:13	TAU
8	08:34	GEM
10	16:34	CAN
12	22:23	LEO
15	02:18	VIR
17	04:41	LIB
19	06:12	SCO
21	08:00	SAG
23	11:35	CAP
25	18:19	AQU
28	04:39	PIS
30	17:19	ARI

JUNE		
2	05:44	TAU
4	15:50	GEM
6	23:02	CAN
9	04:01	LEO
11	07:41	VIR
13	10:44	LIB
15	13:32	SCO
17	16:34	SAG
19	20:45	CAP
22	03:15	AQU
24	12:56	PIS
27	01:13	ARI
29	13:53	TAU

JULY		
2	00:16	GEM
4	07:11	CAN
6	11:13	LEO
8	13:45	VIR
10	16:07	LIB
12	19:07	SCO
14	23:05	SAG
17	04:18	CAP
19	11:22	AQU
21	20:59	PIS
24	09:02	ARI
26	21:57	TAU
29	09:04	GEM
31	16:32	CAN

AUGUST		
2	20:20	LEO
4	21:51	VIR
6	22:50	LIB
9	00:46	SCO
11	04:29	SAG
13	10:15	CAP
15	18:08	AQU
18	04:10	PIS
20	16:14	ARI
23	05:17	TAU
25	17:13	GEM
28	01:54	CAN
30	06:32	LEO

SEPTEMBER		
1	07:57	VIR
3	07:54	LIB
5	08:17	SCO
7	10:36	SAG
9	15:46	CAP
11	23:52	AQU
14	10:26	PIS
16	22:43	ARI
19	11:46	TAU
22	00:06	GEM
24	09:58	CAN
26	16:09	LEO
28	18:42	VIR
30	18:47	LIB

OCTOBER		
2	18:12	SCO
4	18:54	SAG
6	22:29	CAP
9	05:44	AQU
11	16:18	PIS
14	04:50	ARI
16	17:50	TAU
19	06:00	GEM
21	16:18	CAN
23	23:51	LEO
26	04:10	VIR
28	05:37	LIB
30	05:25	SCO

NOVEMBER		
1	05:21	SAG
3	07:23	CAP
5	13:04	AQU
7	22:46	PIS
10	11:13	ARI
13	00:13	TAU
15	12:01	GEM
17	21:53	CAN
20	05:39	LEO
22	11:11	VIR
24	14:25	LIB
26	15:45	SCO
28	16:19	SAG
30	17:51	CAP

DECEMBER		
2	22:13	AQU
5	06:36	PIS
7	18:27	ARI
10	07:28	TAU
12	19:08	GEM
15	04:20	CAN
17	11:17	LEO
19	16:35	VIR
21	20:37	LIB
23	23:30	SCO
26	01:37	SAG
28	03:59	CAP
30	08:09	AQU

1941

JANUARY			FEBRUARY			MARCH			APRIL		
1	15:35	PIS	2	23:41	TAU	2	07:24	TAU	1	03:07	GEM
4	02:35	ARI	5	12:10	GEM	4	20:12	GEM	3	14:44	CAN
6	15:29	TAU	7	21:58	CAN	7	07:04	CAN	5	23:26	LEO
9	03:27	GEM	10	04:08	LEO	9	14:19	LEO	8	04:21	VIR
11	12:34	CAN	12	07:22	VIR	11	17:52	VIR	10	05:55	LIB
13	18:40	LEO	14	09:08	LIB	13	18:52	LIB	12	05:32	SCO
15	22:46	VIR	16	10:53	SCO	15	19:03	SCO	14	05:08	SAG
18	02:00	LIB	18	13:37	SAG	17	20:08	SAG	16	06:39	CAP
20	05:04	SCO	20	17:54	CAP	19	23:25	CAP	18	11:31	AQU
22	08:17	SAG	23	00:02	AQU	22	05:34	AQU	20	20:07	PIS
24	12:01	CAP	25	08:19	PIS	24	14:30	PIS	23	07:35	ARI
26	17:06	AQU	27	18:55	ARI	27	01:40	ARI	25	20:23	TAU
29	00:35	PIS				29	14:14	TAU	28	09:11	GEM
31	11:02	ARI							30	20:56	CAN

MAY			JUNE			JULY			AUGUST		
3	06:34	LEO	1	19:39	VIR	1	06:17	LIB	1	17:50	SAG
5	13:06	VIR	4	00:17	LIB	3	09:34	SCO	3	20:17	CAP
7	16:12	LIB	6	02:14	SCO	5	11:14	SAG	5	23:32	AQU
9	16:34	SCO	8	02:24	SAG	7	12:21	CAP	8	04:51	PIS
11	15:50	SAG	10	02:32	CAP	9	14:36	AQU	10	13:13	ARI
13	16:04	CAP	12	04:42	AQU	11	19:42	PIS	13	00:32	TAU
15	19:15	AQU	14	10:34	PIS	14	04:35	ARI	15	13:10	GEM
18	02:34	PIS	16	20:31	ARI	16	16:30	TAU	18	00:38	CAN
20	13:34	ARI	19	09:03	TAU	19	05:10	GEM	20	09:16	LEO
23	02:27	TAU	21	21:45	GEM	21	16:15	CAN	22	14:53	VIR
25	15:10	GEM	24	08:51	CAN	24	00:48	LEO	24	18:22	LIB
28	02:37	CAN	26	17:55	LEO	26	07:04	VIR	26	20:49	SCO
30	12:16	LEO	29	01:03	VIR	28	11:41	LIB	28	23:13	SAG
						30	15:09	SCO	31	02:18	CAP

SEPTEMBER			OCTOBER			NOVEMBER			DECEMBER		
2	06:39	AQU	1	19:18	PIS	2	22:19	TAU	2	17:00	GEM
4	12:52	PIS	4	04:38	ARI	5	10:53	GEM	5	05:22	CAN
6	21:29	ARI	6	15:52	TAU	7	23:26	CAN	7	16:43	LEO
9	08:32	TAU	9	04:23	GEM	10	10:49	LEO	10	02:13	VIR
11	21:06	GEM	11	16:53	CAN	12	19:29	VIR	12	08:46	LIB
14	09:09	CAN	14	03:29	LEO	15	00:22	LIB	14	11:52	SCO
16	18:36	LEO	16	10:36	VIR	17	01:40	SCO	16	12:10	SAG
19	00:29	VIR	18	13:54	LIB	19	00:54	SAG	18	11:27	CAP
21	03:18	LIB	20	14:26	SCO	21	00:12	CAP	20	11:54	AQU
23	04:24	SCO	22	14:01	SAG	23	01:47	AQU	22	15:33	PIS
25	05:25	SAG	24	14:40	CAP	25	07:09	PIS	24	23:24	ARI
27	07:45	CAP	26	18:03	AQU	27	16:27	ARI	27	10:43	TAU
29	12:17	AQU	29	00:51	PIS	30	04:19	TAU	29	23:27	GEM
			31	10:38	ARI						

1942

JANUARY			FEBRUARY			MARCH			APRIL		
1	11:42	CAN	2	13:58	VIR	1	22:06	VIR	2	14:55	SCO
3	22:33	LEO	4	20:18	LIB	4	03:23	LIB	4	16:05	SAG
6	07:43	VIR	7	00:56	SCO	6	06:50	SCO	6	17:42	CAP
8	14:49	LIB	9	04:07	SAG	8	09:28	SAG	8	20:57	AQU
10	19:25	SCO	11	06:19	CAP	10	12:09	CAP	11	02:20	PIS
12	21:32	SAG	13	08:28	AQU	12	15:31	AQU	13	09:49	ARI
14	22:07	CAP	15	11:51	PIS	14	20:09	PIS	15	19:18	TAU
16	22:53	AQU	17	17:47	ARI	17	02:41	ARI	18	06:37	GEM
19	01:43	PIS	20	02:58	TAU	19	11:39	TAU	20	19:10	CAN
21	08:08	ARI	22	14:48	GEM	21	23:01	GEM	23	07:22	LEO
23	18:19	TAU	25	03:16	CAN	24	11:33	CAN	25	17:03	VIR
26	06:44	GEM	27	14:06	LEO	26	23:05	LEO	27	22:50	LIB
28	19:04	CAN				29	07:37	VIR	30	00:59	SCO
31	05:37	LEO				31	12:37	LIB			

MAY			JUNE			JULY			AUGUST		
2	01:03	SAG	2	11:00	AQU	1	22:46	PIS	2	20:48	TAU
4	01:05	CAP	4	14:14	PIS	4	04:11	ARI	5	07:55	GEM
6	02:56	AQU	6	21:11	ARI	6	13:23	TAU	7	20:31	CAN
8	07:44	PIS	9	07:16	TAU	9	01:10	GEM	10	08:40	LEO
10	15:32	ARI	11	19:12	GEM	11	13:52	CAN	12	19:09	VIR
13	01:37	TAU	14	07:50	CAN	14	02:08	LEO	15	03:31	LIB
15	13:15	GEM	16	20:20	LEO	16	13:09	VIR	17	09:38	SCO
18	01:49	CAN	19	07:34	VIR	18	22:02	LIB	19	13:35	SAG
20	14:21	LEO	21	16:05	LIB	21	04:02	SCO	21	15:47	CAP
23	01:08	VIR	23	20:51	SCO	23	06:58	SAG	23	17:07	AQU
25	08:22	LIB	25	22:09	SAG	25	07:38	CAP	25	18:56	PIS
27	11:32	SCO	27	21:30	CAP	27	07:37	AQU	27	22:39	ARI
29	11:39	SAG	29	21:01	AQU	29	08:49	PIS	30	05:29	TAU
31	10:44	CAP				31	12:56	ARI			

SEPTEMBER			OCTOBER			NOVEMBER			DECEMBER		
1	15:41	GEM	1	12:04	CAN	2	20:19	VIR	2	13:56	LIB
4	04:01	CAN	4	00:36	LEO	5	04:22	LIB	4	19:07	SCO
6	16:16	LEO	6	11:14	VIR	7	08:27	SCO	6	20:34	SAG
9	02:31	VIR	8	18:33	LIB	9	09:47	SAG	8	20:07	CAP
11	10:05	LIB	10	22:47	SCO	11	10:18	CAP	10	19:57	AQU
13	15:19	SCO	13	01:11	SAG	13	11:49	AQU	12	21:56	PIS
15	18:58	SAG	15	03:14	CAP	15	15:28	PIS	15	03:05	ARI
17	21:48	CAP	17	06:01	AQU	17	21:31	ARI	17	11:17	TAU
20	00:27	AQU	19	10:05	PIS	20	05:38	TAU	19	21:46	GEM
22	03:34	PIS	21	15:37	ARI	22	15:35	GEM	22	09:46	CAN
24	07:57	ARI	23	22:52	TAU	25	03:17	CAN	24	22:36	LEO
26	14:35	TAU	26	08:19	GEM	27	16:10	LEO	27	11:11	VIR
29	00:05	GEM	28	20:00	CAN	30	04:30	VIR	29	21:45	LIB
			31	08:49	LEO						

1943

JANUARY			FEBRUARY			MARCH			APRIL		
1	04:40	SCO	1	18:16	CAP	1	02:19	CAP	1	13:27	PIS
3	07:34	SAG	3	18:11	AQU	3	03:57	AQU	3	16:18	ARI
5	07:35	CAP	5	18:08	PIS	5	04:55	PIS	5	20:38	TAU
7	06:42	AQU	7	20:01	ARI	7	06:42	ARI	8	03:42	GEM
9	07:03	PIS	10	01:18	TAU	9	10:54	TAU	10	14:03	CAN
11	10:21	ARI	12	10:25	GEM	11	18:39	GEM	13	02:40	LEO
13	17:22	TAU	14	22:25	CAN	14	05:51	CAN	15	14:59	VIR
16	03:39	GEM	17	11:19	LEO	16	18:41	LEO	18	00:41	LIB
18	15:54	CAN	19	23:20	VIR	19	06:43	VIR	20	07:04	SCO
21	04:44	LEO	22	09:30	LIB	21	16:21	LIB	22	10:57	SAG
23	17:03	VIR	24	17:25	SCO	23	23:23	SCO	24	13:40	CAP
26	03:47	LIB	26	22:59	SAG	26	04:24	SAG	26	16:21	AQU
28	11:51	SCO				28	08:05	CAP	28	19:36	PIS
30	16:34	SAG				30	10:57	AQU	30	23:40	ARI

MAY			JUNE			JULY			AUGUST		
3	04:57	TAU	1	19:30	GEM	1	12:14	CAN	2	19:46	VIR
5	12:16	GEM	4	05:46	CAN	4	00:40	LEO	5	07:52	LIB
7	22:17	CAN	6	18:03	LEO	6	13:45	VIR	7	17:40	SCO
10	10:39	LEO	9	07:04	VIR	9	01:45	LIB	10	00:09	SAG
12	23:22	VIR	11	18:22	LIB	11	10:41	SCO	12	03:10	CAP
15	09:45	LIB	14	01:59	SCO	13	15:37	SAG	14	03:37	AQU
17	16:20	SCO	16	05:36	SAG	15	17:07	CAP	16	03:07	PIS
19	19:33	SAG	18	06:30	CAP	17	16:46	AQU	18	03:33	ARI
21	21:00	CAP	20	06:34	AQU	19	16:31	PIS	20	06:40	TAU
23	22:23	AQU	22	07:37	PIS	21	18:09	ARI	22	13:35	GEM
26	00:58	PIS	24	10:53	ARI	23	22:53	TAU	25	00:07	CAN
28	05:17	ARI	26	16:52	TAU	26	07:04	GEM	27	12:50	LEO
30	11:25	TAU	29	01:27	GEM	28	18:04	CAN	30	01:47	VIR
						31	06:43	LEO			

SEPTEMBER			OCTOBER			NOVEMBER			DECEMBER		
1	13:34	LIB	1	05:05	SCO	1	22:37	CAP	1	08:02	AQU
3	23:21	SCO	3	12:03	SAG	4	02:10	AQU	3	10:36	PIS
6	06:39	SAG	5	17:11	CAP	6	05:16	PIS	5	14:00	ARI
8	11:14	CAP	7	20:40	AQU	8	08:11	ARI	7	18:30	TAU
10	13:18	AQU	9	22:45	PIS	10	11:33	TAU	10	00:33	GEM
12	13:47	PIS	12	00:12	ARI	12	16:32	GEM	12	08:47	CAN
14	14:09	ARI	14	02:26	TAU	15	00:23	CAN	14	19:37	LEO
16	16:15	TAU	16	07:07	GEM	17	11:28	LEO	17	08:23	VIR
18	21:43	GEM	18	15:28	CAN	20	00:22	VIR	19	20:56	LIB
21	07:11	CAN	21	03:13	LEO	22	12:19	LIB	22	06:46	SCO
23	19:34	LEO	23	16:10	VIR	24	21:09	SCO	24	12:44	SAG
26	08:31	VIR	26	03:38	LIB	27	02:35	SAG	26	15:24	CAP
28	19:57	LIB	28	12:15	SCO	29	05:43	CAP	28	16:21	AQU
			30	18:15	SAG				30	17:17	PIS

1944

JANUARY
1 19:34 ARI
3 23:59 TAU
6 06:45 GEM
8 15:48 CAN
11 02:58 LEO
13 15:39 VIR
16 04:29 LIB
18 15:28 SCO
20 22:54 SAG
23 02:27 CAP
25 03:10 AQU
27 02:48 PIS
29 03:15 ARI
31 06:07 TAU

FEBRUARY
2 12:18 GEM
4 21:40 CAN
7 09:20 LEO
9 22:08 VIR
12 10:55 LIB
14 22:24 SCO
17 07:15 SAG
19 12:33 CAP
21 14:27 AQU
23 14:09 PIS
25 13:31 ARI
27 14:36 TAU
29 19:06 GEM

MARCH
3 03:38 CAN
5 15:20 LEO
8 04:19 VIR
10 16:56 LIB
13 04:12 SCO
15 13:31 SAG
17 20:14 CAP
19 23:55 AQU
22 00:59 PIS
24 00:42 ARI
26 01:01 TAU
28 03:59 GEM
30 11:00 CAN

APRIL
1 21:54 LEO
4 10:49 VIR
6 23:22 LIB
9 10:12 SCO
11 19:03 SAG
14 01:56 CAP
16 06:46 AQU
18 09:28 PIS
20 10:36 ARI
22 11:29 TAU
24 13:59 GEM
26 19:49 CAN
29 05:36 LEO

MAY
1 18:05 VIR
4 06:40 LIB
6 17:18 SCO
9 01:27 SAG
11 07:33 CAP
13 12:10 AQU
15 15:35 PIS
17 18:04 ARI
19 20:16 TAU
21 23:27 GEM
24 05:04 CAN
26 14:05 LEO
29 01:59 VIR
31 14:38 LIB

JUNE
3 01:32 SCO
5 09:28 SAG
7 14:41 CAP
9 18:12 AQU
11 20:59 PIS
13 23:41 ARI
16 02:52 TAU
18 07:11 GEM
20 13:29 CAN
22 22:26 LEO
25 09:58 VIR
27 22:40 LIB
30 10:11 SCO

JULY
2 18:39 SAG
4 23:42 CAP
7 02:14 AQU
9 03:39 PIS
11 05:19 ARI
13 08:17 TAU
15 13:12 GEM
17 20:22 CAN
20 05:51 LEO
22 17:25 VIR
25 06:08 LIB
27 18:17 SCO
30 03:50 SAG

AUGUST
1 09:43 CAP
3 12:11 AQU
5 12:35 PIS
7 12:44 ARI
9 14:20 TAU
11 18:39 GEM
14 02:04 CAN
16 12:08 LEO
19 00:01 VIR
21 12:46 LIB
24 01:13 SCO
26 11:52 SAG
28 19:13 CAP
30 22:45 AQU

SEPTEMBER
1 23:15 PIS
3 22:27 ARI
5 22:29 TAU
8 01:14 GEM
10 07:47 CAN
12 17:51 LEO
15 06:01 VIR
17 18:48 LIB
20 07:11 SCO
22 18:17 SAG
25 02:56 CAP
27 08:10 AQU
29 09:58 PIS

OCTOBER
1 09:30 ARI
3 08:46 TAU
5 10:00 GEM
7 14:57 CAN
10 00:04 LEO
12 12:05 VIR
15 00:56 LIB
17 13:04 SCO
19 23:50 SAG
22 08:49 CAP
24 15:19 AQU
26 18:54 PIS
28 19:54 ARI
30 19:45 TAU

NOVEMBER
1 20:29 GEM
4 00:05 CAN
6 07:45 LEO
8 18:59 VIR
11 07:45 LIB
13 19:48 SCO
16 06:02 SAG
18 14:20 CAP
20 20:47 AQU
23 01:19 PIS
25 03:57 ARI
27 05:23 TAU
29 06:55 GEM

DECEMBER
1 10:17 CAN
3 16:53 LEO
6 03:04 VIR
8 15:29 LIB
11 03:42 SCO
13 13:51 SAG
15 21:22 CAP
18 02:44 AQU
20 06:40 PIS
22 09:43 ARI
24 12:25 TAU
26 15:26 GEM
28 19:44 CAN
31 02:20 LEO

1945

JANUARY

2	11:49	VIR
4	23:44	LIB
7	12:13	SCO
9	22:56	SAG
12	06:28	CAP
14	10:57	AQU
16	13:28	PIS
18	15:21	ARI
20	17:48	TAU
22	21:35	GEM
25	03:05	CAN
27	10:33	LEO
29	20:09	VIR

FEBRUARY

1	07:46	LIB
3	20:23	SCO
6	07:58	SAG
8	16:30	CAP
10	21:12	AQU
12	22:53	PIS
14	23:13	ARI
17	00:05	TAU
19	03:01	GEM
21	08:43	CAN
23	16:59	LEO
26	03:14	VIR
28	14:57	LIB

MARCH

3	03:33	SCO
5	15:45	SAG
8	01:38	CAP
10	07:40	AQU
12	09:50	PIS
14	09:33	ARI
16	08:55	TAU
18	10:05	GEM
20	14:32	CAN
22	22:32	LEO
25	09:11	VIR
27	21:15	LIB
30	09:50	SCO

APRIL

1	22:08	SAG
4	08:52	CAP
6	16:29	AQU
8	20:11	PIS
10	20:38	ARI
12	19:40	TAU
14	19:31	GEM
16	22:14	CAN
19	04:52	LEO
21	15:04	VIR
24	03:15	LIB
26	15:53	SCO
29	03:56	SAG

MAY

1	14:40	CAP
3	23:06	AQU
6	04:21	PIS
8	06:25	ARI
10	06:25	TAU
12	06:12	GEM
14	07:51	CAN
16	12:57	LEO
18	21:56	VIR
21	09:43	LIB
23	22:21	SCO
26	10:12	SAG
28	20:25	CAP
31	04:35	AQU

JUNE

2	10:26	PIS
4	13:51	ARI
6	15:24	TAU
8	16:15	GEM
10	18:02	CAN
12	22:20	LEO
15	06:08	VIR
17	17:07	LIB
20	05:36	SCO
22	17:28	SAG
25	03:15	CAP
27	10:37	AQU
29	15:52	PIS

JULY

1	19:30	ARI
3	22:05	TAU
6	00:20	GEM
8	03:11	CAN
10	07:44	LEO
12	14:58	VIR
15	01:13	LIB
17	13:29	SCO
20	01:36	SAG
22	11:29	CAP
24	18:17	AQU
26	22:27	PIS
29	01:08	ARI
31	03:29	TAU

AUGUST

2	06:24	GEM
4	10:23	CAN
6	15:53	LEO
8	23:24	VIR
11	09:21	LIB
13	21:25	SCO
16	09:56	SAG
18	20:31	CAP
21	03:33	AQU
23	07:05	PIS
25	08:30	ARI
27	09:34	TAU
29	11:47	GEM
31	16:00	CAN

SEPTEMBER

2	22:20	LEO
5	06:37	VIR
7	16:49	LIB
10	04:48	SCO
12	17:38	SAG
15	05:12	CAP
17	13:20	AQU
19	17:19	PIS
21	18:11	ARI
23	17:54	TAU
25	18:32	GEM
27	21:39	CAN
30	03:47	LEO

OCTOBER

2	12:34	VIR
4	23:17	LIB
7	11:24	SCO
10	00:18	SAG
12	12:33	CAP
14	22:07	AQU
17	03:34	PIS
19	05:09	ARI
21	04:31	TAU
23	03:50	GEM
25	05:11	CAN
27	09:56	LEO
29	18:12	VIR

NOVEMBER

1	05:08	LIB
3	17:30	SCO
6	06:19	SAG
8	18:36	CAP
11	04:59	AQU
13	12:05	PIS
15	15:25	ARI
17	15:48	TAU
19	15:03	GEM
21	15:14	CAN
23	18:12	LEO
26	01:00	VIR
28	11:19	LIB
30	23:43	SCO

DECEMBER

3	12:30	SAG
6	00:24	CAP
8	10:35	AQU
10	18:21	PIS
12	23:16	ARI
15	01:30	TAU
17	02:03	GEM
19	02:28	CAN
21	04:31	LEO
23	09:44	VIR
25	18:45	LIB
28	06:43	SCO
30	19:33	SAG

1946

JANUARY			FEBRUARY			MARCH			APRIL		
2	07:11	CAP	1	00:24	AQU	2	15:25	PIS	1	04:17	ARI
4	16:38	AQU	3	06:33	PIS	4	18:24	ARI	3	04:57	TAU
6	23:47	PIS	5	10:38	ARI	6	20:09	TAU	5	05:25	GEM
9	04:56	ARI	7	13:47	TAU	8	22:12	GEM	7	07:21	CAN
11	08:26	TAU	9	16:46	GEM	11	01:29	CAN	9	11:38	LEO
13	10:43	GEM	11	19:59	CAN	13	06:15	LEO	11	18:21	VIR
15	12:33	CAN	13	23:51	LEO	15	12:33	VIR	14	03:14	LIB
17	15:04	LEO	16	05:03	VIR	17	20:41	LIB	16	14:04	SCO
19	19:41	VIR	18	12:36	LIB	20	07:05	SCO	19	02:30	SAG
22	03:32	LIB	20	23:05	SCO	22	19:31	SAG	21	15:29	CAP
24	14:40	SCO	23	11:41	SAG	25	08:18	CAP	24	02:57	AQU
27	03:28	SAG	26	00:02	CAP	27	18:51	AQU	26	10:55	PIS
29	15:18	CAP	28	09:35	AQU	30	01:26	PIS	28	14:46	ARI
									30	15:31	TAU

MAY			JUNE			JULY			AUGUST		
2	15:04	GEM	1	01:29	CAN	2	15:45	VIR	1	07:05	LIB
4	15:23	CAN	3	02:40	LEO	4	22:21	LIB	3	16:23	SCO
6	18:05	LEO	5	06:57	VIR	7	08:42	SCO	6	04:37	SAG
8	23:58	VIR	7	14:57	LIB	9	21:21	SAG	8	17:24	CAP
11	08:54	LIB	10	02:05	SCO	12	10:06	CAP	11	04:24	AQU
13	20:09	SCO	12	14:51	SAG	14	21:17	AQU	13	12:41	PIS
16	08:46	SAG	15	03:40	CAP	17	06:16	PIS	15	18:37	ARI
18	21:42	CAP	17	15:16	AQU	19	12:59	ARI	17	23:00	TAU
21	09:32	AQU	20	00:43	PIS	21	17:36	TAU	20	02:23	GEM
23	18:39	PIS	22	07:20	ARI	23	20:19	GEM	22	05:07	CAN
26	00:05	ARI	24	10:56	TAU	25	21:44	CAN	24	07:38	LEO
28	02:04	TAU	26	12:08	GEM	27	22:58	LEO	26	10:54	VIR
30	01:55	GEM	28	12:11	CAN	30	01:33	VIR	28	16:15	LIB
			30	12:48	LEO				31	00:50	SCO

SEPTEMBER			OCTOBER			NOVEMBER			DECEMBER		
2	12:32	SAG	2	09:30	CAP	1	05:37	AQU	3	07:06	ARI
5	01:24	CAP	4	21:28	AQU	3	15:32	PIS	5	10:49	TAU
7	12:42	AQU	7	06:09	PIS	5	21:28	ARI	7	11:30	GEM
9	20:46	PIS	9	11:05	ARI	7	23:49	TAU	9	10:50	CAN
12	01:49	ARI	11	13:21	TAU	10	00:08	GEM	11	10:47	LEO
14	05:04	TAU	13	14:37	GEM	12	00:16	CAN	13	13:09	VIR
16	07:46	GEM	15	16:23	CAN	14	01:53	LEO	15	19:08	LIB
18	10:42	CAN	17	19:35	LEO	16	06:05	VIR	18	04:43	SCO
20	14:13	LEO	20	00:36	VIR	18	13:13	LIB	20	16:49	SAG
22	18:38	VIR	22	07:34	LIB	20	22:58	SCO	23	05:51	CAP
25	00:40	LIB	24	16:41	SCO	23	10:44	SAG	25	18:30	AQU
27	09:13	SCO	27	04:04	SAG	25	23:40	CAP	28	05:44	PIS
29	20:33	SAG	29	17:00	CAP	28	12:30	AQU	30	14:31	ARI
						30	23:30	PIS			

1947

JANUARY
1	20:06	TAU
3	22:26	GEM
5	22:28	CAN
7	21:54	LEO
9	22:45	VIR
12	02:54	LIB
14	11:16	SCO
16	23:03	SAG
19	12:11	CAP
22	00:37	AQU
24	11:23	PIS
26	20:11	ARI
29	02:46	TAU
31	06:52	GEM

FEBRUARY
2	08:39	CAN
4	09:02	LEO
6	09:42	VIR
8	12:40	LIB
10	19:29	SCO
13	06:16	SAG
15	19:12	CAP
18	07:39	AQU
20	17:58	PIS
23	01:58	ARI
25	08:08	TAU
27	12:47	GEM

MARCH
1	15:59	CAN
3	18:00	LEO
5	19:47	VIR
7	22:51	LIB
10	04:51	SCO
12	14:34	SAG
15	03:01	CAP
17	15:36	AQU
20	01:58	PIS
22	09:23	ARI
24	14:29	TAU
26	18:16	GEM
28	21:26	CAN
31	00:22	LEO

APRIL
2	03:31	VIR
4	07:40	LIB
6	13:57	SCO
8	23:13	SAG
11	11:09	CAP
13	23:52	AQU
16	10:48	PIS
18	18:26	ARI
20	22:56	TAU
23	01:28	GEM
25	03:23	CAN
27	05:44	LEO
29	09:16	VIR

MAY
1	14:24	LIB
3	21:36	SCO
6	07:10	SAG
8	18:55	CAP
11	07:41	AQU
13	19:21	PIS
16	03:57	ARI
18	08:52	TAU
20	10:52	GEM
22	11:27	CAN
24	12:18	LEO
26	14:50	VIR
28	19:54	LIB
31	03:43	SCO

JUNE
2	13:54	SAG
5	01:52	CAP
7	14:38	AQU
10	02:47	PIS
12	12:34	ARI
14	18:46	TAU
16	21:22	GEM
18	21:33	CAN
20	21:07	LEO
22	22:02	VIR
25	01:52	LIB
27	09:17	SCO
29	19:46	SAG

JULY
2	08:03	CAP
4	20:50	AQU
7	09:03	PIS
9	19:35	ARI
12	03:12	TAU
14	07:17	GEM
16	08:15	CAN
18	07:35	LEO
20	07:19	VIR
22	09:34	LIB
24	15:41	SCO
27	01:41	SAG
29	14:02	CAP

AUGUST
1	02:50	AQU
3	14:49	PIS
6	01:20	ARI
8	09:44	TAU
10	15:18	GEM
12	17:50	CAN
14	18:07	LEO
16	17:49	VIR
18	19:04	LIB
20	23:45	SCO
23	08:35	SAG
25	20:31	CAP
28	09:18	AQU
30	21:04	PIS

SEPTEMBER
2	07:03	ARI
4	15:11	TAU
6	21:19	GEM
9	01:12	CAN
11	03:03	LEO
13	03:51	VIR
15	05:17	LIB
17	09:11	SCO
19	16:50	SAG
22	03:58	CAP
24	16:38	AQU
27	04:25	PIS
29	13:59	ARI

OCTOBER
1	21:16	TAU
4	02:44	GEM
6	06:47	CAN
8	09:42	LEO
10	11:57	VIR
12	14:32	LIB
14	18:46	SCO
17	01:53	SAG
19	12:14	CAP
22	00:39	AQU
24	12:46	PIS
26	22:31	ARI
29	05:16	TAU
31	09:36	GEM

NOVEMBER
2	12:32	CAN
4	15:04	LEO
6	17:55	VIR
8	21:43	LIB
11	03:03	SCO
13	10:34	SAG
15	20:37	CAP
18	08:45	AQU
20	21:17	PIS
23	07:54	ARI
25	15:06	TAU
27	18:56	GEM
29	20:31	CAN

DECEMBER
1	21:30	LEO
3	23:24	VIR
6	03:14	LIB
8	09:25	SCO
10	17:50	SAG
13	04:14	CAP
15	16:16	AQU
18	04:59	PIS
20	16:37	ARI
23	01:12	TAU
25	05:47	GEM
27	07:03	CAN
29	06:42	LEO
31	06:47	VIR

1948

JANUARY			FEBRUARY			MARCH			APRIL		
2	09:10	LIB	3	05:26	SAG	1	12:42	SAG	2	18:19	AQU
4	14:51	SCO	5	16:30	CAP	3	22:51	CAP	5	06:56	PIS
6	23:41	SAG	8	04:59	AQU	6	11:15	AQU	7	18:29	ARI
9	10:41	CAP	10	17:37	PIS	8	23:54	PIS	10	03:59	TAU
11	22:54	AQU	13	05:38	ARI	11	11:33	ARI	12	11:20	GEM
14	11:36	PIS	15	16:09	TAU	13	21:41	TAU	14	16:42	CAN
16	23:44	ARI	17	23:56	GEM	16	05:46	GEM	16	20:16	LEO
19	09:43	TAU	20	04:09	CAN	18	11:14	CAN	18	22:31	VIR
21	16:02	GEM	22	05:07	LEO	20	13:58	LEO	21	00:17	LIB
23	18:24	CAN	24	04:23	VIR	22	14:43	VIR	23	02:50	SCO
25	18:00	LEO	26	04:06	LIB	24	15:02	LIB	25	07:32	SAG
27	16:56	VIR	28	06:24	SCO	26	16:50	SCO	27	15:22	CAP
29	17:30	LIB				28	21:47	SAG	30	02:16	AQU
31	21:28	SCO				31	06:34	CAP			

MAY			JUNE			JULY			AUGUST		
2	14:44	PIS	1	10:55	ARI	1	05:40	TAU	2	02:21	CAN
5	02:29	ARI	3	20:44	TAU	3	12:48	GEM	4	03:14	LEO
7	11:48	TAU	6	03:07	GEM	5	16:07	CAN	6	02:33	VIR
9	18:20	GEM	8	06:29	CAN	7	16:53	LEO	8	02:30	LIB
11	22:39	CAN	10	08:12	LEO	9	17:04	VIR	10	04:57	SCO
14	01:39	LEO	12	09:49	VIR	11	18:31	LIB	12	10:50	SAG
16	04:15	VIR	14	12:34	LIB	13	22:28	SCO	14	19:52	CAP
18	07:07	LIB	16	17:04	SCO	16	05:11	SAG	17	07:03	AQU
20	10:56	SCO	18	23:29	SAG	18	14:14	CAP	19	19:23	PIS
22	16:22	SAG	21	07:51	CAP	21	01:03	AQU	22	08:06	ARI
25	00:08	CAP	23	18:16	AQU	23	13:13	PIS	24	20:04	TAU
27	10:31	AQU	26	06:24	PIS	26	01:58	ARI	27	05:40	GEM
29	22:46	PIS	28	18:56	ARI	28	13:34	TAU	29	11:34	CAN
						30	22:02	GEM	31	13:42	LEO

SEPTEMBER			OCTOBER			NOVEMBER			DECEMBER		
2	13:21	VIR	1	23:30	LIB	2	13:11	SAG	2	04:17	CAP
4	12:36	LIB	3	23:59	SCO	4	18:40	CAP	4	12:32	AQU
6	13:35	SCO	6	02:55	SAG	7	03:42	AQU	6	23:46	PIS
8	17:52	SAG	8	09:31	CAP	9	15:34	PIS	9	12:30	ARI
11	01:57	CAP	10	19:43	AQU	12	04:13	ARI	12	00:09	TAU
13	12:59	AQU	13	08:04	PIS	14	15:24	TAU	14	08:45	GEM
16	01:27	PIS	15	20:37	ARI	17	00:02	GEM	16	14:01	CAN
18	14:02	ARI	18	07:54	TAU	19	06:12	CAN	18	17:03	LEO
21	01:46	TAU	20	17:15	GEM	21	10:33	LEO	20	19:19	VIR
23	11:40	GEM	23	00:22	CAN	23	13:49	VIR	22	22:00	LIB
25	18:46	CAN	25	05:10	LEO	25	16:33	LIB	25	01:39	SCO
27	22:35	LEO	27	07:54	VIR	27	19:19	SCO	27	06:29	SAG
29	23:41	VIR	29	09:16	LIB	29	22:52	SAG	29	12:47	CAP
			31	10:32	SCO				31	21:08	AQU

1949

JANUARY

3	07:59	PIS
5	20:41	ARI
8	09:03	TAU
10	18:31	GEM
12	23:57	CAN
15	02:08	LEO
17	02:53	VIR
19	04:03	LIB
21	07:00	SCO
23	12:09	SAG
25	19:22	CAP
28	04:27	AQU
30	15:27	PIS

FEBRUARY

2	04:05	ARI
4	16:57	TAU
7	03:41	GEM
9	10:23	CAN
11	13:01	LEO
13	13:06	VIR
15	12:44	LIB
17	13:53	SCO
19	17:50	SAG
22	00:51	CAP
24	10:26	AQU
26	21:54	PIS

MARCH

1	10:36	ARI
3	23:33	TAU
6	11:06	GEM
8	19:22	CAN
10	23:34	LEO
13	00:24	VIR
14	23:40	LIB
16	23:26	SCO
19	01:31	SAG
21	07:05	CAP
23	16:11	AQU
26	03:50	PIS
28	16:42	ARI
31	05:30	TAU

APRIL

2	17:03	GEM
5	02:10	CAN
7	08:00	LEO
9	10:32	VIR
11	10:48	LIB
13	10:28	SCO
15	11:24	SAG
17	15:16	CAP
19	23:00	AQU
22	10:08	PIS
24	23:01	ARI
27	11:41	TAU
29	22:48	GEM

MAY

2	07:44	CAN
4	14:12	LEO
6	18:12	VIR
8	20:07	LIB
10	20:54	SCO
12	21:57	SAG
15	00:57	CAP
17	07:19	AQU
19	17:27	PIS
22	06:02	ARI
24	18:42	TAU
27	05:27	GEM
29	13:39	CAN
31	19:36	LEO

JUNE

2	23:54	VIR
5	02:58	LIB
7	05:14	SCO
9	07:24	SAG
11	10:40	CAP
13	16:27	AQU
16	01:39	PIS
18	13:45	ARI
21	02:31	TAU
23	13:20	GEM
25	21:02	CAN
28	02:01	LEO
30	05:27	VIR

JULY

2	08:22	LIB
4	11:22	SCO
6	14:45	SAG
8	19:03	CAP
11	01:09	AQU
13	10:02	PIS
15	21:43	ARI
18	10:36	TAU
20	21:58	GEM
23	05:52	CAN
25	10:19	LEO
27	12:36	VIR
29	14:20	LIB
31	16:44	SCO

AUGUST

2	20:25	SAG
5	01:36	CAP
7	08:34	AQU
9	17:46	PIS
12	05:20	ARI
14	18:18	TAU
17	06:23	GEM
19	15:15	CAN
21	20:08	LEO
23	21:56	VIR
25	22:25	LIB
27	23:20	SCO
30	02:01	SAG

SEPTEMBER

1	07:05	CAP
3	14:37	AQU
6	00:27	PIS
8	12:14	ARI
11	01:13	TAU
13	13:47	GEM
15	23:52	CAN
18	06:05	LEO
20	08:34	VIR
22	08:42	LIB
24	08:21	SCO
26	09:22	SAG
28	13:07	CAP
30	20:14	AQU

OCTOBER

3	06:20	PIS
5	18:28	ARI
8	07:27	TAU
10	20:03	GEM
13	06:51	CAN
15	14:35	LEO
17	18:43	VIR
19	19:48	LIB
21	19:19	SCO
23	19:08	SAG
25	21:11	CAP
28	02:51	AQU
30	12:22	PIS

NOVEMBER

2	00:35	ARI
4	13:37	TAU
7	01:55	GEM
9	12:35	CAN
11	21:01	LEO
14	02:43	VIR
16	05:36	LIB
18	06:19	SCO
20	06:16	SAG
22	07:20	CAP
24	11:25	AQU
26	19:36	PIS
29	07:18	ARI

DECEMBER

1	20:22	TAU
4	08:29	GEM
6	18:32	CAN
9	02:28	LEO
11	08:32	VIR
13	12:45	LIB
15	15:14	SCO
17	16:32	SAG
19	18:00	CAP
21	21:25	AQU
24	04:20	PIS
26	15:05	ARI
29	03:58	TAU
31	16:13	GEM

1950

JANUARY
3	01:57	CAN
5	08:58	LEO
7	14:06	VIR
9	18:09	LIB
11	21:28	SCO
14	00:16	SAG
16	03:07	CAP
18	07:07	AQU
20	13:42	PIS
22	23:38	ARI
25	12:08	TAU
28	00:43	GEM
30	10:50	CAN

FEBRUARY
1	17:34	LEO
3	21:37	VIR
6	00:19	LIB
8	02:51	SCO
10	05:52	SAG
12	09:45	CAP
14	14:58	AQU
16	22:11	PIS
19	08:01	ARI
21	20:12	TAU
24	09:03	GEM
26	20:03	CAN

MARCH
1	03:31	LEO
3	07:25	VIR
5	09:01	LIB
7	09:56	SCO
9	11:38	SAG
11	15:07	CAP
13	20:53	AQU
16	05:00	PIS
18	15:21	ARI
21	03:33	TAU
23	16:28	GEM
26	04:17	CAN
28	13:05	LEO
30	18:01	VIR

APRIL
1	19:41	LIB
3	19:36	SCO
5	19:37	SAG
7	21:30	CAP
10	02:25	AQU
12	10:38	PIS
14	21:32	ARI
17	10:00	TAU
19	22:55	GEM
22	11:02	CAN
24	20:58	LEO
27	03:30	VIR
29	06:25	LIB

MAY
1	06:38	SCO
3	05:51	SAG
5	06:08	CAP
7	09:22	AQU
9	16:34	PIS
12	03:18	ARI
14	15:59	TAU
17	04:53	GEM
19	16:51	CAN
22	03:07	LEO
24	10:51	VIR
26	15:26	LIB
28	17:01	SCO
30	16:44	SAG

JUNE
1	16:27	CAP
3	18:18	AQU
5	23:57	PIS
8	09:44	ARI
10	22:13	TAU
13	11:05	GEM
15	22:45	CAN
18	08:38	LEO
20	16:32	VIR
22	22:10	LIB
25	01:19	SCO
27	02:26	SAG
29	02:49	CAP

JULY
1	04:20	AQU
3	08:52	PIS
5	17:25	ARI
8	05:14	TAU
10	18:02	GEM
13	05:34	CAN
15	14:53	LEO
17	22:06	VIR
20	03:34	LIB
22	07:27	SCO
24	09:56	SAG
26	11:40	CAP
28	13:56	AQU
30	18:19	PIS

AUGUST
2	02:03	ARI
4	13:06	TAU
7	01:44	GEM
9	13:27	CAN
11	22:37	LEO
14	05:04	VIR
16	09:31	LIB
18	12:49	SCO
20	15:36	SAG
22	18:23	CAP
24	21:53	AQU
27	03:02	PIS
29	10:45	ARI
31	21:19	TAU

SEPTEMBER
3	09:46	GEM
5	21:54	CAN
8	07:34	LEO
10	13:55	VIR
12	17:28	LIB
14	19:27	SCO
16	21:13	SAG
18	23:49	CAP
21	04:00	AQU
23	10:10	PIS
25	18:32	ARI
28	05:09	TAU
30	17:27	GEM

OCTOBER
3	06:00	CAN
5	16:40	LEO
7	23:54	VIR
10	03:29	LIB
12	04:31	SCO
14	04:44	SAG
16	05:56	CAP
18	09:27	AQU
20	15:53	PIS
23	00:59	ARI
25	12:03	TAU
28	00:23	GEM
30	13:04	CAN

NOVEMBER
2	00:38	LEO
4	09:21	VIR
6	14:10	LIB
8	15:29	SCO
10	14:52	SAG
12	14:26	CAP
14	16:15	AQU
16	21:39	PIS
19	06:40	ARI
21	18:08	TAU
24	06:39	GEM
26	19:14	CAN
29	07:02	LEO

DECEMBER
1	16:54	VIR
3	23:29	LIB
6	02:20	SCO
8	02:17	SAG
10	01:17	CAP
12	01:35	AQU
14	05:11	PIS
16	12:59	ARI
19	00:10	TAU
21	12:50	GEM
24	01:18	CAN
26	12:46	LEO
28	22:42	VIR
31	06:20	LIB

1951

JANUARY		
2	10:58	SCO
4	12:39	SAG
6	12:32	CAP
8	12:36	AQU
10	14:56	PIS
12	21:06	ARI
15	07:11	TAU
17	19:36	GEM
20	08:06	CAN
22	19:12	LEO
25	04:26	VIR
27	11:46	LIB
29	17:04	SCO
31	20:17	SAG

FEBRUARY		
2	21:53	CAP
4	23:04	AQU
7	01:29	PIS
9	06:43	ARI
11	15:34	TAU
14	03:19	GEM
16	15:52	CAN
19	03:01	LEO
21	11:43	VIR
23	18:01	LIB
25	22:31	SCO
28	01:50	SAG

MARCH		
2	04:30	CAP
4	07:11	AQU
6	10:46	PIS
8	16:16	ARI
11	00:33	TAU
13	11:36	GEM
16	00:06	CAN
18	11:45	LEO
20	20:39	VIR
23	02:21	LIB
25	05:36	SCO
27	07:41	SAG
29	09:51	CAP
31	13:03	AQU

APRIL		
2	17:45	PIS
5	00:16	ARI
7	08:53	TAU
9	19:41	GEM
12	08:05	CAN
14	20:18	LEO
17	06:07	VIR
19	12:14	LIB
21	14:55	SCO
23	15:40	SAG
25	16:20	CAP
27	18:33	AQU
29	23:14	PIS

MAY		
2	06:27	ARI
4	15:47	TAU
7	02:51	GEM
9	15:13	CAN
12	03:50	LEO
14	14:44	VIR
16	22:06	LIB
19	01:24	SCO
21	01:44	SAG
23	01:08	CAP
25	01:42	AQU
27	05:06	PIS
29	11:54	ARI
31	21:34	TAU

JUNE		
3	09:03	GEM
5	21:32	CAN
8	10:12	LEO
10	21:47	VIR
13	06:31	LIB
15	11:17	SCO
17	12:27	SAG
19	11:38	CAP
21	11:04	AQU
23	12:50	PIS
25	18:14	ARI
28	03:18	TAU
30	14:52	GEM

JULY		
3	03:28	CAN
5	16:01	LEO
8	03:36	VIR
10	13:05	LIB
12	19:19	SCO
14	22:03	SAG
16	22:15	CAP
18	21:42	AQU
20	22:29	PIS
23	02:22	ARI
25	10:07	TAU
27	21:08	GEM
30	09:43	CAN

AUGUST		
1	22:08	LEO
4	09:19	VIR
6	18:35	LIB
9	01:24	SCO
11	05:31	SAG
13	07:19	CAP
15	07:53	AQU
17	08:53	PIS
19	11:59	ARI
21	18:27	TAU
24	04:28	GEM
26	16:45	CAN
29	05:10	LEO
31	16:00	VIR

SEPTEMBER		
3	00:32	LIB
5	06:49	SCO
7	11:12	SAG
9	14:07	CAP
11	16:12	AQU
13	18:22	PIS
15	21:48	ARI
18	03:42	TAU
20	12:47	GEM
23	00:35	CAN
25	13:08	LEO
28	00:06	VIR
30	08:09	LIB

OCTOBER		
2	13:24	SCO
4	16:49	SAG
6	19:30	CAP
8	22:19	AQU
11	01:47	PIS
13	06:20	ARI
15	12:37	TAU
17	21:22	GEM
20	08:43	CAN
22	21:25	LEO
25	09:02	VIR
27	17:26	LIB
29	22:10	SCO

NOVEMBER		
1	00:20	SAG
3	01:40	CAP
5	03:43	AQU
7	07:23	PIS
9	12:53	ARI
11	20:08	TAU
14	05:16	GEM
16	16:28	CAN
19	05:12	LEO
21	17:36	VIR
24	03:09	LIB
26	08:32	SCO
28	10:20	SAG
30	10:23	CAP

DECEMBER		
2	10:45	AQU
4	13:08	PIS
6	18:18	ARI
9	02:05	TAU
11	11:54	GEM
13	23:23	CAN
16	12:05	LEO
19	00:53	VIR
21	11:41	LIB
23	18:39	SCO
25	21:27	SAG
27	21:24	CAP
29	20:36	AQU
31	21:11	PIS

1952

JANUARY		
3	00:42	ARI
5	07:44	TAU
7	17:43	GEM
10	05:35	CAN
12	18:20	LEO
15	07:01	VIR
17	18:20	LIB
20	02:44	SCO
22	07:22	SAG
24	08:39	CAP
26	08:07	AQU
28	07:46	PIS
30	09:33	ARI

FEBRUARY		
1	14:51	TAU
3	23:55	GEM
6	11:44	CAN
9	00:36	LEO
11	13:02	VIR
14	00:01	LIB
16	08:45	SCO
18	14:43	SAG
20	17:50	CAP
22	18:49	AQU
24	19:01	PIS
26	20:12	ARI
29	00:02	TAU

MARCH		
2	07:37	GEM
4	18:41	CAN
7	07:31	LEO
9	19:52	VIR
12	06:17	LIB
14	14:21	SCO
16	20:16	SAG
19	00:20	CAP
21	02:55	AQU
23	04:39	PIS
25	06:34	ARI
27	10:06	TAU
29	16:36	GEM

APRIL		
1	02:39	CAN
3	15:10	LEO
6	03:41	VIR
8	13:56	LIB
10	21:14	SCO
13	02:08	SAG
15	05:42	CAP
17	08:44	AQU
19	11:41	PIS
21	14:57	ARI
23	19:15	TAU
26	01:41	GEM
28	11:06	CAN
30	23:13	LEO

MAY		
3	11:58	VIR
5	22:39	LIB
8	05:49	SCO
10	09:51	SAG
12	12:09	CAP
14	14:15	AQU
16	17:06	PIS
18	21:07	ARI
21	02:30	TAU
23	09:38	GEM
25	19:06	CAN
28	07:00	LEO
30	19:57	VIR

JUNE		
2	07:26	LIB
4	15:20	SCO
6	19:21	SAG
8	20:47	CAP
10	21:27	AQU
12	23:01	PIS
15	02:29	ARI
17	08:11	TAU
19	16:04	GEM
22	02:04	CAN
24	14:03	LEO
27	03:07	VIR
29	15:19	LIB

JULY		
2	00:26	SCO
4	05:27	SAG
6	07:03	CAP
8	06:55	AQU
10	07:00	PIS
12	08:56	ARI
14	13:46	TAU
16	21:38	GEM
19	08:05	CAN
21	20:21	LEO
24	09:25	VIR
26	21:54	LIB
29	08:05	SCO
31	14:38	SAG

AUGUST		
2	17:28	CAP
4	17:42	AQU
6	17:05	PIS
8	17:34	ARI
10	20:46	TAU
13	03:37	GEM
15	13:53	CAN
18	02:19	LEO
20	15:23	VIR
23	03:42	LIB
25	14:11	SCO
27	21:54	SAG
30	02:24	CAP

SEPTEMBER		
1	04:03	AQU
3	04:00	PIS
5	03:58	ARI
7	05:48	TAU
9	11:06	GEM
11	20:24	CAN
14	08:39	LEO
16	21:42	VIR
19	09:42	LIB
21	19:44	SCO
24	03:33	SAG
26	09:06	CAP
28	12:25	AQU
30	13:53	PIS

OCTOBER		
2	14:34	ARI
4	16:06	TAU
6	20:15	GEM
9	04:16	CAN
11	15:51	LEO
14	04:51	VIR
16	16:45	LIB
19	02:10	SCO
21	09:12	SAG
23	14:29	CAP
25	18:28	AQU
27	21:23	PIS
29	23:35	ARI

NOVEMBER		
1	01:59	TAU
3	06:02	GEM
5	13:13	CAN
7	23:57	LEO
10	12:47	VIR
13	00:58	LIB
15	10:19	SCO
17	16:34	SAG
19	20:41	CAP
21	23:52	AQU
24	02:55	PIS
26	06:10	ARI
28	09:55	TAU
30	14:53	GEM

DECEMBER		
2	22:09	CAN
5	08:23	LEO
7	20:58	VIR
10	09:36	LIB
12	19:39	SCO
15	02:00	SAG
17	05:18	CAP
19	07:03	AQU
21	08:46	PIS
23	11:30	ARI
25	15:46	TAU
27	21:48	GEM
30	05:54	CAN

1953

JANUARY		
1	16:18	LEO
4	04:41	VIR
6	17:37	LIB
9	04:44	SCO
11	12:15	SAG
13	15:55	CAP
15	16:58	AQU
17	17:07	PIS
19	18:09	ARI
21	21:21	TAU
24	03:21	GEM
26	12:07	CAN
28	23:06	LEO
31	11:36	VIR

FEBRUARY		
3	00:32	LIB
5	12:21	SCO
7	21:21	SAG
10	02:32	CAP
12	04:17	AQU
14	03:58	PIS
16	03:31	ARI
18	04:51	TAU
20	09:27	GEM
22	17:48	CAN
25	05:06	LEO
27	17:51	VIR

MARCH		
2	06:41	LIB
4	18:31	SCO
7	04:20	SAG
9	11:10	CAP
11	14:38	AQU
13	15:17	PIS
15	14:39	ARI
17	14:45	TAU
19	17:35	GEM
22	00:30	CAN
24	11:15	LEO
27	00:04	VIR
29	12:52	LIB

APRIL		
1	00:20	SCO
3	09:59	SAG
5	17:29	CAP
7	22:28	AQU
10	00:50	PIS
12	01:19	ARI
14	01:32	TAU
16	03:27	GEM
18	08:53	CAN
20	18:27	LEO
23	06:53	VIR
25	19:41	LIB
28	06:52	SCO
30	15:53	SAG

MAY		
2	22:55	CAP
5	04:13	AQU
7	07:47	PIS
9	09:49	ARI
11	11:12	TAU
13	13:27	GEM
15	18:17	CAN
18	02:47	LEO
20	14:31	VIR
23	03:16	LIB
25	14:33	SCO
27	23:09	SAG
30	05:17	CAP

JUNE		
1	09:46	AQU
3	13:12	PIS
5	16:02	ARI
7	18:42	TAU
9	22:03	GEM
12	03:18	CAN
14	11:28	LEO
16	22:37	VIR
19	11:17	LIB
21	22:58	SCO
24	07:48	SAG
26	13:29	CAP
28	16:52	AQU
30	19:09	PIS

JULY		
2	21:24	ARI
5	00:24	TAU
7	04:43	GEM
9	10:55	CAN
11	19:28	LEO
14	06:29	VIR
16	19:04	LIB
19	07:17	SCO
21	16:59	SAG
23	23:07	CAP
26	02:03	AQU
28	03:07	PIS
30	03:56	ARI

AUGUST		
1	05:57	TAU
3	10:11	GEM
5	17:00	CAN
8	02:16	LEO
10	13:34	VIR
13	02:09	LIB
15	14:44	SCO
18	01:30	SAG
20	08:53	CAP
22	12:29	AQU
24	13:12	PIS
26	12:46	ARI
28	13:11	TAU
30	16:07	GEM

SEPTEMBER		
1	22:30	CAN
4	08:05	LEO
6	19:48	VIR
9	08:28	LIB
11	21:06	SCO
14	08:32	SAG
16	17:21	CAP
18	22:30	AQU
21	00:07	PIS
22	23:31	ARI
24	22:45	TAU
27	00:01	GEM
29	04:57	CAN

OCTOBER		
1	13:54	LEO
4	01:41	VIR
6	14:28	LIB
9	02:57	SCO
11	14:20	SAG
13	23:52	CAP
16	06:35	AQU
18	09:56	PIS
20	10:27	ARI
22	09:47	TAU
24	10:05	GEM
26	13:24	CAN
28	20:55	LEO
31	08:05	VIR

NOVEMBER		
2	20:51	LIB
5	09:12	SCO
7	20:07	SAG
10	05:19	CAP
12	12:31	AQU
14	17:18	PIS
16	19:36	ARI
18	20:15	TAU
20	20:55	GEM
22	23:32	CAN
25	05:41	LEO
27	15:41	VIR
30	04:06	LIB

DECEMBER		
2	16:31	SCO
5	03:09	SAG
7	11:33	CAP
9	18:00	AQU
11	22:47	PIS
14	02:07	ARI
16	04:23	TAU
18	06:28	GEM
20	09:40	CAN
22	15:23	LEO
25	00:24	VIR
27	12:11	LIB
30	00:43	SCO

1954

JANUARY

1	11:40	SAG
3	19:46	CAP
6	01:10	AQU
8	04:43	PIS
10	07:27	ARI
12	10:10	TAU
14	13:30	GEM
16	18:01	CAN
19	00:25	LEO
21	09:14	VIR
23	20:30	LIB
26	09:04	SCO
28	20:43	SAG
31	05:27	CAP

FEBRUARY

2	10:38	AQU
4	13:04	PIS
6	14:15	ARI
8	15:47	TAU
10	18:55	GEM
13	00:10	CAN
15	07:36	LEO
17	17:01	VIR
20	04:15	LIB
22	16:44	SCO
25	05:01	SAG
27	14:58	CAP

MARCH

1	21:07	AQU
3	23:33	PIS
5	23:41	ARI
7	23:33	TAU
10	01:07	GEM
12	05:38	CAN
14	13:17	LEO
16	23:22	VIR
19	10:58	LIB
21	23:27	SCO
24	11:57	SAG
26	22:56	CAP
29	06:38	AQU
31	10:17	PIS

APRIL

2	10:40	ARI
4	09:43	TAU
6	09:40	GEM
8	12:29	CAN
10	19:06	LEO
13	05:03	VIR
15	16:58	LIB
18	05:33	SCO
20	17:55	SAG
23	05:12	CAP
25	14:03	AQU
27	19:22	PIS
29	21:09	ARI

MAY

1	20:43	TAU
3	20:07	GEM
5	21:30	CAN
8	02:29	LEO
10	11:23	VIR
12	23:04	LIB
15	11:42	SCO
17	23:54	SAG
20	10:49	CAP
22	19:49	AQU
25	02:09	PIS
27	05:32	ARI
29	06:34	TAU
31	06:41	GEM

JUNE

2	07:46	CAN
4	11:35	LEO
6	19:07	VIR
9	05:59	LIB
11	18:30	SCO
14	06:38	SAG
16	17:06	CAP
19	01:26	AQU
21	07:37	PIS
23	11:44	ARI
25	14:09	TAU
27	15:42	GEM
29	17:36	CAN

JULY

1	21:17	LEO
4	03:56	VIR
6	13:54	LIB
9	02:04	SCO
11	14:19	SAG
14	00:40	CAP
16	08:20	AQU
18	13:33	PIS
20	17:08	ARI
22	19:53	TAU
24	22:31	GEM
27	01:42	CAN
29	06:11	LEO
31	12:50	VIR

AUGUST

2	22:14	LIB
5	10:03	SCO
7	22:33	SAG
10	09:21	CAP
12	16:55	AQU
14	21:17	PIS
16	23:38	ARI
19	01:26	TAU
21	03:57	GEM
23	07:50	CAN
25	13:23	LEO
27	20:44	VIR
30	06:12	LIB

SEPTEMBER

1	17:49	SCO
4	06:33	SAG
6	18:10	CAP
9	02:31	AQU
11	06:55	PIS
13	08:23	ARI
15	08:45	TAU
17	09:55	GEM
19	13:13	CAN
21	19:04	LEO
24	03:11	VIR
26	13:11	LIB
29	00:52	SCO

OCTOBER

1	13:42	SAG
4	02:05	CAP
6	11:46	AQU
8	17:17	PIS
10	18:59	ARI
12	18:32	TAU
14	18:10	GEM
16	19:50	CAN
19	00:41	LEO
21	08:45	VIR
23	19:12	LIB
26	07:11	SCO
28	19:59	SAG
31	08:37	CAP

NOVEMBER

2	19:23	AQU
5	02:35	PIS
7	05:43	ARI
9	05:49	TAU
11	04:51	GEM
13	05:00	CAN
15	08:03	LEO
17	14:53	VIR
20	01:03	LIB
22	13:13	SCO
25	02:02	SAG
27	14:24	CAP
30	01:20	AQU

DECEMBER

2	09:39	PIS
4	14:35	ARI
6	16:23	TAU
8	16:17	GEM
10	16:07	CAN
12	17:49	LEO
14	22:54	VIR
17	07:52	LIB
19	19:44	SCO
22	08:35	SAG
24	20:41	CAP
27	07:01	AQU
29	15:10	PIS
31	20:57	ARI

1955

JANUARY		
3	00:25	TAU
5	02:05	GEM
7	03:01	CAN
9	04:42	LEO
11	08:43	VIR
13	16:15	LIB
16	03:15	SCO
18	16:02	SAG
21	04:10	CAP
23	13:59	AQU
25	21:11	PIS
28	02:20	ARI
30	06:06	TAU

FEBRUARY		
1	09:03	GEM
3	11:37	CAN
5	14:29	LEO
7	18:43	VIR
10	01:34	LIB
12	11:39	SCO
15	00:08	SAG
17	12:35	CAP
19	22:33	AQU
22	05:10	PIS
24	09:06	ARI
26	11:47	TAU
28	14:24	GEM

MARCH		
2	17:40	CAN
4	21:49	LEO
7	03:09	VIR
9	10:20	LIB
11	20:05	SCO
14	08:14	SAG
16	21:02	CAP
19	07:47	AQU
21	14:45	PIS
23	18:10	ARI
25	19:32	TAU
27	20:42	GEM
29	23:06	CAN

APRIL		
1	03:21	LEO
3	09:31	VIR
5	17:34	LIB
8	03:38	SCO
10	15:42	SAG
13	04:41	CAP
15	16:20	AQU
18	00:29	PIS
20	04:30	ARI
22	05:30	TAU
24	05:24	GEM
26	06:09	CAN
28	09:09	LEO
30	14:58	VIR

MAY		
2	23:26	LIB
5	10:04	SCO
7	22:19	SAG
10	11:19	CAP
12	23:30	AQU
15	08:54	PIS
17	14:21	ARI
19	16:12	TAU
21	15:57	GEM
23	15:33	CAN
25	16:53	LEO
27	21:16	VIR
30	05:08	LIB

JUNE		
1	15:54	SCO
4	04:24	SAG
6	17:21	CAP
9	05:30	AQU
11	15:32	PIS
13	22:24	ARI
16	01:50	TAU
18	02:37	GEM
20	02:16	CAN
22	02:37	LEO
24	05:27	VIR
26	11:56	LIB
28	22:05	SCO

JULY		
1	10:34	SAG
3	23:30	CAP
6	11:19	AQU
8	21:09	PIS
11	04:33	ARI
13	09:21	TAU
15	11:43	GEM
17	12:30	CAN
19	13:04	LEO
21	15:07	VIR
23	20:16	LIB
26	05:19	SCO
28	17:24	SAG
31	06:19	CAP

AUGUST		
2	17:52	AQU
5	03:04	PIS
7	10:00	ARI
9	15:03	TAU
11	18:34	GEM
13	20:51	CAN
15	22:34	LEO
18	00:58	VIR
20	05:34	LIB
22	13:38	SCO
25	01:04	SAG
27	13:57	CAP
30	01:36	AQU

SEPTEMBER		
1	10:23	PIS
3	16:24	ARI
5	20:37	TAU
7	23:59	GEM
10	03:01	CAN
12	06:02	LEO
14	09:34	VIR
16	14:36	LIB
18	22:59	SCO
21	09:12	SAG
23	22:01	CAP
26	10:08	AQU
28	19:13	PIS

OCTOBER		
1	00:47	ARI
3	03:52	TAU
5	06:00	GEM
7	08:23	CAN
9	11:42	LEO
11	16:12	VIR
13	22:14	LIB
16	06:24	SCO
18	17:08	SAG
21	05:52	CAP
23	18:33	AQU
26	04:38	PIS
28	10:47	ARI
30	13:30	TAU

NOVEMBER		
1	14:23	GEM
3	15:12	CAN
5	17:20	LEO
7	21:37	VIR
10	04:16	LIB
12	13:13	SCO
15	00:17	SAG
17	12:59	CAP
20	01:59	AQU
22	13:11	PIS
24	20:48	ARI
27	00:27	TAU
29	01:11	GEM

DECEMBER		
1	00:47	CAN
3	01:08	LEO
5	03:50	VIR
7	09:49	LIB
9	19:00	SCO
12	06:34	SAG
14	19:24	CAP
17	08:20	AQU
19	20:02	PIS
22	05:06	ARI
24	10:33	TAU
26	12:33	GEM
28	12:18	CAN
30	11:37	LEO

1956

JANUARY
1	12:31	VIR
3	16:44	LIB
6	01:00	SCO
8	12:33	SAG
11	01:34	CAP
13	14:20	AQU
16	01:48	PIS
18	11:18	ARI
20	18:12	TAU
22	22:06	GEM
24	23:20	CAN
26	23:07	LEO
28	23:18	VIR
31	01:56	LIB

FEBRUARY
2	08:34	SCO
4	19:13	SAG
7	08:09	CAP
9	20:52	AQU
12	07:52	PIS
14	16:49	ARI
16	23:49	TAU
19	04:51	GEM
21	07:50	CAN
23	09:11	LEO
25	10:05	VIR
27	12:21	LIB
29	17:45	SCO

MARCH
3	03:10	SAG
5	15:33	CAP
8	04:20	AQU
10	15:12	PIS
12	23:27	ARI
15	05:33	TAU
17	10:12	GEM
19	13:48	CAN
21	16:31	LEO
23	18:53	VIR
25	22:00	LIB
28	03:19	SCO
30	11:56	SAG

APRIL
1	23:38	CAP
4	12:25	AQU
6	23:38	PIS
9	07:47	ARI
11	13:04	TAU
13	16:31	GEM
15	19:15	CAN
17	22:01	LEO
20	01:17	VIR
22	05:37	LIB
24	11:45	SCO
26	20:26	SAG
29	07:45	CAP

MAY
1	20:28	AQU
4	08:16	PIS
6	17:06	ARI
8	22:24	TAU
11	01:01	GEM
13	02:21	CAN
15	03:52	LEO
17	06:40	VIR
19	11:26	LIB
21	18:27	SCO
24	03:47	SAG
26	15:12	CAP
29	03:52	AQU
31	16:10	PIS

JUNE
3	02:05	ARI
5	08:22	TAU
7	11:10	GEM
9	11:42	CAN
11	11:45	LEO
13	13:04	VIR
15	16:59	LIB
18	00:03	SCO
20	09:56	SAG
22	21:43	CAP
25	10:26	AQU
27	22:55	PIS
30	09:43	ARI

JULY
2	17:26	TAU
4	21:26	GEM
6	22:20	CAN
8	21:42	LEO
10	21:35	VIR
12	23:55	LIB
15	05:57	SCO
17	15:38	SAG
20	03:41	CAP
22	16:29	AQU
25	04:51	PIS
27	15:54	ARI
30	00:41	TAU

AUGUST
1	06:16	GEM
3	08:33	CAN
5	08:27	LEO
7	07:50	VIR
9	08:51	LIB
11	13:21	SCO
13	22:00	SAG
16	09:48	CAP
18	22:38	AQU
21	10:48	PIS
23	21:30	ARI
26	06:24	TAU
28	13:00	GEM
30	16:52	CAN

SEPTEMBER
1	18:14	LEO
3	18:21	VIR
5	19:05	LIB
7	22:27	SCO
10	05:46	SAG
12	16:46	CAP
15	05:28	AQU
17	17:34	PIS
20	03:48	ARI
22	12:01	TAU
24	18:25	GEM
26	23:00	CAN
29	01:49	LEO

OCTOBER
1	03:25	VIR
3	05:02	LIB
5	08:19	SCO
7	14:46	SAG
10	00:48	CAP
12	13:10	AQU
15	01:25	PIS
17	11:36	ARI
19	19:08	TAU
22	00:29	GEM
24	04:24	CAN
26	07:27	LEO
28	10:10	VIR
30	13:10	LIB

NOVEMBER
1	17:25	SCO
3	23:57	SAG
6	09:24	CAP
8	21:20	AQU
11	09:51	PIS
13	20:37	ARI
16	04:13	TAU
18	08:45	GEM
20	11:18	CAN
22	13:10	LEO
24	15:32	VIR
26	19:11	LIB
29	00:35	SCO

DECEMBER
1	07:59	SAG
3	17:36	CAP
6	05:17	AQU
8	17:57	PIS
11	05:37	ARI
13	14:16	TAU
15	19:07	GEM
17	20:52	CAN
19	21:12	LEO
21	21:56	VIR
24	00:39	LIB
26	06:09	SCO
28	14:20	SAG
31	00:37	CAP

1957

JANUARY
2	12:25	AQU
5	01:05	PIS
7	13:23	ARI
9	23:27	TAU
12	05:44	GEM
14	08:06	CAN
16	07:51	LEO
18	07:04	VIR
20	07:55	LIB
22	12:03	SCO
24	19:52	SAG
27	06:33	CAP
29	18:42	AQU

FEBRUARY
1	07:21	PIS
3	19:42	ARI
6	06:38	TAU
8	14:35	GEM
10	18:39	CAN
12	19:19	LEO
14	18:17	VIR
16	17:50	LIB
18	20:06	SCO
21	02:23	SAG
23	12:27	CAP
26	00:43	AQU
28	13:25	PIS

MARCH
3	01:31	ARI
5	12:21	TAU
7	21:04	GEM
10	02:45	CAN
12	05:12	LEO
14	05:20	VIR
16	04:59	LIB
18	06:15	SCO
20	10:54	SAG
22	19:35	CAP
25	07:18	AQU
27	20:00	PIS
30	07:55	ARI

APRIL
1	18:11	TAU
4	02:31	GEM
6	08:38	CAN
8	12:25	LEO
10	14:13	VIR
12	15:09	LIB
14	16:46	SCO
16	20:43	SAG
19	04:09	CAP
21	14:54	AQU
24	03:23	PIS
26	15:22	ARI
29	01:18	TAU

MAY
1	08:47	GEM
3	14:09	CAN
5	17:54	LEO
7	20:37	VIR
9	22:58	LIB
12	01:49	SCO
14	06:14	SAG
16	13:14	CAP
18	23:13	AQU
21	11:21	PIS
23	23:34	ARI
26	09:43	TAU
28	16:47	GEM
30	21:06	CAN

JUNE
1	23:46	LEO
4	02:00	VIR
6	04:46	LIB
8	08:41	SCO
10	14:10	SAG
12	21:37	CAP
15	07:24	AQU
17	19:15	PIS
20	07:46	ARI
22	18:39	TAU
25	02:07	GEM
27	06:01	CAN
29	07:31	LEO

JULY
1	08:24	VIR
3	10:17	LIB
5	14:10	SCO
7	20:21	SAG
10	04:35	CAP
12	14:43	AQU
15	02:33	PIS
17	15:15	ARI
20	02:58	TAU
22	11:34	GEM
24	16:05	CAN
26	17:17	LEO
28	17:00	VIR
30	17:20	LIB

AUGUST
1	20:01	SCO
4	01:48	SAG
6	10:24	CAP
8	21:02	AQU
11	09:02	PIS
13	21:46	ARI
16	10:01	TAU
18	19:52	GEM
21	01:49	CAN
23	03:51	LEO
25	03:26	VIR
27	02:42	LIB
29	03:46	SCO
31	08:08	SAG

SEPTEMBER
2	16:06	CAP
5	02:50	AQU
7	15:04	PIS
10	03:45	ARI
12	15:58	TAU
15	02:27	GEM
17	09:50	CAN
19	13:31	LEO
21	14:12	VIR
23	13:33	LIB
25	13:41	SCO
27	16:28	SAG
29	23:00	CAP

OCTOBER
2	09:04	AQU
4	21:18	PIS
7	09:57	ARI
9	21:48	TAU
12	08:01	GEM
14	15:55	CAN
16	21:00	LEO
18	23:24	VIR
21	00:04	LIB
23	00:31	SCO
25	02:34	SAG
27	07:41	CAP
29	16:33	AQU

NOVEMBER
1	04:19	PIS
3	17:00	ARI
6	04:38	TAU
8	14:09	GEM
10	21:24	CAN
13	02:37	LEO
15	06:07	VIR
17	08:26	LIB
19	10:18	SCO
21	12:52	SAG
23	17:30	CAP
26	01:17	AQU
28	12:16	PIS

DECEMBER
1	00:57	ARI
3	12:48	TAU
5	22:01	GEM
8	04:16	CAN
10	08:24	LEO
12	11:29	VIR
14	14:23	LIB
16	17:36	SCO
18	21:31	SAG
21	02:47	CAP
23	10:19	AQU
25	20:41	PIS
28	09:13	ARI
30	21:38	TAU

1958

JANUARY		
2	07:22	GEM
4	13:22	CAN
6	16:22	LEO
8	17:59	VIR
10	19:52	LIB
12	23:03	SCO
15	03:50	SAG
17	10:13	CAP
19	18:23	AQU
22	04:42	PIS
24	17:03	ARI
27	05:57	TAU
29	16:48	GEM
31	23:41	CAN

FEBRUARY		
3	02:38	LEO
5	03:11	VIR
7	03:24	LIB
9	05:04	SCO
11	09:12	SAG
13	15:56	CAP
16	00:52	AQU
18	11:40	PIS
21	00:02	ARI
23	13:05	TAU
26	00:53	GEM
28	09:17	CAN

MARCH		
2	13:27	LEO
4	14:15	VIR
6	13:36	LIB
8	13:35	SCO
10	15:57	SAG
12	21:37	CAP
15	06:28	AQU
17	17:42	PIS
20	06:17	ARI
22	19:16	TAU
25	07:20	GEM
27	16:53	CAN
29	22:46	LEO

APRIL		
1	01:01	VIR
3	00:54	LIB
5	00:17	SCO
7	01:07	SAG
9	05:01	CAP
11	12:42	AQU
13	23:39	PIS
16	12:23	ARI
19	01:17	TAU
21	13:03	GEM
23	22:47	CAN
26	05:44	LEO
28	09:41	VIR
30	11:07	LIB

MAY		
2	11:15	SCO
4	11:44	SAG
6	14:21	CAP
8	20:30	AQU
11	06:27	PIS
13	18:58	ARI
16	07:50	TAU
18	19:14	GEM
21	04:23	CAN
23	11:15	LEO
25	16:00	VIR
27	18:56	LIB
29	20:34	SCO
31	21:54	SAG

JUNE		
3	00:23	CAP
5	05:34	AQU
7	14:24	PIS
10	02:21	ARI
12	15:13	TAU
15	02:31	GEM
17	11:04	CAN
19	17:04	LEO
21	21:23	VIR
24	00:43	LIB
26	03:31	SCO
28	06:12	SAG
30	09:33	CAP

JULY		
2	14:45	AQU
4	22:57	PIS
7	10:18	ARI
9	23:10	TAU
12	10:47	GEM
14	19:16	CAN
17	00:31	LEO
19	03:42	VIR
21	06:12	LIB
23	08:58	SCO
25	12:26	SAG
27	16:53	CAP
29	22:53	AQU

AUGUST		
1	07:12	PIS
3	18:15	ARI
6	07:05	TAU
8	19:17	GEM
11	04:26	CAN
13	09:44	LEO
15	12:07	VIR
17	13:17	LIB
19	14:50	SCO
21	17:48	SAG
23	22:39	CAP
26	05:28	AQU
28	14:25	PIS
31	01:36	ARI

SEPTEMBER		
2	14:24	TAU
5	03:07	GEM
7	13:23	CAN
9	19:42	LEO
11	22:20	VIR
13	22:45	LIB
15	22:50	SCO
18	00:17	SAG
20	04:13	CAP
22	11:04	AQU
24	20:34	PIS
27	08:08	ARI
29	20:58	TAU

OCTOBER		
2	09:51	GEM
4	21:01	CAN
7	04:51	LEO
9	08:50	VIR
11	09:44	LIB
13	09:12	SCO
15	09:09	SAG
17	11:23	CAP
19	17:04	AQU
22	02:20	PIS
24	14:11	ARI
27	03:08	TAU
29	15:50	GEM

NOVEMBER		
1	03:09	CAN
3	12:03	LEO
5	17:46	VIR
7	20:17	LIB
9	20:30	SCO
11	20:03	SAG
13	20:55	CAP
16	00:53	AQU
18	08:57	PIS
20	20:29	ARI
23	09:31	TAU
25	22:01	GEM
28	08:52	CAN
30	17:41	LEO

DECEMBER		
3	00:18	VIR
5	04:31	LIB
7	06:29	SCO
9	07:02	SAG
11	07:47	CAP
13	10:38	AQU
15	17:12	PIS
18	03:46	ARI
20	16:38	TAU
23	05:09	GEM
25	15:33	CAN
27	23:34	LEO
30	05:41	VIR

1959

JANUARY			FEBRUARY			MARCH			APRIL		
1	10:22	LIB	1	22:11	SAG	1	03:33	SAG	1	17:42	AQU
3	13:42	SCO	4	01:29	CAP	3	07:06	CAP	4	01:23	PIS
5	15:56	SAG	6	05:41	AQU	5	12:17	AQU	6	11:33	ARI
7	17:50	CAP	8	11:51	PIS	7	19:26	PIS	8	23:32	TAU
9	20:52	AQU	10	20:55	ARI	10	04:54	ARI	11	12:25	GEM
12	02:40	PIS	13	08:48	TAU	12	16:37	TAU	14	00:48	CAN
14	12:10	ARI	15	21:40	GEM	15	05:31	GEM	16	10:55	LEO
17	00:33	TAU	18	08:51	CAN	17	17:28	CAN	18	17:28	VIR
19	13:16	GEM	20	16:38	LEO	20	02:23	LEO	20	20:19	LIB
21	23:47	CAN	22	21:06	VIR	22	07:28	VIR	22	20:34	SCO
24	07:14	LEO	24	23:29	LIB	24	09:27	LIB	24	19:59	SAG
26	12:14	VIR	27	01:15	SCO	26	09:54	SCO	26	20:33	CAP
28	15:55	LIB				28	10:32	SAG	28	23:56	AQU
30	19:06	SCO				30	12:49	CAP			

MAY			JUNE			JULY			AUGUST		
1	06:59	PIS	2	11:37	TAU	2	07:06	GEM	1	02:24	CAN
3	17:19	ARI	5	00:36	GEM	4	19:04	CAN	3	12:10	LEO
6	05:39	TAU	7	12:44	CAN	7	05:08	LEO	5	19:30	VIR
8	18:35	GEM	9	23:19	LEO	9	13:16	VIR	8	00:57	LIB
11	06:57	CAN	12	07:51	VIR	11	19:27	LIB	10	05:00	SCO
13	17:41	LEO	14	13:42	LIB	13	23:34	SCO	12	07:59	SAG
16	01:38	VIR	16	16:39	SCO	16	01:42	SAG	14	10:19	CAP
18	06:07	LIB	18	17:15	SAG	18	02:42	CAP	16	12:54	AQU
20	07:25	SCO	20	17:02	CAP	20	04:05	AQU	18	17:00	PIS
22	06:51	SAG	22	18:01	AQU	22	07:41	PIS	20	23:52	ARI
24	06:24	CAP	24	22:10	PIS	24	14:54	ARI	23	09:59	TAU
26	08:10	AQU	27	06:28	ARI	27	01:44	TAU	25	22:19	GEM
28	13:43	PIS	29	18:11	TAU	29	14:24	GEM	28	10:34	CAN
30	23:19	ARI							30	20:34	LEO

SEPTEMBER			OCTOBER			NOVEMBER			DECEMBER		
2	03:31	VIR	1	17:09	LIB	2	05:02	SAG	1	15:11	CAP
4	07:57	LIB	3	18:54	SCO	4	05:05	CAP	3	15:35	AQU
6	10:53	SCO	5	19:55	SAG	6	07:14	AQU	5	19:17	PIS
8	13:21	SAG	7	21:39	CAP	8	12:36	PIS	8	03:00	ARI
10	16:05	CAP	10	01:13	AQU	10	21:10	ARI	10	13:56	TAU
12	19:44	AQU	12	07:06	PIS	13	08:05	TAU	13	02:25	GEM
15	00:54	PIS	14	15:20	ARI	15	20:17	GEM	15	15:01	CAN
17	08:17	ARI	17	01:40	TAU	18	08:57	CAN	18	02:58	LEO
19	18:13	TAU	19	13:40	GEM	20	21:04	LEO	20	13:30	VIR
22	06:16	GEM	22	02:23	CAN	23	07:08	VIR	22	21:29	LIB
24	18:50	CAN	24	14:04	LEO	25	13:42	LIB	25	02:01	SCO
27	05:37	LEO	26	22:49	VIR	27	16:22	SCO	27	03:16	SAG
29	13:04	VIR	29	03:42	LIB	29	16:12	SAG	29	02:38	CAP
			31	05:14	SCO				31	02:15	AQU

1960

JANUARY		
2	04:19	PIS
4	10:22	ARI
6	20:23	TAU
9	08:46	GEM
11	21:24	CAN
14	09:00	LEO
16	19:04	VIR
19	03:15	LIB
21	09:00	SCO
23	12:03	SAG
25	13:00	CAP
27	13:19	AQU
29	14:57	PIS
31	19:40	ARI

FEBRUARY		
3	04:17	TAU
5	15:59	GEM
8	04:38	CAN
10	16:09	LEO
13	01:35	VIR
15	08:56	LIB
17	14:24	SCO
19	18:12	SAG
21	20:40	CAP
23	22:33	AQU
26	01:04	PIS
28	05:38	ARI

MARCH		
1	13:19	TAU
4	00:08	GEM
6	12:37	CAN
9	00:25	LEO
11	09:48	VIR
13	16:20	LIB
15	20:38	SCO
17	23:38	SAG
20	02:15	CAP
22	05:11	AQU
24	09:02	PIS
26	14:30	ARI
28	22:14	TAU
31	08:32	GEM

APRIL		
2	20:46	CAN
5	09:01	LEO
7	19:02	VIR
10	01:36	LIB
12	05:02	SCO
14	06:38	SAG
16	08:01	CAP
18	10:32	AQU
20	14:56	PIS
22	21:23	ARI
25	05:51	TAU
27	16:17	GEM
30	04:23	CAN

MAY		
2	16:59	LEO
5	03:59	VIR
7	11:31	LIB
9	15:07	SCO
11	15:56	SAG
13	15:51	CAP
15	16:52	AQU
17	20:24	PIS
20	02:56	ARI
22	12:00	TAU
24	22:55	GEM
27	11:07	CAN
29	23:51	LEO

JUNE		
1	11:38	VIR
3	20:32	LIB
6	01:20	SCO
8	02:31	SAG
10	01:48	CAP
12	01:23	AQU
14	03:18	PIS
16	08:43	ARI
18	17:34	TAU
21	04:46	GEM
23	17:10	CAN
26	05:52	LEO
28	17:53	VIR

JULY		
1	03:47	LIB
3	10:09	SCO
5	12:43	SAG
7	12:35	CAP
9	11:43	AQU
11	12:19	PIS
13	16:07	ARI
15	23:49	TAU
18	10:41	GEM
20	23:09	CAN
23	11:46	LEO
25	23:32	VIR
28	09:34	LIB
30	16:55	SCO

AUGUST		
1	21:05	SAG
3	22:26	CAP
5	22:21	AQU
7	22:43	PIS
10	01:22	ARI
12	07:36	TAU
14	17:30	GEM
17	05:43	CAN
19	18:18	LEO
22	05:42	VIR
24	15:10	LIB
26	22:24	SCO
29	03:20	SAG
31	06:09	CAP

SEPTEMBER		
2	07:36	AQU
4	08:51	PIS
6	11:26	ARI
8	16:45	TAU
11	01:32	GEM
13	13:11	CAN
16	01:47	LEO
18	13:07	VIR
20	21:59	LIB
23	04:18	SCO
25	08:42	SAG
27	11:54	CAP
29	14:33	AQU

OCTOBER		
1	17:15	PIS
3	20:47	ARI
6	02:09	TAU
8	10:17	GEM
10	21:19	CAN
13	09:55	LEO
15	21:41	VIR
18	06:33	LIB
20	12:06	SCO
22	15:16	SAG
24	17:29	CAP
26	19:58	AQU
28	23:27	PIS
31	04:12	ARI

NOVEMBER		
2	10:28	TAU
4	18:45	GEM
7	05:26	CAN
9	18:00	LEO
12	06:24	VIR
14	16:08	LIB
16	21:54	SCO
19	00:17	SAG
21	01:03	CAP
23	02:05	AQU
25	04:50	PIS
27	09:51	ARI
29	17:00	TAU

DECEMBER		
2	02:01	GEM
4	12:53	CAN
7	01:22	LEO
9	14:14	VIR
12	01:11	LIB
14	08:14	SCO
16	11:07	SAG
18	11:17	CAP
20	10:49	AQU
22	11:48	PIS
24	15:35	ARI
26	22:31	TAU
29	08:02	GEM
31	19:22	CAN

1961

JANUARY			FEBRUARY		
3	07:54	LEO	2	02:49	VIR
5	20:49	VIR	4	14:28	LIB
8	08:32	LIB	6	23:51	SCO
10	17:09	SCO	9	06:02	SAG
12	21:41	SAG	11	08:51	CAP
14	22:42	CAP	13	09:15	AQU
16	21:56	AQU	15	08:53	PIS
18	21:32	PIS	17	09:41	ARI
20	23:27	ARI	19	13:22	TAU
23	04:52	TAU	21	20:52	GEM
25	13:50	GEM	24	07:49	CAN
28	01:22	CAN	26	20:35	LEO
30	14:06	LEO			

MARCH			APRIL		
1	09:12	VIR	2	11:37	SCO
3	20:22	LIB	4	17:34	SAG
6	05:24	SCO	6	21:52	CAP
8	12:04	SAG	9	01:03	AQU
10	16:19	CAP	11	03:32	PIS
12	18:29	AQU	13	05:56	ARI
14	19:27	PIS	15	09:17	TAU
16	20:33	ARI	17	14:55	GEM
18	23:26	TAU	19	23:50	CAN
21	05:33	GEM	22	11:43	LEO
23	15:23	CAN	25	00:31	VIR
26	03:49	LEO	27	11:35	LIB
28	16:30	VIR	29	19:27	SCO
31	03:22	LIB			

MAY			JUNE		
2	00:25	SAG	2	12:45	AQU
4	03:40	CAP	4	14:51	PIS
6	06:24	AQU	6	18:24	ARI
8	09:23	PIS	8	23:38	TAU
10	12:56	ARI	11	06:41	GEM
12	17:26	TAU	13	15:50	CAN
14	23:35	GEM	16	03:16	LEO
17	08:17	CAN	18	16:12	VIR
19	19:45	LEO	21	04:32	LIB
22	08:39	VIR	23	13:51	SCO
24	20:18	LIB	25	19:06	SAG
27	04:35	SCO	27	21:00	CAP
29	09:11	SAG	29	21:18	AQU
31	11:21	CAP			

JULY			AUGUST		
1	21:53	PIS	2	11:19	TAU
4	00:12	ARI	4	18:04	GEM
6	05:02	TAU	7	03:57	CAN
8	12:28	GEM	9	16:00	LEO
10	22:13	CAN	12	05:01	VIR
13	09:57	LEO	14	17:44	LIB
15	22:55	VIR	17	04:45	SCO
18	11:39	LIB	19	12:44	SAG
20	22:05	SCO	21	17:08	CAP
23	04:42	SAG	23	18:26	AQU
25	07:29	CAP	25	18:03	PIS
27	07:42	AQU	27	17:49	ARI
29	07:13	PIS	29	19:37	TAU
31	07:56	ARI			

SEPTEMBER			OCTOBER		
1	00:53	GEM	3	04:44	LEO
3	10:01	CAN	5	17:46	VIR
5	22:01	LEO	8	06:04	LIB
8	11:05	VIR	10	16:20	SCO
10	23:34	LIB	13	00:21	SAG
13	10:23	SCO	15	06:24	CAP
15	18:55	SAG	17	10:37	AQU
18	00:42	CAP	19	13:10	PIS
20	03:44	AQU	21	14:36	ARI
22	04:36	PIS	23	16:07	TAU
24	04:40	ARI	25	19:25	GEM
26	05:42	TAU	28	02:03	CAN
28	09:32	GEM	30	12:30	LEO
30	17:20	CAN			

NOVEMBER			DECEMBER		
2	01:18	VIR	1	22:08	LIB
4	13:43	LIB	4	08:30	SCO
6	23:41	SCO	6	15:25	SAG
9	06:51	SAG	8	19:31	CAP
11	12:00	CAP	10	22:12	AQU
13	16:00	AQU	13	00:42	PIS
15	19:19	PIS	15	03:45	ARI
17	22:11	ARI	17	07:39	TAU
20	01:03	TAU	19	12:48	GEM
22	04:59	GEM	21	19:50	CAN
24	11:21	CAN	24	05:26	LEO
26	21:02	LEO	26	17:30	VIR
29	09:26	VIR	29	06:27	LIB
			31	17:42	SCO

1962

JANUARY		
3	01:24	SAG
5	05:24	CAP
7	07:00	AQU
9	07:54	PIS
11	09:34	ARI
13	13:02	TAU
15	18:42	GEM
18	02:40	CAN
20	12:50	LEO
23	00:54	VIR
25	13:52	LIB
28	01:55	SCO
30	11:00	SAG

FEBRUARY		
1	16:10	CAP
3	17:57	AQU
5	17:53	PIS
7	17:51	ARI
9	19:35	TAU
12	00:19	GEM
14	08:20	CAN
16	19:04	LEO
19	07:27	VIR
21	20:22	LIB
24	08:37	SCO
26	18:47	SAG

MARCH		
1	01:39	CAP
3	04:52	AQU
5	05:17	PIS
7	04:32	ARI
9	04:41	TAU
11	07:36	GEM
13	14:26	CAN
16	00:56	LEO
18	13:33	VIR
21	02:29	LIB
23	14:29	SCO
26	00:49	SAG
28	08:46	CAP
30	13:44	AQU

APRIL		
1	15:43	PIS
3	15:42	ARI
5	15:26	TAU
7	17:00	GEM
9	22:12	CAN
12	07:37	LEO
14	19:57	VIR
17	08:54	LIB
19	20:37	SCO
22	06:27	SAG
24	14:20	CAP
26	20:08	AQU
28	23:40	PIS

MAY		
1	01:12	ARI
3	01:50	TAU
5	03:17	GEM
7	07:28	CAN
9	15:36	LEO
12	03:12	VIR
14	16:03	LIB
17	03:43	SCO
19	13:03	SAG
21	20:09	CAP
24	01:31	AQU
26	05:30	PIS
28	08:15	ARI
30	10:17	TAU

JUNE		
1	12:41	GEM
3	16:57	CAN
6	00:24	LEO
8	11:13	VIR
10	23:51	LIB
13	11:45	SCO
15	21:04	SAG
18	03:30	CAP
20	07:49	AQU
22	10:59	PIS
24	13:43	ARI
26	16:35	TAU
28	20:10	GEM

JULY		
1	01:19	CAN
3	08:56	LEO
5	19:23	VIR
8	07:48	LIB
10	20:06	SCO
13	06:01	SAG
15	12:32	CAP
17	16:08	AQU
19	18:01	PIS
21	19:34	ARI
23	21:57	TAU
26	01:57	GEM
28	08:01	CAN
30	16:21	LEO

AUGUST		
2	02:58	VIR
4	15:18	LIB
7	03:56	SCO
9	14:49	SAG
11	22:18	CAP
14	02:08	AQU
16	03:17	PIS
18	03:26	ARI
20	04:20	TAU
22	07:28	GEM
24	13:34	CAN
26	22:30	LEO
29	09:36	VIR
31	22:01	LIB

SEPTEMBER		
3	10:47	SCO
5	22:27	SAG
8	07:20	CAP
10	12:27	AQU
12	14:02	PIS
14	13:33	ARI
16	13:01	TAU
18	14:29	GEM
20	19:26	CAN
23	04:07	LEO
25	15:31	VIR
28	04:08	LIB
30	16:49	SCO

OCTOBER		
3	04:40	SAG
5	14:35	CAP
7	21:22	AQU
10	00:29	PIS
12	00:41	ARI
13	23:44	TAU
15	23:51	GEM
18	03:05	CAN
20	10:31	LEO
22	21:32	VIR
25	10:14	LIB
27	22:49	SCO
30	10:20	SAG

NOVEMBER		
1	20:18	CAP
4	04:03	AQU
6	08:53	PIS
8	10:46	ARI
10	10:45	TAU
12	10:44	GEM
14	12:49	CAN
16	18:40	LEO
19	04:34	VIR
21	16:58	LIB
24	05:34	SCO
26	16:44	SAG
29	02:01	CAP

DECEMBER		
1	09:26	AQU
3	14:54	PIS
5	18:18	ARI
7	20:00	TAU
9	21:08	GEM
11	23:22	CAN
14	04:21	LEO
16	13:00	VIR
19	00:42	LIB
21	13:18	SCO
24	00:33	SAG
26	09:19	CAP
28	15:43	AQU
30	20:21	PIS

1963

JANUARY
1	23:48	ARI
4	02:34	TAU
6	05:14	GEM
8	08:42	CAN
10	14:01	LEO
12	22:07	VIR
15	09:05	LIB
17	21:36	SCO
20	09:21	SAG
22	18:24	CAP
25	00:14	AQU
27	03:35	PIS
29	05:44	ARI
31	07:55	TAU

FEBRUARY
2	11:03	GEM
4	15:41	CAN
6	22:06	LEO
9	06:36	VIR
11	17:19	LIB
14	05:39	SCO
16	17:58	SAG
19	04:01	CAP
21	10:24	AQU
23	13:18	PIS
25	14:06	ARI
27	14:39	TAU

MARCH
1	16:39	GEM
3	21:08	CAN
6	04:15	LEO
8	13:34	VIR
11	00:35	LIB
13	12:52	SCO
16	01:27	SAG
18	12:35	CAP
20	20:22	AQU
23	00:05	PIS
25	00:38	ARI
26	23:57	TAU
29	00:13	GEM
31	03:14	CAN

APRIL
2	09:46	LEO
4	19:21	VIR
7	06:50	LIB
9	19:14	SCO
12	07:49	SAG
14	19:27	CAP
17	04:35	AQU
19	09:54	PIS
21	11:30	ARI
23	10:51	TAU
25	10:07	GEM
27	11:28	CAN
29	16:25	LEO

MAY
2	01:13	VIR
4	12:43	LIB
7	01:16	SCO
9	13:43	SAG
12	01:14	CAP
14	10:52	AQU
16	17:32	PIS
18	20:48	ARI
20	21:22	TAU
22	20:54	GEM
24	21:29	CAN
27	00:59	LEO
29	08:22	VIR
31	19:10	LIB

JUNE
3	07:39	SCO
5	20:01	SAG
8	07:07	CAP
10	16:22	AQU
12	23:21	PIS
15	03:47	ARI
17	05:55	TAU
19	06:44	GEM
21	07:47	CAN
23	10:45	LEO
25	16:57	VIR
28	02:41	LIB
30	14:48	SCO

JULY
3	03:12	SAG
5	14:03	CAP
7	22:37	AQU
10	04:53	PIS
12	09:17	ARI
14	12:15	TAU
16	14:28	GEM
18	16:45	CAN
20	20:16	LEO
23	02:07	VIR
25	11:03	LIB
27	22:39	SCO
30	11:08	SAG

AUGUST
1	22:13	CAP
4	06:26	AQU
6	11:46	PIS
8	15:07	ARI
10	17:38	TAU
12	20:16	GEM
14	23:40	CAN
17	04:17	LEO
19	10:41	VIR
21	19:26	LIB
24	06:39	SCO
26	19:16	SAG
29	06:58	CAP
31	15:38	AQU

SEPTEMBER
2	20:38	PIS
4	22:53	ARI
7	00:03	TAU
9	01:46	GEM
11	05:08	CAN
13	10:30	LEO
15	17:48	VIR
18	03:00	LIB
20	14:11	SCO
23	02:50	SAG
25	15:16	CAP
28	01:04	AQU
30	06:47	PIS

OCTOBER
2	08:48	ARI
4	08:50	TAU
6	08:59	GEM
8	11:01	CAN
10	15:55	LEO
12	23:35	VIR
15	09:25	LIB
17	20:53	SCO
20	09:33	SAG
22	22:21	CAP
25	09:21	AQU
27	16:37	PIS
29	19:40	ARI
31	19:43	TAU

NOVEMBER
2	18:49	GEM
4	19:09	CAN
6	22:24	LEO
9	05:14	VIR
11	15:08	LIB
14	02:57	SCO
16	15:40	SAG
19	04:23	CAP
21	15:52	AQU
24	00:33	PIS
26	05:25	ARI
28	06:50	TAU
30	06:15	GEM

DECEMBER
2	05:45	CAN
4	07:20	LEO
6	12:27	VIR
8	21:22	LIB
11	09:05	SCO
13	21:54	SAG
16	10:22	CAP
18	21:29	AQU
21	06:29	PIS
23	12:41	ARI
25	15:58	TAU
27	16:59	GEM
29	17:07	CAN
31	18:09	LEO

1964

JANUARY
2	21:48	VIR
5	05:10	LIB
7	16:04	SCO
10	04:50	SAG
12	17:14	CAP
15	03:48	AQU
17	12:04	PIS
19	18:11	ARI
21	22:24	TAU
24	01:05	GEM
26	02:52	CAN
28	04:46	LEO
30	08:09	VIR

FEBRUARY
1	14:26	LIB
4	00:13	SCO
6	12:36	SAG
9	01:11	CAP
11	11:40	AQU
13	19:09	PIS
16	00:10	ARI
18	03:46	TAU
20	06:48	GEM
22	09:50	CAN
24	13:11	LEO
26	17:30	VIR
28	23:47	LIB

MARCH
2	08:54	SCO
4	20:47	SAG
7	09:36	CAP
9	20:36	AQU
12	04:06	PIS
14	08:16	ARI
16	10:31	TAU
18	12:26	GEM
20	15:12	CAN
22	19:15	LEO
25	00:42	VIR
27	07:48	LIB
29	17:04	SCO

APRIL
1	04:41	SAG
3	17:37	CAP
6	05:25	AQU
8	13:47	PIS
10	18:09	ARI
12	19:37	TAU
14	20:06	GEM
16	21:24	CAN
19	00:40	LEO
21	06:18	VIR
23	14:09	LIB
26	00:01	SCO
28	11:46	SAG

MAY
1	00:43	CAP
3	13:07	AQU
5	22:44	PIS
8	04:16	ARI
10	06:09	TAU
12	06:02	GEM
14	05:54	CAN
16	07:32	LEO
18	12:03	VIR
20	19:42	LIB
23	05:58	SCO
25	18:04	SAG
28	07:01	CAP
30	19:33	AQU

JUNE
2	06:02	PIS
4	13:03	ARI
6	16:20	TAU
8	16:50	GEM
10	16:17	CAN
12	16:35	LEO
14	19:28	VIR
17	01:54	LIB
19	11:50	SCO
22	00:04	SAG
24	13:02	CAP
27	01:22	AQU
29	11:57	PIS

JULY
1	19:53	ARI
4	00:43	TAU
6	02:43	GEM
8	02:57	CAN
10	03:01	LEO
12	04:45	VIR
14	09:42	LIB
16	18:33	SCO
19	06:29	SAG
21	19:27	CAP
24	07:31	AQU
26	17:36	PIS
29	01:26	ARI
31	07:01	TAU

AUGUST
2	10:29	GEM
4	12:13	CAN
6	13:11	LEO
8	14:51	VIR
10	18:52	LIB
13	02:32	SCO
15	13:45	SAG
18	02:39	CAP
20	14:40	AQU
23	00:14	PIS
25	07:16	ARI
27	12:24	TAU
29	16:16	GEM
31	19:14	CAN

SEPTEMBER
2	21:37	LEO
5	00:13	VIR
7	04:20	LIB
9	11:20	SCO
11	21:48	SAG
14	10:31	CAP
16	22:48	AQU
19	08:23	PIS
21	14:44	ARI
23	18:47	TAU
25	21:47	GEM
28	00:40	CAN
30	03:53	LEO

OCTOBER
2	07:43	VIR
4	12:45	LIB
6	19:57	SCO
9	06:03	SAG
11	18:32	CAP
14	07:16	AQU
16	17:33	PIS
19	00:05	ARI
21	03:25	TAU
23	05:04	GEM
25	06:38	CAN
27	09:14	LEO
29	13:26	VIR
31	19:25	LIB

NOVEMBER
3	03:25	SCO
5	13:44	SAG
8	02:06	CAP
10	15:09	AQU
13	02:29	PIS
15	10:11	ARI
17	13:57	TAU
19	14:59	GEM
21	15:04	CAN
23	15:59	LEO
25	19:03	VIR
28	00:55	LIB
30	09:31	SCO

DECEMBER
2	20:24	SAG
5	08:54	CAP
7	21:58	AQU
10	10:00	PIS
12	19:13	ARI
15	00:33	TAU
17	02:22	GEM
19	02:03	CAN
21	01:31	LEO
23	02:42	VIR
25	07:05	LIB
27	15:12	SCO
30	02:21	SAG

1965

JANUARY

1	15:07	CAP
4	04:05	AQU
6	16:07	PIS
9	02:09	ARI
11	09:11	TAU
13	12:49	GEM
15	13:35	CAN
17	12:58	LEO
19	12:55	VIR
21	15:28	LIB
23	22:01	SCO
26	08:33	SAG
28	21:22	CAP
31	10:18	AQU

FEBRUARY

2	21:56	PIS
5	07:44	ARI
7	15:24	TAU
9	20:37	GEM
11	23:14	CAN
13	23:55	LEO
16	00:06	VIR
18	01:46	LIB
20	06:46	SCO
22	15:58	SAG
25	04:17	CAP
27	17:15	AQU

MARCH

2	04:39	PIS
4	13:45	ARI
6	20:50	TAU
9	02:15	GEM
11	06:03	CAN
13	08:23	LEO
15	09:56	VIR
17	12:04	LIB
19	16:33	SCO
22	00:37	SAG
24	12:07	CAP
27	00:59	AQU
29	12:32	PIS
31	21:19	ARI

APRIL

3	03:29	TAU
5	07:55	GEM
7	11:25	CAN
9	14:24	LEO
11	17:15	VIR
13	20:39	LIB
16	01:42	SCO
18	09:32	SAG
20	20:24	CAP
23	09:05	AQU
25	21:03	PIS
28	06:13	ARI
30	12:04	TAU

MAY

2	15:27	GEM
4	17:39	CAN
6	19:50	LEO
8	22:48	VIR
11	03:05	LIB
13	09:10	SCO
15	17:32	SAG
18	04:20	CAP
20	16:51	AQU
23	05:15	PIS
25	15:19	ARI
27	21:49	TAU
30	00:59	GEM

JUNE

1	02:06	CAN
3	02:47	LEO
5	04:34	VIR
7	08:30	LIB
9	15:04	SCO
12	00:10	SAG
14	11:21	CAP
16	23:52	AQU
19	12:29	PIS
21	23:30	ARI
24	07:17	TAU
26	11:19	GEM
28	12:20	CAN
30	11:59	LEO

JULY

2	12:12	VIR
4	14:43	LIB
6	20:38	SCO
9	05:54	SAG
11	17:29	CAP
14	06:08	AQU
16	18:45	PIS
19	06:13	ARI
21	15:14	TAU
23	20:49	GEM
25	22:54	CAN
27	22:38	LEO
29	21:55	VIR
31	22:55	LIB

AUGUST

3	03:21	SCO
5	11:50	SAG
7	23:23	CAP
10	12:10	AQU
13	00:38	PIS
15	11:57	ARI
17	21:28	TAU
20	04:21	GEM
22	08:05	CAN
24	09:02	LEO
26	08:37	VIR
28	08:53	LIB
30	11:54	SCO

SEPTEMBER

1	19:00	SAG
4	05:52	CAP
6	18:34	AQU
9	06:57	PIS
11	17:50	ARI
14	02:57	TAU
16	10:07	GEM
18	15:01	CAN
20	17:36	LEO
22	18:30	VIR
24	19:16	LIB
26	21:47	SCO
29	03:43	SAG

OCTOBER

1	13:29	CAP
4	01:49	AQU
6	14:14	PIS
9	00:54	ARI
11	09:17	TAU
13	15:40	GEM
15	20:27	CAN
17	23:52	LEO
20	02:14	VIR
22	04:21	LIB
24	07:32	SCO
26	13:10	SAG
28	22:05	CAP
31	09:50	AQU

NOVEMBER

2	22:23	PIS
5	09:22	ARI
7	17:30	TAU
9	22:55	GEM
12	02:30	CAN
14	05:14	LEO
16	07:55	VIR
18	11:11	LIB
20	15:37	SCO
22	21:57	SAG
25	06:46	CAP
27	18:04	AQU
30	06:40	PIS

DECEMBER

2	18:23	ARI
5	03:12	TAU
7	08:28	GEM
9	10:57	CAN
11	12:09	LEO
13	13:36	VIR
15	16:34	LIB
17	21:41	SCO
20	05:02	SAG
22	14:27	CAP
25	01:45	AQU
27	14:18	PIS
30	02:40	ARI

1966

JANUARY		
1	12:47	TAU
3	19:07	GEM
5	21:41	CAN
7	21:50	LEO
9	21:35	VIR
11	22:53	LIB
14	03:09	SCO
16	10:40	SAG
18	20:45	CAP
21	08:27	AQU
23	20:59	PIS
26	09:33	ARI
28	20:43	TAU
31	04:44	GEM

FEBRUARY		
2	08:41	CAN
4	09:14	LEO
6	08:12	VIR
8	07:51	LIB
10	10:15	SCO
12	16:34	SAG
15	02:26	CAP
17	14:26	AQU
20	03:06	PIS
22	15:31	ARI
25	02:54	TAU
27	12:03	GEM

MARCH		
1	17:48	CAN
3	19:57	LEO
5	19:37	VIR
7	18:49	LIB
9	19:47	SCO
12	00:19	SAG
14	08:56	CAP
16	20:35	AQU
19	09:19	PIS
21	21:34	ARI
24	08:32	TAU
26	17:42	GEM
29	00:24	CAN
31	04:12	LEO

APRIL		
2	05:31	VIR
4	05:40	LIB
6	06:31	SCO
8	09:54	SAG
10	17:02	CAP
13	03:43	AQU
15	16:14	PIS
18	04:28	ARI
20	15:01	TAU
22	23:28	GEM
25	05:48	CAN
27	10:10	LEO
29	12:50	VIR

MAY		
1	14:31	LIB
3	16:24	SCO
5	19:53	SAG
8	02:13	CAP
10	11:52	AQU
12	23:55	PIS
15	12:16	ARI
17	22:50	TAU
20	06:40	GEM
22	12:01	CAN
24	15:37	LEO
26	18:23	VIR
28	21:00	LIB
31	00:12	SCO

JUNE		
2	04:39	SAG
4	11:11	CAP
6	20:21	AQU
9	07:57	PIS
11	20:27	ARI
14	07:30	TAU
16	15:27	GEM
18	20:06	CAN
20	22:29	LEO
23	00:08	VIR
25	02:23	LIB
27	06:04	SCO
29	11:32	SAG

JULY		
1	18:52	CAP
4	04:15	AQU
6	15:40	PIS
9	04:16	ARI
11	16:04	TAU
14	00:52	GEM
16	05:45	CAN
18	07:28	LEO
20	07:47	VIR
22	08:39	LIB
24	11:32	SCO
26	17:05	SAG
29	01:05	CAP
31	11:02	AQU

AUGUST		
2	22:36	PIS
5	11:15	ARI
7	23:38	TAU
10	09:39	GEM
12	15:42	CAN
14	17:51	LEO
16	17:35	VIR
18	17:06	LIB
20	18:25	SCO
22	22:51	SAG
25	06:37	CAP
27	16:56	AQU
30	04:49	PIS

SEPTEMBER		
1	17:28	ARI
4	06:00	TAU
6	16:53	GEM
9	00:27	CAN
11	04:01	LEO
13	04:26	VIR
15	03:33	LIB
17	03:35	SCO
19	06:22	SAG
21	12:53	CAP
23	22:48	AQU
26	10:49	PIS
28	23:30	ARI

OCTOBER		
1	11:48	TAU
3	22:44	GEM
6	07:13	CAN
8	12:25	LEO
10	14:27	VIR
12	14:30	LIB
14	14:22	SCO
16	16:00	SAG
18	20:56	CAP
21	05:41	AQU
23	17:21	PIS
26	06:04	ARI
28	18:06	TAU
31	04:28	GEM

NOVEMBER		
2	12:43	CAN
4	18:37	LEO
6	22:10	VIR
8	23:55	LIB
11	00:54	SCO
13	02:37	SAG
15	06:37	CAP
17	14:04	AQU
20	00:53	PIS
22	13:32	ARI
25	01:37	TAU
27	11:31	GEM
29	18:50	CAN

DECEMBER		
2	00:02	LEO
4	03:49	VIR
6	06:44	LIB
8	09:18	SCO
10	12:14	SAG
12	16:31	CAP
14	23:20	AQU
17	09:18	PIS
19	21:40	ARI
22	10:08	TAU
24	20:14	GEM
27	02:59	CAN
29	06:58	LEO
31	09:34	VIR

1967

JANUARY			FEBRUARY			MARCH			APRIL		
2	12:04	LIB	3	00:56	SAG	2	06:53	SAG	3	02:49	AQU
4	15:17	SCO	5	07:11	CAP	4	12:36	CAP	5	13:29	PIS
6	19:28	SAG	7	15:17	AQU	6	21:04	AQU	8	01:57	ARI
9	00:54	CAP	10	01:19	PIS	9	07:42	PIS	10	14:57	TAU
11	08:06	AQU	12	13:17	ARI	11	19:53	ARI	13	03:15	GEM
13	17:45	PIS	15	02:19	TAU	14	08:55	TAU	15	13:37	CAN
16	05:48	ARI	17	14:16	GEM	16	21:20	GEM	17	20:55	LEO
18	18:40	TAU	19	22:48	CAN	19	07:10	CAN	20	00:43	VIR
21	05:39	GEM	22	03:05	LEO	21	13:04	LEO	22	01:42	LIB
23	12:51	CAN	24	04:04	VIR	23	15:09	VIR	24	01:19	SCO
25	16:21	LEO	26	03:45	LIB	25	14:51	LIB	26	01:27	SAG
27	17:37	VIR	28	04:10	SCO	27	14:11	SCO	28	03:54	CAP
29	18:33	LIB				29	15:09	SAG	30	09:58	AQU
31	20:44	SCO				31	19:11	CAP			

MAY			JUNE			JULY			AUGUST		
2	19:48	PIS	1	15:07	ARI	1	11:43	TAU	2	17:32	CAN
5	08:10	ARI	4	04:05	TAU	3	23:39	GEM	4	23:27	LEO
7	21:10	TAU	6	15:53	GEM	6	08:48	CAN	7	02:36	VIR
10	09:09	GEM	9	01:18	CAN	8	14:59	LEO	9	04:35	LIB
12	19:11	CAN	11	08:19	LEO	10	19:08	VIR	11	06:45	SCO
15	02:49	LEO	13	13:24	VIR	12	22:20	LIB	13	09:53	SAG
17	07:52	VIR	15	16:59	LIB	15	01:18	SCO	15	14:19	CAP
19	10:31	LIB	17	19:26	SCO	17	04:23	SAG	17	20:17	AQU
21	11:30	SCO	19	21:20	SAG	19	08:00	CAP	20	04:18	PIS
23	12:06	SAG	21	23:47	CAP	21	13:00	AQU	22	14:48	ARI
25	13:59	CAP	24	04:11	AQU	23	20:29	PIS	25	03:22	TAU
27	18:44	AQU	26	11:50	PIS	26	07:01	ARI	27	16:09	GEM
30	03:19	PIS	28	22:53	ARI	28	19:41	TAU	30	02:35	CAN
						31	08:01	GEM			

SEPTEMBER			OCTOBER			NOVEMBER			DECEMBER		
1	09:09	LEO	2	23:35	LIB	1	10:27	SCO	2	21:25	CAP
3	12:08	VIR	4	23:15	SCO	3	09:52	SAG	4	23:57	AQU
5	13:04	LIB	6	23:33	SAG	5	10:45	CAP	7	06:20	PIS
7	13:45	SCO	9	02:04	CAP	7	14:46	AQU	9	16:44	ARI
9	15:40	SAG	11	07:46	AQU	9	22:43	PIS	12	05:32	TAU
11	19:43	CAP	13	16:38	PIS	12	09:59	ARI	14	18:19	GEM
14	02:09	AQU	16	03:58	ARI	14	22:53	TAU	17	05:23	CAN
16	10:53	PIS	18	16:42	TAU	17	11:41	GEM	19	14:21	LEO
18	21:47	ARI	21	05:39	GEM	19	23:13	CAN	21	21:22	VIR
21	10:21	TAU	23	17:28	CAN	22	08:48	LEO	24	02:27	LIB
23	23:22	GEM	26	02:41	LEO	24	15:46	VIR	26	05:36	SCO
26	10:46	CAN	28	08:20	VIR	26	19:49	LIB	28	07:10	SAG
28	18:42	LEO	30	10:32	LIB	28	21:14	SCO	30	08:11	CAP
30	22:39	VIR				30	21:11	SAG			

1968

JANUARY			FEBRUARY			MARCH			APRIL		
1	10:24	AQU	2	09:40	ARI	3	05:28	TAU	2	01:41	GEM
3	15:36	PIS	4	21:16	TAU	5	18:17	GEM	4	14:13	CAN
6	00:46	ARI	7	10:09	GEM	8	06:22	CAN	7	00:29	LEO
8	13:03	TAU	9	21:35	CAN	10	15:28	LEO	9	07:04	VIR
11	01:55	GEM	12	05:50	LEO	12	20:52	VIR	11	10:01	LIB
13	12:54	CAN	14	11:03	VIR	14	23:24	LIB	13	10:32	SCO
15	21:10	LEO	16	14:22	LIB	17	00:34	SCO	15	10:24	SAG
18	03:11	VIR	18	17:00	SCO	19	01:54	SAG	17	11:23	CAP
20	07:48	LIB	20	19:48	SAG	21	04:35	CAP	19	14:58	AQU
22	11:28	SCO	22	23:12	CAP	23	09:17	AQU	21	21:46	PIS
24	14:24	SAG	25	03:37	AQU	25	16:16	PIS	24	07:33	ARI
26	16:57	CAP	27	09:43	PIS	28	01:32	ARI	26	19:23	TAU
28	20:06	AQU	29	18:15	ARI	30	12:55	TAU	29	08:12	GEM
31	01:16	PIS									

MAY			JUNE			JULY			AUGUST		
1	20:50	CAN	2	22:53	VIR	2	11:10	LIB	3	00:11	SAG
4	07:54	LEO	5	04:50	LIB	4	15:21	SCO	5	01:58	CAP
6	15:59	VIR	7	07:31	SCO	6	17:05	SAG	7	03:38	AQU
8	20:21	LIB	9	07:43	SAG	8	17:24	CAP	9	06:46	PIS
10	21:30	SCO	11	07:06	CAP	10	18:04	AQU	11	12:54	ARI
12	20:54	SAG	13	07:47	AQU	12	21:03	PIS	13	22:36	TAU
14	20:31	CAP	15	11:43	PIS	15	03:52	ARI	16	10:52	GEM
16	22:22	AQU	17	19:50	ARI	17	14:31	TAU	18	23:16	CAN
19	03:53	PIS	20	07:26	TAU	20	03:13	GEM	21	09:40	LEO
21	13:15	ARI	22	20:23	GEM	22	15:32	CAN	23	17:21	VIR
24	01:16	TAU	25	08:43	CAN	25	01:55	LEO	25	22:45	LIB
26	14:13	GEM	27	19:31	LEO	27	10:10	VIR	28	02:39	SCO
29	02:43	CAN	30	04:27	VIR	29	16:33	LIB	30	05:41	SAG
31	13:54	LEO				31	21:12	SCO			

SEPTEMBER			OCTOBER			NOVEMBER			DECEMBER		
1	08:22	CAP	2	22:21	PIS	1	11:51	ARI	1	03:58	TAU
3	11:20	AQU	5	05:36	ARI	3	22:02	TAU	3	16:06	GEM
5	15:28	PIS	7	15:07	TAU	6	09:48	GEM	6	04:44	CAN
7	21:50	ARI	10	02:44	GEM	8	22:27	CAN	8	17:03	LEO
10	07:06	TAU	12	15:24	CAN	11	10:45	LEO	11	04:00	VIR
12	18:55	GEM	15	03:09	LEO	13	20:55	VIR	13	12:09	LIB
15	07:29	CAN	17	11:59	VIR	16	03:27	LIB	15	16:32	SCO
17	18:26	LEO	19	17:06	LIB	18	06:06	SCO	17	17:28	SAG
20	02:16	VIR	21	19:06	SCO	20	06:04	SAG	19	16:33	CAP
22	07:00	LIB	23	19:33	SAG	22	05:20	CAP	21	16:00	AQU
24	09:39	SCO	25	20:14	CAP	24	06:03	AQU	23	18:01	PIS
26	11:31	SAG	27	22:43	AQU	26	09:53	PIS	26	00:03	ARI
28	13:45	CAP	30	03:55	PIS	28	17:26	ARI	28	09:57	TAU
30	17:11	AQU							30	22:12	GEM

1969

JANUARY

2	10:53	CAN
4	22:55	LEO
7	09:43	VIR
9	18:33	LIB
12	00:32	SCO
14	03:19	SAG
16	03:40	CAP
18	03:17	AQU
20	04:21	PIS
22	08:44	ARI
24	17:13	TAU
27	04:54	GEM
29	17:37	CAN

FEBRUARY

1	05:29	LEO
3	15:41	VIR
6	00:01	LIB
8	06:19	SCO
10	10:24	SAG
12	12:29	CAP
14	13:31	AQU
16	15:04	PIS
18	18:49	ARI
21	02:02	TAU
23	12:42	GEM
26	01:12	CAN
28	13:12	LEO

MARCH

2	23:07	VIR
5	06:34	LIB
7	11:57	SCO
9	15:48	SAG
11	18:41	CAP
13	21:10	AQU
16	00:04	PIS
18	04:27	ARI
20	11:21	TAU
22	21:13	GEM
25	09:19	CAN
27	21:37	LEO
30	07:54	VIR

APRIL

1	15:04	LIB
3	19:23	SCO
5	21:58	SAG
8	00:05	CAP
10	02:47	AQU
12	06:42	PIS
14	12:14	ARI
16	19:44	TAU
19	05:29	GEM
21	17:18	CAN
24	05:51	LEO
26	16:57	VIR
29	00:44	LIB

MAY

1	04:50	SCO
3	06:19	SAG
5	06:57	CAP
7	08:28	AQU
9	12:05	PIS
11	18:09	ARI
14	02:29	TAU
16	12:42	GEM
19	00:31	CAN
21	13:13	LEO
24	01:07	VIR
26	10:08	LIB
28	15:05	SCO
30	16:31	SAG

JUNE

1	16:07	CAP
3	16:04	AQU
5	18:14	PIS
7	23:37	ARI
10	08:06	TAU
12	18:49	GEM
15	06:53	CAN
17	19:36	LEO
20	07:54	VIR
22	18:04	LIB
25	00:31	SCO
27	03:00	SAG
29	02:45	CAP

JULY

1	01:50	AQU
3	02:27	PIS
5	06:17	ARI
7	13:54	TAU
10	00:32	GEM
12	12:48	CAN
15	01:30	LEO
17	13:43	VIR
20	00:20	LIB
22	08:04	SCO
24	12:11	SAG
26	13:10	CAP
28	12:35	AQU
30	12:31	PIS

AUGUST

1	14:55	ARI
3	21:02	TAU
6	06:50	GEM
8	18:58	CAN
11	07:39	LEO
13	19:33	VIR
16	05:51	LIB
18	13:54	SCO
20	19:13	SAG
22	21:49	CAP
24	22:36	AQU
26	23:04	PIS
29	00:58	ARI
31	05:51	TAU

SEPTEMBER

2	14:24	GEM
5	01:58	CAN
7	14:37	LEO
10	02:21	VIR
12	12:02	LIB
14	19:26	SCO
17	00:43	SAG
19	04:14	CAP
21	06:32	AQU
23	08:23	PIS
25	10:56	ARI
27	15:29	TAU
29	23:06	GEM

OCTOBER

2	09:53	CAN
4	22:26	LEO
7	10:22	VIR
9	19:49	LIB
12	02:19	SCO
14	06:34	SAG
16	09:36	CAP
18	12:22	AQU
20	15:26	PIS
22	19:18	ARI
25	00:33	TAU
27	08:01	GEM
29	18:13	CAN

NOVEMBER

1	06:35	LEO
3	19:01	VIR
6	04:59	LIB
8	11:18	SCO
10	14:31	SAG
12	16:09	CAP
14	17:53	AQU
16	20:53	PIS
19	01:32	ARI
21	07:53	TAU
23	15:59	GEM
26	02:11	CAN
28	14:23	LEO

DECEMBER

1	03:14	VIR
3	14:17	LIB
5	21:31	SCO
8	00:43	SAG
10	01:21	CAP
12	01:28	AQU
14	02:57	PIS
16	06:56	ARI
18	13:36	TAU
20	22:28	GEM
23	09:09	CAN
25	21:22	LEO
28	10:21	VIR
30	22:19	LIB

1970

JANUARY		
2	07:04	SCO
4	11:33	SAG
6	12:30	CAP
8	11:48	AQU
10	11:37	PIS
12	13:48	ARI
14	19:21	TAU
17	04:07	GEM
19	15:14	CAN
22	03:41	LEO
24	16:33	VIR
27	04:43	LIB
29	14:35	SCO
31	20:50	SAG

FEBRUARY		
2	23:22	CAP
4	23:20	AQU
6	22:38	PIS
8	23:18	ARI
11	03:00	TAU
13	10:30	GEM
15	21:17	CAN
18	09:54	LEO
20	22:42	VIR
23	10:30	LIB
25	20:24	SCO
28	03:39	SAG

MARCH		
2	07:55	CAP
4	09:35	AQU
6	09:49	PIS
8	10:17	ARI
10	12:44	TAU
12	18:37	GEM
15	04:19	CAN
17	16:40	LEO
20	05:30	VIR
22	16:57	LIB
25	02:11	SCO
27	09:07	SAG
29	14:01	CAP
31	17:09	AQU

APRIL		
2	19:01	PIS
4	20:32	ARI
6	23:03	TAU
9	04:02	GEM
11	12:34	CAN
14	00:16	LEO
16	13:08	VIR
19	00:35	LIB
21	09:16	SCO
23	15:15	SAG
25	19:27	CAP
27	22:44	AQU
30	01:38	PIS

MAY		
2	04:33	ARI
4	08:05	TAU
6	13:18	GEM
8	21:17	CAN
11	08:22	LEO
13	21:11	VIR
16	09:03	LIB
18	17:50	SCO
20	23:12	SAG
23	02:14	CAP
25	04:26	AQU
27	06:59	PIS
29	10:27	ARI
31	15:04	TAU

JUNE		
2	21:10	GEM
5	05:26	CAN
7	16:17	LEO
10	05:02	VIR
12	17:28	LIB
15	03:02	SCO
17	08:39	SAG
19	11:05	CAP
21	12:01	AQU
23	13:12	PIS
25	15:53	ARI
27	20:35	TAU
30	03:25	GEM

JULY		
2	12:21	CAN
4	23:26	LEO
7	12:12	VIR
10	01:03	LIB
12	11:41	SCO
14	18:26	SAG
16	21:20	CAP
18	21:45	AQU
20	21:37	PIS
22	22:43	ARI
25	02:19	TAU
27	08:53	GEM
29	18:14	CAN

AUGUST		
1	05:45	LEO
3	18:35	VIR
6	07:33	LIB
8	18:57	SCO
11	03:08	SAG
13	07:25	CAP
15	08:31	AQU
17	08:02	PIS
19	07:51	ARI
21	09:46	TAU
23	15:04	GEM
25	23:59	CAN
28	11:39	LEO
31	00:36	VIR

SEPTEMBER		
2	13:26	LIB
5	00:55	SCO
7	09:59	SAG
9	15:52	CAP
11	18:34	AQU
13	18:58	PIS
15	18:36	ARI
17	19:21	TAU
19	23:02	GEM
22	06:41	CAN
24	17:55	LEO
27	06:54	VIR
29	19:34	LIB

OCTOBER		
2	06:36	SCO
4	15:32	SAG
6	22:11	CAP
9	02:26	AQU
11	04:31	PIS
13	05:13	ARI
15	06:00	TAU
17	08:44	GEM
19	14:59	CAN
22	01:13	LEO
24	13:58	VIR
27	02:37	LIB
29	13:15	SCO
31	21:25	SAG

NOVEMBER		
3	03:33	CAP
5	08:11	AQU
7	11:33	PIS
9	13:52	ARI
11	15:51	TAU
13	18:49	GEM
16	00:24	CAN
18	09:36	LEO
20	21:50	VIR
23	10:40	LIB
25	21:25	SCO
28	05:03	SAG
30	10:06	CAP

DECEMBER		
2	13:45	AQU
4	16:56	PIS
6	20:04	ARI
8	23:25	TAU
11	03:34	GEM
13	09:33	CAN
15	18:22	LEO
18	06:05	VIR
20	19:02	LIB
23	06:28	SCO
25	14:28	SAG
27	19:02	CAP
29	21:24	AQU
31	23:08	PIS

1971

JANUARY			FEBRUARY			MARCH			APRIL		
3	01:27	ARI	1	10:49	TAU	2	22:02	GEM	1	11:51	CAN
5	05:01	TAU	3	15:35	GEM	5	04:48	CAN	3	21:06	LEO
7	10:09	GEM	5	23:07	CAN	7	14:56	LEO	6	09:17	VIR
9	17:09	CAN	8	09:07	LEO	10	03:11	VIR	8	22:17	LIB
12	02:25	LEO	10	20:58	VIR	12	16:06	LIB	11	10:28	SCO
14	13:58	VIR	13	09:51	LIB	15	04:32	SCO	13	21:04	SAG
17	02:54	LIB	15	22:22	SCO	17	15:24	SAG	16	05:39	CAP
19	15:04	SCO	18	08:46	SAG	19	23:38	CAP	18	11:46	AQU
22	00:16	SAG	20	15:37	CAP	22	04:29	AQU	20	15:08	PIS
24	05:33	CAP	22	18:44	AQU	24	06:08	PIS	22	16:09	ARI
26	07:37	AQU	24	19:06	PIS	26	05:46	ARI	24	16:07	TAU
28	08:02	PIS	26	18:30	ARI	28	05:16	TAU	26	16:59	GEM
30	08:37	ARI	28	18:55	TAU	30	06:44	GEM	28	20:44	CAN

MAY			JUNE			JULY			AUGUST		
1	04:35	LEO	2	12:27	LIB	2	08:47	SCO	1	03:50	SAG
3	16:04	VIR	5	00:37	SCO	4	18:59	SAG	3	11:32	CAP
6	05:00	LIB	7	10:29	SAG	7	02:04	CAP	5	15:47	AQU
8	17:04	SCO	9	17:46	CAP	9	06:27	AQU	7	17:35	PIS
11	03:08	SAG	11	23:03	AQU	11	09:15	PIS	9	18:27	ARI
13	11:10	CAP	14	03:02	PIS	13	11:33	ARI	11	19:56	TAU
15	17:20	AQU	16	06:06	ARI	15	14:11	TAU	13	23:11	GEM
17	21:40	PIS	18	08:39	TAU	17	17:47	GEM	16	04:50	CAN
20	00:12	ARI	20	11:24	GEM	19	22:57	CAN	18	12:58	LEO
22	01:32	TAU	22	15:31	CAN	22	06:17	LEO	20	23:19	VIR
24	03:02	GEM	24	22:13	LEO	24	16:10	VIR	23	11:23	LIB
26	06:27	CAN	27	08:07	VIR	27	04:12	LIB	26	00:10	SCO
28	13:17	LEO	29	20:23	LIB	29	16:51	SCO	28	11:57	SAG
30	23:49	VIR							30	20:55	CAP

SEPTEMBER			OCTOBER			NOVEMBER			DECEMBER		
2	02:05	AQU	1	14:37	PIS	2	00:56	TAU	1	11:26	GEM
4	03:51	PIS	3	14:41	ARI	4	00:28	GEM	3	12:52	CAN
6	03:44	ARI	5	13:42	TAU	6	02:15	CAN	5	17:17	LEO
8	03:38	TAU	7	13:54	GEM	8	07:57	LEO	8	01:41	VIR
10	05:26	GEM	9	17:11	CAN	10	17:45	VIR	10	13:20	LIB
12	10:21	CAN	12	00:31	LEO	13	06:06	LIB	13	02:02	SCO
14	18:38	LEO	14	11:17	VIR	15	18:50	SCO	15	13:38	SAG
17	05:29	VIR	16	23:48	LIB	18	06:30	SAG	17	23:08	CAP
19	17:48	LIB	19	12:31	SCO	20	16:37	CAP	20	06:33	AQU
22	06:34	SCO	22	00:32	SAG	23	00:53	AQU	22	12:10	PIS
24	18:44	SAG	24	11:06	CAP	25	06:48	PIS	24	16:10	ARI
27	04:53	CAP	26	19:12	AQU	27	10:04	ARI	26	18:46	TAU
29	11:39	AQU	28	23:57	PIS	29	11:09	TAU	28	20:39	GEM
			31	01:27	ARI				30	23:02	CAN

1972

JANUARY
2	03:22	LEO
4	10:51	VIR
6	21:34	LIB
9	10:04	SCO
11	21:58	SAG
14	07:26	CAP
16	14:04	AQU
18	18:29	PIS
20	21:36	ARI
23	00:18	TAU
25	03:14	GEM
27	07:02	CAN
29	12:22	LEO
31	19:56	VIR

FEBRUARY
3	06:07	LIB
5	18:18	SCO
8	06:38	SAG
10	16:51	CAP
12	23:37	AQU
15	03:11	PIS
17	04:51	ARI
19	06:12	TAU
21	08:36	GEM
23	12:53	CAN
25	19:15	LEO
28	03:40	VIR

MARCH
1	14:01	LIB
4	02:01	SCO
6	14:37	SAG
9	01:50	CAP
11	09:43	AQU
13	13:40	PIS
15	14:38	ARI
17	14:28	TAU
19	15:13	GEM
21	18:27	CAN
24	00:47	LEO
26	09:48	VIR
28	20:42	LIB
31	08:49	SCO

APRIL
2	21:28	SAG
5	09:21	CAP
7	18:38	AQU
9	23:58	PIS
12	01:33	ARI
14	00:55	TAU
16	00:17	GEM
18	01:47	CAN
20	06:47	LEO
22	15:25	VIR
25	02:35	LIB
27	14:56	SCO
30	03:31	SAG

MAY
2	15:29	CAP
5	01:36	AQU
7	08:28	PIS
9	11:35	ARI
11	11:48	TAU
13	10:58	GEM
15	11:17	CAN
17	14:38	LEO
19	21:57	VIR
22	08:37	LIB
24	21:01	SCO
27	09:34	SAG
29	21:13	CAP

JUNE
1	07:16	AQU
3	14:53	PIS
5	19:28	ARI
7	21:15	TAU
9	21:25	GEM
11	21:45	CAN
14	00:10	LEO
16	06:04	VIR
18	15:39	LIB
21	03:43	SCO
23	16:15	SAG
26	03:37	CAP
28	13:03	AQU
30	20:19	PIS

JULY
3	01:23	ARI
5	04:25	TAU
7	06:05	GEM
9	07:30	CAN
11	10:06	LEO
13	15:17	VIR
15	23:49	LIB
18	11:16	SCO
20	23:47	SAG
23	11:11	CAP
25	20:08	AQU
28	02:29	PIS
30	06:51	ARI

AUGUST
1	09:58	TAU
3	12:34	GEM
5	15:18	CAN
7	18:57	LEO
10	00:23	VIR
12	08:28	LIB
14	19:20	SCO
17	07:50	SAG
19	19:38	CAP
22	04:44	AQU
24	10:29	PIS
26	13:41	ARI
28	15:43	TAU
30	17:56	GEM

SEPTEMBER
1	21:12	CAN
4	01:54	LEO
6	08:16	VIR
8	16:37	LIB
11	03:16	SCO
13	15:43	SAG
16	04:08	CAP
18	14:05	AQU
20	20:10	PIS
22	22:45	ARI
24	23:28	TAU
27	00:15	GEM
29	02:39	CAN

OCTOBER
1	07:26	LEO
3	14:31	VIR
5	23:35	LIB
8	10:28	SCO
10	22:53	SAG
13	11:45	CAP
15	22:52	AQU
18	06:13	PIS
20	09:23	ARI
22	09:38	TAU
24	09:03	GEM
26	09:45	CAN
28	13:15	LEO
30	20:00	VIR

NOVEMBER
2	05:28	LIB
4	16:47	SCO
7	05:17	SAG
9	18:12	CAP
12	06:03	AQU
14	14:57	PIS
16	19:45	ARI
18	20:53	TAU
20	20:06	GEM
22	19:32	CAN
24	21:12	LEO
27	02:25	VIR
29	11:16	LIB

DECEMBER
1	22:43	SCO
4	11:23	SAG
7	00:07	CAP
9	11:54	AQU
11	21:33	PIS
14	04:00	ARI
16	07:00	TAU
18	07:25	GEM
20	06:57	CAN
22	07:35	LEO
24	11:03	VIR
26	18:22	LIB
29	05:11	SCO
31	17:52	SAG

1973

JANUARY			FEBRUARY			MARCH			APRIL		
3	06:31	CAP	2	00:56	AQU	1	09:23	AQU	2	07:49	ARI
5	17:48	AQU	4	09:23	PIS	3	17:32	PIS	4	09:59	TAU
8	03:03	PIS	6	15:29	ARI	5	22:38	ARI	6	11:13	GEM
10	09:58	ARI	8	19:54	TAU	8	01:51	TAU	8	13:05	CAN
12	14:25	TAU	10	23:11	GEM	10	04:31	GEM	10	16:32	LEO
14	16:42	GEM	13	01:45	CAN	12	07:30	CAN	12	21:47	VIR
16	17:39	CAN	15	04:13	LEO	14	11:08	LEO	15	04:51	LIB
18	18:41	LEO	17	07:32	VIR	16	15:43	VIR	17	13:52	SCO
20	21:24	VIR	19	12:59	LIB	18	21:49	LIB	20	01:02	SAG
23	03:17	LIB	21	21:36	SCO	21	06:16	SCO	22	13:50	CAP
25	12:53	SCO	24	09:15	SAG	23	17:27	SAG	25	02:22	AQU
28	01:11	SAG	26	22:04	CAP	26	06:16	CAP	27	12:10	PIS
30	13:55	CAP				28	18:13	AQU	29	17:54	ARI
						31	02:55	PIS			

MAY			JUNE			JULY			AUGUST		
1	20:02	TAU	2	06:22	CAN	1	16:56	LEO	2	08:13	LIB
3	20:16	GEM	4	06:50	LEO	3	18:32	VIR	4	15:36	SCO
5	20:36	CAN	6	09:52	VIR	5	23:24	LIB	7	02:37	SAG
7	22:37	LEO	8	16:16	LIB	8	08:06	SCO	9	15:30	CAP
10	03:13	VIR	11	01:52	SCO	10	19:48	SAG	12	03:53	AQU
12	10:31	LIB	13	13:43	SAG	13	08:46	CAP	14	14:15	PIS
14	20:10	SCO	16	02:37	CAP	15	21:15	AQU	16	22:16	ARI
17	07:42	SAG	18	15:20	AQU	18	08:08	PIS	19	04:14	TAU
19	20:31	CAP	21	02:29	PIS	20	16:44	ARI	21	08:27	GEM
22	09:18	AQU	23	10:49	ARI	22	22:41	TAU	23	11:08	CAN
24	20:06	PIS	25	15:38	TAU	25	01:59	GEM	25	12:50	LEO
27	03:15	ARI	27	17:18	GEM	27	03:11	CAN	27	14:34	VIR
29	06:28	TAU	29	17:09	CAN	29	03:30	LEO	29	17:53	LIB
31	06:53	GEM				31	04:35	VIR			

SEPTEMBER			OCTOBER			NOVEMBER			DECEMBER		
1	00:18	SCO	3	07:03	CAP	2	03:59	AQU	1	23:33	PIS
3	10:25	SAG	5	19:49	AQU	4	15:27	PIS	4	08:51	ARI
5	23:02	CAP	8	06:24	PIS	6	23:20	ARI	6	14:09	TAU
8	11:31	AQU	10	13:29	ARI	9	03:26	TAU	8	15:58	GEM
10	21:41	PIS	12	17:37	TAU	11	05:00	GEM	10	15:52	CAN
13	04:57	ARI	14	20:09	GEM	13	05:47	CAN	12	15:45	LEO
15	10:00	TAU	16	22:29	CAN	15	07:20	LEO	14	17:21	VIR
17	13:48	GEM	19	01:25	LEO	17	10:42	VIR	16	21:54	LIB
19	17:02	CAN	21	05:19	VIR	19	16:16	LIB	19	05:44	SCO
21	19:57	LEO	23	10:29	LIB	22	00:07	SCO	21	16:20	SAG
23	22:59	VIR	25	17:28	SCO	24	10:11	SAG	24	04:42	CAP
26	03:01	LIB	28	02:58	SAG	26	22:13	CAP	26	17:43	AQU
28	09:19	SCO	30	14:58	CAP	29	11:18	AQU	29	06:10	PIS
30	18:48	SAG							31	16:35	ARI

1974

JANUARY			FEBRUARY			MARCH			APRIL		
2	23:38	TAU	1	11:54	GEM	2	22:00	CAN	1	06:41	LEO
5	03:00	GEM	3	14:06	CAN	4	23:49	LEO	3	08:57	VIR
7	03:29	CAN	5	14:12	LEO	7	00:34	VIR	5	11:23	LIB
9	02:43	LEO	7	13:52	VIR	9	01:52	LIB	7	15:26	SCO
11	02:42	VIR	9	15:11	LIB	11	05:40	SCO	9	22:28	SAG
13	05:22	LIB	11	19:58	SCO	13	13:21	SAG	12	08:57	CAP
15	11:55	SCO	14	05:02	SAG	16	00:42	CAP	14	21:35	AQU
17	22:13	SAG	16	17:16	CAP	18	13:39	AQU	17	09:45	PIS
20	10:48	CAP	19	06:21	AQU	21	01:34	PIS	19	19:21	ARI
22	23:50	AQU	21	18:16	PIS	23	11:03	ARI	22	01:54	TAU
25	12:01	PIS	24	04:13	ARI	25	18:10	TAU	24	06:12	GEM
27	22:32	ARI	26	12:12	TAU	27	23:34	GEM	26	09:18	CAN
30	06:42	TAU	28	18:11	GEM	30	03:40	CAN	28	12:04	LEO
									30	15:01	VIR

MAY			JUNE			JULY			AUGUST		
2	18:40	LIB	1	06:11	SCO	3	07:20	CAP	2	01:47	AQU
4	23:44	SCO	3	14:22	SAG	5	19:42	AQU	4	14:27	PIS
7	07:06	SAG	6	00:49	CAP	8	08:26	PIS	7	02:16	ARI
9	17:16	CAP	8	13:03	AQU	10	20:11	ARI	9	12:13	TAU
12	05:35	AQU	11	01:44	PIS	13	05:22	TAU	11	19:16	GEM
14	18:04	PIS	13	12:53	ARI	15	10:55	GEM	13	22:49	CAN
17	04:20	ARI	15	20:47	TAU	17	12:57	CAN	15	23:27	LEO
19	11:11	TAU	18	00:59	GEM	19	12:44	LEO	17	22:43	VIR
21	14:55	GEM	20	02:22	CAN	21	12:10	VIR	19	22:45	LIB
23	16:46	CAN	22	02:30	LEO	23	13:20	LIB	22	01:38	SCO
25	18:13	LEO	24	03:12	VIR	25	17:46	SCO	24	08:35	SAG
27	20:26	VIR	26	05:58	LIB	28	02:00	SAG	26	19:16	CAP
30	00:17	LIB	28	11:41	SCO	30	13:11	CAP	29	07:53	AQU
			30	20:21	SAG				31	20:30	PIS

SEPTEMBER			OCTOBER			NOVEMBER			DECEMBER		
3	07:59	ARI	2	23:40	TAU	1	13:24	GEM	1	01:22	CAN
5	17:51	TAU	5	07:01	GEM	3	18:02	CAN	3	03:32	LEO
8	01:37	GEM	7	12:31	CAN	5	21:31	LEO	5	05:41	VIR
10	06:40	CAN	9	16:03	LEO	8	00:19	VIR	7	08:43	LIB
12	08:55	LEO	11	17:57	VIR	10	02:59	LIB	9	13:14	SCO
14	09:13	VIR	13	19:11	LIB	12	06:24	SCO	11	19:35	SAG
16	09:18	LIB	15	21:24	SCO	14	11:40	SAG	14	04:04	CAP
18	11:15	SCO	18	02:15	SAG	16	19:42	CAP	16	14:49	AQU
20	16:47	SAG	20	10:45	CAP	19	06:39	AQU	19	03:13	PIS
23	02:22	CAP	22	22:21	AQU	21	19:12	PIS	21	15:36	ARI
25	14:39	AQU	25	10:57	PIS	24	07:00	ARI	24	01:45	TAU
28	03:15	PIS	27	22:14	ARI	26	16:05	TAU	26	08:16	GEM
30	14:26	ARI	30	07:01	TAU	28	21:59	GEM	28	11:16	CAN
									30	12:05	LEO

1975

JANUARY
1	12:33	VIR
3	14:22	LIB
5	18:39	SCO
8	01:40	SAG
10	10:59	CAP
12	22:04	AQU
15	10:24	PIS
17	23:04	ARI
20	10:22	TAU
22	18:23	GEM
24	22:21	CAN
26	23:01	LEO
28	22:14	VIR
30	22:13	LIB

FEBRUARY
2	00:54	SCO
4	07:11	SAG
6	16:43	CAP
9	04:17	AQU
11	16:46	PIS
14	05:23	ARI
16	17:10	TAU
19	02:35	GEM
21	08:19	CAN
23	10:14	LEO
25	09:38	VIR
27	08:39	LIB

MARCH
1	09:34	SCO
3	14:06	SAG
5	22:40	CAP
8	10:10	AQU
10	22:50	PIS
13	11:19	ARI
15	22:53	TAU
18	08:44	GEM
20	15:49	CAN
22	19:32	LEO
24	20:22	VIR
26	19:52	LIB
28	20:08	SCO
30	23:10	SAG

APRIL
2	06:09	CAP
4	16:46	AQU
7	05:17	PIS
9	17:45	ARI
12	04:54	TAU
14	14:15	GEM
16	21:28	CAN
19	02:15	LEO
21	04:43	VIR
23	05:42	LIB
25	06:40	SCO
27	09:20	SAG
29	15:09	CAP

MAY
2	00:34	AQU
4	12:35	PIS
7	01:03	ARI
9	12:04	TAU
11	20:45	GEM
14	03:08	CAN
16	07:39	LEO
18	10:46	VIR
20	13:06	LIB
22	15:26	SCO
24	18:52	SAG
27	00:31	CAP
29	09:10	AQU
31	20:33	PIS

JUNE
3	09:02	ARI
5	20:19	TAU
8	04:50	GEM
10	10:22	CAN
12	13:46	LEO
14	16:11	VIR
16	18:41	LIB
18	22:00	SCO
21	02:35	SAG
23	08:57	CAP
25	17:34	AQU
28	04:34	PIS
30	17:03	ARI

JULY
3	04:55	TAU
5	13:59	GEM
7	19:24	CAN
9	21:51	LEO
11	22:56	VIR
14	00:22	LIB
16	03:24	SCO
18	08:33	SAG
20	15:46	CAP
23	00:56	AQU
25	11:59	PIS
28	00:28	ARI
30	12:54	TAU

AUGUST
1	23:03	GEM
4	05:18	CAN
6	07:44	LEO
8	07:54	VIR
10	07:52	LIB
12	09:31	SCO
14	14:00	SAG
16	21:26	CAP
19	07:10	AQU
21	18:33	PIS
24	07:03	ARI
26	19:45	TAU
29	06:54	GEM
31	14:36	CAN

SEPTEMBER
2	18:09	LEO
4	18:30	VIR
6	17:38	LIB
8	17:46	SCO
10	20:41	SAG
13	03:12	CAP
15	12:52	AQU
18	00:32	PIS
20	13:08	ARI
23	01:44	TAU
25	13:14	GEM
27	22:08	CAN
30	03:21	LEO

OCTOBER
2	05:04	VIR
4	04:39	LIB
6	04:09	SCO
8	05:36	SAG
10	10:29	CAP
12	19:10	AQU
15	06:41	PIS
17	19:21	ARI
20	07:44	TAU
22	18:52	GEM
25	03:58	CAN
27	10:20	LEO
29	13:47	VIR
31	14:56	LIB

NOVEMBER
2	15:08	SCO
4	16:11	SAG
6	19:46	CAP
9	03:00	AQU
11	13:43	PIS
14	02:18	ARI
16	14:38	TAU
19	01:15	GEM
21	09:37	CAN
23	15:49	LEO
25	20:05	VIR
27	22:48	LIB
30	00:37	SCO

DECEMBER
2	02:34	SAG
4	05:59	CAP
6	12:13	AQU
8	21:52	PIS
11	10:07	ARI
13	22:40	TAU
16	09:13	GEM
18	16:50	CAN
20	21:54	LEO
23	01:28	VIR
25	04:28	LIB
27	07:29	SCO
29	10:53	SAG
31	15:17	CAP

1976

JANUARY		
2	21:34	AQU
5	06:36	PIS
7	18:22	ARI
10	07:10	TAU
12	18:20	GEM
15	02:01	CAN
17	06:16	LEO
19	08:26	VIR
21	10:11	LIB
23	12:49	SCO
25	16:52	SAG
27	22:25	CAP
30	05:35	AQU

FEBRUARY		
1	14:47	PIS
4	02:18	ARI
6	15:14	TAU
9	03:17	GEM
11	11:59	CAN
13	16:33	LEO
15	18:00	VIR
17	18:15	LIB
19	19:14	SCO
21	22:19	SAG
24	03:55	CAP
26	11:49	AQU
28	21:42	PIS

MARCH		
2	09:23	ARI
4	22:19	TAU
7	10:56	GEM
9	20:59	CAN
12	02:56	LEO
14	04:59	VIR
16	04:45	LIB
18	04:18	SCO
20	05:34	SAG
22	09:49	CAP
24	17:20	AQU
27	03:34	PIS
29	15:38	ARI

APRIL		
1	04:35	TAU
3	17:16	GEM
6	04:07	CAN
8	11:37	LEO
10	15:16	VIR
12	15:55	LIB
14	15:15	SCO
16	15:16	SAG
18	17:44	CAP
20	23:48	AQU
23	09:28	PIS
25	21:37	ARI
28	10:38	TAU
30	23:06	GEM

MAY		
3	09:54	CAN
5	18:10	LEO
7	23:22	VIR
10	01:40	LIB
12	02:03	SCO
14	02:05	SAG
16	03:32	CAP
18	08:03	AQU
20	16:27	PIS
23	04:08	ARI
25	17:08	TAU
28	05:23	GEM
30	15:40	CAN

JUNE		
1	23:38	LEO
4	05:22	VIR
6	09:00	LIB
8	10:59	SCO
10	12:07	SAG
12	13:46	CAP
14	17:32	AQU
17	00:44	PIS
19	11:33	ARI
22	00:22	TAU
24	12:37	GEM
26	22:30	CAN
29	05:40	LEO

JULY		
1	10:47	VIR
3	14:35	LIB
5	17:34	SCO
7	20:06	SAG
9	22:50	CAP
12	02:54	AQU
14	09:37	PIS
16	19:40	ARI
19	08:12	TAU
21	20:41	GEM
24	06:40	CAN
26	13:19	LEO
28	17:24	VIR
30	20:14	LIB

AUGUST		
1	22:56	SCO
4	02:04	SAG
6	05:55	CAP
8	10:58	AQU
10	18:01	PIS
13	03:50	ARI
15	16:06	TAU
18	04:55	GEM
20	15:34	CAN
22	22:31	LEO
25	02:04	VIR
27	03:42	LIB
29	05:06	SCO
31	07:29	SAG

SEPTEMBER		
2	11:30	CAP
4	17:21	AQU
7	01:12	PIS
9	11:19	ARI
11	23:31	TAU
14	12:33	GEM
17	00:07	CAN
19	08:11	LEO
21	12:17	VIR
23	13:28	LIB
25	13:34	SCO
27	14:22	SAG
29	17:14	CAP

OCTOBER		
1	22:50	AQU
4	07:10	PIS
6	17:50	ARI
9	06:12	TAU
11	19:15	GEM
14	07:25	CAN
16	16:50	LEO
18	22:25	VIR
21	00:27	LIB
23	00:18	SCO
24	23:49	SAG
27	00:56	CAP
29	05:06	AQU
31	12:54	PIS

NOVEMBER		
2	23:46	ARI
5	12:24	TAU
8	01:22	GEM
10	13:29	CAN
12	23:37	LEO
15	06:47	VIR
17	10:35	LIB
19	11:32	SCO
21	11:04	SAG
23	11:04	CAP
25	13:31	AQU
27	19:48	PIS
30	06:02	ARI

DECEMBER		
2	18:42	TAU
5	07:39	GEM
7	19:22	CAN
10	05:13	LEO
12	12:56	VIR
14	18:14	LIB
16	21:02	SCO
18	21:55	SAG
20	22:12	CAP
22	23:49	AQU
25	04:37	PIS
27	13:32	ARI
30	01:44	TAU

1977

JANUARY
1 14:43 GEM
4 02:13 CAN
6 11:21 LEO
8 18:24 VIR
10 23:48 LIB
13 03:45 SCO
15 06:19 SAG
17 08:03 CAP
19 10:13 AQU
21 14:31 PIS
23 22:20 ARI
26 09:42 TAU
28 22:38 GEM
31 10:21 CAN

FEBRUARY
2 19:12 LEO
5 01:18 VIR
7 05:37 LIB
9 09:05 SCO
11 12:12 SAG
13 15:14 CAP
15 18:46 AQU
17 23:45 PIS
20 07:23 ARI
22 18:07 TAU
25 06:51 GEM
27 19:03 CAN

MARCH
2 04:26 LEO
4 10:19 VIR
6 13:35 LIB
8 15:38 SCO
10 17:42 SAG
12 20:40 CAP
15 01:01 AQU
17 07:06 PIS
19 15:24 ARI
22 02:06 TAU
24 14:39 GEM
27 03:17 CAN
29 13:41 LEO
31 20:26 VIR

APRIL
2 23:40 LIB
5 00:40 SCO
7 01:09 SAG
9 02:41 CAP
11 06:25 AQU
13 12:50 PIS
15 21:53 ARI
18 09:03 TAU
20 21:38 GEM
23 10:26 CAN
25 21:44 LEO
28 05:53 VIR
30 10:13 LIB

MAY
2 11:24 SCO
4 10:59 SAG
6 10:55 CAP
8 13:00 AQU
10 18:30 PIS
13 03:30 ARI
15 15:05 TAU
18 03:51 GEM
20 16:36 CAN
23 04:14 LEO
25 13:32 VIR
27 19:29 LIB
29 21:57 SCO
31 21:55 SAG

JUNE
2 21:08 CAP
4 21:44 AQU
7 01:36 PIS
9 09:35 ARI
11 20:57 TAU
14 09:50 GEM
16 22:29 CAN
19 09:54 LEO
21 19:30 VIR
24 02:36 LIB
26 06:43 SCO
28 08:03 SAG
30 07:49 CAP

JULY
2 07:57 AQU
4 10:32 PIS
6 17:04 ARI
9 03:34 TAU
11 16:16 GEM
14 04:50 CAN
16 15:52 LEO
19 00:59 VIR
21 08:10 LIB
23 13:14 SCO
25 16:05 SAG
27 17:15 CAP
29 18:05 AQU
31 20:24 PIS

AUGUST
3 01:55 ARI
5 11:19 TAU
7 23:30 GEM
10 12:05 CAN
12 22:57 LEO
15 07:26 VIR
17 13:50 LIB
19 18:36 SCO
21 22:03 SAG
24 00:31 CAP
26 02:41 AQU
28 05:47 PIS
30 11:12 ARI

SEPTEMBER
1 19:52 TAU
4 07:28 GEM
6 20:04 CAN
9 07:14 LEO
11 15:35 VIR
13 21:08 LIB
16 00:46 SCO
18 03:29 SAG
20 06:05 CAP
22 09:13 AQU
24 13:30 PIS
26 19:41 ARI
29 04:22 TAU

OCTOBER
1 15:34 GEM
4 04:10 CAN
6 15:58 LEO
9 00:59 VIR
11 06:30 LIB
13 09:11 SCO
15 10:28 SAG
17 11:51 CAP
19 14:37 AQU
21 19:27 PIS
24 02:35 ARI
26 11:54 TAU
28 23:09 GEM
31 11:41 CAN

NOVEMBER
3 00:04 LEO
5 10:17 VIR
7 16:52 LIB
9 19:43 SCO
11 20:04 SAG
13 19:51 CAP
15 21:01 AQU
18 00:59 PIS
20 08:14 ARI
22 18:10 TAU
25 05:49 GEM
27 18:21 CAN
30 06:54 LEO

DECEMBER
2 18:06 VIR
5 02:18 LIB
7 06:34 SCO
9 07:22 SAG
11 06:27 CAP
13 06:00 AQU
15 08:10 PIS
17 14:12 ARI
19 23:55 TAU
22 11:52 GEM
25 00:31 CAN
27 12:52 LEO
30 00:14 VIR

1978

JANUARY
1	09:32	LIB
3	15:36	SCO
5	18:04	SAG
7	17:55	CAP
9	17:06	AQU
11	17:51	PIS
13	22:06	ARI
16	06:31	TAU
18	18:07	GEM
21	06:51	CAN
23	19:03	LEO
26	05:57	VIR
28	15:08	LIB
30	22:04	SCO

FEBRUARY
2	02:14	SAG
4	03:51	CAP
6	04:05	AQU
8	04:48	PIS
10	07:57	ARI
12	14:51	TAU
15	01:25	GEM
17	13:56	CAN
20	02:10	LEO
22	12:40	VIR
24	21:04	LIB
27	03:29	SCO

MARCH
1	08:03	SAG
3	10:59	CAP
5	12:51	AQU
7	14:46	PIS
9	18:09	ARI
12	00:19	TAU
14	09:49	GEM
16	21:50	CAN
19	10:13	LEO
21	20:50	VIR
24	04:42	LIB
26	10:02	SCO
28	13:38	SAG
30	16:24	CAP

APRIL
1	19:06	AQU
3	22:21	PIS
6	02:52	ARI
8	09:22	TAU
10	18:28	GEM
13	06:00	CAN
15	18:31	LEO
18	05:45	VIR
20	13:54	LIB
22	18:40	SCO
24	21:01	SAG
26	22:28	CAP
29	00:29	AQU

MAY
1	04:01	PIS
3	09:28	ARI
5	16:53	TAU
8	02:19	GEM
10	13:42	CAN
13	02:18	LEO
15	14:16	VIR
17	23:25	LIB
20	04:39	SCO
22	06:32	SAG
24	06:42	CAP
26	07:11	AQU
28	09:37	PIS
30	14:53	ARI

JUNE
1	22:51	TAU
4	08:54	GEM
6	20:31	CAN
9	09:08	LEO
11	21:35	VIR
14	07:56	LIB
16	14:29	SCO
18	17:02	SAG
20	16:53	CAP
22	16:08	AQU
24	16:58	PIS
26	20:54	ARI
29	04:22	TAU

JULY
1	14:38	GEM
4	02:34	CAN
6	15:14	LEO
9	03:45	VIR
11	14:49	LIB
13	22:48	SCO
16	02:50	SAG
18	03:34	CAP
20	02:42	AQU
22	02:27	PIS
24	04:47	ARI
26	10:51	TAU
28	20:31	GEM
31	08:29	CAN

AUGUST
2	21:11	LEO
5	09:30	VIR
7	20:30	LIB
10	05:12	SCO
12	10:43	SAG
14	13:04	CAP
16	13:16	AQU
18	13:05	PIS
20	14:30	ARI
22	19:06	TAU
25	03:32	GEM
27	15:00	CAN
30	03:40	LEO

SEPTEMBER
1	15:47	VIR
4	02:16	LIB
6	10:39	SCO
8	16:40	SAG
10	20:20	CAP
12	22:09	AQU
14	23:10	PIS
17	00:51	ARI
19	04:44	TAU
21	11:57	GEM
23	23:32	CAN
26	11:02	LEO
28	23:12	VIR

OCTOBER
1	09:17	LIB
3	16:49	SCO
5	22:07	SAG
8	01:53	CAP
10	04:43	AQU
12	07:13	PIS
14	10:07	ARI
16	14:23	TAU
18	21:06	GEM
21	06:53	CAN
23	19:05	LEO
26	07:33	VIR
28	17:52	LIB
31	00:53	SCO

NOVEMBER
2	05:04	SAG
4	07:41	CAP
6	10:04	AQU
8	13:07	PIS
10	17:12	ARI
12	22:36	TAU
15	05:45	GEM
17	15:17	CAN
20	03:10	LEO
22	15:58	VIR
25	03:08	LIB
27	10:39	SCO
29	14:24	SAG

DECEMBER
1	15:45	CAP
3	16:36	AQU
5	18:37	PIS
7	22:40	ARI
10	04:51	TAU
12	12:55	GEM
14	22:51	CAN
17	10:38	LEO
19	23:35	VIR
22	11:41	LIB
24	20:33	SCO
27	01:08	SAG
29	02:16	CAP
31	01:54	AQU

1979

JANUARY
2	02:09	PIS
4	04:42	ARI
6	10:18	TAU
8	18:43	GEM
11	05:15	CAN
13	17:17	LEO
16	06:11	VIR
18	18:41	LIB
21	04:51	SCO
23	11:09	SAG
25	13:28	CAP
27	13:13	AQU
29	12:26	PIS
31	13:12	ARI

FEBRUARY
2	17:04	TAU
5	00:34	GEM
7	11:06	CAN
9	23:26	LEO
12	12:18	VIR
15	00:38	LIB
17	11:13	SCO
19	18:52	SAG
21	23:01	CAP
24	00:13	AQU
25	23:53	PIS
27	23:55	ARI

MARCH
2	02:10	TAU
4	07:59	GEM
6	17:35	CAN
9	05:48	LEO
11	18:43	VIR
14	06:42	LIB
16	16:50	SCO
19	00:39	SAG
21	05:57	CAP
23	08:53	AQU
25	10:05	PIS
27	10:48	ARI
29	12:37	TAU
31	17:09	GEM

APRIL
3	01:25	CAN
5	12:58	LEO
8	01:53	VIR
10	13:46	LIB
12	23:16	SCO
15	06:19	SAG
17	11:24	CAP
19	15:03	AQU
21	17:42	PIS
23	19:52	ARI
25	22:28	TAU
28	02:49	GEM
30	10:12	CAN

MAY
2	20:57	LEO
5	09:42	VIR
7	21:48	LIB
10	07:11	SCO
12	13:25	SAG
14	17:26	CAP
16	20:26	AQU
18	23:19	PIS
21	02:31	ARI
23	06:21	TAU
25	11:29	GEM
27	18:51	CAN
30	05:09	LEO

JUNE
1	17:41	VIR
4	06:12	LIB
6	16:06	SCO
8	22:15	SAG
11	01:24	CAP
13	03:07	AQU
15	04:57	PIS
17	07:53	ARI
19	12:19	TAU
21	18:23	GEM
24	02:25	CAN
26	12:48	LEO
29	01:15	VIR

JULY
1	14:09	LIB
4	00:58	SCO
6	07:56	SAG
8	11:08	CAP
10	12:00	AQU
12	12:23	PIS
14	13:58	ARI
16	17:44	TAU
19	00:00	GEM
21	08:41	CAN
23	19:31	LEO
26	08:02	VIR
28	21:07	LIB
31	08:47	SCO

AUGUST
2	17:06	SAG
4	21:23	CAP
6	22:29	AQU
8	22:06	PIS
10	22:11	ARI
13	00:22	TAU
15	05:42	GEM
17	14:18	CAN
20	01:29	LEO
22	14:12	VIR
25	03:14	LIB
27	15:13	SCO
30	00:40	SAG

SEPTEMBER
1	06:34	CAP
3	09:00	AQU
5	09:04	PIS
7	08:30	ARI
9	09:13	TAU
11	12:55	GEM
13	20:28	CAN
16	07:26	LEO
18	20:16	VIR
21	09:11	LIB
23	20:55	SCO
26	06:36	SAG
28	13:41	CAP
30	17:50	AQU

OCTOBER
2	19:24	PIS
4	19:29	ARI
6	19:45	TAU
8	22:08	GEM
11	04:10	CAN
13	14:12	LEO
16	02:52	VIR
18	15:45	LIB
21	03:03	SCO
23	12:10	SAG
25	19:12	CAP
28	00:17	AQU
30	03:30	PIS

NOVEMBER
1	05:10	ARI
3	06:17	TAU
5	08:26	GEM
7	13:24	CAN
9	22:15	LEO
12	10:21	VIR
14	23:17	LIB
17	10:30	SCO
19	18:57	SAG
22	01:02	CAP
24	05:37	AQU
26	09:18	PIS
28	12:17	ARI
30	14:55	TAU

DECEMBER
2	18:03	GEM
4	23:02	CAN
7	07:10	LEO
9	18:34	VIR
12	07:30	LIB
14	19:09	SCO
17	03:37	SAG
19	08:55	CAP
21	12:13	AQU
23	14:51	PIS
25	17:41	ARI
27	21:08	TAU
30	01:33	GEM

1980

JANUARY			FEBRUARY			MARCH			APRIL		
1	07:30	CAN	2	10:22	VIR	3	05:41	LIB	2	00:22	SCO
3	15:48	LEO	4	23:05	LIB	5	18:23	SCO	4	11:35	SAG
6	02:49	VIR	7	11:47	SCO	8	05:39	SAG	6	20:43	CAP
8	15:39	LIB	9	22:20	SAG	10	14:03	CAP	9	03:00	AQU
11	03:56	SCO	12	05:13	CAP	12	18:46	AQU	11	06:07	PIS
13	13:18	SAG	14	08:20	AQU	14	20:11	PIS	13	06:41	ARI
15	18:52	CAP	16	08:55	PIS	16	19:42	ARI	15	06:11	TAU
17	21:26	AQU	18	08:43	ARI	18	19:14	TAU	17	06:42	GEM
19	22:34	PIS	20	09:36	TAU	20	20:48	GEM	19	10:12	CAN
21	23:52	ARI	22	12:59	GEM	23	01:56	CAN	21	17:53	LEO
24	02:32	TAU	24	19:35	CAN	25	10:59	LEO	24	05:13	VIR
26	07:12	GEM	27	05:11	LEO	27	22:53	VIR	26	18:10	LIB
28	14:03	CAN	29	16:54	VIR	30	11:50	LIB	29	06:36	SCO
30	23:09	LEO									

MAY			JUNE			JULY			AUGUST		
1	17:22	SAG	2	14:30	AQU	2	00:49	PIS	2	11:56	TAU
4	02:15	CAP	4	19:11	PIS	4	03:47	ARI	4	15:10	GEM
6	09:04	AQU	6	22:24	ARI	6	06:31	TAU	6	20:13	CAN
8	13:34	PIS	9	00:30	TAU	8	09:34	GEM	9	03:24	LEO
10	15:45	ARI	11	02:23	GEM	10	13:45	CAN	11	12:55	VIR
12	16:25	TAU	13	05:30	CAN	12	20:03	LEO	14	00:33	LIB
14	17:08	GEM	15	11:23	LEO	15	05:12	VIR	16	13:16	SCO
16	19:53	CAN	17	20:48	VIR	17	16:56	LIB	19	01:08	SAG
19	02:15	LEO	20	08:56	LIB	20	05:34	SCO	21	10:12	CAP
21	12:33	VIR	22	21:27	SCO	22	16:43	SAG	23	15:33	AQU
24	01:12	LIB	25	08:02	SAG	25	00:45	CAP	25	17:44	PIS
26	13:37	SCO	27	15:47	CAP	27	05:35	AQU	27	18:12	ARI
29	00:05	SAG	29	21:04	AQU	29	08:11	PIS	29	18:42	TAU
31	08:15	CAP				31	09:54	ARI	31	20:51	GEM

SEPTEMBER			OCTOBER			NOVEMBER			DECEMBER		
3	01:40	CAN	2	14:58	LEO	1	07:19	VIR	1	02:14	LIB
5	09:23	LEO	5	01:20	VIR	3	19:32	LIB	3	15:01	SCO
7	19:32	VIR	7	13:31	LIB	6	08:20	SCO	6	02:58	SAG
10	07:23	LIB	10	02:16	SCO	8	20:26	SAG	8	13:13	CAP
12	20:07	SCO	12	14:38	SAG	11	07:16	CAP	10	21:37	AQU
15	08:29	SAG	15	01:37	CAP	13	16:11	AQU	13	04:04	PIS
17	18:46	CAP	17	09:54	AQU	15	22:22	PIS	15	08:22	ARI
20	01:31	AQU	19	14:32	PIS	18	01:22	ARI	17	10:37	TAU
22	04:28	PIS	21	15:44	ARI	20	01:52	TAU	19	11:40	GEM
24	04:38	ARI	23	14:56	TAU	22	01:28	GEM	21	13:04	CAN
26	03:54	TAU	25	14:18	GEM	24	02:19	CAN	23	16:34	LEO
28	04:22	GEM	27	16:01	CAN	26	06:24	LEO	25	23:33	VIR
30	07:47	CAN	29	21:39	LEO	28	14:38	VIR	28	10:06	LIB
									30	22:37	SCO

1981

JANUARY

2	10:43	SAG
4	20:42	CAP
7	04:13	AQU
9	09:43	PIS
11	13:44	ARI
13	16:46	TAU
15	19:18	GEM
17	22:08	CAN
20	02:22	LEO
22	09:03	VIR
24	18:46	LIB
27	06:49	SCO
29	19:12	SAG

FEBRUARY

1	05:38	CAP
3	12:56	AQU
5	17:22	PIS
7	20:02	ARI
9	22:11	TAU
12	00:52	GEM
14	04:43	CAN
16	10:11	LEO
18	17:35	VIR
21	03:13	LIB
23	14:55	SCO
26	03:30	SAG
28	14:47	CAP

MARCH

2	22:51	AQU
5	03:13	PIS
7	04:49	ARI
9	05:23	TAU
11	06:43	GEM
13	10:06	CAN
15	16:03	LEO
18	00:20	VIR
20	10:31	LIB
22	22:15	SCO
25	10:52	SAG
27	22:53	CAP
30	08:16	AQU

APRIL

1	13:42	PIS
3	15:26	ARI
5	15:05	TAU
7	14:48	GEM
9	16:34	CAN
11	21:37	LEO
14	05:57	VIR
16	16:39	LIB
19	04:40	SCO
21	17:16	SAG
24	05:32	CAP
26	15:58	AQU
28	22:57	PIS

MAY

1	01:58	ARI
3	02:00	TAU
5	01:02	GEM
7	01:18	CAN
9	04:41	LEO
11	11:56	VIR
13	22:25	LIB
16	10:38	SCO
18	23:15	SAG
21	11:21	CAP
23	22:01	AQU
26	06:06	PIS
28	10:44	ARI
30	12:11	TAU

JUNE

1	11:49	GEM
3	11:39	CAN
5	13:44	LEO
7	19:26	VIR
10	04:56	LIB
12	16:55	SCO
15	05:32	SAG
17	17:22	CAP
20	03:37	AQU
22	11:45	PIS
24	17:19	ARI
26	20:17	TAU
28	21:22	GEM
30	21:58	CAN

JULY

2	23:48	LEO
5	04:27	VIR
7	12:43	LIB
10	00:02	SCO
12	12:36	SAG
15	00:20	CAP
17	10:03	AQU
19	17:26	PIS
21	22:44	ARI
24	02:19	TAU
26	04:42	GEM
28	06:42	CAN
30	09:21	LEO

AUGUST

1	13:55	VIR
3	21:25	LIB
6	07:59	SCO
8	20:23	SAG
11	08:21	CAP
13	17:57	AQU
16	00:35	PIS
18	04:50	ARI
20	07:44	TAU
22	10:19	GEM
24	13:17	CAN
26	17:11	LEO
28	22:32	VIR
31	06:03	LIB

SEPTEMBER

2	16:11	SCO
5	04:24	SAG
7	16:49	CAP
10	02:59	AQU
12	09:35	PIS
14	12:56	ARI
16	14:31	TAU
18	16:00	GEM
20	18:40	CAN
22	23:09	LEO
25	05:29	VIR
27	13:41	LIB
29	23:54	SCO

OCTOBER

2	12:00	SAG
5	00:50	CAP
7	12:02	AQU
9	19:33	PIS
11	23:02	ARI
13	23:44	TAU
15	23:42	GEM
18	00:53	CAN
20	04:35	LEO
22	11:06	VIR
24	19:57	LIB
27	06:39	SCO
29	18:49	SAG

NOVEMBER

1	07:47	CAP
3	19:52	AQU
6	04:53	PIS
8	09:39	ARI
10	10:45	TAU
12	10:00	GEM
14	09:38	CAN
16	11:33	LEO
18	16:54	VIR
21	01:34	LIB
23	12:37	SCO
26	01:01	SAG
28	13:53	CAP

DECEMBER

1	02:10	AQU
3	12:17	PIS
5	18:50	ARI
7	21:32	TAU
9	21:31	GEM
11	20:41	CAN
13	21:09	LEO
16	00:39	VIR
18	07:59	LIB
20	18:40	SCO
23	07:12	SAG
25	20:00	CAP
28	07:54	AQU
30	18:02	PIS

1982

JANUARY		
2	01:34	ARI
4	06:03	TAU
6	07:49	GEM
8	08:02	CAN
10	08:22	LEO
12	10:38	VIR
14	16:18	LIB
17	01:47	SCO
19	14:01	SAG
22	02:51	CAP
24	14:26	AQU
26	23:50	PIS
29	06:59	ARI
31	12:04	TAU

FEBRUARY		
2	15:21	GEM
4	17:19	CAN
6	18:51	LEO
8	21:16	VIR
11	02:03	LIB
13	10:17	SCO
15	21:46	SAG
18	10:37	CAP
20	22:16	AQU
23	07:10	PIS
25	13:18	ARI
27	17:33	TAU

MARCH		
1	20:51	GEM
3	23:49	CAN
6	02:51	LEO
8	06:28	VIR
10	11:35	LIB
12	19:17	SCO
15	06:04	SAG
17	18:48	CAP
20	06:54	AQU
22	16:02	PIS
24	21:38	ARI
27	00:40	TAU
29	02:45	GEM
31	05:10	CAN

APRIL		
2	08:37	LEO
4	13:19	VIR
6	19:27	LIB
9	03:34	SCO
11	14:08	SAG
14	02:42	CAP
16	15:19	AQU
19	01:20	PIS
21	07:24	ARI
23	09:59	TAU
25	10:49	GEM
27	11:44	CAN
29	14:10	LEO

MAY		
1	18:46	VIR
4	01:33	LIB
6	10:25	SCO
8	21:17	SAG
11	09:50	CAP
13	22:45	AQU
16	09:47	PIS
18	17:05	ARI
20	20:23	TAU
22	20:55	GEM
24	20:39	CAN
26	21:28	LEO
29	00:44	VIR
31	07:03	LIB

JUNE		
2	16:13	SCO
5	03:32	SAG
7	16:13	CAP
10	05:09	AQU
12	16:45	PIS
15	01:21	ARI
17	06:07	TAU
19	07:35	GEM
21	07:13	CAN
23	06:58	LEO
25	08:37	VIR
27	13:31	LIB
29	22:02	SCO

JULY		
2	09:26	SAG
4	22:16	CAP
7	11:04	AQU
9	22:36	PIS
12	07:50	ARI
14	14:01	TAU
16	17:04	GEM
18	17:47	CAN
20	17:36	LEO
22	18:21	VIR
24	21:46	LIB
27	04:59	SCO
29	15:48	SAG

AUGUST		
1	04:37	CAP
3	17:18	AQU
6	04:24	PIS
8	13:21	ARI
10	20:01	TAU
13	00:23	GEM
15	02:41	CAN
17	03:41	LEO
19	04:41	VIR
21	07:23	LIB
23	13:22	SCO
25	23:12	SAG
28	11:42	CAP
31	00:24	AQU

SEPTEMBER		
2	11:11	PIS
4	19:25	ARI
7	01:28	TAU
9	05:58	GEM
11	09:19	CAN
13	11:47	LEO
15	13:58	VIR
17	17:04	LIB
19	22:33	SCO
22	07:31	SAG
24	19:32	CAP
27	08:22	AQU
29	19:19	PIS

OCTOBER		
2	03:07	ARI
4	08:10	TAU
6	11:40	GEM
8	14:40	CAN
10	17:45	LEO
12	21:10	VIR
15	01:23	LIB
17	07:21	SCO
19	16:03	SAG
22	03:39	CAP
24	16:37	AQU
27	04:13	PIS
29	12:26	ARI
31	17:04	TAU

NOVEMBER		
2	19:23	GEM
4	21:00	CAN
6	23:11	LEO
9	02:41	VIR
11	07:46	LIB
13	14:43	SCO
15	23:52	SAG
18	11:22	CAP
21	00:21	AQU
23	12:43	PIS
25	22:08	ARI
28	03:32	TAU
30	05:36	GEM

DECEMBER		
2	05:58	CAN
4	06:27	LEO
6	08:33	VIR
8	13:11	LIB
10	20:35	SCO
13	06:28	SAG
15	18:16	CAP
18	07:13	AQU
20	19:57	PIS
23	06:35	ARI
25	13:38	TAU
27	16:49	GEM
29	17:13	CAN
31	16:34	LEO

1983

JANUARY

2	16:50	VIR
4	19:45	LIB
7	02:17	SCO
9	12:14	SAG
12	00:27	CAP
14	13:27	AQU
17	02:03	PIS
19	13:09	ARI
21	21:37	TAU
24	02:41	GEM
26	04:29	CAN
28	04:11	LEO
30	03:35	VIR

FEBRUARY

1	04:48	LIB
3	09:33	SCO
5	18:29	SAG
8	06:34	CAP
10	19:41	AQU
13	08:02	PIS
15	18:47	ARI
18	03:31	TAU
20	09:53	GEM
22	13:32	CAN
24	14:47	LEO
26	14:50	VIR
28	15:31	LIB

MARCH

2	18:51	SCO
5	02:16	SAG
7	13:30	CAP
10	02:31	AQU
12	14:48	PIS
15	01:01	ARI
17	09:05	TAU
19	15:21	GEM
21	19:53	CAN
23	22:44	LEO
26	00:19	VIR
28	01:49	LIB
30	04:58	SCO

APRIL

1	11:21	SAG
3	21:30	CAP
6	10:07	AQU
8	22:31	PIS
11	08:38	ARI
13	16:00	TAU
15	21:16	GEM
18	01:15	CAN
20	04:27	LEO
22	07:12	VIR
24	10:05	LIB
26	14:05	SCO
28	20:29	SAG

MAY

1	06:02	CAP
3	18:10	AQU
6	06:44	PIS
8	17:17	ARI
11	00:37	TAU
13	05:04	GEM
15	07:49	CAN
17	10:02	LEO
19	12:37	VIR
21	16:12	LIB
23	21:18	SCO
26	04:28	SAG
28	14:08	CAP
31	02:00	AQU

JUNE

2	14:43	PIS
5	02:00	ARI
7	10:06	TAU
9	14:38	GEM
11	16:33	CAN
13	17:22	LEO
15	18:39	VIR
17	21:37	LIB
20	03:00	SCO
22	10:56	SAG
24	21:09	CAP
27	09:07	AQU
29	21:52	PIS

JULY

2	09:48	ARI
4	19:06	TAU
7	00:42	GEM
9	02:51	CAN
11	02:54	LEO
13	02:44	VIR
15	04:11	LIB
17	08:39	SCO
19	16:32	SAG
22	03:12	CAP
24	15:27	AQU
27	04:12	PIS
29	16:22	ARI

AUGUST

1	02:38	TAU
3	09:44	GEM
5	13:10	CAN
7	13:38	LEO
9	12:50	VIR
11	12:52	LIB
13	15:45	SCO
15	22:34	SAG
18	09:00	CAP
20	21:26	AQU
23	10:11	PIS
25	22:09	ARI
28	08:39	TAU
30	16:50	GEM

SEPTEMBER

1	21:54	CAN
3	23:48	LEO
5	23:37	VIR
7	23:14	LIB
10	00:50	SCO
12	06:09	SAG
14	15:34	CAP
17	03:46	AQU
19	16:31	PIS
22	04:11	ARI
24	14:13	TAU
26	22:25	GEM
29	04:25	CAN

OCTOBER

1	07:55	LEO
3	09:16	VIR
5	09:43	LIB
7	11:07	SCO
9	15:21	SAG
11	23:31	CAP
14	11:01	AQU
16	23:42	PIS
19	11:19	ARI
21	20:48	TAU
24	04:11	GEM
26	09:48	CAN
28	13:51	LEO
30	16:34	VIR

NOVEMBER

1	18:31	LIB
3	20:54	SCO
6	01:10	SAG
8	08:32	CAP
10	19:11	AQU
13	07:42	PIS
15	19:37	ARI
18	05:07	TAU
20	11:46	GEM
22	16:11	CAN
24	19:20	LEO
26	22:03	VIR
29	00:58	LIB

DECEMBER

1	04:41	SCO
3	09:57	SAG
5	17:29	CAP
8	03:40	AQU
10	15:54	PIS
13	04:17	ARI
15	14:34	TAU
17	21:24	GEM
20	01:03	CAN
22	02:45	LEO
24	04:02	VIR
26	06:19	LIB
28	10:27	SCO
30	16:45	SAG

1984

JANUARY			FEBRUARY			MARCH			APRIL		
2	01:08	CAP	3	06:23	PIS	1	12:30	PIS	2	18:56	TAU
4	11:31	AQU	5	19:05	ARI	4	01:08	ARI	5	05:05	GEM
6	23:35	PIS	8	07:06	TAU	6	13:10	TAU	7	13:00	CAN
9	12:16	ARI	10	16:40	GEM	8	23:30	GEM	9	18:02	LEO
11	23:37	TAU	12	22:21	CAN	11	06:49	CAN	11	20:12	VIR
14	07:41	GEM	15	00:10	LEO	13	10:22	LEO	13	20:30	LIB
16	11:48	CAN	16	23:33	VIR	15	10:48	VIR	15	20:42	SCO
18	12:50	LEO	18	22:40	LIB	17	09:52	LIB	17	22:45	SAG
20	12:36	VIR	20	23:45	SCO	19	09:50	SCO	20	04:11	CAP
22	13:08	LIB	23	04:23	SAG	21	12:42	SAG	22	13:28	AQU
24	16:05	SCO	25	12:50	CAP	23	19:37	CAP	25	01:27	PIS
26	22:13	SAG	28	00:03	AQU	26	06:10	AQU	27	14:03	ARI
29	07:13	CAP				28	18:38	PIS	30	01:31	TAU
31	18:12	AQU				31	07:15	ARI			

MAY			JUNE			JULY			AUGUST		
2	11:03	GEM	1	00:54	CAN	2	14:28	VIR	3	01:05	SCO
4	18:27	CAN	3	05:20	LEO	4	16:28	LIB	5	05:30	SAG
6	23:44	LEO	5	08:28	VIR	6	19:29	SCO	7	12:25	CAP
9	03:03	VIR	7	11:04	LIB	9	00:04	SAG	9	21:26	AQU
11	04:55	LIB	9	13:49	SCO	11	06:24	CAP	12	08:14	PIS
13	06:23	SCO	11	17:27	SAG	13	14:42	AQU	14	20:29	ARI
15	08:51	SAG	13	22:49	CAP	16	01:11	PIS	17	09:14	TAU
17	13:44	CAP	16	06:42	AQU	18	13:27	ARI	19	20:32	GEM
19	21:56	AQU	18	17:19	PIS	21	01:53	TAU	22	04:21	CAN
22	09:09	PIS	21	05:41	ARI	23	12:11	GEM	24	08:01	LEO
24	21:40	ARI	23	17:39	TAU	25	18:45	CAN	26	08:33	VIR
27	09:14	TAU	26	03:05	GEM	27	21:42	LEO	28	07:58	LIB
29	18:24	GEM	28	09:10	CAN	29	22:30	VIR	30	08:24	SCO
			30	12:31	LEO	31	23:04	LIB			

SEPTEMBER			OCTOBER			NOVEMBER			DECEMBER		
1	11:30	SAG	1	00:29	CAP	2	02:50	PIS	1	22:43	ARI
3	17:56	CAP	3	09:04	AQU	4	15:21	ARI	4	11:21	TAU
6	03:12	AQU	5	20:20	PIS	7	03:54	TAU	6	22:25	GEM
8	14:25	PIS	8	08:52	ARI	9	15:11	GEM	9	06:57	CAN
11	02:47	ARI	10	21:29	TAU	12	00:32	CAN	11	13:09	LEO
13	15:34	TAU	13	09:15	GEM	14	07:34	LEO	13	17:36	VIR
16	03:27	GEM	15	19:01	CAN	16	12:09	VIR	15	20:53	LIB
18	12:37	CAN	18	01:42	LEO	18	14:30	LIB	17	23:28	SCO
20	17:50	LEO	20	04:57	VIR	20	15:31	SCO	20	01:59	SAG
22	19:20	VIR	22	05:32	LIB	22	16:35	SAG	22	05:22	CAP
24	18:42	LIB	24	05:09	SCO	24	19:18	CAP	24	10:48	AQU
26	18:05	SCO	26	05:44	SAG	27	01:07	AQU	26	19:19	PIS
28	19:33	SAG	28	09:06	CAP	29	10:34	PIS	29	06:50	ARI
			30	16:14	AQU				31	19:37	TAU

1985

JANUARY			FEBRUARY			MARCH			APRIL		
3	07:01	GEM	2	01:00	CAN	1	10:24	CAN	2	05:26	VIR
5	15:18	CAN	4	06:03	LEO	3	16:29	LEO	4	05:54	LIB
7	20:29	LEO	6	08:10	VIR	5	23:43	VIR	6	05:11	SCO
9	23:40	VIR	8	09:11	LIB	7	23:48	LIB	8	05:18	SAG
12	02:14	LIB	10	10:50	SCO	9	23:47	SCO	10	07:58	CAP
14	05:08	SCO	12	14:10	SAG	11	20:30	SAG	12	14:05	AQU
16	08:49	SAG	14	19:28	CAP	14	00:55	CAP	14	23:31	PIS
18	13:30	CAP	17	02:37	AQU	16	08:12	AQU	17	11:19	ARI
20	19:39	AQU	19	11:39	PIS	18	17:51	PIS	20	00:13	TAU
23	04:03	PIS	21	22:43	ARI	21	05:21	ARI	22	13:01	GEM
25	15:06	ARI	24	11:28	TAU	23	18:07	TAU	25	00:27	CAN
28	03:54	TAU	27	00:12	GEM	26	07:03	GEM	27	09:11	LEO
30	16:01	GEM				28	18:14	CAN	29	14:25	VIR
						31	01:52	LEO			

MAY			JUNE			JULY			AUGUST		
1	16:23	LIB	2	02:34	SAG	1	13:23	CAP	2	07:34	PIS
3	16:18	SCO	4	03:35	CAP	3	16:37	AQU	4	16:44	ARI
5	15:57	SAG	6	06:53	AQU	5	22:41	PIS	7	04:42	TAU
7	17:12	CAP	8	13:47	PIS	8	08:21	ARI	9	17:32	GEM
9	21:39	AQU	11	00:25	ARI	10	20:45	TAU	12	04:29	CAN
12	05:57	PIS	13	13:12	TAU	13	09:24	GEM	14	11:58	LEO
14	17:26	ARI	16	01:46	GEM	15	19:55	CAN	16	16:16	VIR
17	06:24	TAU	18	12:23	CAN	18	03:26	LEO	18	18:45	LIB
19	19:02	GEM	20	20:33	LEO	20	08:30	VIR	20	20:52	SCO
22	06:06	CAN	23	02:33	VIR	22	12:11	LIB	22	23:37	SAG
24	14:55	LEO	25	06:48	LIB	24	15:17	SCO	25	03:25	CAP
26	21:07	VIR	27	09:38	SCO	26	18:13	SAG	27	08:32	AQU
29	00:41	LIB	29	11:31	SAG	28	21:22	CAP	29	15:26	PIS
31	02:08	SCO				31	01:26	AQU			

SEPTEMBER			OCTOBER			NOVEMBER			DECEMBER		
1	00:43	ARI	3	08:37	GEM	2	03:32	CAN	1	20:00	LEO
3	12:29	TAU	5	21:00	CAN	4	14:04	LEO	4	04:15	VIR
6	01:28	GEM	8	06:34	LEO	6	21:19	VIR	6	09:34	LIB
8	13:11	CAN	10	12:10	VIR	9	00:53	LIB	8	11:57	SCO
10	21:28	LEO	12	14:13	LIB	11	01:32	SCO	10	12:14	SAG
13	01:53	VIR	14	14:14	SCO	13	00:53	SAG	12	12:00	CAP
15	03:35	LIB	16	14:06	SAG	15	00:54	CAP	14	13:16	AQU
17	04:18	SCO	18	15:36	CAP	17	03:26	AQU	16	17:51	PIS
19	05:41	SAG	20	19:55	AQU	19	09:43	PIS	19	02:37	ARI
21	08:50	CAP	23	03:28	PIS	21	19:43	ARI	21	14:41	TAU
23	14:12	AQU	25	13:48	ARI	24	08:08	TAU	24	03:46	GEM
25	21:51	PIS	28	02:00	TAU	26	21:09	GEM	26	15:45	CAN
28	07:43	ARI	30	15:00	GEM	29	09:24	CAN	29	01:45	LEO
30	19:36	TAU							31	09:44	VIR

1986

JANUARY		
2	15:46	LIB
4	19:45	SCO
6	21:48	SAG
8	22:43	CAP
11	00:02	AQU
13	03:40	PIS
15	11:04	ARI
17	22:14	TAU
20	11:13	GEM
22	23:15	CAN
25	08:48	LEO
27	15:52	VIR
29	21:11	LIB

FEBRUARY		
1	01:20	SCO
3	04:32	SAG
5	07:02	CAP
7	09:36	AQU
9	13:33	PIS
11	20:22	ARI
14	06:39	TAU
16	19:18	GEM
19	07:40	CAN
21	17:26	LEO
23	23:59	VIR
26	04:08	LIB
28	07:07	SCO

MARCH		
2	09:52	SAG
4	12:57	CAP
6	16:43	AQU
8	21:49	PIS
11	05:04	ARI
13	15:05	TAU
16	03:24	GEM
18	16:05	CAN
21	02:39	LEO
23	09:40	VIR
25	13:23	LIB
27	15:06	SCO
29	16:21	SAG
31	18:26	CAP

APRIL		
2	22:12	AQU
5	04:04	PIS
7	12:13	ARI
9	22:37	TAU
12	10:52	GEM
14	23:43	CAN
17	11:11	LEO
19	19:25	VIR
21	23:51	LIB
24	01:16	SCO
26	01:17	SAG
28	01:42	CAP
30	04:07	AQU

MAY		
2	09:31	PIS
4	18:02	ARI
7	05:00	TAU
9	17:27	GEM
12	06:19	CAN
14	18:16	LEO
17	03:46	VIR
19	09:42	LIB
21	12:03	SCO
23	11:58	SAG
25	11:16	CAP
27	12:01	AQU
29	15:55	PIS
31	23:44	ARI

JUNE		
3	10:46	TAU
5	23:27	GEM
8	12:17	CAN
11	00:12	LEO
13	10:19	VIR
15	17:39	LIB
17	21:37	SCO
19	22:37	SAG
21	22:01	CAP
23	21:51	AQU
26	00:13	PIS
28	06:35	ARI
30	16:55	TAU

JULY		
3	05:33	GEM
5	18:20	CAN
8	05:57	LEO
10	15:51	VIR
12	23:41	LIB
15	04:59	SCO
17	07:35	SAG
19	08:11	CAP
21	08:18	AQU
23	10:00	PIS
25	15:03	ARI
28	00:12	TAU
30	12:20	GEM

AUGUST		
2	01:05	CAN
4	12:27	LEO
6	21:45	VIR
9	05:05	LIB
11	10:37	SCO
13	14:18	SAG
15	16:23	CAP
17	17:45	AQU
19	19:53	PIS
22	00:28	ARI
24	08:37	TAU
26	20:01	GEM
29	08:41	CAN
31	20:09	LEO

SEPTEMBER		
3	05:07	VIR
5	11:34	LIB
7	16:13	SCO
9	19:41	SAG
11	22:29	CAP
14	01:08	AQU
16	04:28	PIS
18	09:34	ARI
20	17:26	TAU
23	04:14	GEM
25	16:45	CAN
28	04:40	LEO
30	13:58	VIR

OCTOBER		
2	20:04	LIB
4	23:36	SCO
7	01:49	SAG
9	03:53	CAP
11	06:46	AQU
13	11:04	PIS
15	17:14	ARI
18	01:36	TAU
20	12:16	GEM
23	00:38	CAN
25	13:03	LEO
27	23:21	VIR
30	06:05	LIB

NOVEMBER		
1	09:20	SCO
3	10:20	SAG
5	10:49	CAP
7	12:29	AQU
9	16:30	PIS
11	23:15	ARI
14	08:25	TAU
16	19:27	GEM
19	07:47	CAN
21	20:26	LEO
24	07:47	VIR
26	16:00	LIB
28	20:14	SCO
30	21:09	SAG

DECEMBER		
2	20:29	CAP
4	20:24	AQU
6	22:49	PIS
9	04:50	ARI
11	14:11	TAU
14	01:42	GEM
16	14:10	CAN
19	02:45	LEO
21	14:31	VIR
24	00:06	LIB
26	06:07	SCO
28	08:20	SAG
30	07:55	CAP

1987

JANUARY		
1	06:54	AQU
3	07:37	PIS
5	11:52	ARI
7	20:14	TAU
10	07:40	GEM
12	20:19	CAN
15	08:46	LEO
17	20:16	VIR
20	06:10	LIB
22	13:31	SCO
24	17:36	SAG
26	18:43	CAP
28	18:18	AQU
30	18:25	PIS

FEBRUARY		
1	21:10	ARI
4	03:54	TAU
6	14:24	GEM
9	02:56	CAN
11	15:22	LEO
14	02:27	VIR
16	11:45	LIB
18	19:05	SCO
21	00:10	SAG
23	02:58	CAP
25	04:09	AQU
27	05:08	PIS

MARCH		
1	07:38	ARI
3	13:12	TAU
5	22:27	GEM
8	10:25	CAN
10	22:55	LEO
13	09:56	VIR
15	18:35	LIB
18	00:58	SCO
20	05:33	SAG
22	08:49	CAP
24	11:19	AQU
26	13:46	PIS
28	17:13	ARI
30	22:47	TAU

APRIL		
2	07:17	GEM
4	18:34	CAN
7	07:05	LEO
9	18:29	VIR
12	03:06	LIB
14	08:41	SCO
16	12:02	SAG
18	14:22	CAP
20	16:46	AQU
22	20:03	PIS
25	00:41	ARI
27	07:07	TAU
29	15:44	GEM

MAY		
2	02:40	CAN
4	15:07	LEO
7	03:08	VIR
9	12:30	LIB
11	18:10	SCO
13	20:42	SAG
15	21:37	CAP
17	22:43	AQU
20	01:25	PIS
22	06:24	ARI
24	13:40	TAU
26	22:56	GEM
29	10:00	CAN
31	22:26	LEO

JUNE		
3	10:57	VIR
5	21:25	LIB
8	04:07	SCO
10	06:54	SAG
12	07:06	CAP
14	06:46	AQU
16	07:55	PIS
18	11:57	ARI
20	19:10	TAU
23	04:55	GEM
25	16:23	CAN
28	04:53	LEO
30	17:35	VIR

JULY		
3	04:56	LIB
5	13:04	SCO
7	17:06	SAG
9	17:44	CAP
11	16:50	AQU
13	16:37	PIS
15	19:01	ARI
18	01:05	TAU
20	10:33	GEM
22	22:14	CAN
25	10:51	LEO
27	23:27	VIR
30	11:00	LIB

AUGUST		
1	20:10	SCO
4	01:48	SAG
6	03:52	CAP
8	03:38	AQU
10	03:02	PIS
12	04:10	ARI
14	08:39	TAU
16	17:00	GEM
19	04:20	CAN
21	16:59	LEO
24	05:24	VIR
26	16:36	LIB
29	01:50	SCO
31	08:25	SAG

SEPTEMBER		
2	12:05	CAP
4	13:22	AQU
6	13:38	PIS
8	14:35	ARI
10	17:58	TAU
13	00:55	GEM
15	11:23	CAN
17	23:51	LEO
20	12:14	VIR
22	22:59	LIB
25	07:31	SCO
27	13:50	SAG
29	18:09	CAP

OCTOBER		
1	20:52	AQU
3	22:40	PIS
6	00:36	ARI
8	03:58	TAU
10	10:04	GEM
12	19:32	CAN
15	07:35	LEO
17	20:07	VIR
20	06:51	LIB
22	14:42	SCO
24	19:58	SAG
26	23:34	CAP
29	02:28	AQU
31	05:20	PIS

NOVEMBER		
2	08:41	ARI
4	13:03	TAU
6	19:17	GEM
9	04:11	CAN
11	15:46	LEO
14	04:30	VIR
16	15:49	LIB
18	23:48	SCO
21	04:17	SAG
23	06:33	CAP
25	08:14	AQU
27	10:41	PIS
29	14:37	ARI

DECEMBER		
1	20:06	TAU
4	03:14	GEM
6	12:21	CAN
8	23:41	LEO
11	12:31	VIR
14	00:41	LIB
16	09:42	SCO
18	14:34	SAG
20	16:08	CAP
22	16:21	AQU
24	17:11	PIS
26	20:06	ARI
29	01:37	TAU
31	09:30	GEM

1988

JANUARY			FEBRUARY			MARCH			APRIL		
2	19:17	CAN	1	13:07	LEO	2	08:07	VIR	1	03:06	LIB
5	06:48	LEO	4	01:55	VIR	4	20:33	LIB	3	13:27	SCO
7	19:36	VIR	6	14:37	LIB	7	07:28	SCO	5	21:30	SAG
10	08:18	LIB	9	01:43	SCO	9	16:00	SAG	8	03:20	CAP
12	18:40	SCO	11	09:37	SAG	11	21:32	CAP	10	07:11	AQU
15	00:59	SAG	13	13:37	CAP	14	00:09	AQU	12	09:25	PIS
17	03:16	CAP	15	14:26	AQU	16	00:43	PIS	14	10:48	ARI
19	03:03	AQU	17	13:45	PIS	18	00:46	ARI	16	12:32	TAU
21	02:28	PIS	19	13:36	ARI	20	02:06	TAU	18	16:11	GEM
23	03:32	ARI	21	15:51	TAU	22	06:22	GEM	20	23:05	CAN
25	07:37	TAU	23	21:43	GEM	24	14:28	CAN	23	09:35	LEO
27	15:03	GEM	26	07:13	CAN	27	01:55	LEO	25	22:17	VIR
30	01:12	CAN	28	19:13	LEO	29	14:50	VIR	28	10:38	LIB
									30	20:40	SCO

MAY			JUNE			JULY			AUGUST		
3	03:53	SAG	1	15:59	CAP	1	02:30	AQU	1	12:54	ARI
5	08:55	CAP	3	18:35	AQU	3	03:34	PIS	3	15:25	TAU
7	12:38	AQU	5	21:01	PIS	5	05:38	ARI	5	20:44	GEM
9	15:40	PIS	8	00:05	ARI	7	09:28	TAU	8	04:53	CAN
11	18:24	ARI	10	04:03	TAU	9	15:17	GEM	10	15:27	LEO
13	21:23	TAU	12	09:15	GEM	11	23:09	CAN	13	03:47	VIR
16	01:32	GEM	14	16:20	CAN	14	09:12	LEO	15	16:53	LIB
18	08:06	CAN	17	01:58	LEO	16	21:18	VIR	18	05:13	SCO
20	17:52	LEO	19	14:04	VIR	19	10:23	LIB	20	14:56	SAG
23	06:13	VIR	22	02:58	LIB	21	22:14	SCO	22	20:50	CAP
25	18:50	LIB	24	13:59	SCO	24	06:43	SAG	24	23:06	AQU
28	05:07	SCO	26	21:19	SAG	26	11:08	CAP	26	23:02	PIS
30	11:58	SAG	29	01:01	CAP	28	12:26	AQU	28	22:30	ARI
						30	12:24	PIS	30	23:23	TAU

SEPTEMBER			OCTOBER			NOVEMBER			DECEMBER		
2	03:12	GEM	1	17:39	CAN	2	23:03	VIR	2	19:57	LIB
4	10:38	CAN	4	03:32	LEO	5	12:05	LIB	5	07:52	SCO
6	21:15	LEO	6	16:02	VIR	7	23:47	SCO	7	16:56	SAG
9	09:49	VIR	9	05:04	LIB	10	09:07	SAG	9	23:08	CAP
11	22:52	LIB	11	16:59	SCO	12	16:13	CAP	12	03:26	AQU
14	11:08	SCO	14	02:59	SAG	14	21:37	AQU	14	06:54	PIS
16	21:26	SAG	16	10:45	CAP	17	01:35	PIS	16	10:04	ARI
19	04:46	CAP	18	16:06	AQU	19	04:13	ARI	18	13:12	TAU
21	08:44	AQU	20	18:59	PIS	21	06:03	TAU	20	16:44	GEM
23	09:52	PIS	22	20:00	ARI	23	08:13	GEM	22	21:36	CAN
25	09:30	ARI	24	20:23	TAU	25	12:20	CAN	25	04:58	LEO
27	09:29	TAU	26	21:56	GEM	27	19:53	LEO	27	15:28	VIR
29	11:44	GEM	29	02:29	CAN	30	07:00	VIR	30	04:10	LIB
			31	11:04	LEO						

1989

JANUARY			FEBRUARY			MARCH			APRIL		
1	16:35	SCO	2	18:31	CAP	2	03:59	CAP	2	20:38	PIS
4	02:12	SAG	4	21:52	AQU	4	08:37	AQU	4	20:52	ARI
6	08:15	CAP	6	22:53	PIS	6	10:00	PIS	6	20:08	TAU
8	11:31	AQU	8	23:19	ARI	8	09:37	ARI	8	20:32	GEM
10	13:32	PIS	11	00:46	TAU	10	09:26	TAU	10	23:59	CAN
12	15:36	ARI	13	04:23	GEM	12	11:17	GEM	13	07:32	LEO
14	18:37	TAU	15	10:41	CAN	14	16:28	CAN	15	18:40	VIR
16	22:58	GEM	17	19:34	LEO	17	01:14	LEO	18	07:32	LIB
19	04:58	CAN	20	06:35	VIR	19	12:40	VIR	20	20:14	SCO
21	13:03	LEO	22	19:06	LIB	22	01:25	LIB	23	07:39	SAG
23	23:33	VIR	25	07:58	SCO	24	14:11	SCO	25	17:16	CAP
26	12:02	LIB	27	19:30	SAG	27	01:55	SAG	28	00:34	AQU
29	00:50	SCO				29	11:26	CAP	30	05:04	PIS
31	11:31	SAG				31	17:46	AQU			

MAY			JUNE			JULY			AUGUST		
2	06:51	ARI	2	17:03	GEM	2	04:20	CAN	3	02:20	VIR
4	06:56	TAU	4	19:18	CAN	4	09:38	LEO	5	13:29	LIB
6	07:04	GEM	7	00:29	LEO	6	18:05	VIR	8	02:06	SCO
8	09:20	CAN	9	09:30	VIR	9	05:31	LIB	10	14:03	SAG
10	15:24	LEO	11	21:32	LIB	11	18:10	SCO	12	23:17	CAP
13	01:31	VIR	14	10:12	SCO	14	05:32	SAG	15	05:00	AQU
15	14:08	LIB	16	21:13	SAG	16	14:02	CAP	17	07:46	PIS
18	02:48	SCO	19	05:42	CAP	18	19:36	AQU	19	09:00	ARI
20	13:53	SAG	21	11:58	AQU	20	23:08	PIS	21	10:11	TAU
22	22:55	CAP	23	16:37	PIS	23	01:41	ARI	23	12:40	GEM
25	06:02	AQU	25	20:07	ARI	25	04:11	TAU	25	17:14	CAN
27	11:14	PIS	27	22:46	TAU	27	07:16	GEM	28	00:12	LEO
29	14:26	ARI	30	01:09	GEM	29	11:33	CAN	30	09:30	VIR
31	16:00	TAU				31	17:42	LEO			

SEPTEMBER			OCTOBER			NOVEMBER			DECEMBER		
1	20:48	LIB	1	15:54	SCO	2	21:47	CAP	2	12:43	AQU
4	09:24	SCO	4	04:30	SAG	5	07:10	AQU	4	19:49	PIS
6	21:52	SAG	6	15:46	CAP	7	13:26	PIS	7	00:12	ARI
9	08:14	CAP	9	00:07	AQU	9	16:09	ARI	9	02:00	TAU
11	15:03	AQU	11	04:38	PIS	11	16:10	TAU	11	02:16	GEM
13	18:08	PIS	13	05:42	ARI	13	15:20	GEM	13	02:50	CAN
15	18:39	ARI	15	04:53	TAU	15	15:52	CAN	15	05:42	LEO
17	18:23	TAU	17	04:20	GEM	17	19:46	LEO	17	12:20	VIR
19	19:17	GEM	19	06:10	CAN	20	03:55	VIR	19	22:46	LIB
21	22:51	CAN	21	11:48	LEO	22	15:26	LIB	22	11:19	SCO
24	05:45	LEO	23	21:16	VIR	25	04:14	SCO	24	23:38	SAG
26	15:33	VIR	26	09:12	LIB	27	16:31	SAG	27	10:11	CAP
29	03:16	LIB	28	21:57	SCO	30	03:27	CAP	29	18:39	AQU
			31	10:24	SAG						

1990

JANUARY		
1	01:11	PIS
3	05:57	ARI
5	09:05	TAU
7	11:02	GEM
9	12:53	CAN
11	16:03	LEO
13	21:58	VIR
16	07:18	LIB
18	19:17	SCO
21	07:45	SAG
23	18:28	CAP
26	02:26	AQU
28	07:52	PIS
30	11:35	ARI

FEBRUARY		
1	14:28	TAU
3	17:13	GEM
5	20:28	CAN
8	00:52	LEO
10	07:14	VIR
12	16:10	LIB
15	03:35	SCO
17	16:08	SAG
20	03:31	CAP
22	11:53	AQU
24	16:50	PIS
26	19:17	ARI
28	20:44	TAU

MARCH		
2	22:38	GEM
5	02:03	CAN
7	07:25	LEO
9	14:48	VIR
12	00:10	LIB
14	11:26	SCO
16	23:57	SAG
19	12:02	CAP
21	21:32	AQU
24	03:09	PIS
26	05:16	ARI
28	05:27	TAU
30	05:43	GEM

APRIL		
1	07:51	CAN
3	12:51	LEO
5	20:43	VIR
8	06:45	LIB
10	18:19	SCO
13	06:49	SAG
15	19:16	CAP
18	05:54	AQU
20	12:58	PIS
22	15:59	ARI
24	16:04	TAU
26	15:13	GEM
28	15:40	CAN
30	19:09	LEO

MAY		
3	02:19	VIR
5	12:29	LIB
8	00:23	SCO
10	12:57	SAG
13	01:22	CAP
15	12:31	AQU
17	20:55	PIS
20	01:32	ARI
22	02:43	TAU
24	02:01	GEM
26	01:35	CAN
28	03:30	LEO
30	09:09	VIR

JUNE		
1	18:32	LIB
4	06:22	SCO
6	19:00	SAG
9	07:13	CAP
11	18:10	AQU
14	03:01	PIS
16	08:56	ARI
18	11:44	TAU
20	12:15	GEM
22	12:10	CAN
24	13:26	LEO
26	17:43	VIR
29	01:48	LIB

JULY		
1	13:02	SCO
4	01:36	SAG
6	13:40	CAP
9	00:07	AQU
11	08:30	PIS
13	14:37	ARI
15	18:30	TAU
17	20:33	GEM
19	21:45	CAN
21	23:30	LEO
24	03:18	VIR
26	10:19	LIB
28	20:40	SCO
31	09:01	SAG

AUGUST		
2	21:09	CAP
5	07:20	AQU
7	14:55	PIS
9	20:14	ARI
11	23:56	TAU
14	02:42	GEM
16	05:13	CAN
18	08:12	LEO
20	12:34	VIR
22	19:18	LIB
25	04:57	SCO
27	16:58	SAG
30	05:24	CAP

SEPTEMBER		
1	15:52	AQU
3	23:06	PIS
6	03:24	ARI
8	05:56	TAU
10	08:06	GEM
12	10:54	CAN
14	14:53	LEO
16	20:19	VIR
19	03:35	LIB
21	13:07	SCO
24	00:53	SAG
26	13:37	CAP
29	00:55	AQU

OCTOBER		
1	08:43	PIS
3	12:43	ARI
5	14:07	TAU
7	14:48	GEM
9	16:30	CAN
11	20:17	LEO
14	02:21	VIR
16	10:27	LIB
18	20:25	SCO
21	08:10	SAG
23	21:04	CAP
26	09:15	AQU
28	18:23	PIS
30	23:15	ARI

NOVEMBER		
2	00:32	TAU
4	00:07	GEM
6	00:08	CAN
8	02:25	LEO
10	07:49	VIR
12	16:09	LIB
15	02:40	SCO
17	14:40	SAG
20	03:32	CAP
22	16:08	AQU
25	02:33	PIS
27	09:07	ARI
29	11:38	TAU

DECEMBER		
1	11:23	GEM
3	10:28	CAN
5	11:01	LEO
7	14:40	VIR
9	22:01	LIB
12	08:29	SCO
14	20:45	SAG
17	09:36	CAP
19	22:00	AQU
22	08:49	PIS
24	16:46	ARI
26	21:10	TAU
28	22:27	GEM
30	22:03	CAN

1991

JANUARY		
1	21:55	LEO
3	23:58	VIR
6	05:34	LIB
8	15:00	SCO
11	03:07	SAG
13	16:01	CAP
16	04:05	AQU
18	14:24	PIS
20	22:28	ARI
23	04:02	TAU
25	07:07	GEM
27	08:24	CAN
29	09:04	LEO
31	10:45	VIR

FEBRUARY		
2	15:03	LIB
4	23:02	SCO
7	10:24	SAG
9	23:17	CAP
12	11:17	AQU
14	21:00	PIS
17	04:12	ARI
19	09:25	TAU
21	13:11	GEM
23	15:57	CAN
25	18:13	LEO
27	20:51	VIR

MARCH		
2	01:04	LIB
4	08:09	SCO
6	18:36	SAG
9	07:15	CAP
11	19:32	AQU
14	05:12	PIS
16	11:38	ARI
18	15:41	TAU
20	18:38	GEM
22	21:28	CAN
25	00:44	LEO
27	04:42	VIR
29	09:50	LIB
31	17:02	SCO

APRIL		
3	03:00	SAG
5	15:20	CAP
8	04:00	AQU
10	14:18	PIS
12	20:50	ARI
15	00:06	TAU
17	01:42	GEM
19	03:18	CAN
21	06:05	LEO
23	10:30	VIR
25	16:37	LIB
28	00:35	SCO
30	10:43	SAG

MAY		
2	22:55	CAP
5	11:52	AQU
7	23:05	PIS
10	06:35	ARI
12	10:08	TAU
14	11:03	GEM
16	11:15	CAN
18	12:31	LEO
20	16:01	VIR
22	22:09	LIB
25	06:42	SCO
27	17:22	SAG
30	05:41	CAP

JUNE		
1	18:42	AQU
4	06:37	PIS
6	15:26	ARI
8	20:14	TAU
10	21:37	GEM
12	21:17	CAN
14	21:11	LEO
16	23:04	VIR
19	04:02	LIB
21	12:19	SCO
23	23:17	SAG
26	11:50	CAP
29	00:48	AQU

JULY		
1	12:52	PIS
3	22:34	ARI
6	04:53	TAU
8	07:43	GEM
10	08:04	CAN
12	07:36	LEO
14	08:13	VIR
16	11:35	LIB
18	18:42	SCO
21	05:17	SAG
23	17:56	CAP
26	06:50	AQU
28	18:36	PIS
31	04:21	ARI

AUGUST		
2	11:33	TAU
4	15:55	GEM
6	17:48	CAN
8	18:10	LEO
10	18:36	VIR
12	20:53	LIB
15	02:35	SCO
17	12:12	SAG
20	00:35	CAP
22	13:28	AQU
25	00:52	PIS
27	10:02	ARI
29	17:01	TAU
31	22:03	GEM

SEPTEMBER		
3	01:20	CAN
5	03:14	LEO
7	04:36	VIR
9	06:52	LIB
11	11:43	SCO
13	20:15	SAG
16	08:05	CAP
18	20:59	AQU
21	08:21	PIS
23	16:57	ARI
25	23:00	TAU
28	03:26	GEM
30	06:59	CAN

OCTOBER		
2	09:59	LEO
4	12:46	VIR
6	16:01	LIB
8	21:01	SCO
11	04:59	SAG
13	16:11	CAP
16	05:05	AQU
18	16:54	PIS
21	01:34	ARI
23	06:56	TAU
25	10:10	GEM
27	12:38	CAN
29	15:21	LEO
31	18:48	VIR

NOVEMBER		
2	23:13	LIB
5	05:10	SCO
7	13:22	SAG
10	00:17	CAP
12	13:07	AQU
15	01:34	PIS
17	11:08	ARI
19	16:50	TAU
21	19:23	GEM
23	20:26	CAN
25	21:38	LEO
28	00:13	VIR
30	04:48	LIB

DECEMBER		
2	11:34	SCO
4	20:33	SAG
7	07:42	CAP
9	20:28	AQU
12	09:20	PIS
14	20:07	ARI
17	03:11	TAU
19	06:22	GEM
21	06:55	CAN
23	06:39	LEO
25	07:25	VIR
27	10:38	LIB
29	17:04	SCO

1992

JANUARY		
1	02:31	SAG
3	14:10	CAP
6	03:00	AQU
8	15:53	PIS
11	03:23	ARI
13	12:01	TAU
15	16:56	GEM
17	18:27	CAN
19	17:58	LEO
21	17:23	VIR
23	18:43	LIB
25	23:33	SCO
28	08:21	SAG
30	20:08	CAP

FEBRUARY		
2	09:10	AQU
4	21:52	PIS
7	09:16	ARI
9	18:37	TAU
12	01:09	GEM
14	04:32	CAN
16	05:16	LEO
18	04:48	VIR
20	05:06	LIB
22	08:12	SCO
24	15:27	SAG
27	02:34	CAP
29	15:35	AQU

MARCH		
3	04:12	PIS
5	15:08	ARI
8	00:06	TAU
10	07:04	GEM
12	11:51	CAN
14	14:21	LEO
16	15:14	VIR
18	15:56	LIB
20	18:21	SCO
23	00:14	SAG
25	10:09	CAP
27	22:45	AQU
30	11:24	PIS

APRIL		
1	22:05	ARI
4	06:19	TAU
6	12:34	GEM
8	17:19	CAN
10	20:47	LEO
12	23:10	VIR
15	01:11	LIB
17	04:11	SCO
19	09:41	SAG
21	18:41	CAP
24	06:39	AQU
26	19:21	PIS
29	06:14	ARI

MAY		
1	14:10	TAU
3	19:29	GEM
5	23:10	CAN
8	02:08	LEO
10	04:57	VIR
12	08:06	LIB
14	12:16	SCO
16	18:23	SAG
19	03:14	CAP
21	14:44	AQU
24	03:26	PIS
26	14:53	ARI
28	23:17	TAU
31	04:20	GEM

JUNE		
2	06:58	CAN
4	08:36	LEO
6	10:29	VIR
8	13:34	LIB
10	18:28	SCO
13	01:30	SAG
15	10:51	CAP
17	22:20	AQU
20	11:01	PIS
22	23:04	ARI
25	08:29	TAU
27	14:15	GEM
29	16:43	CAN

JULY		
1	17:16	LEO
3	17:38	VIR
5	19:28	LIB
7	23:54	SCO
10	07:18	SAG
12	17:16	CAP
15	05:04	AQU
17	17:45	PIS
20	06:08	ARI
22	16:37	TAU
24	23:45	GEM
27	03:09	CAN
29	03:40	LEO
31	03:02	VIR

AUGUST		
2	03:18	LIB
4	06:17	SCO
6	12:58	SAG
8	23:01	CAP
11	11:07	AQU
13	23:52	PIS
16	12:12	ARI
18	23:11	TAU
21	07:37	GEM
23	12:37	CAN
25	14:16	LEO
27	13:47	VIR
29	13:12	LIB
31	14:39	SCO

SEPTEMBER		
2	19:51	SAG
5	05:07	CAP
7	17:09	AQU
10	05:57	PIS
12	18:03	ARI
15	04:48	TAU
17	13:41	GEM
19	20:00	CAN
21	23:20	LEO
24	00:09	VIR
25	23:56	LIB
28	00:45	SCO
30	04:34	SAG

OCTOBER		
2	12:30	CAP
4	23:54	AQU
7	12:39	PIS
10	00:37	ARI
12	10:49	TAU
14	19:09	GEM
17	01:37	CAN
19	06:02	LEO
21	08:28	VIR
23	09:40	LIB
25	11:05	SCO
27	14:30	SAG
29	21:19	CAP

NOVEMBER		
1	07:44	AQU
3	20:14	PIS
6	08:20	ARI
8	18:20	TAU
11	01:50	GEM
13	07:20	CAN
15	11:24	LEO
17	14:29	VIR
19	17:04	LIB
21	19:53	SCO
24	00:02	SAG
26	06:39	CAP
28	16:20	AQU

DECEMBER		
1	04:24	PIS
3	16:50	ARI
6	03:17	TAU
8	10:38	GEM
10	15:06	CAN
12	17:48	LEO
14	19:57	VIR
16	22:34	LIB
19	02:21	SCO
21	07:43	SAG
23	15:05	CAP
26	00:44	AQU
28	12:29	PIS
31	01:08	ARI

1993

JANUARY			FEBRUARY			MARCH			APRIL		
2	12:31	TAU	1	06:15	GEM	2	21:17	CAN	1	09:22	LEO
4	20:43	GEM	3	11:57	CAN	5	00:41	LEO	3	11:11	VIR
7	01:11	CAN	5	13:52	LEO	7	00:53	VIR	5	10:55	LIB
9	02:50	LEO	7	13:30	VIR	8	23:47	LIB	7	10:33	SCO
11	03:21	VIR	9	12:59	LIB	10	23:41	SCO	9	12:11	SAG
13	04:31	LIB	11	14:24	SCO	13	02:34	SAG	11	17:25	CAP
15	07:43	SCO	13	19:09	SAG	15	09:29	CAP	14	02:37	AQU
17	13:31	SAG	16	03:21	CAP	17	19:53	AQU	16	14:33	PIS
19	21:47	CAP	18	14:06	AQU	20	08:12	PIS	19	03:15	ARI
22	08:01	AQU	21	02:13	PIS	22	20:52	ARI	21	15:09	TAU
24	19:48	PIS	23	14:51	ARI	25	09:00	TAU	24	01:28	GEM
27	08:29	ARI	26	03:12	TAU	27	19:49	GEM	26	09:46	CAN
29	20:38	TAU	28	13:53	GEM	30	04:15	CAN	28	15:40	LEO
									30	19:01	VIR

MAY			JUNE			JULY			AUGUST		
2	20:21	LIB	1	05:23	SCO	2	20:49	CAP	1	11:37	AQU
4	20:58	SCO	3	08:02	SAG	5	04:15	AQU	3	21:45	PIS
6	22:35	SAG	5	12:27	CAP	7	14:11	PIS	6	09:40	ARI
9	02:52	CAP	7	19:40	AQU	10	02:12	ARI	8	22:23	TAU
11	10:45	AQU	10	05:58	PIS	12	14:38	TAU	11	09:48	GEM
13	21:51	PIS	12	18:15	ARI	15	01:08	GEM	13	17:47	CAN
16	10:25	ARI	15	06:20	TAU	17	08:09	CAN	15	21:44	LEO
18	22:17	TAU	17	16:13	GEM	19	11:48	LEO	17	22:42	VIR
21	08:08	GEM	19	23:06	CAN	21	13:25	VIR	19	22:36	LIB
23	15:39	CAN	22	03:27	LEO	23	14:40	LIB	21	23:28	SCO
25	21:04	LEO	24	06:19	VIR	25	17:01	SCO	24	02:46	SAG
28	00:47	VIR	26	08:46	LIB	27	21:14	SAG	26	08:59	CAP
30	03:19	LIB	28	11:38	SCO	30	03:28	CAP	28	17:43	AQU
			30	15:29	SAG				31	04:19	PIS

SEPTEMBER			OCTOBER			NOVEMBER			DECEMBER		
2	16:22	ARI	2	11:14	TAU	1	05:14	GEM	3	04:34	LEO
5	05:10	TAU	4	23:28	GEM	3	15:26	CAN	5	09:44	VIR
7	17:17	GEM	7	09:43	CAN	5	23:07	LEO	7	13:04	LIB
10	02:38	CAN	9	16:35	LEO	8	03:48	VIR	9	15:05	SCO
12	07:52	LEO	11	19:37	VIR	10	05:43	LIB	11	16:40	SAG
14	09:21	VIR	13	19:48	LIB	12	06:01	SCO	13	19:07	CAP
16	08:45	LIB	15	19:02	SCO	14	06:21	SAG	15	23:52	AQU
18	08:16	SCO	17	19:24	SAG	16	08:35	CAP	18	08:00	PIS
20	09:54	SAG	19	22:43	CAP	18	14:09	AQU	20	19:20	ARI
22	14:55	CAP	22	05:50	AQU	20	23:28	PIS	23	08:06	TAU
24	23:00	AQU	24	16:18	PIS	23	11:31	ARI	25	19:47	GEM
27	10:14	PIS	27	04:40	ARI	26	00:15	TAU	28	04:47	CAN
29	22:30	ARI	29	17:21	TAU	28	11:49	GEM	30	11:00	LEO
						30	21:18	CAN			

1994

JANUARY			FEBRUARY			MARCH			APRIL		
1	15:16	VIR	2	02:50	SCO	1	09:44	SCO	1	22:39	CAP
3	18:32	LIB	4	06:15	SAG	3	11:55	SAG	4	04:46	AQU
5	21:30	SCO	6	11:03	CAP	5	16:25	CAP	6	13:52	PIS
8	00:35	SAG	8	17:17	AQU	7	23:16	AQU	9	01:10	ARI
10	04:17	CAP	11	01:24	PIS	10	08:10	PIS	11	13:49	TAU
12	09:26	AQU	13	11:50	ARI	12	19:00	ARI	14	02:49	GEM
14	17:05	PIS	16	00:21	TAU	15	07:28	TAU	16	14:42	CAN
17	03:43	ARI	18	13:06	GEM	17	20:30	GEM	18	23:46	LEO
19	16:23	TAU	20	23:28	CAN	20	07:55	CAN	21	04:59	VIR
22	04:35	GEM	23	05:48	LEO	22	15:40	LEO	23	06:41	LIB
24	13:56	CAN	25	08:28	VIR	24	19:15	VIR	25	06:19	SCO
26	19:39	LEO	27	09:07	LIB	26	19:47	LIB	27	05:49	SAG
28	22:40	VIR				28	19:16	SCO	29	07:06	CAP
31	00:35	LIB				30	19:42	SAG			

MAY			JUNE			JULY			AUGUST		
1	11:35	AQU	2	13:32	ARI	2	09:24	TAU	1	06:06	GEM
3	19:48	PIS	5	02:15	TAU	4	22:13	GEM	3	17:23	CAN
6	07:02	ARI	7	15:04	GEM	7	09:18	CAN	6	01:32	LEO
8	19:51	TAU	10	02:23	CAN	9	17:44	LEO	8	06:43	VIR
11	08:44	GEM	12	11:30	LEO	11	23:49	VIR	10	10:08	LIB
13	20:28	CAN	14	18:17	VIR	14	04:16	LIB	12	12:57	SCO
16	05:59	LEO	16	22:49	LIB	16	07:36	SCO	14	15:54	SAG
18	12:32	VIR	19	01:21	SCO	18	10:10	SAG	16	19:19	CAP
20	15:55	LIB	21	02:33	SAG	20	12:31	CAP	18	23:35	AQU
22	16:52	SCO	23	03:38	CAP	22	15:39	AQU	21	05:28	PIS
24	16:44	SAG	25	06:11	AQU	24	20:57	PIS	23	13:56	ARI
26	17:18	CAP	27	11:45	PIS	27	05:32	ARI	26	01:14	TAU
28	20:20	AQU	29	21:08	ARI	29	17:14	TAU	28	14:08	GEM
31	03:04	PIS							31	02:01	CAN

SEPTEMBER			OCTOBER			NOVEMBER			DECEMBER		
2	10:38	LEO	2	01:40	VIR	2	15:20	SCO	2	02:14	SAG
4	15:34	VIR	4	03:57	LIB	4	14:47	SAG	4	01:43	CAP
6	17:58	LIB	6	04:23	SCO	6	15:03	CAP	6	02:53	AQU
8	19:27	SCO	8	04:48	SAG	8	17:49	AQU	8	07:25	PIS
10	21:26	SAG	10	06:45	CAP	11	00:05	PIS	10	16:04	ARI
13	00:45	CAP	12	11:10	AQU	13	09:45	ARI	13	03:57	TAU
15	05:43	AQU	14	18:19	PIS	15	21:45	TAU	15	17:01	GEM
17	12:32	PIS	17	03:57	ARI	18	10:42	GEM	18	05:26	CAN
19	21:31	ARI	19	15:35	TAU	20	23:22	CAN	20	16:14	LEO
22	08:48	TAU	22	04:29	GEM	23	10:34	LEO	23	01:02	VIR
24	21:42	GEM	24	17:16	CAN	25	19:10	VIR	25	07:28	LIB
27	10:13	CAN	27	04:06	LEO	28	00:23	LIB	27	11:18	SCO
29	19:56	LEO	29	11:22	VIR	30	02:22	SCO	29	12:46	SAG
			31	14:47	LIB				31	12:58	CAP

1995

JANUARY			FEBRUARY			MARCH			APRIL		
2	13:40	AQU	1	03:06	PIS	2	18:31	ARI	1	12:00	TAU
4	16:50	PIS	3	09:13	ARI	5	03:51	TAU	3	23:50	GEM
6	23:57	ARI	5	19:10	TAU	7	15:56	GEM	6	12:41	CAN
9	10:59	TAU	8	07:45	GEM	10	04:41	CAN	9	00:16	LEO
11	23:58	GEM	10	20:18	CAN	12	15:29	LEO	11	08:40	VIR
14	12:21	CAN	13	06:32	LEO	14	22:55	VIR	13	13:21	LIB
16	22:37	LEO	15	13:53	VIR	17	03:19	LIB	15	15:14	SCO
19	06:40	VIR	17	19:01	LIB	19	05:53	SCO	17	15:52	SAG
21	12:55	LIB	19	22:56	SCO	21	07:58	SAG	19	16:55	CAP
23	17:33	SCO	22	02:14	SAG	23	10:32	CAP	21	19:39	AQU
25	20:38	SAG	24	05:12	CAP	25	14:11	AQU	24	00:52	PIS
27	22:27	CAP	26	08:15	AQU	27	19:19	PIS	26	08:42	ARI
30	00:04	AQU	28	12:17	PIS	30	02:27	ARI	28	18:54	TAU

MAY			JUNE			JULY			AUGUST		
1	06:54	GEM	2	14:18	LEO	2	06:36	VIR	3	02:30	SCO
3	19:46	CAN	5	00:47	VIR	4	14:56	LIB	5	06:15	SAG
6	07:56	LEO	7	08:14	LIB	6	20:20	SCO	7	07:53	CAP
8	17:34	VIR	9	12:04	SCO	8	22:38	SAG	9	08:29	AQU
10	23:31	LIB	11	12:51	SAG	10	22:44	CAP	11	09:47	PIS
13	01:54	SCO	13	12:06	CAP	12	22:22	AQU	13	13:42	ARI
15	01:59	SAG	15	11:53	AQU	14	23:38	PIS	15	21:26	TAU
17	01:37	CAP	17	14:14	PIS	17	04:24	ARI	18	08:41	GEM
19	02:40	AQU	19	20:30	ARI	19	13:21	TAU	20	21:25	CAN
21	06:41	PIS	22	06:36	TAU	22	01:24	GEM	23	09:14	LEO
23	14:14	ARI	24	19:03	GEM	24	14:17	CAN	25	18:51	VIR
26	00:47	TAU	27	07:57	CAN	27	02:08	LEO	28	02:16	LIB
28	13:08	GEM	29	20:03	LEO	29	12:13	VIR	30	07:52	SCO
31	02:00	CAN				31	20:24	LIB			

SEPTEMBER			OCTOBER			NOVEMBER			DECEMBER		
1	11:58	SAG	2	23:00	AQU	1	08:18	PIS	3	04:41	TAU
3	14:46	CAP	5	02:36	PIS	3	14:22	ARI	5	15:36	GEM
5	16:48	AQU	7	07:43	ARI	5	22:36	TAU	8	03:45	CAN
7	19:09	PIS	9	15:06	TAU	8	08:56	GEM	10	16:25	LEO
9	23:15	ARI	12	01:11	GEM	10	20:58	CAN	13	04:27	VIR
12	06:22	TAU	14	13:21	CAN	13	09:38	LEO	15	14:10	LIB
14	16:49	GEM	17	01:47	LEO	15	21:03	VIR	17	20:08	SCO
17	05:17	CAN	19	12:12	VIR	18	05:19	LIB	19	22:14	SAG
19	17:20	LEO	21	19:16	LIB	20	09:41	SCO	21	21:47	CAP
22	03:02	VIR	23	23:07	SCO	22	10:57	SAG	23	20:53	AQU
24	09:51	LIB	26	00:57	SAG	24	10:49	CAP	25	21:46	PIS
26	14:21	SCO	28	02:16	CAP	26	11:16	AQU	28	02:07	ARI
28	17:31	SAG	30	04:24	AQU	28	14:00	PIS	30	10:22	TAU
30	20:11	CAP				30	19:52	ARI			

1996

JANUARY		
1	21:30	GEM
4	09:57	CAN
6	22:31	LEO
9	10:30	VIR
11	20:56	LIB
14	04:31	SCO
16	08:26	SAG
18	09:08	CAP
20	08:16	AQU
22	08:03	PIS
24	10:38	ARI
26	17:17	TAU
29	03:43	GEM
31	16:12	CAN

FEBRUARY		
3	04:47	LEO
5	16:23	VIR
8	02:31	LIB
10	10:36	SCO
12	15:59	SAG
14	18:30	CAP
16	19:01	AQU
18	19:10	PIS
20	20:59	ARI
23	02:09	TAU
25	11:15	GEM
27	23:11	CAN

MARCH		
1	11:48	LEO
3	23:14	VIR
6	08:41	LIB
8	16:06	SCO
10	21:33	SAG
13	01:09	CAP
15	03:16	AQU
17	04:51	PIS
19	07:16	ARI
21	12:00	TAU
23	20:00	GEM
26	07:07	CAN
28	19:38	LEO
31	07:16	VIR

APRIL		
2	16:27	LIB
4	22:58	SCO
7	03:22	SAG
9	06:31	CAP
11	09:10	AQU
13	12:01	PIS
15	15:44	ARI
17	21:06	TAU
20	04:55	GEM
22	15:26	CAN
25	03:45	LEO
27	15:50	VIR
30	01:28	LIB

MAY		
2	07:43	SCO
4	11:06	SAG
6	12:55	CAP
8	14:40	AQU
10	17:30	PIS
12	22:01	ARI
15	04:26	TAU
17	12:49	GEM
19	23:17	CAN
22	11:29	LEO
24	23:59	VIR
27	10:34	LIB
29	17:31	SCO
31	20:44	SAG

JUNE		
2	21:30	CAP
4	21:46	AQU
6	23:20	PIS
9	03:24	ARI
11	10:12	TAU
13	19:17	GEM
16	06:09	CAN
18	18:23	LEO
21	07:08	VIR
23	18:38	LIB
26	02:54	SCO
28	07:02	SAG
30	07:48	CAP

JULY		
2	07:06	AQU
4	07:08	PIS
6	09:43	ARI
8	15:44	TAU
11	00:53	GEM
13	12:09	CAN
16	00:32	LEO
18	13:17	VIR
21	01:15	LIB
23	10:44	SCO
25	16:25	SAG
27	18:18	CAP
29	17:48	AQU
31	17:02	PIS

AUGUST		
2	18:06	ARI
4	22:34	TAU
7	06:50	GEM
9	17:58	CAN
12	06:30	LEO
14	19:08	VIR
17	06:56	LIB
19	16:51	SCO
21	23:49	SAG
24	03:23	CAP
26	04:11	AQU
28	03:50	PIS
30	04:16	ARI

SEPTEMBER		
1	07:21	TAU
3	14:09	GEM
6	00:30	CAN
8	12:55	LEO
11	01:29	VIR
13	12:52	LIB
15	22:21	SCO
18	05:32	SAG
20	10:13	CAP
22	12:40	AQU
24	13:44	PIS
26	14:47	ARI
28	17:25	TAU
30	23:02	GEM

OCTOBER		
3	08:15	CAN
5	20:13	LEO
8	08:50	VIR
10	20:01	LIB
13	04:47	SCO
15	11:08	SAG
17	15:38	CAP
19	18:52	AQU
21	21:23	PIS
23	23:51	ARI
26	03:12	TAU
28	08:36	GEM
30	16:57	CAN

NOVEMBER		
2	04:17	LEO
4	16:58	VIR
7	04:30	LIB
9	13:03	SCO
11	18:27	SAG
13	21:45	CAP
16	00:15	AQU
18	03:01	PIS
20	06:35	ARI
22	11:13	TAU
24	17:21	GEM
27	01:38	CAN
29	12:31	LEO

DECEMBER		
2	01:12	VIR
4	13:24	LIB
6	22:40	SCO
9	03:59	SAG
11	06:16	CAP
13	07:15	AQU
15	08:45	PIS
17	11:56	ARI
19	17:11	TAU
22	00:18	GEM
24	09:15	CAN
26	20:10	LEO
29	08:46	VIR
31	21:33	LIB

1997

JANUARY			FEBRUARY			MARCH			APRIL		
3	08:03	SCO	1	23:52	SAG	1	07:02	SAG	1	23:00	AQU
5	14:28	SAG	4	03:45	CAP	3	12:39	CAP	4	00:43	PIS
7	16:56	CAP	6	04:22	AQU	5	14:55	AQU	6	01:20	ARI
9	17:01	AQU	8	03:35	PIS	7	14:58	PIS	8	02:21	TAU
11	16:52	PIS	10	03:30	ARI	9	14:34	ARI	10	05:29	GEM
13	18:23	ARI	12	05:57	TAU	11	15:38	TAU	12	12:04	CAN
15	22:41	TAU	14	11:54	GEM	13	19:49	GEM	14	22:23	LEO
18	05:54	GEM	16	21:14	CAN	16	03:52	CAN	17	11:01	VIR
20	15:30	CAN	19	08:53	LEO	18	15:09	LEO	19	23:37	LIB
23	02:51	LEO	21	21:39	VIR	21	04:00	VIR	22	10:20	SCO
25	15:27	VIR	24	10:24	LIB	23	16:36	LIB	24	18:33	SAG
28	04:22	LIB	26	21:58	SCO	26	03:43	SCO	27	00:33	CAP
30	15:49	SCO				28	12:41	SAG	29	04:51	AQU
						30	19:08	CAP			

MAY			JUNE			JULY			AUGUST		
1	07:51	PIS	1	19:40	TAU	1	06:36	GEM	2	05:28	LEO
3	10:00	ARI	3	23:56	GEM	3	13:34	CAN	4	17:16	VIR
5	12:05	TAU	6	06:03	CAN	5	22:46	LEO	7	06:18	LIB
7	15:22	GEM	8	14:59	LEO	8	10:23	VIR	9	18:51	SCO
9	21:14	CAN	11	02:44	VIR	10	23:22	LIB	12	04:46	SAG
12	06:34	LEO	13	15:36	LIB	13	11:21	SCO	14	10:43	CAP
14	18:44	VIR	16	02:52	SCO	15	20:03	SAG	16	12:59	AQU
17	07:28	LIB	18	10:40	SAG	18	00:46	CAP	18	13:02	PIS
19	18:13	SCO	20	15:03	CAP	20	02:30	AQU	20	12:46	ARI
22	01:52	SAG	22	17:21	AQU	22	03:01	PIS	22	13:58	TAU
24	06:52	CAP	24	19:10	PIS	24	04:04	ARI	24	17:57	GEM
26	10:21	AQU	26	21:39	ARI	26	06:54	TAU	27	01:12	CAN
28	13:19	PIS	29	01:24	TAU	28	12:05	GEM	29	11:20	LEO
30	16:19	ARI				30	19:39	CAN	31	23:28	VIR

SEPTEMBER			OCTOBER			NOVEMBER			DECEMBER		
3	12:31	LIB	3	06:58	SCO	1	23:28	SAG	1	13:39	CAP
6	01:11	SCO	5	17:44	SAG	4	07:32	CAP	3	18:59	AQU
8	11:55	SAG	8	02:05	CAP	6	13:34	AQU	5	23:08	PIS
10	19:24	CAP	10	07:30	AQU	8	17:36	PIS	8	02:25	ARI
12	23:11	AQU	12	10:00	PIS	10	19:45	ARI	10	05:01	TAU
15	00:00	PIS	14	10:26	ARI	12	20:46	TAU	12	07:36	GEM
16	23:26	ARI	16	10:17	TAU	14	22:06	GEM	14	11:26	CAN
18	23:22	TAU	18	11:27	GEM	17	01:33	CAN	16	17:59	LEO
21	01:40	GEM	20	15:46	CAN	19	08:39	LEO	19	04:01	VIR
23	07:34	CAN	23	00:11	LEO	21	19:34	VIR	21	16:36	LIB
25	17:13	LEO	25	12:00	VIR	24	08:30	LIB	24	05:08	SCO
28	05:28	VIR	28	01:06	LIB	26	20:44	SCO	26	15:08	SAG
30	18:33	LIB	30	13:16	SCO	29	06:29	SAG	28	21:49	CAP
									31	01:59	AQU

1998

JANUARY		
2	04:57	PIS
4	07:44	ARI
6	10:53	TAU
8	14:43	GEM
10	19:44	CAN
13	02:46	LEO
15	12:32	VIR
18	00:45	LIB
20	13:35	SCO
23	00:26	SAG
25	07:40	CAP
27	11:28	AQU
29	13:09	PIS
31	14:22	ARI

FEBRUARY		
2	16:26	TAU
4	20:10	GEM
7	01:58	CAN
9	09:58	LEO
11	20:11	VIR
14	08:18	LIB
16	21:14	SCO
19	08:57	SAG
21	17:30	CAP
23	22:11	AQU
25	23:43	PIS
27	23:43	ARI

MARCH		
2	00:01	TAU
4	02:16	GEM
6	07:28	CAN
8	15:47	LEO
11	02:36	VIR
13	14:59	LIB
16	03:52	SCO
18	15:57	SAG
21	01:44	CAP
23	08:02	AQU
25	10:44	PIS
27	10:50	ARI
29	10:07	TAU
31	10:39	GEM

APRIL		
2	14:11	CAN
4	21:37	LEO
7	08:26	VIR
9	21:05	LIB
12	09:57	SCO
14	21:53	SAG
17	08:06	CAP
19	15:42	AQU
21	20:07	PIS
23	21:31	ARI
25	21:10	TAU
27	20:56	GEM
29	22:58	CAN

MAY		
2	04:50	LEO
4	14:48	VIR
7	03:20	LIB
9	16:11	SCO
12	03:49	SAG
14	13:40	CAP
16	21:31	AQU
19	03:04	PIS
21	06:07	ARI
23	07:07	TAU
25	07:26	GEM
27	08:59	CAN
29	13:39	LEO
31	22:22	VIR

JUNE		
3	10:18	LIB
5	23:07	SCO
8	10:35	SAG
10	19:51	CAP
13	03:04	AQU
15	08:32	PIS
17	12:24	ARI
19	14:48	TAU
21	16:27	GEM
23	18:40	CAN
25	23:05	LEO
28	06:55	VIR
30	18:06	LIB

JULY		
3	06:46	SCO
5	18:25	SAG
8	03:28	CAP
10	09:53	AQU
12	14:23	PIS
14	17:46	ARI
16	20:34	TAU
18	23:19	GEM
21	02:44	CAN
23	07:50	LEO
25	15:35	VIR
28	02:15	LIB
30	14:45	SCO

AUGUST		
2	02:49	SAG
4	12:19	CAP
6	18:32	AQU
8	22:05	PIS
11	00:11	ARI
13	02:05	TAU
15	04:47	GEM
17	08:56	CAN
19	15:02	LEO
21	23:22	VIR
24	10:03	LIB
26	22:26	SCO
29	10:56	SAG
31	21:24	CAP

SEPTEMBER		
3	04:22	AQU
5	07:49	PIS
7	08:53	ARI
9	09:17	TAU
11	10:41	GEM
13	14:21	CAN
15	20:49	LEO
18	05:53	VIR
20	16:58	LIB
23	05:23	SCO
25	18:06	SAG
28	05:31	CAP
30	13:54	AQU

OCTOBER		
2	18:24	PIS
4	19:33	ARI
6	18:58	TAU
8	18:45	GEM
10	20:49	CAN
13	02:26	LEO
15	11:33	VIR
17	23:03	LIB
20	11:37	SCO
23	00:17	SAG
25	12:06	CAP
27	21:45	AQU
30	03:59	PIS

NOVEMBER		
1	06:28	ARI
3	06:13	TAU
5	05:12	GEM
7	05:40	CAN
9	09:34	LEO
11	17:38	VIR
14	04:59	LIB
16	17:42	SCO
19	06:14	SAG
21	17:46	CAP
24	03:44	AQU
26	11:15	PIS
28	15:35	ARI
30	16:54	TAU

DECEMBER		
2	16:31	GEM
4	16:29	CAN
6	18:56	LEO
9	01:22	VIR
11	11:44	LIB
14	00:17	SCO
16	12:48	SAG
18	23:56	CAP
21	09:18	AQU
23	16:46	PIS
25	22:05	ARI
28	01:06	TAU
30	02:23	GEM

1999

JANUARY

1	03:16	CAN
3	05:32	LEO
5	10:50	VIR
7	19:54	LIB
10	07:50	SCO
12	20:24	SAG
15	07:30	CAP
17	16:12	AQU
19	22:41	PIS
22	03:26	ARI
24	06:53	TAU
26	09:30	GEM
28	11:58	CAN
30	15:17	LEO

FEBRUARY

1	20:38	VIR
4	04:57	LIB
6	16:07	SCO
9	04:39	SAG
11	16:11	CAP
14	00:58	AQU
16	06:41	PIS
18	10:07	ARI
20	12:30	TAU
22	14:55	GEM
24	18:10	CAN
26	22:45	LEO

MARCH

1	05:06	VIR
3	13:35	LIB
6	00:23	SCO
8	12:47	SAG
11	00:55	CAP
13	10:33	AQU
15	16:31	PIS
17	19:14	ARI
19	20:10	TAU
21	21:06	GEM
23	23:34	CAN
26	04:23	LEO
28	11:35	VIR
30	20:50	LIB

APRIL

2	07:50	SCO
4	20:08	SAG
7	08:40	CAP
9	19:25	AQU
12	02:36	PIS
14	05:47	ARI
16	06:08	TAU
18	05:40	GEM
20	06:28	CAN
22	10:07	LEO
24	17:05	VIR
27	02:47	LIB
29	14:13	SCO

MAY

2	02:37	SAG
4	15:13	CAP
7	02:41	AQU
9	11:17	PIS
11	15:54	ARI
13	16:57	TAU
15	16:08	GEM
17	15:40	CAN
19	17:38	LEO
21	23:16	VIR
24	08:30	LIB
26	20:06	SCO
29	08:38	SAG
31	21:07	CAP

JUNE

3	08:38	AQU
5	18:02	PIS
8	00:09	ARI
10	02:45	TAU
12	02:49	GEM
14	02:15	CAN
16	03:08	LEO
18	07:13	VIR
20	15:11	LIB
23	02:19	SCO
25	14:52	SAG
28	03:13	CAP
30	14:20	AQU

JULY

2	23:35	PIS
5	06:22	ARI
7	10:23	TAU
9	12:01	GEM
11	12:28	CAN
13	13:27	LEO
15	16:40	VIR
17	23:20	LIB
20	09:31	SCO
22	21:49	SAG
25	10:09	CAP
27	20:55	AQU
30	05:28	PIS

AUGUST

1	11:48	ARI
3	16:10	TAU
5	18:58	GEM
7	20:54	CAN
9	22:57	LEO
12	02:23	VIR
14	08:25	LIB
16	17:41	SCO
19	05:33	SAG
21	18:00	CAP
24	04:50	AQU
26	12:51	PIS
28	18:10	ARI
30	21:42	TAU

SEPTEMBER

2	00:26	GEM
4	03:11	CAN
6	06:30	LEO
8	10:58	VIR
10	17:17	LIB
13	02:09	SCO
15	13:36	SAG
18	02:15	CAP
20	13:39	AQU
22	21:52	PIS
25	02:35	ARI
27	04:52	TAU
29	06:22	GEM

OCTOBER

1	08:32	CAN
3	12:14	LEO
5	17:41	VIR
8	00:53	LIB
10	10:02	SCO
12	21:20	SAG
15	10:05	CAP
17	22:18	AQU
20	07:34	PIS
22	12:42	ARI
24	14:26	TAU
26	14:34	GEM
28	15:10	CAN
30	17:48	LEO

NOVEMBER

1	23:08	VIR
4	06:58	LIB
6	16:47	SCO
9	04:16	SAG
11	17:01	CAP
14	05:47	AQU
16	16:22	PIS
18	22:58	ARI
21	01:27	TAU
23	01:15	GEM
25	00:30	CAN
27	01:20	LEO
29	05:12	VIR

DECEMBER

1	12:30	LIB
3	22:36	SCO
6	10:28	SAG
8	23:15	CAP
11	12:00	AQU
13	23:19	PIS
16	07:31	ARI
18	11:46	TAU
20	12:40	GEM
22	11:53	CAN
24	11:33	LEO
26	13:35	VIR
28	19:15	LIB
31	04:37	SCO

2000

JANUARY		
2	16:33	SAG
5	05:25	CAP
7	17:54	AQU
10	05:00	PIS
12	13:49	ARI
14	19:39	TAU
16	22:26	GEM
18	23:02	CAN
20	22:59	LEO
23	00:08	VIR
25	04:10	LIB
27	12:02	SCO
29	23:19	SAG

FEBRUARY		
1	12:11	CAP
4	00:32	AQU
6	11:03	PIS
8	19:18	ARI
11	01:22	TAU
13	05:24	GEM
15	07:46	CAN
17	09:12	LEO
19	10:54	VIR
21	14:22	LIB
23	20:59	SCO
26	07:11	SAG
28	19:46	CAP

MARCH		
2	08:15	AQU
4	18:31	PIS
7	01:55	ARI
9	07:02	TAU
11	10:47	GEM
13	13:52	CAN
15	16:44	LEO
17	19:49	VIR
19	23:58	LIB
22	06:19	SCO
24	15:44	SAG
27	03:52	CAP
29	16:35	AQU

APRIL		
1	03:13	PIS
3	10:23	ARI
5	14:30	TAU
7	16:59	GEM
9	19:17	CAN
11	22:17	LEO
14	02:20	VIR
16	07:37	LIB
18	14:36	SCO
20	23:59	SAG
23	11:48	CAP
26	00:43	AQU
28	12:07	PIS
30	19:56	ARI

MAY		
2	23:55	TAU
5	01:24	GEM
7	02:15	CAN
9	04:02	LEO
11	07:42	VIR
13	13:28	LIB
15	21:17	SCO
18	07:10	SAG
20	19:02	CAP
23	08:01	AQU
25	20:08	PIS
28	05:09	ARI
30	10:03	TAU

JUNE		
1	11:35	GEM
3	11:31	CAN
5	11:47	LEO
7	13:58	VIR
9	19:00	LIB
12	02:56	SCO
14	13:19	SAG
17	01:28	CAP
19	14:27	AQU
22	02:53	PIS
24	12:56	ARI
26	19:20	TAU
28	22:00	GEM
30	22:10	CAN

JULY		
2	21:39	LEO
4	22:20	VIR
7	01:48	LIB
9	08:49	SCO
11	19:07	SAG
14	07:29	CAP
16	20:28	AQU
19	08:45	PIS
21	19:10	ARI
24	02:45	TAU
26	07:02	GEM
28	08:31	CAN
30	08:25	LEO

AUGUST		
1	08:28	VIR
3	10:32	LIB
5	16:05	SCO
8	01:31	SAG
10	13:45	CAP
13	02:44	AQU
15	14:42	PIS
18	00:45	ARI
20	08:32	TAU
22	13:56	GEM
24	17:01	CAN
26	18:18	LEO
28	18:56	VIR
30	20:34	LIB

SEPTEMBER		
2	00:56	SCO
4	09:09	SAG
6	20:48	CAP
9	09:45	AQU
11	21:35	PIS
14	07:01	ARI
16	14:06	TAU
18	19:23	GEM
20	23:17	CAN
23	02:01	LEO
25	04:03	VIR
27	06:23	LIB
29	10:31	SCO

OCTOBER		
1	17:51	SAG
4	04:43	CAP
6	17:34	AQU
9	05:37	PIS
11	14:52	ARI
13	21:07	TAU
16	01:20	GEM
18	04:38	CAN
20	07:43	LEO
22	10:53	VIR
24	14:31	LIB
26	19:24	SCO
29	02:41	SAG
31	13:03	CAP

NOVEMBER		
3	01:42	AQU
5	14:14	PIS
8	00:03	ARI
10	06:13	TAU
12	09:28	GEM
14	11:22	CAN
16	13:20	LEO
18	16:16	VIR
20	20:36	LIB
23	02:34	SCO
25	10:34	SAG
27	20:58	CAP
30	09:28	AQU

DECEMBER		
2	22:24	PIS
5	09:18	ARI
7	16:28	TAU
9	19:51	GEM
11	20:50	CAN
13	21:10	LEO
15	22:31	VIR
18	02:02	LIB
20	08:13	SCO
22	16:58	SAG
25	03:55	CAP
27	16:26	AQU
30	05:28	PIS

★ **4** ★

The Mercury Tables

How to Find the Planet Mercury at the Time of Your Birth

Locate the year of your birth, then find the range of dates that includes your birth date. The sign indicated next to this range is your Mercury Sign.

1900		1901	
Jan. 1–Jan. 8	Sagittarius	Jan. 2–Jan. 20	Capricorn
Jan. 9–Jan. 28	Capricorn	Jan. 21–Feb. 6	Aquarius
Jan. 29–Feb. 14	Aquarius	Feb. 7–Apr. 14	Pisces
Feb. 15–Mar. 2	Pisces	Apr. 15–May 2	Aries
Mar. 3–Apr. 7	Aries	May 3–May 16	Taurus
Apr. 8–Apr. 16	Pisces	May 17–May 31	Gemini
Apr. 17–May 9	Aries	Jun. 1–Aug. 9	Cancer
May 10–May 24	Taurus	Aug. 10–Aug. 24	Leo
May 25–Jun. 7	Gemini	Aug. 25–Sep. 10	Virgo
Jun. 8–Jun. 26	Cancer	Sep. 11–Sep. 30	Libra
Jun. 27–Aug. 2	Leo	Oct. 1–Dec. 5	Scorpio
Aug. 3–Sep. 17	Virgo	Dec. 6–Dec. 25	Sagittarius
Sep. 18–Oct. 5	Libra	Dec. 26–Jan. 12	Capricorn
Oct. 6–Oct. 28	Scorpio		
Oct. 29–Nov. 18	Sagittarius		
Nov. 19–Dec. 19	Scorpio		
Dec. 20–Jan. 1	Sagittarius		

1902

Jan. 1–Jan. 12	Capricorn
Jan. 13–Jan. 31	Aquarius
Feb. 1–Feb. 17	Pisces
Feb. 18–Mar. 18	Aquarius
Mar. 19–Apr. 8	Pisces
Apr. 9–Apr. 24	Aries
Apr. 25–May 8	Taurus
May 9–May 28	Gemini
May 29–Jun. 25	Cancer
Jun. 26–Jul. 12	Gemini
Jul. 13–Aug. 1	Cancer
Aug. 2–Aug. 16	Leo
Aug. 17–Sep. 3	Virgo
Sep. 4–Sep. 27	Libra
Sep. 28–Oct. 14	Scorpio
Oct. 15–Nov. 9	Libra
Nov. 10–Nov. 29	Scorpio
Nov. 30–Dec. 18	Sagittarius
Dec. 19–Dec. 31	Capricorn

1903

Jan. 1–Jan. 5	Capricorn
Jan. 6–Mar. 13	Aquarius
Mar. 14–Apr. 1	Pisces
Apr. 2–Apr. 15	Aries
Apr. 16–May 1	Taurus
May 2–Jul. 9	Gemini
Jul. 10–Jul. 24	Cancer
Jul. 25–Aug. 8	Leo
Aug. 9–Aug. 28	Virgo
Aug. 29–Nov. 3	Libra
Nov. 4–Nov. 21	Scorpio
Nov. 22–Dec. 11	Sagittarius
Dec. 12–Dec. 31	Capricorn

1904

Jan. 1	Capricorn
Jan. 2–Jan. 13	Aquarius
Jan. 14–Feb. 14	Capricorn
Feb. 15–Mar. 6	Aquarius
Mar. 7–Mar. 22	Pisces
Mar. 23–Apr. 6	Aries
Apr. 7–Jun. 13	Taurus
Jun. 14–Jun. 30	Gemini
Jul. 1–Jul. 15	Cancer
Jul. 16–Jul. 31	Leo
Aug. 1–Aug. 27	Virgo
Aug. 28–Sep. 6	Libra
Sep. 7–Oct. 8	Virgo
Oct. 9–Oct. 25	Libra
Oct. 26–Nov. 13	Scorpio
Nov. 14–Dec. 3	Sagittarius
Dec. 4–Dec. 31	Capricorn

1905

Jan. 1–Feb. 8	Capricorn
Feb. 9–Feb. 26	Aquarius
Feb. 27–Mar. 14	Pisces
Mar. 15–Mar. 31	Aries
Apr. 1–Apr. 27	Taurus
Apr. 28–May 14	Aries
May 15–Jun. 7	Taurus
Jun. 8–Jun. 22	Gemini
Jun. 23–Jul. 6	Cancer
Jul. 7–Jul. 26	Leo
Jul. 27–Jul. 30	Virgo
Oct. 1–Oct. 18	Libra
Oct. 19–Nov. 6	Scorpio
Nov. 7–Dec. 1	Sagittarius
Dec. 2–Dec. 9	Capricorn
Dec. 10–Dec. 31	Sagittarius

1906

Jan. 1–Jan. 11	Sagittarius
Jan. 12–Feb. 1	Capricorn
Feb. 2–Feb. 19	Aquarius
Feb. 20–Mar. 7	Pisces
Mar. 8–May 14	Aries
May 15–May 30	Taurus
May 31–Jun. 13	Gemini
Jun. 14–Jun. 29	Cancer
Jun. 30–Sep. 6	Leo
Sep. 7–Sep. 23	Virgo
Sep. 24–Oct. 10	Libra
Oct. 11–Oct. 31	Scorpio
Nov. 1–Dec. 5	Sagittarius
Dec. 6–Dec. 11	Scorpio
Dec. 12–Dec. 31	Sagittarius

1907

Jan. 1–Jan. 6	Sagittarius
Jan. 7–Jan. 25	Capricorn
Jan. 26–Feb. 11	Aquarius
Feb. 12–Mar. 2	Pisces
Mar. 3–Mar. 13	Aries
Mar. 14–Apr. 17	Pisces
Apr. 18–May 7	Aries
May 8–May 22	Taurus
May 23–Jun. 5	Gemini
Jun. 6–Jun. 26	Cancer
Jun. 27–Jul. 25	Leo
Jul. 26–Aug. 11	Cancer
Aug. 12–Aug. 30	Leo
Aug. 31–Sep. 15	Virgo
Sep. 16–Oct. 4	Libra
Oct. 5–Dec. 10	Scorpio
Dec. 11–Dec. 30	Sagittarius
Dec. 31	Capricorn

1908

Jan. 1–Jan. 17	Capricorn
Jan. 18–Feb. 4	Aquarius
Feb. 5–Apr. 11	Pisces
Apr. 12–Apr. 28	Aries
Apr. 29–May 12	Taurus
May 13–May 29	Gemini
May 30–Aug. 5	Cancer
Aug. 6–Aug. 21	Leo
Aug. 22–Sep. 6	Virgo
Sep. 7–Sep. 27	Libra
Sep. 28–Oct. 31	Scorpio
Nov. 1–Nov. 10	Libra
Nov. 11–Dec. 2	Scorpio
Dec. 3–Dec. 21	Sagittarius
Dec. 22–Dec. 31	Capricorn

1909

Jan. 1–Jan. 9	Capricorn
Jan. 10–Mar. 16	Aquarius
Mar. 17–Apr. 5	Pisces
Apr. 6–Apr. 20	Aries
Apr. 21–May 4	Taurus
May 5–Jul. 12	Gemini
Jul. 13–Jul. 29	Cancer
Jul. 30–Aug. 12	Leo
Aug. 13–Aug. 31	Virgo
Sep. 1–Nov. 6	Libra
Nov. 7–Nov. 25	Scorpio
Nov. 26–Dec. 14	Sagittarius
Dec. 15–Dec. 31	Capricorn

1910

Jan. 1–Jan. 2	Capricorn
Jan. 3–Jan. 30	Aquarius
Jan. 31–Feb. 14	Capricorn
Feb. 15–Mar. 10	Aquarius
Mar. 11–Mar. 28	Pisces
Mar. 29–Apr. 12	Aries
Apr. 13–Apr. 29	Taurus
Apr. 30–May 31	Gemini
Jun. 1–Jun. 11	Taurus
Jun. 12–Jul. 6	Gemini
Jul. 7–Jul. 20	Cancer
Jul. 21–Aug. 5	Leo
Aug. 6–Aug. 26	Virgo
Aug. 27–Sep. 27	Libra
Sep. 28–Oct. 11	Virgo
Oct. 12–Oct. 30	Libra
Oct. 31–Nov. 18	Scorpio
Nov. 19–Dec. 7	Sagittarius
Dec. 8–Dec. 31	Capricorn

1911

Jan. 1–Feb. 12	Capricorn
Feb. 13–Mar. 3	Aquarius
Mar. 4–Mar. 20	Pisces
Mar. 21–Apr. 4	Aries
Apr. 5–Jun. 12	Taurus
Jun. 13–Jun. 27	Gemini
Jun. 28–Jul. 12	Cancer
Jul. 13–Jul. 29	Leo
Jul. 30–Oct. 5	Virgo
Oct. 6–Oct. 23	Libra
Oct. 24–Nov. 11	Scorpio
Nov. 12–Dec. 2	Sagittarius
Dec. 3–Dec. 26	Capricorn
Dec. 27–Dec. 31	Sagittarius

1912

Jan. 1–Jan. 14	Sagittarius
Jan. 15–Feb. 6	Capricorn
Feb. 7–Feb. 24	Aquarius
Feb. 25–Mar. 11	Pisces
Mar. 12–May 15	Aries
May 16–Jun. 4	Taurus
Jun. 5–Jun. 18	Gemini
Jun. 19–Jul. 3	Cancer
Jul. 4–Jul. 25	Leo
Jul. 26–Aug. 20	Virgo
Aug. 21–Sep. 9	Leo
Sep. 10–Sep. 27	Virgo
Sep. 28–Oct. 14	Libra
Oct. 15–Nov. 3	Scorpio
Nov. 4–Dec. 31	Sagittarius

1913

Jan. 1–Jan. 9	Sagittarius
Jan. 10–Jan. 29	Capricorn
Jan. 30–Feb. 15	Aquarius
Feb. 16–Mar. 3	Pisces
Mar. 4–Apr. 6	Aries
Apr. 7–Apr. 13	Pisces
Apr. 14–May 11	Aries
May 12–May 27	Taurus
May 28–Jun. 9	Gemini
Jun. 10–Jun. 27	Cancer
Jun. 28–Sep. 3	Leo
Sep. 4–Sep. 19	Virgo
Sep. 20–Oct. 7	Libra
Oct. 8–Oct. 29	Scorpio
Oct. 30–Nov. 22	Sagittarius
Nov. 23–Dec. 12	Scorpio
Dec. 13–Dec. 31	Sagittarius

1914

Jan. 1–Jan. 21	Capricorn
Jan. 22–Feb. 7	Aquarius
Feb. 8–Apr. 15	Pisces
Apr. 16–May 4	Aries
May 5–May 18	Taurus
May 19–Jun. 2	Gemini
Jun. 3–Aug. 10	Cancer
Aug. 11–Aug. 26	Leo
Aug. 27–Sep. 11	Virgo
Sep. 12–Oct. 1	Libra
Oct. 2–Dec. 7	Scorpio
Dec. 8–Dec. 26	Sagittarius
Dec. 27–Dec. 31	Capricorn

1915

Jan. 1–Jan. 14	Capricorn
Jan. 15–Feb. 1	Aquarius
Feb. 2–Feb. 22	Pisces
Feb. 23–Mar. 18	Aquarius
Mar. 19–Apr. 9	Pisces
Apr. 10–Apr. 25	Aries
Apr. 26–May 9	Taurus
May 10–May 28	Gemini
May 29–Aug. 3	Cancer
Aug. 4–Aug. 18	Leo
Aug. 19–Sep. 4	Virgo
Sep. 5–Sep. 27	Libra
Sep. 28–Oct. 20	Scorpio
Oct. 21–Nov. 10	Libra
Nov. 11–Nov. 30	Scorpio
Dec. 1–Dec. 19	Sagittarius
Dec. 20–Dec. 31	Capricorn

1916

Jan. 1–Jan. 7	Capricorn
Jan. 8–Mar. 14	Aquarius
Mar. 15–Apr. 1	Pisces
Apr. 2–Apr. 16	Aries
Apr. 17–May 1	Taurus
May 2–Jul. 9	Gemini
Jul. 10–Jul. 25	Cancer
Jul. 26–Aug. 9	Leo
Aug. 10–Aug. 28	Virgo
Aug. 29–Nov. 3	Libra
Nov. 4–Nov. 22	Scorpio
Nov. 23–Dec. 11	Sagittarius
Dec. 12–Dec. 31	Capricorn

1917

Jan. 1–Jan. 17	Aquarius
Jan. 18–Feb. 14	Capricorn
Feb. 15–Mar. 7	Aquarius
Mar. 8–Mar. 24	Pisces
Mar. 25–Apr. 8	Aries
Apr. 9–Jun. 13	Taurus
Jun. 14–Jul. 2	Gemini
Jul. 3–Jul. 16	Cancer
Jul. 17–Aug. 1	Leo
Aug. 2–Aug. 25	Virgo
Aug. 26–Sep. 13	Libra
Sep. 14–Oct. 9	Virgo
Oct. 10–Oct. 27	Libra
Oct. 28–Nov. 14	Scorpio
Nov. 15–Dec. 4	Sagittarius
Dec. 5–Dec. 31	Capricorn

1918

Jan. 1–Feb. 9	Capricorn
Feb. 10–Feb. 28	Aquarius
Mar. 1–Mar. 16	Pisces
Mar. 17–Apr. 1	Aries
Apr. 2–Jun. 9	Taurus
Jun. 10–Jun. 23	Gemini
Jun. 24–Jul. 8	Cancer
Jul. 9–Jul. 27	Leo
Jul. 28–Oct. 2	Virgo
Oct. 3–Oct. 19	Libra
Oct. 20–Nov. 7	Scorpio
Nov. 8–Nov. 30	Sagittarius
Dec. 1–Dec. 14	Capricorn
Dec. 15–Dec. 31	Sagittarius

1919

Jan. 1–Jan. 12	Sagittarius
Jan. 13–Feb. 2	Capricorn
Feb. 3–Feb. 20	Aquarius
Feb. 21–Mar. 8	Pisces
Mar. 9–May 15	Aries
May 16–Jun. 1	Taurus
Jun. 2–Jun. 15	Gemini
Jun. 16–Jul. 1	Cancer
Jul. 2–Sep. 8	Leo
Sep. 9–Sep. 24	Virgo
Sep. 25–Oct. 12	Libra
Oct. 13–Nov. 1	Scorpio
Nov. 2–Dec. 31	Sagittarius

1920

Jan. 1–Jan. 7	Sagittarius
Jan. 8–Jan. 27	Capricorn
Jan. 28–Feb. 13	Aquarius
Feb. 14–Mar. 2	Pisces
Mar. 3–Mar. 19	Aries
Mar. 20–Apr. 17	Pisces
Apr. 18–May 8	Aries
May 9–May 23	Taurus
May 24–Jun. 6	Gemini
Jun. 7–Jun. 26	Cancer
Jun. 27–Aug. 2	Leo
Aug. 3–Aug. 10	Cancer
Aug. 11–Aug. 31	Leo
Sep. 1–Sep. 16	Virgo
Sep. 17–Oct. 4	Libra
Oct. 5–Oct. 30	Scorpio
Oct. 31–Nov. 9	Sagittarius
Nov. 10–Dec. 10	Scorpio
Dec. 11–Dec. 30	Sagittarius
Dec. 31	Capricorn

1921

Jan. 1–Jan. 18	Capricorn
Jan. 19–Feb. 4	Aquarius
Feb. 5–Apr. 14	Pisces
Apr. 15–Apr. 30	Aries
May 1–May 14	Taurus
May 15–May 30	Gemini
May 31–Aug. 7	Cancer
Aug. 8–Aug. 22	Leo
Aug. 23–Sep. 8	Virgo
Sep. 9–Sep. 28	Libra
Sep. 29–Dec. 4	Scorpio
Dec. 5–Dec. 23	Sagittarius
Dec. 24–Dec. 31	Capricorn

1922

Jan. 1–Jan. 10	Capricorn
Jan. 11–Jan. 31	Aquarius
Feb. 1–Feb. 8	Pisces
Feb. 9–Mar. 17	Aquarius
Mar. 18–Apr. 6	Pisces
Apr. 7–Apr. 21	Aries
Apr. 22–May 6	Taurus
May 7–May 31	Gemini
Jun. 1–Jun. 9	Cancer
Jun. 10–Jul. 12	Gemini
Jul. 13–Jul. 30	Cancer
Jul. 31–Aug. 14	Leo
Aug. 15–Sep. 1	Virgo
Sep. 2–Sep. 30	Libra
Oct. 1–Oct. 4	Scorpio
Oct. 5–Nov. 7	Libra
Nov. 8–Nov. 26	Scorpio
Nov. 27–Dec. 16	Sagittarius
Dec. 17–Dec. 31	Capricorn

1923

Jan. 1–Jan. 3	Capricorn
Jan. 4–Feb. 5	Aquarius
Feb. 6–Feb. 12	Capricorn
Feb. 13–Mar. 12	Aquarius
Mar. 13–Mar. 29	Pisces
Mar. 30–Apr. 13	Aries
Apr. 14–Apr. 30	Taurus
May 1–Jul. 7	Gemini
Jul. 8–Jul. 22	Cancer
Jul. 23–Aug. 6	Leo
Aug. 7–Aug. 26	Virgo
Aug. 27–Oct. 3	Libra
Oct. 4–Oct. 10	Virgo
Oct. 11–Nov. 1	Libra
Nov. 2–Nov. 19	Scorpio
Nov. 20–Dec. 9	Sagittarius
Dec. 10–Dec. 31	Capricorn

1924

Jan. 1–Feb. 13	Capricorn
Feb. 14–Mar. 4	Aquarius
Mar. 5–Mar. 20	Pisces
Mar. 21–Apr. 4	Aries
Apr. 5–Jun. 12	Taurus
Jun. 13–Jun. 28	Gemini
Jun. 29–Jul. 12	Cancer
Jul. 13–Jul. 29	Leo
Jul. 30–Oct. 6	Virgo
Oct. 7–Oct. 23	Libra
Oct. 24–Nov. 11	Scorpio
Nov. 12–Dec. 1	Sagittarius
Dec. 2–Dec. 30	Capricorn
Dec. 31	Sagittarius

1925

Jan. 1–Jan. 13	Sagittarius
Jan. 14–Feb. 6	Capricorn
Feb. 7–Feb. 24	Aquarius
Feb. 25–Mar. 12	Pisces
Mar. 13–Mar. 31	Aries
Apr. 1–Apr. 14	Taurus
Apr. 15–May 16	Aries
May 17–Jun. 5	Taurus
Jun. 6–Jun. 19	Gemini
Jun. 20–Jul. 4	Cancer
Jul. 5–Jul. 25	Leo
Jul. 26–Aug. 26	Virgo
Aug. 27–Sep. 10	Leo
Sep. 11–Sep. 28	Virgo
Sep. 29–Oct. 16	Libra
Oct. 17–Nov. 4	Scorpio
Nov. 5–Dec. 31	Sagittarius

1926

Jan. 1–Jan. 10	Sagittarius
Jan. 11–Jan. 30	Capricorn
Jan. 31–Feb. 16	Aquarius
Feb. 17–Mar. 5	Pisces
Mar. 6–May 12	Aries
May 13–May 28	Taurus
May 29–Jun. 11	Gemini
Jun. 12–Jun. 28	Cancer
Jun. 29–Sep. 4	Leo
Sep. 5–Sep. 20	Virgo
Sep. 21–Oct. 8	Libra
Oct. 9–Oct. 30	Scorpio
Oct. 31–Nov. 27	Sagittarius
Nov. 28–Dec. 12	Scorpio
Dec. 13–Dec. 31	Sagittarius

1927

Jan. 1–Jan. 4	Sagittarius
Jan. 5–Jan. 23	Capricorn
Jan. 24–Feb. 9	Aquarius
Feb. 10–Apr. 16	Pisces
Apr. 17–May 5	Aries
May 6–May 20	Taurus
May 21–Jun. 3	Gemini
Jun. 4–Jun. 27	Cancer
Jun. 28–Jul. 13	Leo
Jul. 14–Aug. 11	Cancer
Aug. 12–Aug. 27	Leo
Aug. 28–Sep. 13	Virgo
Sep. 14–Oct. 2	Libra
Oct. 3–Dec. 8	Scorpio
Dec. 9–Dec. 28	Sagittarius
Dec. 29–Dec. 31	Capricorn

1928

Jan. 1–Jan. 15	Capricorn
Jan. 16–Feb. 2	Aquarius
Feb. 3–Feb. 28	Pisces
Feb. 29–Mar. 17	Aquarius
Mar. 18–Apr. 10	Pisces
Apr. 11–Apr. 26	Aries
Apr. 27–May 10	Taurus
May 11–May 27	Gemini
May 28–Aug. 3	Cancer
Aug. 4–Aug. 18	Leo
Aug. 19–Sep. 4	Virgo
Sep. 5–Sep. 26	Libra
Sep. 27–Oct. 23	Scorpio
Oct. 24–Nov. 10	Libra
Nov. 11–Nov. 30	Scorpio
Dec. 1–Dec. 19	Sagittarius
Dec. 20–Dec. 31	Capricorn

1929

Jan. 1–Jan. 7	Capricorn
Jan. 8–Mar. 15	Aquarius
Mar. 16–Apr. 2	Pisces
Apr. 3–Apr. 18	Aries
Apr. 19–May 2	Taurus
May 3–Jul. 10	Gemini
Jul. 11–Jul. 26	Cancer
Jul. 27–Aug. 10	Leo
Aug. 11–Aug. 29	Virgo
Aug. 30–Nov. 4	Libra
Nov. 5–Nov. 23	Scorpio
Nov. 24–Dec. 12	Sagittarius
Dec. 13–Dec. 31	Capricorn

1930

Jan. 1	Capricorn
Jan. 2–Jan. 22	Aquarius
Jan. 23–Feb. 14	Capricorn
Feb. 15–Mar. 8	Aquarius
Mar. 9–Mar. 25	Pisces
Mar. 26–Apr. 9	Aries
Apr. 10–Apr. 30	Taurus
May 1–May 16	Gemini
May 17–Jun. 13	Taurus
Jun. 14–Jul. 3	Gemini
Jul. 4–Jul. 18	Cancer
Jul. 19–Aug. 3	Leo
Aug. 4–Aug. 25	Virgo
Aug. 26–Sep. 19	Libra
Sep. 20–Oct. 10	Virgo
Oct. 22–Oct. 28	Libra
Oct. 29–Nov. 16	Scorpio
Nov. 17–Dec. 5	Sagittarius
Dec. 6–Dec. 31	Capricorn

1931

Jan. 1–Feb. 10	Capricorn
Feb. 11–Mar. 1	Aquarius
Mar. 2–Mar. 17	Pisces
Mar. 18–Apr. 2	Aries
Apr. 3–Jun. 10	Taurus
Jun. 11–Jun. 25	Gemini
Jun. 26–Jul. 9	Cancer
Jul. 10–Jul. 27	Leo
Jul. 28–Oct. 3	Virgo
Oct. 4–Oct. 21	Libra
Oct. 22–Nov. 9	Scorpio
Nov. 10–Dec. 1	Sagittarius
Dec. 2–Dec. 19	Capricorn
Dec. 20–Dec. 31	Sagittarius

1932

Jan. 1–Jan. 13	Sagittarius
Jan. 14–Feb. 4	Capricorn
Feb. 5–Feb. 22	Aquarius
Feb. 23–Mar. 8	Pisces
Mar. 9–May 14	Aries
May 15–Jun. 1	Taurus
Jun. 2–Jun. 15	Gemini
Jun. 16–Jul. 26	Leo
Jul. 27–Aug. 9	Virgo
Aug. 10–Sep. 8	Leo
Sep. 9–Sep. 25	Virgo
Sep. 26–Oct. 12	Libra
Oct. 13–Nov. 1	Scorpio
Nov. 2–Dec. 31	Sagittarius

1933

Jan. 1–Jan. 7	Sagittarius
Jan. 8–Jan. 26	Capricorn
Jan. 27–Feb. 13	Aquarius
Feb. 14–Mar. 2	Pisces
Mar. 3–Mar. 24	Aries
Mar. 25–Apr. 16	Pisces
Apr. 17–May 9	Aries
May 10–May 24	Taurus
May 25–Jun. 7	Gemini
Jun. 8–Jun. 26	Cancer
Jun. 27–Sep. 1	Leo
Sep. 2–Sep. 17	Virgo
Sep. 18–Oct. 5	Libra
Oct. 6–Oct. 29	Scorpio
Oct. 30–Nov. 15	Sagittarius
Nov. 16–Dec. 11	Scorpio
Dec. 12–Dec. 31	Sagittarius

1934

Jan. 1–Jan. 19	Capricorn
Jan. 20–Feb. 5	Aquarius
Feb. 6–Apr. 15	Pisces
Apr. 16–May 1	Aries
May 2–May 15	Taurus
May 16–May 31	Gemini
Jun. 1–Aug. 8	Cancer
Aug. 9–Aug. 24	Leo
Aug. 25–Sep. 9	Virgo
Sep. 10–Sep. 29	Libra
Sep. 30–Dec. 5	Scorpio
Dec. 6–Dec. 24	Sagittarius
Dec. 25–Dec. 31	Capricorn

1935

Jan. 1–Jan. 12	Capricorn
Jan. 13–Jan. 31	Aquarius
Feb. 1–Feb. 14	Pisces
Feb. 15–Mar. 17	Aquarius
Mar. 18–Apr. 7	Pisces
Apr. 8–Apr. 23	Aries
Apr. 24–May 7	Taurus
May 8–May 28	Gemini
May 29–Jun. 19	Cancer
Jun. 20–Jul. 12	Gemini
Jul. 13–Aug. 1	Cancer
Aug. 2–Aug. 15	Leo
Aug. 16–Sep. 2	Virgo
Sep. 3–Sep. 27	Libra
Sep. 28–Oct. 11	Scorpio
Oct. 12–Nov. 9	Libra
Nov. 10–Nov. 28	Scorpio
Nov. 29–Dec. 17	Sagittarius
Dec. 18–Dec. 31	Capricorn

1936

Jan. 1–Jan. 5	Capricorn
Jan. 6–Mar. 12	Aquarius
Mar. 13–Mar. 30	Pisces
Mar. 31–Apr. 14	Aries
Apr. 15–Apr. 30	Taurus
May 1–Jul. 7	Gemini
Jul. 8–Jul. 22	Cancer
Jul. 23–Aug. 6	Leo
Aug. 7–Aug. 26	Virgo
Aug. 27–Nov. 1	Libra
Nov. 2–Nov. 20	Scorpio
Nov. 21–Dec. 9	Sagittarius
Dec. 10–Dec. 31	Capricorn

1937

Jan. 1–Jan. 8	Aquarius
Jan. 9–Feb. 13	Capricorn
Feb. 14–Mar. 5	Aquarius
Mar. 6–Mar. 22	Pisces
Mar. 23–Apr. 6	Aries
Apr. 7–Jun. 12	Taurus
Jun. 13–Jun. 30	Gemini
Jul. 1–Jul. 14	Cancer
Jul. 15–Jul. 30	Leo
Jul. 31–Oct. 7	Virgo
Oct. 8–Oct. 25	Libra
Oct. 26–Nov. 12	Scorpio
Nov. 13–Dec. 2	Sagittarius
Dec. 3–Dec. 31	Capricorn

1938

Jan. 1–Jan. 5	Capricorn
Jan. 6–Jan. 11	Sagittarius
Jan. 12–Feb. 7	Capricorn
Feb. 8–Feb. 26	Aquarius
Feb. 27–Mar. 31	Aries
Apr. 1–Apr. 22	Taurus
Apr. 23–May 15	Aries
May 16–Jun. 7	Taurus
Jun. 8–Jun. 21	Gemini
Jun. 22–Jul. 6	Cancer
Jul. 7–Jul. 25	Leo
Jul. 26–Sep. 2	Virgo
Sep. 3–Sep. 9	Leo
Sep. 10–Sep. 30	Virgo
Oct. 1–Oct. 17	Libra
Oct. 18–Nov. 5	Scorpio
Nov. 6–Dec. 31	Sagittarius

1939

Jan. 1–Jan. 11	Sagittarius
Jan. 12–Jan. 31	Capricorn
Feb. 1–Feb. 18	Aquarius
Feb. 19–Mar. 6	Pisces
Mar. 7–May 13	Aries
May 14–May 30	Taurus
May 31–Jun. 12	Gemini
Jun. 13–Jun. 29	Cancer
Jun. 30–Sep. 6	Leo
Sep. 7–Sep. 22	Virgo
Sep. 23–Oct. 10	Libra
Oct. 11–Oct. 31	Scorpio
Nov. 1–Dec. 2	Sagittarius
Dec. 3–Dec. 12	Scorpio
Dec. 13–Dec. 31	Sagittarius

1940

Jan. 1–Jan. 5	Sagittarius
Jan. 6–Jan. 24	Capricorn
Jan. 25–Feb. 10	Aquarius
Feb. 11–Mar. 3	Pisces
Mar. 4–Mar. 7	Aries
Mar. 8–Apr. 16	Pisces
Apr. 17–May 5	Aries
May 6–May 20	Taurus
May 21–Jun. 3	Gemini
Jun. 4–Jun. 25	Cancer
Jun. 26–Jul. 20	Leo
Jul. 21–Aug. 10	Cancer
Aug. 11–Aug. 28	Leo
Aug. 29–Sep. 13	Virgo
Sep. 14–Oct. 2	Libra
Oct. 3–Dec. 8	Scorpio
Dec. 9–Dec. 28	Sagittarius
Dec. 29–Dec. 31	Aquarius

1941

Jan. 1–Feb. 2	Aquarius
Feb. 3–Mar. 6	Pisces
Mar. 7–Mar. 15	Aquarius
Mar. 16–Apr. 11	Pisces
Apr. 12–Apr. 27	Aries
Apr. 28–May 12	Taurus
May 13–May 28	Gemini
May 29–Aug. 5	Cancer
Aug. 6–Aug. 20	Leo
Aug. 21–Sep. 5	Virgo
Sep. 6–Sep. 27	Libra
Sep. 28–Oct. 28	Scorpio
Oct. 29–Nov. 10	Libra
Nov. 11–Dec. 2	Scorpio
Dec. 3–Dec. 21	Sagittarius
Dec. 22–Dec. 31	Capricorn

1942

Jan. 1–Jan. 8	Capricorn
Jan. 9–Mar. 16	Aquarius
Mar. 17–Apr. 4	Pisces
Apr. 5–Apr. 19	Aries
Apr. 20–May 4	Taurus
May 5–Jul. 11	Gemini
Jul. 12–Jul. 28	Cancer
Jul. 29–Aug. 12	Leo
Aug. 13–Nov. 6	Virgo
Nov. 7–Nov. 24	Scorpio
Nov. 25–Dec. 13	Sagittarius
Dec. 14–Dec. 31	Capricorn

1943

Jan. 1–Jan. 2	Capricorn
Jan. 3–Jan. 26	Aquarius
Jan. 27–Feb. 14	Capricorn
Feb. 15–Mar. 10	Aquarius
Mar. 11–Mar. 27	Pisces
Mar. 28–Apr. 11	Aries
Apr. 12–Apr. 29	Taurus
Apr. 30–May 25	Gemini
May 26–Jun. 13	Taurus
Jun. 14–Jul.5	Gemini
Jul. 6–Jul. 19	Cancer
Jul. 20–Aug. 4	Leo
Aug. 5–Aug. 26	Virgo
Aug. 27–Sep. 24	Libra
Sep. 25–Oct. 10	Virgo
Oct. 11–Oct. 29	Libra
Oct. 30–Nov. 17	Scorpio
Nov. 18–Dec. 7	Sagittarius
Dec. 8–Dec. 31	Capricorn

1944

Jan. 1–Feb. 11	Capricorn
Feb. 12–Mar. 2	Aquarius
Mar. 3–Mar. 18	Pisces
Mar. 19–Apr. 2	Aries
Apr. 3–Jun. 10	Taurus
Jun. 11–Jul. 27	Gemini
Jul. 28–Oct. 4	Virgo
Oct. 5–Oct. 21	Libra
Oct. 22–Nov. 9	Scorpio
Nov. 10–Nov. 30	Sagittarius
Dec. 1–Dec. 22	Capricorn
Dec. 23–Dec. 31	Sagittarius

1945

Jan. 1–Jan. 13	Sagittarius
Jan. 14–Feb. 4	Capricorn
Feb. 5–Feb. 22	Aquarius
Feb. 23–Mar. 10	Pisces
Mar. 11–May 15	Aries
May 16–Jun. 3	Taurus
Jun. 4–Jun. 17	Gemini
Jun. 18–Jul. 2	Cancer
Jul. 3–Jul. 25	Leo
Jul. 26–Aug. 16	Virgo
Aug. 17–Sep. 9	Leo
Sep. 10–Sep. 26	Virgo
Sep. 27–Oct. 14	Libra
Oct. 15–Nov. 2	Scorpio
Nov. 3–Dec. 31	Sagittarius

1946

Jan. 1–Jan. 8	Sagittarius
Jan. 9–Jan. 28	Capricorn
Jan. 29–Feb. 14	Aquarius
Feb. 15–Mar. 3	Pisces
Mar. 4–Mar. 31	Aries
Apr. 1–Apr. 15	Pisces
Apr. 16–May 10	Aries
May 11–May 26	Taurus
May 27–Jun. 9	Gemini
Jun. 10–Jun. 26	Cancer
Jun. 27–Sep. 2	Leo
Sep. 3–Sep. 18	Virgo
Sep. 19–Oct. 6	Libra
Oct. 7–Oct. 29	Scorpio
Oct. 30–Nov. 19	Sagittarius
Nov. 20–Dec. 12	Scorpio
Dec. 13–Dec. 31	Sagittarius

1947

Jan. 1–Jan. 2	Sagittarius
Jan. 3–Jan. 20	Capricorn
Jan. 21–Feb. 7	Aquarius
Feb. 8–Apr. 15	Pisces
Apr. 16–May 3	Aries
May 4–May 17	Taurus
May 18–Jun. 1	Gemini
Jun. 2–Aug. 9	Cancer
Aug. 10–Aug. 25	Leo
Aug. 26–Sep. 10	Virgo
Sep. 11–Sep. 30	Libra
Oct. 1–Dec. 6	Scorpio
Dec. 7–Dec. 25	Sagittarius
Dec. 26–Dec. 31	Capricorn

1948

Jan. 1–Jan. 13	Capricorn
Jan. 14–Feb. 1	Aquarius
Feb. 2–Feb. 19	Pisces
Feb. 20–Mar. 17	Aquarius
Mar. 18–Apr. 8	Pisces
Apr. 9–Apr. 24	Aries
Apr. 25–May 8	Taurus
May 9–May 27	Gemini
May 28–Jun. 27	Cancer
Jun. 28–Jul. 10	Gemini
Jul. 11–Aug. 1	Cancer
Aug. 2–Aug. 16	Leo
Aug. 17–Sep. 2	Virgo
Sep. 3–Sep. 26	Libra
Sep. 27–Oct. 16	Scorpio
Oct. 17–Nov. 9	Libra
Nov. 10–Nov. 28	Scorpio
Nov. 29–Dec. 17	Sagittarius
Dec. 18–Dec. 31	Capricorn

1949

Jan. 1–Jan. 5	Capricorn
Jan. 6–Mar. 13	Aquarius
Mar. 14–Mar. 31	Pisces
Apr. 1–Apr. 15	Aries
Apr. 16–May 1	Taurus
May 2–Jul. 9	Gemini
Jul. 10–Jul. 24	Cancer
Jul. 25–Aug. 8	Leo
Aug. 9–Aug. 27	Virgo
Aug. 28–Nov. 2	Libra
Nov. 3–Nov. 21	Scorpio
Nov. 22–Dec. 10	Sagittarius
Dec. 11–Dec. 31	Capricorn

1950

Jan. 1–Jan. 14	Aquarius
Jan. 15–Feb. 13	Capricorn
Feb. 14–Mar. 6	Aquarius
Mar. 7–Mar. 23	Pisces
Mar. 24–Apr. 7	Aries
Apr. 8–Jun. 13	Taurus
Jun. 14–Jul. 1	Gemini
Jul. 2–Jul. 15	Cancer
Jul. 16–Aug. 1	Leo
Aug. 2–Aug. 26	Virgo
Aug. 27–Sep. 9	Libra
Sep. 10–Oct. 8	Virgo
Oct. 9–Oct. 26	Libra
Oct. 27–Nov. 14	Scorpio
Nov. 15–Dec. 4	Sagittarius
Dec. 5–Dec. 31	Capricorn

1951

Jan. 1–Feb. 8	Capricorn
Feb. 9–Feb. 27	Aquarius
Feb. 28–Mar. 15	Pisces
Mar. 16–Apr. 1	Aries
Apr. 2–Apr. 31	Taurus
May 1–May 14	Aries
May 15–Jun. 8	Taurus
Jun. 9–Jun. 23	Gemini
Jun. 24–Jul. 7	Cancer
Jul. 8–Jul. 26	Leo
Jul. 27–Oct. 1	Virgo
Oct. 2–Oct. 18	Libra
Oct. 19–Nov. 7	Scorpio
Nov. 8–Nov. 30	Sagittarius
Dec. 1–Dec. 11	Capricorn
Dec. 12–Dec. 31	Sagittarius

1952

Jan. 1–Jan. 12	Sagittarius
Jan. 13–Feb. 2	Capricorn
Feb. 3–Feb. 19	Aquarius
Feb. 20–Mar. 6	Pisces
Mar. 7–May 13	Aries
May 14–May 30	Taurus
May 31–Jun. 13	Gemini
Jun. 14–Jun. 29	Cancer
Jun. 30–Sep. 6	Leo
Sep. 7–Sep. 22	Virgo
Sep. 23–Oct. 10	Libra
Oct. 11–Oct. 31	Scorpio
Nov. 1–Dec. 31	Sagittarius

1953

Jan. 1–Jan. 5	Sagittarius
Jan. 6–Jan. 24	Capricorn
Jan. 25–Feb. 10	Aquarius
Feb. 11–Mar. 1	Pisces
Mar. 2–Mar. 14	Aries
Mar. 15–Apr. 16	Pisces
Apr. 17–May 7	Aries
May 8–May 22	Taurus
May 23–Jun. 5	Gemini
Jun. 6–Jun. 25	Cancer
Jun. 26–Jul. 27	Leo
Jul. 28–Aug. 10	Cancer
Aug. 11–Aug. 29	Leo
Aug. 30–Sep. 14	Virgo
Sep. 15–Oct. 3	Libra
Oct. 4–Oct. 30	Scorpio
Oct. 31–Nov. 5	Sagittarius
Nov. 6–Dec. 9	Scorpio
Dec. 10–Dec. 29	Sagittarius
Dec. 30–Dec. 31	Capricorn

1954

Jan. 1–Jan. 7	Capricorn
Jan. 8–Feb. 3	Aquarius
Feb. 4–Apr. 12	Pisces
Apr. 13–Apr. 29	Aries
Apr. 30–May 13	Taurus
May 14–May 29	Gemini
May 30–Aug. 6	Cancer
Aug. 7–Aug. 21	Leo
Aug. 22–Sep. 7	Virgo
Sep. 8–Sep. 28	Libra
Sep. 29–Nov. 3	Scorpio
Nov. 4–Nov. 10	Libra
Nov. 11–Dec. 3	Scorpio
Dec. 4–Dec. 22	Sagittarius
Dec. 23–Dec. 31	Capricorn

1955

Jan. 1–Jan. 9	Capricorn
Jan. 10–Mar. 16	Aquarius
Mar. 17–Apr. 5	Pisces
Apr. 6–Apr. 21	Aries
Apr. 22–May 5	Taurus
May 6–Jul. 12	Gemini
Jul. 13–Jul. 29	Cancer
Jul. 30–Aug. 13	Leo
Aug. 14–Aug. 31	Virgo
Sep. 1–Nov. 7	Libra
Nov. 8–Nov. 26	Scorpio
Nov. 27–Dec. 15	Sagittarius
Dec. 16–Dec. 31	Capricorn

1956

Jan. 1–Jan. 3	Capricorn
Jan. 4–Feb. 1	Aquarius
Feb. 2–Feb. 14	Capricorn
Feb. 15–Mar. 10	Aquarius
Mar. 11–Mar. 27	Pisces
Mar. 28–Apr. 11	Aries
Apr. 12–Apr. 28	Taurus
Apr. 29–Jul. 5	Gemini
Jul. 6–Jul. 20	Cancer
Jul. 21–Aug. 4	Leo
Aug. 5–Aug. 25	Virgo
Aug. 26–Sep. 28	Libra
Sep. 29–Oct. 10	Virgo
Oct. 11–Oct. 30	Libra
Oct. 31–Nov. 17	Scorpio
Nov. 18–Dec. 7	Sagittarius
Dec. 8–Dec. 31	Capricorn

1957

Jan. 1–Feb. 11	Capricorn
Feb. 12–Mar. 3	Aquarius
Mar. 4–Mar. 19	Pisces
Mar. 20–Apr. 3	Aries
Apr. 4–Jun. 11	Taurus
Jun. 12–Jul. 29	Leo
Jul. 30–Oct. 5	Virgo
Oct. 6–Oct. 22	Libra
Oct. 23–Nov. 10	Scorpio
Nov. 11–Dec. 1	Sagittarius
Dec. 2–Dec. 27	Capricorn
Dec. 28–Dec. 31	Sagittarius

1958

Jan. 1–Jan. 13	Sagittarius
Jan. 14–Feb. 5	Capricorn
Feb. 6–Feb. 23	Aquarius
Feb. 24–Mar. 11	Pisces
Mar. 12–Apr. 1	Aries
Apr. 2–Apr. 9	Taurus
Apr. 10–May 16	Aries
May 17–Jun. 4	Taurus
Jun. 5–Jun. 19	Gemini
Jun. 20–Jul. 3	Cancer
Jul. 4–Jul. 25	Leo
Jul. 26–Aug. 22	Virgo
Aug. 23–Sep. 10	Leo
Sep. 11–Sep. 27	Virgo
Sep. 28–Oct. 15	Libra
Oct. 16–Nov. 4	Scorpio
Nov. 5–Dec. 31	Sagittarius

1959

Jan. 1–Jan. 9	Sagittarius
Jan. 10–Jan. 29	Capricorn
Jan. 30–Feb. 16	Aquarius
Feb. 17–Mar. 4	Pisces
Mar. 5–May 11	Aries
May 12–May 27	Taurus
May 28–Jun. 10	Gemini
Jun. 11–Jun. 27	Cancer
Jun. 28–Sep. 4	Leo
Sep. 5–Sep. 20	Virgo
Sep. 21–Oct. 8	Libra
Oct. 9–Oct. 30	Scorpio
Oct. 31–Nov. 24	Sagittarius
Nov. 25–Dec. 12	Scorpio
Dec. 13–Dec. 31	Sagittarius

1960

Jan. 1–Jan. 3	Sagittarius
Jan. 4–Jan. 22	Capricorn
Jan. 23–Feb. 8	Aquarius
Feb. 9–Apr. 15	Pisces
Apr. 16–May 3	Aries
May 4–May 18	Taurus
May 19–Jun. 1	Gemini
Jun. 2–Jun. 30	Cancer
Jul. 1–Jul. 5	Leo
Jul. 6–Aug. 9	Cancer
Aug. 10–Aug. 26	Leo
Aug. 27–Sep. 11	Virgo
Sep. 12–Sep. 30	Libra
Oct. 1–Dec. 6	Scorpio
Dec. 7–Dec. 26	Sagittarius
Dec. 27–Dec. 31	Capricorn

1961

Jan. 1–Jan. 13	Capricorn
Jan. 14–Jan. 31	Aquarius
Feb. 1–Feb. 23	Pisces
Feb. 24–Mar. 17	Aquarius
Mar. 18–Apr. 9	Pisces
Apr. 10–Apr. 25	Aries
Apr. 26–May 9	Taurus
May 10–May 27	Gemini
May 28–Aug. 3	Cancer
Aug. 4–Aug. 17	Leo
Aug. 18–Sep. 3	Virgo
Sep. 4–Sep. 26	Libra
Sep. 27–Oct. 21	Scorpio
Oct. 22–Nov. 9	Libra
Nov. 10–Nov. 29	Scorpio
Nov. 30–Dec. 19	Sagittarius
Dec. 20–Dec. 31	Capricorn

1962

Jan. 1–Jan. 6	Capricorn
Jan. 7–Mar. 14	Aquarius
Mar. 15–Apr. 2	Pisces
Apr. 3–Apr. 17	Aries
Apr. 18–May 2	Taurus
May 3–Jul. 10	Gemini
Jul. 11–Jul. 25	Cancer
Jul. 26–Aug. 9	Leo
Aug. 10–Aug. 28	Virgo
Aug. 29–Nov. 4	Libra
Nov. 5–Nov. 22	Scorpio
Nov. 23–Dec. 11	Sagittarius
Dec. 12–Dec. 31	Capricorn

1963

Jan. 1	Capricorn
Jan. 2–Jan. 19	Aquarius
Jan. 20–Feb. 14	Capricorn
Feb. 15–Mar. 8	Aquarius
Mar. 9–Mar. 25	Pisces
Mar. 26–Apr. 8	Aries
Apr. 9–May 2	Taurus
May 3–May 9	Gemini
May 10–Jun. 13	Taurus
Jun. 14–Jul. 3	Gemini
Jul. 4–Jul. 17	Cancer
Jul. 18–Aug. 2	Leo
Aug. 3–Aug. 25	Virgo
Aug. 26–Sep. 15	Libra
Sep. 16–Oct. 9	Virgo
Oct. 10–Oct. 27	Libra
Oct. 28–Nov. 15	Scorpio
Nov. 16–Dec. 5	Sagittarius
Dec. 6–Dec. 31	Capricorn

1964

Jan. 1–Feb. 9	Capricorn
Feb. 10–Feb. 28	Aquarius
Feb. 29–Mar. 15	Pisces
Mar. 16–Apr. 1	Aries
Apr. 2–Jun. 8	Taurus
Jun. 9–Jun. 23	Gemini
Jun. 24–Jul. 8	Cancer
Jul. 9–Jul. 26	Leo
Jul. 27–Oct. 2	Virgo
Oct. 3–Oct. 19	Libra
Oct. 20–Nov. 7	Scorpio
Nov. 8–Nov. 29	Sagittarius
Nov. 30–Dec. 15	Capricorn
Dec. 16–Dec. 31	Sagittarius

1965

Jan. 1–Jan. 12	Sagittarius
Jan. 13–Feb. 2	Capricorn
Feb. 3–Feb. 20	Aquarius
Feb. 21–Mar. 8	Pisces
Mar. 9–May 14	Aries
May 15–Jun. 1	Taurus
Jun. 2–Jun. 15	Gemini
Jun. 16–Jun. 30	Leo
Jul. 1–Aug. 2	Virgo
Aug. 3–Sep. 7	Leo
Sep. 8–Sep. 24	Virgo
Sep. 25–Oct. 11	Libra
Oct. 12–Nov. 1	Scorpio
Nov. 2–Dec. 31	Sagittarius

1966

Jan. 1–Jan. 6	Sagittarius
Jan. 7–Jan. 26	Capricorn
Jan. 27–Feb. 12	Aquarius
Feb. 13–Mar. 2	Pisces
Mar. 3–Mar. 21	Aries
Mar. 22–Apr. 16	Pisces
Apr. 17–May 8	Aries
May 9–May 23	Taurus
May 24–Jun. 6	Gemini
Jun. 7–Jun. 25	Cancer
Jun. 26–Jul. 31	Leo
Sep. 1–Sep. 16	Virgo
Sep. 17–Oct. 4	Leo
Oct. 5–Oct. 29	Scorpio
Oct. 30–Nov. 12	Sagittarius
Nov. 13–Dec. 10	Scorpio
Dec. 11–Dec. 31	Sagittarius

1967

Jan. 1–Jan. 18	Capricorn
Jan. 19–Feb. 5	Aquarius
Feb. 6–Apr. 13	Pisces
Apr. 14–Apr. 30	Aries
May 1–May 15	Taurus
May 16–May 30	Gemini
May 31–Aug. 7	Cancer
Aug. 8–Aug. 23	Leo
Aug. 24–Sep. 8	Virgo
Sep. 9–Sep. 29	Cancer
Sep. 30–Dec. 4	Scorpio
Dec. 5–Dec. 23	Sagittarius
Dec. 24–Dec. 31	Capricorn

1968

Jan. 1–Jan. 11	Capricorn
Jan. 12–Jan. 31	Aquarius
Feb. 1–Feb. 10	Pisces
Feb. 11–Mar. 16	Aquarius
Mar. 17–Apr. 6	Pisces
Apr. 7–Apr. 21	Aries
Apr. 22–May 5	Taurus
May 6–May 28	Gemini
May 29–Jun. 12	Cancer
Jun. 13–Jul. 12	Gemini
Jul. 13–Jul. 30	Cancer
Jul. 31–Aug. 14	Leo
Aug. 15–Aug. 31	Virgo
Sep. 1–Sep. 27	Libra
Sep. 28–Oct. 6	Scorpio
Oct. 7–Nov. 7	Libra
Nov. 8–Nov. 26	Scorpio
Nov. 27–Dec. 15	Sagittarius
Dec. 16–Dec. 31	Capricorn

1969

Jan. 1–Jan. 2	Capricorn
Jan. 3–Mar. 11	Aquarius
Mar. 12–Mar. 29	Pisces
Mar. 30–Apr. 13	Aries
Apr. 14–Apr. 29	Taurus
Apr. 30–Jul. 7	Gemini
Jul. 8–Jul. 21	Cancer
Jul. 22–Aug. 6	Leo
Aug. 7–Aug. 26	Virgo
Aug. 27–Oct. 6	Libra
Oct. 7–Oct. 8	Virgo
Oct. 9–Oct. 31	Libra
Nov. 1–Nov. 19	Scorpio
Nov. 20–Dec. 8	Sagittarius
Dec. 9–Dec. 31	Capricorn

1970

Jan. 1–Feb. 12	Capricorn
Feb. 13–Mar. 4	Aquarius
Mar. 5–Mar. 21	Pisces
Mar. 22–Apr. 5	Aries
Apr. 6–Jun. 12	Taurus
Jun. 13–Jun. 29	Gemini
Jun. 30–Jul. 13	Cancer
Jul. 14–Jul. 30	Leo
Jul. 21–Oct. 6	Virgo
Oct. 7–Oct. 24	Libra
Oct. 25–Nov. 12	Scorpio
Nov. 13–Dec. 2	Sagittarius
Dec. 3–Dec. 31	Capricorn

1971

Jan. 1	Capricorn
Jan. 2–Jan. 13	Sagittarius
Jan. 14–Feb. 6	Capricorn
Feb. 7–Feb. 25	Aquarius
Feb. 26–Mar. 13	Pisces
Mar. 14–Mar. 31	Aries
Apr. 1–Apr. 17	Taurus
Apr. 18–May 16	Aries
May 17–Jun. 6	Taurus
Jun. 7–Jun. 20	Gemini
Jun. 21–Jul. 5	Cancer
Jul. 6–Jul. 25	Leo
Jul. 26–Aug. 28	Virgo
Aug. 29–Sep. 10	Leo
Sep. 11–Sep. 29	Virgo
Sep. 30–Oct. 16	Libra
Oct. 17–Nov. 5	Scorpio
Nov. 6–Dec. 31	Sagittarius

1972

Jan. 1–Jan. 10	Sagittarius
Jan. 11–Jan. 30	Capricorn
Jan. 31–Feb. 17	Aquarius
Feb. 18–Mar. 4	Pisces
Mar. 5–May 11	Aries
May 12–May 28	Taurus
May 29–Jun. 11	Gemini
Jun. 12–Jun. 27	Cancer
Jun. 28–Sep. 4	Leo
Sep. 5–Sep. 20	Virgo
Sep. 21–Oct. 8	Libra
Oct. 9–Oct. 29	Scorpio
Oct. 30–Nov. 28	Sagittarius
Nov. 29–Dec. 11	Scorpio
Dec. 12–Dec. 31	Sagittarius

1973

Jan. 1–Jan. 3	Sagittarius
Jan. 4–Jan. 22	Capricorn
Jan. 23–Feb. 8	Aquarius
Feb. 9–Apr. 15	Pisces
Apr. 16–May 5	Aries
May 6–May 19	Taurus
May 20–Jun. 3	Gemini
Jun. 4–Jun. 26	Cancer
Jun. 27–Jul. 15	Leo
Jul. 16–Aug. 10	Cancer
Aug. 11–Aug. 27	Leo
Aug. 28–Sep. 12	Virgo
Sep. 13–Oct. 1	Libra
Oct. 2–Dec. 7	Scorpio
Dec. 8–Dec. 27	Sagittarius
Dec. 28–Dec. 31	Capricorn

1974

Jan. 1–Jan. 15	Capricorn
Jan. 16–Feb. 1	Aquarius
Feb. 2–Mar. 1	Pisces
Mar. 2–Mar. 16	Aquarius
Mar. 17–Apr. 10	Pisces
Apr. 11–Apr. 27	Aries
Apr. 28–May 11	Taurus
May 12–May 28	Gemini
May 29–Aug. 4	Cancer
Aug. 5–Aug. 19	Leo
Aug. 20–Sep. 5	Virgo
Sep. 6–Sep. 27	Libra
Sep. 28–Oct. 25	Scorpio
Oct. 26–Nov. 10	Libra
Nov. 11–Dec. 1	Scorpio
Dec. 2–Dec. 20	Sagittarius
Dec. 21–Dec. 31	Capricorn

1975

Jan. 1–Jan. 7	Capricorn
Jan. 8–Mar. 15	Aquarius
Mar. 16–Apr. 3	Pisces
Apr. 4–Apr. 18	Aries
Apr. 19–May 3	Taurus
May 4–Jul. 11	Gemini
Jul. 12–Jul. 27	Cancer
Jul. 28–Aug. 11	Leo
Aug. 12–Aug. 29	Virgo
Aug. 30–Nov. 5	Libra
Nov. 6–Nov. 24	Scorpio
Nov. 25–Dec. 13	Sagittarius
Dec. 14–Dec. 31	Capricorn

1976

Jan. 1	Capricorn
Jan. 2–Jan. 24	Aquarius
Jan. 25–Feb. 14	Capricorn
Feb. 15–Mar. 8	Aquarius
Mar. 9–Mar. 25	Pisces
Mar. 26–Apr. 9	Aries
Apr. 10–Apr. 28	Taurus
Apr. 29–May 18	Gemini
May 19–Jun. 12	Taurus
Jun. 13–Jul. 3	Gemini
Jul. 4–Jul. 17	Cancer
Jul. 18–Aug. 2	Leo
Aug. 3–Aug. 24	Virgo
Aug. 25–Sep. 20	Libra
Sep. 21–Oct. 9	Virgo
Oct. 10–Oct. 28	Libra
Oct. 29–Nov. 15	Scorpio
Nov. 16–Dec. 5	Sagittarius
Dec. 6–Dec. 31	Capricorn

1977

Jan. 1–Feb. 9	Capricorn
Feb. 10–Mar. 1	Aquarius
Mar. 2–Mar. 17	Pisces
Mar. 18–Apr. 2	Aries
Apr. 3–Jun. 9	Taurus
Jun. 10–Jun. 25	Gemini
Jun. 26–Jul. 9	Cancer
Jul. 10–Jul. 27	Leo
Jul. 28–Oct. 3	Virgo
Oct. 4–Oct. 20	Libra
Oct. 21–Nov. 8	Scorpio
Nov. 9–Nov. 30	Sagittarius
Dec. 1–Dec. 20	Capricorn
Dec. 21–Dec. 31	Sagittarius

1978

Jan. 1–Jan. 12	Sagittarius
Jan. 13–Feb. 4	Capricorn
Feb. 5–Feb. 21	Aquarius
Feb. 22–Mar. 9	Pisces
Mar. 10–May 15	Aries
May 16–Jun. 3	Taurus
Jun. 4–Jun. 16	Gemini
Jun. 17–Jul. 1	Cancer
Jul. 2–Jul. 26	Leo
Jul. 27–Aug. 12	Virgo
Aug. 13–Sep. 8	Leo
Sep. 9–Sep. 25	Virgo
Sep. 26–Oct. 13	Libra
Oct. 14–Nov. 2	Scorpio
Nov. 3–Dec. 31	Sagittarius

1979

Jan. 1–Jan. 7	Sagittarius
Jan. 8–Jan. 28	Capricorn
Jan. 29–Feb. 13	Aquarius
Feb. 14–Mar. 2	Pisces
Mar. 3–Mar. 27	Aries
Mar. 28–Apr. 17	Pisces
Apr. 18–May 9	Aries
May 10–May 25	Taurus
May 26–Jun. 8	Gemini
Jun. 9–Jun. 26	Cancer
Jun. 27–Sep. 1	Leo
Sep. 2–Sep. 18	Virgo
Sep. 19–Oct. 6	Libra
Oct. 7–Oct. 29	Scorpio
Oct. 30–Nov. 17	Sagittarius
Nov. 18–Dec. 11	Scorpio
Dec. 12–Dec. 31	Sagittarius

1980

Jan. 1	Sagittarius
Jan. 2–Jan. 20	Capricorn
Jan. 21–Feb. 6	Aquarius
Feb. 7–Apr. 13	Pisces
Apr. 14–May 1	Aries
May 2–May 15	Taurus
May 16–May 30	Gemini
May 31–Aug. 8	Cancer
Aug. 9–Aug. 23	Leo
Aug. 24–Sep. 29	Virgo
Sep. 30–Dec. 4	Scorpio
Dec. 5–Dec. 24	Sagittarius
Dec. 25–Dec. 31	Capricorn

1981

Jan. 1–Jan. 11	Capricorn
Jan. 12–Jan. 30	Aquarius
Jan. 31–Feb. 15	Pisces
Feb. 16–Mar. 17	Aquarius
Mar. 18–Apr. 7	Pisces
Apr. 8–Apr. 23	Aries
Apr. 24–May 7	Taurus
May 8–May 27	Gemini
May 28–Jun. 21	Cancer
Jun. 22–Jul. 11	Gemini
Jul. 12–Jul. 31	Cancer
Aug. 1–Aug. 15	Leo
Aug. 16–Sep. 1	Virgo
Sep. 2–Sep. 26	Libra
Sep. 27–Oct. 13	Scorpio
Oct. 14–Nov. 8	Libra
Nov. 9–Nov. 27	Scorpio
Nov. 28–Dec. 16	Sagittarius
Dec. 17–Dec. 31	Capricorn

1982

Jan. 1–Jan. 4	Capricorn
Jan. 5–Mar. 12	Aquarius
Mar. 13–Mar. 30	Pisces
Mar. 31–Apr. 14	Aries
Apr. 15–Apr. 30	Taurus
May 1–Jul. 8	Gemini
Jul. 9–Jul. 23	Cancer
Jul. 24–Aug. 7	Leo
Aug. 8–Aug. 27	Virgo
Aug. 28–Nov. 2	Libra
Nov. 3–Nov. 20	Scorpio
Nov. 21–Dec. 9	Sagittarius
Dec. 10–Dec. 31	Capricorn

1983

Jan. 1–Jan. 11	Aquarius
Jan. 12–Feb. 13	Capricorn
Feb. 14–Mar. 6	Aquarius
Mar. 7–Mar. 22	Pisces
Mar. 23–Apr. 6	Aries
Apr. 7–Jun. 13	Taurus
Jun. 14–Jun. 30	Gemini
Jul. 1–Jul. 14	Cancer
Jul. 15–Jul. 31	Leo
Aug. 1–Aug. 28	Virgo
Aug. 29–Sep. 5	Libra
Sep. 6–Oct. 7	Virgo
Oct. 8–Oct. 25	Libra
Oct. 26–Nov. 13	Scorpio
Nov. 14–Dec. 3	Sagittarius
Dec. 4–Dec. 31	Capricorn

1984

Jan. 1–Feb. 8	Capricorn
Feb. 9–Feb. 26	Aquarius
Feb. 27–Mar. 13	Pisces
Mar. 14–Mar. 30	Aries
Mar. 31–Apr. 24	Taurus
Apr. 25–May 14	Aries
May 15–Jun. 6	Taurus
Jun. 7–Jun. 21	Gemini
Jun. 22–Jul. 5	Cancer
Jul. 6–Jul. 25	Leo
Jul. 26–Sep. 29	Virgo
Sep. 30–Oct. 17	Libra
Oct. 18–Nov. 5	Scorpio
Nov. 6–Nov. 30	Sagittarius
Dec. 1–Dec. 6	Capricorn
Dec. 7–Dec. 31	Sagittarius

1985

Jan. 1–Jan. 10	Sagittarius
Jan. 11–Jan. 31	Capricorn
Feb. 1–Feb. 17	Aquarius
Feb. 18–Mar. 6	Pisces
Mar. 7–May 13	Aries
May 14–May 29	Taurus
May 30–Jun. 12	Gemini
Jun. 13–Jun. 28	Cancer
Jun. 29–Sep. 5	Leo
Sep. 6–Sep. 21	Virgo
Sep. 22–Oct. 9	Libra
Oct. 10–Oct. 30	Scorpio
Oct. 31–Dec. 3	Sagittarius
Dec. 4–Dec. 11	Scorpio
Dec. 12–Dec. 31	Sagittarius

1986

Jan. 1–Jan. 4	Sagittarius
Jan. 5–Jan. 24	Capricorn
Jan. 25–Feb. 10	Aquarius
Feb. 11–Mar. 2	Pisces
Mar. 3–Mar. 10	Aries
Mar. 11–Apr. 16	Pisces
Apr. 17–May 6	Aries
May 7–May 21	Taurus
May 22–Jun. 4	Gemini
Jun. 5–Jun. 25	Cancer
Jun. 26–Jul. 22	Leo
Jul. 23–Aug. 10	Cancer
Aug. 11–Aug. 29	Leo
Aug. 30–Sep. 14	Virgo
Sep. 15–Oct. 3	Libra
Oct. 4–Dec. 9	Scorpio
Dec. 10–Dec. 28	Sagittarius
Dec. 29–Dec. 31	Capricorn

1987

Jan. 1–Jan. 16	Capricorn
Jan. 17–Feb. 3	Aquarius
Feb. 4–Mar. 10	Pisces
Mar. 11–Mar. 12	Aquarius
Mar. 13–Apr. 11	Pisces
Apr. 12–Apr. 28	Aries
Apr. 29–May 12	Taurus
May 13–May 29	Gemini
May 30–Aug. 5	Cancer
Aug. 6–Aug. 20	Leo
Aug. 21–Sep. 6	Virgo
Sep. 7–Sep. 27	Libra
Sep. 28–Oct. 31	Scorpio
Nov. 1–Nov. 10	Libra
Nov. 11–Dec. 2	Scorpio
Dec. 3–Dec. 21	Sagittarius
Dec. 22–Dec. 31	Capricorn

1988

Jan. 1–9	Capricorn
Jan. 10–Mar. 15	Aquarius
Mar. 16–Apr. 4	Pisces
Apr. 5–Apr. 19	Aries
Apr. 20–May 4	Taurus
May 5–Jul. 10	Gemini
Jul. 11–Jul. 28	Cancer
Jul. 29–Aug. 11	Leo
Aug. 12–Aug. 30	Virgo
Aug. 31–Nov. 6	Libra
Nov. 7–Nov. 24	Scorpio
Nov. 25–Dec 13	Sagittarius
Dec. 14–Dec 31	Capricorn

1989

Jan. 1	Capricorn
Jan. 2–Jan. 28	Aquarius
Jan. 29–Feb. 13	Capricorn
Feb. 14–Mar. 9	Aquarius
Mar. 10–Mar. 27	Pisces
Mar. 28–Apr. 10	Aries
Apr. 11–Apr. 28	Taurus
Apr. 29–May 27	Gemini
May 28–Jun. 11	Taurus
Jun. 12–Jul. 5	Gemini
Jul. 6–Jul. 19	Cancer
Jul. 20–Aug. 4	Leo
Aug. 5–Aug. 25	Virgo
Aug. 26–Sep. 25	Libra
Sep. 26–Oct. 10	Virgo
Oct. 11–Oct. 29	Libra
Oct. 30–Nov. 17	Scorpio
Nov. 18–Dec. 6	Sagittarius
Dec. 7–Dec. 31	Capricorn

1990

Jan. 1–Feb. 11	Capricorn
Feb. 12–Mar. 2	Aquarius
Mar. 3–Mar. 19	Pisces
Mar. 20–Apr. 3	Aries
Apr. 4–Jun. 11	Taurus
Jun. 12–Jun. 26	Gemini
Jun. 27–Jul. 10	Cancer
Jul. 11–Jul. 28	Leo
Jul. 29–Oct. 4	Virgo
Oct. 5–Oct. 22	Libra
Oct. 23–Nov. 10	Scorpio
Nov. 11–Dec. 1	Sagittarius
Dec. 2–Dec. 24	Capricorn
Dec. 25–Dec. 31	Sagittarius

1991

Jan. 1–Jan. 13	Sagittarius
Jan. 14–Feb. 4	Capricorn
Feb. 5–Feb. 23	Aquarius
Feb. 24–Mar. 10	Pisces
Mar. 11–May 15	Aries
May 16–Jun. 4	Taurus
Jun. 5–Jun. 18	Gemini
Jun. 19–Jul. 3	Cancer
Jul. 4–Jul. 25	Leo
Jul. 26–Aug. 18	Virgo
Aug. 19–Sep. 9	Leo
Sep. 10–Sep. 27	Virgo
Sep. 28–Oct. 14	Libra
Oct. 15–Nov. 3	Scorpio
Nov. 4–Dec. 31	Sagittarius

1992

Jan. 1–Jan. 9	Sagittarius
Jan. 10–Jan. 28	Capricorn
Jan. 29–Feb. 15	Aquarius
Feb. 16–Mar. 2	Pisces
Mar. 3–Apr. 2	Aries
Apr. 3–Apr. 13	Pisces
Apr. 14–May 10	Aries
May 11–May 25	Taurus
May 26–Jun. 8	Gemini
Jun. 9–Jun. 26	Cancer
Jun. 27–Sep. 2	Leo
Sep. 3–Sep. 18	Virgo
Sep. 19–Oct. 6	Libra
Oct. 7–Oct. 28	Scorpio
Oct. 29–Nov. 20	Sagittarius
Nov. 21–Dec. 11	Scorpio
Dec. 12–Dec. 31	Sagittarius

1993

Jan. 1	Sagittarius
Jan. 2–Jan. 20	Capricorn
Jan. 21–Feb. 6	Aquarius
Feb. 7–Apr. 14	Pisces
Apr. 15–May 2	Aries
May 3–May 17	Taurus
May 18–Jun. 1	Gemini
Jun. 2–Aug. 9	Cancer
Aug. 10–Aug. 25	Leo
Aug. 26–Sep. 10	Virgo
Sep. 11–Sep. 30	Libra
Oct. 1–Dec. 6	Scorpio
Dec. 7–Dec. 25	Sagittarius
Dec. 26–Dec. 31	Capricorn

1994

Jan. 1–Jan. 13	Capricorn
Jan. 14–Jan. 31	Aquarius
Feb. 1–Feb. 20	Pisces
Feb. 21–Mar. 17	Aquarius
Mar. 18–Apr. 8	Pisces
Apr. 9–Apr. 24	Aries
Apr. 25–May 8	Taurus
May 9–May 27	Gemini
May 28–Jul. 1	Cancer
Jul. 2–Jul. 9	Gemini
Jul. 10–Aug. 2	Cancer
Aug. 3–Aug. 17	Leo
Aug. 18–Sep. 3	Virgo
Sep. 4–Sep. 26	Libra
Sep. 27–Oct. 18	Scorpio
Oct. 19–Nov. 9	Libra
Nov. 10–Nov. 29	Scorpio
Nov. 30–Dec. 18	Sagittarius
Dec. 19–Dec. 31	Capricorn

1995

Jan. 1–Jan. 5	Capricorn
Jan. 6–Mar. 13	Aquarius
Mar. 14–Apr. 2	Pisces
Apr. 3–Apr. 16	Aries
Apr. 17–May 1	Taurus
May 2–Jul. 9	Gemini
Jul. 10–Jul. 24	Cancer
Jul. 25–Aug. 9	Leo
Aug. 10–Aug. 28	Virgo
Aug. 29–Nov. 3	Libra
Nov. 4–Nov. 21	Scorpio
Nov. 22–Dec. 11	Sagittarius
Dec. 12–Dec. 31	Capricorn

1996

Jan. 1–Jan. 16	Aquarius
Jan. 17–Feb. 14	Capricorn
Feb. 15–Mar. 6	Aquarius
Mar. 7–Mar. 23	Pisces
Mar. 24–Apr. 7	Aries
Apr. 8–Jun. 12	Taurus
Jun. 13–Jul. 1	Gemini
Jul. 2–Jul. 15	Cancer
Jul. 16–Jul. 31	Leo
Aug. 1–Aug. 25	Virgo
Aug. 26–Sep. 11	Leo
Sep. 12–Oct. 8	Virgo
Oct. 9–Oct. 26	Libra
Oct. 27–Nov. 13	Scorpio
Nov. 14–Dec. 3	Sagittarius
Dec. 4–Dec. 31	Capricorn

1997

Jan. 1–Feb. 8	Capricorn
Feb. 9–Feb. 27	Aquarius
Feb. 28–Mar. 15	Pisces
Mar. 16–Mar. 31	Aries
Apr. 1–May 4	Taurus
May 5–May 11	Aries
May 12–Jun. 7	Taurus
Jun. 8–Jun. 22	Gemini
Jun. 23–Jul. 7	Cancer
Jul. 8–Jul. 26	Leo
Jul. 27–Oct. 1	Virgo
Oct. 2–Oct. 18	Libra
Oct. 19–Nov. 6	Scorpio
Nov. 7–Nov. 29	Sagittarius
Nov. 30–Dec. 12	Capricorn
Dec. 13–Dec. 31	Sagittarius

1998

Jan. 1–Jan. 11	Sagittarius
Jan. 12–Feb. 1	Capricorn
Feb. 2–Feb. 19	Aquarius
Feb. 20–Mar. 7	Pisces
Mar. 8–May 14	Aries
May 15–May 31	Taurus
Jun. 1–Jun. 14	Gemini
Jun. 15–Jun. 29	Cancer
Jun. 30–Sep. 7	Leo
Sep. 8–Sep. 23	Virgo
Sep. 24–Oct. 11	Libra
Oct. 12–Oct. 31	Scorpio
Nov. 1–Dec. 31	Sagittarius

1999

Jan. 1–Jan. 6	Sagittarius
Jan. 7–Jan. 25	Capricorn
Jan. 26–Feb. 11	Aquarius
Feb. 12–Mar. 1	Pisces
Mar. 2–Mar. 17	Aries
Mar. 18–Apr. 16	Pisces
Apr. 17–May 7	Aries
May 8–May 22	Taurus
May 23–Jun. 6	Gemini
Jun. 7–Jun. 25	Cancer
Jun. 26–Jul. 30	Leo
Jul. 31–Aug. 10	Cancer
Aug. 11–Aug. 30	Leo
Aug. 31–Sep. 15	Virgo
Sep. 16–Oct. 4	Libra
Oct. 5–Oct. 29	Scorpio
Oct. 30–Nov. 8	Sagittarius
Nov. 9–Dec. 10	Scorpio
Dec. 11–Dec. 30	Sagittarius
Dec. 31	Capricorn

2000

Jan. 1–Jan. 17	Capricorn
Jan. 18–Feb. 4	Aquarius
Feb. 5–Apr. 13	Pisces
Apr. 14–Apr. 29	Aries
Apr. 30–May 13	Taurus
May 14–May 29	Gemini
May 30–Aug. 6	Cancer
Aug. 7–Aug. 21	Leo
Aug. 22–Sep. 6	Virgo
Sep. 7–Sep. 27	Libra
Sep. 28–Nov. 6	Scorpio
Nov. 7	Libra
Nov. 8–Dec. 2	Scorpio
Dec. 3–Dec. 22	Sagittarius
Dec. 23–Dec. 31	Capricorn

5

The Venus Tables

How to Find the Planet Venus at the Time of Your Birth

Locate the year of your birth. Find the range of dates that includes your birth date. The sign indicated to the right of this range is your Venus Sign.

1900		1901	
Jan. 1–Jan. 19	Aquarius	Jan. 1–Jan. 14	Sagittarius
Jan. 20–Feb. 12	Pisces	Jan. 15–Feb. 7	Capricorn
Feb. 13–Mar. 8	Aries	Feb. 8–Mar. 3	Aquarius
Mar. 9–Apr. 3	Taurus	Mar. 4–Mar. 27	Pisces
Apr. 4–May 3	Gemini	Mar. 28–Apr. 21	Aries
May 4–Sep. 6	Cancer	Apr. 22–May 15	Taurus
Sep. 7–Oct. 6	Leo	May 16–Jun. 8	Gemini
Oct. 7–Nov. 1	Virgo	Jun. 9–Jul. 3	Cancer
Nov. 2–Nov. 26	Libra	Jul. 4–Jul. 27	Leo
Nov. 27–Dec. 21	Scorpio	Jul. 28–Aug. 21	Virgo
Dec. 22–Dec. 31	Sagittarius	Aug. 22–Sep. 15	Libra
		Sep. 16–Oct. 10	Scorpio
		Oct. 11–Nov. 5	Sagittarius
		Nov. 6–Dec. 3	Capricorn
		Dec. 4–Dec. 31	Aquarius

1902

Jan. 1–Jan. 7	Aquarius
Jan. 8–Feb. 11	Pisces
Feb. 12–Apr. 1	Aquarius
Apr. 2–May 4	Pisces
May 5–Jun. 1	Aries
Jun. 2–Jun. 28	Taurus
Jun. 29–Jul. 23	Gemini
Jul. 24–Aug. 17	Cancer
Aug. 18–Sep. 11	Leo
Sep. 12–Oct. 5	Virgo
Oct. 6–Oct. 29	Libra
Oct. 30–Nov. 22	Scorpio
Nov. 23–Dec. 16	Sagittarius
Dec. 17–Dec. 31	Capricorn

1903

Jan. 1–Jan. 9	Capricorn
Jan. 10–Feb. 2	Aquarius
Feb. 3–Feb. 26	Pisces
Feb. 27–Mar. 22	Aries
Mar. 23–Apr. 16	Taurus
Apr. 17–May 11	Gemini
May 12–Jun. 6	Cancer
Jun. 7–Jul. 5	Leo
Jul. 6–Aug. 12	Virgo
Aug. 13–Sep. 11	Libra
Sep. 12–Nov. 5	Virgo
Nov. 6–Dec. 7	Libra
Dec. 8–Dec. 31	Scorpio

1904

Jan. 1–Jan. 2	Scorpio
Jan. 3–Jan. 28	Sagittarius
Jan. 29–Feb. 22	Capricorn
Feb. 23–Mar. 17	Aquarius
Mar. 18–Apr. 11	Pisces
Apr. 12–May 5	Aries
May 6–May 30	Taurus
May 31–Jun. 23	Gemini
Jun. 24–Jul. 18	Cancer
Jul. 19–Aug. 12	Leo
Aug. 13–Sep. 4	Virgo
Sep. 5–Sep. 28	Libra
Sep. 29–Oct. 23	Scorpio
Oct. 24–Nov. 17	Sagittarius
Nov. 18–Dec. 12	Capricorn
Dec. 13–Dec. 31	Aquarius

1905

Jan. 1–Jan. 5	Aquarius
Jan. 6–Jan. 31	Pisces
Feb. 1–Mar. 3	Aries
Mar. 4–Jul. 6	Taurus
Jul. 7–Aug. 4	Gemini
Aug. 5–Aug. 30	Cancer
Aug. 31–Sep. 25	Leo
Sep. 26–Oct. 19	Virgo
Oct. 20–Nov. 12	Libra
Nov. 13–Dec. 6	Scorpio
Dec. 7–Dec. 31	Sagittarius

1906

Jan. 1	Sagittarius
Jan. 2–Jan. 25	Capricorn
Jan. 26–Feb. 18	Aquarius
Feb. 19–Mar. 14	Pisces
Mar. 15–Apr. 7	Aries
Apr. 8–May 1	Taurus
May 2–May 26	Gemini
May 27–Jun. 20	Cancer
Jun. 21–Jul. 15	Leo
Jul. 16–Aug. 10	Virgo
Aug. 11–Sep. 6	Libra
Sep. 7–Oct. 8	Scorpio
Oct. 9–Dec. 17	Sagittarius
Dec. 18–Dec. 25	Scorpio
Dec. 26–Dec. 31	Sagittarius

1907

Jan. 1–Feb. 5	Sagittarius
Feb. 6–Mar. 5	Capricorn
Mar. 6–Apr. 1	Aquarius
Apr. 2–Apr. 26	Pisces
Apr. 27–May 22	Aries
May 23–Jun. 16	Taurus
Jun. 17–Jul. 10	Gemini
Jul. 11–Aug. 4	Cancer
Aug. 5–Aug. 28	Leo
Aug. 29–Sep. 21	Virgo
Sep. 22–Oct. 15	Libra
Oct. 16–Nov. 8	Scorpio
Nov. 9–Dec. 2	Sagittarius
Dec. 3–Dec. 26	Capricorn
Dec. 27–Dec. 31	Aquarius

1908

Jan. 1–Jan. 20	Aquarius
Jan. 21–Feb. 13	Pisces
Feb. 14–Mar. 9	Aries
Mar. 10–Apr. 4	Taurus
Apr. 5–May 4	Gemini
May 5–Sep. 7	Cancer
Sep. 8–Oct. 7	Leo
Oct. 8–Nov. 2	Virgo
Nov. 3–Nov. 27	Libra
Nov. 28–Dec. 22	Scorpio
Dec. 23–Dec. 31	Sagittarius

1909

Jan. 1–Jan. 15	Sagittarius
Jan. 16–Feb. 8	Capricorn
Feb. 9–Mar. 4	Aquarius
Mar. 5–Mar. 28	Pisces
Mar. 29–Apr. 22	Aries
Apr. 23–May 16	Taurus
May 17–Jun. 9	Gemini
Jun. 10–Jul. 4	Cancer
Jul. 5–Jul. 28	Leo
Jul. 29–Aug. 22	Virgo
Aug. 23–Sep. 16	Libra
Sep. 17–Oct. 11	Scorpio
Oct. 12–Nov. 6	Sagittarius
Nov. 7–Dec. 4	Capricorn
Dec. 5–Dec. 31	Aquarius

1910

Jan. 1–Jan. 8	Aquarius
Jan. 9–Feb. 12	Pisces
Feb. 13–Apr. 2	Aquarius
Apr. 3–May 5	Pisces
May 6–Jun. 2	Aries
Jun. 3–Jun. 29	Taurus
Jun. 30–Jul. 24	Gemini
Jul. 25–Aug. 18	Cancer
Aug. 19–Sep. 12	Leo
Sep. 13–Oct. 6	Virgo
Oct. 7–Oct. 30	Libra
Oct. 31–Nov. 23	Scorpio
Nov. 24–Dec. 17	Sagittarius
Dec. 18–Dec. 31	Capricorn

1911

Jan. 1–Jan. 10	Capricorn
Jan. 11–Feb. 3	Aquarius
Feb. 4–Feb. 27	Pisces
Feb. 28–Mar. 23	Aries
Mar. 24–Apr. 17	Taurus
Apr. 18–May 12	Gemini
May 13–Jun. 7	Cancer
Jun. 8–Jul. 6	Leo
Jul. 7–Aug. 13	Virgo
Aug. 14–Sep. 12	Libra
Sep. 13–Nov. 6	Virgo
Nov. 7–Dec. 8	Libra
Dec. 9–Dec. 31	Scorpio

1912

Jan. 1–Jan. 3	Scorpio
Jan. 4–Jan. 29	Sagittarius
Jan. 30–Feb. 23	Capricorn
Feb. 24–Mar. 18	Aquarius
Mar. 19–Apr. 12	Pisces
Apr. 13–May 6	Aries
May 7–May 31	Taurus
Jun. 1–Jun. 24	Gemini
Jun. 25–Jul. 19	Cancer
Jul. 20–Aug. 13	Leo
Aug. 14–Sep. 5	Virgo
Sep. 6–Sep. 29	Libra
Sep. 30–Oct. 24	Scorpio
Oct. 25–Nov. 18	Sagittarius
Nov. 19–Dec. 13	Capricorn
Dec. 14–Dec. 31	Aquarius

1913

Jan. 1–Jan. 6	Aquarius
Jan. 7–Feb. 1	Pisces
Feb. 2–Mar. 4	Aries
Mar. 5–Jul. 7	Taurus
Jul. 8–Aug. 5	Gemini
Aug. 6–Aug. 31	Cancer
Sep. 1–Sep. 26	Leo
Sep. 27–Oct. 20	Virgo
Oct. 21–Nov. 13	Libra
Nov. 14–Dec. 7	Scorpio
Dec. 8–Dec. 31	Sagittarius

1914

Jan. 1–Jan. 24	Capricorn
Jan. 25–Feb. 17	Aquarius
Feb. 18–Mar. 13	Pisces
Mar. 14–Apr. 6	Aries
Apr. 7–Apr. 30	Taurus
May 1–May 25	Gemini
May 26–Jun. 19	Cancer
Jun. 20–Jul. 14	Leo
Jul. 15–Aug. 11	Virgo
Aug. 12–Sep. 5	Libra
Sep. 6–Oct. 10	Scorpio
Oct. 11–Dec. 31	Sagittarius

1915

Jan. 1–Feb. 4	Sagittarius
Feb. 5–Mar. 4	Capricorn
Mar. 5–Mar. 31	Aquarius
Apr. 1–Apr. 25	Pisces
Apr. 26–May 21	Aries
May 22–Jun. 15	Taurus
Jun. 16–Jul. 9	Gemini
Jul. 10–Aug. 3	Cancer
Aug. 4–Aug. 27	Leo
Aug. 28–Sep. 20	Virgo
Sep. 21–Oct. 14	Libra
Oct. 15–Nov. 7	Scorpio
Nov. 8–Dec. 1	Sagittarius
Dec. 2–Dec. 25	Capricorn
Dec. 26–Dec. 31	Aquarius

1916

Jan. 1–Jan. 19	Aquarius
Jan. 20–Feb. 12	Pisces
Feb. 13–Mar. 8	Aries
Mar. 9–Apr. 3	Taurus
Apr. 4–May 3	Gemini
May 4–Sep. 6	Cancer
Sep. 7–Oct. 6	Leo
Oct. 7–Nov. 1	Virgo
Nov. 2–Nov. 26	Libra
Nov. 27–Dec. 21	Scorpio
Dec. 22–Dec. 31	Sagittarius

1917

Jan. 1–Jan. 14	Sagittarius
Jan. 15–Feb. 7	Capricorn
Feb. 8–Mar. 3	Aquarius
Mar. 4–Mar. 27	Pisces
Mar. 28–Apr. 21	Aries
Apr. 22–May 15	Taurus
May 16–Jun. 8	Gemini
Jun. 9–Jul. 3	Cancer
Jul. 4–Jul. 27	Leo
Jul. 28–Aug. 21	Virgo
Aug. 22–Sep. 15	Libra
Sep. 16–Oct. 10	Scorpio
Oct. 11–Nov. 5	Sagittarius
Nov. 6–Dec. 3	Capricorn
Dec. 4–Dec. 31	Aquarius

1918

Jan. 1–Jan. 7	Aquarius
Jan. 8–Feb. 11	Pisces
Feb. 12–Apr. 1	Aquarius
Apr. 2–May 4	Pisces
May 5–Jun. 1	Aries
Jun. 2–Jun. 28	Taurus
Jun. 29–Jul. 23	Gemini
Jul. 24–Aug. 17	Cancer
Aug. 18–Sep. 11	Leo
Sep. 12–Oct. 5	Virgo
Oct. 6–Oct. 29	Libra
Oct. 30–Nov. 22	Scorpio
Nov. 23–Dec. 16	Sagittarius
Dec. 17–Dec. 31	Capricorn

1919

Jan. 1–Jan. 9	Capricorn
Jan. 10–Feb. 2	Aquarius
Feb. 3–Feb. 26	Pisces
Feb. 27–Mar. 22	Aries
Mar. 23–Apr. 16	Taurus
Apr. 17–May 11	Gemini
May 12–Jun. 6	Cancer
Jun. 7–Jul. 5	Leo
Jul. 6–Aug. 12	Virgo
Aug. 13–Sep. 11	Libra
Sep. 12–Nov. 5	Virgo
Nov. 6–Dec. 7	Libra
Dec. 8–Dec. 31	Scorpio

1920

Jan. 1–Jan. 2	Scorpio
Jan. 3–Jan. 28	Sagittarius
Jan. 29–Feb. 22	Capricorn
Feb. 23–Mar. 17	Aquarius
Mar. 18–Apr. 11	Pisces
Apr. 12–May 5	Aries
May 6–May 30	Taurus
May 31–Jun. 23	Gemini
Jun. 24–Jul. 18	Cancer
Jul. 19–Aug. 12	Leo
Aug. 13–Sep. 4	Virgo
Sep. 5–Sep. 28	Libra
Sep. 29–Oct. 23	Scorpio
Oct. 24–Nov. 17	Sagittarius
Nov. 18–Dec. 12	Capricorn
Dec. 13–Dec. 31	Aquarius

1921

Jan. 1–Jan. 5	Aquarius
Jan. 6–Jan. 31	Pisces
Feb. 1–Mar. 3	Aries
Mar. 4–Jul. 6	Taurus
Jul. 7–Aug. 4	Gemini
Aug. 5–Aug. 30	Cancer
Aug. 31–Sep. 25	Leo
Sep. 26–Oct. 19	Virgo
Oct. 20–Nov. 12	Libra
Nov. 13–Dec. 6	Scorpio
Dec. 7–Dec. 31	Sagittarius

1922

Jan. 1–Jan. 24	Capricorn
Jan. 25–Feb. 17	Aquarius
Feb. 18–Mar. 13	Pisces
Mar. 14–Apr. 6	Aries
Apr. 7–Apr. 30	Taurus
May 1–May 25	Gemini
May 26–Jun. 19	Cancer
Jun. 20–Jul. 14	Leo
Jul. 15–Aug. 11	Virgo
Aug. 12–Sep. 5	Libra
Sep. 6–Oct. 10	Scorpio
Oct. 11–Dec. 31	Sagittarius

1923

Jan. 1–Feb. 4	Sagittarius
Feb. 5–Mar. 4	Capricorn
Mar. 5–Mar. 31	Aquarius
Apr. 1–Apr. 25	Pisces
Apr. 26–May 21	Aries
May 22–Jun. 15	Taurus
Jun. 16–Jul. 9	Gemini
Jul. 10–Aug. 3	Cancer
Aug. 4–Aug. 27	Leo
Aug. 28–Sep. 20	Virgo
Sep. 21–Oct. 14	Libra
Oct. 15–Nov. 7	Scorpio
Nov. 8–Dec. 1	Sagittarius
Dec. 2–Dec. 25	Capricorn
Dec. 26–Dec. 31	Aquarius

1924

Jan. 1–Jan. 19	Aquarius
Jan. 20–Feb. 12	Pisces
Feb. 13–Mar. 8	Aries
Mar. 9–Apr. 3	Taurus
Apr. 4–May 3	Gemini
May 4–Sep. 6	Cancer
Sep. 7–Oct. 6	Leo
Oct. 7–Nov. 1	Virgo
Nov. 2–Nov. 26	Libra
Nov. 27–Dec. 21	Scorpio
Dec. 22–Dec. 31	Sagittarius

1925

Jan. 1–Jan. 14	Sagittarius
Jan. 15–Feb. 7	Capricorn
Feb. 8–Mar. 3	Aquarius
Mar. 4–Mar. 27	Pisces
Mar. 28–Apr. 21	Aries
Apr. 22–May 15	Taurus
May 16–Jun. 8	Gemini
Jun. 9–Jul. 3	Cancer
Jul. 4–Jul. 27	Leo
Jul. 28–Aug. 21	Virgo
Aug. 22–Sep. 15	Libra
Sep. 16–Oct. 10	Scorpio
Oct. 11–Nov. 5	Sagittarius
Nov. 6–Dec. 3	Capricorn
Dec. 4–Dec. 31	Aquarius

1926

Jan. 1–Jan. 7	Aquarius
Jan. 8–Feb. 11	Pisces
Feb. 12–Apr. 1	Aquarius
Apr. 2–May 4	Pisces
May 5–Jun. 1	Aries
Jun. 2–Jun. 28	Taurus
Jun. 29–Jul. 23	Gemini
Jul. 24–Aug. 17	Cancer
Aug. 18–Sep. 11	Leo
Sep. 12–Oct. 5	Virgo
Oct. 6–Oct. 29	Libra
Oct. 30–Nov. 22	Scorpio
Nov. 23–Dec. 16	Sagittarius
Dec. 17–Dec. 31	Capricorn

1927

Jan. 1–Jan. 9	Capricorn
Jan. 10–Feb. 2	Aquarius
Feb. 3–Feb. 26	Pisces
Feb. 27–Mar. 22	Aries
Mar. 23–Apr. 16	Taurus
Apr. 17–May 11	Gemini
May 12–Jun. 6	Cancer
Jun. 7–Jul. 5	Leo
Jul. 6–Aug. 12	Virgo
Aug. 13–Sep. 11	Libra
Sep. 12–Nov. 5	Virgo
Nov. 6–Dec. 7	Libra
Dec. 8–Dec. 31	Scorpio

1928

Jan. 1–Jan. 2	Scorpio
Jan. 3–Jan. 28	Sagittarius
Jan. 29–Feb. 22	Capricorn
Feb. 23–Mar. 17	Aquarius
Mar. 18–Apr. 11	Pisces
Apr. 12–May 5	Aries
May 6–May 30	Taurus
May 31–Jun. 23	Gemini
Jun. 24–Jul. 18	Cancer
Jul. 19–Aug. 12	Leo
Aug. 13–Sep. 4	Virgo
Sep. 5–Sep. 28	Libra
Sep. 29–Oct. 23	Scorpio
Oct. 24–Nov. 17	Sagittarius
Nov. 18–Dec. 12	Capricorn
Dec. 13–Dec. 31	Aquarius

1929

Jan. 1–Jan. 5	Aquarius
Jan. 6–Jan. 31	Pisces
Feb. 1–Mar. 3	Aries
Mar. 4–Jul. 6	Taurus
Jul. 7–Aug. 4	Gemini
Aug. 5–Aug. 30	Cancer
Aug. 31–Sep. 25	Leo
Sep. 26–Oct. 19	Virgo
Oct. 20–Nov. 12	Libra
Nov. 13–Dec. 6	Scorpio
Dec. 7–Dec. 31	Sagittarius

1930

Jan. 1–Jan. 23	Capricorn
Jan. 24–Feb. 16	Aquarius
Feb. 17–Mar. 12	Pisces
Mar. 13–Apr. 5	Aries
Apr. 6–Apr. 29	Taurus
Apr. 30–May 24	Gemini
May 25–Jun. 18	Cancer
Jun. 19–Jul. 13	Leo
Jul. 14–Aug. 9	Virgo
Aug. 10–Sep. 6	Libra
Sep. 7–Oct. 12	Scorpio
Oct. 13–Nov. 22	Sagittarius
Nov. 23–Dec. 31	Scorpio

1931

Jan. 1–Feb. 3	Sagittarius
Feb. 4–Mar. 3	Capricorn
Mar. 4–Mar. 30	Aquarius
Mar. 31–Apr. 24	Pisces
Apr. 25–May 20	Aries
May 21–Jun. 14	Taurus
Jun. 15–Jul. 8	Gemini
Jul. 9–Aug. 2	Cancer
Aug. 3–Aug. 26	Leo
Aug. 27–Sep. 19	Virgo
Sep. 20–Oct. 13	Libra
Oct. 14–Nov. 6	Scorpio
Nov. 7–Nov. 30	Sagittarius
Dec. 1–Dec. 24	Capricorn
Dec. 25–Dec. 31	Aquarius

1932

Jan. 1–Jan. 18	Aquarius
Jan. 19–Feb. 11	Pisces
Feb. 12–Mar. 7	Aries
Mar. 8–Apr. 2	Taurus
Apr. 3–May 2	Gemini
May 3–Sep. 5	Cancer
Sep. 6–Oct. 5	Leo
Oct. 6–Oct. 31	Virgo
Nov. 1–Nov. 25	Libra
Nov. 26–Dec. 20	Scorpio
Dec. 21–Dec. 31	Sagittarius

1933

Jan. 1–Jan. 13	Sagittarius
Jan. 14–Feb. 6	Capricorn
Feb. 7–Mar. 2	Aquarius
Mar. 3–Mar. 26	Pisces
Mar. 27–Apr. 20	Aries
Apr. 21–May 14	Taurus
May 15–Jun. 7	Gemini
Jun. 8–Jul. 2	Cancer
Jul. 3–Jul. 26	Leo
Jul. 27–Aug. 20	Virgo
Aug. 21–Sep. 16	Libra
Sep. 17–Oct. 9	Scorpio
Oct. 10–Nov. 4	Sagittarius
Nov. 5–Dec. 2	Capricorn
Dec. 3–Dec. 31	Aquarius

1934

Jan. 1–Jan. 6	Aquarius
Jan. 7–Feb. 10	Pisces
Feb. 11–Mar. 31	Aquarius
Apr. 1–May 3	Pisces
May 4–May 31	Aries
Jun. 1–Jun. 27	Taurus
Jun. 28–Jul. 22	Gemini
Jul. 23–Aug. 16	Cancer
Aug. 17–Sep. 10	Leo
Sep. 11–Oct. 4	Virgo
Oct. 5–Oct. 28	Libra
Oct. 29–Nov. 21	Scorpio
Nov. 22–Dec. 15	Sagittarius
Dec. 16–Dec. 31	Capricorn

1935

Jan. 1–Jan. 8	Capricorn
Jan. 9–Feb. 1	Aquarius
Feb. 2–Feb. 25	Pisces
Feb. 26–Mar. 21	Aries
Mar. 22–Apr. 15	Taurus
Apr. 16–May 10	Gemini
May 11–Jun. 5	Cancer
Jun. 6–Jul. 4	Leo
Jul. 5–Aug. 11	Virgo
Aug. 12–Sep. 10	Libra
Sep. 11–Nov. 4	Virgo
Nov. 5–Dec. 6	Libra
Dec. 7–Dec. 31	Scorpio

1936

Jan. 1	Scorpio
Jan. 2–Jan. 27	Sagittarius
Jan. 28–Feb. 21	Capricorn
Feb. 22–Mar. 16	Aquarius
Mar. 17–Apr. 10	Pisces
Apr. 11–May 4	Aries
May 5–May 29	Taurus
May 30–Jun. 22	Gemini
Jun. 23–Jul. 17	Cancer
Jul. 18–Aug. 11	Leo
Aug. 12–Sep. 3	Virgo
Sep. 4–Sep. 27	Libra
Sep. 28–Oct. 22	Scorpio
Oct. 23–Nov. 16	Sagittarius
Nov. 17–Dec. 11	Capricorn
Dec. 12–Dec. 31	Aquarius

1937

Jan. 1–Jan. 4	Aquarius
Jan. 5–Jan. 30	Pisces
Jan. 31–Mar. 2	Aries
Mar. 3–Jul. 5	Taurus
Jul. 6–Aug. 3	Gemini
Aug. 4–Aug. 29	Cancer
Aug. 30–Sep. 24	Leo
Sep. 25–Oct. 18	Virgo
Oct. 19–Nov. 11	Libra
Nov. 12–Dec. 5	Scorpio
Dec. 6–Dec. 31	Sagittarius

1938

Jan. 1–Jan. 22	Capricorn
Jan. 23–Feb. 15	Aquarius
Feb. 16–Mar. 11	Pisces
Mar. 12–Apr. 4	Aries
Apr. 5–Apr. 28	Taurus
Apr. 29–May 23	Gemini
May 24–Jun. 17	Cancer
Jun. 18–Jul. 12	Leo
Jul. 13–Aug. 9	Virgo
Aug. 10–Sep. 3	Libra
Sep. 4–Oct. 13	Scorpio
Oct. 14–Dec. 31	Sagittarius

1939

Jan. 1–Feb. 2	Sagittarius
Feb. 3–Mar. 2	Capricorn
Mar. 3–Mar. 29	Aquarius
Mar. 30–Apr. 23	Pisces
Apr. 24–May 19	Aries
May 20–Jun. 13	Taurus
Jun. 14–Jul. 7	Gemini
Jul. 8–Aug. 1	Cancer
Aug. 2–Aug. 25	Leo
Aug. 26–Sep. 18	Virgo
Sep. 19–Oct. 12	Libra
Oct. 13–Nov. 5	Scorpio
Nov. 6–Nov. 29	Sagittarius
Nov. 30–Dec. 23	Capricorn
Dec. 24–Dec. 31	Aquarius

1940

Jan. 1–Jan. 17	Aquarius
Jan. 18–Feb. 10	Pisces
Feb. 11–Mar. 6	Aries
Mar. 7–Apr. 1	Taurus
Apr. 2–May 1	Gemini
May 2–Sep. 4	Cancer
Sep. 5–Oct. 4	Leo
Oct. 5–Oct. 30	Virgo
Oct. 31–Nov. 24	Libra
Nov. 25–Dec. 19	Scorpio
Dec. 20–Dec. 31	Sagittarius

1941

Jan. 1–Jan. 12	Sagittarius
Jan. 13–Feb. 5	Capricorn
Feb. 6–Mar. 1	Aquarius
Mar. 2–Mar. 25	Pisces
Mar. 26–Apr. 19	Aries
Apr. 20–May 13	Taurus
May 14–Jun. 6	Gemini
Jun. 7–Jul. 1	Cancer
Jul. 2–Jul. 25	Leo
Jul. 26–Aug. 19	Virgo
Aug. 20–Sep. 15	Libra
Sep. 16–Oct. 8	Scorpio
Oct. 9–Nov. 3	Sagittarius
Nov. 4–Dec. 1	Capricorn
Dec. 2–Dec. 31	Aquarius

1942

Jan. 1–Jan. 5	Aquarius
Jan. 6–Feb. 9	Pisces
Feb. 10–Mar. 30	Aquarius
Mar. 31–May 2	Pisces
May 3–May 30	Aries
May 31–Jun. 26	Taurus
Jun. 27–Jul. 21	Gemini
Jul. 22–Aug. 15	Cancer
Aug. 16–Sep. 9	Leo
Sep. 10–Oct. 3	Virgo
Oct. 4–Oct. 27	Libra
Oct. 28–Nov. 20	Scorpio
Nov. 21–Dec. 16	Sagittarius
Dec. 17–Dec. 31	Capricorn

1943

Jan. 1–Jan. 7	Capricorn
Jan. 8–Jan. 31	Aquarius
Feb. 1–Feb. 24	Pisces
Feb. 25–Mar. 20	Aries
Mar. 21–Apr. 14	Taurus
Apr. 15–May 9	Gemini
May 10–Jun. 4	Cancer
Jun. 5–Jul. 3	Leo
Jul. 4–Aug. 10	Virgo
Aug. 11–Sep. 9	Libra
Sep. 10–Nov. 3	Virgo
Nov. 4–Dec. 5	Libra
Dec. 6–Dec. 31	Scorpio

1944

Jan. 1–Jan. 26	Sagittarius
Jan. 27–Feb. 20	Capricorn
Feb. 21–Mar. 15	Aquarius
Mar. 16–Apr. 9	Pisces
Apr. 10–May 3	Aries
May 4–May 28	Taurus
May 29–Jun. 21	Gemini
Jun. 22–Jul. 16	Cancer
Jul. 17–Aug. 10	Leo
Aug. 11–Sep. 2	Virgo
Sep. 3–Sep. 26	Libra
Sep. 27–Oct. 21	Scorpio
Oct. 22–Nov. 15	Sagittarius
Nov. 16–Dec. 10	Capricorn
Dec. 11–Dec. 31	Aquarius

1945

Jan. 1–Jan. 3	Aquarius
Jan. 4–Jan. 29	Pisces
Jan. 30–Mar. 1	Aries
Mar. 2–Jul. 4	Taurus
Jul. 5–Aug. 2	Gemini
Aug. 3–Aug. 28	Cancer
Aug. 29–Sep. 23	Leo
Sep. 24–Oct. 17	Virgo
Oct. 18–Nov. 10	Libra
Nov. 11–Dec. 4	Scorpio
Dec. 5–Dec. 31	Sagittarius

1946

Jan. 1–Jan. 22	Capricorn
Jan. 23–Feb. 15	Aquarius
Feb. 16–Mar. 11	Pisces
Mar. 12–Apr. 4	Aries
Apr. 5–Apr. 28	Taurus
Apr. 29–May 23	Gemini
May 24–Jun. 17	Cancer
Jun. 18–Jul. 12	Leo
Jul. 13–Aug. 9	Virgo
Aug. 10–Sep. 6	Libra
Sep. 7–Oct. 16	Scorpio
Oct. 17–Dec. 31	Sagittarius

1947

Jan. 1–Feb. 2	Sagittarius
Feb. 3–Mar. 2	Capricorn
Mar. 3–Mar. 29	Aquarius
Mar. 30–Apr. 23	Pisces
Apr. 24–May 19	Aries
May 20–Jun. 13	Taurus
Jun. 14–Jul. 7	Gemini
Jul. 8–Aug. 1	Cancer
Aug. 2–Aug. 25	Leo
Aug. 26–Sep. 18	Virgo
Sep. 19–Oct. 12	Libra
Oct. 13–Nov. 5	Scorpio
Nov. 6–Nov. 29	Sagittarius
Nov. 30–Dec. 23	Capricorn
Dec. 24–Dec. 31	Aquarius

1948

Jan. 1–Jan. 17	Aquarius
Jan. 18–Feb. 10	Pisces
Feb. 11–Mar. 6	Aries
Mar. 7–Apr. 1	Taurus
Apr. 2–May 1	Gemini
May 2–Sep. 4	Cancer
Sep. 5–Oct. 4	Leo
Oct. 5–Oct. 30	Virgo
Oct. 31–Nov. 24	Libra
Nov. 25–Dec. 19	Scorpio
Dec. 20–Dec. 31	Sagittarius

1949

Jan. 1–Jan. 12	Sagittarius
Jan. 13–Feb. 5	Capricorn
Feb. 6–Mar. 1	Aquarius
Mar. 2–Mar. 25	Pisces
Mar. 26–Apr. 19	Aries
Apr. 20–May 13	Taurus
May 14–Jun. 6	Gemini
Jun. 7–Jul. 1	Cancer
Jul. 2–Jul. 25	Leo
Jul. 26–Aug. 19	Virgo
Aug. 20–Sep. 15	Libra
Sep. 16–Oct. 8	Scorpio
Oct. 9–Nov. 3	Sagittarius
Nov. 4–Dec. 1	Capricorn
Dec. 2–Dec. 31	Aquarius

1950

Jan. 1–Jan. 5	Aquarius
Jan. 6–Feb. 9	Pisces
Feb. 10–Mar. 30	Aquarius
Mar. 31–May 2	Pisces
May 3–May 30	Aries
May 31–Jun. 26	Taurus
Jun. 27–Jul. 21	Gemini
Jul. 22–Aug. 15	Cancer
Aug. 16–Sep. 9	Leo
Sep. 10–Oct. 3	Virgo
Oct. 4–Oct. 27	Libra
Oct. 28–Nov. 20	Scorpio
Nov. 21–Dec. 16	Sagittarius
Dec. 17–Dec. 31	Capricorn

1951

Jan. 1–Jan. 7	Capricorn
Jan. 8–Jan. 31	Aquarius
Feb. 1–Feb. 24	Pisces
Feb. 25–Mar. 20	Aries
Mar. 21–Apr. 14	Taurus
Apr. 15–May 9	Gemini
May 10–Jun. 4	Cancer
Jun. 5–Jul. 3	Leo
Jul. 4–Aug. 10	Virgo
Aug. 11–Sep. 9	Libra
Sep. 10–Nov. 3	Virgo
Nov. 4–Dec. 5	Libra
Dec. 6–Dec. 31	Scorpio

1952

Jan. 1–Jan. 26	Sagittarius
Jan. 27–Feb. 20	Capricorn
Feb. 21–Mar. 15	Aquarius
Mar. 16–Apr. 9	Pisces
Apr. 10–May 3	Aries
May 4–May 28	Taurus
May 29–Jun. 21	Gemini
Jun. 22–Jul. 16	Cancer
Jul. 17–Aug. 10	Leo
Aug. 11–Sep. 2	Virgo
Sep. 3–Sep. 26	Libra
Sep. 27–Oct. 21	Scorpio
Oct. 22–Nov. 15	Sagittarius
Nov. 16–Dec. 10	Capricorn
Dec. 11–Dec. 31	Aquarius

1953

Jan. 1–Jan. 3	Aquarius
Jan. 4–Jan. 29	Pisces
Jan. 30–Mar. 1	Aries
Mar. 2–Jul. 4	Taurus
Jul. 5–Aug. 2	Gemini
Aug. 3–Aug. 28	Cancer
Aug. 29–Sep. 23	Leo
Sep. 24–Oct. 17	Virgo
Oct. 18–Nov. 10	Libra
Nov. 11–Dec. 4	Scorpio
Dec. 5–Dec. 31	Sagittarius

1954

Jan. 1–Jan. 21	Capricorn
Jan. 22–Feb. 14	Aquarius
Feb. 15–Mar. 10	Pisces
Mar. 11–Apr. 3	Aries
Apr. 4–Apr. 27	Taurus
Apr. 28–May 22	Gemini
May 23–Jun. 16	Cancer
Jun. 17–Jul. 11	Leo
Jul. 12–Aug. 8	Virgo
Aug. 9–Sep. 6	Libra
Sep. 7–Oct. 23	Scorpio
Oct. 24–Oct. 26	Sagittarius
Oct. 27–Dec. 31	Scorpio

1955

Jan. 1–Feb. 1	Sagittarius
Feb. 2–Mar. 1	Capricorn
Mar. 2–Mar. 28	Aquarius
Mar. 29–Apr. 22	Pisces
Apr. 23–May 18	Aries
May 19–Jun. 12	Taurus
Jun. 13–Jul. 6	Gemini
Jul. 7–Jul. 31	Cancer
Aug. 1–Aug. 24	Leo
Aug. 25–Sep. 17	Virgo
Sep. 18–Oct. 11	Libra
Oct. 12–Nov. 4	Scorpio
Nov. 5–Nov. 28	Sagittarius
Nov. 29–Dec. 22	Capricorn
Dec. 23–Dec. 31	Aquarius

1956

Jan. 1–Jan. 16	Aquarius
Jan. 17–Feb. 9	Pisces
Feb. 10–Mar. 5	Aries
Mar. 6–Mar. 31	Taurus
Apr. 1–Apr. 30	Gemini
May 1–Sep. 3	Cancer
Sep. 4–Oct. 3	Leo
Oct. 4–Oct. 29	Virgo
Oct. 30–Nov. 23	Libra
Nov. 24–Dec. 18	Scorpio
Dec. 19–Dec. 31	Sagittarius

1957

Jan. 1–Feb. 12	Capricorn
Feb. 13–Feb. 28	Aquarius
Mar. 1–Mar. 24	Pisces
Mar. 25–Apr. 18	Aries
Apr. 19–May 12	Taurus
May 13–Jun. 5	Gemini
Jun. 6–Jun. 30	Cancer
Jul. 1–Jul. 24	Leo
Jul. 25–Aug. 18	Virgo
Aug. 19–Sep. 14	Libra
Sep. 15–Oct. 7	Scorpio
Oct. 8–Nov. 2	Sagittarius
Nov. 3–Nov. 30	Capricorn
Dec. 1–Dec. 31	Aquarius

1958

Jan. 1–Jan. 4	Aquarius
Jan. 5–Feb. 8	Pisces
Feb. 9–Mar. 29	Aquarius
Mar. 30–May 1	Pisces
May 2–May 29	Aries
May 30–Jun. 25	Taurus
Jun. 26–Jul. 20	Gemini
Jul. 21–Aug. 14	Cancer
Aug. 15–Sep. 8	Leo
Sep. 9–Oct. 2	Virgo
Oct. 3–Oct. 26	Libra
Oct. 27–Nov. 19	Scorpio
Nov. 20–Dec. 15	Sagittarius
Dec. 16–Dec. 31	Capricorn

1959

Jan. 1–Jan. 6	Capricorn
Jan. 7–Jan. 30	Aquarius
Jan. 31–Feb. 23	Pisces
Feb. 24–Mar. 19	Aries
Mar. 20–Apr. 13	Taurus
Apr. 14–May 10	Gemini
May 11–Jun. 3	Cancer
Jun. 4–Jul. 2	Leo
Jul. 3–Aug. 9	Virgo
Aug. 10–Sep. 8	Libra
Sep. 9–Nov. 2	Virgo
Nov. 3–Dec. 4	Libra
Dec. 5–Dec. 31	Scorpio

1960

Jan. 1–Jan. 25	Sagittarius
Jan. 26–Feb. 19	Capricorn
Feb. 20–Mar. 14	Aquarius
Mar. 15–Apr. 8	Pisces
Apr. 9–May 2	Aries
May 3–May 27	Taurus
May 28–Jun. 20	Gemini
Jun. 21–Jul. 15	Cancer
Jul. 16–Aug. 9	Leo
Aug. 10–Sep. 1	Virgo
Sep. 2–Sep. 25	Libra
Sep. 26–Oct. 20	Scorpio
Oct. 21–Nov. 14	Sagittarius
Nov. 15–Dec. 9	Capricorn
Dec. 10–Dec. 31	Aquarius

1961

Jan. 1–Jan. 2	Aquarius
Jan. 3–Jan. 28	Pisces
Jan. 29–Feb. 28	Aries
Mar. 1–Jul. 3	Taurus
Jul. 4–Aug. 1	Gemini
Aug. 2–Aug. 27	Cancer
Aug. 28–Sep. 22	Leo
Sep. 23–Oct. 16	Virgo
Oct. 17–Nov. 9	Libra
Nov. 10–Dec. 3	Scorpio
Dec. 4–Dec. 31	Sagittarius

1962

Jan. 1–Jan. 21	Capricorn
Jan. 22–Feb. 14	Aquarius
Feb. 15–Mar. 10	Pisces
Mar. 11–Apr. 3	Aries
Apr. 4–Apr. 27	Taurus
Apr. 28–May 22	Gemini
May 23–Jun. 16	Cancer
Jun. 17–Jul. 11	Leo
Jul. 12–Aug. 8	Virgo
Aug. 9–Sep. 2	Libra
Sep. 3–Dec. 31	Scorpio

1963

Jan. 1–Feb. 1	Sagittarius
Feb. 2–Mar. 1	Capricorn
Mar. 2–Mar. 28	Aquarius
Mar. 29–Apr. 22	Pisces
Apr. 23–May 18	Aries
May 19–Jun. 12	Taurus
Jun. 13–Jul. 6	Gemini
Jul. 7–Jul. 31	Cancer
Aug. 1–Aug. 24	Leo
Aug. 25–Sep. 17	Virgo
Sep. 18–Oct. 11	Libra
Oct. 12–Nov. 4	Scorpio
Nov. 5–Nov. 28	Sagittarius
Nov. 29–Dec. 22	Capricorn
Dec. 23–Dec. 31	Aquarius

1964

Jan. 1–Jan. 16	Aquarius
Jan. 17–Feb. 9	Pisces
Feb. 10–Mar. 5	Aries
Mar. 6–Mar. 31	Taurus
Apr. 1–Apr. 30	Gemini
May 1–Sep. 3	Cancer
Sep. 4–Oct. 3	Leo
Oct. 4–Oct. 29	Virgo
Oct. 30–Nov. 23	Libra
Nov. 24–Dec. 18	Scorpio
Dec. 19–Dec. 31	Sagittarius

1965

Jan. 1–Jan. 11	Sagittarius
Jan. 12–Feb. 4	Capricorn
Feb. 5–Feb. 28	Aquarius
Mar. 1–Mar. 21	Pisces
Mar. 22–Apr. 18	Aries
Apr. 19–May 12	Taurus
May 13–Jun. 5	Gemini
Jun. 6–Jun. 30	Cancer
Jul. 1–Jul. 24	Leo
Jul. 25–Aug. 18	Virgo
Aug. 19–Sep. 14	Libra
Sep. 15–Oct. 7	Scorpio
Oct. 8–Nov. 2	Sagittarius
Nov. 3–Nov. 30	Capricorn
Dec. 1–Dec. 31	Aquarius

1966

Jan. 1–Jan. 4	Aquarius
Jan. 5–Feb. 8	Pisces
Feb. 9–Mar. 29	Aquarius
Mar. 30–May 1	Pisces
May 2–May 29	Aries
May 30–Jun. 25	Taurus
Jun. 26–Jul. 20	Gemini
Jul. 21–Aug. 14	Cancer
Aug. 15–Sep. 8	Leo
Sep. 9–Oct. 2	Virgo
Oct. 3–Oct. 26	Libra
Oct. 27–Nov. 19	Scorpio
Nov. 20–Dec. 15	Sagittarius
Dec. 16–Dec. 31	Capricorn

1967

Jan. 1–Jan. 6	Capricorn
Jan. 7–Jan. 30	Aquarius
Jan. 31–Feb. 23	Pisces
Feb. 24–Mar. 19	Aries
Mar. 20–Apr. 13	Taurus
Apr. 14–May 10	Gemini
May 11–Jun. 3	Cancer
Jun. 4–Jul. 2	Leo
Jul. 3–Aug. 9	Virgo
Aug. 10–Sep. 8	Libra
Sep. 9–Nov. 2	Virgo
Nov. 3–Dec. 4	Libra
Dec. 5–Dec. 31	Scorpio

1968

Jan. 1–Jan. 25	Sagittarius
Jan. 26–Feb. 19	Capricorn
Feb. 20–Mar. 14	Aquarius
Mar. 15–Apr. 8	Pisces
Apr. 9–May 2	Aries
May 3–May 27	Taurus
May 28–Jun. 20	Gemini
Jun. 21–Jul. 15	Cancer
Jul. 16–Aug. 9	Leo
Aug. 10–Sep. 1	Virgo
Sep. 2–Sep. 25	Libra
Sep. 26–Oct. 20	Scorpio
Oct. 21–Nov. 14	Sagittarius
Nov. 15–Dec. 9	Capricorn
Dec. 10–Dec. 31	Aquarius

1969

Jan. 1–Jan. 2	Aquarius
Jan. 3–Jan. 28	Pisces
Jan. 29–Feb. 28	Aries
Mar. 1–Jul. 3	Taurus
Jul. 4–Aug. 1	Gemini
Aug. 2–Aug. 27	Cancer
Aug. 28–Sep. 22	Leo
Sep. 23–Oct. 16	Virgo
Oct. 17–Nov. 9	Libra
Nov. 10–Dec. 3	Scorpio
Dec. 4–Dec. 31	Sagittarius

1970

Jan. 1–Jan. 20	Capricorn
Jan. 21–Feb. 13	Aquarius
Feb. 14–Mar. 9	Pisces
Mar. 10–Apr. 2	Aries
Apr. 3–Apr. 26	Taurus
Apr. 27–May 21	Gemini
May 22–Jun. 15	Cancer
Jun. 16–Jul. 10	Leo
Jul. 11–Aug. 7	Virgo
Aug. 8–Sep. 1	Libra
Sep. 2–Oct. 22	Scorpio
Oct. 23–Dec. 31	Sagittarius

1971

Jan. 1–Jan. 7	Scorpio
Jan. 8–Feb. 5	Sagittarius
Feb. 6–Mar. 4	Capricorn
Mar. 5–Mar. 29	Aquarius
Mar. 30–Apr. 23	Pisces
Apr. 24–May 18	Aries
May 19–Jun. 10	Taurus
Jun. 11–Jul. 6	Gemini
Jul. 7–Jul. 31	Cancer
Aug. 1–Aug. 24	Leo
Aug. 25–Sep. 17	Virgo
Sep. 18–Oct. 11	Libra
Oct. 12–Nov. 5	Scorpio
Nov. 6–Nov. 29	Sagittarius
Nov. 30–Dec. 23	Capricorn
Dec. 24–Dec. 31	Aquarius

1972

Jan. 1–Jan. 16	Aquarius
Jan. 17–Feb. 10	Pisces
Feb. 11–Mar. 7	Aries
Mar. 8–Apr. 3	Taurus
Apr. 4–May 10	Gemini
May 11–Jun. 11	Cancer
Jun. 12–Aug. 6	Gemini
Aug. 7–Sep. 7	Cancer
Sep. 8–Oct. 5	Leo
Oct. 6–Oct. 30	Virgo
Oct. 31–Nov. 24	Libra
Nov. 25–Dec. 18	Scorpio
Dec. 19–Dec. 31	Sagittarius

1973

Jan. 1–Jan. 11	Sagittarius
Jan. 12–Feb. 4	Capricorn
Feb. 5–Feb. 28	Aquarius
Mar. 1–Mar. 24	Pisces
Mar. 25–Apr. 18	Aries
Apr. 19–May 12	Taurus
May 13–Jun. 5	Gemini
Jun. 6–Jun. 30	Cancer
Jul. 1–Jul. 25	Leo
Jul. 26–Aug. 19	Virgo
Aug. 20–Sep. 14	Libra
Sep. 15–Oct. 9	Scorpio
Oct. 10–Nov. 5	Sagittarius
Nov. 6–Dec. 7	Capricorn
Dec. 8–Dec. 31	Aquarius

1974

Jan. 1–Jan. 29	Aquarius
Jan. 30–Feb. 28	Capricorn
Mar. 1–Apr. 6	Aquarius
Apr. 7–May 4	Pisces
May 5–May 31	Aries
Jun. 1–Jun. 25	Taurus
Jun. 26–Jul. 21	Gemini
Jul. 22–Aug. 14	Cancer
Aug. 15–Sep. 8	Leo
Sep. 9–Oct. 2	Virgo
Oct. 3–Oct. 26	Libra
Oct. 27–Nov. 19	Scorpio
Nov. 20–Dec. 13	Sagittarius
Dec. 14–Dec. 31	Capricorn

1975

Jan. 1–Jan. 6	Capricorn
Jan. 7–Jan. 30	Aquarius
Jan. 31–Feb. 23	Pisces
Feb. 24–Mar. 19	Aries
Mar. 20–Apr. 13	Taurus
Apr. 14–May 9	Gemini
May 10–Jun. 6	Cancer
Jun. 7–Jul. 9	Leo
Jul. 10–Sep. 2	Virgo
Sep. 3–Oct. 4	Leo
Oct. 5–Nov. 9	Virgo
Nov. 10–Dec. 7	Libra
Dec. 8–Dec. 31	Scorpio

1976

Jan. 1–Jan. 2	Virgo
Jan. 3–Jan. 26	Sagittarius
Jan. 27–Feb. 19	Capricorn
Feb. 20–Mar. 15	Aquarius
Mar. 16–Apr. 8	Pisces
Apr. 9–May 2	Aries
May 3–May 26	Taurus
May 27–Jun. 20	Gemini
Jun. 21–Jul. 14	Cancer
Jul. 15–Aug. 8	Leo
Aug. 9–Sep. 1	Virgo
Sep. 2–Sep. 26	Libra
Sep. 27–Oct. 20	Scorpio
Oct. 21–Nov. 14	Sagittarius
Nov. 15–Dec. 9	Capricorn
Dec. 10–Dec. 31	Aquarius

1977

Jan. 1–Jan. 4	Aquarius
Jan. 5–Feb. 2	Pisces
Feb. 3–Jun. 6	Aries
Jun. 7–Jul. 6	Taurus
Jul. 7–Aug. 2	Gemini
Aug. 3–Aug. 28	Cancer
Aug. 29–Sep. 22	Leo
Sep. 23–Oct. 17	Libra
Oct. 18–Nov. 10	Virgo
Nov. 11–Dec. 4	Scorpio
Dec. 5–Dec. 27	Sagittarius
Dec. 28–Dec. 31	Capricorn

1978

Jan. 1–Jan. 20	Capricorn
Jan. 21–Feb. 13	Aquarius
Feb. 14–Mar. 9	Pisces
Mar. 10–Apr. 2	Aries
Apr. 3–Apr. 27	Taurus
Apr. 28–May 22	Gemini
May 23–Jun. 16	Cancer
Jun. 17–Jul. 12	Leo
Jul. 13–Aug. 8	Virgo
Aug. 9–Sep. 7	Libra
Sep. 8–Dec. 31	Scorpio

1979

Jan. 1–Jan. 7	Scorpio
Jan. 8–Feb. 5	Sagittarius
Feb. 6–Mar. 3	Capricorn
Mar. 4–Mar. 29	Aquarius
Mar. 30–Apr. 23	Pisces
Apr. 24–May 18	Aries
May 19–Jun. 11	Taurus
Jun. 12–Jul. 6	Gemini
Jul. 7–Jul. 30	Cancer
Jul. 31–Aug. 24	Leo
Aug. 25–Sep. 17	Virgo
Sep. 18–Oct. 11	Libra
Oct. 12–Nov. 4	Scorpio
Nov. 5–Nov. 28	Sagittarius
Nov. 29–Dec. 22	Capricorn
Dec. 23–Dec. 31	Aquarius

1980

Jan. 1–Jan. 16	Aquarius
Jan. 17–Feb. 9	Pisces
Feb. 10–Mar. 6	Aries
Mar. 7–Apr. 3	Taurus
Apr. 4–May 12	Gemini
May 13–Jun. 5	Cancer
Jun. 6–Aug. 6	Gemini
Aug. 7–Sep. 7	Cancer
Sep. 8–Oct. 4	Leo
Oct. 5–Oct. 30	Virgo
Oct. 31–Nov. 24	Libra
Nov. 25–Dec. 18	Scorpio
Dec. 19–Dec. 31	Sagittarius

1981

Jan. 1–Jan. 11	Sagittarius
Jan. 12–Feb. 4	Capricorn
Feb. 5–Feb. 28	Aquarius
Mar. 1–Mar. 24	Pisces
Mar. 25–Apr. 17	Aries
Apr. 18–May 11	Taurus
May 12–Jun. 6	Gemini
Jun. 7–Jun. 30	Cancer
Jul. 1–Jul. 24	Leo
Jul. 25–Aug. 18	Virgo
Aug. 19–Sep. 12	Libra
Sep. 13–Oct. 8	Scorpio
Oct. 9–Nov. 5	Sagittarius
Nov. 6–Dec. 7	Capricorn
Dec. 8–Dec. 31	Aquarius

1982

Jan. 1–Jan. 22	Aquarius
Jan. 23–Mar. 2	Capricorn
Mar. 3–Apr. 6	Aquarius
Apr. 7–May 4	Pisces
May 5–May 30	Aries
May 31–Jun. 25	Taurus
Jun. 26–Jul. 20	Gemini
Jul. 21–Aug. 14	Cancer
Aug. 15–Sep. 7	Leo
Sep. 8–Oct. 2	Virgo
Oct. 3–Oct. 26	Libra
Oct. 27–Nov. 18	Scorpio
Nov. 19–Dec. 12	Sagittarius
Dec. 13–Dec. 31	Capricorn

1983

Jan. 1–Jan. 5	Capricorn
Jan. 6–Jan. 29	Aquarius
Jan. 30–Feb. 22	Pisces
Feb. 23–Mar. 19	Aries
Mar. 20–Apr. 13	Taurus
Apr. 14–May 9	Gemini
May 10–Jun. 6	Cancer
Jun. 7–Jul. 10	Leo
Jul. 11–Aug. 28	Virgo
Aug. 29–Oct. 5	Leo
Oct. 6–Nov. 9	Virgo
Nov. 10–Dec. 6	Libra
Dec. 7–Dec. 31	Scorpio

1984

Jan. 1	Scorpio
Jan. 2–Jan. 25	Sagittarius
Jan. 26–Feb. 19	Capricorn
Feb. 20–Mar. 14	Aquarius
Mar. 15–Apr. 7	Pisces
Apr. 8–May 2	Aries
May 3–May 26	Taurus
May 27–Jun. 20	Gemini
Jun. 21–Jul. 14	Cancer
Jul. 15–Aug. 7	Leo
Aug. 8–Sep. 1	Virgo
Sep. 2–Sep. 24	Libra
Sep. 25–Oct. 20	Scorpio
Oct. 21–Nov. 15	Sagittarius
Nov. 16–Dec. 9	Capricorn
Dec. 10–Dec. 31	Aquarius

1985

Jan. 1–Jan. 4	Aquarius
Jan. 5–Feb. 2	Pisces
Feb. 3–Jun. 6	Aries
Jun. 7–Jul. 6	Taurus
Jul. 7–Aug. 22	Gemini
Aug. 23–Sep. 2	Libra
Sep. 3–Sep. 28	Cancer
Sep. 29–Nov. 9	Leo
Nov. 10–Dec. 3	Scorpio
Dec. 4–Dec. 27	Sagittarius
Dec. 28–Dec. 31	Capricorn

1986

Jan. 1–Jan. 15	Capricorn
Jan. 16–Feb. 9	Aquarius
Feb. 10–Mar. 9	Pisces
Mar. 10–Apr. 2	Aries
Apr. 3–Apr. 26	Taurus
Apr. 27–May 21	Gemini
May 22–Jun. 15	Cancer
Jun. 16–Jul. 11	Leo
Jul. 12–Aug. 7	Virgo
Aug. 8–Sep. 7	Libra
Sep. 8–Dec. 31	Scorpio

1987

Jan. 1–Jan. 7	Scorpio
Jan. 8–Feb. 4	Sagittarius
Feb. 5–Mar. 3	Capricorn
Mar. 4–Mar. 28	Aquarius
Mar. 29–Apr. 22	Pisces
Apr. 23–May 17	Aries
May 18–Jun. 11	Taurus
Jun. 12–Jul. 5	Gemini
Jul. 6–Jul. 30	Cancer
Jul. 31–Aug. 23	Leo
Aug. 24–Oct. 10	Libra
Oct. 11–Nov. 3	Scorpio
Nov. 4–Nov. 28	Sagittarius
Nov. 29–Dec. 22	Capricorn
Dec. 23–Dec. 31	Aquarius

1988

Jan. 1–Jan. 15	Aquarius
Jan. 16–Feb. 9	Pisces
Feb. 10–Mar. 6	Aries
Mar. 7–Apr. 4	Taurus
Apr. 5–May 17	Gemini
May 18–May 28	Cancer
May 29–Aug. 6	Gemini
Aug. 7–Sep. 7	Cancer
Sep. 8–Oct. 4	Leo
Oct. 5–Oct. 29	Virgo
Oct. 30–Nov. 23	Libra
Nov. 24–Dec. 17	Scorpio
Dec. 18–Dec. 31	Sagittarius

1989

Jan. 1–Jan. 10	Sagittarius
Jan. 11–Feb. 3	Capricorn
Feb. 4–Feb. 27	Aquarius
Feb. 28–Apr. 2	Pisces
Apr. 3–Apr. 26	Taurus
Apr. 27–May 21	Gemini
May 22–Jun. 15	Cancer
Jun. 16–Jul. 11	Leo
Jul. 12–Aug. 7	Virgo
Aug. 8–Sep. 7	Libra
Sep. 8–Dec. 31	Scorpio

1990

Jan. 1–Jan. 16	Aquarius
Jan. 17–Mar. 3	Capricorn
Mar. 4–Apr. 6	Aquarius
Apr. 7–May 4	Pisces
May 5–May 30	Aries
May 31–Jun. 25	Taurus
Jun. 26–Jul. 20	Gemini
Jul. 21–Aug. 13	Cancer
Aug. 14–Sep. 7	Leo
Sep. 8–Oct. 2	Virgo
Oct. 3–Oct. 26	Libra
Oct. 27–Nov. 18	Scorpio
Nov. 19–Dec. 12	Sagittarius
Dec. 13–Dec. 31	Capricorn

1991

Jan. 1–Jan. 4	Capricorn
Jan. 5–Jan. 28	Aquarius
Jan. 29–Feb. 21	Pisces
Feb. 22–Mar. 17	Aries
Mar. 18–Apr. 12	Taurus
Apr. 13–May 8	Gemini
May 9–Jun. 5	Cancer
Jun. 6–Jul. 10	Leo
Jul. 11–Aug. 20	Virgo
Aug. 21–Oct. 5	Leo
Oct. 6–Nov. 8	Virgo
Nov. 9–Dec. 5	Libra
Dec. 6–Dec. 30	Scorpio
Dec. 31	Sagittarius

1992

Jan. 1–Jan. 24	Sagittarius
Jan. 25–Feb. 17	Capricorn
Feb. 18–Mar. 12	Aquarius
Mar. 13–Apr. 6	Pisces
Apr. 7–Apr. 30	Aries
May 1–May 25	Taurus
May 26–Jun. 18	Gemini
Jun. 19–Jul. 12	Cancer
Jul. 13–Aug. 6	Leo
Aug. 7–Aug. 30	Virgo
Aug. 31–Sep. 24	Libra
Sep. 25–Oct. 18	Scorpio
Oct. 19–Nov. 12	Sagittarius
Nov. 13–Dec. 7	Capricorn
Dec. 8–Dec. 31	Aquarius

1993

Jan. 1–Jan. 2	Aquarius
Jan. 3–Feb. 1	Pisces
Feb. 2–Jun. 5	Aries
Jun. 6–Jul. 5	Taurus
Jul. 6–Jul. 31	Gemini
Aug. 1–Aug. 26	Cancer
Aug. 27–Sep. 20	Leo
Sep. 21–Oct. 15	Virgo
Oct. 16–Nov. 8	Libra
Nov. 9–Dec. 1	Scorpio
Dec. 2–Dec. 25	Sagittarius
Dec. 26–Dec. 31	Capricorn

402 LINDA GOODMAN'S RELATIONSHIP SIGNS

1994

Jan. 1–Jan. 18	Capricorn
Jan. 19–Feb. 11	Aquarius
Feb. 12–Mar. 7	Pisces
Mar. 8–Mar. 31	Aries
Apr. 1–Apr. 25	Taurus
Apr. 26–May 20	Gemini
May 21–Jun. 14	Cancer
Jun. 15–Jul. 10	Leo
Jul. 11–Aug. 6	Virgo
Aug. 7–Sep. 6	Libra
Sep. 7–Dec. 31	Scorpio

1995

Jan. 1–Jan. 6	Scorpio
Jan. 7–Feb. 3	Sagittarius
Feb. 4–Mar. 1	Capricorn
Mar. 2–Mar. 27	Aquarius
Mar. 28–Apr. 21	Pisces
Apr. 22–May 15	Aries
May 16–Jun. 9	Taurus
Jun. 10–Jul. 4	Gemini
Jul. 5–Jul. 28	Cancer
Jul. 29–Aug. 22	Leo
Aug. 23–Sep. 15	Virgo
Sep. 16–Oct. 9	Libra
Oct. 10–Nov. 2	Scorpio
Nov. 3–Nov. 26	Sagittarius
Nov. 27–Dec. 20	Capricorn
Dec. 21–Dec. 31	Aquarius

1996

Jan. 1–Jan. 14	Aquarius
Jan. 15–Feb. 8	Pisces
Feb. 9–Mar. 5	Aries
Mar. 6–Apr. 2	Taurus
Apr. 3–Aug. 6	Gemini
Aug. 7–Sep. 6	Cancer
Sep. 7–Oct. 3	Leo
Oct. 4–Oct. 28	Virgo
Oct. 29–Nov. 22	Libra
Nov. 23–Dec. 16	Scorpio
Dec. 17–Dec. 31	Sagittarius

1997

Jan. 1–Jan. 9	Sagittarius
Jan. 10–Feb. 2	Capricorn
Feb. 3–Feb. 26	Aquarius
Feb. 27–Mar. 22	Pisces
Mar. 23–Apr. 15	Aries
Apr. 16–May 9	Taurus
May 10–Jun. 3	Gemini
Jun. 4–Jun. 27	Cancer
Jun. 28–Jul. 22	Leo
Jul. 23–Aug. 16	Virgo
Aug. 17–Sep. 11	Libra
Sep. 12–Oct. 7	Scorpio
Oct. 8–Nov. 4	Sagittarius
Nov. 5–Dec. 11	Capricorn
Dec. 12–Dec. 31	Aquarius

1998

Jan. 1–Jan. 8	Aquarius
Jan. 9–Mar. 3	Capricorn
Mar. 4–Apr. 5	Aquarius
Apr. 6–May 2	Pisces
May 3–May 28	Aries
May 29–Jun. 23	Taurus
Jun. 24–Jul. 18	Gemini
Jul. 19–Aug. 12	Cancer
Aug. 13–Sep. 5	Leo
Sep. 6–Sep. 29	Virgo
Sep. 30–Oct. 23	Libra
Oct. 24–Nov. 16	Scorpio
Nov. 17–Dec. 10	Sagittarius
Dec. 11–Dec. 31	Capricorn

1999

Jan. 1–Jan. 3	Capricorn
Jan. 4–Jan. 27	Aquarius
Jan. 28–Feb. 20	Pisces
Feb. 21–Mar. 17	Aries
Mar. 18–Apr. 11	Taurus
Apr. 12–May 7	Gemini
May 8–Jun. 4	Cancer
Jun. 5–Jul. 11	Leo
Jul. 12–Aug. 14	Virgo
Aug. 15–Oct. 6	Leo
Oct. 7–Nov. 8	Virgo
Nov. 9–Dec. 4	Libra
Dec. 5–Dec. 30	Scorpio
Dec. 31	Sagittarius

2000

Jan. 1–Jan. 23	Sagittarius
Jan. 24–Feb. 17	Capricorn
Feb. 18–Mar. 12	Aquarius
Mar. 13–Apr. 5	Pisces
Apr. 6–Apr. 30	Aries
May 1–May 24	Taurus
May 25–Jun. 17	Gemini
Jun. 18–Jul. 12	Cancer
Jul. 13–Aug. 5	Leo
Aug. 6–Aug. 30	Virgo
Aug. 31–Sep. 23	Libra
Sep. 24–Oct. 18	Scorpio
Oct. 19–Nov. 12	Sagittarius
Nov. 13–Dec. 7	Capricorn
Dec. 8–Dec. 31	Aquarius

★

★ 6 ★

The Mars Tables

How to Find the Planet Mars at the Time of Your Birth

Locate the year of your birth. Then find the range of dates that includes your birthdate. The sign to the right of this range is your Mars Sign.

1900	
Jan. 1–Jan. 22	Capricorn
Jan. 23–Mar. 1	Aquarius
Mar. 2–Apr. 7	Pisces
Apr. 8–May 16	Aries
May 17–Jun. 26	Taurus
Jun. 27–Aug. 9	Gemini
Aug. 10–Sep. 26	Cancer
Sep. 27–Nov. 22	Leo
Nov. 23–Dec. 31	Virgo

1901	
Jan. 1–Mar. 1	Virgo
Mar. 2–May 10	Leo
May 11–Jul. 13	Virgo
Jul. 14–Aug. 31	Libra
Sep. 1–Oct. 14	Scorpio
Oct. 15–Nov. 23	Sagittarius
Nov. 24–Dec. 31	Capricorn

1902

Jan. 1	Capricorn
Jan. 2–Feb. 8	Aquarius
Feb. 9–Mar. 17	Pisces
Mar. 18–Apr. 26	Aries
Apr. 27–Jun. 6	Taurus
Jun. 7–Jul. 20	Gemini
Jul. 21–Sep. 4	Cancer
Sep. 5–Oct. 23	Leo
Oct. 24–Dec. 19	Virgo
Dec. 20–Dec. 31	Libra

1903

Jan. 1–Apr. 19	Libra
Apr. 20–May 30	Virgo
May 31–Aug. 6	Libra
Aug. 7–Sep. 22	Scorpio
Sep. 23–Nov. 2	Sagittarius
Nov. 3–Dec. 11	Capricorn
Dec. 12–Dec. 31	Aquarius

1904

Jan. 1–Jan. 19	Aquarius
Jan. 20–Feb. 26	Pisces
Feb. 27–Apr. 6	Aries
Apr. 7–May 17	Taurus
May 18–Jun. 30	Gemini
Jul. 1–Aug. 14	Cancer
Aug. 15–Oct. 1	Leo
Oct. 2–Nov. 19	Virgo
Nov. 20–Dec. 31	Libra

1905

Jan. 1–Jan. 13	Libra
Jan. 14–Aug. 21	Scorpio
Aug. 22–Oct. 7	Sagittarius
Oct. 8–Nov. 17	Capricorn
Nov. 18–Dec. 27	Aquarius
Dec. 28–Dec. 31	Pisces

1906

Jan. 1–Feb. 4	Pisces
Feb. 5–Mar. 16	Aries
Mar. 17–Apr. 28	Taurus
Apr. 29–Jun. 11	Gemini
Jun. 12–Jul. 27	Cancer
Jul. 28–Sep. 12	Leo
Sep. 13–Oct. 29	Virgo
Oct. 30–Dec. 16	Libra
Dec. 17–Dec. 31	Scorpio

1907

Jan. 1–Feb. 4	Scorpio
Feb. 5–Apr. 1	Sagittarius
Apr. 2–Oct. 13	Capricorn
Oct. 14–Nov. 28	Aquarius
Nov. 29–Dec. 31	Pisces

1908

Jan. 1–Jan. 10	Pisces
Jan. 11–Feb. 22	Aries
Feb. 23–Apr. 6	Taurus
Apr. 7–May 22	Gemini
May 23–Jul. 7	Cancer
Jul. 8–Aug. 23	Leo
Aug. 24–Oct. 9	Virgo
Oct. 10–Nov. 25	Libra
Nov. 26–Dec. 31	Scorpio

1909

Jan. 1–Jan. 9	Scorpio
Jan. 10–Feb. 23	Sagittarius
Feb. 24–Apr. 9	Capricorn
Apr. 10–May 25	Aquarius
May 26–Jul. 20	Pisces
Jul. 21–Sep. 26	Aries
Sep. 27–Nov. 20	Pisces
Nov. 21–Dec. 31	Aries

1910

Jan. 1–Feb. 22	Aries
Feb. 23–Mar. 13	Taurus
Mar. 14–May 1	Gemini
May 2–Jun. 18	Cancer
Jun. 19–Aug. 5	Leo
Aug. 6–Sep. 21	Virgo
Sep. 22–Nov. 6	Libra
Nov. 7–Dec. 19	Scorpio
Dec. 20–Dec. 31	Sagittarius

1911

Jan. 1–Jan. 31	Sagittarius
Feb. 1–Mar. 13	Capricorn
Mar. 14–Apr. 22	Aquarius
Apr. 23–Jun. 2	Pisces
Jun. 3–Jul. 15	Aries
Jul. 16–Sep. 5	Taurus
Sep. 6–Nov. 29	Gemini
Nov. 30–Dec. 31	Taurus

1912

Jan. 1–Jan. 30	Taurus
Jan. 31–Apr. 4	Gemini
Apr. 5–May 27	Cancer
May 28–Jul. 16	Leo
Jul. 17–Sep. 2	Virgo
Sep. 3–Oct. 17	Libra
Oct. 18–Nov. 29	Scorpio
Nov. 30–Dec. 31	Sagittarius

1913

Jan. 1–Jan. 10	Sagittarius
Jan. 11–Feb. 18	Capricorn
Feb. 19–Mar. 29	Aquarius
Mar. 30–May 7	Pisces
May 8–Jun. 16	Aries
Jun. 17–Jul. 28	Taurus
Jul. 29–Sep. 15	Gemini
Sep. 16–Dec. 31	Cancer

1914

Jan. 1–May 1	Cancer
May 2–Jun. 25	Leo
Jun. 26–Aug. 14	Virgo
Aug. 15–Sep. 28	Libra
Sep. 29–Nov. 10	Scorpio
Nov. 11–Dec. 21	Sagittarius
Dec. 22–Dec. 31	Capricorn

1915

Jan. 1–Jan. 29	Capricorn
Jan. 30–Mar. 9	Aquarius
Mar. 10–Apr. 16	Pisces
Apr. 17–May 25	Aries
May 26–Jul. 5	Taurus
Jul. 6–Aug. 18	Gemini
Aug. 19–Oct. 7	Cancer
Oct. 8–Dec. 31	Leo

1916

Jan. 1–May 28	Leo
May 29–Jul. 22	Virgo
Jul. 23–Sep. 8	Libra
Sep. 9–Oct. 21	Scorpio
Oct. 22–Dec. 1	Sagittarius
Dec. 2–Dec. 31	Capricorn

1917

Jan. 1–Jan. 9	Capricorn
Jan. 10–Feb. 16	Aquarius
Feb. 17–Mar. 26	Pisces
Mar. 27–May 4	Aries
May 5–Jun. 14	Taurus
Jun. 15–Jul. 27	Gemini
Jul. 28–Sep. 11	Cancer
Sep. 12–Nov. 1	Leo
Nov. 2–Dec. 31	Virgo

1918

Jan. 1–Jan. 10	Virgo
Jan. 11–Feb. 25	Libra
Feb. 26–Jun. 23	Virgo
Jun. 24–Aug. 16	Libra
Aug. 17–Sep. 30	Scorpio
Oct. 1–Nov. 10	Sagittarius
Nov. 11–Dec. 19	Capricorn
Dec. 20–Dec. 31	Aquarius

1919

Jan. 1–Jan. 26	Aquarius
Jan. 27–Mar. 6	Pisces
Mar. 7–Apr. 14	Aries
Apr. 15–May 25	Taurus
May 26–Jul. 8	Gemini
Jul. 9–Aug. 22	Cancer
Aug. 23–Oct. 9	Leo
Oct. 10–Nov. 29	Virgo
Nov. 30–Dec. 31	Libra

1920

Jan. 1–Jan. 31	Libra
Feb. 1–Apr. 23	Scorpio
Apr. 24–Jul. 10	Libra
Jul. 11–Sep. 4	Scorpio
Sep. 5–Oct. 18	Sagittarius
Oct. 19–Nov. 27	Capricorn
Nov. 28–Dec. 31	Aquarius

1921

Jan. 1–Jan. 4	Aquarius
Jan. 5–Feb. 12	Pisces
Feb. 13–Mar. 24	Aries
Mar. 25–May 5	Taurus
May 6–Jun. 10	Gemini
Jun. 11–Aug. 2	Cancer
Aug. 3–Sep. 18	Leo
Sep. 19–Nov. 6	Virgo
Nov. 7–Dec. 25	Libra
Dec. 26–Dec. 31	Scorpio

1922

Jan. 1–Feb. 18	Scorpio
Feb. 19–Sep. 13	Sagittarius
Sep. 14–Oct. 30	Capricorn
Oct. 31–Dec. 11	Aquarius
Dec. 12–Dec. 31	Pisces

1923

Jan. 1–Jan. 20	Pisces
Jan. 21–Mar. 3	Aries
Mar. 4–Apr. 15	Taurus
Apr. 16–May 30	Gemini
May 31–Jul. 15	Cancer
Jul. 16–Aug. 31	Leo
Sep. 1–Oct. 17	Virgo
Oct. 18–Dec. 3	Libra
Dec. 4–Dec. 31	Scorpio

1924

Jan. 1–Feb. 19	Scorpio
Feb. 20–Mar. 6	Sagittarius
Mar. 7–Apr. 24	Capricorn
Apr. 25–Jun. 24	Aquarius
Jun. 25–Aug. 24	Pisces
Aug. 25–Oct. 19	Aquarius
Oct. 20–Dec. 18	Pisces
Dec. 19–Dec. 31	Aries

1925

Jan. 1–Feb. 4	Aries
Feb. 5–Mar. 23	Taurus
Mar. 24–May 9	Gemini
May 10–Jun. 25	Cancer
Jun. 26–Aug. 12	Leo
Aug. 13–Sep. 28	Virgo
Sep. 29–Nov. 13	Libra
Nov. 14–Dec. 27	Scorpio
Dec. 28–Dec. 31	Sagittarius

1926

Jan. 1–Feb. 8	Sagittarius
Feb. 9–Mar. 22	Capricorn
Mar. 23–May 3	Aquarius
May 4–Jun. 14	Pisces
Jun. 15–Jul. 31	Aries
Aug. 1–Dec. 31	Taurus

1927

Jan. 1–Feb. 21	Taurus
Feb. 22–Apr. 16	Gemini
Apr. 17–Jun. 5	Cancer
Jun. 6–Jul. 24	Leo
Jul. 25–Sep. 10	Virgo
Sep. 11–Oct. 25	Libra
Oct. 26–Dec. 7	Scorpio
Dec. 8–Dec. 31	Sagittarius

1928

Jan. 1–Jan. 18	Sagittarius
Jan. 19–Feb. 27	Capricorn
Feb. 28–Apr. 7	Aquarius
Apr. 8–May 16	Pisces
May 17–Jun. 25	Aries
Jun. 26–Aug. 8	Taurus
Aug. 9–Oct. 2	Gemini
Oct. 3–Dec. 19	Cancer
Dec. 20–Dec. 31	Gemini

1929

Jan. 1–Mar. 10	Gemini
Mar. 11–May 12	Cancer
May 13–Jul. 3	Leo
Jul. 4–Aug. 21	Virgo
Aug. 22–Oct. 5	Libra
Oct. 6–Nov. 18	Scorpio
Nov. 19–Dec. 28	Sagittarius
Dec. 29–Dec. 31	Capricorn

1930

Jan. 1–Feb. 6	Capricorn
Feb. 7–Mar. 16	Aquarius
Mar. 17–Apr. 24	Pisces
Apr. 25–Jun. 2	Aries
Jun. 3–Jul. 14	Taurus
Jul. 15–Aug. 27	Gemini
Aug. 28–Oct. 20	Cancer
Oct. 21–Dec. 31	Leo

1931

Jan. 1–Feb. 15	Leo
Feb. 16–Mar. 29	Cancer
Mar. 30–Jun. 9	Leo
Jun. 10–Jul. 31	Virgo
Aug. 1–Sep. 16	Libra
Sep. 17–Oct. 29	Scorpio
Oct. 30–Dec. 9	Sagittarius
Dec. 10–Dec. 31	Capricorn

1932

Jan. 1–Jan. 17	Capricorn
Jan. 18–Feb. 24	Aquarius
Feb. 25–Apr. 2	Pisces
Apr. 3–May 11	Aries
May 12–Jun. 21	Taurus
Jun. 22–Aug. 3	Gemini
Aug. 4–Sep. 19	Cancer
Sep. 20–Nov. 12	Leo
Nov. 13–Dec. 31	Virgo

1933

Jan. 1–Jul. 5	Virgo
Jul. 6–Aug. 25	Libra
Aug. 26–Oct. 8	Scorpio
Oct. 9–Nov. 18	Sagittarius
Nov. 19–Dec. 27	Capricorn
Dec. 28–Dec. 31	Aquarius

1934

Jan. 1–Feb. 3	Aquarius
Feb. 4–Mar. 13	Pisces
Mar. 14–Apr. 21	Aries
Apr. 22–Jun. 1	Taurus
Jun. 2–Jul. 14	Gemini
Jul. 15–Aug. 29	Cancer
Aug. 30–Oct. 17	Leo
Oct. 18–Dec. 10	Virgo
Dec. 11–Dec. 31	Libra

1935

Jan. 1–Jul. 28	Libra
Jul. 29–Sep. 15	Scorpio
Sep. 16–Oct. 27	Sagittarius
Oct. 28–Dec. 6	Capricorn
Dec. 7–Dec. 31	Aquarius

1936

Jan. 1–Jan. 13	Aquarius
Jan. 14–Feb. 21	Pisces
Feb. 22–Mar. 31	Aries
Apr. 1–May 12	Taurus
May 13–Jun. 24	Gemini
Jun. 25–Aug. 9	Cancer
Aug. 10–Sep. 25	Leo
Sep. 26–Nov. 13	Virgo
Nov. 14–Dec. 31	Libra

1937

Jan. 1–Mar. 12	Scorpio
Mar. 13–May 13	Sagittarius
May 14–Aug. 7	Scorpio
Aug. 8–Sep. 29	Sagittarius
Sep. 30–Nov. 10	Capricorn
Nov. 11–Dec. 20	Aquarius
Dec. 21–Dec. 31	Pisces

1938

Jan. 1–Jan. 29	Pisces
Jan. 30–Mar. 11	Aries
Mar. 12–Apr. 22	Taurus
Apr. 23–Jun. 6	Gemini
Jun. 7–Jul. 21	Cancer
Jul. 22–Sep. 6	Leo
Sep. 7–Oct. 24	Virgo
Oct. 25–Dec. 10	Libra
Dec. 11–Dec. 31	Scorpio

1939

Jan. 1–Jan. 28	Scorpio
Jan. 29–Mar. 30	Sagittarius
Mar. 31–May 23	Capricorn
May 24–Jul. 20	Aquarius
Jul. 21–Sep. 23	Capricorn
Sep. 24–Nov. 18	Aquarius
Nov. 19–Dec. 31	Pisces

1940

Jan. 1–Jan. 2	Pisces
Jan. 3–Feb. 16	Aries
Feb. 17–Mar. 31	Taurus
Apr. 1–May 16	Gemini
May 17–Jul. 2	Cancer
Jul. 3–Aug. 18	Leo
Aug. 19–Oct. 4	Virgo
Oct. 5–Nov. 19	Libra
Nov. 20–Dec. 31	Scorpio

1941

Jan. 1–Jan. 3	Scorpio
Jan. 4–Feb. 16	Sagittarius
Feb. 17–Apr. 1	Capricorn
Apr. 2–May 15	Aquarius
May 16–Jul. 1	Pisces
Jul. 2–Dec. 31	Aries

1942

Jan. 1–Jan. 10	Aries
Jan. 11–Mar. 6	Taurus
Mar. 7–Apr. 25	Gemini
Apr. 26–Jun. 13	Cancer
Jun. 14–Jul. 31	Leo
Aug. 1–Sep. 16	Virgo
Sep. 17–Oct. 31	Libra
Nov. 1–Dec. 14	Scorpio
Dec. 15–Dec. 31	Sagittarius

1943

Jan. 1–Jan. 25	Sagittarius
Jan. 26–Mar. 7	Capricorn
Mar. 8–Apr. 16	Aquarius
Apr. 17–May 26	Pisces
May 27–Jun. 6	Aries
Jun. 7–Aug. 22	Taurus
Aug. 23–Dec. 31	Gemini

1944

Jan. 1–Mar. 27	Gemini
Mar. 28–May 21	Cancer
May 22–Jul. 11	Leo
Jul. 12–Aug. 28	Virgo
Aug. 29–Oct. 12	Libra
Oct. 13–Nov. 24	Scorpio
Nov. 25–Dec. 31	Sagittarius

1945

Jan. 1–Jan. 4	Sagittarius
Jan. 5–Feb. 13	Capricorn
Feb. 14–Mar. 24	Aquarius
Mar. 25–May 1	Pisces
May 2–Jun. 10	Aries
Jun. 11–Jul. 22	Taurus
Jul. 23–Sep. 6	Gemini
Sep. 7–Nov. 10	Cancer
Nov. 11–Dec. 25	Leo
Dec. 26–Dec. 31	Cancer

1946

Jan. 1–Apr. 21	Cancer
Apr. 22–Jun. 19	Leo
Jun. 20–Aug. 8	Virgo
Aug. 9–Sep. 23	Libra
Sep. 24–Nov. 5	Scorpio
Nov. 6–Dec. 16	Sagittarius
Dec. 17–Dec. 31	Capricorn

1947

Jan. 1–Jan. 24	Capricorn
Jan. 25–Mar. 3	Aquarius
Mar. 4–Apr. 10	Pisces
Apr. 11–May 20	Aries
May 21–Jun. 30	Taurus
Jul. 1–Aug. 12	Gemini
Aug. 13–Sep. 30	Cancer
Oct. 1–Nov. 30	Leo
Dec. 1–Dec. 31	Virgo

1948

Jan. 1–Feb. 11	Virgo
Feb. 12–May 17	Leo
May 18–Jul. 16	Virgo
Jul. 17–Sep. 2	Libra
Sep. 3–Oct. 16	Scorpio
Oct. 17–Nov. 25	Sagittarius
Nov. 26–Dec. 31	Capricorn

1949

Jan. 1–Jan. 3	Capricorn
Jan. 4–Feb. 10	Aquarius
Feb. 11–Mar. 20	Pisces
Mar. 21–Apr. 29	Aries
Apr. 30–Jun. 9	Taurus
Jun. 10–Jul. 22	Gemini
Jul. 23–Sep. 6	Cancer
Sep. 7–Oct. 26	Leo
Oct. 27–Dec. 25	Virgo
Dec. 26–Dec. 31	Libra

1950

Jan. 1–Mar. 27	Libra
Mar. 28–Jun. 10	Virgo
Jun. 11–Aug. 9	Libra
Aug. 10–Sep. 24	Scorpio
Sep. 25–Nov. 5	Sagittarius
Nov. 6–Dec. 14	Capricorn
Dec. 15–Dec. 31	Aquarius

1951

Jan. 1–Jan. 21	Aquarius
Jan. 22–Feb. 28	Pisces
Mar. 1–Apr. 9	Aries
Apr. 10–May 20	Taurus
May 21–Jul. 2	Gemini
Jul. 3–Aug. 17	Cancer
Aug. 18–Oct. 3	Leo
Oct. 4–Nov. 23	Virgo
Nov. 24–Dec. 31	Libra

1952

Jan. 1–Jan. 19	Libra
Jan. 20–Aug. 26	Scorpio
Aug. 27–Oct. 11	Sagittarius
Oct. 12–Nov. 20	Capricorn
Nov. 21–Dec. 29	Aquarius
Dec. 30–Dec. 31	Pisces

1953

Jan. 1–Feb. 7	Pisces
Feb. 8–Mar. 19	Aries
Mar. 20–Apr. 30	Taurus
May 1–Jun. 13	Gemini
Jun. 14–Jul. 28	Cancer
Jul. 29–Sep. 13	Leo
Sep. 14–Oct. 31	Virgo
Nov. 1–Dec. 19	Libra
Dec. 20–Dec. 31	Scorpio

1954

Jan. 1–Feb. 8	Scorpio
Feb. 9–Apr. 11	Sagittarius
Apr. 12–Jul. 2	Capricorn
Jul. 3–Aug. 23	Sagittarius
Aug. 24–Oct. 20	Capricorn
Oct. 21–Dec. 3	Aquarius
Dec. 4–Dec. 31	Pisces

1955

Jan. 1–Jan. 14	Pisces
Jan. 15–Feb. 25	Aries
Feb. 26–Apr. 9	Taurus
Apr. 10–May 25	Gemini
May 26–Jul. 10	Cancer
Jul. 11–Aug. 26	Leo
Aug. 27–Oct. 12	Virgo
Oct. 13–Nov. 28	Libra
Nov. 29–Dec. 31	Scorpio

1956

Jan. 1–Jan. 13	Scorpio
Jan. 14–Feb. 27	Sagittarius
Feb. 28–Apr. 13	Capricorn
Apr. 14–Jun. 2	Aquarius
Jun. 3–Dec. 5	Pisces
Dec. 6–Dec. 31	Aries

1957

Jan. 1–Feb. 27	Aries
Feb. 28–Mar. 16	Taurus
Mar. 17–May 3	Gemini
May 4–Jun. 20	Cancer
Jun. 21–Aug. 7	Leo
Aug. 8–Sep. 23	Virgo
Sep. 24–Nov. 7	Libra
Nov. 8–Dec. 22	Scorpio
Dec. 23–Dec. 31	Sagittarius

1958

Jan. 1–Feb. 2	Sagittarius
Feb. 3–Mar. 16	Capricorn
Mar. 17–Apr. 26	Aquarius
Apr. 27–Jun. 6	Pisces
Jun. 7–Jul. 20	Aries
Jul. 21–Sep. 20	Taurus
Sep. 21–Oct. 28	Gemini
Oct. 29–Dec. 31	Taurus

1959

Jan. 1–Feb. 9	Taurus
Feb. 10–Apr. 9	Gemini
Apr. 10–May 31	Cancer
Jun. 1–Jul. 19	Leo
Jul. 20–Sep. 4	Virgo
Sep. 5–Oct. 20	Libra
Oct. 21–Dec. 2	Scorpio
Dec. 3–Dec. 31	Sagittarius

1960

Jan. 1–Jan. 13	Sagittarius
Jan. 14–Feb. 22	Capricorn
Feb. 23–Apr. 1	Aquarius
Apr. 2–May 10	Pisces
May 11–Jun. 19	Aries
Jun. 20–Aug. 1	Taurus
Aug. 2–Sep. 20	Gemini
Sep. 21–Dec. 31	Cancer

1961

Jan. 1–May 5	Cancer
May 6–Jun. 27	Leo
Jun. 28–Aug. 16	Virgo
Aug. 17–Sep. 30	Libra
Oct. 1–Nov. 12	Scorpio
Nov. 13–Dec. 23	Sagittarius
Dec. 24–Dec. 31	Capricorn

1962

Jan. 1–Jan. 31	Capricorn
Feb. 1–Mar. 11	Aquarius
Mar. 12–Apr. 18	Pisces
Apr. 19–May 27	Aries
May 28–Jul. 8	Taurus
Jul. 9–Aug. 21	Gemini
Aug. 22–Oct. 10	Cancer
Oct. 11–Dec. 31	Leo

1963

Jan. 1–Jun. 2	Leo
Jun. 3–Jul. 26	Virgo
Jul. 27–Sep. 11	Libra
Sep. 12–Oct. 24	Scorpio
Oct. 25–Dec. 4	Sagittarius
Dec. 5–Dec. 31	Capricorn

1964

Jan. 1–Jan. 12	Capricorn
Jan. 13–Feb. 19	Aquarius
Feb. 20–Mar. 28	Pisces
Mar. 29–May 6	Aries
May 7–Jun. 16	Taurus
Jun. 17–Jul. 29	Gemini
Jul. 30–Sep. 14	Cancer
Sep. 15–Nov. 5	Leo
Nov. 6–Dec. 31	Virgo

1965

Jan. 1–Jun. 28	Virgo
Jun. 29–Aug. 19	Libra
Aug. 20–Oct. 3	Scorpio
Oct. 4–Nov. 13	Sagittarius
Nov. 14–Dec. 22	Capricorn
Dec. 23–Dec. 31	Aquarius

1966

Jan. 1–Jan. 29	Aquarius
Jan. 30–Mar. 8	Pisces
Mar. 9–Apr. 16	Aries
Apr. 17–May 27	Taurus
May 28–Jul. 10	Gemini
Jul. 11–Aug. 24	Cancer
Aug. 25–Oct. 11	Leo
Oct. 12–Dec. 3	Virgo
Dec. 4–Dec. 31	Libra

1967

Jan. 1–Feb. 11	Libra
Feb. 12–Mar. 31	Scorpio
Apr. 1–Jul. 18	Libra
Jul. 19–Sep. 9	Scorpio
Sep. 10–Oct. 22	Sagittarius
Oct. 23–Nov. 30	Capricorn
Dec. 1–Dec. 31	Aquarius

1968

Jan. 1–Jan. 8	Aquarius
Jan. 9–Feb. 16	Pisces
Feb. 17–Mar. 26	Aries
Mar. 27–May 7	Taurus
May 8–Jun. 20	Gemini
Jun. 21–Aug. 4	Cancer
Aug. 5–Sep. 20	Leo
Sep. 21–Oct. 8	Virgo
Oct. 9–Dec. 28	Libra
Dec. 29–Dec. 31	Scorpio

1969

Jan. 1–Feb. 24	Scorpio
Feb. 25–Sep. 20	Sagittarius
Sep. 21–Nov. 3	Capricorn
Nov. 4–Dec. 13	Aquarius
Dec. 14–Dec. 31	Pisces

1970

Jan. 1–Jan. 23	Pisces
Jan. 24–Mar. 6	Aries
Mar. 7–Apr. 17	Taurus
Apr. 18–Jun. 1	Gemini
Jun. 2–Jul. 17	Cancer
Jul. 18–Sep. 2	Leo
Sep. 3–Oct. 19	Virgo
Oct. 20–Dec. 5	Libra
Dec. 6–Dec. 31	Scorpio

1971

Jan. 1–Jan. 23	Scorpio
Jan. 24–Mar. 12	Sagittarius
Mar. 13–May 3	Capricorn
May 4–Nov. 6	Aquarius
Nov. 7–Dec. 26	Pisces
Dec. 27–Dec. 31	Aries

1972

Jan. 1–Feb. 10	Aries
Feb. 11–Mar. 27	Taurus
Mar. 28–May 12	Gemini
May 13–Jun. 28	Cancer
Jun. 29–Aug. 15	Leo
Aug. 16–Sep. 30	Virgo
Oct. 1–Nov. 15	Libra
Nov. 16–Dec. 30	Scorpio
Dec. 31	Sagittarius

1973

Jan. 1–Feb. 12	Sagittarius
Feb. 13–Mar. 26	Capricorn
Mar. 27–May 8	Aquarius
May 9–Jun. 20	Pisces
Jun. 21–Aug. 12	Aries
Aug. 13–Oct. 29	Taurus
Oct. 30–Dec. 24	Aries
Dec. 25–Dec. 31	Taurus

1974

Jan. 1–Feb. 27	Taurus
Feb. 28–Apr. 20	Gemini
Apr. 21–Jun. 9	Cancer
Jun. 10–Jul. 27	Leo
Jul. 28–Sep. 12	Virgo
Sep. 13–Oct. 28	Libra
Oct. 29–Dec. 10	Scorpio
Dec. 11–Dec. 31	Sagittarius

1975

Jan. 1–Jan. 21	Sagittarius
Jan. 22–Mar. 3	Capricorn
Mar. 4–Apr. 11	Aquarius
Apr. 12–May 21	Pisces
May 22–Jul. 1	Aries
Jul. 2–Aug. 14	Taurus
Aug. 15–Oct. 17	Gemini
Oct. 18–Nov. 25	Cancer
Nov. 26–Dec. 31	Gemini

1976

Jan. 1–Mar. 18	Gemini
Mar. 19–May 16	Cancer
May 17–Jul. 6	Leo
Jul. 7–Aug. 24	Virgo
Aug. 25–Oct. 8	Libra
Oct. 9–Nov. 20	Scorpio
Nov. 21–Dec. 31	Sagittarius

1977

Jan. 1–Jan. 2	Sagittarius
Jan. 3–Feb. 9	Capricorn
Feb. 10–Mar. 20	Aquarius
Mar. 21–Apr. 27	Pisces
Apr. 28–Jun. 6	Aries
Jun. 7–Jul. 17	Taurus
Jul. 18–Sep. 1	Gemini
Sep. 2–Oct. 26	Cancer
Oct. 27–Dec. 31	Leo

1978

Jan. 1–Jan. 26	Leo
Jan. 27–Apr. 10	Cancer
Apr. 11–Jun. 14	Leo
Jun. 15–Aug. 4	Virgo
Aug. 5–Sep. 19	Libra
Sep. 20–Nov. 2	Scorpio
Nov. 3–Dec. 12	Sagittarius
Dec. 13–Dec. 31	Capricorn

1979

Jan. 1–Jan. 20	Capricorn
Jan. 21–Feb. 27	Aquarius
Feb. 28–Apr. 7	Pisces
Apr. 8–May 16	Aries
May 17–Jun. 26	Taurus
Jun. 27–Aug. 8	Gemini
Aug. 9–Sep. 24	Cancer
Sep. 25–Nov. 19	Leo
Nov. 20–Dec. 31	Virgo

1980

Jan. 1–Mar. 11	Virgo
Mar. 12–May 4	Libra
May 5–Jul. 10	Scorpio
Jul. 11–Aug. 29	Sagittarius
Aug. 30–Oct. 12	Capricorn
Oct. 13–Nov. 22	Aquarius
Nov. 23–Dec. 31	Pisces

1981

Jan. 1–Feb. 9	Aquarius
Feb. 10–Mar. 17	Pisces
Mar. 18–Apr. 25	Aries
Apr. 26–Jun. 6	Taurus
Jun. 7–Jul. 19	Gemini
Jul. 20–Sep. 2	Cancer
Sep. 3–Oct. 21	Leo
Oct. 22–Dec. 16	Virgo
Dec. 17–Dec. 31	Libra

1982

Jan. 1–Aug. 3	Libra
Aug. 4–Sep. 20	Scorpio
Sep. 21–Nov. 1	Sagittarius
Nov. 2–Dec. 12	Capricorn
Dec. 13–Dec. 31	Aquarius

1983

Jan. 1–Jan. 17	Aquarius
Jan. 18–Feb. 22	Pisces
Feb. 23–Apr. 5	Aries
Apr. 6–May 16	Taurus
May 17–Jun. 29	Gemini
Jun. 30–Aug. 13	Cancer
Aug. 14–Sep. 29	Leo
Sep. 30–Oct. 18	Virgo
Oct. 19–Dec. 31	Libra

1984

Jan. 1–Jan. 12	Libra
Jan. 13–Aug. 17	Scorpio
Aug. 18–Oct. 5	Sagittarius
Oct. 6–Nov. 13	Capricorn
Nov. 14–Dec. 25	Aquarius
Dec. 26–Dec. 31	Pisces

1985

Jan. 1–Feb. 2	Pisces
Feb. 3–Mar. 15	Aries
Mar. 16–Apr. 26	Taurus
Apr. 27–Jun. 10	Gemini
Jun. 11–Jul. 26	Cancer
Jul. 27–Aug. 10	Leo
Aug. 11–Oct. 27	Virgo
Oct. 28–Dec. 14	Libra
Dec. 15–Dec. 31	Scorpio

1986

Jan. 1–Feb. 2	Scorpio
Feb. 3–Mar. 28	Sagittarius
Mar. 29–Oct. 9	Capricorn
Oct. 10–Nov. 26	Aquarius
Nov. 27–Dec. 31	Pisces

1987

Jan. 1–Jan. 8	Pisces
Jan. 9–Feb. 20	Aries
Feb. 21–Apr. 5	Taurus
Apr. 6–May 21	Gemini
May 22–Jul. 6	Cancer
Jul. 7–Aug. 22	Leo
Aug. 23–Oct. 8	Virgo
Oct. 9–Nov. 24	Libra
Nov. 25–Dec. 31	Scorpio

1988

Jan. 1–Jan. 8	Scorpio
Jan. 9–Feb. 22	Sagittarius
Feb. 23–Apr. 6	Capricorn
Apr. 7–May 23	Virgo
May 24–Jul. 13	Pisces
Jul. 14–Dec. 31	Aries

1989

Jan. 1–Jan. 19	Aries
Jan. 20–Mar. 11	Taurus
Mar. 12–Apr. 29	Gemini
Apr. 30–Jun. 16	Cancer
Jun. 17–Aug. 3	Leo
Aug. 4–Sep. 19	Virgo
Sep. 20–Nov. 4	Libra
Nov. 5–Dec. 18	Scorpio
Dec. 19–Dec. 31	Sagittarius

1990

Jan. 1–Jan. 29	Sagittarius
Jan. 30–Mar. 11	Capricorn
Mar. 12–Apr. 20	Aquarius
Apr. 21–May 31	Pisces
Jun. 1–Jul. 12	Aries
Jul. 13–Aug. 31	Taurus
Sep. 1–Dec. 14	Gemini
Dec. 15–Dec. 31	Taurus

1991

Jan. 1–Jan. 21	Gemini
Jan. 22–Apr. 3	Cancer
Apr. 4–May 26	Leo
May 27–Jul. 15	Virgo
Jul. 16–Sep. 1	Libra
Sep. 2–Oct. 15	Scorpio
Oct. 16–Nov. 29	Sagittarius
Nov. 30–Dec. 31	Capricorn

1992

Jan. 1–Jan. 8	Sagittarius
Jan. 9–Feb. 17	Capricorn
Feb. 18–Mar. 27	Aquarius
Mar. 28–May 4	Pisces
May 5–Jun. 13	Aries
Jun. 14–Jul. 25	Taurus
Jul. 26–Sep. 12	Gemini
Sep. 13–Dec. 31	Cancer

1993

Jan. 1–Apr. 26	Cancer
Apr. 27–Jun. 22	Leo
Jun. 23–Aug. 11	Virgo
Aug. 12–Sep. 26	Libra
Sep. 27–Nov. 8	Scorpio
Nov. 9–Dec. 20	Sagittarius
Dec. 21–Dec. 31	Capricorn

1994

Jan. 1–Mar. 6	Aquarius
Mar. 7–Apr. 13	Pisces
Apr. 14–May 22	Aries
May 23–Jul. 2	Taurus
Jul. 3–Aug. 15	Gemini
Aug. 16–Oct. 3	Cancer
Oct. 4–Dec. 11	Leo
Dec. 12–Dec. 31	Virgo

1995

Jan. 1–Jan. 22	Virgo
Jan. 23–May 24	Leo
May 25–Jul. 20	Virgo
Jul. 21–Sep. 6	Libra
Sep. 7–Oct. 20	Scorpio
Oct. 21–Nov. 30	Sagittarius
Dec. 1–Dec. 31	Capricorn

1996

Jan. 1–Jan. 7	Capricorn
Jan. 8–Feb. 15	Aquarius
Feb. 16–Mar. 24	Pisces
Mar. 25–May 1	Aries
May 2–Jun. 11	Taurus
Jun. 12–Jul. 24	Gemini
Jul. 25–Sep. 8	Cancer
Sep. 9–Oct. 29	Leo
Oct. 30–Dec. 31	Virgo

1997

Jan. 1–Jan. 3	Virgo
Jan. 4–Mar. 8	Libra
Mar. 9–Jun. 17	Virgo
Jun. 18–Aug. 13	Libra
Aug. 14–Sep. 27	Scorpio
Sep. 28–Nov. 8	Sagittarius
Nov. 9–Dec. 17	Capricorn
Dec. 18–Dec. 31	Aquarius

1998

Jan. 1–Jan. 24	Aquarius
Jan. 25–Mar. 3	Pisces
Mar. 4–Apr. 12	Aries
Apr. 13–May 23	Taurus
May 24–Jul. 5	Gemini
Jul. 6–Aug. 19	Cancer
Aug. 20–Oct. 6	Leo
Oct. 7–Nov. 26	Virgo
Nov. 27–Dec. 31	Libra

1999

Jan. 1–Jan. 25	Libra
Jan. 26–May 4	Scorpio
May 5–Jul. 4	Libra
Jul. 5–Sep. 1	Scorpio
Sep. 2–Oct. 16	Sagittarius
Oct. 17–Nov. 25	Capricorn
Nov. 26–Dec. 31	Aquarius

2000

Jan. 1–Jan. 3	Aquarius
Jan. 4–Feb. 11	Pisces
Feb. 12–Mar. 22	Aries
Mar. 23–May 2	Taurus
May 3–Jun. 15	Gemini
Jun. 16–Jul. 31	Cancer
Aug. 1–Sep. 16	Leo
Sep. 17–Nov. 3	Virgo
Nov. 4–Dec. 22	Libra
Dec. 23–Dec. 31	Scorpio

7

The Jupiter Tables

How to Find the Planet Jupiter at the Time of Your Birth

Locate the range of dates (month, day, and year) that includes your birthdate. The sign noted to the right of this range is your Jupiter Sign.

Jan. 1, 1901–Jan. 18, 1901	Sagittarius
Jan. 19, 1901–Feb. 6, 1902	Capricorn
Feb. 7, 1902–Feb. 19, 1903	Aquarius
Feb. 20, 1903–Feb. 29, 1904	Pisces
Mar. 1, 1904–Aug. 8, 1904	Aries
Aug. 9, 1904–Aug. 31, 1904	Taurus
Sep. 1, 1904–Mar. 7, 1905	Aries
Mar. 8, 1905–Jul. 20, 1905	Taurus
Jul. 21, 1905–Dec. 4, 1905	Gemini
Dec. 5, 1905–Mar. 9, 1906	Taurus
Mar. 10, 1906–Jul. 30, 1906	Gemini
Jul. 31, 1906–Aug. 18, 1907	Cancer
Aug. 19, 1907–Sep. 11, 1908	Leo
Sep. 12, 1908–Oct. 11, 1909	Virgo
Oct. 12, 1909–Nov. 11, 1910	Libra
Nov. 12, 1910–Dec. 9, 1911	Scorpio
Dec. 10, 1911–Jan. 2, 1913	Sagittarius
Jan. 3, 1913–Jan. 21, 1914	Capricorn

Jan. 22, 1914–Feb. 3, 1915	Aquarius
Feb. 4, 1915–Feb. 11, 1916	Pisces
Feb. 12, 1916–Jun. 25, 1916	Aries
Jun. 26, 1916–Oct. 26, 1916	Taurus
Oct. 27, 1916–Feb. 12, 1917	Aries
Feb. 13, 1917–Jun. 29, 1917	Taurus
Jun. 30, 1917–Jul. 12, 1918	Gemini
Jul. 13, 1918–Aug. 1, 1919	Cancer
Aug. 2, 1919–Aug. 26, 1920	Leo
Aug. 27, 1920–Sep. 25, 1921	Virgo
Sep. 26, 1921–Oct. 26, 1922	Libra
Oct. 27, 1922–Nov. 24, 1923	Scorpio
Nov. 25, 1923–Dec. 17, 1924	Sagittarius
Dec. 18, 1924–Jan. 5, 1926	Capricorn
Jan. 6, 1926–Jan. 17, 1927	Aquarius
Jan. 18, 1927–Jun. 5, 1927	Pisces
Jun. 6, 1927–Sep. 10, 1927	Aries
Sep. 11, 1927–Jan. 22, 1928	Pisces
Jan. 23, 1928–Jun. 3, 1928	Aries
Jun. 4, 1928–Jun. 11, 1929	Taurus
Jun. 12, 1929–Jun. 26, 1930	Gemini
Jun. 27, 1930–Jul. 16, 1931	Cancer
Jul. 17, 1931–Aug. 10, 1932	Leo
Aug. 11, 1932–Sep. 9, 1933	Virgo
Sep. 10, 1933–Oct. 10, 1934	Libra
Oct. 11, 1934–Nov. 8, 1935	Scorpio
Nov. 9, 1935–Dec. 1, 1936	Sagittarius
Dec. 2, 1936–Dec. 19, 1937	Capricorn
Dec. 20, 1937–May 13, 1938	Aquarius
May 14, 1938–Jul. 29, 1938	Pisces
Jul. 30, 1938–Dec. 28, 1938	Aquarius
Dec. 29, 1938–May 10, 1939	Pisces
May 11, 1939–Oct. 29, 1939	Aries
Oct. 30, 1939–Dec. 19, 1939	Pisces
Dec. 20, 1939–May 15, 1940	Aries
May 16, 1940–May 25, 1941	Taurus
May 26, 1941–Jun. 9, 1942	Gemini
Jun. 10, 1942–Jun. 29, 1943	Cancer
Jun. 30, 1943–Jul. 25, 1944	Leo
Jul. 26, 1944–Aug. 24, 1945	Virgo
Aug. 25, 1945–Sep. 24, 1946	Libra

Sep. 25, 1946–Oct. 23, 1947	Scorpio
Oct. 24, 1947–Nov. 14, 1948	Sagittarius
Nov. 15, 1948–Apr. 11, 1949	Capricorn
Apr. 12, 1949–Jun. 26, 1949	Aquarius
Jun. 27, 1949–Nov. 29, 1949	Capricorn
Nov. 30, 1949–Apr. 14, 1950	Aquarius
Apr. 15, 1950–Sep. 14, 1950	Pisces
Sep. 15, 1950–Dec. 1, 1950	Aquarius
Dec. 2, 1950–Apr. 20, 1951	Pisces
Apr. 21, 1951–Apr. 27, 1952	Aries
Apr. 28, 1952–May 8, 1953	Taurus
May 9, 1953–May 23, 1954	Gemini
May 24, 1954–Jun. 11, 1955	Cancer
Jun. 12, 1955–Nov. 16, 1955	Leo
Nov. 17, 1955–Jan. 17, 1956	Virgo
Jan. 18, 1956–Jul. 6, 1956	Leo
Jul. 7, 1956–Dec. 11, 1956	Virgo
Dec. 12, 1956–Feb. 18, 1957	Libra
Feb. 19, 1957–Aug. 5, 1957	Virgo
Aug. 6, 1957–Jan. 12, 1958	Libra
Jan. 13, 1958–Mar. 19, 1958	Scorpio
Mar. 20, 1958–Sep. 6, 1958	Libra
Sep. 7, 1958–Feb. 9, 1959	Scorpio
Feb. 10, 1959–Apr. 23, 1959	Sagittarius
Apr. 24, 1959–Oct. 4, 1959	Scorpio
Oct. 5, 1959–Feb. 29, 1960	Sagittarius
Mar. 1, 1960–Jun. 9, 1960	Capricorn
Jun. 10, 1960–Oct. 24, 1960	Sagittarius
Oct. 25, 1960–Mar. 14, 1961	Capricorn
Mar. 15, 1961–Aug. 11, 1961	Aquarius
Aug. 12, 1961–Nov. 3, 1961	Capricorn
Nov. 4, 1961–Mar. 24, 1962	Aquarius
Mar. 25, 1962–Apr. 3, 1963	Pisces
Apr. 4, 1963–Apr. 11, 1964	Aries
Apr. 12, 1964–Apr. 21, 1965	Taurus
Apr. 22, 1965–Sep. 20, 1965	Gemini
Sep. 21, 1965–Nov. 16, 1965	Cancer
Nov. 17, 1965–May 4, 1966	Gemini
May 5, 1966–Sep. 26, 1966	Cancer
Sep. 27, 1966–Jan. 15, 1967	Leo
Jan. 16, 1967–May 22, 1967	Cancer

May 23, 1967–Oct. 18, 1967	Leo
Oct. 19, 1967–Feb. 26, 1968	Virgo
Feb. 27, 1968–Jun. 14, 1968	Leo
Jun. 15, 1968–Nov. 14, 1968	Virgo
Nov. 15, 1968–Mar. 29, 1969	Libra
Mar. 30, 1969–Jul. 14, 1969	Virgo
Jul. 15, 1969–Dec. 15, 1969	Libra
Dec. 16, 1969–Apr. 29, 1970	Scorpio
Apr. 30, 1970–Aug. 14, 1970	Libra
Aug. 15, 1970–Jan. 13, 1971	Scorpio
Jan. 14, 1971–Jun. 4, 1971	Sagittarius
Jun. 5, 1971–Sep. 10, 1971	Scorpio
Sep. 11, 1971–Feb. 5, 1972	Sagittarius
Feb. 6, 1972–Jul. 23, 1972	Capricorn
Jul. 24, 1972–Sep. 24, 1972	Sagittarius
Sep. 25, 1972–Feb. 22, 1973	Capricorn
Feb. 23, 1973–Mar. 7, 1974	Aquarius
Mar. 8, 1974–Mar. 17, 1975	Pisces
Mar. 18, 1975–Mar. 25, 1976	Aries
Mar. 26, 1976–Aug. 22, 1976	Taurus
Aug. 23, 1976–Oct. 15, 1976	Gemini
Oct. 16, 1976–Apr. 2, 1977	Taurus
Apr. 3, 1977–Aug. 19, 1977	Gemini
Aug. 20, 1977–Dec. 29, 1977	Cancer
Dec. 30, 1977–Apr. 11, 1978	Gemini
Apr. 12, 1978–Sep. 4, 1978	Cancer
Sep. 5, 1978–Feb. 27, 1979	Leo
Feb. 28, 1979–Apr. 19, 1979	Cancer
Apr. 20, 1979–Sep. 28, 1979	Leo
Sep. 29, 1979–Oct. 26, 1980	Virgo
Oct. 27, 1980–Nov. 26, 1981	Libra
Nov. 27, 1981–Dec. 25, 1982	Scorpio
Dec. 26, 1982–Jan. 18, 1984	Sagittarius
Jan. 19, 1984–Feb. 5, 1985	Capricorn
Feb. 6, 1985–Feb. 19, 1986	Aquarius
Feb. 20, 1986–Mar. 1, 1987	Pisces
Mar. 2, 1987–Mar. 7, 1988	Aries
Mar. 8, 1988–Jul. 21, 1988	Taurus
Jul. 22, 1988–Nov. 29, 1988	Gemini
Nov. 30, 1988–Mar. 10, 1989	Taurus
Mar. 11, 1989–Jul. 29, 1989	Gemini

Jul. 30, 1989–Aug. 17, 1990	Cancer
Aug. 18, 1990–Sep. 11, 1991	Leo
Sep. 12, 1991–Oct. 9, 1992	Virgo
Oct. 10, 1992–Nov. 9, 1993	Libra
Nov. 10, 1993–Dec. 8, 1994	Scorpio
Dec. 9, 1994–Jan. 2, 1996	Sagittarius
Jan. 3, 1996–Jan. 20, 1997	Capricorn
Jan. 21, 1997–Feb. 3, 1998	Aquarius
Feb. 4, 1998–Feb. 12, 1999	Pisces
Feb. 13, 1999–Jun. 27, 1999	Aries
Jun. 28, 1999–Oct. 22, 1999	Taurus
Oct. 23, 1999–Dec. 31, 1999	Aries

8

The Saturn Tables

How to Find the Planet Saturn at the Time of Your Birth

Find the range of dates (month, day, and year) that includes your birth date. The sign indicated to the right of this range is your Saturn Sign.

Jan. 1, 1900–Jan. 20, 1900	Sagittarius
Jan. 21, 1900–Jul. 18, 1900	Capricorn
Jul. 19, 1900–Oct. 16, 1900	Sagittarius
Oct. 17, 1900–Jan. 19, 1903	Capricorn
Jan. 20, 1903–Apr. 12, 1905	Aquarius
Apr. 13, 1905–Aug. 16, 1905	Pisces
Aug. 17, 1905–Jan. 7, 1906	Aquarius
Jan. 8, 1906–Mar. 18, 1908	Pisces
Mar. 19, 1908–May 16, 1910	Aries
May 17, 1910–Dec. 14, 1910	Taurus
Dec. 15, 1910–Jan. 19, 1911	Aries
Jan. 20, 1911–Jul. 6, 1912	Taurus
Jul. 7, 1912–Nov. 30, 1912	Gemini
Dec. 1, 1912–Mar. 25, 1913	Taurus
Mar. 26, 1913–Aug. 24, 1914	Gemini
Aug. 25, 1914–Dec. 6, 1914	Cancer
Dec. 7, 1914–May 11, 1915	Gemini

May 12, 1915–Oct. 16, 1916	Cancer
Oct. 17, 1916–Dec. 7, 1916	Leo
Dec. 8, 1916–Jun. 23, 1917	Cancer
Jun. 24, 1917–Aug. 11, 1919	Leo
Aug. 12, 1919–Oct. 7, 1921	Virgo
Oct. 8, 1921–Dec. 19, 1923	Libra
Dec. 20, 1923–Apr. 5, 1924	Scorpio
Apr. 6, 1924–Sep. 13, 1924	Libra
Sep. 14, 1924–Dec. 2, 1926	Scorpio
Dec. 3, 1926–Mar. 29, 1929	Sagittarius
Mar. 30, 1929–May 4, 1929	Capricorn
May 5, 1929–Nov. 29, 1929	Sagittarius
Nov. 30, 1929–Feb. 22, 1932	Capricorn
Feb. 23, 1932–Aug. 12, 1932	Aquarius
Aug. 13, 1932–Nov. 18, 1932	Capricorn
Nov. 19, 1932–Feb. 13, 1935	Aquarius
Feb. 14, 1935–Apr. 24, 1937	Pisces
Apr. 25, 1937–Oct. 17, 1937	Aries
Oct. 18, 1937–Jan. 13, 1938	Pisces
Jan. 14, 1938–Jul. 5, 1939	Aries
Jul. 6, 1939–Sep. 21, 1939	Taurus
Sep. 22, 1939–Mar. 19, 1940	Aries
Mar. 20, 1940–May 7, 1942	Taurus
May 8, 1942–Jun. 19, 1944	Gemini
Jun. 20, 1944–Aug. 1, 1946	Cancer
Aug. 2, 1946–Sep. 18, 1948	Leo
Sep. 19, 1948–Apr. 2, 1949	Virgo
Apr. 3, 1949–May 28, 1949	Leo
May 29, 1949–Nov. 19, 1950	Virgo
Nov. 20, 1950–Mar. 6, 1951	Libra
Mar. 7, 1951–Aug. 12, 1951	Virgo
Aug. 13, 1951–Oct. 21, 1953	Libra
Oct. 22, 1953–Jan. 11, 1956	Scorpio
Jan. 12, 1956–May 13, 1956	Sagittarius
May 14, 1956–Oct. 9, 1956	Scorpio
Oct. 10, 1956–Jan. 4, 1959	Sagittarius
Jan. 5, 1959–Jan. 9, 1962	Capricorn
Jan. 10, 1962–Dec. 16, 1964	Aquarius
Dec. 17, 1964–Mar. 2, 1967	Pisces
Mar. 3, 1967–Apr. 28, 1969	Aries
Apr. 29, 1969–Jun. 18, 1971	Taurus
Jun. 19, 1971–Jan. 10, 1972	Gemini

Jan. 11, 1972–Feb. 21, 1972	Taurus
Feb. 22, 1972–Aug. 1, 1973	Gemini
Aug. 2, 1973–Jan. 7, 1974	Cancer
Jan. 8, 1974–Apr. 18, 1974	Gemini
Apr. 19, 1974–Sep. 17, 1975	Cancer
Sep. 18, 1975–Jan. 14, 1976	Leo
Jan. 15, 1976–Jun. 5, 1976	Cancer
Jun. 6, 1976–Nov. 17, 1977	Leo
Nov. 18, 1977–Jan. 5, 1978	Virgo
Jan. 6, 1978–Jul. 26, 1978	Leo
Jul. 27, 1978–Sep. 21, 1980	Virgo
Sep. 22, 1980–Nov. 30, 1982	Libra
Dec. 1, 1982–May 6, 1983	Scorpio
May 7, 1983–Aug. 24, 1983	Libra
Aug. 25, 1983–Nov. 17, 1985	Scorpio
Nov. 18, 1985–Feb. 13, 1988	Sagittarius
Feb. 14, 1988–Jun. 10, 1988	Capricorn
Jun. 11, 1988–Nov. 12, 1988	Sagittarius
Nov. 13, 1988–Feb. 7, 1991	Capricorn
Feb. 8, 1991–May 21, 1993	Aquarius
May 22, 1993–Jun. 30, 1993	Pisces
Jul. 1, 1993–Jan. 28, 1994	Aquarius
Jan. 29, 1994–Apr. 6, 1996	Pisces
Apr. 7, 1996–Jun. 9, 1998	Aries
Jun. 10, 1998–Oct. 25, 1998	Taurus
Oct. 26, 1998–Mar. 1, 1999	Aries
Mar. 2, 1999–Dec. 31, 1999	Taurus

★ # 9 ★

The Uranus Tables

How to Find the Planet Uranus at the Time of Your Birth

Find the range of dates (month, day, and year) that includes your birth date. The sign indicated to the right of the range is your Uranus Sign.

Sep. 11, 1898–Dec. 19, 1904	Sagittarius
Dec. 20, 1904–Jan. 30, 1912	Capricorn
Jan. 31, 1912–Sep. 4, 1912	Aquarius
Sep. 5, 1912–Nov. 11, 1912	Capricorn
Nov. 12, 1912–Mar. 31, 1919	Aquarius
Apr. 1, 1919–Aug. 16, 1919	Pisces
Aug. 17, 1919–Jan. 21, 1920	Aquarius
Jan. 22, 1920–Mar. 30, 1927	Pisces
Mar. 31, 1927–Nov. 4, 1927	Aries
Nov. 5, 1927–Jan. 12, 1928	Pisces
Jan. 13, 1928–Jun. 6, 1934	Aries
Jun. 7, 1934–Oct. 9, 1934	Taurus
Oct. 10, 1934–Mar. 28, 1935	Aries
Mar. 29, 1935–Aug. 6, 1941	Taurus
Aug. 7, 1941–Oct. 4, 1941	Gemini
Oct. 5, 1941–May 13, 1942	Taurus
May 14, 1942–Aug. 29, 1948	Gemini
Aug. 30, 1948–Nov. 11, 1948	Cancer

Nov. 12, 1948–Jun. 9, 1949	Gemini
Jun. 10, 1949–Aug. 23, 1955	Cancer
Aug. 24, 1955–Jan. 27, 1956	Leo
Jan. 28, 1956–Jun. 8, 1956	Cancer
Jun. 9, 1956–Oct. 31, 1961	Leo
Nov. 1, 1961–Jan. 11, 1962	Virgo
Jan. 12, 1962–Aug. 8, 1962	Leo
Aug. 9, 1962–Sep. 27, 1968	Virgo
Sep. 28, 1968–May 20, 1969	Libra
May 21, 1969–Jun. 23, 1969	Virgo
Jun. 24, 1969–Nov. 22, 1974	Libra
Nov. 23, 1974–May 2, 1975	Scorpio
May 3, 1975–Sep. 5, 1975	Libra
Sep. 6, 1975–Feb. 18, 1981	Scorpio
Feb. 19, 1981–Mar. 21, 1981	Sagittarius
Mar. 22, 1981–Nov. 16, 1981	Scorpio
Nov. 17, 1981–Dec. 2, 1988	Sagittarius
Dec. 3, 1988–Apr. 1, 1995	Capricorn
Apr. 2, 1995–Jun. 9, 1995	Aquarius
Jun. 10, 1995–Jan. 12, 1996	Capricorn
Jan. 13, 1996–Jan. 1, 2000	Aquarius

★

★ 10 ★

The Neptune Tables

How to Find the Planet Neptune at the Time of Your Birth

Find the range of dates (month, day, and year) that includes your birth date. The sign indicated to the right is your Neptune Sign.

Jan. 1, 1890–Jul. 19, 1901	Gemini
Jul. 20, 1901–Dec. 25, 1901	Cancer
Dec. 26, 1901–May 19, 1902	Gemini
May 20, 1902–Sep. 22, 1914	Cancer
Sep. 23, 1914–Dec. 14, 1914	Leo
Dec. 15, 1914–Jul. 18, 1915	Cancer
Jul. 19, 1915–Mar. 19, 1916	Leo
Mar. 20, 1916–May 1, 1916	Cancer
May 2, 1916–Sep. 20, 1928	Leo
Sep. 21, 1928–Feb. 19, 1929	Virgo
Feb. 20, 1929–Jul. 23, 1929	Leo
Jul. 24, 1929–Oct. 3, 1942	Virgo
Oct. 4, 1942–Apr. 16, 1943	Libra
Apr. 17, 1943–Aug. 2, 1943	Virgo
Aug. 3, 1943–Dec. 24, 1955	Libra
Dec. 25, 1955–Mar. 12, 1956	Scorpio
Mar. 13, 1956–Oct. 19, 1956	Libra
Oct. 20, 1956–Jun. 14, 1957	Scorpio

Jun. 15, 1957–Aug. 5, 1957	Libra
Aug. 6, 1957–Jan. 4, 1970	Scorpio
Jan. 5, 1970–May 3, 1970	Sagittarius
May 4, 1970–Nov. 5, 1970	Scorpio
Nov. 6, 1970–Jan. 19, 1984	Sagittarius
Jan. 20, 1984–Jun. 22, 1984	Capricorn
Jun. 23, 1984–Nov. 21, 1984	Sagittarius
Nov. 22, 1984–Jan. 28, 1998	Capricorn
Jan. 29, 1998–Aug. 22, 1998	Aquarius
Aug. 23, 1998–Nov. 27, 1999	Capricorn
Nov. 28, 1999–Dec. 31, 1999	Aquarius

★
★ 11 ★

The Pluto Tables

How to Find the Planet Pluto at the Time of Your Birth

Find the range of dates (month, day, and year) that includes your birth date. The sign to the right of this range is your Pluto Sign.

Jan. 1, 1900–Aug. 23, 1912	Gemini
Aug. 24, 1912–Sep. 23, 1912	Cancer
Sep. 24, 1912–Jun. 20, 1913	Gemini
Jun. 21, 1913–Dec. 31, 1913	Cancer
Jan. 1, 1914–Jun. 15, 1914	Gemini
Jun. 16, 1914–Nov. 1, 1937	Cancer
Nov. 2, 1937–Nov. 30, 1937	Leo
Dec. 1, 1937–Aug. 31, 1938	Cancer
Sep. 1, 1938–Dec. 31, 1938	Leo
Jan. 1, 1939–Mar. 6, 1939	Cancer
Mar. 7, 1939–Oct. 1, 1956	Leo
Oct. 2, 1956–Jan. 31, 1957	Virgo
Feb. 1, 1957–Sep. 1, 1957	Leo
Sep. 2, 1957–Oct. 5, 1971	Virgo
Oct. 6, 1971–Apr. 18, 1972	Libra
Apr. 19, 1972–Jul. 30, 1972	Virgo
Jul. 31, 1972–Nov. 4, 1983	Libra
Nov. 5, 1983–May 18, 1984	Scorpio

May 19, 1984–Jun. 1, 1984	Libra
Jun. 2, 1984–Jul. 8, 1984	Scorpio
Jul. 9, 1984–Jul. 31, 1984	Libra
Aug. 1, 1984–Jan. 15, 1995	Scorpio
Jan. 16, 1995–Apr. 21, 1995	Sagittarius
Apr. 22, 1995–Nov. 9, 1995	Scorpio
Nov. 10, 1995–Dec. 31, 2000	Sagittarius

★ Appendices ★

★

★ Blessing ★
for a Marriage
─────────────

May your marriage bring you all the exquisite excitements
a marriage should bring,
and may life grant you also patience, tolerance, and
understanding.
May you always need one another—
not so much to fill your emptiness as to help you to know
your fullness.
A mountain needs a valley to be complete;
the valley does not make the mountain less but more;
and the valley is more a valley because it has a mountain
towering over it.
So let it be with you and you.
May you need one another, but not out of weakness.
May you want one another, but not out of lack.
May you entice one another, but not compel one another.
May you embrace one another, but not encircle one another.
May you succeed in all important ways with one another,
and not fail in the little graces.
May you look for things to praise, often say, "I love you!"
and take no notice of small faults.
If you have quarrels that push you apart,
May both of you hope to have good sense enough to take
the first step back.

*May you enter into the mystery which is the awareness of
one another's presence—
no more physical than spiritual, warm and near when you
are side by side,
and warm and near when you are in separate rooms
or even distant cities.
May you have happiness, and may you find it making
one another happy.
May you have love, and may you find it loving one another!
Thank You, God,
for Your presence here with us
and Your blessing on this marriage.
Amen.*

— JAMES DILLET FREEMAN

My favorite part, and the reason I wanted to share this
with you is: "May you have happiness, and may you find it
making each other happy." It's a nice thought regardless of
the level of commitment.

Permission to reprint from *A Book of Marriage Charts*, by Emylu Lander Hughes,
The American Federation of Astrologers, 1986.

★ Wedding ★ Dates to Rethink When Mercury Is Retrograde R$_x$

A word about Mercury Retrograde. When we say Mercury is Retrograde we are talking about the apparent backward movement of the planet Mercury. Mercury rules language, our intellect, and all things contractual. The planet's motion, when retrograde, can cause delays and misinformation since its movement is contrary to best astrological results. Things become complicated and confusing. When I think of Mercury Retrograde I think of Re. Re-do, re-organize, re-figure, re-write, etc. Yes becomes no. Reservations, correspondence, and travel get fouled up. Who wants this for a wedding date? Or a move-in date?

Thankfully, Mercury is only Retrograde a few times a year. Avoid it if you can. Work around Mercury Retrograde and your important days will be memorable for the right reasons. Why fight it?

1989	Jan. 16 to Feb. 5
	May 12 to Jun. 5
	Sep. 11 to Oct. 3

1990	Jan. 30 to Feb. 20
	Apr. 23 to May 17
	Aug. 25 to Sep. 17
	Dec. 14 to Jan. 3

1991	Apr. 4 to Apr. 28
	Aug. 7 to Sep. 31
	Nov. 28 to Dec. 18

1992	Mar. 17 to Apr. 9
	Jul. 20 to Aug. 13
	Nov. 11 to Dec. 1

1993	Mar. 27 to Apr. 22
	Jul. 1 to Jul. 25
	Oct. 25 to Nov. 15

1994	Feb. 11 to Mar. 5
	Jun. 12 to Jul. 6
	Oct. 9 to Nov. 30

1995	Jan. 26 to Feb. 15
	May 24 to Jun. 17
	Sep. 22 to Oct. 14

1996	Jan. 9 to Feb. 29
	May 3 to May 27
	Sep. 4 to Sep. 26
	Dec. 23 to Jan. 12

1997	Apr. 15 to May 8
	Aug. 17 to Sep. 10
	Dec. 7 to Dec. 27

1998	Mar. 27 to Apr. 20
	Jul. 31 to Aug. 23
	Nov. 21 to Dec. 11

1999	Mar. 10 to Apr. 2
	Jul. 12 to Aug. 6
	Nov. 5 to Nov. 25

2000	Feb. 21 to Mar. 14
	Jun. 23 to Jul. 17
	Oct. 18 to Nov. 8

✦ Sources ✦

The History of Astrology, Zolar, Arco Publishing Co., Inc.

Llewellyn's 1994 Moon Sign Book, Llewellyn's Publication Worldwide.

★ Disclaimer ★

★

"To err is human," and so with all best intentions there may be an error in the planetary tables. We couldn't find one. If you do, please let us know. Thank you.

★ Final ★
Words
from Linda

The Sun	Our character
The Moon	Our emotional needs
Mercury	Communication: "Can we talk?"
Venus	Our ability to love and be loved
Mars	Basic energies
Jupiter	Where we get lucky
Saturn	Commitment
Uranus	The need for space and how much
Neptune	Romantic ideals
Pluto	Our power to transform, to attract, and repel
Rising Sign or Ascendant	Our personality

"Remember, love can conquer the influences of the planets....
It can even eliminate karma."

— LINDA GOODMAN

LINDA GOODMAN has been called the modern-day Nostradamus. She is the largest-selling author of books on astrology in the world. Her first book, *Sun Signs*, is responsible for bringing astrology into the mainstream and was so well received by the public that it hit the *New York Times* bestseller list immediately—the first astrology book ever to achieve this. Her next book, *Love Signs*, made nine bestseller lists, and with *Star Signs*—another bestseller—Linda brought the world an understanding of metaphysics and numerology. Because of her universal appeal, her books have been translated into many different languages and are available worldwide. Most homes have at least one of her books, and most of today's astrologers confirm that she had some part in inspiring them to study astrology. Although very sought-after for interviews, Linda preferred to be something of a recluse, making her home 10,000 feet above sea level in Cripple Creek, Colorado, where she spent her days researching and writing about the mysteries of the universe until her death in October 1995. Linda's other works include *Venus Trines at Midnight* and *Gooberz,* books of poetry and prose. One of her greatest wishes was to be remembered not solely for astrology, but also for her poetry, and at this, too, she excelled.

CAROLYN REYNOLDS has been a professional astrologer for over twenty years. Her background in journalism and social work has helped her provide a unique approach to astrology for her clients and for the readers of her daily forecasts. Living in the Palm Springs area with her husband, Patrick, and their dog, Stevie, she gets daily inspiration from the Santa Rosa mountains. She is also the author of *The Book of Lovers*.

CRYSTAL BUSH currently lives in California and has the worldwide responsibility for all future Linda Goodman–related projects. At present Crystal is developing the Linda Goodman School of Astrology in Los Angeles, which intends to offer courses and seminars in astrology throughout the world. For more information, write to: GMI, 1007 Montana Avenue #721, Santa Monica, CA 90403.

Our e-mail address is:
LGStarVision@msn.com

And please visit our web site at:
www.LindaGoodman.net